MO●N
HANDBOOKS

BELIZE

JOSHUA BERMAN

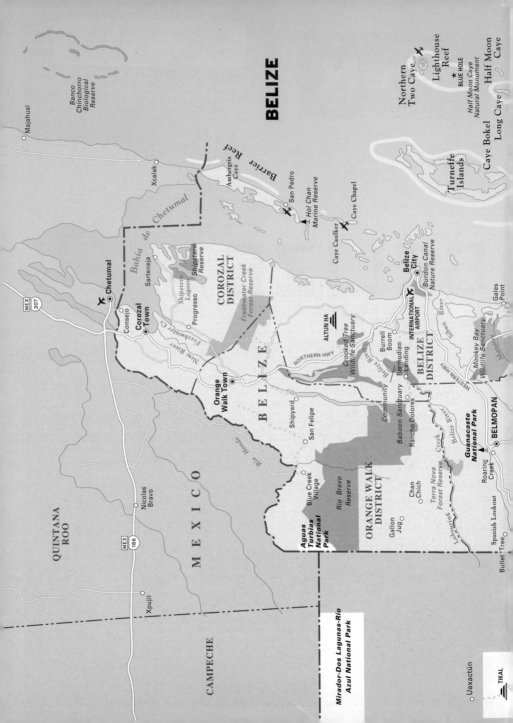

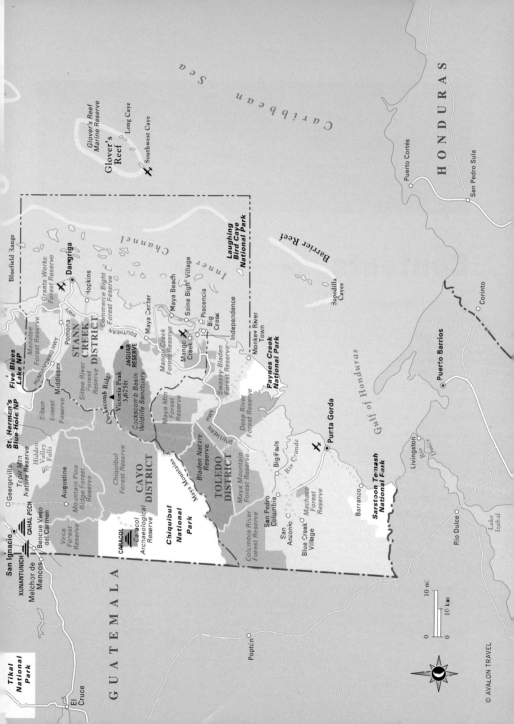

Contents

Discover Belize

The first morning I awoke in Belize, it was raining and warm. I got up before dawn and followed the crowds to the water's edge in Belize City. There, a gray dawn delivered a festooned flotilla of wooden dories to the dock in Haulover Creek. It was November 19, Settlement Day, the Garifuna people's annual reenactment of their ancestors' 1832 arrival to Belizean shores. Drums, smiles, and biting belts of *gífit*, a drink also known as "bitters," were on hand as I walked with the clump of celebrants through Belize City's narrow streets. People were singing and drumming, dancing and marching. There were shouts and umbrellas, black-and-yellow flags, babies crying. And the rain.

The parade marched across the old Swing Bridge. The first light of day had become a bright white suffused in a light drizzle, and masts of fishing boats were reflected on the water's glassy surface. The smell of low tide, fish, and gasoline completed the scene. As we turned onto Front Street, a man next to me beat on a string of turtle shells dangling from his neck, the drums thumping below him. When we arrived at the entrance to the church, I stepped aside and watched waves of wet, shiny people wash up the stairs with drums and flags, music never ceasing as they crammed inside for a blessing.

My first day in Belize delivered this damp, convivial experience. My

second day, driving inland, gave me a different experience entirely – river crossings, pyramids, and the roar of "baboons." On my fifth day, in the cayes, I saw Belize through a curtain of grouper fish and reef sharks.

If you've traveled in other parts of Central America or the Caribbean, forget them all. Belize is different: It is coconut shavings in your rice and beans. It is butter pooling in your conch soup – with a squirt of lime and a splash of hot sauce to make it bite. Belize is the hemisphere's largest barrier reef; it is massive forests of giant cohune palms and prehistoric tree ferns, some amid ancient Maya plazas. There are birds, big cats, and strange rodents in Belize's ample backabush. And, of course, there are the Belizeans – about 300,000 of them, each family line hailing from a uniquely Creolized collection of cultures.

It's a country that is always new to me, as new as it was that first morning in the rain. Your experience will be just as personal. And it will begin the moment you decide to go to Belize.

Planning Your Trip

▶ WHERE TO GO

Belize District

This stretch of coastline, islands, and swampy lowlands includes former capital Belize City. Scattered sights and events make it worth a quick visit. If you don't appreciate the city's unique grit and texture, focus on attractions like the Belize Zoo, Community Baboon Sanctuary, Crooked Tree Wildlife Sanctuary, and Altun Ha ruins.

The Northern Cayes

This group of islands includes Ambergris Caye, with swanky beach resorts. Caye Caulker, just down the reef, offers a slower pace with a cheaper vibe. Turneffe Islands and Lighthouse Reef Atoll offer spectacular wall diving and include Jacques Cousteau's old favorite, the Blue Hole.

Belmopan and the Hummingbird Highway

For most travelers, Belize's capital, Belmopan, is nothing more than an annoying bus layover. The surrounding countryside, however— and the beautiful Hummingbird Highway that snakes through the district—is not to be missed. Some of the country's most famous adventure lodges occupy riverbanks in the area, as does Belize's only working golf course, along Roaring Creek.

Cayo and the Mountain Pine Ridge

Bordering Guatemala's Petén wilderness, Belize's interior offers a remarkable selection of lodges and camps. Sights include the Xunantunich and Caracol archaeological sites, the Belize Botanic Gardens, and the

IF YOU HAVE . . .

waiting for the water taxi at Caye Caulker

- **ONE WEEK:** Visit Caye Caulker and Cayo (three days each).

- **TWO WEEKS:** Add the Mountain Pine Ridge.

- **THREE WEEKS:** Add Punta Gorda and the Toledo District.

- **FOUR WEEKS:** Add a five-day side trip to Tikal in Guatemala.

Mountain Pine Ridge. Explore by foot, canoe, or horseback.

Southern Coast: Dangriga to Placencia

Stann Creek District offers hiking in several protected areas in the Maya Mountains, and

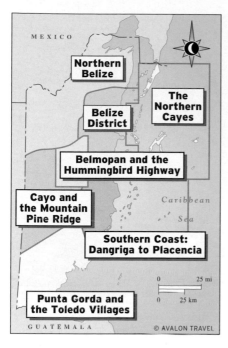

MEXICO

Northern Belize

The Northern Cayes

Belize District

Belmopan and the Hummingbird Highway

Cayo and the Mountain Pine Ridge

Caribbean Sea

Southern Coast: Dangriga to Placencia

0   25 mi

0   25 km

Punta Gorda and the Toledo Villages

GUATEMALA   © AVALON TRAVEL

kayaking, diving, and sailing out in the cayes. Dangriga is the cultural center of Belize's Garifuna population. Just down the coast, lazy Hopkins has empty beaches and fine

dining, both of which you'll also find along the Placencia Peninsula and the low-key village of Placencia.

Punta Gorda and the Toledo Villages

Forest, reef, river, ruins, and ridges await the handful of visitors who get off the beaten path and onto the "cacao trail" in southern Belize. Consider signing up with a guesthouse or homestay program in the up-country villages, where you can learn how to make a corn tortilla and speak a few phrases of the local Mayan tongue.

Northern Belize

Orange Walk and Corozal Districts are not a focus for most travelers—unless, of course, they've heard about the Chan Chich Lodge or Lamanai Outpost Lodge, gorgeous accommodations amid remote, vast archaeological ruins. Both are set deep in the bush and are as popular with birders and naturalists as they are with archaeologists and biologists. You can also stroll the sleepy streets of gentle and affordable Corozal, a possible launching pad to Ambergris Caye.

▶ WHEN TO GO

High season is mid-December through May, a period many travel agents will tell you is the "dry season," in a vain effort to neatly contain Belize's weather patterns. In many years, this is true, with sunny skies and green vegetation throughout the country during the North American winter. However, November can be dry as a bone and sunny, while December, January, and even February can play host to wet cold fronts that either blow right through or sit around for days.

June, July, and August technically form the rainy season—which may mean just

house gecko in a hammock

Tranquility Bay Resort on northern Ambergris Caye is one of the few beach hotels in the country with walk-in snorkeling.

a quick afternoon shower or rain for days. This often means significantly discounted accommodations. August is the most popular with European backpackers, while December and February are dominated by North Americans. Some tourism businesses shut down completely during the months of September and October, the peak of hurricane season.

Your best bet? Be prepared for clouds or sun at any time of year. A week of stormy weather may ruin a vacation planned solely around snorkeling, but it could also provide the perfect setting for exploring the rainforests or enjoying a hot tub and fireplace in the Mountain Pine Ridge. For current conditions, check the Belize National Meteorological Service's website (www.hydromet.gov.bz).

► BEFORE YOU GO

Passports and Visas
You must have a passport that is valid for the duration of your stay in Belize. You may be asked at the border (or airport immigration) to show a return ticket or ample money to leave the country. You do *not* need a visa if you are a British Commonwealth subject or a citizen of Belgium, Denmark, Finland, Greece, Iceland, Italy, Liechtenstein, Luxembourg, Mexico, Spain, Switzerland, Tunisia, Turkey, the United States, or Uruguay. Visitors for purposes other than tourism must obtain a visa.

Vaccinations
Technically, a certificate of vaccination against yellow fever is required for travelers aged above one year arriving from an affected area, though immigration officials rarely, if ever, ask to see one.

In general, before traveling anywhere in Central America, your routine

scarlet macaw at the Belize Zoo

vaccinations—tetanus, diphtheria, measles, mumps, rubella, and polio—should be up to date. Hepatitis A vaccine is recommended for all travelers over age two and should be given at least two weeks (preferably four weeks or more) before departure. Hepatitis B vaccine is recommended for travelers who will have intimate contact with local residents or potentially need blood transfusions or injections while abroad, especially if visiting for more than six months. It is also recommended for all health care personnel and volunteers. Typhoid and rabies vaccines are recommended for those headed for rural areas.

Transportation

The vast majority of travelers arrive in Belize by air at Philip Goldson International Airport (BZE), nine miles from Belize City. From there, short domestic connections are available around the country. A few travelers fly into Cancún as a cheaper back door to Belize; once there, they board a bus or rent a car and head south through the Yucatán Peninsula to get to Belize.

Belize is small and extremely manageable, especially if you fly the domestic airline from tiny airstrip to tiny airstrip. You can also get around by rental car, hired taxi, or bus, experiences that make the country seem larger. Another option is to simply let your resort or lodge arrange your airport transfer and all tours.

Water taxis are another way people get around in Belize, especially to and from Ambergris Caye and Caye Caulker; there are regular routes between Belize City and these islands.

Explore Belize

▶ THE BEST OF BELIZE

A week and a half provides just enough time to see a few of Belize's major destinations and get a taste for just how much more there is to discover. Following is an active and mobile 10-day tour; you can double or triple the time allotted to any of the areas listed below and still remain busy. Feel free to follow this itinerary in any order and, when you tire, stop where you are and soak it in.

Day 1
Arrive at Philip Goldson International Airport and transfer to Cayo on the San Ignacio shuttle. Settle into a family guesthouse and spend the evening strolling the mellow, misty village of San Ignacio. Or you can just as easily base yourself at one of the many area jungle lodges throughout Cayo and still hit all the best sights.

Day 2
Rise early for a canoe trip up the Macal River. Depending on the water level, you may make it to The Lodge at Chaa Creek or duPlooy's Jungle Lodge, both with a number of attractions, including a nature center, a butterfly farm, and the Belize Botanic Gardens. Float back downstream for another relaxed San Ignacio evening—book a massage for those well-worked shoulders.

Day 3
Visit Xunantunich or El Pilar, either by foot, mountain bike, or horseback. When you get back from the archaeological site, ask your host to help plan a trip to Caracol the next day.

Day 4
Enjoy the ride along the Mountain Pine Ridge to the ruins of Caracol, then try the swimming hole tour on the way back. Stop for an organic salad or gourmet pizza at Blancaneaux Lodge or a photo op at Thousand Foot Falls, one of the highest in Central America.

wall tents at the Macal River Camp, the budget-friendly accommodation option at The Lodge at Chaa Creek

The Turtleman's House, Bacalar Chico Marine Reserve, northern Ambergris Caye

Day 5

Transfer to Belize City in the morning, but be sure to stop for a hike at Guanacaste National Park or the Belize Zoo. When you arrive in the city, buy your water taxi ticket to Ambergris Caye for the last boat of the afternoon, then stash your bags at the water taxi terminal while you explore Belize City's Fort George, the Image Factory Art Foundation, and the Museum of Belize. Get on the boat and arrive in San Pedro in time for a fancy seafood dinner.

Day 6

Diving or snorkeling, anyone? How about window shopping along the dusty lanes or soaking in one of several spas? Repeat this day as often as needed, maybe even for the duration of your trip.

Day 7

Two quick puddle-jumper flights plop you in Dangriga. From there, cruise out to Tobacco Caye or South Water Caye for more sun, ocean, diving, and conviviality.

Day 8

Back on the mainland, spend the morning at the Gulisi Garifuna Museum and Marie Sharp's hot sauce factory, then ride south to Sittee River (or Hopkins) and arrange for a night canoe safari.

Day 9

Stay put, or take a day trip to Cockscomb Basin Wildlife Sanctuary, where you can hike through the jungle and float the river under a sky of birdsong and green canopy.

Day 10

Transfer to Philip Goldson International Airport for your departure. Plan on coming back next year to explore the southern and northern parts of Belize.

MUNDO MAYA

Archaeologists estimate that at one time, as many as one million or more Maya lived in the area that is now called Belize, part of a loose empire of city-states that extended into present-day Guatemala, Belize, Mexico, and Honduras. Today, some 10 million Maya remain in those countries, speaking two dozen Mayan languages. Meanwhile, the ruins of their ancestors serve as stark reminders of another time.

MAYA ARCHAEOLOGICAL SITES

There's a giddy, childlike feeling you get when climbing thousand-year-old stone pyramids in the middle of the jungle – a fairy-tale, Tolkienesque mood of mystery as you scramble up crooked staircases while strange creatures howl in the surrounding forest. Belize has dozens of accessible, lushly vegetated archaeological sites, some fully excavated and restored, others barely peeking through centuries of ferns, trees, and monkeys. New archaeological sites are discovered each year in Belize, and it's common for rural families to have ruins and mounds in their backyards that are not officially known to archaeologists.

There will be a huge celebration at Xunantunich during the winter solstice in 2012.

The most spectacular, extensive, and exciting sites in Belize are **Caracol, Xunantunich,** and **Lamanai,** where ongoing excavations, combined with new technology, turn up exciting discoveries each year. Other sites include **El Pilar,** whose main attraction is its *lack* of excavation, the **Cahal Pech Archaeological Site** in San Ignacio, and the southern sites of **Nim Li Punit** and **Lubaantun,** each with its own architectural flair.

The **Belize Institute of Archaeology** manages all archaeological sites. It is part of the government's **National Institute of Culture and History** (NICH, www.nichbelize.org).

2012: THE YEAR OF THE MAYA

On December 21, 2012, the 13th baktun in the Great Cycle of the Mayan calendar will come to an end and another 13-baktun cycle, or "era of man," will begin (each baktun is approximately 400 years). Mayan astronomers calculated and recorded this length of time more than 5,000 years ago, a precise count of 1,872,000 days that began on the summer solstice in the year 3114 B.C. and will end on the winter solstice in 2012.

There are hundreds of books and theories about what this new cycle will mean and how it will happen. Most agree that the date signifies some kind of transition for humanity, but argue about the details. The various theories include a vengeful Mother Nature, societal collapse, solar flares, galactic shifts, the angle of the Earth's spin, and/or extraterrestrials. Some say it's all bunk, that there is no "Maya Prophecy."

The old royal residence at the Cahal Pech Archaeological Site in San Igancio will host the reenactment of an ancient Maya feast in 2012.

Dr. Jaime Awe, director of Belize's Institute of Archaeology, says such sensational talk around 2012 "has very little to do with the reality of what the Maya calendar and Long Count calculations are all about. This represents the ending of one cosmological cycle and the beginning of another. It's very much the way most people would look at the end of one year and the beginning of another, but over a very, very long period of time. It is a time for reflection, and for considering future direction," he said.

Celebration of the New Era

Belize's official 2012 tourism slogan is phrased as a challenge: "Where will you be when the world begins anew?" Though 2012 hysteria is based on a single day – the shortest day of the year – expect a full year-long, nationwide celebration of Maya culture leading up to the 21st of December and beyond.

"Imagine a New Year's party that comes only once every 52,000 years, and you'll get an idea of what this means to those of us living in the Maya heartland," says Dr. Awe.

There will be sporting events like temple-to-temple cycling races, torch relays, La Ruta Maya River Challenge, and reenactments of the ancient Maya ball game on the old courts. There will also be archaeology symposiums, lecture series, and school programs in a veritable 12-month feast of Maya nerditude. Above all, 2012 will be a year to honor the living Maya, who will be hosting ceremonies, herbal healings, dances, and teachings.

And of course, many of the best lodges and resorts in the country are offering Maya-themed packages throughout the year to place you in the middle of it all. You'll find the complete collection of events at www.travel-belize.org.

MAYA ARCHAEOLOGICAL SITES

To Tulum

MEXICO

Corozal Town

SANTA RITA

AVENTURA

CERROS

NOHMUL

COROZAL DISTRICT

SAN ANTONIO RIO HONDA

SHIPSTERN

Orange Walk Town

Ambergris Caye

CUELLO

Rio Hondo

EL POSITO

ORANGE WALK DISTRICT

LAS MILPAS

LAMANAI

ALTUN HA

EL INFIERNO

KAKABISH

CHAN CHICH

SAN JOSE

BELIZE DISTRICT

Belize City

BELIZE

Northern Two Caye

Turneffe Islands

EL PILAR

BARTON RAMIE

BELMOPAN

San Ignacio

XUNANTUNICH

CAHAL PECH

TIPU

CAYO DISTRICT

MUCNAL TUNICH

POMONA

Dangriga

To Tikal

KUCHIL BALUM

KENDAL

Glover's Reef

TZIMIN KAX

STANN CREEK DISTRICT

CARACOL

ACTUN BALAM

TOLEDO DISTRICT

ALABAMA

Placencia

Caribbean Sea

NIM LI PUNIT

XNAHEB

LUBAANTUN

San Pedro Columbia

UXBENKA

PUSILHA

HOKEB HA

Punta Gorda

Gulf of Honduras

0   30 mi

0   30 km

GUATEMALA

© AVALON TRAVEL

▶ BACKABUSH BELIZE

Even with Belize's increased name recognition around the world, it still doesn't take much to drop off the beaten path, and for those whose preferred "scene" is no scene at all, here are some ideas. The two-week adventure suggested below is an entirely mainland one. To add more Caribbean time to your trip, consider inserting several days on Caye Caulker, followed by Raggamuffin Tours' three-day sailing trip to Placencia, a unique fishing, snorkeling, and camping trip. From Placencia, you can visit Laughing Bird Caye National Park, spend a night in Monkey River, or hop a boat bound for Puerto Cortés, Honduras. Others figure out a way to get to Glover's Reef Atoll, an unparalleled Caribbean experience. Another alternative is to make it to Punta Gorda, as mentioned in day 10, then instead of the village homestay, head for the Sapodilla Cayes or to Livingston, Guatemala, for a few nights.

Of course, the most important items you'll want to pack for any of these trips are an open mind, extra patience, and the ability to scrap the entire plan when you feel the adventure pulling you in its own direction.

Day 1

Transfer to a riverside Belize City guesthouse and enjoy your first heaping plate of rice, beans, and stew chicken while reggae blasts all around you.

Day 2

Catch a bus to the Community Baboon Sanctuary at Bermuda Landing, where you are guaranteed howler monkey sightings and can stay in a tent, a cabin, or with a local family.

Day 3

After a morning hike, take a bus down the

kayaks on the beach in Placencia

DIVING BLISS

There's nothing like the raw excitement of swimming among curious and brazen fish, combined with the sensation of zero gravity. Belize was a Western Hemisphere diving mecca decades before it became the romantic and trendy destination it is today. Hundreds of miles of reefs, atolls, caves, coral patches, and coastline harbor entire alien worlds to explore, as do shipwrecks with centuries of secrets.

Belizean dive stories often involve dolphins, swarms of horse-eye jacks and massive tarpon, or dozens of spotted eagle rays at a time. Some divers go strictly to photograph the Dr. Seussian coral life or to get that elusive whale shark shot in March, April, or May.

Dive shops exist everywhere there is access to the reef and cayes in Belize – this means San Pedro and Caye Caulker, Belize City, Sittee River, Placencia – and then there are more shops and dive resorts scattered throughout the islands and atolls. Options are much more limited in Punta Gorda, which means you'll have the ocean to yourself when diving the southern hook of the barrier reef.

No matter which path to diving you choose, your first order of business is choosing a **dive shop.** You'll have no trouble finding a shop; in fact, you may have a difficult time choosing between so many options. In most cases, prices are more or less the same between shops, but it pays to do a bit of comparing. Expect to pay US$60-75 for a two-tank fun dive, possibly extra for gear rental or for longer boat trips. Know that the bigger a shop's boats, the more comfortable a long ride will be, but also the bigger your group will be, a serious consideration; small groups (6-10) ensure more personalized attention from your dive masters. Also, to beat the crowds at more popular sights, choose a dive shop with early start times.

BEST DIVE SITES

Phenomenal dives are abundant up and down the entire **Belize Barrier Reef,** which begins off the northern tip of Ambergris Caye and extends southward to the Sapodilla Cayes in Belize's southernmost reaches. Except for a few overused or storm-damaged spots, the barrier reef's coral is in excellent condition.

Beyond the reef are Belize's three amazing atolls:

- **Glover's Reef:** Belize's southernmost atoll, Glover's Reef is a ring of beautiful coral reef that spans nearly 80 square miles.

- **Turneffe Islands:** Not far from Belize City, the Turneffe Islands are a diver's dream, encompassing some of Belize's not-to-be-missed dive sites, such as The Elbow and Gales Point.

- **Lighthouse Reef:** Accessible from Belize City, Ambergris Caye, and Caye Caulker, the Lighthouse Reef Atoll is a favorite diving destination – home to the famous **Blue Hole** and **Half Moon Caye Wall,** where the diving is second to none.

dive shop on Ambergris Caye

Belize has the largest barrier reef in the western hemisphere.

While these dive sites might top the list, know that your options include literally hundreds of other sites. Of particular note is the diving in **southern Belize,** where you'll find some of Belize's most exclusive and remote dive opportunities amid the Sapodilla Cayes.

CERTIFICATION COURSES

Courses accredited by the **Professional Association of Diving Instructors (PADI)** and **National Association of Underwater Instructors (NAUI)** are offered at most dive shops in Belize. Expect to pay about US$250–400 for **Open Water** or **Advanced** certification courses. Belize diving prices are roughly on par with diving prices in Roatán in the Honduran Bay Islands, but more expensive than they are in Utila, another of the Bay Islands.

INTRODUCTORY DIVE COURSES

You're in Belize on vacation and want to dive – but you don't want to spend four precious days (and US$400) getting certified. What can you do? How about a **"resort course"** – a one-day introduction to scuba. Also called "discovery" courses, these usually include one tank of air and cost around US$75.

LIVE-ABOARD DIVE BOATS

If you want to guarantee the most diving time possible, several live-aboard vessels based in Belize City are designed for serious divers but can also accommodate an avid diver's companion if he or she is a sea lover or a casual angler. Your own luxury hotel and chef travel with you to some of the best diving spots in the tropical world. Most of the rates are weekly and all-inclusive (plus a few hundred dollars of extra charges, of course). Options include the **Belize Aggressor III** (120 feet, U.S. tel. 800/348-2628, www.aggressor.com, US$2,295) and Dancer Fleet's **Sun Dancer II** (138 feet, U.S. tel. 800/932-6237, www.dancerfleet.com, US$1,895-2,595).

Many boats, including Ras Creek's *Heritage Cruze,* based in Caye Caulker, catch and prepare fresh *ceviche* while you are snorkeling.

Western Highway and catch another ride to San Ignacio in Cayo District. Continue through town and stay at the Trek Stop, where you should have time for a round of disc golf and a tour of the butterfly farm at Tropical Wings Nature Center before bedtime.

Bullet Tree Falls via canoe or kayak—plan on five hours of easy paddling and mellow riffles down the Mopan River; when you arrive, have a cabin and meal waiting for you at the Cohune Palms Cabañas or Parrot Nest Lodge.

Day 4

Spend the morning at the Xunantunich archaeological site, climbing pyramids and convening with the spirits. In the afternoon, arrange a pickup in Benque Viejo to take you to one of the funky places down the Hydro Road: Martz Farm or Chechem Ha.

Day 5

Spend the day hiking, horseback riding, caving, and spouting poetry inspired by the awesome views of the upper Macal River Gorge. Spend a second night in your tent, cabin, or waterfall-enhanced treehouse.

Day 6

Get a ride back to Benque, then travel to

trail to a sacred cave

Garifuna drummers

Day 7

Spend at least a night at Barton Creek Outpost, a campsite near the entrance to Barton Creek Cave with one of the country's best swimming holes; then catch a southbound bus in Belmopan and get off in the village of Armenia for a cozy night with a mestizo family.

Day 8

Make your way to Hopkins for a few beers and a Garifuna drumming workshop. You'll likely have to spend a few hours in Dangriga on the way, so feel free to get sidetracked out to Tobacco Caye for a night or two.

Day 9

Spend the day hiking the trails and splashing in the waterfalls of Mayflower Bocawina National Park, one of Belize's newest national parks.

Day 10

Continue south to Punta Gorda and check into one of several lovely new accommodations, such as Hickatee Cottages or Coral House Inn. From Punta Gorda, go on trips into the countryside and cayes, or arrange a homestay in the hills before dining on a vegetarian feast at Gomier's Restaurant.

Days 11-13

Go deep into the Toledo bush, living among the Maya or Garifuna. Hire guides and listen to stories, music, and the river. On the last day, transfer back to Punta Gorda. You can do this through the homestay program or based at one of the backabush accommodations in the area.

Day 14

Fly back north to Philip Goldson International Airport and begin writing your memoirs as your return flight takes off.

▶ BIRDING IN BELIZE

Because of its extensive protected forests, varied wetland habitat, and location on a major migratory route, Belize is a major hotspot for both novice and experienced birders, who arrive throughout the year and from all over the world. The Belize Audubon Society (BAS, www.belizeaudubon.org) reports 587 recorded bird species in Belize, about 20 percent of which are migrants from other parts of North America. BAS helps manage many of the country's wildlife reserves and maintains bird checklists for these areas. Always check with BAS for the latest sightings, and you can purchase several bird guides in the central BAS office in the historic Fort George area of Belize City.

A number of lodges throughout the country cater specifically to birders. A sure sign is if they have downloadable bird checklists on their websites. Another is whether or not they employ guides; many inland resorts have brilliant Belizean birders on their staff for daily sunrise walks and other activities. Belizean park rangers also generally have excellent bird identification skills, notably Israel Manzanero, who works at Blue Hole National Park.

Twitchers on a serious mission can choose from several bird-centric tour operators; this is for those who'd rather let someone else (someone who knows where the birds are) handle the logistics of a countrywide tour, so you can keep your eyes glued to those binocs. The Tut brothers lead multiday birding tours throughout the country. Find them at Paradise Expeditions, based at the Crystal Paradise Resort in Cayo.

Bring binoculars; wear boots, a lightweight long-sleeved shirt, and lightweight trousers; and carry a field guide. *Birds of Belize*, by H. Lee Jones, illustrated by Dana Gardner, is the most comprehensive guide available, but not the most practical book to carry in the field. *Peterson Field Guides: Mexican Birds* is an excellent choice, and National Geographic's *Field Guide to the Birds of North America* is a good companion guide.

For details about species you're likely to encounter, or to participate in the annual Christmas Bird Count, consult the Belize Audubon Society's website, particularly the "Birds of Belize" section. These are the most popular spots for birders:

• **Crooked Tree Wildlife Sanctuary:** Designated a wetland of international importance, the mosaic of wetland habitats attracts a spectacular variety of wading birds, especially during the dry season (Mar.–May). This is the last Central American stronghold of the jabiru stork—the tallest flying bird in the Americas. The surrounding landscape hosts Yucatán endemics.

bird-watchers in Lamanai Archaeological Zone

BUTTERFLY SAFARI

A number of butterfly "farms" or "ranches" have been built around Belize, and a visit to one is always a pleasant, educational, and colorful experience. Many began as export businesses, to raise butterflies for foreign zoos and classrooms, but now feature screened-in rooms where you'll see the creatures fluttering about your head as you walk through.

Butterfly farms pay as much attention to the plants that provide the larval food as to the pupae and winged creatures. Different species often have different tastes and needs. Depending on where you are in the country, you'll see the intense **blue morpho** as well as the **white morpho,** which is white but shot with iridescent blue. Three species of the **owl butterfly** (genus *Caligo*) love to come and lunch on the overripe fruit. You'll also see tiny **heliconians** and large yellow and white **pierids,** among many, many more.

A butterfly goes from tiny teardroplike egg to colorful caterpillar, to pupae, and then graceful adult. Butterfly farms gather breeding populations of typical Belizean species in the pupal stage, and then the pupae are carefully hung in what is called an "emerging cage" with a simulated jungle atmosphere – hot and humid (not hard to do in Belize). A short time later they shed their pupal skin, and a tiny bit of Belize flutters away to the amazement and joy of anyone who happens to be present.

Depending on the species, butterflies live anywhere from seven days to six weeks. If you plan to visit a farm, or to go into the rainforest on a butterfly safari, you'll see much more butterfly activity on a sunny day than on an overcast day. If it's raining, forget it!

In many areas of Belize, butterfly populations have been almost totally depleted for many reasons, including habitat destruction (from logging, for instance) and changing farming practices, particularly the use of pesticides. Belize's steamy marshes, swamps, and rainforest have been a natural breeding ground for beautiful butterflies for thousands of years and hopefully will continue to be so.

In the Cayo District, **Green Hills Butterfly Ranch and Botanical Collections** on the Mountain Pine Ridge Road is a butterfly breeding, educational, and interpretive center. Another readily accessible butterfly farm, with one of the highest numbers of species, is **Tropical Wings Nature Center,** just outside San José Succotz. There's an excellent interpretive center, a guided tour, and a disc golf course and café for when you've finished. Down the road from Tropical Wings, **The Lodge at Chaa Creek** has the **Blue Morpho Butterfly Breeding Center.** Naturalists gladly explain the various stages of life the butterfly goes through, with a wonderful little flight room.

In Punta Gorda, you'll find a small but diverse butterfly reserve at the entrance road to the **Cockscomb Basin Wildlife Sanctuary.** It's right across the creek from the women's craft co-op in Maya Centre. And there is a treat for butterfly lovers who stay at **Hickatee Cottages.**

blue morpho butterfly

Lamanai Archaeological Zone

- **Lamanai Archaeological Zone:** Enjoy the extensive river and lagoon sections as you travel to and from the ruins of Lamanai; look for northern jacanas and pygmy kingfishers. All four species of trogon found in Belize can be seen here, along with many woodcreepers and woodpeckers. Be sure to watch for both blue-crowned and tody motmots, which burrow into unexcavated ruins to nest.

- **Mountain Pine Ridge:** Overlapping microclimates and habitats are favored by several species that are difficult to find elsewhere, including lovely cotinga, ocellated turkey, and the rare orange-breasted falcon, which nests near Thousand Foot Falls. At the Caracol ruins, you can spot a keel-billed motmot, especially in March and April.

- **Cockscomb Basin Wildlife Sanctuary:** Belize's preeminent birding destination offers a good introduction to neotropical birding and a shot at a "big day"—spotting 100 species in a single day. Listen for the early morning call of tinamous and watch parrots

and toucans fly overhead; around the visitor center and hiking trails expect to see woodcreepers, honeycreepers, manakins, tanagers, orioles, and much more.

- **The Northern Cayes:** The mangroves and littoral forests of Caye Caulker and Ambergris Caye are disappearing, but these islands are still a stopover for many neotropical migrants, plus they are home to the black catbird and white-crowned pigeon. Be sure to make a pilgrimage to the red-footed booby colony on Half Moon Caye National Monument.

- **Red Bank:** This small Maya village in southern Belize is home to an annual gathering of over 100 scarlet macaws (Jan.–Mar.). The birds feast on the fruits of the annatto tree, which are also used in making red recado seasoning. Swallow-tailed and plumbeous kites can be seen over the peaks around the village during the dry season.

- **Aguacaliente Wildlife Sanctuary:** In Toledo District, near the village of Laguna, this reserve features breeding colonies of unique wading birds.

BELIZE DISTRICT

Home of the Maya archaeological site of Altun Ha, the cashews of Crooked Tree, and the baboons of Burrell Boom, Belize District includes the low-simmering commotion of Belize City, as well as a number of nearby cayes and protected areas. This wide, low coastal region of mangroves, pine savanna, marshes, and cayes is the most populated district in the country, encompassing nearly a quarter of all Belizeans, most of them clustered on a tiny peninsula jutting into the Caribbean (on land partly composed, some say, of centuries worth of rum bottles).

Belize City is the hub of the nation, only a couple hours' traveling time from anywhere in the country. Because of this access, Belize City is where you'll find the headquarters of the bus lines, rental car agencies, and airlines, as well as water taxis to the cayes. It used to be the capital of Belize, but the government now sits inland, in Belmopan.

Belize City is worth a day for its handful of attractions and restaurants. Many excellent diving, snorkeling, and marine reserves are a short boat ride away from downtown Belize City, where there are a couple of dive shops. But for those wishing to avoid the bustle, traffic, and rising crime rate of the city, there are accommodations in the farther reaches of Belize District on par with many more well-known upland or island resorts.

PLANNING YOUR TIME

A self-guided daytime walking tour of Belize City is a must for anyone interested in the

HIGHLIGHTS

◖ Museum of Belize: Housed in the old prison, this museum has rotating exhibitions and an incredible stamp collection that make it worth a visit (page 32).

◖ Fort George Area: Take a stroll through this breezy neighborhood with its ramshackle colonial homes and old wooden hotels (page 35).

◖ Old Belize and Cucumber Beach: Go for a meal, and stay for the beach, boats, waterslide, and zip line. This entertainment center is a few miles down the Western Highway from Belize City and features a historical heritage tour and museum (page 35).

◖ Altun Ha Ruins: Head north to this ancient Maya trading center, the most extensively excavated ruins in Belize (page 47).

◖ The Community Baboon Sanctuary: The area is thick with black howler monkeys around a few simple Creole villages. This community-managed ecotourism venture offers an adventurous menu of wildlife hikes and canoe trips (page 50).

◖ Crooked Tree Wildlife Sanctuary: Drive an hour north of Belize City, to this habitat for hundreds of resident and migratory birds, for a full day of birding and a boat tour (page 53).

LOOK FOR ◖ TO FIND RECOMMENDED SIGHTS, ACTIVITIES, DINING, AND LODGING.

bigger picture of the country—even if you have only a few hours between bus and boat connections. You can see all the sights in one rushed day or two relaxed ones. Although Belize City doesn't have the dining scene of some of the touristy parts of the country, there are enough decent restaurants and many cheap local eateries to get you by.

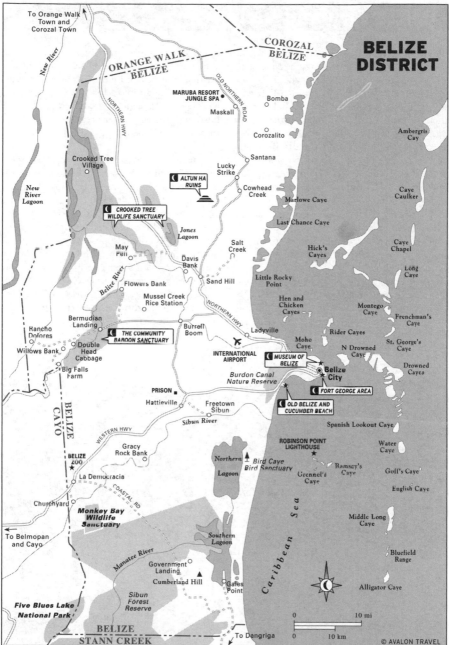

To Orange Walk
Town and
Corozal Town

New River

ORANGE WALK
BELIZE

CfOROZAL
BELIZE

BELIZE
DISTRICT

NORTHERN HWY

OLD NORTHERN ROAD

MARUBA RESORT
JUNGLE SPA

Maskall

Bomba

Corozalito

Santana

Ambergris
Cay

Crooked Tree
Village

New
River
Lagoon

ALTUN HA
RUINS

Lucky
Strike

Cowhead
Creek

Marlowe Caye

Caye
Caulker

CROOKED TREE
WILDLIFE SANCTUARY

Last Chance Caye

Jones
Lagoon

Salt
Creek

Hick's
Cayes

Caye
Chapel

May
Pen

Davis
Bank

Belize River

Flowers Bank

Sand Hill

Little Rocky
Point

Long
Caye

Mussel Creek
Rice Station

Hen and
Chicken
Cayes

Montego
Caye

Frenchman's
Caye

Bermudian
Landing

Burrell
Boom

NORTHERN HWY

Ladyville

Rider Cayes

St. George's
Caye

Rancho
Dolores

THE COMMUNITY
BABOON SANCTUARY

Moho
Caye

N Drowned
Caye

Willows Bank

Double
Head
Cabbage

INTERNATIONAL
AIRPORT

MUSEUM OF
BELIZE

Belize
City

Drowned
Cayes

Big Falls
Farm

BELIZE CAYO

PRISON

Hattieville

Freetown
Sibun

Sibun River

Burdon Canal
Nature Reserve

OLD BELIZE AND
CUCUMBER BEACH

FORT GEORGE AREA

Spanish Lookout Caye

WESTERN HWY

BELIZE
ZOO

Gracy
Rock Bank

La Democracia

COASTAL RD

Churchyard

Monkey Bay
Wildlife
Sanctuary

Northern
Lagoon

Bird Caye
Bird Sanctuary

ROBINSON POINT
LIGHTHOUSE

Grennel's
Caye

Ramsey's
Caye

Water
Caye

Golf's Caye

English Caye

Middle Long
Caye

To Belmopan
and Cayo

Manatee River

Southern
Lagoon

Caribbean Sea

Bluefield
Range

Government
Landing

Cumberland Hill

Gales
Point

Alligator Caye

Five Blues Lake
National Park

Sibun
Forest
Reserve

BELIZE
STANN CREEK

To Dangriga

0   10 mi

0   10 km

© AVALON TRAVEL

Belize City and Vicinity

Okay, so "city" might be stretching it, but there is no doubt that the biggest concentration of Belizeans in the world (about 70,000) live on a relatively small peninsula. Belizeans throughout the country refer to Belize City, their former capital, as "Belize," which can be disorienting until you get used to it. And while there are no high-rises, only three traffic lights, and more faded paint and rotten wood than you'd expect, Belize City is an exciting cluster of cultures throbbing under tropical sun, wind, and rain.

The town straddles Haulover Creek (named when cattle were attached to one another by a rope around the horns and hauled across) and sprawls loosely north to the Belize River and the international airport. For tourists, Belize City is certainly no Caribbean paradise—not by a long shot. Indeed, the banks of the Haulover Creek, meandering through the middle of the city, are often foul. The city is run-down and, though perched on the edge of the Caribbean, it is without beaches (except the artificial one at Old Belize, just outside town). Antiquated clapboard buildings on stilts—weathered, tilted, and streaked with age—line narrow streets. In other areas, the old buildings are slowly being replaced by uninspired concrete boxes.

The people of Belize City are friendly, though the hucksters who prey on cruise ship passengers are sometimes a little too friendly. In general, Belize City residents are better off and more optimistic than those in other developing world cities—in large part because Belize City is *so* much smaller. It has its problems (from petty gang crime to government corruption), but it doesn't have sprawling slums and shantytowns like other cities in Central America. Schools and uniformed students are plentiful, little shops are everywhere (often referred to locally as the "Hindu," "Arab," or

Belize City pedestrian traffic

© JOSHUA BERMAN

"Chinese" store, based on the ancestry of the proprietors), and some of the simplest bars are gathering places for truly interesting and important people.

ORIENTATION

The old **Swing Bridge** spans Haulover Creek, connecting Belize City's "Northside" to its "Southside," and it is the most distinct landmark in the city. North of the creek, Queen and Front Streets are the crucial thoroughfares. On this side of the bridge, you'll find the **Caye Caulker Water Taxi Terminal,** an important transportation and information hub. Across Front Street are the post office and library (with a quiet sitting room). Walking east on Front Street (toward the sea), you'll find several art galleries and shops before you come to "Tourism Village," the hopeful, Disneyesque name for the cruise ship passenger arrival area. The minimalls and decorations that garnish this area of docks and shops are contrived and overpriced, and owned in part by the cruise ship companies. The rest of the adjoining Fort George historic area and the lighthouse are, in contrast, quite genuine and interesting to see.

On the Swing Bridge's south end, Regent and Albert Streets make a V-shaped split and are the core of the city's banking and shopping activity. There are a few old government buildings here, too, as well as Battlefield (Central) Park and a couple of guesthouses. Southside has a seedier reputation than Northside, which is monitored more closely by the police.

SIGHTS

An early morning stroll through the weathered buildings of Belize City, starting in the Fort George Lighthouse area and toward the Swing Bridge, gives you a feel for this seaside population center. This is when people are rushing off to work, kids are spiffed up on their way to school, and folks are out doing their daily shopping. The streets are crammed with small shops, a stream of pedestrians, and lots of traffic.

There are decent art shops and galleries in

CRIME AND THE CITY

Like other Central American countries, Belize has its share of problems with drugs, gangs, and violent street crime. Because of its extremely low population, however – 70,000 inhabitants, compared to millions in most Central American capitals – Belize City's problems are nowhere near as severe as those of El Salvador, Honduras, and Guatemala's cities. Still, over the last several years, violent crime has increased in Belize City, mostly in the form of petty theft, beatings, stabbings, and shootings. Much of the violent gang culture is imported from the United States by deported Belizean youths.

Most – but not all – violent crime occurs in downtown Belize City or deep in the Southside part of the city, many blocks away from the traditional walking paths of tourists, but occasional sprees have occurred throughout the city and in broad daylight. Use the same common sense you would apply in any city in the world. Before you venture out, have a clear idea of how to get where you're going and ask a local Belizean – like your hotel desk clerk or a restaurant waiter – whether your plan is reasonable.

The government has taken steps to battle crime, including stiffer enforcement of the law and deployment of a force of tourist police, recognizable by their khaki shirts and green pants.

At night, don't walk if you are at all unsure; taxis are plentiful, but only those with a green license plate should be considered. In fact, most Belizeans have a personal taxi driver whom they know and trust. Ask if they would be willing to call for you and get the "Belizean price."

Don't flash money, jewelry, or other temptations, and if threatened, hand them over. Report all crimes to the local police and your country's embassy.

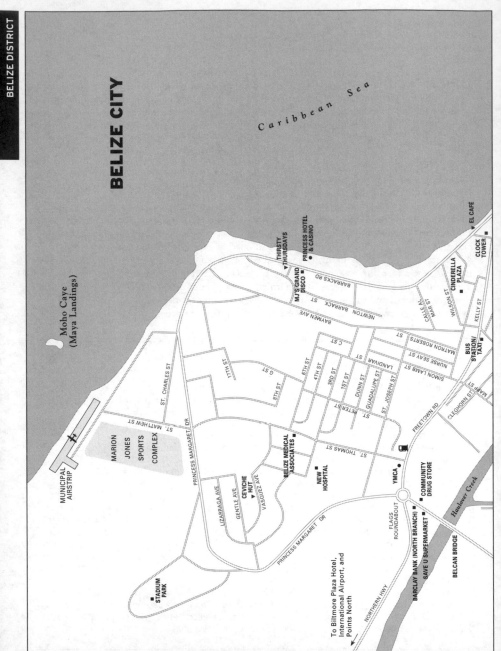

BELIZE CITY

Caribbean Sea

Moho Caye
(Maya Landings)

MUNICIPAL
AIRSTRIP

MARION
JONES
SPORTS
COMPLEX

ST. MATTHEW ST

ST. CHARLES ST

PRINCESS MARGARET DR

17TH ST

8TH ST

G ST

6TH ST

4TH ST

3RD ST

1ST ST

C ST

PETER ST

DUNN ST

GUADALUPE ST

ST. JOSEPH ST

NURSE SEAY ST

MATRON ROBERTS ST

SIMON LAMB ST

LANDIVAR ST

NEWTON BARRACK ST

BAYMEN AVE

CALLE AL MAR ST

WILSON ST

KELLY ST

MAR ST

BARRACKS RD

MA'S GRAND
DISCO

THIRSTY
THURSDAYS

PRINCESS HOTEL
& CASINO

EL CAFÉ

CLOCK
TOWER

CINDERELLA
PLAZA

BUS
STATION/
TAXI

FREETOWN RD

CLEGHORN ST

MARY ST

LIZARRAGA AVE

GENTLE AVE

VASQUEZ AVE

CEVICHE
HUT

BELIZE MEDICAL
ASSOCIATES

NEW
HOSPITAL

ST. THOMAS ST

YMCA

COMMUNITY
DRUG STORE

FLAGS
ROUNDABOUT

BARCLAY BANK (NORTH BRANCH)

SAVE U SUPERMARKET

BELCAN BRIDGE

Haulover Creek

STADIUM
PARK

PRINCESS MARGARET DR

To Biltmore Plaza Hotel,
International Airport, and
Points North

NORTHERN HWY

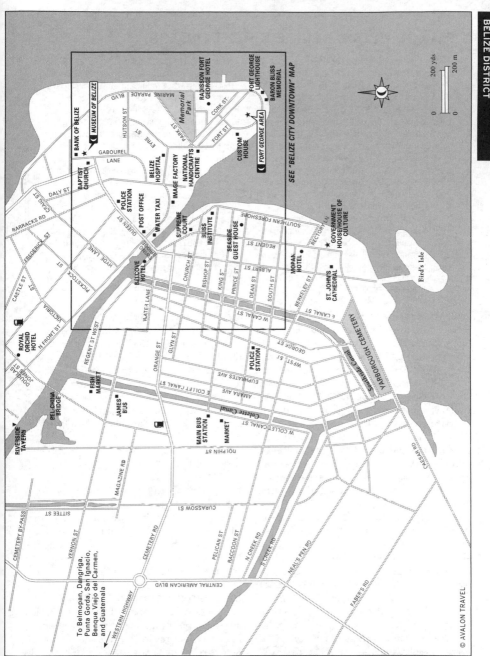

© AVALON TRAVEL

BARON BLISS, BELIZE'S BENEFACTOR

Henry Edward Ernest Victor Bliss, also known as the "Fourth Baron Bliss of the Former Kingdom of Portugal," was born in the county of Buckingham in England. He first sailed into the harbor of Belize in 1926, though he was too ill to go ashore because of food poisoning he had contracted while visiting Trinidad. Bliss spent several months aboard his yacht, the *Sea King*, in the harbor, fishing in Belizean waters. Although he never got well enough to go ashore, Bliss learned to love the country from the sea, and its habitués – the fishermen and officials in the harbor – all treated him with great respect and friendliness. On the days that he was able only to languish on deck, he made every effort to learn about the small country. He was apparently so impressed with what he learned and the people he met that before his death, he drew up

a will that established a trust of nearly US$2 million for projects to benefit the people of Belize.

More than US$1 million in interest from the trust has been used for the erection of the Bliss Institute, Bliss School of Nursing, and Bliss Promenade, plus contributions to the Belize City water supply, the Corozal Town Board and Health Clinic, and land purchase for the building of Belmopan.

An avid yachtsman, Bliss stipulated that money be set aside for a regatta to be held in Belizean waters, now a focal point of the gala Baron Bliss Day celebrations each March, an important holiday that is now called National Heroes and Benefactors Day. The baron's white granite tomb is at the point of Fort George in Belize City, guarded by the Bliss Lighthouse and the occasional pair of late-night Belizean lovers.

and around the Fort George area and Tourism Village, including the **Fine Arts Gallery** (Fort Street Tourism Village, tel. 503/752-8634, www.fineartsgallerybelize.com, 9:30 A.M.–4 P.M. Mon.–Fri.), on Front Street, which has a nice collection of paintings and crafts. Inside the Fort George compound is **Rachel's Art Gallery**, which carries prints and original art by various artists, including Rachel herself. Around the corner, next to Memorial Park, look for the **National Handicrafts Center** (8 A.M.–5 P.M. Mon.–Fri., 8 A.M.–4 P.M. Sat.), an official Chamber of Commerce–sponsored shop with fine crafts purchased directly from artisans around the country.

As you cross to the Southside, you'll encounter even more traffic and local color. Vendors sell fruits, vegetables, clothing, incense, jewelry, and cold drinks along the southeast side of Swing Bridge. Bliss Promenade skirts the waterfront and brings you to the **Bliss Center for Performing Arts** (Southern Foreshore, tel. 501/227-2110), which hosts social functions, seminars, arts festivals, and drama series. It is also the location of a theater, museum, and library, as well as the Institute of Creative Arts.

(Museum of Belize

Housed in the old city jail (Her Majesty's Prison was built in 1857 and served as the nation's only prison until the 1990s), this small but worthwhile museum (8 Gabourel Ln., tel. 501/223-4524, 8 A.M.–5 P.M. Mon.–Thurs., till 4 P.M. on Fri., US$5) includes city history artifacts, indigenous relics, and rotating displays, such as Insects of Belize, Maya Jade, and Pirates of Belize. Philatelists and bottle collectors will love the 150 years of stamps and bottles on display.

Supreme Court Building

On Regent Street, in front of Battlefield (Central) Park, this structure is decorated with a graceful white metal filigree stairway that leads to the long veranda overlooking the square. An antiquated town clock is perched atop the white clapboard building.

St. John's Anglican Cathedral

On South Albert Street at Regent Street, this lovely old building, one of the few typically British structures in the city, is surrounded by well-kept green lawns and next to a lively

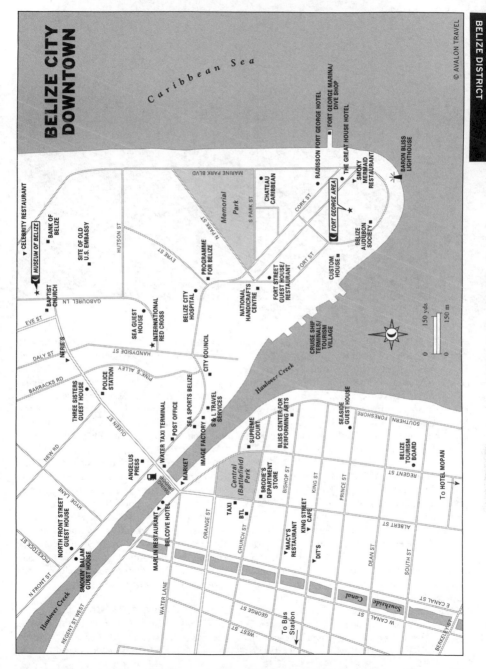

BELIZE CITY DOWNTOWN

© AVALON TRAVEL

Caribbean Sea

- CELEBRITY RESTAURANT
- MUSEUM OF BELIZE
- BANK OF BELIZE
- SITE OF OLD U.S. EMBASSY
- BAPTIST CHURCH
- SEA GUEST HOUSE
- INTERNATIONAL RED CROSS
- THREE SISTERS GUEST HOUSE
- POLICE STATION
- WATER TAXI TERMINAL
- POST OFFICE
- SEA SPORTS BELIZE
- ANGELUS PRESS
- NORTH FRONT STREET GUEST HOUSE
- SMOKIN' BALAM GUEST HOUSE
- MARLIN RESTAURANT
- BELCOVE HOTEL
- IMAGE FACTORY
- MARKET
- S & L TRAVEL SERVICES
- CITY COUNCIL
- BELIZE CITY HOSPITAL
- PROGRAMME FOR BELIZE
- NATIONAL HANDICRAFTS CENTRE
- FORT STREET GUEST HOUSE/ RESTAURANT
- CHATEAU CARIBBEAN
- RADISSON FORT GEORGE HOTEL
- FORT GEORGE MARINA/ DIVE SHOP
- THE GREAT HOUSE HOTEL
- SMOKY MERMAID RESTAURANT
- BARON BLISS LIGHTHOUSE
- FORT GEORGE AREA
- BELIZE AUDUBON SOCIETY
- CUSTOM HOUSE
- CRUISE SHIP TERMINALS/ TOURISM VILLAGE
- SUPREME COURT
- BLISS CENTER FOR PERFORMING ARTS
- SEASIDE GUEST HOUSE
- BELIZE TOURISM BOARD
- BRODIE'S DEPARTMENT STORE
- TAXI
- BTL
- MACY'S RESTAURANT
- KING STREET CAFE
- DIT'S

MARINE PARK BLVD
Memorial Park
S PARK ST
CORK ST
FORT ST
N PARK ST
HUTSON ST
EYRE ST
GABOUREL LN
EVE ST
NERIE'S
DALY ST
BARRACKS RD
NEW RD
QUEEN ST
HYDE LANE
N FRONT ST
PICKSTOCK ST
REGENT ST WEST
WATER LANE
WEST ST
GEORGE ST
N FRONT ST
PINK'S ALLEY
HANDYSIDE ST
SWING BRIDGE
ORANGE ST
CHURCH ST
BISHOP ST
KING ST
PRINCE ST
REGENT ST
ALBERT ST
DEAN ST
SOUTH ST
SOUTHERN FORESHORE
Central (Battlefield) Park
Haulover Creek
Southside Canal
W CANAL ST
E CANAL ST
BERKELEY ST

To HOTEL MOPAN →
To Bus Station ↓

150 yds
150 m

0
0

© JOSHUA BERMAN

view of Belize City, from the Swing Bridge

schoolyard. In 1812, slaves helped erect this graceful piece of architecture, using bricks brought as ballast on sailing ships from Europe. Several Mosquito Coast kings from Nicaragua and Honduras were crowned in this cathedral with ultimate pomp and grandeur; the last was in 1815. It's usually okay to walk right in and take a moment; put something in the donation box on your way out.

Government House and House of Culture

Behind St. John's Cathedral, at the southern end of Regent Street and facing the Southern Foreshore, is the House of Culture museum in the old Government House (www.nichbelize. org, 8:30 A.M.–4:30 P.M. Mon.–Fri., US$5), which, before Hurricane Hattie and the ensuing construction of Belmopan, was the home and office of the governor general, the official representative of the Queen of England. (Today's governor general can be found in Belmopan, at Belize House.) For a long time these grounds were used as a guesthouse for visiting VIPs and a venue for social functions. Queen Elizabeth and Prince Philip stayed here in 1994. The elegant wooden buildings (built 1812–1814) are said to have been designed by acclaimed English architect Christopher Wren. Sprawling lawns and wind-brushed palms facing the sea surround government House; outdoor functions and ceremonies are still held here.

Wander through the wood structure and enjoy the period furniture, silverware, and glassware collections—plus a selection of paintings and sculptures by modern Belizean artists. There are special events, concerts, and art shows throughout the year. Stroll the grounds, on the water's edge, and enjoy the solitude. Also on-site is the headquarters of the National Kriol Council, whose resource center you may find interesting; it includes a few Kriol language phrasebooks for sale.

Luba Garifuna Museum

This small house museum on Jasmine Street showcases Garifuna culture and history. Admission is US$5 and includes a guided tour

(St. Martin Depores area, tel. 501/202-4331, 8 A.M.–5 P.M. Mon.–Sat.).

ℂ Fort George Area

In general, the Fort George area, a peninsula ringed by Marine Parade Boulevard and Fort Street, is one of the most pleasant in Belize City (especially on days when it is *not* flooded with thousands of cruise ship passengers and their associated entourages of taxi drivers and would-be tour guides). Meander the neighborhood and you'll pass some impressive homes and buildings, including a few charming old guesthouses. The **Baron Bliss Memorial** and **Fort George Lighthouse** stand guard over it all.

The sea breeze can be pleasant here, and you can glimpse cayes and ships offshore. Once you round the point, the road becomes Marine Parade and runs past the modern Radisson Fort George Hotel and **Memorial Park,** a grassy salute to the 40 Belizeans who lost their lives in World War I. The old U.S. Embassy sits at the end of the block on the right; the house was built in New England, dismantled, and transported to Belize as ship's ballast. It was reconstructed in 1840 and served as the U.S. Embassy until 2006, when operations were moved to Belmopan.

From the Radisson Fort George dock, you'll get a good view of the harbor. Originally this was Fort George Island; the strait separating the island from the mainland (the site of today's Memorial Park) was filled in during the early 1920s.

The Image Factory Shop and Gallery

A few doors up from the Swing Bridge, the **Image Factory Art Foundation** (91 N. Front St., www.imagefactorybelize.com, 9 A.M.–5 P.M. Mon.–Fri., 9 A.M.–noon Sat.) is the official pulse of the Belizean art and literary scene. In addition to offering the best book selection in the country (both local authors and some foreign titles), the shop offers gallery space for semiregular art events, usually held on Friday evenings at happy hour.

ℂ Old Belize and Cucumber Beach

In addition to Cucumber Beach, a swimming lagoon, a zip line, a waterslide, and other water sports, Old Belize (Western Highway, tel. 501/222-4153, www.oldbelize.com. US$2.50 museum tour, US$20 zip line) also features the impressive **Cultural and Historical Center** (10 A.M.–8:30 P.M. daily), a 45-minute tour through a thousand years of Belizean history. It's kind of like a walk-through museum, but with all kinds of fascinating relics and simulations. Some of the displays from the former Maritime Museum are now housed here and include models of boats used in Belize, as well as photos and bios of local fishers and boat builders. On cruise ship days (usually Tuesday and Thursday), a Belizean cabaret showcases the dances and songs of Belize's cultural groups. There's also a boat marina, a helipad, and an excellent restaurant, bar, and grill (11 A.M.–10 P.M. daily). It's five miles out of the city on the Western Highway and gets more Belizean clients than foreign tourists; it's definitely worth the trip. A snorkel pool containing ocean water, a manmade reef, and exotic fish is being planned. Bring a bathing suit and plan to spend half a day or more.

RECREATION
Sportfishing

Fantastic river, reef, flats, and deep-sea fishing is available from Belize City. You can fish for tarpon in the morning and bonefish in the afternoon. Deep-sea opportunities include mackerel, wahoo, kingfish, and bill fish. Most lodges in the area can set up fishing trips, or contact fishing guide and local expert **Richard Young** (tel. 501/624-3510, richardyoungjr@yahoo. com). **Sea Sports Belize** (tel. 501/223-5505) also runs professional custom sportfishing trips to stunning sights offshore.

Diving and Snorkeling

The Belize Barrier Reef is less than 30 minutes away and offers excellent wall dives and idyllic snorkeling. Turneffe Islands Atoll and Lighthouse Atoll are one and two hours away, respectively, by boat. These sites are perfect for anyone trapped in the city on business, or for tourists staying in Belize City. There are also excellent manatee trips available, as well as outings to Swallow Caye Marine Reserve.

Belize City has two dive shops: **Sea Sports Belize** (83 N. Front St., tel. 501/223-5505, www.seasportsbelize.com) is across from the post office, two buildings east of the Swing Bridge; Sea Sports has been in business 15 years and is a PADI 5-Star Instructor Development Center, offering equipment sales, scuba instruction, and daily dive, snorkel, fishing, and manatee encounter trips. They use small boats and take groups of no more than eight people per guide. They can also arrange overnight packages with lodging at St. George's Caye, Belize's first capital.

Hugh Parkey's Dive Connection (tel. 501/223-5086 or 501/223-4526, U.S. tel. 888/223-5403, www.belizediving.com) is based at the Radisson Fort George Marina and offers all manner of trips and certification courses. Hugh Parkey's has the newest and biggest day-trip boat fleet around and provides diving services for the cruise ships that call on Belize; they can arrange accommodations at nearby Spanish Lookout Caye.

Sailing

Ask at any of the tour companies, marinas, or dive shops to see what's available; there should be a decent range of charter opportunities, plus day trips and sunset cruises. Sailing/snorkeling trips to Caye Caulker (US$65) are offered, as well as sunset cruises to Ambergris Caye (US$35) on a "Belizean Authentic Gaff Rig Sloop" (tel. 501/610-3240 or 501/226-2340, ask for George Eiley).

Spectator Sports

The basketball court on Bird Isle used to be packed to the gills during local championship games. Ask around to see if any games are coming up. Catch a soccer (called "football" here) match at the stadium Sundays at 3:30 P.M. through mid-December or so. There's loud,

booming pregame music and lots of security. The stadium is across the street from the Princess Hotel on Barrack Road.

Massage and Bodywork

If you're in a bind and can't make it to any of the resort spas around the country, try some "traditional Maya therapy" at the **Oltsil Day Spa** (173 Juliet Soberanis St., tel. 501/223-7722, oltsil@yahoo.com), located in the residential Belama neighborhood, three miles north of downtown; or just go for a pedicure. Or put yourself in the hands of **Harold Zuniga,** a U.S.–trained physical therapist, masseur, and acupuncturist (85 Amara Ave., tel. 501/227-6753 or 501/604-5679, haroldzuniga@yahoo. com).

NIGHTLIFE

Thursday nights are the biggest for dancing in Belize City, followed by Fridays, especially those that fall on payday. Nightclubs come and go like hurricanes in Belize City; at the moment, the best places for dancing are **Palm Island** (on the Northern Highway) and **Club Next** (in the Princess Hotel). Serious dancing usually doesn't get started till after 11 P.M. Keep your wits about you and ask whether there have been recent shootings or stabbings in a place before selecting a club.

Ask around to find out where the best happy hours are being held—they often feature live music and free *bocas* (deep-fried something, probably). The bars at the **Radisson** (2 Marine Parade, tel. 501/223-3333), Biltmore (tel. 501/223-2302), and **Princess Hotel** (tel. 501/223-2670) are popular and provide safe, contained venues—and some of the highest drink prices in the city. **Bird's Isle** (south end of Albert St., tel. 501/207-2179) is popular for karaoke on Thursdays.

SHOPPING

There are gift shops, craft stalls, and street vendors lining Front Street near Tourism Village, as well as just south of the Swing Bridge. In the Fort George area, check out the **National Handicrafts Center** (Memorial Park,

8 A.M.–5 P.M. Mon.–Fri., 8 A.M.–4 P.M. Sat.). It's near the Radisson. There is a **flea market** at the Catholic Church on North Front Street on Saturdays at 7 A.M. Seek out the **Mennonite Furniture Market** (47 N. Front St., open Friday and Saturday during daylight hours); they won't arrange shipping, but you can get nice, basic handmade wooden furniture for reasonable prices.

Rum

At the **Traveller's Liquors Heritage Center** (Northern Highway mile 2.5, tel. 501/223-2855, www.onebarrelrum.com, 10 A.M.–6 P.M. Mon.–Fri., bar open till midnight on weekends), a couple miles north on the Northern Highway, Belize's premier rum producer offers a fun stop on your way in or out of town. Ask about the "vintage edition rum" to bring home some premium spirits. The Heritage Center consists of a historical display, a selection of their many products at bargain prices, an open-air bar and restaurant, and most importantly, a tasting bar where you can sample all 27 varieties of Traveller's Liquors rum.

ACCOMMODATIONS

Just a reminder: All room rates are for double occupancy in the high season and may or may not include the 9 percent hotel tax. If you're traveling alone or between May and November, expect discounts at some (but not all) of the following hotels.

Under US$25

The **Seaside Guest House** (3 Prince St., tel. 501/605-3786 or 501/607-8534, seaside-belize@btl.gmail.com, US$20–40) is popular among budget travelers. The couple of rooms are tiny, barely bigger than the beds, but the common spaces are good for meeting travelers from the world over. Choose from shared bunk space or private rooms. There is hot water in the community bathroom, a breeze on its ocean-facing porch, and a friendly, family-run atmosphere in this former Quaker house. Three cheap meals a day are available for US$5

© JOSHUA BERMAN

simple wooden room at the budget-friendly Seaside Guest House, Belize City

each. If you know you're coming to town, make a reservation—the Seaside can sometimes fill up fast.

On North Front Street, **(Smokin' Balam Guest House** (59 N. Front St., tel. 501/601-4510, smokinbalam2@yahoo.com, single US$15, double US$20–25) has four rooms, all airy with fans, two with private bathroom; all have access to a caged balcony over Haulover Creek as well as the nice café (meals from US$2). There's a gift shop, a pay phone, and Internet access downstairs. The guesthouse also offers weekly/monthly rates, bag storage, and a friendly atmosphere.

North Front Street Guest House (124 N. Front St., tel. 501/227-7595, US$15) offers seven spartan rooms with shared basement bath. It's a bit decrepit, but it's worth considering if the other places are booked up; eight rooms have foam mattresses and fans. The back porch overlooking the neighborhood is the high point.

US$25-50

The **(Belcove Hotel** (9 Regent St., tel. 501/227-3054, www.belcove.com, US$33–52), centrally located on the southern bank of Haulover Creek, just west of the Swing Bridge, is well taken care of, clean and bright, and easy to recommend. There are 13 rooms on three stories; options include shared or private bath with fan or the works (a/c and TV). The porch over the creek is fun to watch boats from, and cheap, lively eats are right next door at Deep Sea Marlin's Restaurant & Bar. Tour packages will keep you busy on the reef or at inland sights. The only downside is the seedy two blocks on Regent Street between the hotel and the Swing Bridge; take a cab to and from the hotel door.

Three Sisters Guest House (36 Queen St., tel. 501/207-3139 or 501/203-5729, US$32) has three big, clean rooms with private baths and fans, plus a massive, cavernous common space, all on the second floor of an old building on Queen Street. It's good for groups, friendly, and has lots of beds. Additional rooms are also for rent in an annex on Albert Street.

On the Northside, **Sea Breeze Guest House** (18 Gabourel Ln., tel. 501/203-0043 or 501/621-9651, http://seabreeze-belize.com, US$25–40) has nine small, clean rooms with fan and TV, some with shared bath, others with private baths and air-conditioning, all in a rickety building with a nice common space and an Internet café downstairs. It's very secure (behind razor wire).

US$50-100

The **(Hotel Mopan** (55 Regent St., tel. 501/227-7351, www.hotelmopan.com, US$50–65) is an old standby (built in 1973) with a very pleasant rooftop lounge area. There are 12 rooms, some with ocean view, all with tile floor, private baths, TV, free wireless Internet, minifridge, and air-conditioning. Balcony rooms are worth the extra couple of dollars. **Coningsby Inn** (76 Regent St., tel. 501/227-1566, www.coningsby-inn.com, US$60–75) has 10 rooms with TV, private baths, air-conditioning, wireless Internet, and minibars. There's a second-story bar and restaurant; breakfast is US$6. Staff can help plan your tours as well as your wedding! Both Hotel Mopan and Coningsby Inn are in Southside, near the House of Culture.

On the Northside, toward "the Flags" roundabout, the **Bakadeer Inn** (74 Cleghorn St., tel. 501/223-0659, www.bakadeerinn.com, US$55 includes breakfast) has 12 clean, well-kept rooms with comfy beds, private baths, ceiling fans, TV, and optional air-conditioning in any of the rooms (singles, doubles, triples, and quads available), as well as laundry service, a dining area, high-speed Internet access, and a cozy common space. Another functional place, run by a second-generation Belizean-Chinese family, is the **Royal Orchid Hotel** (153 New Rd., corner of Douglas Jones St., tel. 501/223-2783, US$50), a four-story hotel across the street from a pizza shop; the 21 rooms have hot and cold water, private baths, air-conditioning, and TV.

Near the Fort George Radisson, the **Chateau Caribbean** (6 Marine Parade, tel. 501/223-0800, www.chateaucaribbean.com, from

US$89) resides in an 84-year-old wooden building with wide porches, ocean breezes, and plenty of character, but it is overall in need of some TLC. The 16 rooms are well worn but have private baths, cable TV, fridges, wireless Internet, and air-conditioning. The lounge areas, restaurant, and bar have big east-facing bay windows; definitely ask for an upstairs room.

Located in Buttonwood Bay, a residential area three miles north of downtown and seven miles south of the international airport, **Villa Boscardi Bed & Breakfast** (6043 Manatee Dr., tel. 501/223-1691, www.villaboscardi.com, US$75 plus tax, includes breakfast) is an excellent option, only a block away from the sea. Its seven rooms are spotless, with white tile and white paint, bathtubs, and secure parking; the place is popular with business travelers, but it also has a honeymoon suite and dinner special. There's easy access to the international airport, and it's a short ride to downtown Belize City. Several restaurants are within walking distance, including a mellow oceanfront bar.

In the same area as Villa Boscardi, but a few blocks on the other side of the highway, in the Belama neighborhood, **D'Nest Inn** (475 Cedar St., tel. 501/223-5416, www.dnestinn.com, US$70–80) is a two-story Caribbean-style bed-and-breakfast surrounded by an English garden and run by one of the sweetest, most accommodating couples in Belize. Gaby and Oty offer five comfortable rooms decorated with Belizean antiques, all equipped with private baths, air-conditioning, TV, and wireless Internet. Wonderful multicourse breakfasts feature lots of fresh fruit and conversation with your hosts.

US$100-150

The **Princess Hotel and Casino** (Barrack Rd., tel. 501/223-2670, U.S. tel. 800/233-9784, www.princessbelize.com, from US$120) has 170 concrete rooms, all with the same air-conditioning, cable TV, and breakfast. Overall, you'll find much better value elsewhere, particularly at the B&Bs mentioned above. But if you're looking for lots of on-site entertainment,

the Princess houses Belize's only cinema and bowling alley; there's also a pool, a gift shop, a beauty salon, a conference room, bars, restaurants, and a tour desk. The on-site marina has docking facilities and water sports, and the popular casino and disco are open midnight–4 A.M.

Over US$150

The Great House (13 Cork St., tel. 501/223-3400, www.greathousebelize.com, from US$150) is a beautiful colonial-style boutique hotel, built in 1927 and recently renovated to show off its 16 unique, colorful rooms. Both tiled and hardwood floors offset the pastel walls and modern furniture; the rooms in back have more charm than the rest. Downstairs, you'll find car rental and tour services, plus a high-end real estate company, a business service center, and the Smoky Mermaid restaurant.

After World War II, visiting dignitaries from England came to Belize with plans for various agricultural projects, but they couldn't find a place to stay. As a result, the **Radisson Fort George Hotel** (2 Marine Parade, tel. 501/223-3333, U.S. tel. 800/333-3333, www.radisson.com/belizecitybz, US$139–174 plus tax) was built, and it remains the premier accommodation in town. The Radisson's 102 nicely appointed, full-service rooms sport all the amenities you'd expect, including outrageously priced minibars. This grand resort-style hotel has two swimming pools, a poolside bar, the Stone Grill (an outdoor restaurant where you grill your own meat), and fine dining and a massive breakfast buffet in St. George's Dining Room. All the restaurants host special events and happy hours. Full catering facilities and banquet rooms are available. All kinds of tours, from diving to caving to golfing, are organized right out of the hotel. Renovation in the Villa Wing includes bathrooms, a new business center, a gym, and an expansion of Le Petit Café, connecting it to the Villa Lobby with expanded seating and wireless Internet.

The Belize Biltmore Plaza (tel. 501/223-2302, U.S. tel. 800/528-1234, www.belizebiltmore.com, from US$140) is the local

Best Western branch, three miles north of the city center (seven miles south of the international airport) on the Northern Highway. The Biltmore is popular with business travelers; its 75 midsize rooms surround a garden, pool, and bar and have cable TV, phones, and modern baths. There's also Internet service, an excellent gift shop, and an overpriced dining room (US$12–20 per entrée of mediocre international food) and lounge. The hotel may be convenient for flights, but the Biltmore is walking distance to nothing, so you may feel a bit trapped.

FOOD

Belize City is not known for its fine dining. Residents' priority is a big lunch of stew chicken and beans. Expect many authentic Belizean options but only a small handful of recommended restaurants.

Cafés

Southside's **King Street Café** (King St., 6:30 A.M.–4:30 P.M. Mon.–Sat.) is a low-key Belizean espresso bar, ice-cream shop, and tamale joint, with breakfasts from under US$3. A bit more European in flavor is **Le Petit Café** (6 A.M.–8 P.M. daily), attached to the Radisson Hotel in the Fort George area; it offers delicious pastries, cakes, and ham-and-cheese croissants and possibly the best cup of freshly brewed coffee in town.

The **Smokin' Balam** (59 N. Front St., tel. 501/601-4510, 7 A.M.–5 P.M. daily) is a café, gift shop, guest house, and Internet hub. They have a comfortable little space, plus a back porch over Haulover Creek. Up on Marine Parade, **Pandora Café** (daily lunch and dinner) has all sorts of coffee drinks, smoothies, teas, Chinese and Belizean plates (US$4–10 entrée). There is also an espresso bar in the Caye Caulker Water Taxi terminal while you wait for your boat.

Belizean

The city is packed with traditional Creole eateries. **(Macy's Cafe** (18 Bishop St., tel. 501/207-3419, 11:30 A.M.–9:30 P.M. Mon.–Sat.) is one of the best, long-standing options

for Creole food at reasonable prices; Miss Macy still welcomes guests and oversees the kitchen after nearly three decades in business! Another excellent local option is **Dit's** (King St., tel. 501/227-3330, 8 A.M.–5 P.M. Mon.–Sat., 8 A.M.–3 P.M. Sun.); it's always packed with Belizeans—a good sign. **Nerie's** (corner of Queen and Daly Sts., tel. 501/223-4028, 7:30 A.M.–10 P.M. daily) was featured on the Travel Channel in a feature on traditional Belizean fare; stew chicken, fish fillets, soups, and daily specials for about US$5–9.

A fantastic Belize City neighborhood experience is a trip to the **(Ceviche Hut** (5672 Vasquez Ave., tel. 501/223-6426, 11:30 A.M.–10 P.M. Thurs.–Sat.). The proprietor, Don Enrique, works for the fishermen's cooperative, and he doesn't mess around about freshness. There's no menu, just ceviche: shout out "shrimp," "conch," or "mixed" as you take your seat (also lobster in season); about US$11 gets you a large plate that feeds three or four people. It's very popular with locals—fun and friendly. Ask Enrique to arrange a taxi to and from so you don't have to negotiate the confusing streets in this neighborhood.

Deep Sea Marlin's Restaurant & Bar (Regent St. W., 7 A.M.–9 P.M. Mon.–Sat.) is on Haulover Creek, next to the Belcove Hotel. It's a cheap and sometimes raucous fishermen's joint, with Belizean and American staples for US$4; the breakfast fry jacks are said to be out of this world. **Thirsty Thursdays** (164 Newtown Barrack St., tel. 501/223-1677, 10 A.M.–10 P.M. Mon.–Thurs., till midnight Fri.–Sat., closed) is a popular pre-party joint with a savory menu and breezy patio overlooking the ocean, just north of the Princess Hotel complex. Entrées are US$8–15, appetizers about US$6.

Bird's Isle Restaurant (tel. 501/207-2179, open Mon.–Sat. 10 A.M.–midnight) has a long reputation and an excellent waterfront location on a small islet to the south of downtown Belize City. Any taxi driver will know it, or just walk south past the Anglican Church (Albert St.) until you can't walk any more. It's a casual affair in a gorgeous outdoor setting. Large portions of local comfort dishes are served, from stew beans to hamburgers.

In Buttonwood Bay, three miles north of central Belize City, the **Seashore Restaurant** (5865 Seashore Dr., tel. 501/620-6645, 11 A.M.–10 P.M. Mon.–Sat. with a 2-hour break between lunch and dinner) has an excellent waterfront location. You sometimes see dolphins from the dock as you eat your big Belizean lunch and down a few Belikins.

International

Pepper's Pizza (tel. 501/223-5000, 11 A.M.–10 P.M. daily, US$17 large pizza) offers free delivery within city limits.

There are more authentic Chinese restaurants in Belize City than you can fathom. They all make decent, greasy dishes, but a few stand out, including **Chon Saan Palace** (1 Kelly St., tel. 501/223-3008, 11 A.M.–11:30 P.M. Mon.–Sat., 5–11:30 P.M. Sun.). In addition to Chinese standards, there are many seafood and steak dishes. **Mama Chen's** (5 Eve St., tel. 501/223-4568, 10 A.M.–6 P.M. Mon.–Sat.) is good for vegetarians, serving very inexpensive Chinese dishes (US$4–6); it's on the corner of Eve and Queen Streets. Choose from veggie chow mein, spicy beef dumplings, crispy spring rolls, sushi, and bubble tea (the "bubbles" are sweet seaweed balls that are slurped up through a thick straw). For authentic dim sum, head to **Mei Xing** (Freetown Rd.), also known as "the green place." She also has four rooms for rent (US$30 with private bath and a/c).

Belize City's small but hungry Arab community ensures a few authentic Lebanese restaurants in town: start with **Sahara Grill** (tel. 501/202-3031, 11 A.M.–3 P.M. and 5–10 P.M. Mon.–Sat., 5–10 P.M. Sun.), right across the Northern Highway from the Best Western Biltmore Hotel. They have a long menu of kabobs, hummus, and falafel (US$5–7), plus shwarma wraps and gyros for only US$4 and sheesha water pipes for US$15. There's also **Manatee Landing** (tel. 501/225-3461, noon–midnight daily, US$6), near the entrance to the international airport, about 15 minutes north of the city; watch dolphins swim by in

the Belize River while you enjoy your hummus, kabobs, burgers, or wings.

Eight white-cloth tables and a gorgeous wine list await at the only true Italian restaurant in Belize City: **La Tavernetta Italian Ice Cream and Restaurant** (2 Dolphin Dr., tel. 501/223-7998, www.latavernettabelize.com, 11:30 A.M.–9:30 P.M. Wed.–Sun.), is just north of downtown in Buttonwood Bay; the homemade ice cream is unbelievable. Pasta and meat entrées cost US$12–15.

For East Indian curries and dal, **《 Sumathi** is by far the best (31 Eve St., tel. 501/223-1172 or 501/223-3655, 11 A.M.–3 P.M. and 6–11 P.M. Tues.–Sun.). They've got a great lunch buffet for only US$5 during the week, plus air-conditioning and a large Indian menu. They offer takeout and delivery anywhere in the city, and their food is so good that expats as far away as San Pedro or PG order takeout via airplane.

Fine Dining

Belize's Belikin brewing family runs the **《 Riverside Tavern** (2 Mapp St., tel. 501/223-5640, 11 A.M.–10 P.M. Mon.–Thurs., later on weekends, closed Sun.), an upscale sports bar whose massive "gourmet burger" is one of the best in Belize (US$9 for a 10-oz. patty, US$12.50 for the super-sized 16-oz. patty, made of Belizean beef from the Bowens' Gallon Jug Estate). Or go for the coconut-crusted shrimp or other bar foods. There's beer on tap, and the very convivial atmosphere is a popular meeting place for Belize's who's who crowd.

Celebrity Restaurant and Bar (Marine Parade Blvd., Volta Building, tel. 501/223-2826 or 501/223-7272, www.celebritybelize.com, 11 A.M.–10 P.M. daily) is near the water, next to the national bank and museum. You enter through a dark, swanky lounge into a bright restaurant with a huge variety of seafood, pasta, steaks, and salads (burgers US$9, entrées US$12–20). The best deal is Celebrity's US$5 takeout menu and the giant plate of fish and chips. They're also open for hearty breakfasts on Saturday and Sunday (8 A.M.–3 P.M.).

Just outside town, but worth the trip, the **Sibun Bite Bar & Grill** (tel. 501/222-4153, www.oldbelize.com, 11 A.M.–9 P.M. daily, a bit later on weekends) is part of the **Old Belize** complex, 10 minutes west of downtown Belize City on the Western Highway. The tasty, varied menu and excellent service complement the open setting with lots of activities available.

The **Smoky Mermaid** (opposite the Radisson, tel. 501/223-4759, 6:30 A.M.–10 P.M., entrées US$12–20) specializes in smoked fish, meats, and assorted fresh breads. Breakfast, lunch, and dinner feature Belizean cuisine and freshly baked Creole bread, served on a dining patio under thatch roofs surrounding a porcelain mermaid.

The **St. George's Restaurant** (2 Marine Parade, tel. 501/223-3333, 6:30–10 A.M., 11:30 A.M.–2 P.M., and 6:30–10 P.M. daily, US$20) at the Radisson Fort George Hotel serves a grand buffet and has a standard menu of international fare and seafood. Outside around the bar, the **Stonegrill Restaurant** (10 A.M.–10 P.M. daily, US$ 15–20) is a fun, meat-sizzlin' meal on the heavily vegetated outdoor patio.

INFORMATION AND SERVICES
Tourist Information
The central office of the **Belize Tourism Board** (BTB, 64 Regent St., tel. 501/227-2420, U.S. tel. 800/624-0686, info@travelbelize.org, www.travelbelize.org) is in the Southside, near the Mopan Hotel. The **Belize Tourism Industry Association** (10 N. Park St., tel. 501/227-5717 or 501/223-3507, www.btia.org) can also answer many of your questions and give you lodging suggestions. The **Belize Hotel Association** (BHA, 13 Cork St., tel. 501/223-0669, www.belizehotels.org) is a nonprofit NGO of some of the country's most respected resorts and lodges; they can help you decide where to stay.

Money
Most of the city's banking is clustered in one strip along Albert Street, just south of the Swing Bridge, and includes **Atlantic Bank** (tel. 501/227-1225), **Bank of Nova Scotia** (tel. 501/227-7027), **Barclay's Bank** (tel. 501/227-7211), and **Belize Bank** (tel. 501/227-7132). Most banks have ATMs and keep the same hours: 8 A.M.–1 P.M. Monday–Thursday, 8 A.M.–1 P.M. and 3–6 P.M. Friday.

Health and Emergencies
For police, fire, or ambulance, dial 90 or 911. Another ambulance service is **B.E.R.T** (tel. 501/223-3292). **Belize Medical Associates** (5791 St. Thomas St., tel. 501/223-0302, 501/223-0303, or 501/223-0304, bzmedasso@btl.net, www.belizemedical.com) is the only private hospital in Belize City. The fairly modern 25-bed facility provides 24-hour assistance and a wide range of specialties. Or try **Karl Heusner Memorial Hospital** (Princess Margaret Dr., tel. 501/223-1548 or 501/223-1564).

Internet Access
As elsewhere in the country, an increasing number of hotels and guesthouses offer at least a single computer for guests or even wireless Internet for your laptop. There are a few broadband Internet cafés in Belize City, though not as many as in San Ignacio or San Pedro.

The **Community Computer Center** (9 A.M.–7 P.M. Mon.–Fri., 9 A.M.–1 P.M. Sat., sometimes closed for lunch), in a narrow, tucked-away, air-conditioned room above the library, has nine speedy computers; they are the cheapest in town at US$1.25/hour. On the Southside, try the mothball-smelling **KGS Internet** (near the corner of King and E. Canal Sts., 8 A.M.–7 P.M. Mon.–Fri., reduced hours on weekends, US$3/hr.). It's a bit dark and dingy but has fast cable connections. Check **Angelus Press**, on Queen Street, which has a few available machines. More expensive options are available in Tourism Village and in fancier hotels' business centers.

Library and Bookstores
A reading room and two stories of books are found on Front Street at **Turton Library**

(tel. 501/227-3401, 9 A.M.–7 P.M. Mon.–Fri., 9 A.M.–1 P.M. Sat.), a wonderfully quiet respite from the chaotic rush just outside. Stop in to enjoy the day's newspaper at one of the long, open tables, or dig into their archives for a look at the past.

A few stores have small but pertinent book selections, featuring several shelves of Belizean and about-Belize books. The **Image Factory** (91 N. Front St., www.imagefactorybelize.com, 9 A.M.–5 P.M. Mon.–Fri., 9 A.M.–noon Sat.) has the best collection. **Angelus Press,** right around the corner from the Image Factory on Queen Street, has a complete corner of books and maps, back behind all the office supplies. Across the Swing Bridge, you'll want to hit the second-story **Book Center** (8 A.M.–5:30 P.M. Mon.–Thurs. and Sat., 8 A.M.–9 P.M. Fri.).

Groceries and Sundries

Brodie's (Albert and Regent Sts., tel. 501/227-7070, 8 A.M.–7 P.M. weekdays, closes earlier on weekends) is a department store, supermarket, deli, drugstore, and more—a Belizean institution. Stock up on your way into or out of the north edge of town at **Sav U Supermarket.** This modern, air-conditioned market sells everything any supermarket in the United States would carry, and it's reasonably priced. There's also a new, massive Brodie's on the Northern Highway, just before you reach the Biltmore Hotel.

Post Office

The old post office in the Paslow Building (at the corner of Queen and Front Sts., by the north end of the Swing Bridge) was burned down in 2002 by an embezzling employee trying to hide the evidence (he's now serving time in the "Hattieville Marriott" for his efforts), but the new one is right next door to the razed lot (tel. 501/227-2201, 8 A.M.–4 P.M. Mon.–Fri.). There is a smaller branch around the corner on Queen Street, called the Philatelic Bureau (tel. 501/227-2201, ext. 35, same hours but closed for lunch); a third post office is at Queens Square in the Southside (tel. 501/227-1155).

Tours and Travel Agents

If you prefer to delegate the logistics of your trip, local travel agencies can book local and international transportation, tours, and accommodations across the country. **S & L Travel and Tours** (91 N. Front St., tel. 501/227-7514 or 501/227-7593, www.sltravelbelize.com) is easy to find, next door to the Image Factory. Belizean owners Sarita and Lascelle Tillet run a first-class and very personable operation; they've been in business for more than 30 years. They can get as creative as you like, whether you want a custom vacation, a photo safari, a bird-watching adventure, or anything else you can imagine.

Belize Global Travel Services (41 Albert St., tel. 501/227-7185 or 501/227-7363, www.belizeglobal.com) is one of the more established travel consultants in the city, offering a full range of Belizean tours, packages, and custom trips. A TACA Airlines counter and the country's only official American Express window are located in the same office. The Continental Airlines office is found at 80 Regent Street (tel. 501/227-8309 or U.S. tel. 800/266-3822, 8 A.M.–5 P.M. Mon.–Fri., 8 A.M.–noon Sat.).

Laundry

G's Laundry (22 Dean St., between Albert and Canal, tel. 501/297-4461, 8 A.M.–8 P.M. Mon.–Sat., 8 A.M.–1 P.M. Sun.) charges US$4 to wash and dry.

Luggage Lockers

Check with the travel agencies in the main Caye Caulker Water Taxi Terminal; they may be able to rent a locker for your pack or arrange for longer storage (US$1/hr, US$5/day). Ask your guesthouse if you can leave a bag there as well.

Haircuts

How 'bout a little reggae with your haircut? Loud music blasts all day long at the **Ras Tash Barber Shop** on King Street (8:30 A.M.–8 P.M. Mon.–Sat., plus Sun. mornings, cut and shave US$5). Don't be surprised if your barber sings and bops while sculpting your 'do. If you're not into incredibly loud reggae music, choose from one of the (seemingly) hundreds of other barber shops within a three-block radius.

GETTING THERE
By Air

From the international airport, it's a 20-minute drive to downtown Belize City, a trip that costs US$25 in a taxi (less in the opposite direction). The Municipal Airport (a.k.a. "Muni") is on the waterfront, practically in downtown Belize City. Belizean commuter planes provide steady service in and out of Belize City to outlying airports all over the country. It's cheaper to fly to local destinations out of Municipal.

By Bus

Domestic bus service is handled almost entirely out of **Novelo's Terminal,** at the western terminus of King Street. If you arrive by bus and want to walk downtown, it's about 10 blocks to the Swing Bridge (from Novelo's, cross the canal and stay on King Street till you reach Albert Street, then make a left; continue for three blocks to the Swing Bridge and Water Taxi Terminal). This walk should not be attempted at night but is usually safe during the day (remember; when in doubt, always take a cab). International bus service to Guatemala and Mexico is offered by a handful of companies with offices in the Caye Caulker Water Taxi Terminal.

By Boat

There are three companies with regular service to San Pedro and Caye Caulker. The **Caye Caulker Water Taxi Terminal** is at the north end of the Swing Bridge, with boats leaving between 8 A.M. and 4:30 P.M. (San Pedro tel. 501/226-4646, Caye Caulker tel. 501/226-0992, Belize City tel. 501/223-5752, www. cayecaulkerwatertaxi.com).

San Pedro Express departs from the Tourism Village (tel. 501/223-2225, www. belizewatertaxi.com) between 9 A.M. and 5:30 P.M. express.

Water Jets Express (tel. 501/207-1000, www.sanpedrowatertaxi.com) leaves from

Belize City water taxi to the islands

© JOSHUA BERMAN

Bird's Isle Water Taxi and Marina between 7 A.M. and 6 P.M. daily.

Boat transit to Caye Caulker takes about 45 minutes, then it's another half hour to Ambergris Caye. The trip to Caulker costs about US$10 one-way; to San Pedro costs US$15 one-way. The trip is pleasant on calm, sunny days, but be prepared for a cold and wet ride if the sky to the east is dark. A few of the boats are covered; others will pass out plastic tarps if it's really coming down.

GETTING AROUND

Most sights are relatively close together in Belize City, and you can walk from the Southside's House of Culture to the National Museum in about 20 leisurely minutes. This route is generally safe during the day, especially if you are traveling in a group.

To hail a taxi, look for the green license plates, or ask your hotel to call you one. From the international airport to Belize City, the flat fare is US$25; from the municipal airstrip expect to pay US$5 or less. The fare for one passenger carried between any two points within Belize City (or any other district town) is US$3–7. If you plan to make several stops, tell the cabbie in advance and ask what the total will be; this eliminates lots of misunderstandings. Taxis can be hired by the hour (about US$25) for long trips out of town.

GALES POINT

This tiny, unique Creole settlement occupies a thin, two-mile-long peninsula jutting north into the Southern Lagoon. Gales Point is 15 miles north of Dangriga or 25 miles southwest of Belize City, but getting there makes it feel farther. Depending on which accounts you read, the 400 or so modern inhabitants are descended from either logwood cutters or escaped slaves known as "maroons" who settled here in the 1700s. Gales Point is a traditional Creole culture stronghold. If you're lucky, your visit to Gales Point will coincide with the full moon, when the entire village often participates in a roaming call-and-response drumming and dance circle. In the weeks before Christmas, the frequency of *sambaii* drumming events increases, reaching a crescendo on Christmas Day and Boxing Day with a unique village-wide celebration called *bram*. Gales Point is also known for its homemade cashew wine.

The Southern Lagoon (which surrounds Gales Point on three sides) is part of an extensive estuary bordered by thick mangroves. Their tangled roots provide the perfect breeding grounds for sport fish, crabs, shrimp, lobster, and a host of other marine life. Rich beds of sea grass line the bottom of the lagoon and support a population of manatees. These gentle mammals are often seen basking on the surface of the water or coming up for air (which they must do about every four minutes). This is a popular spot to observe the manatees, often spotted close to a warm, spring-fed hole in the lagoon. Tours to see manatees can be arranged through any of the Gales Point accommodations; trips are also available to see birds and caves in the region and to go fishing.

In July 2008 Gales Point experienced the most devastating floods in its history, as the entire lagoon rose and covered much of the peninsula, a phenomenon that did not occur even during Hurricane Hattie in 1961. It has since recovered, and remains just as remote as ever.

Accommodations

There are some loose homestay programs and places to camp in the village; call the community phone at 501/209-8031 for the latest. **Gentle's Cool Spot** (tel. 501/609-4991) is one local service, providing traditional *fiyah haat* (fire hearth) cooking, plus a few stuffy, depressing clapboard rooms (US$15–20). Gentle's veranda is a favorite gathering place for locals and Gentle provides tours.

Manatee Lodge (tel. 501/220-8040, U.S. tel. 877/462-6283, www.manateelodge.com, US$85) is at the very northern tip of the peninsula and caters to birders, sport fishers, and independent nature-loving travelers and families. The eight rooms have nice wood furnishings, private bathrooms, 24-hour electricity, and a veranda with views of the surrounding lagoon and sunsets behind the Maya Mountains; rooms

BELIZE DISTRICT

© JOSHUA BERMAN

Gales Point

sleep up to four. The lodge offers access to a wildlife habitat completely different from the rest of Belize, living in the shallow brackish water and mangroves of the Southern Lagoon. The number of shorebirds and waterfowl is impressive, and to encourage guests to see local wildlife, the lodge provides each room with a canoe. Binoculars and bug repellent are a must. Children under six are free, ages 6–12 half price. Moderately priced and delicious home-cooked Creole (and continental) meals are available; so are transfers and multiday packages.

Getting There

To get to Gales Point by car, either choose the Manatee Highway (a.k.a. the Coastal Road)

and expect rough muddy roads if it's raining, or take the Hummingbird Highway, which is about 25 miles longer but smoother (for most of the way anyway). The most enjoyable—and expensive—way to reach Gales Point is the 90-minute boat ride from Belize City; you'll wind through bird-filled canals, rivers, and lagoons, and you may spot crocodiles, manatees, or dolphins. Manatee Lodge can arrange a boat transfer, but it is very expensive; it's worth it if you have a group. There used to be several weekly buses from Belize City, but they were not running regularly at last check; call the community phone (tel. 501/209-8031) or Manatee Lodge for current schedules or possible rides.

Along the Northern Highway

After escaping the city's traffic and passing the international airport, you'll cruise up the Northern Highway to either ruins or monkeys. Take your pick.

◖ ALTUN HA RUINS

Altun Ha, a Maya trading center as well as a religious ceremonial site, is believed to have accommodated about 10,000 people. Archaeologists, working amid a Maya community that has been living here for several centuries, have dated construction to about 1,500–2,000 years ago. It wasn't until the archaeologists came in 1964 that the old name "Rockstone Pond" was translated into the Maya words "Altun Ha." The site spans an area of about 25 square miles, most of which is covered by trees, vines, and jungle.

A team led by Dr. David Pendergast of the Royal Ontario Museum began work in 1965 on the central part of the ancient city, where upwards of 250 structures have been found in an area of about 1,000 square yards. So far, this is the most extensively excavated of all the Maya sites in Belize. For a trading center, Altun Ha was strategically located—a few miles from Little Rocky Point on the Caribbean and a few miles from Moho Caye at the mouth of the Belize River, both believed to have been major centers for the large trading canoes that worked up and down the coasts of Guatemala, Honduras, Belize, Mexico's Yucatán, and all the way to Panama.

Near Plaza B, the **Reservoir,** also known as **Rockstone Pond,** is fed by springs and rain runoff. It demonstrates the advanced knowledge of the Maya in just one of their many fields: engineering. Archaeologists say that an insignificant little stream ran through the jungle for centuries. No doubt it had been a source of fresh water for the Maya—but maybe not enough. The Maya diverted the creek and then began a major engineering project, digging and enlarging a deep, round hole that was then plastered with limestone cement. Once the cement dried and hardened, the stream was rerouted to its original course and the newly built reservoir filled and overflowed at the east end, allowing the stream to continue on its age-old track. This made the area livable. Was all of this done before or after the temple structures were built? Is the completion of this reservoir what made the Maya elite choose to locate themselves in this area? We may never know for sure. Today Rockstone Pond is surrounded by thick brush, and the pond is alive with jungle creatures, including tarpon, small fish, and turtles and other reptiles.

The concentration of structures includes palaces and temples surrounding two main plazas.

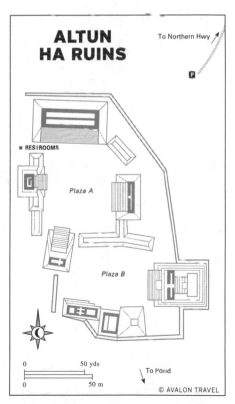

ALTUN HA RUINS

To Northern Hwy

▣ RESTROOMS

Plaza A

Plaza B

0   50 yds

0   50 m

To Pond

© AVALON TRAVEL

The tallest building (the **Sun God Temple**) is 59 feet above the plaza floor. At Altun Ha, the structure bases are oval and terraced. The small temples on top have typical small rooms built with the Maya trademark—the corbel arch.

Pendergast's team uncovered many valuable finds, such as unusual green obsidian blades, pearls, and more than 300 jade pieces—beads, earrings, and rings. Seven funeral chambers were discovered, including the **Temple of the Green Tomb,** rich with human remains and traditional funerary treasures. Maya scholars believe the first man buried was someone of great importance. He was draped with jade beads, pearls, and shells. And it was next to his right hand that the most exciting find was located—a solid jade head now referred to as **Kinich Ahau** ("The Sun God"). Kinich Ahau is, to date, the largest jade carving found in any Maya country. The head weighs nine pounds and measures nearly six inches from base to crown. It is reportedly now housed far away, in a museum in Canada. The two men who discovered the jade head some 40 years ago, Winston Herbert and William Leslie, still reside in Rockstone Pond and Lucky Strike villages. On November 29, 2006, they were honored by the National Institute of Culture and History for their discovery.

Altun Ha was rebuilt several times during the Pre-Classic, Classic, and Post-Classic Periods. The desecration of the structures leads scientists believe that the site may have been abandoned because of violence.

Visiting the Ruins

From the Northern Highway, continue past the Burrell Boom turnoff (to the Baboon Sanctuary) and continue to about Mile 19, where the road forks; the right fork is the Old Northern Highway and leads to Altun Ha and Maskall Village. Ten and a half miles from the intersection, you'll reach the Altun Ha entrance. The road is in horrible condition and is not getting any better with the increased traffic, mainly from long parades of buses carrying cruise ship passengers.

The ruins of Altun Ha have become one of the more popular day trips for groups and individuals venturing from Belize City, Ambergris Caye, and Caye Caulker. A gift shop and toilet facilities are at the entrance (tel. 501/609-3540, 9 A.M.–5 P.M., US$10).

Note that Altun Ha is a popular destination for cruise ship passengers (usually Tuesday and Thursday), so if you don't want to share your experience with 40 busloads of gawking cruisers, be sure to check with the park before coming. In general, it's easy to avoid the crowds if you get there when the park first opens. You'll see more birds and wildlife that way as well.

A couple of local tour guides will be waiting for you at the entrance. They charge about US$10 per group per half hour and are well worth it, especially Ann-Marie Avona. If you're coming to Altun Ha as part of a package, consider insisting that your tour provider use a local guide. This is important to ensure that local communities receive something other than a crumbling road. To that end, you'll most likely also find tables of artisans with decent crafts for sale.

Accommodations and Food

There are several budget-oriented lodgings in the area around Lucky Strike and Rockstone Pond villages, but few travelers choose to stay here, probably because there's not much offered in the area, apart from a short hike through the nearby ruins and the tranquil sounds of the jungle. The best option is only about a mile from the entrance to the ruins. There's a small casita at the **Mayan Wells Restaurant** (tel. 501/205-5641 or 501/225-5505, www.mayanwells.com, US$40); it has a kitchenette, a screened porch, and hammocks. You can also camp out for US$5 per person. Meals at the restaurant cost US$6–10. Mayan Wells is set on a nice-size chunk of forest, walking distance from the Altun Ha ruins, and offers meals and tours, and free admission to their butterfly house.

MARUBA RESORT JUNGLE SPA

By any standard, Maruba Resort Jungle Spa (tel. 501/225-5555, U.S. tel. 800/627-8227,

HATTIEVILLE CENTRAL PRISON GIFT SHOP

In 2002, management of Hattieville Central Prison was transferred from the government of Belize to the **Kolbe Foundation** (tel. 501/225-6190, www.kolbe.bz), a private, nonprofit Christian organization. The Hattieville facility had been in operation for less than a decade and was horribly constructed and disastrously overcrowded. The Kolbe Foundation's vision of a secure, humane facility based on meaningful rehabilitation and reintegration has had astonishing results in the short time they've been there.

A major part of the foundation's approach (in addition to piping Bible readings over the PA system) is education and skill building, including the creation and development of workshops and classroom courses. Inmates learn woodworking, jewelry making, tailoring, and welding. There is an agricultural program, which includes a large vegetable garden, a farm where chickens and pigs are raised, and a cement-block shop.

The **Prison Gift Shop** (tel. 501/225-6218 or 501/225-6190, ext. 235, open 8 A.M.-3 P.M.) features items made exclusively at the prison by the inmates in all the aforementioned workshops. You'll find furniture, jewelry, hammocks, carvings, handicrafts, and many other items.

The Prison Gift Shop is a step into the future for inmates, offering the means for their rehabilitation and for the prison itself to become economically self-sustainable. Your patronage will go a long way to assist in these goals.

To get to the gift shop, leave Belize City and follow the Western Highway until you reach the Hattieville roundabout at Mile 14. Turn right (north onto Burrell Boom Road) and travel for approximately two miles. The prison and gift shop are on the left side of the road.

---

www.maruba-belize.com, US$130–700 per night) is an interesting sight in the middle of the forest, located at Mile 40½ on the Old Northern Highway, about a mile out of Maskall Village. Many visitors come just for the day—it's a popular stopover for Altun Ha explorers who decide to enjoy lunch and a mud mask before heading back to San Pedro, Belize City, or other nearby destinations. The resort's verdant landscaping is enhanced by intriguing focal points spread around the grounds: a tiny, glass-decorated chapel, a palapa-covered stone chess table, a pool that seems to spring from the jungle, complete with waterfalls. The uniquely named rooms—Moon, Fertility, Mayan Loft, and Bondage, to name a few—continue the eclectic motif with carved masks, mosaic-tile floors, standing candles, concrete fountains, tiled tubs, screened windows, and fresh flowers on the massive feather beds and in the bathrooms.

The restaurant often offers tasty international fusion fare, and at the bar you will find viper rum ("for real men only"), an insanely strong shot of liquor infused with snake venom. Instructions on how to properly down a shot will be given by owner/bartender Nicky. Massages, mud wraps, manicures, and pedicures are available, as well as a free-weight gym. Packages are available with tours to the reefs, ruins, and inland destinations.

Getting to Altun Ha and Maruba

If you want to bus it, ask at your hotel for current schedules and make sure there is a return bus the same day if you do not plan on staying in the area. Altun Ha is close enough to the city that a taxi is your best bet, or try a tour operator that specializes in these trips.

BURRELL BOOM

This village of about 1,200 people is named after the Scottish logger who built a boom across the river to catch his logs. Today, Burrell Boom is inhabited by subsistence farmers, fishermen, cashew growers, and fruit wine makers. It is the gateway to the Community Baboon Sanctuary, but also conveniently close to the international airport and a good way to avoid staying in Belize City if you don't want to.

Accommodations

Black Orchid Resort (tel. 501/225-9158, www.blackorchidresort.com, US$120–140) is a relaxed riverside resort within striking distance of a number of area attractions. Guests rave about this place, which is a mere 11 miles from the international airport, but feels as remote as other upcountry jungle lodges. Black Orchid's owner, Doug Thompson, is a native Belizean who lived in the United States for 36 years, and is currently the president of the Belize Hotel Association, so he is very savvy about what guests want. He also runs a tour company to whisk you around the region (and free airport shuttle); or stay on the grounds and enjoy the swimming pool, volleyball net, shaded picnic tables, kayaks, and canoes. Sixteen spacious rooms are comfortable, have all basic amenities, and there is an excellent on-site restaurant and bar. Ask about the Jaguar Eco-house and 3-bedroom villa for longer term rental, or for families.

A few blocks from the river, **El Chiclero Inn** (tel. 501/225-9005, www.elchicleroinn.com, US$60) is a six-room hotel known mostly for its huge American-style menu (US$8–11), with everything from chili dogs to pizza to pastas, steaks, Cajun pork chops, and cashew pie. The restaurant is open 7 A.M.–9 P.M. daily. The rooms are bright, with air-conditioning, TVs, and private bathrooms. El Chiclero is often used by business travelers as an alternative to staying in Belize City.

◖ THE COMMUNITY BABOON SANCTUARY (CBS)

The sanctuary (tel. 501/660-3545, www.howlermonkeys.org) consists of 220 members in seven local communities who have voluntarily agreed to manage their land in ways that will preserve their beloved "baboon" (the local term for the black howler monkey). Because of community-based efforts to preserve the creature, there are now 3,000 individual baboons living freely in the forests and buffer zones between

people's farms. CBS feels remote but is less than an hour's drive from Belize City, making it both a popular day trip *and* a destination for anyone who'd rather wake up to the throaty roars of Belizean baboons than the smelly bustle of Belize City.

History

One of the six species of howler monkeys in the world, the black howlers, or *Alouatta caraya,* are the largest monkeys in the Americas. Robert Horwich, from the University of Wisconsin at Milwaukee, was the first zoologist to spend extended time in the howler's range, which covered southern Mexico, northeast Guatemala, and Belize. The results of his study were disturbing. In Mexico, the monkeys were being hunted for food, and their habitat was fast disappearing. Conditions in Guatemala were only slightly better. Here, too, the monkeys were hunted by locals in the forests around Tikal, and as the forest habitat shrank, so too did the number of howler monkeys.

In the Belizean village of Bermudian Landing, however, the communities of monkeys were strong and healthy, the forest was intact, and the locals seemed genuinely fond of the noisy creatures. This was definitely the place to start talking about a wildlife reserve. Horwich, with the help of Jon Lyon, a botanist from the State University of New York, began a survey of the village in 1984. After many meetings with the town leaders, excitement grew about the idea of saving the "baboon." Homeowners agreed to leave the monkey's food trees—hogplums and sapodillas—and small strips of forest between cleared fields as aerial pathways for the primates, as well as 60 feet of forest along both sides of waterways.

An application was made to World Wildlife Fund USA in 1985 for funds to set up the reserve. Local landowners signed a voluntary management agreement set forth by Horwich and Lyon—and a sanctuary was born.

Continuing Results

According to sanctuary manager Fallett Young, who passed away in 2010, there have been

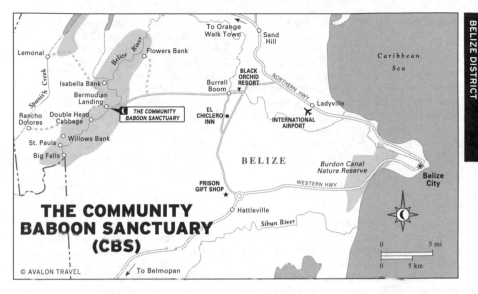

THE COMMUNITY BABOON SANCTUARY (CBS)

© AVALON TRAVEL

successful relocations of some of the thriving monkey troops around the country, including to the Cockscomb Basin Wildlife Sanctuary, where howlers hadn't been heard since they were decimated by yellow fever decades ago.

In the case of CBS, educating people about conservation and encouraging their fondness for nature was more successful than stringent hunting laws. The managers of the sanctuary are villagers who understand their neighbors; much of their time is spent with schoolchildren and adults in interested villages. Part of their education includes basic farming and sustained land use techniques that eliminate the constant need to cut forest for new *milpas* (cornfields).

Another result is the unhindered growth of 100 species of trees, vines, and epiphytes. The animal life is thriving—anteaters, armadillos, iguanas, hicatee turtles, deer, coatis, amphibians, reptiles, and about 200 species of birds all live here.

A lively debate continues among traditional conservationists about allowing people to live within a wildlife preserve. However, Belize's grassroots conservation is proving that it can succeed. Other countries, such as Australia and Sierra Leone, are watching carefully to see how this concept can be adapted to the needs of their own endangered species without disturbing the people who have lived on the land for many generations.

Recreation

There are enough trails, rivers, and guided tours to keep you busy here for a couple of days. Or you can settle for the standard 45-minute walking tour with a "99 percent chance to see wild monkeys." All activities are arranged through the CBS Visitor Center in Bermudian Landing (group trips and guides from local hotels are also available). The basic nature walk is included with your US$7 entrance fee to the visitors center and museum (feel free to tip your guide).

There is a three-hour canoe tour and a two-hour walking tour of some of the different sanctuary villages. Overnighters should absolutely take advantage of the nighttime trips, including a 3.5-hour crocodile canoe trip up Mussell Creek and a two-hour night hike into the surrounding forest.

If you're lucky, you might catch a village softball game or cricket match, between February and August.

Accommodations and Food

A popular choice for adventurous travelers is the homestay program, where you'll stay with a local family in primitive conditions, bathing with a bucket and talking with your host family in the evening. The **Women's Bed and Breakfast Group** has established a network of accommodations throughout the seven sanctuary villages, offering visitors a traditional Creole-style stay. Arrange your stay in one of these "bed-and-breakfasts" (US$39 pp includes all meals) at least 24 hours in advance through the visitors center at Bermudian Landing.

If you've got a tent, you can pitch it on the visitors center grounds or down by the river for US$5 per person. Arrange a meal with a local family; both options are less than US$5 per meal. There are privies and showers available.

A couple notches up in comfort and price, and right next to the visitors center, is the **Nature Resort** (tel. 501/624-6896, US$30–75), with 12 free-standing cabanas scattered across a gorgeous lawn near the river; the wooden structures have shared baths and it's US$75 for a full kitchenette and private bathroom. The cabins are clean, well kept, and well equipped.

Next door, the **Howler Monkey Resort** (tel. 501/220-2158, www.howlermonkeyresort.bz, US$91–126) has a selection of cabins, and a screened restaurant and path to the river.

Getting There and Away

Bermudian Landing is only 26 miles from Belize City, or about a 45-minute drive. Drive north on the Northern Highway for 13 miles, then turn left toward Burrell Boom and follow signs to the CBS Museum and Visitor's Center.

Two bus companies travel to and from Bermuda Landing and Belize City: McFadzean buses depart from the corner of Cemetery Rd. and Amara Ave. and Russell leaves from Euphrates St. and Cairo Street. Monday–Friday, seven buses depart Belize City between noon and 9 P.M.; there's a shortened schedule on Saturday. There are no buses in either direction on Sunday. The bus takes about an hour. Four early-morning buses leave Bermudian Landing 5:30–7 A.M., and there are two in the afternoon at 3:30 P.M. and 4 P.M.

The sanctuary is close enough to the city or either airport that you can consider a taxi or an escorted tour for a day trip. Negotiate taxi prices ahead of time. The Community Baboon Sanctuary can arrange airport transfers for reasonable prices; just call.

SPANISH CREEK WILDLIFE SANCTUARY

Spanish Creek Wildlife Sanctuary is near Rancho Dolores, due west along the Burrell Boom Road, beyond the Community Baboon Sanctuary. This new protected area is rich in wildlife but short on infrastructure so far. It's operated by the Rancho Dolores Environmental and Development Group and is accessible by bus from Belize City (call Leonard Russell, tel. 510/610-5164, to arrange bus transport).

Crooked Tree

The island village and the wildlife sanctuary of Crooked Tree are only a 36-mile drive from Belize City and a primary destination for all serious bird-watchers who visit Belize. Others will enjoy paddling through the water, hiking various trails, or reveling at the annual cashew festival. Most visitors to the area also enjoy the simple pleasure of mingling with the islanders, perhaps at one of the weekly cricket matches.

Crooked Tree is a network of inland lagoons, swamps, and waterways. The sanctuary also encompasses the freshwater lagoon that surrounds the area. **Crooked Tree Lagoon** is up to a mile wide and more than 20 miles long. Along its banks lies the town of Crooked Tree. An island surrounded by fresh water, accessible only by boats traveling up the Belize River and Black Creek, it was settled during the early days of the logwood era. The waterways were used to float the logs out to the sea.

◖ CROOKED TREE WILDLIFE SANCTUARY

The 16,400 acres of waterways, logwood swamps, and lagoon provide habitat for a diverse array of hundreds of resident and migratory birds—all year long. Explore the area by paddle power in a rented canoe or kayak, motor through on a guided tour, or hike the system of boardwalks through lowland savanna and logwood forests, with observation towers providing wide views across the lagoons.

The reserve was established by the Belize Audubon Society to protect its most famous habitant, the jabiru stork. It's the largest flying bird in the Western Hemisphere, with a wingspan of up to eight feet. Multitudes of other birds (285 species, at last count) find the sanctuary a safe resting spot during the dry season, with enormous food resources along the shorelines and in the trees. After a rain, thousands of minuscule frogs (no more than an inch long) seem to drop from the sky. They're fair game for the agami heron, snowy egret, and great egret—quick hunters with their long beaks. A fairly large bird, the snail kite uses its particular beak to hook meat out of the apple snails.

Two varieties of ducks, the black-bellied whistling duck and the Muscovy, nest in trees along the swamp. All five species of kingfishers live in the sanctuary, and you can see ospreys and black-collared hawks diving for their morning catch.

On one trip, we watched from our dory (dugout canoe) as a peregrine falcon repeatedly tried but failed to nab one of a flock of floating American coots. Black Creek, with its forests of large trees, provides homes to monkeys, Morelet's crocodiles, coatimundis, turtles, and iguanas. A profusion of wild ocher pokes up from the water, covered with millions of pale pink snail eggs. Grazing Brahma cattle wade into the shallows of the lagoon to munch on the tum tum (water lilies), a delicacy that keeps them fat and fit when the grasses turn brown in the dry season.

Hunting and fishing are not permitted.

Visiting the Sanctuary

Although several organizations had a financial hand in founding the park, **Belize Audubon Society** (tel. 501/223-5004, www.belizeaudubon.org) runs the show. The organization, with the continued help of devoted volunteers, maintains a small visitors center on the right just after you cross the causeway. Do sign in; this validates the sanctuary and gives the society a reason to sponsor it. It's also obligatory, as is the US$5 per person entrance fee; the office

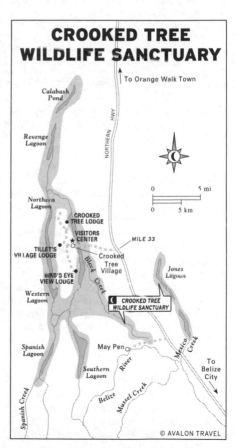

CROOKED TREE WILDLIFE SANCTUARY

To Orange Walk Town

Calabash Pond

NORTHERN HWY

Revenge Lagoon

0   5 mi
0   5 km

Northern Lagoon

CROOKED TREE LODGE

VISITORS CENTER   MILE 33

TILLET'S VILLAGE LODGE

Crooked Tree Village

BIRD'S EYE VIEW LODGE

Black Creek

Jones Lagoon

Western Lagoon

◖ CROOKED TREE WILDLIFE SANCTUARY

Spanish Lagoon

May Pen

Southern Lagoon

Belize River

Mexico Creek

To Belize City

Spanish Creek

Mussel Creek

© AVALON TRAVEL

CROOKED TREE CASHEW FESTIVAL

The namesake of this relaxed inland island village is the cashew tree, which grows prolifically throughout the area. The unique nut has always contributed to the community's economy, especially for its women, who have been able to secure additional income for their households by selling cashew products. The situation is even better today, as the products are more often sold directly to local consumers and tourists than to distributors in Belize City, as they were in the past.

To celebrate the bent branches and their heavy fruit, the people of Crooked Tree Village throw a big cashew harvest festival the second weekend in May. It's a lot of fun, a hometown fair with regional arts, music, folklore, dance, and crafts. And of course it's a chance to sample cashew wine, cashew jellies, stewed cashews...you get the picture. Just make sure the "hometown fair" picture in your head includes *punta* music, fry jacks, and johnnycakes.

Seek out the demonstrations showing how the cashew nut is processed – interesting stuff. The fruit, or the cashew "apple," is either red or yellow, with the seed hanging from the bottom of the apple. The meat of the apple can be stewed or made into jam or wine, while the seedpod is roasted in an open fire on the ground. Roasting the cashew stabilizes the highly acidic oil and at the same time makes the pod brittle enough to crack. The nut is partially cooked during this step in the processing. The seeds are then raked so they cool evenly and quickly.

The cashews are then cracked by hand, one at a time. Those who handle the nuts wear gloves, as the shell contains a highly irritating poison that for most people causes blisters and inflammation. Processing removes all the poison.

is open 8 A.M.–4:30 P.M. 365 days a year. You will always find a knowledgeable curator willing to answer questions about the birds and flora encountered at the sanctuary.

THE VILLAGE

The village is divided into three neighborhoods: Crooked Tree, Pine Ridge, and Stain, with a total population of about 1,000. Villagers operate farms, raise livestock, and have a small fishery. Visitors will find the village spread out on the island, with more cattle trails, half roads, and fence line than roads. There are a few well-grazed athletic fields, four churches, and scores of stilted wooden houses, each with its own tank to catch rainwater. It's a tranquil community with children playing football, racing horses, or whacking a ball around the cricket pitch.

Chau Hiix Ruins

Archaeological site Chau Hiix is being studied nearby. Archaeologists have made some startling discoveries, including a ball court and ball-court marker, along with small artifacts. Preliminary studies indicate the site was occupied from 1200 B.C. to A.D. 1500. **Sapodilla Lagoon** is south of Crooked Tree on Spanish Creek.

GUIDES AND TOURS

The best way to really experience the lagoon is by boat, and there are all kinds available at each hotel. Belize Audubon Society will be happy to have a guide and boat waiting for you when you arrive at Crooked Tree. All three accommodations in the village also arrange birding and village tours.

ACCOMMODATIONS AND FOOD

There are only a few options in this low-key village, starting with the **Tillet's Village Lodge** (tel. 501/671-7100, www.tilletvillage. com, US$40–80). The famous Sam Tillet, renowned as one of the premier Belizean naturalists, passed away in 2007, but his family is carrying on the tradition. They are in the middle of the village (not on the water), and the rooms are small, plain, and clean with private baths and tiled floors. Nature walks are US$15, and you can also go horseback riding or do a "jungle survival" trip.

On the shore of the lagoon to the north of the causeway, **(Crooked Tree Lodge** (tel. 501/626-3820 or 501/623-5035, michael-cjwebb@hotmail.com, www.crookedtreelodgebelize.com, US$40–60) is a peaceful family-run retreat of 11 acres and six stilted en-suite wooden cabanas, including a bigger one for families (US$120, sleeps up to 7). Your hosts, Angie, a Crooked Tree native, and Mick, an ex-helicopter pilot for the British Army, loved it here so much, they got married, stayed, and have two boys. Camping is welcome (US$10), and so are pets and children. Three daily meals are available for reasonable prices. Wide-ranging boat and birding tours are available with local guides. There is wireless Internet, a restaurant and small bar, and it's all on the water's edge.

As you approach the island on the causeway, on the shoreline off to your left, you'll see Crooked Tree's most upscale property: **Bird's Eye View Lodge** (tel. 501/225-7027 or 501/203-2040, www.birdseyeviewbelize.com, US$80–120 for a couple). This hotel stands above the rest in modernity and service, and this is reflected in its higher rates. The 20 rooms all have private baths and various comforts, including air-conditioning. Miss Verna will take good care of you—she's been hosting nature-loving visitors for nearly two decades! The rooftop bar and patio is a wonderful spot to take in the breeze and keep on bird-watching, even after your four-hour, daybreak bird-watching boat cruise on the lagoon. Meals are US$7 for breakfast and lunch; dinner is US$10. Boat rentals, tours, and airport pickups can be arranged. Boat tours for up to four people cost about US$100; ask about village tours and cashew-making tours in season (Mar.–June).

In the village dine at **Triple J's** or **Suzette's Burger Bar,** which is a fine little spot for burgers and hot dogs. Both are found by walking into Crooked Tree Village, and their hours vary depending on demand.

GETTING THERE

By car, drive north to Mile 33, turn left, and continue until the dirt road turns into the earthen causeway that will carry you into Crooked Tree. Or catch the **Jex Bus** to Crooked Tree in Belize City (at 34 Regent St., next to Mike's Club); they leave promptly at 10:55 A.M. Monday–Friday, arriving in Crooked Tree at 12:30 P.M.; there's also a 5 P.M. bus from the Poundyard Bridge. From Crooked Tree to Belize City, buses depart only in the mornings; ask about times. This is fine for those who plan to spend the night; other options are to go by taxi or with a local tour operator. Check with the Audubon Society for further transportation information, rates, and an updated schedule.

THE NORTHERN CAYES

By the 17th century, pirates discovered that the plentiful cayes (islands, pronounced "keys") around the Belizean mainland were perfect for lying low, riding out a storm, drinking rum, and replenishing water and food supplies before setting sail for another round of pillaging and sacking. No doubt modern-day travelers to Belize's largest, most visited islands engage in at least a few of these activities. The more popular cayes are Caulker, Ambergris, St. George's, Half Moon, and Lighthouse.

The Northern Cayes are the crown jewels of Belize's tourist attractions. They have the most experience catering to visitors, have developed several different scenes between them, and continue to be the most popular destinations in the country. By one estimate, more than 70 percent of visitors to Belize come to at least one of these islands during their trip. It's not hard to imagine why—namely, immediate access to world-class diving, fishing, and snorkeling; hospitable Belizean islanders and fellow travelers from around the world; and an amazing selection of small, personable resorts and restaurants. Then, of course, there are palms, rum punches, boat rides, clear blue ocean, and island time. Enjoy, and repeat after the locals: "Go slow!"

PLANNING YOUR TIME

What to do? Dive? Snorkel? Kayak around the island? How about a sailing cruise at sunset? Day trip to the mainland? Massage? Shopping? Deep-sea fishing? Or you can just lie back and read by the pool. Many visitors to Caye Caulker, Ambergris, and the outlying

© JOSHUA BERMAN

HIGHLIGHTS

Hol Chan Marine Reserve: The famous Belize Barrier Reef, less than a mile offshore from both Caye Caulker and Ambergris Caye, is marked by this famous "cut," or break, in the reef, where the mixing water from the open ocean (and bait thrown in from tour boats) ensures plenty of wildlife (page 62).

Bacalar Chico Marine Reserve: This UNESCO World Heritage Site occupies the northern tip of Ambergris Caye and boasts amazing snorkeling and diving; the area is rich with history and lore (page 64).

Swallow Caye Wildlife Sanctuary: One of many ocean-bound excursions available from Belize's Northern Cayes, this protected area offers glimpses of manatees and shorebirds (page 87).

The Elbow: The steep drop-off and clashing currents at the Turneffe Islands' southern tip make for a unique dive site because of the deep-water fish that frequent the area, as well as a thriving population of interesting sponges (page 96).

Half Moon Caye Wall: The beautiful crescent-shaped island is at the southeast corner of Lighthouse Reef Atoll. The wall just offshore is one of Belize's most fascinating sites, with numerous tunnels and canyons in the reef crest, all swimming with wildlife (page 99).

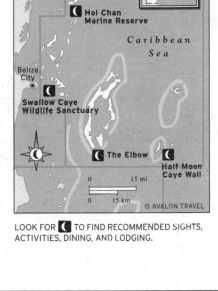

LOOK FOR (TO FIND RECOMMENDED SIGHTS, ACTIVITIES, DINING, AND LODGING.

atolls book their entire vacations on a single island—especially fishing and diving freaks on a mission. You can easily while away 7–10 days on any of these islands. Then there are the surf-and-turf tourists who do five days in the cayes and five days inland. Backpackers often include only a couple of days in the Northern Cayes (or at least enough time to get scuba certified) before continuing on their Central American tours. Even if you focus your vacation elsewhere in the country and have only a day or two, it's still worth the trip to either Caulker or Ambergris, which are both less than an hour by boat from Belize City and worthy of the quickest of glimpses.

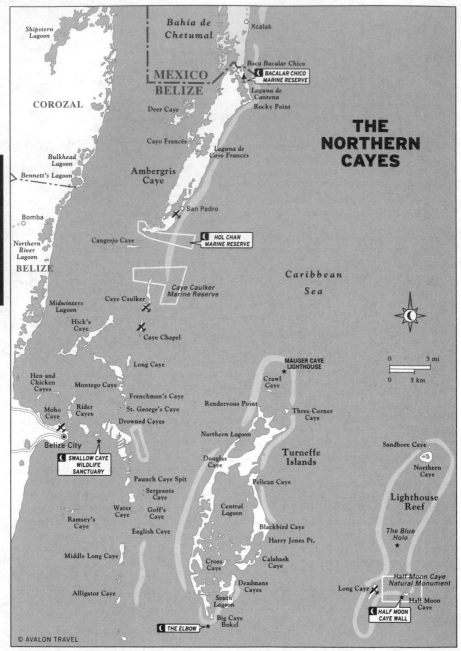

Shipstern
Lagoon

Bahía de
Chetumal

Xcalak

Boca Bacalar Chico

MEXICO
BELIZE

BACALAR CHICO
MARINE RESERVE

COROZAL

Deer Caye

Laguna de
Cantena

Rocky Point

**THE
NORTHERN
CAYES**

Cayo Francés

Bulkhead
Lagoon

Laguna de
Cayo Francés

Bennett's Lagoon

Ambergris
Caye

Bomba

San Pedro

Northern
River
Lagoon

Cangrejo Caye

HOL CHAN
MARINE RESERVE

BELIZE

*Caribbean
Sea*

Caye Caulker
Marine Reserve

Midwinters
Lagoon

Caye Caulker

Hick's
Caye

Caye Chapel

Long Caye

MAUGER CAYE
LIGHTHOUSE

0   5 mi

Hen and
Chicken
Cayes

Montego Caye

Crawl
Caye

0   5 km

Frenchman's Caye

Moho
Caye

Rider
Cayes

St. George's Caye

Rendezvous Point

Three Corner
Caye

Drowned Cayes

Northern Lagoon

Belize City

Turneffe
Islands

Sandbore Caye

SWALLOW CAYE
WILDLIFE
SANCTUARY

Douglas
Caye

Northern
Caye

Paunch Caye Spit

Pelican Caye

**Lighthouse
Reef**

Sergeants
Caye

Water
Caye

Goff's
Caye

Central
Lagoon

Ramsey's
Caye

*The Blue
Hole*

English Caye

Blackbird Caye

Harry Jones Pt.

Middle Long Caye

Cross
Caye

Calabash
Caye

Half Moon Caye
Natural Monument

Alligator Caye

Deadmans
Cayes

Long Caye

South
Lagoon

Half Moon
Caye

HALF MOON
CAYE WALL

Big Caye
Bokel

THE ELBOW

© AVALON TRAVEL

San Pedro and Ambergris Caye

Ambergris Caye is Belize's largest island, just south of the Mexican Yucatán mainland, and stretching southward for 24 miles into Belizean waters. Ambergris (pronounced "AM-bur-giss") is a waxy secretion that originates in the intestines of the sperm whale before it is regurgitated. Don't laugh—this rare and valuable substance used to be a global commodity, used in the manufacture of perfume and going for top dollar.

The island is 35 miles east of Belize City and about three-quarters of a mile west of the Belize Barrier Reef. Ambergris Caye was formed by an accumulation of coral fragments and silt from the Río Hondo as it emptied from what is now northern Belize. The caye is made up of mangrove swamps, a dozen lagoons, a plateau, and a series of low sand ridges. The largest lagoon, fed by 15 creeks, is 2.5-mile-long **Laguna de San Pedro** on the western side of the village.

San Pedro Town sits on a sand ridge at the southern end of the island, the only actual town on the island and the most-visited destination in Belize. It is chock-full of accommodations, restaurants, golf carts, and services. San Pedro is also the most expensive part of Belize, with prices for some basic goods and foods double the mainland prices and sometimes even more than similar services and restaurants in the United States.

HISTORY
The Maya
As in the rest of Belize, the first people on the caye were the Maya. They managed to fight off invading Spaniards as early as 1508. A small Post-Classic site in the Basil Jones area and a few jade ornaments have been found along with obsidian flakes and fragments of pottery. Remnants indicate that Ambergris Caye was an important hub for trading. It is possible to visit these sites; transportation and guides are widely available. It is presumed that because of the location of Ambergris Caye (in the center

of the sea-lane) it was a stopover for Maya traders traveling up and down the coast.

Four and a half miles north of Rocky Point, at Boca Bacalar Chico, a narrow channel separates Belize and Mexico. The Maya dug this strait by hand so that they could bring their canoes through rather than go all the way around the peninsula (which is now Ambergris Caye). In dry years, when the water receded it was impossible to get a boat through, so in 1899 the Mexican government expanded the channel.

The Blakes
Between 1848 and 1849, during the Caste War on the Yucatán Peninsula, Yucatecan mestizos migrated to Belize, and four families were the first permanent residents of present-day San Pedro. Before long, there was a population of

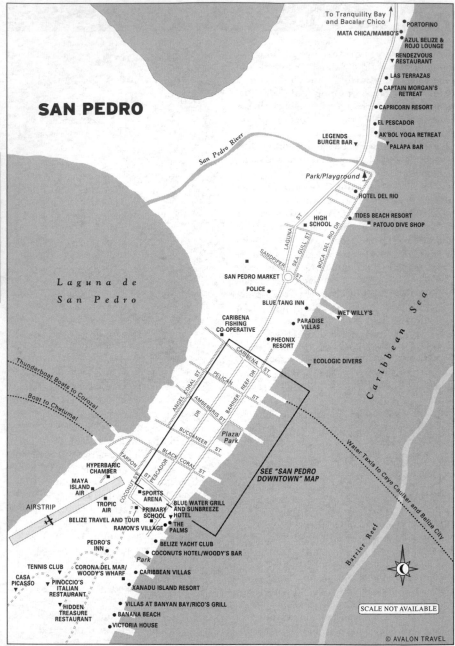

THE NORTHERN CAYES

SAN PEDRO

To Tranquility Bay
and Bacalar Chico
• PORTOFINO
MATA CHICA/MAMBO'S •
• AZUL BELIZE &
ROJO LOUNGE
▼ RENDEZVOUS
RESTAURANT
• LAS TERRAZAS
• CAPTAIN MORGAN'S
RETREAT
• CAPRICORN RESORT
• EL PESCADOR
• AK'BOL YOGA RETREAT
LEGENDS
BURGER BAR ▼
▼ PALAPA BAR

San Pedro River

Park/Playground ▼
• HOTEL DEL RIO
LAGUNA ST
HIGH
SCHOOL ■
SEA GULL ST
BOCA DEL RIO DR
• TIDES BEACH RESORT
■ PATOJO DIVE SHOP
SANDPIPER ST
SAN PEDRO MARKET ◯
• POLICE
*Laguna de
San Pedro*
• BLUE TANG INN
WET WILLY'S •
CARIBENA
FISHING
CO-OPERATIVE
• PARADISE
VILLAS
• PHEONIX
RESORT
CARIBENA ST
• ECOLOGIC DIVERS
Thunderboat Boats to Corozal
Boat to Chetumal
ANGEL CORAL ST
PELICAN ST
BARRIER REEF DR
ST
Caribbean Sea
AMBERGRIS ST
DR
BUCCANEER ST
Plaza/
Park
SEE "SAN PEDRO
DOWNTOWN" MAP
TARPON ST
BLACK CORAL ST
Water Taxis to Caye Caulker and Belize City
HYPERBARIC
CHAMBER ■
MAYA
ISLAND ■
AIR
PESCADOR ST
COCONUT ST
■ SPORTS
ARENA
TROPIC
AIR ■
AIRSTRIP
■ PRIMARY
SCHOOL
BELIZE TRAVEL AND TOUR
BLUE WATER GRILL
AND SUNBREEZE
▼ HOTEL
■ THE
PALMS
RAMON'S VILLAGE ●
PEDRO'S
INN ●
Park
• BELIZE YACHT CLUB
• COCONUTS HOTEL/WOODY'S BAR
TENNIS CLUB
▼ CORONA DEL MAR/
WOODY'S WHARF
CASA
PICASSO ▼
▼ PINOCCIO'S
ITALIAN
RESTAURANT
• CARIBBEAN VILLAS
■ XANADU ISLAND RESORT
▼ HIDDEN
TREASURE
RESTAURANT
• VILLAS AT BANYAN BAY/RICO'S GRILL
• BANANA BEACH
• VICTORIA HOUSE
Barrier Reef
SCALE NOT AVAILABLE
© AVALON TRAVEL

about 50 self-sufficient fishermen, who were also growing corn and vegetables. Life was idyllic for these people—until 1874 and the coming of the Blake family, the first of many foreign real estate developers who would transform the island.

James Blake paid the Belize government BZE$650 for Ambergris Caye (taking over every parcel of land except one set aside for the Catholic church) and began collecting rent from people who had been there for many years. After this, the history of the island was tied up with the fortunes of the Blakes and their in-laws, the Parhams and Alamillas. Their story reads like a novel, including love affairs, illegitimate children, and unlikely marriages. The Blakes controlled everybody and everything on the island, including the coconut and fishing industries; after almost 100 years of this, the Belizean government stepped in and made a "forced purchase" of San Pedro. It redistributed the land, selling lots and parcels to the same islanders who had been living on the land for generations.

The Fishing Industry

The caye's main industry has shifted from logwood to chicle to coconuts, then to lobsters, fish, and conch. Before 1920, the spiny lobster was considered a nuisance, constantly getting caught in fishing nets, and thrown away. That all changed in 1921 when the lobster became a valuable export item. Though the fishermen were getting only a penny a pound, the business became lucrative when freezer vessels and freezer-equipped seaplanes began flying between the cayes and Florida.

Today's Ambergris

The establishment of a fishermen's co-op enabled the population to develop a middle-class economy over the years. The financial upswing allowed the town to improve the infrastructure of the island, which in turn has created a welcoming atmosphere for tourists. The earliest tourists came to Ambergris Caye aboard the boat *Pamelayne* in the 1920s. By 1965, the first hotel was established, and the industry has been growing ever since. The caye boasts 24-hour-a-day electricity (most of the time), modern communication to anywhere in the world, a few banks, and basic medical services. At last count, there were 141 registered hotels on the island employing about 1,100 Belizeans.

There is a steady, mellow buzz to San Pedro Town, which becomes a bit hectic and trendy at holiday times, especially El Día de San Pedro (June 26–29) and the Costa Maya Festival in August.

ORIENTATION

Whether arriving by air or sea, your trip to Ambergris begins in San Pedro Town. There are three roads running north–south and paralleling the beach on the island's east side. Most locals still refer to the streets by their historic names: **Front Street** (Barrier Reef Drive), **Middle Street** (Pescador Drive), and **Back Street** (Angel Coral Street). Another common landmark is at the north end of town, where the San Pedro River flows through a navigable cut. This spot is often referred to as **"the cut"** or "the split," or more recently, "the bridge," referring to the toll bridge that replaced the hand-drawn ferry. You'll often hear the term "south of town," referring to the continually developing area south of the airstrip, accessed by Coconut Drive.

SIGHTS
Beaches

Don't expect the wide-open clean beaches you've seen in other Caribbean destinations. A few hotels on Ambergris Caye have nice soft, white sand (some natural, others dredged from the lagoon side, an ecologically questionable activity); most only have short strips of sand and seagrass shallows. But even if the "beach" serves as a pedestrian walkway and an open market in most of San Pedro, the ocean is as beautiful as ever, and small docks and pools give access where swimming might otherwise be difficult. One of the better natural swimming and snorkeling beaches is 12 miles north of San Pedro at Tranquility Bay Resort.

THE NORTHERN CAYES

SNORKEL SITES NEAR AMBERGRIS CAYE

You don't need a license or a certification to snorkel; just put your face in the water and enjoy. Be sure to observe snorkel and reef etiquette. Expect to pay about US$40 per person for a 2.5-hour snorkel tour, or US$70 per person for a full day (9 A.M.–3 P.M., lunch included). You'll save a few bucks if you have your own gear (rentals are about US$8/day).

For starters, grab your snorkel and mask for a swim around the dock at **Ramon's Village Resort.** With an artificial reef that is home to a wide variety of small reef fish, this spot is a favorite swimming hole for locals. For live coral, book a half-day trip to one or all of the following sites.

Mexico Rocks is on the reef north of town and is the place to go to see a huge diversity of coral formations. Only 12 feet at its deepest, it offers an abundance of coral, and the channel nearby brings in a lot of marine life, especially small reef fish. There aren't as many big fish here as in Hol Chan, but for some that's a plus. Near the northern tip of Ambergris Caye, **Bacalar Chico Marine Reserve** is another incredible site with a stunning diversity of wildlife and coral – at least 187 species of fish and several important spawning aggregation sites, plus loggerhead, green, and hawksbill sea turtles.

A little bit south of this area is **Tres Cocos,** a site popular for spotted eagle rays.

The crown jewel of San Pedro snorkeling is the **Hol Chan Marine Reserve,** four miles southeast of San Pedro Town. Visitors are taken to the Hol Chan cut, a 30-foot-deep natural break in the Belize Barrier Reef. Snor-kelers stay in the shallow inner reef area but can swim through the cut. Because of the movement between the ocean and the inner reef lagoon through this area, it is high in nutrients and allows for marine animals of all types to thrive and increase in size. Be on the lookout for spiny lobsters, black groupers, nurse sharks, moray eels, and a plethora of reef fish showing off their bright colors. Rangers patrol the area during the day and help ensure the safety of visitors. Listen to your guide, though – the current at Hol Chan can be strong!

A mile south of the Hol Chan cut, **Shark Ray Alley** is also part of the reserve and offers visitors the rare opportunity to snorkel alongside southern stingrays and nurse sharks that frequent the area in search of food (which is kindly provided by your tour operator). Large schools of horse-eyed jack and snapper also come here for the free handouts. There are spectacular coral formations on the back reef for snorkelers, and the fore reef gives scuba divers the chance to dive the *Amigos Del Mar* tugboat wreck.

When you step back onto dry land, stop in at the Hol Chan Marine Reserve office, on Caribena Street in the center of town. The interactive visitors center has information on the reserve, as well as displays detailing the various zones of the reserve and species. Not sure what you saw? First ask your guide, and if you still have questions, stop in and ask the staff – they're happy to answer questions and give more details on the reserve.

◀ Hol Chan Marine Reserve

Once a traditional fishing ground, back when San Pedro was a sleepy village of a few hundred people, Hol Chan Marine Reserve (www.holchanbelize.org, US$12.50 pp) is now the most popular dive and snorkel site in Belize, with tens of thousands of visitors each year. The site is four miles south of San Pedro, but in town, they have a small visitors center on Caribena Street with information on the reserve. Nearly all tour operators on Ambergris and Caye Caulker offer trips to the Hol Chan cut and Shark Ray Alley.

Once you visit, you'll quickly understand the popularity of the reserve—and why it is important to help preserve it. Established as a marine park in 1987, which banned fishing, the site boasts an amazing diversity of species. The reserve focuses its energy on creating a sustainable link between tourism and conservation, protecting the coral reef while allowing visitors to experience and learn about the

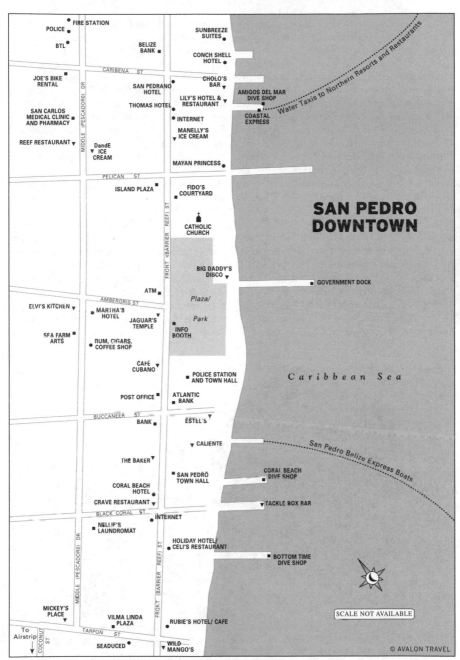

SAN PEDRO
DOWNTOWN

POLICE
FIRE STATION
BTL
BELIZE BANK
SUNBREEZE SUITES
CONCH SHELL HOTEL

CARIBENA ST

JOE'S BIKE RENTAL
SAN PEDRANO HOTEL
THOMAS HOTEL
CHOLO'S BAR
LILY'S HOTEL & RESTAURANT
AMIGOS DEL MAR DIVE SHOP

MIDDLE (PESCADORO) DR

SAN CARLOS MEDICAL CLINIC AND PHARMACY
INTERNET
COASTAL EXPRESS

REEF RESTAURANT
DandE ICE CREAM
MANELLY'S ICE CREAM

Water Taxis to Northern Resorts and Restaurants

PELICAN ST

ISLAND PLAZA
MAYAN PRINCESS

FIDO'S COURTYARD

FRONT (BARRIER REEF) ST

CATHOLIC CHURCH

BIG DADDY'S DISCO

GOVERNMENT DOCK

ATM

AMBERGRIS ST

ELVI'S KITCHEN
MARTHA'S HOTEL
JAGUAR'S TEMPLE
Plaza/ Park
INFO BOOTH

SFA FARM ARTS
RUM, CIGARS, COFFEE SHOP

CAFÉ CUBANO

C a r i b b e a n   S e a

POLICE STATION AND TOWN HALL

POST OFFICE
ATLANTIC BANK

BUCCANEER ST

BANK
ESTEL'S

CALIENTE

San Pedro Belize Express Boats

THE BAKER

SAN PEDRO TOWN HALL
CORAL BEACH DIVE SHOP

CORAL BEACH HOTEL

CRAVE RESTAURANT

TACKLE BOX BAR

BLACK CORAL ST
INTERNET

MIDDLE (PESCADORO) DR

NELLIE'S LAUNDROMAT

FRONT (BARRIER REEF) ST

HOLIDAY HOTEL/ CELI'S RESTAURANT

BOTTOM TIME DIVE SHOP

MICKEY'S PLACE

VILMA LINDA PLAZA

RUBIE'S HOTEL/ CAFE

SCALE NOT AVAILABLE

To Airstrip

COCONUT ST

TARPON ST

SEADUCED

WILD MANGO'S

© AVALON TRAVEL

marine life living there. Some guides think the more daring poses they strike with the rays, the bigger tip they'll get. Please note that officially, it is illegal to feed or touch the fish! Even if your guide tells you differently, and even if you see other groups fondling the nurse sharks and rays—this is against the reserve rules and regulations and against all normal protocol for interacting with wildlife. That said, San Pedro fishers and tour guides have been feeding the animals in this spot every day for over 15 years, so some argue that an exception should be made, or that there is some educational benefit to interacting with the animals. What do you think?

❰ Bacalar Chico Marine Reserve

Located on and around the northern tip of Ambergris Caye, Bacalar Chico National Park and Marine Reserve hosts an incredibly diverse array of wildlife, offers excellent snorkeling and diving, and is rich with history. The Bacalar Chico Canal is reputed to have been dug by Maya traders between A.D. 700 and 900,

creating Ambergris Caye by separating it from the Yucatán Peninsula. The reserve has a wide range of wildlife habitat; 194 species of birds have been sighted there. The landscape consists in part of sinkholes and cenotes created by the effects of weathering on the limestone bedrock of Ambergris Caye. On the eastern side of the reserve is **Rocky Point,** the only location in the Belize Barrier Reef Reserve System where the reef touches the shore. This is one of Belize's most important and prolific sea turtle nesting sites, home to at least 10 threatened species. In 1997, Bacalar Chico—along with the Belize Barrier Reef Reserve System—was designated a World Heritage Site by UNESCO.

Bacalar Chico also contains at least nine archaeological sites: Maya trading, fishing, and agricultural settlements that were inhabited from at least A.D. 300–900. A 10th site just outside the reserve boundary is regarded as especially important for its remaining wall network throughout the settlement and its potential to provide missing information about the transition from the Classic Maya period

© JOSHUA BERMAN

The Turtleman's House in Bacalar Chico Marine Reserve

to modern times. The reserve also contains evidence of Spanish and English habitation during the colonial period, including several Spanish-period shipwrecks offshore.

VISITING THE RESERVE

There is a ranger station in the northwest area of the park with a **visitors center** (tel. 501/226-2833, www.bacalarchico.org) and displays of area history, including old glass bottles and Maya relics found within the reserve. There is a picnic area with a barbecue and grill. Most Ambergris dive shops and a few tour companies do dive/snorkel trips to Bacalar Chico based in San Pedro. Start with **SEAduced by Belize** (tel. 501/226-3221) and **Searious Adventures** (tel. 501/226-4202, www.seariousadventures. com), or arrange a trip with **Tranquility Bay Resort** (U.S. tel. 800/843-2293, www.tranquilitybayresort.com) or **The Turtleman's House** (tel. 501/664-9661, http://turtlemanshouse.com).

ACCOMMODATIONS

The two places to stay are on a fabulous hard-packed white-sand beach 12 miles north of San Pedro. The boat ride from town takes anywhere from 30 to 40 minutes, well past the last stop on the water taxi. These options are for folks who want to feel like they are on another island, not for people who want to drive golf carts and party (though all the standard tours are still available, probably with a little extra transport cost).

Tranquility Bay Resort (U.S. tel. 800/843-2293, www.tranquilitybayresort.com, from US$139) is the only resort on the island where you can snorkel directly from the beach to the reef. Every evening, tarpon, barracudas, and eagle rays swim under the lights of their dock-side restaurant, appropriately named The Aquarium. They have a budget room just off the beach, along with seven brightly painted two-bedroom cabanas and three one-bedrooms with lofts, lining one of the nicest white-sand beaches on the island. Bedrooms are air-conditioned and each cabana is equipped with refrigerator and microwave. The cabins have

Belizean hardwoods, Mexican tiles, and spectacular ocean views. They offer free use of kayaks (which can cover a lot of ground at this site), an on-site dive shop, and a handful of fishing, snorkeling, scuba, and sailing trips.

One of the most distinctive accommodations I've seen, **The Turtleman's House** (tel. 501/664-9661, http://turtlemanshouse.com) is a stilted shack above the water built out of salvaged material (much of it pieces of destroyed docks that wash ashore after hurricanes) by Greg "Turtleman" Smith, a resident of this beach for three decades and the man who is partly responsible for the creation of the reserve and protection of its wildlife. At first glance, US$80 a night (three-night minimum) seems overpriced, but you're paying for the location. Plus, meals are cheap, and you'll have the sunrise all to yourself. Guests sleep in the primitive room with a solar bag shower and seagrass compost bucket toilet, then join Greg, his wife, Rosemary, and their children in their home on the island (50 feet away) for delicious home-cooked meals and cinnamon buns. Guests can also take advantage of Tranquility Bay's restaurant and dive shop, a stone's throw down the beach.

NIGHTLIFE

San Pedro boasts the best nightlife in the country, whether your idea of fun is dancing up a storm, drowning in alcohol, listening to live music, or watching chickens poop—it's all here. Wednesdays and Saturdays are the biggest nights out, and water taxis actually change their schedules to accommodate revelers. The chicken drop is now on Thursdays. In general, the hot spots don't get going until 11 P.M. or midnight, with lots of warming up in various bars before the bumpin' and grindin' begins.

Bars

Diving by day and drinking by night is the standard Ambergris scene—although a number of proud underachievers substitute a full day of cocktails for diving. **Cholo's Sport Bar,** on the beach in the center of town, is a mellow local hangout and heart of San Pedro's social scene. A few stumbles down the beach, **Fido's Courtyard** (open 10 A.M.–midnight, till 2 A.M. on weekends) the largest bar-restaurant complex in town, with live music every night in the high season and one of the only sushi bars in the country. They also have a great app menu and friendly barkeeps.

The bar at **BC's** (on the beach, just east of the airstrip, tel. 501/226-3289) is popular, open from 9 A.M. daily with live music on Sundays, and serving great nachos and burritos all day (US$7.50). The **Rehab Bar,** a small patio bar on Front Street next to the Jaguar's Temple disco, is open daily and great for people-watching.

Place your bets at the weekly **Chicken Drop,** Thursdays at 6 P.M. in front of **Wahoo's Bar** (beachside in the Spindrift Hotel, tel. 501/226-2002) and **Caliente Restaurant** (tel. 501/226-2170, 11 A.M.–9:30 P.M. Tues.–Sun.): A chicken is let loose on a numbered grid and revelers place bets on which numbered square the chicken will choose to soil. Warm up at

Wahoo's Bar and Caliente Restaurant's two-for-one happy hour, 4–6 P.M.

South of San Pedro, **Crazy Canuck's Beach Bar** (S. Coconut Dr.) has live music and dancing on Mondays and Thursdays, and a jam session Sunday afternoons. You'll find happy customers playing cards, horseshoes, dominoes, and other games. Across Coconut Drive from Canuck's, look for the **Roadkill Bar** (S. Coconut Dr.), another popular hangout. Continuing south, you'll find the **Sandbar Restaurant & Grill** (1 Seagrape Dr., US$10–20) on the beach a few hundred yards past Victoria House.

North of San Pedro, the legendary ◖ **Palapa Bar** (tel. 501/226-3111, 10 A.M.–9 P.M.-ish) is a must-stop, whether for lunch, sunset, or a lazy evening of appetizers (US$4–6), barbecue, beer, and cocktails (try the Banango with rum). For the full Palapa experience, bring a bathing suit so you can float in an anchored inner tube and have the bartender lower you down a bucket of beer. It's a short golf cart ride north of the bridge, or US$3.50 by water taxi.

© JOSHUA BERMAN

The famous Palapa Bar, just north of San Pedro, is worth the trip.

Dancing

Wednesday is ladies' night at **Wet Willy's,** and Saturdays get going when Fido's closes at midnight and everyone wanders across the street to **Jaguar's Temple** (open at 9:30 P.M. Thursday, Friday, and Saturday) and **Big Daddy's Disco,** located across from Jaguar's Temple, next to the park. Music and dancing get started around 11 P.M.–midnight and can go until 3 A.M. or later.

SHOPPING

Gift shops abound in San Pedro, especially on Front and Middle Streets; they've got your postcards, beach apparel, towels, hats, T-shirts, hot sauces, and the usual knickknacks. **Orange** has gorgeous hand-carved art and other crafts in its two island locations. Artisans sell their works on Front Street, mainly handmade zirlcote wood carvings and bowls and Guatemalan jewelry and textiles.

For sinful gifts, the **Cigar and Rum Shop** (on Middle Street, across from Elvi's Kitchen, 9 A.M.–9 P.M.) has a walk-in humidor with Cuban and Belizean cigars, interesting rum and liquor products, and dark-roasted Guatemalan Arabica coffee—for sale and sampling.

A decent book selection is available at **Blue,** across from San Pedro Holiday Hotel, open daily at 8 A.M. **Pages** (in Vilma Linda Plaza on Tarpon St., www.pagesbookstorebelize. com, Mon.–Sat.) is another option with a decent stock, but a bit expensive.

Belizean Arts in **Fido's Courtyard** (tel. 501/226-2056, daily) sells art, jewelry, ceramics, and carvings by local and Belizean artists. The well-established shop has the largest selection of original paintings in Belize. Also in Fido's Courtyard is **Bambar,** offering handcrafted jewelry made with resin ambers, Maya jade, shells, and silver. **Mambo Chill** imports expensive women's clothing.

Ambergris Art Gallery is worth a look, with two stores: one on Middle Street near the men's clothing store Moonbreeze, the other in the Sunbreeze Hotel.

Get your rocks at **Ambergris Maya Jade and History Museum** (across from town hall,

9 A.M.–6 P.M. daily). Also a retail jade shop, it's designed "to give visitors an overview of 3,000 years of Mesoamerican jade and its importance to the cultures in the region." When you're finished, check out **The Emerald Mine,** a few doors down.

RECREATION
Diving

Almost every hotel on Ambergris either employs local dive shops or has its own on-site shop and dive masters. They all offer pretty much the same thing: resort courses, PADI or NAUI certification classes, day trips, and snorkel trips. Some also offer things like night dives, and a few have Nitrox capabilities. What really makes the difference is the experience of the instructor or dive master, the quality of the equipment, the size of the boat, and the size of the groups. Prices are pretty standard around the island: local two-tank dive US$60–75, plus rental fee and tax; resort course US$150; open water certification US$450–470; advanced certification US$380; three-tank dive to the Blue Hole US$250, to Turneffe US$185.

dive shop on Ambergris Caye

Amigos del Mar (tel. 501/226-2706, www. amigosdive.com), based on the pier near Cholo's Bar, is a bustling place with top-notch gear and a solid reputation for safety. Many clients return year after year to dive with the same long-term and friendly staff. At press time, Amigos is the only San Pedro operation running trips to the Blue Hole in their 52-foot boat (important for the long journey to and from the famous site). Other extremely reputable dive shops are **Hugh Parkey's Diving** (at the SunBreeze Hotel beachfront in central San Pedro, tel. 501/220-4024, www.belize-diving.com), **Ecologic Divers** (tel. 501/226-4118, www.ecologicdivers.com), and **Patojo's** (tel. 501/206-2283, patojos99@yahoo.com), all with proven reputations for safety and service.

Sailing Charters and Cruising

Explore the Caribbean the way it was meant to be traveled: by wind. Just go to www.ambergriscaye.com and click on "boat charters" to get an updated list of your options. Old standby boats include the *Winnie Estelle* (tel. 501/226-2427, US$55 per adult for day trips) and the "old-school sailing trip" aboard the *Rum Punch II* (tel. 501/226-2340), which offers snorkel tours, beach barbecues, and sunset charters.

Spend the day with the Rubio brothers, snorkeling, fishing, drinking, and relaxing aboard *No Rush*, a 36-foot catamaran that can be booked through **Unity Tours** (tel. 501/226-4551, www.ambergriscaye.com/unitytours). Other cat cruises can be found at **Searious Adventures** (tel. 501/226-4202, www.seariousadventures.com) and **SEAduced by Belize** (tel. 501/226-3221), both of which offer many different activities in addition to sailing. The *Katkandu* (www.belizecharters.com) is a 42-foot luxury cat that provides catered upscale cruises and multiday charters.

Fishing

The area within the reef is a favorite for tarpon and bonefish. Outside the reef, the choice of big game is endless. Most hotels and dive shops will make arrangements for fishing, including boat and guide. Ask around the docks (and your hotel) for the best guides. Serious anglers should consider Abner Marin at **Go Fish Belize** (tel. 501/226-3121, www.gofishbelize.com), one of the most qualified and reputable guides around. Or try Richard French at **Belize Flats Fishing Expeditions** (tel. 501/226-2799, www.belizeflatsfishing.com). **Ruby's Hotel** has a shack on the beach, and the guys working there are rumored to be excellent guides. Another sure bet is **Fishing San Pedro** (tel. 501/226-2835, www.fishingsanpedro.com), where half- or full-day chartered fishing trips are relatively affordable (US$295 full day for two people includes tackle, bait, soda, and water); a fish/lobster barbecue adds a bit extra.

Fitness, Massage, and Yoga

If your hotel lacks a proper gym and you'd rather pump iron than dive, the **Train Station** (tel. 501/226-4222, www.trainstationfitness.com) is 2.5 blocks south of the bridge. In San Pedro, you'll find both scheduled yoga classes (US$15 drop-in) and private sessions at **Sol Spa** (Phoenix Hotel, tel. 501/226-2410, www.belizesolspa.com), which also offers a range of treatments and massages like Honeymoon Bliss, Solar Therapy, and Maya Abdominal Massage.

The **Asian Garden Day Spa** (Coconut Drive, across from Ramon's Village, tel. 501/226-4072, www.asiangardenspasalon.com) is a family-run spa in a lovely courtyard, specializing in Thai massage, hot stone therapy, reflexology, facials, scrubs, and specials like sunset or starlight couples massage.

Tropical Touch (tel. 501/226-4666, www.tropicaltouchspaworks.com) is a full-service massage and day spa right on the water with all kinds of body treatments, including Maya Abdominal Massage. **The Art of Touch** (tel. 501/226-3357) is in the entrance to the Sunbreeze Hotel.

Not far north of the bridge is the **Maya Secrets Spa** (tel. 501/610-3775, belize5@me.com), where you'll find a lovely, romantic

© JOSHUA BERMAN

There are many places to get pampered in Ambergris Caye.

setting for tropical treatments, massage, and facials, all using the owner's own line of Tropical Secret products; this is a great spot for couples. A bit farther north, **Ak'Bol Yoga Retreat** (yogawithkirsten@gmail.com, www.akbol.com) is one of the few places in Belize offering daily yoga classes (usually 9 A.M.) in a gorgeous wood-floor palapa on the beach. They also do full moon gatherings and host a 2012 discussion group.

ACCOMMODATIONS
Under US$25

San Pedro's got slim pickings in this category. The hands-down best is **❰ Ruby's Hotel** (tel. 501/226-2063, rubys@btl.net, US$18–40), with 23 rooms in a building right on the water in the heart of the village. Ruby's Café and pastry shop downstairs are excellent, and you can sit on your room's balcony or the common deck space and watch the beach traffic below. There are rooms with either shared or private bath.

Your only youth hostel option is **Pedro's Inn** (tel. 501/226-3825, www.backpackersbelize.

com, US$12.50 s, US$22.50 d), with two rows of 14 wooden stalls, each with bed, ceiling fans, locker, and access to shared bath facilities. The rooms are right above Pedro's Sports Bar and poker room, so you've got an on-site nightly social scene with a lively cast of characters and pizza available for delivery. Pedro's has a small pool, deck, and shaded picnic area. It's back by the airstrip (you'll wake up to the morning's flights taking off overhead), a seven-minute walk from the town center (or US$3.50 taxi). Across the street, Pedro's has 30 functional hotel rooms for US$50–65 each with air-conditioning, TV, private bath, and fan.

US$25-50

❰ Hotel San Pedrano (Front St., tel. 501/226-2054, sanpedrano@btl.net, US$35 with fan, US$45 with a/c) has six rooms that make up the island's self-proclaimed "top of the low end." From the breezy upstairs veranda, it's easy to eat a bite, read a book, or watch the street below. Each room has hot and cold water, private bath, ceiling fan, and optional air-conditioning. **Thomas Hotel** (Front St., tel. 501/226-2061, US$33–43) has six cheap rooms with private bath, fan, and air-conditioning, a hundred feet from the beach; this humble *hotelito* is 40 years old. **Martha's Hotel** (Middle St., across from Elvi's Kitchen, tel. 501/206-2053, julian@btl.net, US$30) is two blocks from the waterfront. The nine upstairs rooms have private baths, ceiling fans, dirty walls, and cracked-linoleum floors. This is a cheap place to crash, not much else.

US$50–100

The **Coral Beach Hotel** (Front St., tel. 501/266-2013, www.coralbeachhotel.com, US$57 with fan, US$12 more for a/c) offers 19 clean, small rooms, each with private bath, hot and cold water, and air-conditioning or fan. There's a nice veranda overlooking the action on Front Street. Meal plans are available.

Lily's Hotel and Restaurant (tel. 501/226-2650, www.ambergriscaye.com/lilys, US$65–75) has six good-value rooms with private bath, air-conditioning, and very nice verandas on the beach; there are a few apartments too. This simple hotel is run by Felipe Paz and family—friendly longtime residents of San Pedro. Lily's has been known for years for offering excellent local food in plentiful family-style servings.

The beachfront **Conch Shell Inn** (tel. 501/226-2062, belizeanmark@hotmail.com, US$49–99) is in the heart of San Pedro, beside Sunbreeze Suites. It was the third hotel to open in the early days of tourism. Renovated in 2008, the five upstairs single and double rooms have great views and tiled floors, and the cheaper downstairs rooms are steps from the sea. British owners Dr. Mark and Joan are well known for providing the free "Smiles" dental clinics to islanders.

Another quaint and homey option south of town is **Changes in Latitudes Bed and Breakfast** (36 Coconut Dr., tel. 501/226-2986, U.S. tel. 800/631-9834, www.ambergriscaye.com/latitudes, US$95), with six cozy rooms with air-conditioning, ceiling fan, private bath, and pool privileges at Exotic Caye Beach Resort. They're serious about the breakfast, which is served daily in the common room.

On the north end of town, toward the cut, **Hotel del Rio** (tel. 501/226-2286, www.ambergriscaye.com/hoteldelrio, US$50–145) offers great value. Accommodations range from basic economy rooms with shared baths and cold water to bigger casitas built of natural materials (some with king or two queen beds).

CHOOSING A HOTEL IN THE CAYES

At last count, Ambergris had about 140 licensed hotels, mostly midrange to upscale lodging. The couple of places geared toward backpackers and budget travelers are located either right in San Pedro Town or on the outskirts by the airstrip. Otherwise, here are a few things to keep in mind when deciding on a hotel.

First off, in downtown San Pedro, the word "beachside" refers to the very narrow strip of sand on the island's east side. It is used more as a pathway for pedestrians and boats than for lounging in the sand. As you move farther from town, either to the north or south along the island, the beaches fronting the resorts become wider, softer, and more exclusive.

Of course, what you give up in beach quality, you get back in location: "In town" means in the middle of cafés, bars, boutiques, dive shops, dancing, and dining. If you're more into privacy, all this action is easily accessible from any resort on the island by boat, taxi, or golf cart.

Keep in mind that rates across the board are subject to seasonal rate fluctuations, service charges, and government taxes. Always verify and ask about discounts before booking. Remember that rates reported in *Moon Belize* are for double occupancy during the high season.

THE NORTHERN CAYES

© JOSHUA BERMAN

Many beachfront hotels in San Pedro have pleasant rooftop verandas.

Apart from the Turtleman's House in Bacalar Chico Marine Reserve, the only budget option north of the bridge is the **Ak'Bol** retreat center (a.k.a. the "yoga barracks") on the lagoon side, which has 30 fantastic value rooms (US$35 s, US$50 d) in a long wooden building with a massive shared bathroom/shower/locker room. The lagoon here is unspoiled and full of wildlife, and it's on a narrow strip of the island so that the beach (and yoga deck and bar/restaurant) is only a 30-second walk away.

US$100-150

The cheerful **San Pedro Holiday Hotel** (Front. St., tel. 501/226-2014 or 501/226-2103, www. sanpedroholiday.com, US$110–125), the island's first hotel (still under the original family's management), keeps getting better. The 17 clean, spacious rooms have air-conditioning and fans, private baths, and beachfront verandas. Lots of water sports and boats are available. This hotel is very central to restaurants and nightlife in town.

Inside an elegant three-story building of tropical colonial design, on the corner of Sandpiper Street and the ocean, is the 【 **Blue Tang Inn** (tel. 501/226-2326, U.S. tel. 866/881-1020, www.bluetanginn.com, US$120–225). The 14 tasteful rooms sport lots of warm, rich wood paneling and have kitchens, private baths, ceiling fans, and air-conditioning; third floor rooms have whirlpool tubs. The grounds are well kept and the rooftop balcony is breezy and pleasant.

Popular with birders and nature lovers, **Caribbean Villas** (Seagrape Dr., tel. 501/226-2715, U.S. tel. 866/522-9960, www.caribbean-villashotel.com, US$105–220) has a fantastic spot on the beach just south of town, offering a range of economy rooms and luxury suites. The property's small bird sanctuary is one of the few remaining areas of original littoral forest on the island and has a "people perch." Water heating is supplemented by rooftop solar panels; irrigation is from rainwater catchment tanks. In addition, the rooms are designed to catch the cooling trade winds to reduce the need for air-conditioning.

One of Belize's only dedicated yoga resorts, **☾ Ak'Bol** (1 mile north of the bridge, www. akbol.com, US$145–165) has seven cabanas on the beach in a naturally landscaped garden, a small pool, and a shaded yoga garden in earshot of the ocean. This is both a yoga retreat and a great place for travelers who want a new experience that does *not* remind them of home, as the owner Kirsten says. The cabanas have raised beds, local decor, a loft for the kids, unique conch shell sinks, and private outdoor jungle showers. An on-site beach bar sells local meals as cheap as US$3. There are also daily yoga classes and retreat packages.

US$150-200

The **☾ SunBreeze Beach Hotel** (tel. 501/226-2191, U.S. 800/688-0191, www. sunbreeze.net, US$170–225) is a full-service oceanfront hotel with 42 rooms built around an open sand area and pool. Rooms have two queen beds, air-conditioning, tile floors, local artwork, private baths, and direct-dial phones; Front Street starts next door, and the entrance is yards from the airstrip. There's an on-site dive shop, a top-notch restaurant (Blue Water Grill), and many other services. The SunBreeze has some of the few fully handicapped accessible rooms I've seen in the country. They also rent suites at the other end of Front Street; on the beach across from the Belize Bank, **SunBreeze Suites** (tel. 501/226-4675, www. sunbreezesuites.com, US$150–200) offers one-bedroom suites with full kitchens, guest queen sofa beds, and air-conditioning, and they can sleep up to four adults per room; families and children are welcome. They feel more like small condos than hotel rooms.

A full-service resort with 71 rooms, **Ramon's Village** (tel. 501/226-2071, U.S. tel. 800/624-4215, www.ramons.com) has standard rooms from US$155 and a presidential suite for US$400; the rooms are nice, though the "kitchenettes" are not much more than a sink and microwave. The property's 500-foot beach is practically in San Pedro Town and has decent walk-in snorkeling; there is a restaurant and bar and a pool, as well as on-site

dive shops, guides, and an inland tour operator. You can rent sailboards, aquacycles, speedboats, and golf carts.

Xanadu Island Resort (tel. 501/226-2814, www.xanaduresort-belize.com, from US$170) is a cluster of luxury monolithic domes with thatched overlay roofs nestled in lush landscaping. There is a beachfront pool, as well as a private nature walk and bird sanctuary. Nineteen suites are available with fully equipped kitchens, and there is a choice of studios and one-, two-, and three-bedrooms.

Mata Rocks Resort (tel. 501/226-2336, U.S. tel. 888/628-2757, www.matarocks.com, US$135–220) has six beautiful suites and 11 rooms with ocean views around a pool; the rooms, while not huge, have plenty of basic amenities, such as air-conditioning, cable, wireless Internet, bikes, transfers, and continental breakfast. The style is white, clean, and Mediterranean.

Over US$200
SAN PEDRO
The **Phoenix Resort** (U.S. tel. 877/822-5512, tel. 501/226-2083, www.thephoenixbelize. com, US$360–650) takes the luxury thing up a couple of notches in San Pedro. This condo resort has 27 of the largest furnished suites on the island, with every amenity you can imagine both in and out of your room. It has a pool, restaurant, gym, and spa, all in a big white-walled compound toward the north of town, on the beach side, as well as full concierge for activities on and off the island.

SOUTH OF SAN PEDRO
Still one of the island's top class acts, **☾ Victoria House** (tel. 501/226-2067, U.S. tel. 800/247-5159, www.victoria-house.com, US$175–1,650) has a luxurious selection of suites and several multifamily mansion-like villas. Expect grand, colonial elegance on a well-manicured, tranquil piece of property about two miles south of San Pedro. The stucco and thatched casitas with tile floors are placed around several sleek infinity pools; you also get a full-service dive shop with private guides,

the Admiral Nelson Bar, and one of the top-rated restaurants in the country (Restaurant Palmilla).

The Villas at Banyan Bay (tel. 501/226-3739, U.S. tel. 866/466-2179, www.banyanbay.com, from US$300) is a "luxury family resort" with all the amenities in its 40 suites, including a whirlpool tubs. Lots of activities and lessons for children are available; full dive/inland trips can be arranged. There's also a respected on-site dock restaurant, Rico's.

NORTH OF SAN PEDRO

Amid the boxy construction projects north of the split, you'll find some of Belize's most well-known and well-run properties, all only a few hundred yards from Belize's famous barrier reef.

Less than three miles north of San Pedro, **El Pescador** (tel. 501/226-2975, U.S. tel. 800/242-2017, www.elpescador.com, from US$200) was constructed in 1974 as one of the world's premier sportfishing lodges, and it has evolved into a modern resort for sportspeople and their families. There are 14 rooms in the colonial-style mahogany lodge and private one-, two-, and three-bedroom villa accommodations around stunning swimming pools and palms.

Capricorn Resort and Restaurant (tel. 501/226-2809, www.capricornresort.net, US$200) offers a more intimate experience. Stay in one of three cabanas decorated in tropical colors with private bathrooms and showers made for two. Rates include a continental breakfast, bikes, and kayaks.

Las Terrazas (U.S. tel. 800/447-1553, www.lasterrazasresort.com, US$225) is a slick affair of 39 fully equipped "residential townhomes" around a pool area and restaurant serving "southwestern cuisine with Caribbean flair." This is a full-service luxury resort with many activities and packages.

A little more than four miles north of San Pedro is the small, stylish **Mata Chica Beach Resort** (tel. 501/220-5010, www.matachica.com, from US$256), with 24 spacious casitas, suites, and luxury villas, all styled with

the beach at Mata Chica Beach Resort

local art and Oriental-tinged decor. It offers a full range of amenities, a spa, bar-side Jacuzzi, infinity pool, plus a vast swanky lounge, which connects to the Mambo restaurant. The resort does "grand or intimate weddings, honeymoons, and secluded getaways." Their six-person beach mansion goes for a cool US$1,015 a night, plus taxes.

Next door, go for the full rock star treatment in one of two 3,000-square-foot villas at **Azul Belize** (tel. 501/226-4012, www.azulbelize.com, from US$1,000, all inclusive); watch the horizon from your private rooftop Jacuzzi with one of Azul's famous frozen mojitos in hand. Your enormous three-floor crib boasts a full Viking kitchen, ladywood beams, wraparound balconies, flatscreen TV, and wireless Internet throughout the property. Or, unplug at the infinity pool or adjoining Rojo Lounge, where world-class chef Jeff Spiegel prepares some of the island's best cuisine. In 2011, Azul expanded to include several high-luxury options, including a massive 14,400-square-foot villa with its own pool, patio, swim-up bar, and beer on tap.

(Portofino (tel. 501/226-5096, www.portofinobelize.com, US$250–335) is another longstanding luxury lodge, right on the beach, but with a deep swimming pool and an excellent on-site restaurant (meal plan US$55 per day). They have 15 units, including two treetop suites, and a honeymoon/VIP villa with full amenities. You can use their sporting equipment to play around all day—it's only a 15-minute kayak paddle to excellent snorkeling at Mexico Rocks.

Apartment and Condo Rentals

In addition to accommodations listed in these pages, there are many, many apartment and house rentals available across the island. Start by downloading the classifieds from the *San Pedro Sun* website (www.sanpedrosun.net) and checking the classifieds at *San Pedro Daily* (sanpedrodaily.com).

Other sources for vacation homes are **M&M Rentals** (U.S. tel. 949/258-5268, www.mandmrentalsbelize.com) and **Caye Management**

(tel. 501/226-3077, www.cayemanagement.com), which has an office on the north edge of town at Casa Coral and can arrange for cooking and other services in your temporary home.

FOOD

Dining out is very expensive in San Pedro, but there are cheap meals and snacks at the fast food carts in the central park, and at many bakeries.

Bakeries, Cafés, and Ice Cream

This is a category where San Pedro excels. You can smell the freshly baked bread and rolls as you walk down Front Street early in the morning, starting with Ruby's and Celi's, which for decades have been bustling every morning with people eating breakfast and stocking up for day trips. A block north, **The Baker** makes grilled sandwiches for only US$3.50, and has espresso drinks and smoothies.

(Café Cubano (tel. 501/620-1166, 7 A.M.–midnight daily) is hard to miss, on the main street across from the park. You'll find don Pedro slinging some of the strongest, best coffee in town, with beans from his homeland and a large variety of food as well, including a US$10 multi-course breakfast.

Toni's Café Paradise (7 A.M.–3 P.M., closed Sun.) is a nice café offering all-day breakfast, salads, sandwiches, burgers, and pies. It is at the entrance to the purple Vilma Linda Plaza, a peaceful oasis in the bustle of downtown—the tiled courtyard is filled with lush plants and a small fishpond.

Go to **Manelly's** on Front Street for homemade ice cream—they are most proud of their "coconut creation." Or sample the frozen custard at **(DandE's Ice Cream** on Pescador Street, where a couple from dairy country in Pennsylvania turn out fresh flavors every day, including soursop, from a local fruit that makes for a tart Belizean treat.

Barbecue

Besides the informal street barbecues (which offer the best value food around), a rotating schedule ensures a beach barbecue nearly every night of the week, starting with **BC's** (on the beach, just east of the airstrip, tel. 501/226-3289, 11 A.M.–3 P.M. Sun.). Your choice of chicken, ribs, or fish runs US$5–10. Also on Sunday, **Crazy Canuck's** throws in live music and a horseshoe tournament. The **San Pedro Holiday Hotel** has live music to accompany its beach barbecue on Wednesday night; the **Lions Club** donates the money it makes from its Friday and Saturday night barbecues to those who need medical help and can't afford it; and **Ramon's Village** has Tuesday and Friday barbecues.

The island's only falafel joint, **Alibaba's** (across Coconut Dr. from Tropic Air terminal and Moncho's Golf Carts, tel. 501/226-4042, US$5–12, 10 A.M.–10 P.M. daily), is run by two brothers from Jordan and is best known for its takeout rotisserie chicken, served Lebanese style with hummus and tabouli; there are also kabobs, veggie plates, and sometimes hookahs to smoke.

Burgers

You can get a decent burger at many restaurants in San Pedro, but only **Legends Burger Bar,** a half mile or so north of the bridge, specializes totally in beef (and chicken) patties (tel. 501/226-2113, Mon.–Sat. noon–9 P.M.). It's worth the trip. The atmosphere is tropical frat-house, with live music till midnight on weekends. The menu is entertaining, with each burger dedicated to the owner's various heroes. The most Belizean is the "Sir Barry Burger," a tribute to local legend Barry Bowen, a widely admired businessman who was tragically killed in a plane crash in 2010; it's a beef patty topped with Belikin beer–battered shrimp, representing three of the commodities Bowen produced and sold.

Pizza

Pizza is available for delivery or dine-in at dozens of places on the island. **Pepperoni's Pizza** (Coconut Dr., tel. 501/226-4515, 5–10 P.M., closed Mon.) is the most popular for both quality and price—a large 16-inch specialty pie

goes for US$20 and is served deep-dish style. **Pirates** (Middle St., tel. 501/226-4663) is also good, and does slices in the evenings.

Belizean and Mexican

On the back side of the island, you'll find a few fast-food and local eateries offering the cheapest burritos, rice and beans, and stew chicken dishes on the island. **El Fogón** (Trigger Fish St., tel. 501/206-2121, closed Sun., US$4–6) is an authentic family-style eatery serving home-cooked Creole and mestizo dishes in a small, shaded space. Tucked toward the back side of the island, just north of the airstrip, it won't let you down.

On the beach side, **Estel's** (on the beach behind Atlantic Bank, tel. 501/226-2019, 6 A.M.–5 P.M. Wed.–Mon.) is relaxed, and the breakfast menu is perfect (US$7 for a breakfast burrito). The rest of the day, Estel's is good for ribs, barbecue, burgers, seafood, and sangria happy hours.

Ruby's (Front. St.) has pastries and coffee early in the morning. Other reputable spots are **Ambergris Delights** (Front. St.) and **Celi's Deli** (Hicaco Ave., tel. 501/226-0346). **Mickey's Place** (on Tarpon St., tel. 501/226-2223, open for all three meals with breaks in between) is home of the huge Wednesday burrito for US$6; Mickey's has an ample menu of local fare, especially seafood and conch fritters, and offers a bit more ambience than the other Belizean places.

For top-notch Latin Caribbean cuisine, **Wild Mango's** (sandwiched between Ruby's Hotel and the library on the beach, tel. 501/226-2859, noon–3 P.M. and 6–9 P.M. Mon.–Sat., US$12–20) serves amazing versions of local favorites (ceviche, fish tacos, quesadillas, etc., around US$12) prepared by one of Belize's most distinguished chefs, Amy Knox; you cannot go wrong here, from Mango's Mongo Burrito to seafood specials, to rum-glazed bacon shrimp (US$16–24).

Celi's Restaurant (tel. 501/226-2014, 6 A.M.–6 P.M. daily, US$7–17), at San Pedro Holiday Hotel, delivers icy piña coladas and some of the best conch ceviche on the island, plus a full menu, of course. It's been locally owned for many years.

For fun, sandy-floored ambience, try ¶ **Elvi's Kitchen** (on the corner of Middle St. and Ambergris St., tel. 501/226-2176, 11 A.M.–10 P.M., closed Sun., entrées US$10–40), open since 1974. The seafood specials, such as Maya fish, are especially good, and both the conch fritters and frozen key lime pie are locally famous. There's live music on Thursday and a Maya buffet Friday (US$25 pp).

High-end-yet-casual, **Caliente** (in Spindrift Hotel on Front St., tel. 501/226-2170, 11 A.M.–9:30 P.M. Tues.–Sun.) offers creative Mexican and seafood on an open porch or waterfront dining room. They're famous for the lime soup at lunch (good for hangovers, only US$4.50) and generous lobster dinners and other entrées (US$12–22).

South of town, **Blue Iguana Grille** is upstairs at **Crazy Canuck's,** with nice ocean views, and it offers lunch sandwiches and dinners starting at US$16.

Fine Island Cuisine
SAN PEDRO
San Pedro is blessed with an ever-evolving selection of trendy restaurants offering international fare and flair; if you don't pay for such indulgence with an expanded waistline, you'll surely pay for it in cash. If you're *really* dining out—appetizer, a couple of drinks, entrée, and dessert—expect to pay as much as you would in New York City: US$40–80 per person, more if you like your wine. Remember: Many fancy restaurants add a tax and service charge (and a credit card charge), so bring plenty of cash. Reservations are recommended at all of the following restaurants, especially in the high season.

Of the finer restaurants, ¶ **Blue Water Grill** (on the beach behind the SunBreeze Hotel, tel. 501/226-3347, 7 A.M.–9:30 P.M. daily) is known to offer some of the best values and biggest portions. The menu has hints of Hawaiian and Southeast Asian cuisine; try the coconut shrimp stick with black bean sweet and sour sauce. Sushi is offered on Tuesday

and Thursday; there are dishes like snook with banana curry and comfort plates like lasagna (entrées from US$19).

In central San Pedro, **Crave** (tel. 501/226-3211, www.cravebelize.com, Mon.–Sat. 11 A.M.–9:30 P.M., Sun. from 5 P.M.) has a nice corner location on Barrier Reef Drive and Black Coral Street, serving Latin American and Caribbean cuisine. There's an air-conditioned dining room and a bar open to the street, and it serves savory fish and meat dishes, including an entire lobster tail appetizer for US$11, Caribbean jerk snapper (US$20), and a towering Seafood Treasure (US$35).

Red Ginger (tel. 501/226-4623, 7:30–10:30 A.M., 11:30 A.M.–2:30 P.M., and 6–9:30 P.M., closed Tues.), in the Phoenix Resort toward the north part of San Pedro, has an indoor air-conditioned dining room and trellised outdoor patio. They specialize in local cuisine with an international twist—grouper ceviche with mango, empanadas with pork, and plantains with buffalo mozzarella and sautéed basil. There are homemade bagel sandwiches for breakfast, Indian chicken curry and Cajun gumbo for lunch, and a variety of appetizers, salads, pastas, seafood, and steaks (entrées US$9–37), plus a five-course tasting menu (US$45), big wine list, half price wine on Monday, and tapas on Wednesday and Sunday.

SOUTH OF SAN PEDRO
For authentic Italian dishes and gourmet 12-inch pies (US$12), try **Pinocchio Italian Restaurant and Pizza** (Seagrape Dr., tel. 501/226-4447, http://pinocchioitalianrestaurant.com, 5:30–11:30 P.M. Thurs.–Tues.), a US$4 taxi ride or 10-minute walk south of San Pedro. On Sting Ray Street past the gas station, **Casa Picasso** (tel. 501/670-5326, hours vary, US$38–50) is an exclusive supper club, serving tapas (mini crabcakes with chili lime sauce), pastas, and locally made wine and spirits—including the owner's special absinthe verde, a.k.a. The Green Fairy. It's prix fixe, including proprietary cocktail pairings with each course; reservations only.

◖ **Hidden Treasure Restaurant** (4088 Sarstoon St., tel. 501/226-4111, 5:30–9:30 P.M. daily, US$15–22) is an open-air intimate restaurant under a palapa roof. They have a long list of appetizers, lunches, dinner, and desserts; from seafood bisque for US$16 to Maya accented snapper and spare *buhurie* (Garifuna spiced ribs, US$20).

The chef at Victoria House's ◖ **Restaurant Palmilla** (at Victoria House two miles south of San Pedro, tel. 501/226-2067, 6:30 A.M.– 2:30 P.M. and 6–9 P.M. daily, US$24–50) was born in Mexico City, trained in the United States, and comes from a family of renowned chefs. His unique style is "Mayan Bistro," which combines the chili peppers of Mexico with fresh local produce, seafood, and meats. Start with crispy snapper cakes with chipotle beurre blanc, black bean, and roasted corn succotash; follow with black bean or *chilapachole* (corn) soup; then savor main dishes like cashew-crusted grouper.

NORTH OF SAN PEDRO

A common Ambergris evening involves taking a golf cart, bicycle, or water ferry to one of the beach restaurants north of the bridge. The cheapest, most casual places are Palapa Bar and Ak'Bol. Then there's a handful of expensive options that require reservations, most serving dinner 6–9 P.M. at tables with stunning settings on the beach. Many (but not all) do not turn tables, so you can stay until the water taxi comes to take you home.

Glen and Colleen at the **Rendezvous Restaurant and Winery** (tel. 501/226-3426, lunch and dinner) offer free wine tasting to anyone wandering by. They blend, ferment, and bottle their own wine in recycled bottles. The restaurant has a stellar 12-year reputation for its blend of Thai and French cuisine. Start with escargot with lemon-garlic butter sauce for an appetizer (US$10); then have grilled shrimp (US$22) or chicken with coconut red-curry sauce (US$15).

A couple more miles up the coast, **Mambo's** (Mata Chica Beach Resort, tel. 501/220-5010, www.matachica.com, lunch and dinner) is

pure indulgence, serving rich and artful heaps of snapper, scallops, shrimp, lobster, and calamari—you can try them all in the amazing Deep Blue entrée (US$34). Appetizers like soy-glazed snapper carpaccio are US$10–16; save room for the chocolate mousse.

◖ **Rojo Lounge** (at Azul Belize, www.azulbelize.com, tel. 501/226-4012 or 501/226-4013, lunch and dinner Tues.–Sat., entrées from US$27) has a succulent, sophisticated menu that will leave you grasping for adjectives. Or maybe you'll just reach for your peppered cocktail in stunned silence after each bite of shrimp-stuffed grouper or conch pizza; it's spendy but worth every savory cent. The self-made chef, Jeff Spiegel, is a former punk record producer from California.

Portofino Restaurant and Green Parrot Beach Bar (tel. 501/226-5096, lunch and dinner) is six miles north of San Pedro and they'll give you a complimentary boat ride to join them for dinner; expect local cuisine with a European flair including spider crab–laced snapper and other creative seafood specials (US$18–35 entrées). Lunch is also excellent with out-of-this-world quesadillas and an enormous vegetarian selection (US$6–14), and they'll set up a romantic table on the end of their pier if you like.

Supermarkets and Specialty Foods

There are plentiful medium-sized supermarkets throughout San Pedro; the cheapest is **Super Buy** on Back Street. The best selection is at **Island Supermarket** (on Coconut Dr., tel. 501/226-2972), which is large and modern, and offers free delivery.

Wine de Vine (tel. 501/226-3430, www.winedevine.com) has the finest selection of imported wines in all of Belize and a worldwide selection of cheeses and meats. They offer free wine tastings and also sell by the glass. The new location is on Coconut Drive before Island Supermarket. **Pinguino Wine Company** (tel. 501/226-2930, www.pinguinobelize.com) sells Napa Valley wine on its private Pinguino label, as well as gourmet olives and olive oil.

THE NORTHERN CAYES

SAN PEDRO'S PETS: A HEARTENING SAGA

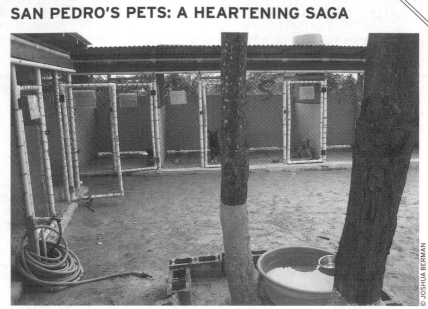

Fort Dog at the Saga Humane Society

Belize's government-sanctioned animal control measures used to consist of tossing strychnine-laced meat onto the streets. The **Saga Humane Society** (tel. 501/226-3266, www.sagahumanesociety.org) was founded in March 1999, partly in response to this practice and to improve the poor conditions of Belize's stray animals. Saga Humane Society's mission is "promoting kindness and preventing cruelty to all animals, achieved through humane education, subsidized spay and neuter programs, and low-cost veterinary services."

Saga started out in a little building with a fenced-in yard that served as the only animal shelter in all of Belize. After much work and dedication, a proper shelter was built on land purchased by the Humane Society, and it was called "Fort Dog." Fort Dog houses lost, unwanted, and homeless animals who receive treatment and care until they are found adoptive families. The Humane Society headquarters on Sea Star Street houses the Saga cattery, where there are always plenty of kittens and cats looking for homes. Fort Dog received a facelift in 2007 – including puppy and isolation areas and new storage and sanitation facilities.

Saga can always use a helping hand and appreciates the generosity of visitors. It is a nonprofit organization funded solely by donations from the public and visitors to the island. Saga maintains an ongoing wish list of needed items for the clinic, so please check in before your trip and see what you can bring down.

The island's only private practice veterinarian is found in the same neighborhood at the **San Pedro Animal Hospital** (tel. 501/610-3647, sanpedroanimalhospital.com), created in 2009 to offer "modern veterinary care similar to that found in the United States, Canada and Europe" on Ambergris Caye. They offer regular office hours, emergency visits, and house calls for your pets.

Premium Wines (tel. 501/226-3700) on Front Street has a selection from seven countries and offers wholesale pricing: Buy 12 bottles and get a 17 percent discount. Prices range from a US$12.50 California wine to US$130 for a French white table wine.

INFORMATION

Things change quickly in San Pedro, especially prices. Before your trip, always take a good look at **www.ambergriscaye.com,** by far the best portal for all things Ambergris, including a lively message board filled with opinionated characters. You'll find links to hundreds of island businesses, as well as Ambergris's two weekly papers, the *San Pedro Sun* (tel. 501/226-2070, www.sanpedrosun.net) and *Ambergris Today* (tel. 501/226-3462), both important resources themselves. Also check **San Pedro Daily** (http://sanpedrodaily.com).

SERVICES

The **post office** is on the corner of Front and Buccaneer Streets (8 A.M.–4 P.M. Mon.–Thurs., 8 A.M.–3:30 P.M. Fri.). It's fun to choose from Belize's beautiful, artistic, and often very large postage stamps; they make great gifts and are perfect for framing or for the traditional stamp collector.

Nellie's Laundromat (on Pescador Dr., tel. 501/226-2454, 7 A.M.–5 P.M. daily, US$1/lb) is a superb value and offers free pickup and delivery in town.

Travel & Tour Belize (just north of the airstrip, tel. 501/226-2137 or 501/226-2031, www. traveltourbelize.com, 8 A.M.–5 P.M. Mon.–Fri., plus Sat. morning) is the oldest and only full-service travel agent in San Pedro; they'll handle all your bookings, both local and international, and can help with weddings and events too.

Money

There are plenty of banks in town. Belize, Scotia, Atlantic, and First Caribbean have international ATMs. There's also an ATM in the big supermarket just south of Ramon's Village. **Milo's Money Exchange** is another option (on Middle St., tel. 501/226-2196). It exchanges

Belizean, U.S., Guatemalan, Mexican, Canadian, and British currencies (and is also a Western Union branch).

Medical

Prescriptions and other medicines can be found at **R&L Pharmacy** (tel. 501/226-2890, open daily) by the airstrip, and there are plenty of smaller Viagra-slinging pharmacies around town. If you need medical attention, all hotels and resorts keep a list of doctors and transport options to call in the middle of the night, including a helicopter to take you to the hospital in Belize City for a major emergency. For other medical concerns, go to the **San Pedro PolyClinic** (tel. 501/226-2536, 8 A.M.–noon and 2–5 P.M. Mon.–Fri.), located behind Wine de Vine and the Island Supermarket, facing the airstrip.

Dr. Daniel Gonzalez's **Ambergris Hope Clinic** (tel. 501/226-2660) is another option, located next to Castillo's hardware store. For diving emergencies, the island's sole hyperbaric chamber can be reached at tel. 501/226-2851 or 501/226-3197.

Police and Fire

The police department (tel. 501/226-2022, or just 911) and fire department (tel. 501/226-2372) are both located in San Pedro Town, near the big BTL antennae on Middle Street.

Internet Access

Many resorts and hotels have free computers and wireless Internet for guests; ask before checking in. **Caribbean Connection** (tel. 501/226-4664, www.sanpedrointernet. com, 7 A.M.–10 P.M. daily, US$5/hour), with its speedy DSL line, wireless Internet access, central location, coffee drinks, and air-conditioning, is a no-brainer, charging less than half as much as other providers.

At **Island Internet** (on the road south of town, 8 A.M.–10 P.M. daily, though hours may vary, US$10/hour), surf their speedy machines (DSL with satellite backup) and receive a complimentary beer, rum drink, espresso, or other beverage for every 20 minutes you're logged on—you do the math.

GETTING THERE

By Air

The 2,600-foot-long runway is located practically in downtown San Pedro. Belize's two airlines (Maya Island Air and Tropic Air) fly more than a dozen daily flights between San Pedro, Caye Caulker, and Belize City—and another five to and from Corozal. Tropic Air has a computerized system and offers more reliable service; they just started flights from San Pedro to Belmopan, offering quicker access to the Cayo District. Maya Island Air is good too, and sometimes gives 50 percent discounts on cash purchases; be sure to ask if a discount is available. The flight from Belize City's international airport to San Pedro takes about 15 minutes and costs US$120 round-trip. Flying in and out of Belize City's Municipal Airport is much cheaper (US$35 each way, not much more expensive than the water taxi).

By Boat

There are three companies providing scheduled water taxi service between Belize City and the islands: **Caye Caulker Water Taxi Association** (San Pedro tel. 501/226-2194, Caye Caulker tel. 501/226-0992, Belize City tel. 501/223-5752, www.cayecaulkerwatertaxi.com) and the San Pedro Water Taxi Express alternate schedules, each offering four daily trips between Belize City and Ambergris Caye, a 75-minute ride that costs US$15 one-way.

In Belize City, the Caye Caulker Water Taxi Terminal is at the north end of the Swing Bridge, with boats leaving between 8 A.M. and 4:30 P.M. The San Pedro Water Taxi Express departs from the Tourism Village in Belize City. Boats depart San Pedro from Wet Willy's Pier from 8 A.M. to 3:30 P.M. Always check the schedule before making plans; usually there are extra boats on weekends and holidays.

Thunderbolt Travels (tel. 501/226-2904 or 501/614-9074, thunderbolttravels@yahoo.com) runs two daily trips to Corozal (7 A.M. and 3 P.M., US$22.50 one-way, same schedule from Corozal).

GETTING AROUND

Walking is feasible within the town of San Pedro itself; it's about a 20-minute stroll from the airstrip to the split. Once you start traveling between resorts to the south or north, however, you may wish to go by bike, golf cart, taxi, or boat. At one time, cars were a rarity, but together with golf carts they are taking over the town streets and even onto the north side of Ambergris. Most of the electric golf carts have been replaced by gas-powered ones, and hundreds ply San Pedro's rutted roads. Cobbled streets mean less dust and fewer potholes downtown.

By Taxi

Minivan taxis (green license plates) run north and south along the island at most hours; just wave one down and climb in. Expect to pay about US$4–7 to travel between town and points south. At press time, the ban on taxis north of the bridge had been lifted by the town council, causing a major kerfuffle with property owners north of the cut, some of whom want to keep the road to golf carts and bicycles only (and the occasional bulldozer). Within town, you'll pay around US$4. There are several drivers that you (or your accommodation's front desk) can call, as well, including **Island Taxi** (tel. 501/226-3125) and **Jesus Wiltshire** (tel. 501/614-8732).

By Bicycle

Many resorts have free bicycles for their guests, and others have them for rent, as do a handful of outside shops. Rentals are available by the hour (about US$5), day (US$10), and week (US$25). **Joe's Bikes** (tel. 501/226-4371) is the most well-used local service; he has a ton of bikes for rent, including kids' sizes and baby seats for family outings.

By Boat

Usually the smoothest and quickest way to travel up and down Ambergris Caye, water taxi service is available from **Coastal Express** (tel. 501/226-2007, or 501/226-3007). Boats share a dock with Amigos del Mar Dive Shop, in front of Lily's Hotel and Restaurant, departing for points north and south from 5:30 A.M.

THE GOLF CARTS OF SAN PEDRO

© JOSHUA BERMAN

Golf carts are one way to explore Ambergris Caye.

Carts are most useful for people staying at one of the many resorts south of San Pedro, especially if you plan on coming into town often to shop, eat, and explore. The road to the north end of Ambergris, however, gets pretty bad in the rainy season, and most companies won't allow you to drive farther north than the Palapa Bar or Grand Caribe Resort, 1.5 miles north of town. To explore farther north, you'll either hike or take the water taxi. If you're staying right in San Pedro, everything is pretty walkable. A golf cart could be fun for an expedition south one day, but otherwise, it's not a necessity.

Ambergris's carts used to be all electric, but now most companies have gas-powered carts. It'll set you back as much as renting an automobile on the mainland, but if you're staying south of town and have multiple passengers (for example, a family), it's probably worth it. Expect to pay more than US$75 for 24 hours, and at least US$250 for a week. Drivers must be 17 and have a valid driver's license. Expect to leave a security deposit of your credit card imprint or cash.

In the high season, you may wish to reserve a cart in advance. Most companies will deliver to your hotel or pick you up at the

airstrip. Your choices begin with **Moncho's** (tel. 501/226-3262, www.monchosrentals. com) and **Carts Belize** (tel. 501/226-4090, www.CARTSbelize.com), both close to the airstrip with relatively large fleets. Toward the north end of town, **Cholo's** (on Jewfish St. in town, tel. 501/226-2406, www.choloscartrental.com) is reliable with a small fleet of carts, and **Island Adventures Golf Cart Rentals** (tel. 501/226-4343, islandadventure@btl.net) has weekly deals and will deliver your cart.

When driving your cart, carry your valid driver's license and follow all normal traffic laws, including one-way street rules! Front Street closes to all but pedestrian traffic on Friday, Saturday, and Sunday evenings. Make sure you park on the correct side of the street (it alternates every few weeks; just do what the locals are doing). Be sure to pay attention to the map you are given.

As the old *Green Guide* advised: "Don't count on the golf carts around you to have brakes. They're designed for lush fairways with a few sprinklers, not for high tides and potholes. When driving, please don't run over the children or splash pedestrians, and note all the one-way streets on the town map."

THE NORTHERN CAYES

to 11:30 P.M., with special late-night schedules on big party nights (Wed.–Sat.). The price depends on how far you are going (US$3.50–10 each way). Most restaurants will radio the ferry to arrange your ride back to San Pedro Town.

Crossing the Bridge
The toll bridge connecting San Pedro Town with Ambergris's north side is free for pedestrians. From 6 A.M. to 10 P.M., bicycles pay a buck to cross and golf carts US$5 round-trip.

Caye Caulker

About 1,500 or so native Hicaqueños (hee-kaw-KEN-yos; or "Caulker Islanders") reside on this island 21 miles northeast of Belize City, just south of Ambergris Caye and less than a mile west of the reef. The island is four miles long from north to south. The developed and inhabited part is only a mile long, from the split to the airstrip.

Yes, there have been many changes and much development on the island as it has figured out its place in Belize's evolving tourism economy, but Caye Caulker remains less expensive than San Pedro and as *tranquilo* and friendly as everybody told you it was.

HISTORY
Most historians agree that Caye Caulker was not permanently inhabited during the time of the pirates, but they did stop here—an anchor dating from the 19th century was found in the channel on the southern end of the island, and a wreck equally old was discovered off the southern end of Caye Chapel. The island was visited by Mexican fishermen during those centuries—for generations they handed down stories of putting ashore at Caye Caulker for fresh water from a "big hole" on the caye.

The island was uninhabited as late as the 1830s. It wasn't until the outbreak of the Yucatán Caste War in 1848, when refugees fled Mexico by the thousands, that people permanently settled on Ambergris Caye, a few finding their way south to Caye Caulker. Many of today's Hicaqueños can trace their family histories back to the Caste War and even know from which region in Mexico their ancestors originated.

Exact dates of settlement on Caye Caulker

are uncertain. The Reyes family tells of their great-grandfather, Luciano, who arrived in Mexico from Spain and worked as a logwood cutter along the coast. He fled with the rest and, after settling in San Pedro, eventually purchased Caye Caulker for BZE$300. Over the years, land was sold to various people; many descendants of the original landholders are still prominent families on Caye Caulker.

Early Economy
The town developed into a fishing village, and *cocales* (coconut plantations) were established from one end of the caye to the other. Though no written records have been found, it is believed the original trees were planted in the 1880s and 1890s, at about the same time as those planted on Ambergris Caye. It took a lot of capital to plant a *cocal* and involved a great deal of time-consuming, laborious work. Reyes was one of the original planters. His workers would begin at the northern end of the island and stack the coconuts all along the shore, where boats picked them up. When the workers finished their sweep of the island, it was time to begin again—the trees produced continually.

Slavery was never a part of the Caulker economy, which prevented the development of the plantation hierarchy common in other parts of the Caribbean. Laborers earned a small cash wage, enabling them to use their incomes to buy the necessities to supplement their subsistence fishing. The people were very poor. Some of the older folks remember their grandparents and great-grandparents working long days and making only pennies.

Maybe because of the economic conditions,

CAYE CAULKER

Caribbean Sea

The Split

LAZY LIZARD BAR AND GRILL

MARA'S PLACE

CAYE CAULKER CONDOS

SEA DREAMS

TSUNAMI TOURS

FRENCHIE'S DIVING

OCEAN PEARL ROYALE HOTEL

Children's Park

CHOCOLATE TOURS/SHOP/ROOM

DON CORLEONE'S CARIBBEAN TRATTORIA

RAGGAMUFFIN TOURS

TAJ

AVENIDA HICACO (FRONT ST)

DISCO

DE REAL MACAW

RAINBOW HOTEL

RAINBOW BAR AND GRILL

IGUANA REEF INN

Football Field

OCEANSIDE BAR & GRILL

BELIZE DIVING SERVICE

MIRA MAR HOTEL

WATER JETS EXPRESS TO BELIZE CITY

BARRIER REEF SPORTS BAR AND GRILL

SAN PEDRO BELIZE EXPRESS BOATS

ATM/BANK

MARIE'S LAUNDRY

BACK BRIDGE

POLICE

BAKERY

INTERNET

YUMA'S HOUSE BELIZE

CHAN'S

SANDBOX RESTAURANT

BLUE MOON HOTEL

HABANEROS

SEASIDE CABANAS

GLENDA'S

BANK

AMOR Y CAFÉ

VEGA INN

WATER TAXI TO SAN PEDRO AND BELIZE CITY

SYD'S

CARLOS TOURS

POPEYE'S RESTAURANT AND BAR

TOWN HALL/ POST OFFICE/ LIBRARY

MARIN'S UPSTAIRS DINER

DAISY'S

I & I BAR

LENA'S GUEST HOUSE

MORGAN'S INN

MAXAPAN

Cemetery

C & N GOLF CARTS

TROPICAL PARADISE HOTEL

YOUNG'S INTERNET

TREE TOPS HOTEL

MORNING STAR GUEST HOUSE

TOM'S HOTEL

LAZY IGUANA B&B

CATHOLIC CHURCH

AVENIDA LANGOSTA (MIDDLE ST)

AVENIDA MARGLE (BACK ST)

BAREFOOT BEACH BELIZE

Caribbean Sea

To Ocean Academy, Coco Plum Garden, and Airstrip

ANCHORAGE HOTEL

To Ignacio's Cabins, Shirley's Guesthouse, and CCBTIA Mini-Reserve

0   1 mi
0   1 km

Caye Caulker Forest Reserve

Caye Caulker

The Split
Caye Caulker

MAP AREA

0   100 yds
0   100 m

© AVALON TRAVEL

the families on the caye began helping each other early on. When one man got a large catch, his family and neighbors helped him with it and, in turn, always went home with some. When one man's fruit trees were bearing, he would share the fruit, knowing that he would benefit later. This created very strong ties, especially between families and extended families.

Independent fishermen liked being their own bosses. As a result, to this day, Hicaqueños consider themselves independent thinkers. They take pride in their early roots on the island. Today, longtime fishing and lobstering families on Caulker continue to earn a living on the sea, whether by fishing, providing tourist services and tours, or a little of both.

ORIENTATION

Caye Caulker is cut into two pieces. The "split" or "cut" separates the southern inhabited part of the island from the northern mangrove swamps. This feature earned its name after Hurricane Hattie widened the channel in 1961. Travelers and locals come to the split to swim, snorkel, and sunbathe on the concrete blocks (there is no beach).

Moving south on **Front Street,** the street that skirts the eastern shore (there are two more north–south streets: Middle and Back), you'll find seven sandy roads that cross three blocks to the other side of the island and Back Street.

On the western pier, there's a fuel pump. Sailors exploring nearby cayes can anchor in the shallow protected waters offshore; the body of water here is open ocean but is still often referred to as a "lagoon."

Front Street's south terminus dead-ends by the **cemetery,** and you have two choices: Follow the narrow beach path along the water, or turn right and then left, and you'll find another dusty avenue that leads to the airstrip. Bordering the airstrip is a rapidly developing neighborhood called Bahia Puesta del Sol, which has a grocery store, a fruit stand, and a new high school. The land north of the split consists mostly of mangrove swamps, with a

WHERE THE STREETS HAVE TWO NAMES

In 2004, the growing village of Caye Caulker decided to name the island's tiny handful of streets after plants, animals, and historical events. Avenida Mangle (Mangrove Avenue), Crocodile Street, Luciana Reyes Street (named for an early settler of Caye Caulker), and Hattie Street (named after the 1961 hurricane that created the split) were among the names chosen. Old Front Street is now Hicaco Avenue (for the cocoplum fruit), and Middle Street is Avenida Langosta, honoring the role of lobster in the island's economic development.

Don't expect to hear too many of the new names in casual conversation, though – people still commonly refer to Front, Middle, and Back Streets (or Way Back Street and "Back-a-bush," if you make it farther from town). There are no house numbers on Caye Caulker, so mail is addressed "General Post," and to receive parcels, residents look for their names scrawled on a poster outside the post office door.

(Contributed by Joni Miller-Valencia.)

narrow strip of land along the east coast; this hasn't stopped people from building off-the-grid homes, though.

SPORTS AND RECREATION
Diving

The reef you see from Caulker's eastern shore provides fantastic diving right in your front yard. The most popular sites are Hol Chan Marine Park, Caye Chapel Canyons, and the reefs around St. George's Caye, Long Caye Wall, and Sergeant's Caye. Many visitors are willing to brave four hours (two each way) on a boat in mostly open ocean to dive the Blue Hole and Turneffe Islands sites. There is no "best" dive site, as every diver is looking for something different—just be sure to discuss the options before booking the trip (and make sure you're comfortable with the boat, guides, and gear).

Caye Caulker's three dive shops offer similarly priced tours: Hol Chan (US$100 for two tanks); Blue Hole, Half Moon, and Lighthouse (US$190 for three tanks); Turneffe day trips (US$125 North and US$150 South); certification courses (US$325 for open water and US$300 for advanced, US$100 for a Discover Scuba single-tank dive); as well as a variety of snorkeling excursions and other trips.

Frenchie's (tel. 501/226-0234, frenchies@btl.net, www.frenchiesdivingbelize.com) has a rock-solid reputation for quality service. Owner and operator Abel Novelo has been diving these waters since he was a child. **Belize Diving Services** (behind the soccer field, tel. 501/226-0143, www.belizedivingservices. net) is another excellent operation that is all computerized and offers both recreational and technical dives at Miner's Gold and Treasure

Hunt dive sites. **Big Fish Dive Center** (tel. 501/226-0450, info@bigfishdivecenter.com, www.bigfishdivecenter.com) is a PADI Dive Resort with a 45-foot dive boat with an on-board restroom and shower that is ideal for farther destinations, such as the Blue Hole. Albert Pacheco's **Extreme Tours** (tel. 501/226-0127) offers small private certification classes (three students with one instructor).

Snorkeling and Swimming

Masks and fins are available for US$5 per day and can be used off almost any dock or at the island's most popular beach and snorkel spot: the split. You'll see flocks of sunbathers here on any given day, lounging like reptiles atop the various chunks of sand and cement, getting up only to splash on some more oil or order another Panty Ripper at the Lazy Lizard Bar, which provides mellow music for the scene. Be aware that swimming in the channel can be dangerous; this is a shallow and heavily trafficked area. The pull of the current can be

---

SHORE TO SEA: CONSERVATION EFFORTS ON CAYE CAULKER

Forest and Marine Reserves Association of Caye Caulker (FAMRACC, www.famracc.org) is a nongovernmental organization composed of representatives from different island organizations and service groups, including tour guides, schools, and the police. FAMRACC co-manages the Caye Caulker Marine Reserves with the Fisheries and Forests Departments and works on projects like mangrove restoration, reef rapid assessments, community reef-technician training, and environmental education field trips for local children.

FAMRACC sometimes accepts volunteers to work with the mangrove and littoral forest restoration projects (Forest Reserve), as well as maintenance of reef mooring lines and buoys (Marine Reserve). Guest researchers and scientists are also welcome.

The Caye Caulker branch of the Belize Tourism Industry Association (CCBTIA) manages

a 1.5-acre private **Forest Reserve** (www.go-cayecaulker.com/forest.html), which is just before the airstrip. This tiny but lush littoral forest nature reserve has a nice walking trail that winds to the mangroves on the beach, and flora and fauna along the way are identified with hand-painted signs. CCBTIA has published a trail guide to the reserve, as well as two books about the plants and birds of Caye Caulker; these are for sale at Cayeboard Connection or from CCBTIA. There is no charge to walk the trails. Guided tours are also available and there is a small interpretation center.

FAMRACC can help you plan a tour in the Forest Reserve. Birding tours leave very early (US$32, three hours), and natural history tours can be booked of the project sites, followed by snorkeling in the North Channel (US$50-70 depending on duration). Contact Ellen McRae to arrange details (tel. 501/226-0178).

enough to overpower children or weak swimmers. Also be aware of boat traffic, as serious accidents have occurred here. Around the bend, only a few yards out of the channel, the water is calm and safer. However, old construction materials have been dumped here for fill, so be careful where you step or dive.

Snorkel and Boat Tours

At least a dozen shops on the island rent gear and offer half-day snorkeling trips to the local reef and full-day trips to Hol Chan Marine Reserve (with snorkel stops at Shark and Sting Ray Alley and the Coral Gardens; lunch, not included, is in San Pedro). Many guides conclude their tours with a visit to the tiny Sea Horse Sanctuary behind the split.

The cheerful, capable guides at € **Raggamuffin Tours** (tel. 501/226-0348, www.raggamuffintours.com) will take you out on *RaggaGal, Ragga Prince, RaggaQueen,* or *RaggaKing*—beautiful, Belizean-built boats designed especially to access shallow snorkeling spots. Raggamuffin regularly sails to Hol Chan (full-day trip includes lunch and rum punch on board) and offers sunset island cruises. The best adventure tour has to be the utterly unique overnight sailing trip south to Placencia (Tuesday and Friday departures), where you'll be dropped off to continue your travels; three days of sun and sea, and two nights camping out in style on idyllic cayes (US$300 pp includes all gear, food, snorkeling, and fishing).

Belizean guide Shedrack Ash offers friendly, professional snorkeling, manatee watching, and fishing trips through his company, **French Angel Expeditions** (tel. 501/670-7506 or 501/670-9155, www.frenchangelexp.com), which gets rave reviews from past clients. Walk straight down the street from the water taxi, on Calle del Sol.

For a reggae vibe, join **Ras Creek** on his boat *Heritage Cruze,* docked at the Lazy Lizard Bar when not plying the reef with happy, reggae-crazy customers; this is one of the best ways to tour the Caye Caulker Marine Reserve (US$30). Ras Creek was the first to guide tourists to the Sea Horse Sanctuary behind the split.

Climb aboard the *Gypsy* with **Carlos Tours** (tel. 501/226-0458 or 501/600-1654, carlosayala@hotmail.com), which has an excellent reputation for personal attention and a focus on safety. Carlos loves underwater photography and will share and sell photo CDs immediately after a trip. His office is on Front Street next to the Sand Box.

A pair of local brothers run **Anwar Tours** (tel. 501/226-0327, www.anwartours.page.tl) and, with 15 years experience, they get positive reviews for both snorkel trips and inland tours. **Tsunami Adventures** (tel. 501/226-0462, www.tsunamiadventures.com) is located near the split, books snorkel and inland trips, and rents underwater cameras. **EZ Boy Tours** (tel. 501/226-0349, ezboytours-bze@yahoo.com) offers all the standard snorkel tours as well as overnight camping trips and night snorkeling.

Other Water Sports

Toucan Canoe and Kayaks (Palapa Gardens on Front St.) has the most comprehensive canoe and kayak tours and rentals on the island (US$5/hour single, US$7.50/hour double, US$10/hour triple canoe). Private and group lessons are offered by Canadian-Belizean owner Allie Ifield, who is a top-placing international canoe racer and licensed tour guide and naturalist. All two-hour tours are US$25. Ask Allie about moonlight or stargazing options, mangrove and seahorse tours, and individual custom tours.

Rudolfo can teach you windsurfing and kite-boarding at **Kitexplorer** (www.kitexplorer.com), located on Front Street near the split (seasonal). **Stuart Trent Adventures** (on the beach in front of Sandbox Restaurant, tel. 501/631-9134, trenteesh@yahoo.com) offers instruction and rentals of small sailing boats.

Fishing

Try to catch your dinner off one of the island's many piers. You can buy bait and rent fishing rods at the Badillos' house near the soccer field (look for a small porch sign). Or fish like a local with a hook, line, and weight. Or take a walk to the back side of the island, where you'll find fishers cleaning their fish, working on lobster traps, or mending their nets in the morning. Many will be willing to take you out for a reasonable fee. The main trophies are groupers, barracuda, snapper, and amberjack—all good eating. Small boats are available for rent by the hour.

For professional fishing tours, go to **Anglers Abroad** (tel. 501/226-0602, www.anglersabroad.com) near the split. Owner Haywood Curry rents and sells a complete selection of fly and spin gear, and he is happy to give advice for the novice or expert fisher. He offers lessons and DIY instruction by canoe or foot and sets up half-day, full-day, and overnight adventure trips. Group tours, as well as private lessons, are available. The shop works with well-known and experienced reefs and flats fishing guides, including Parnel and Kenan Coc, Rafael Alamilla, and Eloy Badillo.

Shadrack Ash, owner of **French Angel Expeditions** (tel. 501/670-7506 or 501/670-9155, www.frenchangelexp.com), can take you fly fishing (catch and release), spin casting (with an option to grill your catch for you), and lobster fishing (seasonal June 15 to February 15).

◖ Swallow Caye Wildlife Sanctuary

The protected area comprises nearly 9,000 acres of sea and mangrove at the north end of the Drowned Cayes, just a few miles east of Belize City. The sanctuary is co-managed by Friends of Swallow Caye and the Belize Forest Department. Check out www.swallowcayemanatees.org for more information, including membership, tours, and manatee facts.

Many tour operators will take you to Swallow Caye, usually for US$60 per person, but **Chocolate's Manatee Tours** (tel. 501/226-0151, chocolateseashore@gmail.com) is the original. Chocolate is a local legend in the ecotourism trade; he was the first guide to take people on trips to Swallow Caye to see manatees, and he was instrumental in the

creation of this sanctuary in July 2002. He has also earned environmental and tourism awards for providing quality trips to hundreds of tourists per season. The all-day excursion stops first in an open area where it is possible to approach manatees in their element. After viewing the manatees for an hour or two, Chocolate heads to the tiny white-sand island of Sergeant's Caye for snorkeling. If Chocolate is not going out, try other tour guides on the island—they offer similar trips.

From Belize City this trip is combined with snorkeling on the barrier reef and looking for Atlantic bottlenose dolphins. Park fees are US$5 pp.

Massage, Yoga, and Fitness

You'll feel like a new person after a session at Eva McFarlane's **Healing Touch Day Spa** (tel. 501/601-9731 or 501/226-0208, cdenbelize@hotmail.com) on Front Street. She does everything from deep tissue and Swedish massage to reiki, reflexology, aura cleansing, waxing, manicures, and facials. All treatments are US$30 for 30 minutes and US$50 for a full hour.

Coco Plum Garden Cafe, Spa & Gallery (Ave. Mulche, tel. 501/226-0226, www.cocoplum.typepad.com) offers massage by Chriss Roggema (US$65 for 90 minutes), tarot readings, and spa services.

Great Island Yoga (www.greatislandyoga.com) offers classes from Christmas to Easter at a beautiful oceanfront location (Coco Plum can provide a schedule and map). Drop-in classes are US$6, and organized groups are also welcome. **RandOM Yoga** (www.randomyoga.com) is a donation-based outdoor yoga studio; for schedules look for their sign on Front Street by Anwar Tours (seasonal).

For those feeling more energetic, there is Louise's **step aerobics** Monday to Thursday (5–6 P.M.), upstairs from the Village Council Office. You can register or just drop in for US$1.

NIGHTLIFE

The biggest show in town is definitely the daily joining of sun and western horizon.

Lazy Lizard Bar, at the split, is a fun place to be for this moment. For something more intimate, walk down the west side of the island before sunset and choose an appropriate cocktail spot.

Oceanside (Front St.) is the happening hot spot for *punta* dancing on Friday and Saturday, with dancing till 4 A.M. (since they soundproofed the place). Tuesday is ladies night, Wednesday and Thursday offer karaoke. There is occasionally a late-night dancehall scene at a ramshackle disco near the back side of town.

Team Trivia Night at the **Barrier Reef Sports Bar and Grill** (Sunday, Wednesday, and Friday at 7:30 P.M.) can get competitive, with the top teams winning money off their bar tabs, not to mention bragging rights. In case of a tie, teams select their top drinker (rather than thinker) for a beer chug race. Barrier Reef also has large-screen TVs with lots of sports.

Outdoor movies are shown at the **Paradiso** on the beach on Monday, Wednesday, and Friday at 6:30 P.M. and 8:30 P.M. with a onedrink minimum. Dinner is also served.

Do not leave the island without enjoying a beverage in **The I & I Bar** (Traveler's Palm St.), a three-story tower of reggae located in the middle of the island. We could try to explain the swing-seats and Monkey Walk, but you're better off just going yourself.

SHOPPING

All shops on the island are open daily. You'll find **Toucan** and a sprinkling of small gift shops on and around Front Street selling T-shirts, hot sauce, hammocks, sarongs, beach wear, postcards, photo albums, and other typical Belizean souvenirs. Caye Caulker's sandy streets are starting to attract several skilled artisan vendors. On Front Street is a collection of numbered stalls called **Palapa Gardens.** Here you can find hand-carved ziricote and rosewood, hand-painted T-shirts, Guatemalan textiles and handicrafts, beautiful model sailboats complete with rigging, jewelry, and music CDs.

Jewelry is a popular craft on the island and often sold from tables set up in the street.

Calvin sells cool island necklaces at his table set up on the corner of Habaneros and Sandbox. **Celi's Music** (Front St.) is where Mr. August can be found at a small table beside the shop, cutting and polishing conch shell pieces. There's a good selection of popular Belizean music and videos.

Cooper's Art Gallery (tel. 501/226-0330, www.debbiecooperart.com) on Front Street sells colorful Caribbean primitive art and posters, many in funky frames hand-painted by artist Debbie Cooper and her husband. Lee Vanderwalker-Alamina's **Caribbean Colors Art Gallery and Cafe** (www.caribbean-colors. com) is upstairs, beside the police station. The **Go Slow Art Gallery,** in Palapa Gardens stalls #6 and #7, encourages the Belizean art community and sells paintings of different styles, including acrylic on canvas, realism, and primitive. Seek out pieces by well-known local artists Nelson Young and Marcos Manzanero.

Hair braiders create "head art" with their lightning-fast fingers, braiding intricate designs and adding colorful beads and extensions. Anita Baker and her daughter are very skilled and set up their outdoor salon across the street from Palapa Gardens.

For clothing, **Chocolate's Gift Shop** (Front St.), run by Annie Seashore, sells high-quality Balinese sarongs, bags, and Guatemalan textiles. Several small shops sell a limited selection of imported women's clothing.

ACCOMMODATIONS

Prices given are for high-season double occupancy, but you can often get discounts, especially if staying for five or more days. Note that in Caye Caulker the "beach" is little more than a sandy sidewalk for foot traffic and golf carts. At last count, there were 79 registered hotels on the island. During high season (late December, mid-February, and Easter week), rooms are quickly filled as water taxis arrive from Belize City; throughout the rest of the year, reservations are rarely necessary. When you step off your boat or plane, ignore any pushy tout who grabs your bag and yells out a hotel name; they are trying to get commissions, and locals wish they would stop their overly assertive tactics.

Under US$25

If these places are full, don't worry; there are many plain-Jane budget rooms along Front Street that are easy to find. **[(Yuma's House** (tel. 501/206-0019, yumahousebelize@gmail.com) is a converted private home to your right as you walk off the town dock. It offers dorm-style rooms (US$12.50), plus a few private rooms (US$28–30) with shared bathroom and kitchen and a relaxed community atmosphere. Hang out on the funky little dock or garden benches and hammocks. The rooms are small, clean, and colorful.

Edith's Hotel (tel. 501/206-0069, US$20–25), with small and tidy rooms, is a landmark on the center street of the island. Rooms come with hot and cold water, ceiling fans, communal kitchen area, and shared or private bath. Daisy's and Lena's are also old-school family-run guesthouses towards the south end of town.

In the heart of the village by the soccer field, there are two great options for reasonable rooms and cabanas. **Sandy Lane** (tel. 501/226-0117) has nine rooms (US$11–13 with shared outside shower/facilities, US$16 with private bath) and four cabanas with kitchenette and TV (US$25). There is a communal outside cooking area as well. Across the lane is **M and N Apartments** (tel. 501/226-0229), which has 10 rooms (US$15, shared bath), three cabanas (US$30), and one upstairs apartment (US$60).

A bit farther south along the beach, you'll find **[(Tom's Hotel** (tel. 501/226-0102, toms@btl.net, US$18–30), popular with budget travelers. There are many options—32 rooms, plus a few simple bungalows. Tom's is well kept and clean, with hot and cold water, fans, louvered windows, tile floors, wireless Internet, and a sea view.

If you're packing a tent, the only place to camp is on the beach at **Vega Inn and Gardens** (www.vegabelize.com, US$12 pp). The site provides communal hot and cold showers, flush toilets, luggage storage, and security. They also have comfortable hotel rooms with all the amenities.

US$25-50

For a relaxed dose of "old Caye Caulker," check into one of the funky beachfront cabins at **Morgan's Inn** (tucked away in a cluster of palms near the old cemetery, tel. 501/226-0178, siwaban@gmail.com, US$28–40); cabins are spacious and rustic. Kayaks and windsurfing are available. Owner Ellen McRae is a marine biologist and birder who can guide interested groups.

The colorful building on your right as you get off of the water taxi is **Trends Beachfront Hotel** (tel. 501/226-0094, www.trendsbze.com, US$35–40), with seven rooms, comfortable queen-sized beds, refrigerators, fans, and private baths.

The bright **[(Rainbow Hotel** (Front. St., tel. 501/226-0123, www.rainbowhotel-cayecaulker.com, US$35–52) has 17 clean, stucco rooms with hot and cold water, private baths, TV, and tile floors; there are also two suites: La Casita and Cielo Azul. The popular Rainbow Bar and Grill is across the street on a dock over the water.

The seven wood cabins at **Mara's Place** (by the split, tel. 501/600-0080, from US$43) are a great value, with private hot-water baths and small porches with hammocks. The property has a private dock with lounge chairs for guests to use and an outdoor communal kitchen. **Ocean Pearl Royale Hotel** (tel. 501/226-0074, oceanpearl@btl.net, US$25) is on a side street before the split. There are 10 rooms, with wireless Internet, around a communal living area and kitchen with fridge, microwave, and coffeemaker. In the pretty garden is a cabana for rent by the week (US$250) or month (US$600).

The **Blue Wave Guest House** (Front. St., tel. 501/206-0114, www.bluewaveguesthouse.com, US$20) has rooms with shared bath, an outdoor communal kitchen, wireless Internet and a private dock.

US$50-100

Sea Dreams Hotel and Guest Houses (Hattie St., tel. 501/226-0602, www.seadreamsbelize.com, US$90 and up) is in a great location beside the split. There are five rooms, three apartments, and a private cabana. The rooms have air-conditioning, wireless Internet, TV, coffeemakers, and continental breakfast; the larger accommodations include full kitchens. Complimentary bikes, use of a canoe, and access to a rooftop deck and sunset pier make this an excellent choice.

De Real Macaw (Front St., tel. 501/226-0459, www.derealmacaw.biz, US$50–70 rooms) is a small, pet-friendly place whose eight units have private baths, mini-kitchens, TV, spacious verandas, and quality beds; US$130 for condo-apartment and beach house.

Tina's Blue Moon Hotel (on the beach near the dock, tel. 501/206-0091, www.bluemoonhotelbelize.blogspot.com, US$75) has a handful of beach suites that sleep up to six for US$75 (or US$850/month); the suites have various amenities and offer excellent value, especially for small groups and families. Divers who stay here get a discount at Frenchie's.

Popeye's Beach Resort (right on the beach near the dock, tel. 501/226-0032, www.popeyesbeachresort.com, US$55–75) is quiet and family friendly and has four cabanas and three family rooms (with two double beds); all rooms have private baths, hot and cold water, and air-conditioning. There is a small beach bar with hammocks (8 A.M.–6 P.M.). Popeye's has an on-site travel agent for Tropic Air and bus tickets.

The **Jaguar Morning Star Guest House** (tel. 501/626-4538, www.jaguarmorningstar.com, US$53) is a big white building with a jungle mural, across from the Catholic church and primary school. It is an excellent bargain, with two modern top-floor rooms each with private bath, fridge, coffeemaker, and TV. There is a shared deck with a great ocean view and breeze. The owners planted many tropical trees and flowers to create a lovely garden.

The southernmost beachfront option on Caye Caulker consists of the five cabins at **Shirley's Guest House** (on the south end of the beach, tel. 501/226-0145 or 501/600-0069, www.shirleysguesthouse.com, US$50–90, adults only), built with beautiful tropical

woods. They are clean, quiet, and comfortable, with a range of amenities.

You'll find six bright and colorful accommodations at the front and seven at the back of **Barefoot Beach Resort Belize** (on the beach, tel. 501/226-0161, www.barefootcariberesort.com, US$69–89), all clustered on the beach; a few bigger suites go for US$129–145. The quaint, cozy rooms have comfortable queen or king beds, ceiling fans, sitting areas, small refrigerators, private baths with hot showers, and air-conditioning, plus their own deck or patio with seating and access to a sunning dock.

The ◖ **Tree Tops Hotel** (tel. 501/226-0240, www.treetopsbelize.com, US$55–140) is tucked back from the water near Tom's Hotel, and is a luxurious little gem in a tall white building. The owner has created a nice ambience with colorful ceramics and thematically decorated rooms—including two suites (the Sunrise and Sunset) that have private balconies, TV, fridge, and hot and cold water bathrooms. Two cheaper rooms share a bath and each has TV, fan, and fridge.

Oasi (tel. 501/226-0384, www.holidaybelize.com, US$70–80) is outside the main buzz of town, toward the airstrip. There are four self-contained, homey, quiet apartments with air-conditioning and ceiling fan, hot and cold rainwater shower, equipped kitchen, and wireless Internet. The entrance is a tropical garden with fountain. Your hosts, Luciana Essenziale and Michael Joseph, will help plan your days; complimentary bikes make the five-minute ride to town easy. There are a few other similarly priced and equipped apartments and rooms for rent in this area, including **Picololo** (tel. 501/226-0371, US$75) and **Maxapan Cabañas** (tel. 501/226-0118, US$60).

US$100-150

Located at the foot of the town dock, ◖ **Seaside Cabanas** (Calle al Sol, tel. 501/226-0498, www.seasidecabanas.com, US$115–130) is a brightly painted 16-room miniresort. The smart rooms and cabanas are equipped with air-conditioning, cable TV, and cheerful decor, surrounding a fine swimming pool and sporting lots of rooftop hang space. The **Uno Mas** bar is open daily to 10 P.M. and upstairs seating has ocean views.

The Lazy Iguana B&B (Alamina Dr., tel. 501/226-0350, www.lazyiguana.net, US$105) is a three-story secluded home. The four spacious rooms have private baths, hot water, air-conditioning, and wireless Internet. The top floor is a deck for lounging with a 360-degree view of the island. Rates include a breakfast spread in the owners' kitchen. It's a short walk from the village center, toward the back side of the island. There are rainwater showers; bikes are available.

Just up from the main dock, you'll see **Sailwinds Beach Suites** (tel. 501/226-0286, www.staycayecaulker.com, US$129), which has colorful, upscale beachfront suites with full amenities.

The **Iguana Reef Inn** (tel. 501/226-0213, www.iguanareefinn.com, US$139–164) continues to raise the bar with its 13 large, upscale rooms built around a well-kept complex on the west side of the island, behind the soccer field. Its rooms are spacious and colorful, some with vaulted ceilings and all with comfortable touches like minifridge, porch, bathtub, hot and cold water, and other modern conveniences. Continental breakfast is included. The bar, swimming pool, and clean beach area face the sunset and are more private and quiet than those on the island's windward side.

Apartment-style accommodations are found at **Caye Caulker Condos** (tel. 501/226-0072, www.cayecaulkercondos.com, US$120–135), near the north end of the village; seven fully furnished suites have all the amenities, including a small pool. The balconies and rooftop hangout are very nice.

Vacation Home Rentals

Caye Caulker Rentals (tel. 501/226-0029 or 501/630-1008, www.cayecaulkerrentals.com) rents over 20 holiday houses, cabanas, and cottages. The website sorts homes by price, location, and size, and provides photos. Nightly rentals range from US$60 to US$379, and one luxury villa sleeps six for US$379 per night.

Minimum booking days are required, and monthly rentals are available.

Caye Caulker Accommodations (tel. 501/226-0381 or 501/610-0240, www.cayecaulkeraccommodations.com) manages nine vacation properties and books suites for two upscale hotels. You can see photos and make reservations through the website.

FOOD
Bakeries and Belizean

Caye Caulker's famous walking bakeries begin with Lloyd, a.k.a. **"The Cake Man,"** balancing his basket of homemade chocolate macaroon and cheesecake brownies, banana bread, and key lime pie; he begins his daily rounds at 4:30 P.M. at the split and works south through the village. **Toni** rides her bike down Front Street at lunchtime with tasty jalapeño bread, ham and cheese rollups, hummus and pita, chicken pilaf, and carrot cake. **Errol** will sell you meat pies and banana bread from his rolling cart. And don't forget to support local kids who are selling their mothers' johnnycakes, fudge, and Creole buns.

One of the few places where you truly are inside someone's home, **Glenda's** on Back Street, on the west side of the island, is as good as ever, with delicious buns. She serves inexpensive food and cheap lobster burritos in a very homey atmosphere. In the morning, try her homemade cinnamon rolls and fresh-squeezed orange juice—by the glass or in a recycled bottle—the best two bucks you'll spend on the island. Affectionately known as "Auntie's," **Chan's Fast Food** (Calle al Sol, tel. 501/226-0478) is a small window-service establishment selling cheap Belizean favorites like stew chicken and fry chicken, rice and beans, beef stew, and the like.

A little farther south on Back Street is **Little Kitchen,** where you can get excellent *salbutes, garnaches, panades* (3 for US$1), burritos, and home-cooked seafood and main dishes as well, all for very cheap. Seating is casual at outdoor picnic tables and the kitchen, while indeed little, is in the front room, and the cook is the friendly owner, Ms. Elba. Similarly,

(El Paso on Middle Street opposite the bakery has excellent low-priced Mexican snacks, meals, and even breakfast. For a cheap early-morning bite, seek out the **taco lady** in front of Habaneros—you'll have to queue up behind the hungry construction workers.

Marin's Upstairs Diner (Traveler's Palm St.) has a nice menu and always-fresh fish. Across the street is **Tortilleria Asunción,** for fresh tortillas and chips.

Paradiso, at Jan's Place on Front Street, has deluxe baguette sandwiches for US$5–8.

Barbecue

Belizeans love their barbecues. They often set up grills right on the beach and serve chicken, lobster, fish, or shrimp for a few bucks; the sides are tortillas, white rice and beans, stew beans, mashed potato, macaroni, or coleslaw. **Jolly Roger's Grill,** in Palapa Gardens on Front Street, is a favorite, grilling up whole lobster (in season; US$12.50), chicken, fish, and shrimp (US$10). Roger is proud of his 2007 silver medal for "Best Food in All Central America." Private beach barbecues with entertainment can be arranged for your group.

(Rose's Grill and Bar, on Front Street behind Habaneros, is always filled with satisfied customers; it's very popular for the dinner barbecue grilled right in front of you and specializes in fresh seafood; chips and ceviche are free. **Fran's,** on Front Street opposite Oceanside, is always packed with tourists seated at outside picnic benches.

Cafés

Two blocks south of the dock, **(Amor y Cafe** (6–11:30 A.M.) specializes in breakfast: eggs, yogurt, granola, waffles, grilled sandwiches, and coffee and juices. It's a friendly place to have breakfast on the raised porch. **Coco Plum Garden Cafe, Spa & Gallery** (9 A.M.–4 P.M., www.cocoplum.typepad.com) is well worth the walk south of the village and toward the airstrip; you'll find all kinds of organic, whole, gourmet food, including a lobster pizza, sushi, and great salads. Exquisite omelets are US$12 and "pancrepes"

are US$6. There's a Belizean craft and art store as well as massage and healing work in the lovely new spa.

Femi's Café and Lounge (Front St., 8 A.M.–10 P.M. daily) serves smoothies and coffees, as well as meals, from a small kitchen. The deck is right beside the sea, and bar swings and hammocks add a nice ambience.

Casual Dining

At the **Sand Box** (7 A.M.–10 P.M. daily), right at the end of the water taxi dock, you'll find an indoor sand floor and a relaxed atmosphere. There are hearty breakfast offerings in the morning and seafood all day: fish with curry rice, conch ceviche, seafood salad, plus stuffed eggplant and mushrooms (meals US$3–10).

The **Barrier Reef Sports Bar and Grill** (9 A.M.–midnight daily), on Front Street, opens onto the beach and serves breakfast, lunch, and dinner. Steaks, seafood, and pasta entrées go for US$12–25. And, oh yeah, there are lots of televisions showing sports, via HD satellite. Barrier Reef has opened up **Los Cocos Cantina and Giftshop** next door, for Mexican snack foods and breakfasts.

Happy Lobster (6 A.M.–5 P.M. daily) on Front Street is a popular choice for breakfast and people-watching. **Sobre Las Olas** (7 A.M.–10 P.M. daily) is opposite Barefoot Caribe on Front Street. The most popular meal is the US$23 combo special—crab claw, shrimp, and lobster.

Sandro's Piccolo Cucina has beachfront picnic tables and serves Italian pasta specialties (US$8–12).

WishWilly's Bar and Grill is in a ramshackle yard with extremely laid-back dinner service, happy hours, and seafood prepared by Chicago-Belizean chef Maurice. His sign on Front Street, two blocks from the split, points the way, and all dinners are US$7.50.

(Syd's, on Middle Street, makes heavy burritos and has a tasty Saturday night barbecue; prices are very reasonable, and the place is popular with locals. The seating has been expanded to include a lovely garden patio in the back.

Fine Island Dining

Don Corleone's Caribbean Trattoria (Front St. across from Raggamuffin Tours, tel. 501/226-0025, 5–9 P.M. Mon.–Sat.) has an elegant oceanview ambience and friendly, attentive staff. Italian dishes start at US$10–15 and choices include gnocchi, pizza, pastas, seafood, and specialty Italian desserts.

⟨ Habanero's (Front St., tel. 501/226-0487, 6–9 P.M.) offers an "eclectic international" menu and lounge bar. Meals are lavishly presented with an international flair.

The **⟨ Rainbow Bar and Grill** (off of Front. St., tel. 501/226-0281, 10:30 A.M.–9 P.M. Tues.–Sun., US$10–25) offers diners perfect seaside ambience—the deck stretches over the water—and consistently excellent food. Lunch is very popular with day-trippers to the island.

Groceries, Fruit, and Fish

Chan's Mini Mart (tel. 501/226-0165) on Middle Street is pretty much the heart of "downtown" Caulker—check the bulletin board for ads and events or go inside for canned goods, meats, cereals, beverages, and snacks. **Chinatown Grocery** (Ave. Langosta and Estrella St.) also has a good selection. There are a few fruit, vegetable, and juice stalls around town (look near the bakery and Atlantic Bank). **Julia's Juice,** on southern Front Street, sells watermelon, orange, lime, soursop, and mixed-fruit juice in recycled plastic bottles (US$2.50). If you want fresh fish or lobster, go to the **Lobstermen's Co-op Dock** (Calle al Sol) on the back side of the island and ask what time the fishing boats come in with their catch. This is always a good place to buy fresh fish.

INFORMATION

There is plenty of online research you can do while planning your trip. The official site of the Caye Caulker Belize Tourism Industry Association (CCBTIA) is **www. gocayecaulker.com.** The most well-run and active site is probably **www.ambergriscaye. com.** The forum has a section for Caye Caulker

where you'll find a large community of knowledgeable folks. There is no general information booth on the island; just walk off the dock and ask around.

SERVICES

Alliance Bank and Atlantic Bank are both on Middle Street (9 A.M.–4:30 P.M. Mon.–Fri., 9 A.M.–noon Sat.). Atlantic's ATM accepts international cards. A Western Union office is located in the bank, and another is down the street inside **Syd's.**

There are a couple of reliable laundry places in town. The best are **Marie** (across from Atlantic Bank, US$5 for 8 lb.) and **Ruby's Wash and Fold,** near Rose's Grill and Bar.

At the south end of Front Street is the Village Council office (community center upstairs) and community library, health clinic, and post office (9 A.M.–noon and 1–5 P.M. Mon.–Thurs., closes a bit earlier on Fri.). The mail goes out three times a week (Monday, Wednesday, and Friday). **FedEx** services are available at the **Tropic Air** cargo office at the airstrip.

The health clinic will help you with meds *if* they have the supplies; it is staffed by a Cuban doctor and Belizean nurse. For any serious emergency, your best bet is an emergency flight to the mainland; all hotels keep a list of emergency boat captains and pilots.

Internet Access

Many hotels offer wireless Internet to guests. **Cayeboard Connection** on Front Street is both an Internet café and bookstore with an extensive collection of guidebooks and novels (8 A.M.–9 P.M. daily) and will burn CDs and print photos; they also have a photocopier. **Island Link** on Front Street near the Split combines Internet access (8 A.M.–9 P.M. daily, US$6/hour) with a small ice-cream parlor. **Young's Internet** is on the southern edge of town, one block before the primary school, but is worth the short walk for US$3 per hour Internet access.

Travel Agencies

Tsunami Adventures (tel. 501/226-0462,

CAYE CAULKER OCEAN ACADEMY

Ocean Academy is Caye Caulker's secondary school.

Caye Caulker's first nonprofit community high school, Ocean Academy (located near airstrip, tel. 501/226-0321, www.cayecaulkerschool.com), opened in 2008. Prior, only a few privileged families could finance the daily water-taxi commute to mainland schools, in addition to fees, uniforms, and books, and many island children quit their schooling at age 12. In Belize only 40 percent of high-school aged youth currently attend high school, so Ocean Academy is committed to youth engagement and equitable access to education.

In addition to core academics, students can study marine biology, tour guiding, graphic design, scuba certifications, windsurfing, kayaking, entrepreneurship, and more. Environmental education projects include composting, mangrove restoration, and eco-art. Current apprenticeship placements are with wedding photographers, scuba and kayak shops, construction, and office reception. Rotary's Interact Club of Ocean Academy pro-

motes community involvement and student volunteerism. The Youth Environmental Club is multi-aged and meets at the community library.

Travelers can get involved in a variety of ways. Ocean Academy can help host service-learning groups, volunteer teachers, and mentors for students in the after-school tutoring program. The school website is updated regularly and has a wish list of volunteer skills and school supplies. Cash donations and student sponsorships are tremendously appreciated, and can be easily made through the school website.

Ocean Academy welcomes visitors on campus for guided school tours (US$5 contribution per person requested for the Student Tuition Scholarship Fund), which include a short video, classroom visits, project viewing, and an opportunity to meet students and staff. *(Contributed by Joni Miller-Valencia, co-founder and Projects Director of Ocean Academy.)*

www.tsunamiadventures.com), up toward the split, acts as a local travel agency and can book your dive trip as well. **Seaside Cabanas** and **Popeye's Beach Resort** also have reliable travel agents. The town's Internet cafés can arrange bus tickets to Guatemala or Mexico and boat trips to Honduras.

GETTING THERE
By Air
Maya Island Air and Tropic Air make daily flights to Caye Caulker, flying to and from Belize City's municipal and international airports as part of their San Pedro run. The airstrip on Caulker is simple—you wait under a tree or on the veranda of the small building that serves all flights. Fares are US$35 one-way to the municipal airport (about 8 minutes) and US$65 one-way to the international airport (10 minutes).

By Boat
The short cruise between Caye Caulker and either Belize City or San Pedro is the most common way to get to the island. There are three competing water taxi companies with alternating schedules and similar fares: **Caye Caulker Water Taxi** (San Pedro tel. 501/226-2194, Caye Caulker tel. 501/226-0992, Belize City tel. 501/223-5752, www.cayecaulkerwatertaxi.com), **San Pedro Express** (San Pedro tel. 501/226-3535, Caye Caulker tel. 501/226-0225, Belize City tel. 501/223-2225, www.belizewatertaxi.com), and **Water Jets Express** (San Pedro tel. 501/226-2194, Caye Caulker tel. 501/206-0234, Belize City tel. 501/207-1000, www.sanpedrowatertaxi.com). The Belize City–Caye Caulker trip costs US$10 one-way, and Caye Caulker–San Pedro is also US$10 one-way. Many boats are partially open-air; a light wrap or rain jacket is handy for windy trips. The boats are often packed to the point of being overloaded. They are supposed to have a passenger limit, but it isn't always observed.

DEPARTING IN BELIZE CITY
You'll find the Caye Caulker Water Taxi

Terminal at the north end of the Swing Bridge, with boats leaving between 8 A.M. and 4:30 P.M.

San Pedro Express has its terminal in the Tourism Village, with boats leaving between 9 A.M. and 5:30 P.M. express.

Water Jets Express leaves from Bird's Isle Water Taxi and Marina, 7 A.M. and 6 P.M.

DEPARTING CAYE CAULKER
Caye Caulker Water Taxi boats depart Caye Caulker from the main pier on the east side of the island; buy tickets at the office right on the dock before boarding the boat. Departures to Belize City run 8:30 A.M.–4 P.M.; to San Pedro 8:45 A.M.–5:15 P.M. daily.

San Pedro Water Taxi has its ticket office on Caye Caulker's Front Street, and boats depart from the police station dock. Express departures to Belize City run 7:30 A.M.–5 P.M.; to San Pedro 6:30 A.M.–6:15 P.M. daily.

Water Jets Express boats depart from the back bridge on the west side to Belize City 6:30 A.M.–6 P.M.; to San Pedro 7:45 A.M.–6:45 P.M. daily.

TO OTHER CAYES AND MEXICO
No regularly scheduled trips are available between cayes other than Ambergris and Caye Caulker, but you can request a stop at St. George's Caye.

San Pedro Water Taxi also offers service to the Muelle Fiscal in **Chetumal, Mexico.** The boat departs from San Pedro at 7:30 A.M. and returns from Chetumal at 3:30 P.M. Caye Caulker connections are available. The 2.5-hour one-way trip costs US$35.

Water Jets Express also offers service to Chetumal and departs San Pedro at 8:15 A.M. and returns at 3 P.M. They also have a boat that leaves San Pedro at 3 P.M. for Corozal and Sarteneja, and returns at 7 A.M.

GETTING AROUND
The navigable part of town—from the airstrip north to the split—is a mile long and easily traversed on foot. Still, a bicycle will make things easier, especially if you're staying in one

of the more southern accommodations. Ask if your hotel provides one, or rent at **Friendship Center** on Front Street or beside the bakery on Middle Street. **Island Boy Rental** near the soccer field also has bikes (US$2/hour or US$40/week).

If you're staying south of the village, you might consider renting a golf cart from **C&N, Island Boy Rental** (Traveler's Palm St., tel.

501/226-0252) or **CC Golf Cart Rentals** (Ave. Mangle, tel. 501/226-0237), about US$12.50/ hour or US$62.50/day.

A golf cart taxi could be very helpful when moving around the island with luggage, but otherwise is not necessary. Taxi guy **George Deicid** (tel. 501/601-4330) is responsive, friendly, and accommodating, and taxis operate from the Rainbow Hotel front desk (tel. 501/226-0123).

Turneffe Islands Atoll

This is a renowned diving and fishing destination about 30 miles east of Belize City. Most of the Turneffe islands are small dots of sand, mangrove clusters, and swamp, home only to seabirds and wading birds, ospreys, manatees, and crocodiles; a few support small colonies of fishers and shellfish divers. Only **Blackbird Caye** and **Douglas Caye** are of habitable size.

If you're looking to hook a bonefish or permit, miles of crystal flats are alive with the hard-fighting fish. Tarpon are abundant late March–June within the protected creeks and channels throughout the islands. Those who seek larger trophies will find a grand choice of marlin, sailfish, wahoo, groupers, blackfin tuna, and many more.

Most visitors to Turneffe are day-tripping divers based in Ambergris Caye or Caye Caulker; a select few choose to book an island vacation package. There are a couple of upscale resorts and one research facility where visitors can stay.

DIVING
Rendezvous Point
This is a popular first dive for overnighters out of Ambergris Caye. It provides a great opportunity for divers who haven't been under in a while. The depth is about 40–50 feet and affords sufficient bottom time for you to get a good look at a wide variety of reef life. Angelfish, butterfly fish, parrot fish, yellowtails, and morays are represented well. This will whet appetites for the outstanding diving to come.

❮ The Elbow
Most divers have heard of the Elbow (just 10 minutes from Turneffe Island Lodge), a point of coral that juts out into the ocean. This now-famous dive site offers a steep sloping drop-off covered with tube sponges and deep-water gorgonians, along with shoals of snappers (sometimes numbering in the hundreds) and other pelagic creatures. Predators such as bar jacks, wahoo, and permits cruise the reef, and the drop-off is impressive. Currents sweep the face of the wall most of the time, and they typically run from the north. However, occasionally they reverse or cease all together.

Lefty's Ledge
A short distance farther up the eastern side of the atoll from the Elbow is another dive to excite even those with a lot of bottom time under their weight belts. Lefty's Ledge features dramatic spur-and-groove formations that create a wealth of habitats. Correspondingly, divers will see a head-turning display of undersea life, both reef and pelagic species. Jacks, mackerels, permits, and groupers are present in impressive numbers. Wrasses, rays, parrot fish, and butterfly fish are evident around the sandy canyons. Cleaning stations are also evident, where you'll see large predators allowing themselves to be groomed by small cleaner shrimp or fish. The dive begins at about 50 feet and the bottom slopes to about 100 feet before dropping off into the blue.

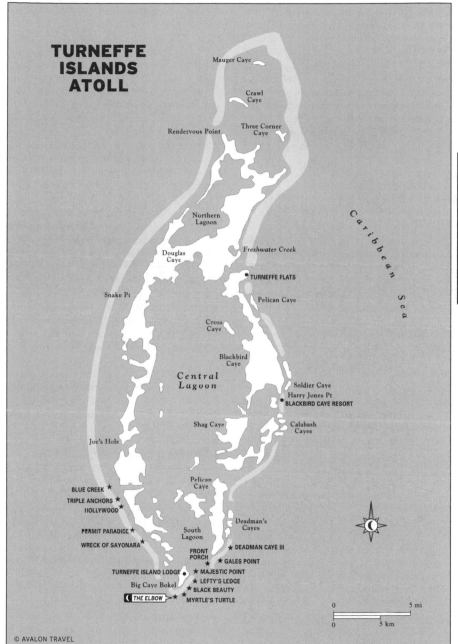

TURNEFFE
ISLANDS
ATOLL

Mauger Caye

Crawl
Caye

Three Corner
Caye

Rendezvous Point

Northern
Lagoon

Douglas
Caye

Freshwater Creek

● TURNEFFE FLATS

Snake Pt

Pelican Caye

Cross
Caye

Blackbird
Caye

*Central
Lagoon*

Soldier Caye
Harry Jones Pt
● BLACKBIRD CAYE RESORT

Shag Caye

Calabash
Cayes

Joe's Hole

Pelican
Caye

BLUE CREEK ★
TRIPLE ANCHORS ★
HOLLYWOOD ★

Deadman's
Cayes

PERMIT PARADICE ★
WRECK OF SAYONARA ★

South
Lagoon

FRONT
PORCH ★
★ DEADMAN CAYE III
★ GALES POINT

TURNEFFE ISLAND LODGE ●
Big Caye Bokel

★ MAJESTIC POINT
★ LEFTY'S LEDGE
★ BLACK BEAUTY

◖ THE ELBOW ★
MYRTLE'S TURTLE

Caribbean Sea

0   5 mi
0   5 km

Gales Point

Another "don't-miss" dive, Gales Point is a short distance farther up the eastern side of the atoll from Lefty's Ledge. Here the reef juts out into the current at a depth of about 45 feet, sloping to about 100 feet before the drop-off. Along the wall and the slope just above it are numerous ledges and cavelike formations. Rays and groupers are especially common here—some say this may be a grouper breeding area. Corals and sponges are everywhere in numerous varieties.

Sayonara

On the leeward, or eastern, side of the atoll, the wreck of the *Sayonara*, a tender sunk by Dave Bennett of Turneffe Island Lodge, lies in about 30 feet of water. Close by is a sloping ledge with interesting tunnels and spur-and-groove formations. Healthy numbers of reef fish play among the coral, and some barracudas tag along. Divers' bubbles often draw down large schools of permit.

Hollywood

A bit farther up the atoll from the *Sayonara,* Hollywood offers divers a relatively shallow dive (30–40 feet) with moderate visibility, unless the currents have reversed. Here you'll find lots of basket and tube sponges and lush coral growth. Many angelfish, parrot fish, grunts, and snappers swim here. Although not as dramatic as an eastern side dive, Hollywood has plenty to see.

ACCOMMODATIONS

Turneffe Island Lodge (tel. 501/220-4011 or 501/220-4142, U.S. tel. 800/874-0118, www.turneffelodge.com) is on Little Caye Bokel, 12 acres of beautiful palm-lined beachfront and mangroves. Book a seven-night dive or fishing package and stay in one of eight ground-floor deluxe rooms, four second-floor superior rooms, and eight stand-alone cabanas. It's a popular location for divers, anglers, and those who just want a hammock under the palms. At the southern tip of the atoll, the lodge is a short distance north of its larger relative, Big Caye Bokel. This strategic location offers enthusiasts a wide range of underwater experiences—it's within minutes of nearly 200 dive sites. Shallow areas are perfect for photography or snorkeling; you can see nurse sharks, rays, reef fish, and dolphins in the flats a few hundred yards from the dock. All the dives mentioned earlier and many more lie within 15 minutes by boat. The dive operation is first rate, and advanced instruction and equipment rentals are available. Anglers have a choice of fishing for snappers, permit, jacks, mackerel, and billfish from the drop-offs. They can stalk the near-record numbers of snook, bonefish, and tarpon in the flats and mangroves. The lodge's fishing guide has an uncanny way of knowing where the fish will be.

On the eastern side of the Turneffe Islands, **Blackbird Caye Resort** (tel. 501/223-2772, U.S. tel. 888/271-3483, www.blackbirdresort.com) encompasses 166 acres of beach and jungle. It can accommodate 36 guests (double occupancy) with hot-water showers, private baths, and double and queen beds, as well as a duplex and triplex featuring private rooms and air-conditioning. Snorkeling, fishing, and diving packages are offered for about US$2,000–3,000 per week (depending on activities and accommodations) and include three dives a day, all meals, lodging, and airport transfers.

Turneffe Flats (tel. 501/220-4046, U.S. tel. 800/512-8812, www.tflats.com) is famous among international saltwater fly fishers who know the value of being able to sight fish in wadeable flats for permit, bonefish, and tarpon. Or go for barracuda, snapper, jacks, or snook, and eat it up at night. Guided fishing is in the lodge's 16-foot Super Skiff flats boats. Divers are welcome and will enjoy daily forays to scores of sites throughout Turneffe Atoll and Lighthouse Reef. Varied beach accommodations are comfortable and well-appointed, and meals are eaten family-style.

Lighthouse Reef Atoll

The most easterly of Belize's three atolls, Lighthouse Reef lies 50 miles southeast of Belize City. The 30-mile-long, 8-mile-wide lagoon is the location of the Blue Hole, a dive spot that was made famous by Jacques Cousteau and that is a favorite destination of dive boats from Belize City, Ambergris Caye, and Caye Caulker. The best dive spots, however, are along the walls of Half Moon Caye and Long Caye, where the diving rivals that of any in the world.

Think of the atoll as a large spatula with a short handle and a long blade. At the northern tip of the spatula-shaped atoll, **Sandbore Caye** is home to a rusty lighthouse and a few fishing shacks. It is also the favorite anchorage of several of the dive boats that do overnight stops, including *Reef Roamer II*.

Big Northern Caye, across a narrow strait, has a landing strip that used to serve the closed resort here. There are long stretches of beach to walk, beautiful vistas, mangroves, and lagoons, home to snowy egrets and crocodiles.

Halfway down the spatula-shaped atoll, about where the blade meets the handle, lies the magnificent Blue Hole, a formation best appreciated from the air, but also impressive from the bridge of a boat.

At the elbow of the handle is **Half Moon Caye,** a historical natural monument and protected area with its lighthouse, bird sanctuary, shipwrecks, and incredible diving offshore. Finally, on the handle, we come upon **Long Caye,** a lonely outpost with a small dock, large palms, and glassy water.

DIVING
Blue Hole

This circular underwater formation, with its magnificent blue-to-black hues surrounded by neon water, is emblematic of Belize itself; this submerged shaft is a karst-eroded sinkhole with depths exceeding 400 feet. In the early 1970s, Jacques Cousteau and his crew explored the tunnels, caverns, and stalactites that were angled by past earthquakes.

Most dive groups descend to a depth of about 135 feet. Technically, this is not a dive for novices or even intermediate divers, though many intermediate divers do it. It requires a rapid descent, a very short period at depth, and a careful ascent. For a group of 10 or more, at least three dive masters should be present. Critics write the Blue Hole off as a "hyped-up macho dive," but my personal experience there—descending with an entourage of 15 circling reef sharks and turtles—was extraordinary. The lip of the crater down to about 60–80 feet has the most life: fat midnight parrot fish, stingrays, angelfish, butterfly fish, and other small reef fish cluster around coral heads and outcroppings.

◖ Half Moon Caye Wall

They just don't come much better than this. Here on the eastern side of the atoll, the reef has a shallow shelf in about 15 feet of water where garden eels are plentiful. The sandy area broken with corals extends downward till you run into the reef wall, which rises some 20 feet toward the surface. Most boats anchor in the sandy area above the reef wall. Numerous fissures in the reef crest form canyons or tunnels leading out to the vertical face. In this area, sandy shelves and valleys frequently harbor nurse sharks and gigantic stingrays. Divers here are sure to return with a wealth of wonderful pictures.

Tres Cocos

On the western wall, "Three Coconuts" refers to trees on nearby Long Caye. The sandy bottom slopes from about 30 feet to about 40 feet deep before it plunges downward. Overhangs here are common features, and sponges and soft corals adorn the walls. Another fish lover's paradise, Tres Cocos does not have the outstanding coral formations you'll see at several other dives in the area, but who cares? There's a rainbow of marine life all about. Turtles, morays, jacks, coral, shrimp, cowfish, rays, and

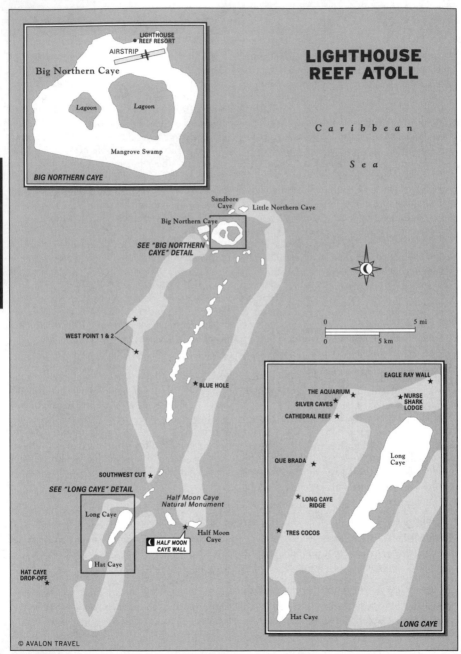

BIG NORTHERN CAYE

LIGHTHOUSE REEF RESORT
AIRSTRIP
Big Northern Caye
Lagoon
Lagoon
Mangrove Swamp
BIG NORTHERN CAYE

LIGHTHOUSE REEF ATOLL

C a r i b b e a n

S e a

Sandbore Caye
Little Northern Caye
Big Northern Caye
SEE "BIG NORTHERN CAYE" DETAIL

WEST POINT 1 & 2

★ BLUE HOLE

0   5 mi
0   5 km

EAGLE RAY WALL

THE AQUARIUM ★   ★ NURSE SHARK LODGE
SILVER CAVES ★
CATHEDRAL REEF ★

QUE BRADA ★   Long Caye

SOUTHWEST CUT ★

SEE "LONG CAYE" DETAIL

Long Caye

Half Moon Caye Natural Monument

★ LONG CAYE RIDGE

★ HALF MOON CAYE WALL
Half Moon Caye

★ TRES COCOS

Hat Caye

HAT CAYE DROP-OFF ★

Hat Caye

LONG CAYE

© AVALON TRAVEL

angelfish are among the actors on this colorful stage.

Silver Caves

The shoals of silversides (small gleaming minnows) that gave this western atoll site its name are gone. But Silver Caves is still impressive and enjoyable. The coral formations are riddled with large crevices and caves that cut clear through the reef. As you enter the water above the sandy slope where most boats anchor, you'll be in about 30 feet of water and surrounded by friendly yellowtail snappers. Once again you'll see the downwardly sloping bottom, the rising reef crest, and the stomach-flipping drop into the blue.

West Point

Farther north and about even with the Blue Hole, West Point is well worth a dive. Visibility may be a bit more limited than down south, but it's still very acceptable. The reef face here is stepped. The first drop plunges from about 30 feet to well over 100 feet deep. Another coral and sand slope at that depth extends a short distance before dropping vertically into very deep water. The first shallow wall has pronounced overhangs and lush coral and sponge growth.

HALF MOON CAYE NATIONAL MONUMENT

Dedicated as a monument in 1982, this crescent-shaped island was the first protected area in Belize. Half Moon Caye, at the southeast corner of Lighthouse Reef, measures 45 square acres, half of which is a thriving (but endangered) littoral forest; the other half is a stunning palm-dotted beach. This is also the only red-footed booby sanctuary in the Western Hemisphere besides the Galápagos. The US$40 per person admission fee is sometimes included in your dive boat fee, but sometimes you'll pay it directly to the park ranger when you disembark.

As you approach Half Moon Caye, you'll believe you have arrived at some South Sea paradise. Offshore, boaters use the rusted hull of a wreck, the *Elksund*, as a landmark in these waters. Its dark hulk looms over the surreal blue

and black of the reef world. The caye, eight feet above sea level, was formed by the accretion of coral bits, shells, and calcareous algae. It's divided into two ecosystems: The section on the western side has dense vegetation with rich fertile soil, while the eastern section primarily supports coconut palms and little other vegetation.

Besides offshore waters that are among the clearest in Belize, the caye's beaches are wonderful. You must climb the eight-foot-high central ridge that divides the island and gaze south before you see the striking half-moon beach with its unrelenting surf erupting against limestone rocks. Half Moon Caye's first lighthouse was built in 1820, modernized and enlarged in 1931, decommissioned in 1997, then felled by the elements in 2010. A newer lighthouse was built in 1998 and is still functioning.

The Tower

Everyone should go to the observation tower, built by the Audubon Society in the ziricote forest; climb above the forest canopy for an unbelievable view. Every tree is covered with perched booby birds in some stage of growth or mating. In the right season, you'll have a close-up view of nests where feathered parents tend their hatchlings. The air is filled with boobies coming and going, attempting to make their usually clumsy landings (those webbed feet weren't designed for landing in trees). Visitors also have a wonderful opportunity to see the other myriad inhabitants of the caye. Magnificent thieving frigates (the symbol of the Belize Audubon Society) swoop in to steal eggs, and iguanas crawl around in the branches, also looking for a snack.

Accommodations

The only place to stay in Lighthouse Reef Atoll is on Long Caye, at **Huracan Diving** (tel. 501/603-2930, www.huracandiving.com), where you can choose from either a four- or seven-night all-inclusive dive package. The four rooms connected to the main lodge have private baths, king beds, ceiling fans, and screened windows. Pickup and transfer from Belize City is included in your package. There is also a home for rent on the same island, **BluHole Lodging** (www.bluholelodge.com), but you'll need to arrange meals and activities beforehand.

Getting There

It's 52 miles to the mainland, a long boat trip

over open ocean. Most visitors make the trip through one of the bigger dive shops, like Amigo's on Ambergris Caye. Otherwise, only chartered or privately owned boats and seaplanes travel to Half Moon Caye. Or check with the Belize Audubon Society in Belize City for other suggestions.

Other Northern Cayes

CAYE CHAPEL

Just one by three miles in size, Caye Chapel is about 15 miles and 25 minutes by boat from Belize City. Until recently, the caye was owned by a wealthy Kentuckian trying to attract corporate America to the island's exclusive 18-hole golf course and retreat. The island is currently closed, but still selling lots.

ST. GEORGE'S CAYE

This small caye, nine miles from Belize City, is shaped something like a boomerang, with its open ends facing the mainland. St. George's Caye Mangrove Reserve was established in 2005 and covers 12.5 acres on the southernmost point of the island. The caye is steeped in history and was the first capital of the British settlement (1650–1784). It was also the scene of the great sea battle between the Spaniards and the British settlers. Today, the small cemetery gives evidence of St. George's heroic past. The historic cemetery on St. George's Caye is Belize's smallest archaeology reserve.

The St. George's Caye Research Station and Field School, founded by ECOMAR in 2009, hosts a group of Texas State University professors and students who spend a month on the island to conduct research digs. They also conduct coral reef research and educational trips based here.

St. George's Caye is far from commercialized—on the contrary, it's very quiet, with mostly residential homes and their docks. There is one upscale resort with accommodations and full-service dive shop here, plus the vacation homes of quite a few of Belize's

elite. Check **St. George's Caye Resort** (tel. 800/813-8498 or 501/220-4444, www.gooddiving.com, US$168 pp includes meals).

THE BLUEFIELD RANGE

Scattered along the coast is a constellation of small cayes, some accessible by tourists, others only by drug traffickers. Seeking out accommodations on any of these islands is guaranteed to get you a unique Belize experience, as you'll be well away from the crowds of the more standard island destinations.

The Bluefield Range is a group of cayes a short distance south of Belize City. On one of the islands, 21 miles south of the city, is **Ricardo's Beach Huts and Lobster Camp** (tel. 501/227-8469 or 501/203-4970), the ultimate in funky. At last check, the accommodations were quite rustic and reasonably priced. Expect campout conditions: outhouse, bucket shower, bugs. Bring mosquito coils, repellent, and a mosquito net bed/tent. On the upside, this is one of the few chances to experience outer island living just as it has been for the people who spend their lives fishing these waters.

ENGLISH CAYE

Though this is just a small collection of palm trees, sand, and coral, an important lighthouse sits here at the entrance to the Belize City harbor from the Caribbean Sea. Large ships stop at English Caye to pick up one of the two pilots who navigate the 10 miles in and out of the busy harbor. Overnights are not allowed here, but it's a pleasant day-trip location.

THE GRAY LADY

The ghost of the famed buccaneer Henry Morgan, it is said, used to roam the waters of the Caribbean, frequently off the coast of Belize City. In his wanderings, Henry brought his fair lady with him, an independent miss. It's easy to imagine that lovers occasionally get testy living in such close quarters aboard a caravel. And though Henry and his lady usually kissed and made up, one lightning-slashed night, just off the coast of St. George's Caye, they were unable to settle a nasty argument – something to do with the seaman standing watch the night before? Morgan was the captain after all; his word was law! The lady ended up walking the plank into the stormy sea, gray gossamer gown whipping around her legs in the angry wind. Since that fateful night, the lady in gray has been roaming the small caye of St. George, trying to find her blackguard lover. Don't scoff; some islanders will speak no ill of the Gray Lady, and on stormy nights they stay safely behind closed doors.

GOFF'S CAYE

Near English Caye, Goff's Caye is a favorite little island stop for picnics and day trips out of Caye Caulker and Belize City, thanks to a beautiful sandy beach and promising snorkeling areas. Sailboats often stop overnight; camping can be arranged from Caye Caulker by talking with any reputable guide. Bring your own tent and supplies. Goff's is a protected caye, so note the rules posted by the pier. Goff's has seen a major impact by the cruise ship industry, which sometimes sends thousands of people per week to snorkel around and party on the tiny piece of sand, and a few reports have said this is destroying the coral.

SPANISH LOOKOUT CAYE

This is a 187-acre mangrove island, located at the southern tip of the Drowned Cayes, only 10 miles east of Belize City. There are many day trip possibilities to Spanish Lookout Caye, including the country's first and only "dolphin encounter" program, a beach, kayaks, and snorkeling.

If you're not researching manatees or mangroves with Earthwatch Institute, you're most likely coming to meet the dolphins or stay at **Belize Adventure Lodge** (tel. 501/220-4024, U.S. reservations 888/223-5403, www.belizeadventurelodge.com), a full-service island facility offering 12 quasi-colonial cabanas over the water, two student dormitories, classrooms, a restaurant, a bar, a gift shop, and a dive center. Five colorful cabanas with 10 rooms, hot showers, and private baths are connected to the island by a dock. The resort offers popular three-night packages that include all meals and transfers to the island.

Diving is one of the favorite activities here, and guests can participate in educational and research programs. Manatees and dolphins are regularly seen foraging near the island. Juvenile reef fish, seahorses, lobster, and mollusks live among the red mangrove roots and sea grass beds. Tarpon and barracudas often come into the bay to feed on the abundant silversides. The resort is only one mile west of the main barrier reef and about eight miles west of central Turneffe Island.

THE NORTHERN CAYES

BELMOPAN AND THE HUMMINGBIRD HIGHWAY

Driving west from Belize City, you'll pass from wetlands to pine savanna, with the Maya Mountains draped across the horizon through your windshield. Most of this region is drained by the Sibun and Caves Branch Rivers, which empty out into a large, lowland wetland before arriving at the sea.

This central chunk of Belize is mostly wild, dotted by a handful of small villages, jungle lodges, and natural attractions and parks. The most popular of these are the Belize Zoo and Guanacaste National Park, both easy road-side stops along the Western Highway, even if you only visit this area en route between the coast and Cayo. Another reason to visit this region is to play a round or two at Roaring River Golf Course, an utterly unique set of tropical links, only a couple of miles west of Belmopan.

Belmopan is the smallest, most unassuming capital in Central America. Rarely a destination for travelers, Belmopan has many services, including an important bus station, a fantastic coffee shop, and a couple of decent restaurants. You'll also find most country embassies here, as well as most important Belize government services, including immigration. Beyond Belmopan, the Hummingbird Highway is one of the most beautiful roads in the region, snaking through densely forested hills, which are riddled with trails, rivers, cenotes, and caves. Start your exploration at the St. Herman's Cave and Blue Hole National Park, whose visitors center is right on the highway. You can stay a night with a local family in Armenia, book a day trip or stylin' treehouse at the world-famous

© JOSHUA BERMAN

HIGHLIGHTS

LOOK FOR (TO FIND RECOMMENDED SIGHTS, ACTIVITIES, DINING, AND LODGING.

(The Belize Zoo: This famous, lush home for animal ex-movie stars and more is an easy stopover as you travel between Belize City and points south and west. It is also home to the Belize Tropical Education Center, where educational and study opportunities abound (page 107).

(Guanacaste National Park: An easy stop along the Western Highway, this 50-acre patch of forest has flat, well-maintained hiking trails through massive trees and ferns that the whole family will enjoy (page 109).

(Roaring River Golf Course: Shoot a leisurely 18 holes at this relaxed set of links, just west of Belmopan (page 112).

(George Price Centre for Peace and Development: This museum and library is an educational, air-conditioned homage to Belize's first prime minister (page 113).

(Blue Hole National Park: Get out the hiking boots, binoculars, flashlight, and a bathing suit for a visit to this park and St. Herman's Cave, halfway down the Hummingbird Highway (page 116).

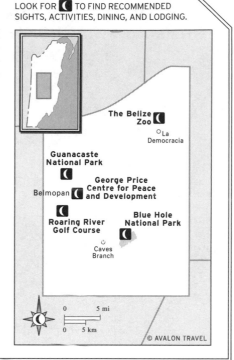

© AVALON TRAVEL

BELMOPAN

Ian Anderson's Caves Branch Adventure Company and Jungle Lodge, or just drive through and enjoy the passing palm trees and orange groves.

PLANNING YOUR TIME

The city of Belmopan certainly doesn't require much of your time, but the rest of the region may warrant a day or two. As you drive the Western Highway out of Belize City, save at least an hour to visit the Belize Zoo, and another half hour for the hike in Guanacaste National Park. Some people spend their entire vacations (or at least the inland portion of them) in one of the adventure lodges in this region.

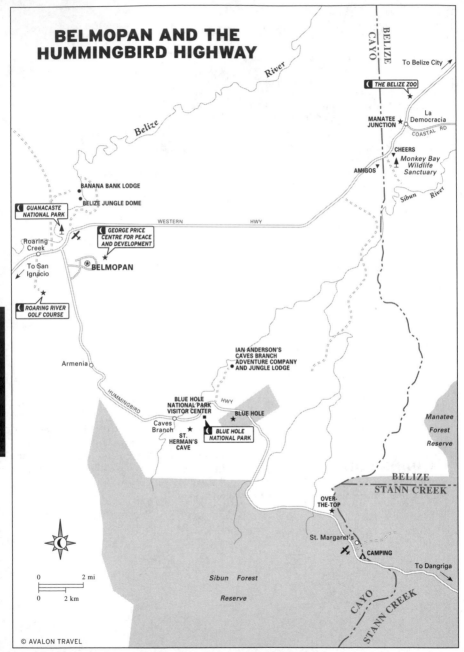

BELMOPAN AND THE HUMMINGBIRD HIGHWAY

BELIZE

CAYO

To Belize City

THE BELIZE ZOO

MANATEE
JUNCTION

La
Democracia

COASTAL RD

CHEERS

Monkey Bay
Wildlife
Sanctuary

AMIGOS

Sibun River

BANANA BANK LODGE

BELIZE JUNGLE DOME

GUANACASTE
NATIONAL PARK

Belize River

WESTERN   HWY

GEORGE PRICE
CENTRE FOR PEACE
AND DEVELOPMENT

Roaring
Creek

To San
Ignacio

BELMOPAN

ROARING RIVER
GOLF COURSE

BELMOPAN

Armenia

IAN ANDERSON'S
CAVES BRANCH
ADVENTURE COMPANY
AND JUNGLE LODGE

HUMMINGBIRD   HWY

BLUE HOLE
NATIONAL PARK
VISITOR CENTER

BLUE HOLE

Caves
Branch

ST.
HERMAN'S
CAVE

BLUE HOLE
NATIONAL PARK

Manatee

Forest

Reserve

BELIZE

STANN CREEK

OVER-
THE-TOP

St. Margaret's

CAMPING

To Dangriga

0   2 mi

0   2 km

Sibun   Forest

Reserve

CAYO

STANN CREEK

© AVALON TRAVEL

Along the Western Highway

FROM BELIZE CITY TO BELMOPAN

As you depart Belize City along the Western Highway, savanna and scraggly pines border the road. The milepost markers between Belize City and San Ignacio will help you find your way around the countryside. If you're driving, you can match the markers as you go by setting your odometer to zero as you turn onto Cemetery Road at the western edge of Belize City.

Freetown Sibun

Three miles south of Hattieville, this small village (community tel. 501/209-6006) has a population of less than 100. Runaway slaves founded the village back in the day, and its population used to peak around 2,000 during big logging runs. Today, you may find campsites, canoe rentals, and hiking trails. Taxis to the village are plentiful from the roundabout in Hattieville.

Manatee Junction

Driving west, note the junction with **Manatee Road** on your left at about Mile 29. (Look for the **Midway Resting Place,** a service station and motel of sorts on the southeast corner of the junction; its tall Texaco sign makes an especially good landmark at night, when the sign glows with bright colors.) This improved dirt road is the shortcut to Gales Point, Dangriga, and the Southern Highway. It's always a good idea to top off your tank, stock up on cold drinks, and ask for current road conditions here. Heavy rains can cause washouts on a lot of these "highways." This is a drive best done in daylight because of the picturesque views of jungle, Maya villages, and the Maya Mountains in the distance.

◖ THE BELIZE ZOO

Established in 1983, the Belize Zoo (tel. 501/220-8004, www.belizezoo.org, 8:30 a.m.–4 p.m. daily, US$15) is settled on 29 acres of tropical savanna and exhibits more than 125 animals, all native to Belize. The zoo keeps only orphaned animals, those injured and rehabilitated, those born in the zoo, and those received as gifts from other zoos. The environment is as natural as possible, with thick native vegetation, and each animal lives in its own wild-looking compound. New displays include the rare harpy eagle; ask about the zoo's restoration program to put these raptors back into forested areas in Belize.

The zoo is at Mile 29 on the Western Highway. It is included in many day tours from Belize City and often as a stop during your airport transfer to or from your lodge in the western or southern parts of Belize. Independent travelers can jump off the bus from Belize City or Cayo (bus fare from Belize City is only US$1–2).

History

Zoo director Sharon Matola's accidental career began when, as a former lion tamer, she agreed to manage a backyard collection of local animals for a nature film company next door. However, after she had worked only five months on the project, funds were severely reduced, and it became evident that the group of animal "film stars" would have to be disbanded. Sharon says that not only had these wild cats, birds, anteaters, and snakes become her friends and companions, but semi-tame animals, dependent on people for care, could not just be released back into the wild. As an alternative, she thought, "This country has never had a zoo. Perhaps if I offered the chance for Belizeans to see these unique animals, their existence here could be permanently established."

A zoo was born. From the very beginning, the amount of local interest in the zoo was incredible. The majority of the people in Belize live in urban areas, and their knowledge of the local fauna is minimal. The Belize Zoo offers Belizeans and tourists alike the opportunity

© JOSHUA BERMAN

The Belize Zoo only has animals that are native to Belize, like this ocelot, one of seven feline species in Belize.

to see the native animals of Belize. Today, the Belize Zoo receives over 10,000 Belizean schoolchildren every year as part of its progressive education programs.

In 2010, Hurricane Richard tore through the zoo, destroying many of the cages and structures. With super-human efforts, the zoo staff and an army of volunteers participated in the immediate reconstruction. (Literally an army—in addition to Belizean volunteers, tour operators, students, ambassadors, and Belize Zoo fans from abroad, U.S. Special Forces and British Forces Belize took part.) The zoo was up and running again in only six weeks, but still has a lot of work to do. The zoo continues to do amazing work with Belizean wildlife, but needs all the help—and visitors—it can get. Enjoy your time there.

Jaguar Rehabilitation

In collaborations with the organization Panthera, the government of Belize, and the U.S. Fish and Wildlife Service, the Belize Zoo runs the only problem jaguar rehabilitation

program and in situ jaguar research program in the world. Problem jaguars (which prey on livestock and domestic animals) are trapped and brought to the zoo for behavior modification training—instead of a bullet. In difficult cases, the animals are transferred to zoos in the United States (the Milwaukee and Philadelphia zoos have received problem cats from Belize).

The Belize Tropical Education Center

Across the street from the zoo, the Belize Tropical Education Center (tel. 501/220-8003, tec@belizezoo.org) was created to promote environmental education and scientific research. Meetings are held here for zoological news, reports, and educational seminars attended and given by people involved in zoology from around the world. The center is equipped with a classroom, a library, a kitchen and dining area, and dormitories that can accommodate as many as 30 people (rates from US$15 pp). Great nature trails weave through the 84-acre site, and bird-watchers can avail themselves of a bird-viewing deck. Also available are canoe trips, nocturnal zoo tours (a real treat), and natural history lectures. Cafeteria-style meals (cooked for the zoo staff) are available for purchase.

MONKEY BAY WILDLIFE SANCTUARY

Monkey Bay Wildlife Sanctuary consists of tropical forest and riparian and savanna habitats, stretching from the Western Highway down to the Sibun River, which flows from the Maya Mountains through the coastal savanna on its path to the Caribbean Sea. Located at Mile 31 on the Western Highway, the 3,300-acre wildlands of Monkey Bay (tel. 501/820-3032, www.monkeybaybelize.org) include the natural habitat of nearly all the animals represented at the Belize Zoo, just east on the Western Highway.

This is a fantastic retreat—for student groups, families, naturalists, and paddlers alike (though most of the sanctuary's business is with study-abroad and service groups). The sanctuary maintains field stations in the Mountain Pine Ridge and Tobacco Caye. The main campus is home to exotic mammal species, including tapirs, pumas, jaguars, and Morelet's crocodiles. More than 250 species of birds have been recorded. The sanctuary borders the Sibun River biological corridor and contains documented remains of ancient Maya settlements and ceremonial caves. A newly built trail system carries you through it all; you can hike, rent a canoe, or hire a caving guide—this is serious spelunking country as well. One option is a three-night camping expedition, where you'll hike to Five Blues Lake National Park.

You'll find two miles of trails and good swimming at nearby Sibun River. With the government's 1992 declaration of the 2,250-acre **Monkey Bay Nature Reserve** across the river, there now exists a wildlands corridor between the **Manatee Forest Reserve** to the south and the sanctuary.

Accommodations

Some travelers find themselves so intrigued by the goings-on at this environmental education center and tropical watershed research station that they opt to stay in one of Monkey Bay's primitively rustic rooms longer than they had planned. The accommodations share the grounds with a screened-in dining area and a shared barnlike library and study space (more than 500 titles are available for reference, with lots of local information).

Choose from a campground in a grove of pine trees with sturdy wooden tent platforms (US$7 pp) or dormitories (US$15 pp); they all share common composting toilets and solar showers. You can also stay in one of the primitive wooden field station rooms in the central building (US$25) or one of three cabins with private baths, air-conditioning, and kitchenettes. Including all the bunks in the dormitory, there are 52 beds here. Freshly prepared meals are available, plus a range of learning and adventure activities throughout Belize.

Monkey Bay offers various cultural learning programs that include homestays with Maya, Creole, and Garifuna communities; it also has a curriculum of tropical watershed ecology field courses. Groups and individuals are welcome for internships and volunteer programs as well.

PIT STOPS AND FOOD

There are a few notable restaurants clustered around Mile 31, right around where you first see the sleeping Maya giant in the hills to the south (the hill formations in this area look like a person laying on their back). You'll first come to **Cheers** (tel. 501/614-9311, 6 A.M.–8:30 P.M. daily), with its interesting collection of orchids, license plates, and T-shirts. A bit farther, just past the turnoff for Monkey Bay, is **Amigos** (tel. 501/802-8000, 8 A.M.–9 P.M. daily), another friendly, screened-in bar and restaurant with excellent Belizean and continental food, US$5–9 per plate.

◀ GUANACASTE NATIONAL PARK

Located at the T junction on the Western Highway where the Hummingbird Highway

begins, the 50-acre Guanacaste National Park is probably one of the most overlooked small attractions in Belize. I recommend planning an hour into your day to stop here for a hike, a picnic, and a dip. Managed by the Belize Audubon Society and the government, the park gets its name from a massive 360-year-old guanacaste, or *tubroos,* tree on the property. The original tree is no longer living and they had to cut the limbs off for safety, but the park is also filled with ceibas, cohune palms, mammee apple, mahogany, quamwood, and other trees, as well as wildlife like agoutis, armadillos, coatis, deer, iguanas, jaguarundis, kinkajous, and more than 100 species of birds. Among the rarer finds are resident blue-crowned motmots.

There are three easy trail loops; bring a swimsuit and take a dip at the quiet spot in the Roaring River just before it enters the Belize River. This is a perfect place for a picnic and a dip on your way to or from Belize City.

The *amate* fig also grows profusely on the water's edge and provides an important part of the howler monkey's diet. Park hours are 8 A.M.–4:30 P.M.; entrance is US$2.50 per person, and naturalist guides are free. Contact the park through the Belize Audubon Society at 501/223-4987.

© JOSHUA BERMAN

It's a short walk through Guanacaste National Park to a clean swimming hole in the Roaring River.

JUNGLE LODGES
NORTH OF BELMOPAN

When they first arrived in Belize more than 30 years ago, Montana cowboy John Carr and his wife, Carolyn, ran **Banana Bank Lodge and Jungle Equestrian Adventure** (tel. 501/820-2020, www.bananabank.com, US$77–175) as a working cattle ranch. Today, most of the pastures have been converted to fields for growing corn and beans (or allowed to turn back to jungle), and the ranch now hosts their lodge. Half of the 4,000-acre ranch is covered in jungle, and within its borders guests will discover not only a wide variety of wildlife but a small Maya ruin. Rooms, suites, cabanas, and chalets are fanciful—no two are alike—and most have beautifully funky bathtubs. The food is served family style. Five cabanas each sleep up to six people, and there are five rooms in the main house, three with shared bathroom, to accommodate guests. Breakfast is included in the room rate. Lunch is US$10, dinner US$15. With 150 saddle horses in its stables and 25 miles of horse trails, Banana Bank features

horseback riding but is also a place to birdwatch, fish, hike, or take a boat trip down the Belize River, with plenty of time left for a cooling swim in the river or pool. Carolyn is considered one of the country's premier artists, and if you admire her on-site studio and gallery, be sure to seek out her paintings in the House of Culture in Belize City. Banana Bank is across the Belize River, about 10–15 minutes by car from the Western Highway (turn in Roaring Creek, next to the big gas station and hotel on the right).

Next door to Banana Bank Lodge, the **Belize Jungle Dome Hotel Resort** (tel. 501/822-2124, www.belizejungledome.com, US$105–200) has five rooms in a unique geodesic dome setting; it's just across the Belize River from Belmopan, but it feels very remote. The rooms are fully equipped with queen beds, air-conditioning, private baths, and wireless Internet; there is a lovely pool and a separate four-bedroom villa. The Jungle Dome serves three meals and caters to all dietary requirements. The resort is a licensed tour operator and runs a full range of tours, as well as airport transfers.

◖ ROARING RIVER GOLF COURSE

The only functioning golf course in all of Belize is the Roaring River Golf Course (Mile 50¼ Western Highway, tel. 501/664-5441 or 501/820-2031, www.belizegolfcourses.com), an unpretentious, executive-type 18-holer (3,892 yards, par 64, slope rating 116). It's a short drive from Belmopan and a worthy activity for anyone staying in an area lodge or resort, whether you're a seasoned slugger or just golf curious (free lessons are offered for beginners). The feel of the course, clubhouse, and restaurant is tranquil, the staff is friendly, and the greens fees are reasonable (US$18 per round or US$25 all-you-can-play).

This is a unique jungle-golf opportunity, by any measure. Over 120 bird species have been identified on and around the property, there are crocodiles in the water hazards, and you'll hear the sound of the nearby river, which flows from Thousand Foot Falls in the Mountain Pine Ridge. After sweating out a round, take a dip in one of the cool, clean, shady pools of the river.

Roaring River Golf Course is well maintained with a level layout and interesting landscaping dividing the fairways; greens boast Bermuda grass, grown from seed. Paul, the South African owner, notes that his course uses chemicals very sparingly, almost not at all—"just a bit of spraying for the ants," he says. The property uses water from a natural spring flowing from within the mountain.

Plant your non-golfing family members in the river for the day while you hit those links. The "Meating Place" restaurant has earned several "best steak in Belize" comments from reviewers (Paul's wife, Jennie, who hails from South Carolina, cures and ages the meat herself); their top filet goes for US$18, if you want to judge for yourself.

Guests can stay in one of four well-furnished villas with air-conditioning, Internet, TV, queen beds, fridge, coffeemaker, work counters, lounge suites, and stunning back porches over the river. Staying here is a perfect option for someone who really wants to get some early rounds in, or for anyone trapped by an assignment in Belmopan, which is only 10 or 15 minutes away.

hitting the links at the Roaring River Golf Course, the only golf course in Belize

© JOSHUA BERMAN

Belmopan

After Hurricane Hattie destroyed government buildings (and records) in Belize City in 1961, Belmopan was built far away from the coast to keep it safe from storm damage, with the expectation that large numbers of the population of Belize City would move with the government center. They didn't. Industry stayed behind, and so did most jobs. Today, though there is some growth in Belmopan, the masses are still in Belize City, which remains the cultural and commercial hub of the country. Some capital employees live in Belize City and commute 50 miles back and forth each day. However, Belmopan was designed for growth and continues to expand, with the population around 9,000 souls (plus a surge of several thousand commuters during weekdays). Today, the feel inside the city grid (within Ring Road) has been compared to a lower-middle-class suburb, with rows of small cement homes and chain-link fencing.

Some students and scientists come to Belmopan to do research in the **Belize Archives Department** (tel. 501/822-2097, archives@btl.net), a closed-stacks library popular with both local students and foreign researchers.

The majority of travelers, however, see only Belmopan's bus terminal and, if they have time, the small open-air market right next door. Some jog across the market to take a peek at the government buildings (only a couple hundred yards away)—an incredibly gray, squat, post-apocalyptic bit of architecture. Their intentionally Maya-influenced arrangement—built around a central plaza—gives the scene just enough strange irony to make it worth the visit.

ORIENTATION

Belmopan is just east of the Hummingbird Highway (and just south of the Western Highway) and is usually accessed by Constitution Drive, which leads straight into the center from a roundabout. Banks, buses,

the market, and government buildings are tightly clustered within easy walking distance of one another. Turning right on Bliss Parade from Constitution Drive, you'll find the dilapidated Belmopan Hotel on your right and the Novelo's bus station and the market on your left. Bliss Parade joins Ring Road, which loops around the central town district. Ring Road passes various government buildings and embassies on the left before meeting back up with Constitution Drive.

◖ GEORGE PRICE CENTRE FOR PEACE AND DEVELOPMENT

This homage to the founding father of Belize is an impressive and modern air-conditioned museum, library, and center for conflict resolution and peace. The George Price Centre (Price Centre Rd., tel. 501/822-1054, www.gpcbelize.com, 8 A.M.–6 P.M. Mon.–Fri., closed Sat., 9 A.M.–11:30 A.M. Sun., free) is just off the eastern part of the Loop Road, near the Catholic church. Set aside at least 30 minutes to tour the display, watch some historical videos, and admire the original flag that flew at Belize's independence ceremony in 1981. The website features a list of events and some fascinating information on George Price's legacy and Belizean history. Born in 1919, at press time Mr. Price was alive and kickin' at the age of 92. He lives in Belize City.

MARKET SQUARE

This is where the action is for local shoppers; the lines of stalls are alive with the commerce and gossip of the area. Hang out here for a little while and you are sure to see a parade of local farmers, government workers, and colorful characters going about their business. Try a tasty tamale or a plate of *garnaches* (crispy tortillas topped with tomato, cabbage, cheese, and hot sauce) for next to nothing. Bananas, oranges, mangoes, tomatoes, chilies, and carrots are cheap, too; stock up before heading deeper into Belize.

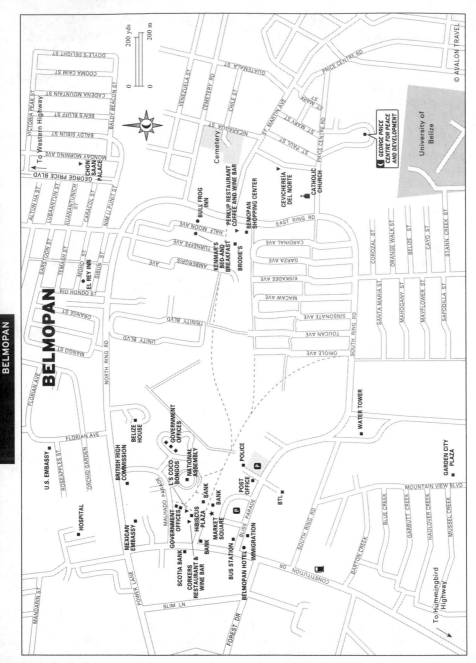

ENTERTAINMENT

Despite Belmopan's reputation for being a "dead" town, weekends can be quite alive in the capital city. **Perkup Café** (4 Shopping Center, tel. 501/822-0001, www.perkupcoffeeshop.com, 11 A.M. to 8 or 9 P.M. during the week, 10 A.M.–5:30 P.M. Sat.) has been a boon for local musicians, hosting live acoustic music and open mic nights Wednesday–Saturday. Thursdays start with karaoke at the **Bull Frog Inn's Restaurant & Bar** (25 Half Moon Ave., tel. 501/822-2111, www.bullfroginn.com) but turn into a rockin' dance party around 11 P.M., when the place gets packed. The rest of the weekend is ruled by **Twilight Lounge,** located on the northeast corner of the traffic circle on the Hummingbird Highway. For a mellow, unpretentious bar, be sure to hit **La Cabaña,** in the western part of town on a hill above Hummingbird Highway by Las Flores, with cheap bar food and a friendly vibe. **Barrio Fino Night Club** (5 P.M.–3 A.M. Thurs.–Sat.) is a local cool spot, dance club, and bar, with popular pool tables, off of Constitution Drive opposite the gas station.

SHOPPING

Besides Market Square, you'll find a few handy stores in Belmopan. **Angelus Press** has a good office supply and bookstore right by the bus station. **The Art Box** is on the Western Highway and has an excellent selection of woodworking, watercolors, and picture frames, in addition to the standard gift shop fare (as well as Christian books and CDs).

Garden City Plaza (Mountain View Blvd., about US$2.50 by taxi from the city center) has a helpful collection of shops, including a Birkenstock store with its own reflexology/massage studio (US$40 one-hour massage), a bakery, Internet café, health food store, and a bank.

ACCOMMODATIONS

If you're staying in Belmopan, you're either a businessperson, a diplomat, a development worker—or just lost. The most reasonably priced beds are found at **El Rey Inn** (23 Moho St., tel. 501/822-3438, hibiscus@btl.net, US$27 plus key deposit), with 11 tidy, white, austere rooms with private baths, hot and cold water, and fans.

KenMar's Bed & Breakfast (on the side street behind the Bull Frog Inn, 22/24 Halfmoon Ave., tel. 501/822-0118, www.kenmar.bz, US$60–100) is an excellent option, with 10 air-conditioned rooms in a large house, each with en suite bathroom and plenty of amenities (there's a luxury suite for US$140). There is a very nice common living area, full Internet access, and, sometimes, the smell of fresh baking from the kitchen.

The **Bull Frog Inn** (25 Half Moon Ave., tel. 501/822-2111, www.bullfroginn.com, US$85 plus tax) has 28 rooms that could be mistaken for those of any basic roadside hotel in the States. The inn reports that 80 percent of the guests are businesspeople doing work for the government or private businesses. The on-site restaurant is solid, and the bar turns into an all-night disco on Thursdays.

FOOD

Even if you're not staying in Belmopan, it is a common lunch stop for anyone traveling to or from Belize City. The cheapest meals are at the market stalls and small restaurants that surround the bus terminal. There are also numerous Chinese bakeries in the area, including the **Golden Tree Bakery** (tel. 501/822-0110, 8 A.M.–7 P.M. daily, closing at 5 P.M. Sun.), just across the main road from the bus terminal; they serve an enormous Chinese vegetarian menu with soy-based "meat."

Also near the bus station, just behind the Belize Bank, **L's Coco Bongos** (tel. 501/802-0666, 11:30 A.M.–8 P.M. Mon.–Wed., till 11 P.M. on Thurs. and Fri.) is a little barbecue joint in a cramped kitchen, with a nice outdoor patio and brisk takeout business. They offer a "Caribbean meets Latin" menu of fajitas, burgers, shrimp tacos, and veg options.

Perkup Restaurant Coffee and Wine Bar (4 Shopping Center, tel. 501/822-0001, www.perkupcoffeeshop.com, 11 A.M. to 8 or 9 P.M. during the week, 10 A.M.–5:30 P.M. Sat.) is an oasis in the desert of Belmopan for the comfortable vibe and unique menu. Choose from a savory roast chicken panini sandwich with garlic sauce (US$8.50) and other sandwiches, stuffed jacks, bagels and cream cheese, wings, espresso drinks, and smoothies, all in a comfy space to kick back and use the free wireless Internet. The owners are savvy to what international travelers and development workers like, and they offer a mellow, musician-friendly vibe some evenings from Wednesdays to Saturdays when the place converts into a lounge scene with jalapeño margaritas and a nice wine list.

Cevichería del Norte (11 A.M.–11 P.M., Wed.–Sun.) is on the east side of town, with fresh ceviche (US$3–10), nachos, tacos, and beer. What else do you need? It's in a purple house on a residential street just north of the George Price Centre.

Pepper's Pizza (on St. Martin Ave., across from Bull Frog Inn, tel. 501/822-0666, US$16) delivers free anywhere in town. And **Pasquale's Pizzeria** (corner of Forest Dr. and Slim Ln., delivery tel. 501/822-4663) offers a large hand-tossed New York–style pizza for US$24.

The open-air restaurant and bar at the **Bull Frog Inn** (25 Half Moon Ave., tel. 501/822-2111, www.bullfroginn.com, 7 A.M.–9:30 P.M.) has a longstanding reputation among the elite of Belmopan, and this is one of the most popular spots in town to dine. The fish fillet, chicken, and burgers are all good here and moderately priced (entrées from US$10, much cheaper lunches and appetizers). For an international menu prepared by a chef from the United Kingdom, **Corkers Restaurant & Wine Bar** (top floor of Hibiscus Plaza, tel. 501/822-0400 or 501/633-5323, www.corkersbelize.com, lunch and dinner Thurs.–Tues.) has salads like tuna Niçoise, wraps, burgers, steaks, pastas, and a lot more (US$4–18).

Among the many Chinese restaurants, **Chon Saan Palace** (7069 George Price Blvd., tel. 501/822-3388) is rated the best place to eat, and **Quang Dong** (right across from the bus terminal) is the most fun to say.

For ice cream, head to **Jolina's** (Mountain View Blvd. and Hummingbird Ave., across from Garden City Plaza).

GETTING THERE AND AWAY

If you are traveling Belize by bus, it's nearly impossible *not* to visit Belmopan, as all buses traveling between Belize City and points west and south—even expresses—pull into the main Belmopan terminal for 5–30 minutes as they rustle up new passengers (and the driver takes a lunch and smoke break).

It's US$2 from Belize City to Belmopan (4 A.M.–8:30 P.M., every 15 minutes). Belmopan to Benque (Guatemalan border) buses leave 5:40 A.M.–11 P.M. every 15 or 30 minutes. Belmopan to Dangriga/Punta Gorda (points south) buses leave 6:30 A.M.–7:30 P.M. (departures hourly).

Along the Hummingbird Highway

This famous stretch of road was paved only a few years ago and boasts some of the most scenic driving in Central America (in my humble opinion). The drive from Belmopan southeast toward Dangriga is an awesome reminder of just how green and wild Belize really is. Some of the canopy took a hit during Hurricane Richard's strange inland rampage in 2010, but the forest grows quickly in these parts, and it is still most impressive.

The highway passes through towering karst hills and long views of broadleaf jungle as you cross the Caves Branch Bridge and enter the Valley of Caves. It climbs into the Maya Mountains, then descends toward the sea. The junction with the Southern Highway is 20 miles east of "Over the Top" pass—Dangriga is another 5 miles from there.

◖ BLUE HOLE NATIONAL PARK

Covering 575 acres, Blue Hole National Park encompasses this water-filled sink, St. Herman's Cave, and the surrounding jungle.

(Belize's other Blue Hole lies in the ocean at Lighthouse Reef.) Rich in wildlife, Blue Hole National Park harbors the jaguar, ocelot, tapir, peccary, tamandua, boa constrictor, fer-de-lance, toucan, crested guan, blue-crowned motmot, and red-legged honeycreeper. You'll find a parking area and a changing room for a dip in the deep blue waters of the Blue Hole.

The pool of the **Blue Hole** is an oblong collapsed karst sinkhole, 300 feet across in some places and about 100 feet deep. Water destined for the nearby Sibun River surfaces briefly here only to disappear once more beneath the ground. Steps lead down to the swimming area, a pool 25 feet deep or so. It is a 45-minute hike from the visitors center, or you can cheat and park closer a little farther down the highway. You can also go tubing and caving here.

St. Herman's Cave requires a hike of a little more than a mile and a half over rugged ground. The trail begins by the changing room. A flashlight and rugged shoes are necessities (they rent flashlights there), and a light windbreaker or sweater is a wise choice for extended stays if you visit in the winter. The nearest of the three entrances to the cave is a huge sinkhole measuring nearly 200 feet across, funneling down to about 65 feet at the cave's lip. Concrete steps laid over the Maya originals aid explorers who wish to descend. The cave doesn't offer the advanced spelunker a real challenge, but neophytes will safely explore it to a distance of about a mile. Pottery, spears, and the remains of torches have been found in many caves in the area. The pottery was used to collect the clear water of cave drippings, called *zuh uy ha* (sacred water) by the Maya. For a guided trip (recommended), call 501/633-7008 (US$30).

It's best to visit most caves with a guide, and at the least, don't visit the park unless the wardens are there (8:30 A.M.–4:30 P.M.). The entrance fee is US$5 per person.

If you're interested in bird-watching, Mr. Israel Manzanero, a park ranger at St. Herman's Blue Hole National Park, is considered one of the most knowledgeable birders in Belize.

FIVE BLUES LAKE NATIONAL PARK

Located on the Hummingbird Highway at Mile 32, the park can be reached by taking a local bus from the terminal in Belmopan to St. Margaret's Village. Within the village, the park office is on the way to the park, but when I stopped there last it was closed up and surrounded by weeds. When you can find them, local rangers are both knowledgeable and willing to help with questions that you may have. From the park office, a rutted, four-kilometer road leads to the park. This road can be hiked, or the rangers will be more than willing to provide transportation.

Within Five Blues Lake National Park, several Maya sites are accessible to visitors. Within the Duende Caves, ceremonial pottery can still be found. While some of the more significant sites are heavily regulated by the Belizean Institute of Archaeology, Five Blues Lake provides ample opportunity for visitors to witness Maya writings and pottery. In 2006, a mysterious draining of some of the lakes occurred as the earth sucked some of the famous blue water back into the limestone. In 2010, the water returned. Spooky. There are many birds and wildlife species here, including coatamundis, collared peccaries, and agoutis.

Entrance fees (US$5 pp) go toward supporting the park and can be paid to the ranger on duty. At the park's entrance, a visitors center with maps of the trails is available, along with picnic tables. In addition, bathroom facilities are available behind the visitors center. From the visitors center, you can take any of the park's trails or go directly to the lake. Be sure to explore St. Margaret's Village and ask about camping and homestay accommodations.

BILLY BARQUEDIER NATIONAL PARK

This 1,500-acre parcel of crucial watershed was declared a protected area in 2001 and is co-managed by the Forestry Department and a unique community-based nonprofit organization called the Steadfast Tourism and Conservation Association (STACA,

BELMOPAN

office in Steadfast village, tel. 501/603-9936, hya172003@yahoo.com). This gorgeous park impacts two major watersheds: North Stann Creek and the Mullins River. There are hiking trails to waterfalls and swimming holes. The entrance to the jungle trail is at Mile 16½, and the entrance to the main waterfall is at Mile 17; camping is permitted at the park warden's camp (US$5 pp). STACA is working on homestay (bed-and-breakfast) options and more campgrounds, so ask about your options. Entrance to the park is US$4 per person, and you are required to hire a trained BBNP park guide (even if you come with an outside guide), who all live in the village of Steadfast.

To visit BBNP from Dangriga, contact **C & G Tours and Charters** (29 Oak St., Dangriga, tel. 501/522-3641 or 501/610-2277, www.cg-tourscharters.com).

IAN ANDERSON'S CAVES BRANCH ADVENTURE COMPANY AND JUNGLE LODGE

One of the premier adventure lodges in Belize, Ian Anderson's Caves Branch Adventure Company and Jungle Lodge (Mile 41½ Hummingbird Hwy., tel. 501/673-3454, www.cavesbranch.com) offers expeditions that can be strenuous and exciting, and is also a hub for social, active travelers. As Ian said a few years ago, "We're certainly not for everyone—thank God!" On the 58,000 acres of this private estate are 68 known caves, and Ian has discovered and explored them all, developing a variety of trips around many of them. The longest and deepest of these Maya ceremonial caves extends seven miles. Pristine dry caves glisten with crystal formations. Some caves still have pottery shards, skeletal remains, and footprints coated with an icing of rock crystals. Ian offers expeditions ranging 1–7 days, including tubing trips through river caves. All expedition guides have received intensive training in cave and wilderness rescue/evacuation and first aid. Popular excursions include the black hole drop, waterfall trips, river caves, and tubing. Their honeymoon packages are particularly creative and adventurous.

Budget travelers pay only US$20 per person for a bed in Caves Branch's fine-screened thatched co-ed dormitory with eight bunk beds, linen provided; the shared jungle showers are fun. The lodge offers their brand of "rustic luxury" in their 25 units, which include jungle cabanas and suites (US$118–205), all the way up to spectacular 800-square-foot treehouse suites (US$245–305) with views to write home about. The screened accommodations are open to the sights and sounds of the surrounding wildness. Lighting is still by the glow of kerosene lamps and the moon—flush toilets and hot and cold water are available throughout (actually, the warm "jungle shower" is the highlight of many a guest's stay). The accommodations have electricity too—for lights and wicker fans—but there are no outlets or appliances. New additions include a spa, wedding facilities, and a helipad. The orchid collection alone has over 400 species of rescued specimens, less than a quarter of which have bloomed yet. Guests dine together in the main open-air lodge, where they discuss the day's stories and next day's plans over family-style meals (breakfast and lunch US$12, dinner US$24).

Access to Ian Anderson's Caves Branch is on the Hummingbird Highway between the Blue Hole National Park visitors center and the parking lot for the Blue Hole itself; turn left (if headed south) and continue to the end of the mile-long dirt road. If traveling by bus, you'll have to hike in from here if you haven't arranged to be picked up by lodge staff.

ACCOMMODATIONS AND FOOD

Bed-and-breakfast homestay options are sometimes available in several villages up and down the Hummingbird Highway, notably Armenia. This is a quiet settlement, eight miles south of Belmopan, with a Maya and Latino population offering **Rock of Excellence Homestays** (call Maria "Betty" Gonzalez, tel. 501/630-7033, or community tel. 501/809-2036, hummingbirdhomestays@gmail.com). There are about a dozen participating families, with a wide range

© JOSHUA BERMAN

one of the tree houses at Ian Anderson's Caves Branch Adventure Company and Jungle Lodge

of accommodations, though all are simple, rustic, and usually within the home of your hosts (US$24 for a night's lodging and three meals).

St. Margaret's, at Mile 32, is the entrance to Five Blues Lake National Park and may have some of the same services as Armenia, including accommodations. A much surer bet is to continue to Mile 29½, where you'll find **Alma and Albert's** (or just "A&A's," tel. 501/606-2765), offering a tent site (US$5 pp with your own gear, or US$10 more to rent) and a two-room cabin (US$40) at a gorgeous bend in the river. Alma and Albert are very friendly people with a lovely property, and they'll cook you typical Belizean food in their little roadside eatery and bar.

The **Green Acres Ranch and Horseback Adventures** (Mile 36 Hummingbird Hwy., tel. 501/670-5698, www.upclosebelize.com) offers a variety of riding and nonriding opportunities; they are run by the tour company UpClose Belize. There are accommodations next door at the **Yamwits'** (six rooms with private baths, hot and cold water, and fans are US$50 per night). It's 17 miles south of Belmopan; turn off the highway after the

Sibun Bridge. A quick drive through the orange orchard, across the brook, and up the hill, and you'll find well-built, healthy quarter horses waiting to take you into the countryside. Green Acres welcomes inexperienced riders (including children) and offers a high level of personalized attention from their guides. Rides vary from one to two hours depending on rider experience. Hourly rides, day rides, and even overnight camping rides are available. A US$85 per person fee includes round-trip transfer from Belize City (or equal distance), two to three hours of on-site riding, and a farm-fresh lunch served under the thatched palapa, including grilled meats, homemade tortillas, salads, and drinks.

As you keep driving south, around mile 16½ you can't miss the **Café Casita De Amour,** or "Little House of Love" (tel. 501/660-2879, Tues.–Sun. 7:30 A.M.–5 P.M.). It is a heart-shaped eatery serving both German and local dishes for breakfast and lunch, everything from milkshakes, coffee, and smoothies to burgers and sandwiches (from US$4). Campers are welcome to pitch a tent, and the Billy Barquedier waterfall is just down the road.

CAYO AND THE MOUNTAIN PINE RIDGE

Between the Caribbean coast "and the inhabited part of Central America is a wilderness, unbroken even by an Indian path. There is no communication with the interior except by the Golfo Dolce or the Balize River; and, from the want of roads, a residence there is more confining than living on an island."

Thus wrote John Lloyd Stephens of Belize's western highlands in the 19th century, well before the construction of the Western Highway, which now zips travelers from Belize City to the Guatemalan border in under two hours. Still, there remains a remote feeling to the largest and most temperate of Belize's six districts. And, as you move away from the highway, Stephens's words are as true as ever.

Cayo District's western side runs the length of the border with Guatemala and comprises some of Belize's steepest, most remote landscape. San Ignacio, a cool town with low-key international restaurants and a great Saturday outdoor market, is the central hub for the area. Cayo's tourism scene is based on a long and varied menu of day trips and a unique selection of accommodations, from remote river resorts and upscale jungle lodges to the guesthouses in San Ignacio. There are also a few favorite backpacker stops in the area. Activities include caving, biking, horseback riding, and paddling expeditions, in addition to archaeological sites and waterfalls.

The Maya Mountains, Vaca Plateau, and Mountain Pine Ridge are important geological features, and several major rivers drain these highlands, including the Branch, Macal, Mopan, and Sibun Rivers. Savanna, broadleaf

© JOSHUA BERMAN

HIGHLIGHTS

◖ **Medicinal Jungle Trail and Iguana Exhibit:** A pleasant and informative guided walk, it's less than an hour long and a short walk from downtown San Ignacio (page 126).

◖ **Cahal Pech Archaeological Site:** The site is unique for both its archaeological intrigue and its location within the city limits of San Ignacio, and the walk up the hill is well worth it (page 127).

◖ **Actun Tunichil Muknal:** Spelunk it in any of Cayo's fascinating caves, especially this one. The "Cave of the Crystal Maiden" is the wettest, dirtiest, most adventurous underground trip available. More caving action is available at Barton Creek, Río Frio, and Chechem Há Caves (page 136).

◖ **Belize Botanic Gardens:** This unique, low-key attraction features hiking trails through a variety of habitats; the operation is totally organic (zero chemicals) and the orchid house is magical (page 140).

◖ **Green Hills Butterfly Ranch and Botanical Collections:** This butterfly breeding, education, and interpretive center also has a fascinating hummingbird observation garden; it's well worth an hour or two of your time as you head to or from the Mountain Pine Ridge (page 145).

◖ **Caracol Archaeological Site:** One of the more difficult major ruins to access in Belize, Caracol is rife with discovery, beauty, and long, peaceful views of the wild countryside from atop its newly excavated temples (page 149).

◖ **Xunantunich Archaeological Site:** It's definitely worth crossing the river to spend a long morning or a lazy afternoon in this ancient Maya city (page 154).

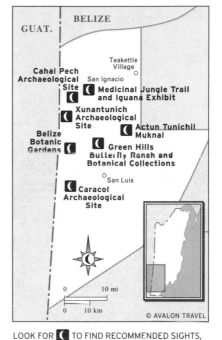

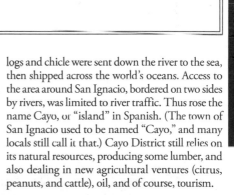

LOOK FOR ◖ TO FIND RECOMMENDED SIGHTS, ACTIVITIES, DINING, AND LODGING.

jungle, and pinelands form a patchwork of habitats for a wide diversity of flora and fauna.

At one time, the majority of the people in Cayo were mestizos from Guatemala. Today, Cayo boasts a rich mixture of people that also includes Mayans, Mennonites, gringos, Lebanese, Creoles, and Chinese, all commingling in government, commerce, agriculture, and tourism.

Cayo's economy has always depended on the forests, especially at the port of San Ignacio, where logs and chicle were sent down the river to the sea, then shipped across the world's oceans. Access to the area around San Ignacio, bordered on two sides by rivers, was limited to river traffic. Thus rose the name Cayo, or "island" in Spanish. (The town of San Ignacio used to be named "Cayo," and many locals still call it that.) Cayo District still relies on its natural resources, producing some lumber, and also dealing in new agricultural ventures (citrus, peanuts, and cattle), oil, and of course, tourism.

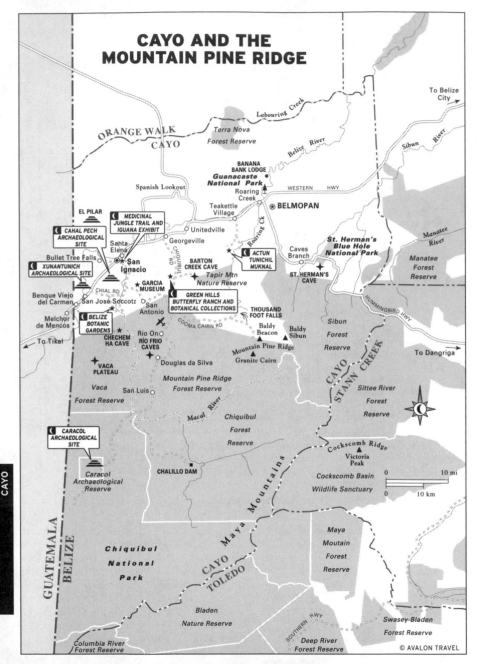

CAYO AND THE MOUNTAIN PINE RIDGE

© AVALON TRAVEL

Cayo

PLANNING YOUR TIME

Budget travelers are always pleased to see that their dollar goes farther in Cayo than in other parts of Belize. Days go by differently here than they do at the beach—maybe because of how busy most Cayo visitors find themselves, signing up for a new activity every day. But there's no rush, and you can easily bop around the area for weeks without getting weary (unless you're the kind of person who gets bored by too many old trees, ruins, and spectacular waterfalls).

Begin in San Ignacio—strike up a friendship with fellow guests at your hotel, enjoy the narrow streets and cafés, then set off early in the morning for a local tour with a packed lunch

CAYO GUIDES AND TOUR OPERATORS

Cayo is famous for both the quantity and quality of its guides, naturalists, and tour operators. Signing up for a tour is as easy as contacting your hotel's front desk or walking up Burns Avenue, where most of Cayo's tour operator offices are located (also look across from the outdoor market). It's often the same price to book a trip through your hotel as it is directly with the tour company, but if you'd like to handle it on your own, here are a few options.

In addition to the Actun Tunichil Muknal cave trip, **Pacz Tours** (tel. 501/604-6921 or 501/824-0536, www.pacztours.net) offers overnight camping options involving some combination of river running, waterfall, ruins, caves, and rappelling. As for their professionalism and gear – well, put it this way: When National Geographic or the Travel Channel comes to Belize, they call Pacz. Equally reputable, **Hun Chi'ik Tours** (tel. 501/600-9192, www. hunchiik.com) has experienced guides and a creative range of trips. They are conscious about the importance of "oral tradition and local knowledge" to enhance the educational value of their tours.

Yute Expeditions (office on Burns Ave. opposite Hotel Casa Blanca, tel. 501/824-2076, yuteexp@btl.net, www.inlandbelize.com) is run by a very experienced Cayo family. They're especially good for families and groups and have a top-notch fleet of air-conditioned vehicles. **Cayo Adventure Tours** (CAT, tel. 501/824-3246, www.cayoadventure.com) is another option, offering all kinds of day trips in the area.

River Rat (tel. 501/625-4636, www.river-ratbelize.com) specializes in Actun Tunichil Muknal, kayak expeditions, and overnight float trips; ask around town for "Gonzo," the amiable Chief Rat who was last seen working on his archaeology degree so he can offer "archaeo-tourism" trips to active excavations.

The tour operator shacks in a row near the open market are all small, Belizean-owned operations and may be cheaper. Among these, **David's Tours** (tel. 501/824-3674) is one of the old standbys, offering volumes of local knowledge and the full range of tours.

Tony's Guided Tours (tel. 501/824-3292) is probably the most economical independent trip on the river at US$17.50 per person. For the more adventurous, Tony also offers a five-day canoe/camp trip to Belize City (US$65 pp per day, all-inclusive). He provides everything except your personal effects.

For a totally unique caving expedition, contact **Belizean Sun Tours** (tel. 501/601-2630, www.belizeansun.com), based in San José de Succotz, just west of San Ignacio. Their Actun Chapat and Halal Caving Adventure runs US$95 per person (includes everything) and begins with an eight-mile Land Rover ride through the jungle, then a hike to several sites, including Actun Chapat, a huge cave with 60-foot ceilings and huge formations. The Maya used this cave extensively for rituals and left behind altars, terraces, carved faces, and artifacts. Since it's on private property, this is an exclusive trip and you will be the only people there.

and plenty of water. Save one day for caving, one for canoeing, one for Maya ruins, and one for a hike—how many's that? Add one or two more days to rest and recuperate before heading back to the Caribbean. And even if you've only got a day or two, San Ignacio is close enough to the coast and worth a trip; the forest runs right up to the city limits, where you'll find several trails and a fascinating archaeological site.

Many visitors skip San Ignacio town entirely, staying up the Macal River, in the Mountain Pine Ridge, down the Hydro Road, or at one of the campgrounds west or south of town—all of which get you even closer to nature.

SPORTS AND RECREATION

Cayo District is home to a beautiful lattice of trails, from short **nature walks** and **medicine trails** to a range of **hiking trips** through the surrounding hills. **Mountain biking** the Cayo District is fun, beautiful, and a great way to burn off a few Belikins (but can be dusty in the dry season). Equestrians will find **horseback riding** at a growing number of resorts and tour operators in and outside San Ignacio.

Many Cayo resorts offer excellent guided **cave trips** of varying levels of difficulty, for everyone from the beginning spelunker to the professional speleologist; day and overnight trips are available. Ask about the varied experiences to be had in Handprint Cave, Yaxsahau (Cave of the Ceiba Tree Lord), Actun Tunichil Muknal, Barton Creek Cave, Chechem Ha

Cave, or any of the most recently discovered ones that are as yet unnamed.

A wise man once said, "The only way to float is downstream." **Canoeing, kayaking,** and **tubing** are all popular ways to enjoy the Macal and Mopan Rivers. Actually, one popular trip is to paddle *up* the Macal River from downtown San Ignacio, making your way to the Ix Chel Medicine Trail or Belize Botanic Gardens.

SHOPPING

There are small gift and supply shops along Burns Avenue in San Ignacio, but the best shopping in the area (some would say in all of Belize) is a few miles east of San Ignacio at **Orange Gifts & Gallery** (Mile 60 Western Hwy., tel. 501/824-2341, www.orangegifts. com). Orange Gifts (there's also a shop in San Pedro) has an enormous collection of original and imported arts and crafts, including the custom hardwood furniture and art of proprietor Julian Sherrard. You'll also find jewelry, paintings, textiles, and practical travelers' items like laminated maps, books, postcards, and Gallon Jug Coffee. Orange has an excellent restaurant and bar.

Nearly across the highway from Orange, **Hot Mama's Belize** (tel. 501/824-0444 or 501/610-1624, www.hotmamasfoods.biz) makes some of the finest and spiciest condiments in the country. Gift packages and other sundries, as well as tours, are available.

San Ignacio

There is something indescribably alluring about the capital of Belize's western district. Maybe it's some remnant Maya magic trickling downhill from the ruins of Cahal Pech, or maybe it's the soft mist itself, quieting the village on rainy-season mornings and blanketing the floodplains to the east. Maybe it's the raw vitality of the surrounding wilderness that bumps right up against the town and breathes so much healthy energy through San Ignacio's

streets—or maybe it's what happens when all of these factors combine with a kind, good-hearted, diverse community of people.

There is budget lodging galore in San Ignacio, as well as a broad range of food—from rice and beans to curried lamb, from veggie burgers to pork ribs. And, of course, there is more to do than anyone—even permanent residents—has time for, with all manner of active expeditions leaving from Burns Avenue each and every morning.

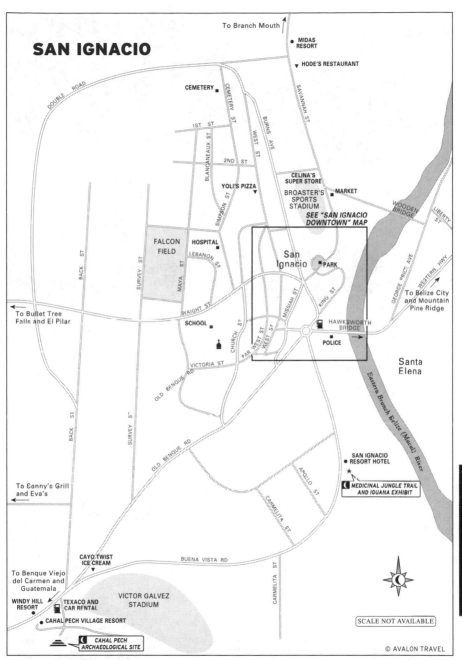

SAN IGNACIO

To Branch Mouth

- MIDAS RESORT
- HODE'S RESTAURANT

DOUBLE ROAD

CEMETERY
CEMETERY ST
BURNS AVE
SAVANNAH ST

1ST ST
BLANCANEAUX ST
WEST ST
2ND ST

CELINA'S SUPER STORE

YOLI'S PIZZA
SIMPSON ST
BROASTER'S SPORTS STADIUM
MARKET

WOODEN BRIDGE
LIBERTY ST

SEE "SAN IGNACIO DOWNTOWN" MAP

FALCON FIELD
HOSPITAL
LEBANON ST
MAYA ST
SURVEY ST
BACK ST

San Ignacio
PARK

MISSIAH ST
KING ST

GEORGE PRICE AVE
WESTERN HWY

To Belize City and Mountain Pine Ridge

WAIGHT ST

To Bullet Tree Falls and El Pilar

SCHOOL
CHURCH ST
FAR WEST ST
WEST ST

HAWKSWORTH BRIDGE

POLICE

Santa Elena

VICTORIA ST
OLD BENQUE RD

Eastern Branch Belize (Macal) River

BACK ST
SURVEY S

OLD BENQUE RD

SAN IGNACIO RESORT HOTEL

APOLLO ST

MEDICINAL JUNGLE TRAIL AND IGUANA EXHIBIT

CARMELITA ST

To Sonny's Grill and Eva's

CAYO TWIST ICE CREAM

BUENA VISTA RD

CARMELITA ST

To Benque Viejo del Carmen and Guatemala

WINDY HILL RESORT
TEXACO AND CAR RENTAL

VICTOR GALVEZ STADIUM

CAHAL PECH VILLAGE RESORT

CAHAL PECH ARCHAEOLOGICAL SITE

SCALE NOT AVAILABLE

CAYO

© AVALON TRAVEL

© JOSHUA BERMAN

bathing in the Macal River, by the old Wooden Bridge in San Ignacio

CAYO

ORIENTATION

Driving to San Ignacio from Belize City, you'll first pass through its sister city of Santa Elena, turning right at the Social Security building and continuing across the **Wooden Bridge** to the San Ignacio side of the Macal River, close to the open market grounds. From there, turning left will take you directly into "downtown" San Ignacio, marked by a five-pronged intersection that is nearly always abuzz with activity. **Burns Avenue** crosses here and is the main drag for locals and tourists alike. Within two or three blocks in any direction of that intersection, you'll find most of San Ignacio's budget accommodations, restaurants, Internet cafés, and tour operators.

The town's three banks are on the block of Burns Avenue that stems east (toward the river) from the big intersection, and at the end of that block you'll find a tiny traffic circle in front of the police station, which guards the western abutment of the **Hawksworth Bridge.** Built in 1949, the Hawksworth is the only suspension bridge in Belize; it is also the starting line of the big canoe race in March. Normally, only eastbound traffic is allowed on the one-lane bridge from Santa Elena to San Ignacio (except when the lower bridge floods and traffic is diverted, as it was several times in 2008 during the highest recorded river levels since 1961). Any of the roads that lead uphill from downtown San Ignacio will eventually place you back on the Western Highway heading toward Benque and the Guatemalan border.

SIGHTS
◖ Medicinal Jungle Trail and Iguana Exhibit

When the local iguana population was on a noticeable downward cycle, the folks at the San Ignacio Resort Hotel created this successful breeding and release project to bring the animals back and protect the riverside from further development. Groups go on hunts for eggs, capture the females, and hijack the eggs, which they raise in a predator-free, food-rich environment before releasing the iguanas back into the wild. The program has also trained

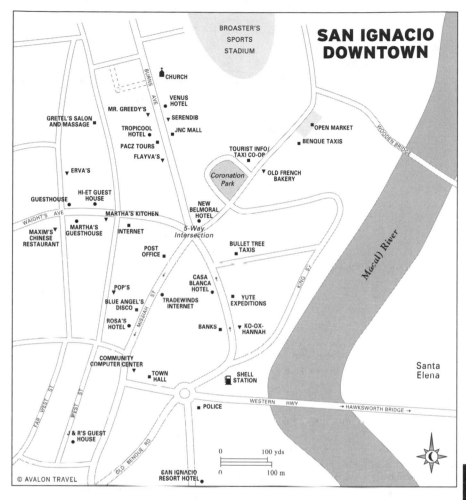

SAN IGNACIO DOWNTOWN

BROASTER'S SPORTS STADIUM

CHURCH

BURNS AVE

VENUS HOTEL

MR. GREEDY'S

GRETEL'S SALON AND MASSAGE

SERENDIB

TROPICOOL HOTEL

JNC MALL

OPEN MARKET

BENQUE TAXIS

WOODEN BRIDGE

PACZ TOURS

FLAYVA'S

TOURIST INFO/ TAXI CO-OP

ERVA'S

Coronation Park

OLD FRENCH BAKERY

HI-ET GUEST HOUSE

GUESTHOUSE

WAIGHT'S AVE

MARTHA'S KITCHEN

NEW BELMORAL HOTEL

MAXIM'S CHINESE RESTAURANT

MARTHA'S GUESTHOUSE

INTERNET

5-Way Intersection

BULLET TREE TAXIS

POST OFFICE

KING ST

Macal River

POP'S

CASA BLANCA HOTEL

BLUE ANGEL'S DISCO

TRADEWINDS INTERNET

YUTE EXPEDITIONS

ROSA'S HOTEL

BANKS

KO-OX-HANNAH

MISSIAH ST

COMMUNITY COMPUTER CENTER

TOWN HALL

SHELL STATION

Santa Elena

FAR WEST ST

WEST ST

POLICE

WESTERN HWY

HAWKSWORTH BRIDGE →

J & R'S GUEST HOUSE

OLD BENQUE RD

0   100 yds

0   100 m

SAN IGNACIO RESORT HOTEL

© AVALON TRAVEL

CAYO

former iguana hunters to become iguana guides, a far more profitable and sustainable endeavor, and hosts many school groups, featuring their "Adopt an Iguana" program.

The Green Iguana Conservation Project and interpretive herb trail is accessed through the San Ignacio Resort Hotel (perched above the Macal River a short downhill walk from the town center, tel. 501/824-2034, 501/824-2125, or 800/822-3274, www.sanignaciobelize.com). To date, 175 species of birds have been observed here (including a rare family pair of black hawk eagles), plus a number of mammals. Tours of the herb trail or the iguana project are offered on the hour 7 A.M.–4 P.M. (US$7 pp; 30 minutes for either talk).

◖ Cahal Pech Archaeological Site

A 10-minute uphill walk from downtown San Ignacio, Cahal Pech is a great, tree-shaded destination, where your imagination can run wild

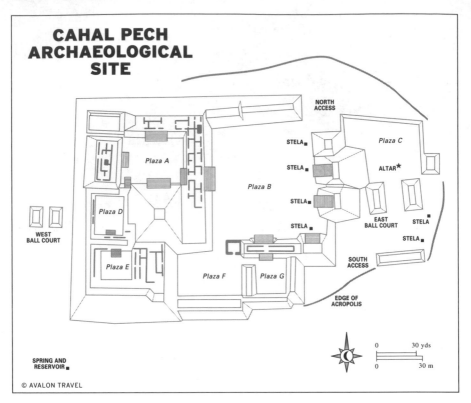

CAHAL PECH ARCHAEOLOGICAL SITE

© AVALON TRAVEL

with all that once occurred here. The ruins of Cahal Pech (Place of the Ticks) features an excavated series of plazas and royal residences. The site was discovered in the early 1950s, but research did not begin until 1988, when a team from San Diego State University's anthropology department began work with local archaeology guru Dr. Jaime Awe. Thirty-four structures were built in a three-acre area. Excavation is ongoing and visitors are welcome. It is well worth your trip and admission fee (US$10 at Cahal Pech Visitor Center, tel. 501/824-4236, 6 A.M.–6 P.M. daily). The visitors center also houses a small museum of artifacts found at the site (and a skeleton from Xunantunich). Nearby **Tipu** was a Christian Maya town during the early years of colonization. Tipu was as far as the Spanish were able to penetrate in the 16th century.

RECREATION
Horseback Riding

Book your horseback riding trip at **Easy Rider** (tel. 501/824-3310), an independent operator who charges reasonable rates and gives good service, based out of an office in San Ignacio next door to Flayva's on Burns Avenue; novices are welcome. Expect to pay about US$20–30 for two hours, US$30–40 for a trip to Xunantunich.

Outside of San Ignacio, **Mountain Rider** (tel. 501/820-4036) is a small operation run by the Tzul family, just past the village of San Antonio as you drive toward the Mountain Pine Ridge; US$35 per horse for a three-hour trip to local caves and medicine trails. Off the Chiquibul Road, **Mountain Equestrian Trails** (tel. 501/669-1124) is the area's premier riding

LA RUTA MAYA BELIZE RIVER CHALLENGE

Belize's Super Bowl is La Ruta Maya Belize River Challenge (www.larutamayabelize. com), an exciting and convivial canoe race held during the first week of March and timed to coincide with National Heroes and Benefactors Day (formerly Baron Bliss Day) celebrations. If you are in San Ignacio for the start of the race, you'll watch 100 teams of paddlers mass together in the Macal River, then bolt downstream – racing five days down the 175-mile length of the Belize River, all the way to Belize City. Increasingly popular since its inception in 1998, La Ruta Maya has many divisions in which to compete (including women's, mixed gender, amateur, dory, and pleasure craft) and offers more than US$15,000 in prize money. The race is part athletic event, part tourism draw, and several parts fiesta.

center, with one of the biggest trail systems in the Pine Ridge.

Boating

Canoe five miles up the Macal River to Chaa Creek and the Botanic Gardens at duPlooy's; rent a boat and guide from **Tony's Guided Tours** (tel. 501/824-3292, US$20 pp). If you're here in March, you won't miss the excitement of La Ruta Maya Belize River Challenge, a long-distance paddle race to the ocean celebrated all week long along the route.

Massage, Bodywork, and Yoga

Eva's Massage Therapy (16 Collins Blvd., tel. 501/824-3423, ebuhler@btl.net) offers an hour-long full body massage for US$35, or a 30–40 minute "back and neck therapy session" for only US$20. Right in San Ignacio, you can find reasonably priced massages (US$40/hr), pedicures, manicures, facials, and body waxing at **Gretel's Salon and Spa** (7 Far West St., tel. 501/604-1126 or

501/666-4576), a locally owned and oriented beauty salon.

Hatha-certified yoga instructor Kate Devine owns and runs **Enlighten-up Yoga Studio** (tel. 510/665-1972, devineyoga@gmail.com), on the third floor of the JNC mall on Burns Avenue. You'll find a range of yoga, meditation, and dance classes for US$7.50, including for children.

Of course, there are full spa services at some of the upscale resorts in the area, notably **Hilltop Spa** at The Lodge at Chaa Creek, which may have the best vistas from a massage table I've ever seen; combine a visit here with a trip to the nearby botanic gardens or a paddle on the river. **Ka'ana Resort and Spa** (Mile 69¼, tel. 501/824-0430, US$80/ hour) offers massages, facials, and body scrubs with homegrown brown sugar, cacao and coffee; they also offer energy work with a Maya healer.

NIGHTLIFE

San Ignacio is not necessarily known for its nightlife, but that doesn't mean you won't find a place for a drink after a long day exploring the countryside. It's a small town, so finding the party is not difficult. Just follow the masses as they trek between bars. Start your evening with the popular happy hour at **Mr. Greedy's** (34 Burns Ave.) or one of the copy-cat happy hours at other restaurants on Burns Avenue. For a more upscale bar scene and occasional live music, check the Stork Club Bar at San Ignacio Resort Hotel.

Meluchi's (across from the cemetery, next to the Big H Juice factory) is another good bet for happy hour and nightly events like movie night (and they serve tasty local dishes). **Mi Cocina** (across from the Victor Galvez Stadium, on the left side of the climb up to Cahal Pech) is a clean bar with reasonably priced drinks. One mile east of town, **Happy's** is another popular bar and gathering spot, with reasonably priced cold drinks and a pool table.

For dancing, you can try the loud DJ mix at **Club Next,** in the casino, or downtown at **Blue Angel's** (on Post Office Rd.), which can be a bit dicey late at night. On weekends, ask if there is a party up at **Cahal Pech Village.**

ACCOMMODATIONS AND CAMPING

Choices abound for such a small town, many of them cheap, clean, converted family homes, and most within a few blocks of each other. Cayo can get hot at times, but remember that it's generally cooler than the rest of the country, so air-conditioning may not be a big priority, especially between June and February. Also, note that most (but not all) accommodations in Cayo quote prices with tax and service charges inclusive; most also offer deep discounts in low season and for multiple nights. As always, I've reported high-season double-occupancy rates only throughout this chapter.

Under US$25

The **(Hi-Et Guest House** (tel. 501/824-2828, thehiet@yahoo.com, US$10–25) is an excellent option on West Street, built right into the owner's large home. The five rooms with shared baths and cold water are clean and comfortable with hardwood floors. The five rooms with private baths in the next building are a big step up in quality and not much in price—they're well kept, with tiled floors and balconies.

The **Tropicool Hotel** (30A Burns Ave., tel. 501/804-3052, US$15–38) has seven simple, clean rooms with shared bath and four nicely kept and furnished cabins around a peaceful garden, each with private bath, TV, and fan.

Find quiet, friendly lodging at **J & R's Guest House** (20 Far West St., tel. 501/626-3604, jrguesthouse@yahoo.com, US$10–23); there are five rooms, one with private bath, and breakfast is included.

US$25-50

One of the best value midrange hotels is the **(Casa Blanca Guest House** (Burns Ave., tel. 501/824-2080, www.casablancaguesthouse.com, US$20–50), with eight immaculate, cozy rooms with private baths, hot and cold water, and TV, as well as access to a beautiful

common living room, kitchen, balcony, and rooftop deck. It's on Burns Avenue near the banks.

Rosa's Hotel (65 Hudson St., tel. 501/804-2265, rosashotel@yahoo.com, from US$28) has a selection of rooms with private baths and fans or air-conditioning (US$38); rooms range from small and stuffy to high and airy—check out a few before deciding. A longtime standard is **Venus Hotel** (tel. 501/824-3203, www.venushotelbelize.com, US$30–43) on Burns Avenue, with 32 rooms. The budget rooms with shared bath are a bit run-down, with no windows. The rooms with private baths are in better condition, and you can take your pick of those overlooking the park or the street.

US$50-100

(Martha's Guesthouse (10 West St., tel. 501/804-3647, www.marthasbelize.com, US$50–80) continues to offer a charming, tasteful atmosphere in the center of San Ignacio, with an abundance of common lounging areas for guests to mingle in if they so desire. The 16 rooms are classy, with hardwood floors and furniture, private baths, fans, hot water, wireless Internet, and cable television. Laundry services are available. There's an excellent restaurant downstairs, as well as a front desk to arrange tours. Martha's just expanded into a six-room annex, about a three-minute walk up Burns Avenue, with beautiful apartment-style options, several with kitchenettes and porches (US$50–65, weekly rates available).

About a quarter mile out of town, **Midas Resort** (tel. 501/824-3172, www.midasbelize.com, US$59–135) is a constantly improving family-run accommodation. You'll find seven cool and airy cottages with private baths (air-conditioning available), situated on seven acres along the banks of the Macal River (down a 300-yard path from the cottages). There is a new lodge with modernly equipped rooms and a pool. A restaurant serves breakfast and lunch.

Talk about a vista! **Cahal Pech Village** (tel. 501/824-3740, www.cahalpech.com, US$79–119) offers a variety of rooms and cabanas spread out on a spacious hillside with stunning views of San Ignacio and the valley below. The 15 rooms have private baths and air-conditioning, or choose a thatch-and-wood cabana with private bath, hot and cold water, and porch. Family suites and cabanas are available too. A restaurant, bar, and creative swimming pool round out the resort, in addition to its quick access to the Cahal Pech ruins right next door.

Over US$150

Fit for royalty, **☾ San Ignacio Resort Hotel** (tel. 501/824-2034, 501/824-2125, or 800/822-3274, www.sanignaciobelize.com, US$170–200) is rightly proud of having hosted Her Majesty Queen Elizabeth II in 1994, and has never stopped improving the property toward the luxury side of things. From the grand marble lobby and reception hall to the lap pool and range of services, this is definitely an excellent upscale option that is both in town and remote-feeling. The hotel is perched above the Macal River and is a short downhill walk from the town center. There are 24 deluxe air-conditioned rooms, some with their own secluded balconies; the rooms have private tiled baths, TV, comfy furniture, and telephones. There is also a honeymoon suite on the second floor. The hotel hosts the Stork Club Bar & Grill, Running W Steakhouse & Restaurant, a jungle-view patio deck ideal for bird-watching, a tennis court, disco, casino, and convention and wedding facilities. Bird-watching tours are available with the on-site guide, who can also show you the Green Iguana Conservation Project and Medicinal Jungle Trail on the hotel's grounds (tours on the hour).

Camping

Smith's Family Farm (tel. 501/604-2227) is a peaceful 25-acre retreat up Branch Mouth Road with a shaded campground (US$5 pp) and collection of cabins (US$20–30), all with private baths, hot and cold water, and simple furniture. Weekly rates are available, and the owner, Roy, sometimes lets you trade labor on his organic farm for a stay at the place. On

the same road, **Cosmos Camping** (15 Branch Mouth Rd., tel. 501/824-2116, cosmoscamping@btl.net, US$5 pp) is a 15-minute walk from town and has pretty grounds, many big trees, and mowed lawns where you can pitch your tent. It's on the Mopan River and has shared baths and showers, but is kind of isolated, as the office is back up the road toward town.

A couple of miles outside San Ignacio on the Western Highway, **Inglewood** (tel. 501/824-3555, www.inglewoodcampinggrounds.com) offers full hookups for RVs. Following the same road, you'll find campgrounds at the **Clarissa Falls Resort** (tel. 501/824-3916, www.clarissafalls.com) and the **Trek Stop** (tel. 501/823-2265, www.thetrekstop.com) in San José de Succotz.

FOOD
Fast and Cheap

San Ignacio has a higher than average number of cheap Mexican fast-food places, and a few *pupuserías* (serving an El Salvadorean dish: fried tortillas stuffed with beans, cheese, and meat) for good measure. Check out the stalls in the basement of the Burns Avenue Mall or across from the Belize Bank. Saturday morning, super early, is the best bet for cheap eats, as organic farmers, local cooks, and produce vendors congregate at the outdoor market. This is the best place to chow down before catching a bus to other areas.

On the road right before the market, the **Old French Bakery** (7 A.M.–6 P.M. Mon.–Sat.) serves delicious breads and pastries with a semi-outdoor patio. The tiny **coffee shop** connected to the Serendib Restaurant (27 Burns Ave.) sells ice cream as well as meat pies and generous vegetable patties: a perfect meal on the go.

The best **barbecue** chefs set up in Santa Elena, just over the Hawksworth Bridge, and they cater especially to weekend party crowds, offering greasy mounds of meat, rice, and beans used by many customers to soak up all that beer sloshing around in their stomachs.

For ice cream, go to **Cayo Twist** (near the

western exit to town, nearly across from the Texaco station, tel. 501/667-7717, 6–9:30 P.M. Thurs.–Sun.), which has delicious soy ice cream.

Low-Key Belizean

Some say **Ⅽ Erva's** (4 Far West St., 8 A.M.–3 P.M. and 6–10 P.M. Mon.–Sat., US$3–10) dishes out the best, most reasonably priced Belizean food in the country. It is a cozy, quality, family-run restaurant that often caters to groups. Dine inside or out and choose from breakfast, stew chicken, rice and beans, burritos, and a full menu of comfort dinners, including chicken cordon bleu.

Pop's (tel. 501/824-3266, 6:30 A.M.–2:30 P.M. daily, US$3–6) may be the closest Belize comes to a small-town, cramped American-style diner, with booths, bottomless cups of coffee, and customers watching CNN and talking religion and politics—except Pop's is owned by a 100 percent Belizean Hemingway look-alike. It's just to the south, around the corner from the five-way intersection; ask anyone nearby for directions.

International

Ⅽ Ko-Ox-Han-Nah (5 Burns Ave., tel. 501/824-3014, 6 A.M.–9 P.M. daily), which means "let's go eat," offers Belizean fare plus a huge, cosmopolitan menu that includes Asian, Indian, and vegetarian dishes (and an ample wine list), all prepared with organic ingredients and meat raised by the owner himself. Entrées are in the US$5–12 range.

Serendib Restaurant (27 Burns Ave., tel. 501/824-2302, 10 A.M.–10 P.M. with a break 3–6 P.M., closed Sun.) is owned by a Sri Lankan family and serves excellent curries and dal, along with reliable hamburgers, steaks, and chow mein,. It's reasonably priced; a broiled lobster dinner or San Ignacio Giant Steak for US$12. **Ⅽ Mr. Greedy's** (34 Burns Ave., tel. 501/804-4688, 5:30 A.M.–midnight daily) understands the importance of a super-hot oven in the production of succulent pizza crust (US$14 for a large cheese pie). They also do a kick-ass breakfast, burger platter, wings,

sandwiches, and a long cocktail menu. The environment is very casual, and wireless Internet is available.

Maxim's Chinese Restaurant (23 Far West St.) has a good reputation among the locals; a family-run café, it serves mainly lunch and dinner. Prices are moderate; you won't pay much over US$10 for the best meal in the house and a beer.

Martha's Kitchen (10 West St., tel. 501/804-3647) has some of the best pizza in Cayo, plus a full menu including stir-fried vegetables (about US$6), T-bone steak with gravy and fries (US$8), and a simple club sandwich (US$4). Visitors also give high praise to **Yoli's Pizza** (West St. next to Plaza del Rio Mall, tel. 501/804-4187), which also delivers.

Flayva's (22 Burns Ave., tel. 501/804-2267, 6:30 A.M.–10:30 P.M., closed Tuesday) is the place for hearty breakfasts and, later in the day, creative comfort dishes like stew sheep, mango shrimp, nachos, sandwiches, and curries. Check out the patio through the back door; there's Internet access and you can book tomorrow's tour while you wait.

For ambience, you'll want to try **Sanny's Grill** (E. 23rd St., US$6–10), which is a bit out of the way (toward the western exit to Benque, just down from the Texaco station) but well worth it for the fine menu and nice lighting and music.

In addition to steaks, pork chops, and seafood entrées from US$10, the **Running W Steakhouse & Restaurant** (in the San Ignacio Resort Hotel, tel. 501/824-2125) also serves up an open-air dining patio above the Macal River. Belizean classic plates start at US$5 and feature meat from the restaurant's own ranch.

INFORMATION

There is an official tourist information post at the Cahal Pech Visitor Center (tel. 501/824-4236), and the Belize Tourism Industry Association, offering brochures for local resorts, taxi charters, and a town map, has a stand near the Savannah Taxi Co-op downtown. However, you'll find out much more by reading the posters and advertisements at the

BUSH MEDICINE IN BELIZE

Herbal medicine is a part of Belize's collective cultural heritage, and is here most commonly referred to as "bush medicine." Most Belizeans still know at least a thing or two about home remedies and medicinal plants. Even those who do not may fondly remember a parent or grandparent who would treat their childhood ills with herbs from the garden. People use medicinal plants to treat a range of maladies, from fever to the "evil eye." Plants are used to treat headache, cough, stomach ailments, arthritis, diabetes, and for virility, fertility, and much more!

The traditional medicine practiced in Belize has ancient roots, which took on distinct specializations, including doctor-priest, bush doctor, village healer, grannie healer, midwife, snake doctor, and bonesetter. Today these specializations are represented by only a few living practitioners, most of whom are getting late in their years.

As a traveler in Belize, you can get into fascinating talks with Belizeans on these topics, if you only bring them up. Belizean medicinal plants have all sorts of chuckle-inducing local names, like piss-a-bed or grandpa's balls or stinking toe. Want to learn more than just the names? Get a copy of *Rainforest Remedies: One Hundred Healing Herbs of Belize*, by Dr. Rosita Arvigo and Dr. Michael Balick.

Don Elijio Panti of the Cayo District, Belize's most revered and acclaimed Maya healer and herbalist, passed away in 1996 at the age of 103. His legacy lives on with those who learned from his vast knowledge. The book *Sastun* recounts Dr. Rosita Arvigo's decade-long apprenticeship with this master healer. The book is a fun, interesting read for anyone traveling through Belize interested in traditional medicine and medicinal plants.

While you're in Cayo, check out the **Rainforest Medicine Trail at Chaa Creek,** which features many of the medicinal plants Don Elijio used in his practice. Guided hour-long tours run every hour on the hour 8 A.M.–4 P.M. for US$10 per person. Or you can walk the trail on a self-guided tour for US$5. In town, at the San Ignacio Hotel, you can also take a guided 30-minute tour of their **Medicinal Jungle Trail.**

© JOSHUA BERMAN

Many Belizeans still make teas, medicine, salves, and other remedies from plants in the forests.

Add a tour of their **Iguana Conservation Project** if you like. Tours leave every hour on the hour 7 A.M.–4 P.M. and cost US$6 per person.

In Toledo District, in the south, many bush doctors still reside in the remote villages, but here as well, the numbers of healers are dwindling, and with their passing disappears their invaluable wisdom. **Remedia** (tel. 501/636-1040, info@remedia.bz) is a nonprofit organization that works in partnerships with Belizeans to revitalize practices of traditional medicine and other forms of traditional knowledge. You can contact the organization to arrange a medicinal plant walk or herbal medicine workshop with a traditional healer in Toledo. The organization also arranges traditional cooking classes and lessons in Belize's indigenous languages.

Popular Belizean remedies include allspice leaf tea for digestive upsets, contribo vine (as a tea or soaked in rum) to treat colds and flu, a bath made with gumbolimbo bark for sunburn and insect bites, and fresh sliced scoggineal tied to the forehead for headaches and fever. Finally, if you're prone to traveler's sickness, pick up a bottle of Rainforest Remedies' **Traveler's Tonic,** made from local jackass bitters leaf and guava leaf. This has helped many a friend while traversing the tropics!

(Contributed by Jillian De Gezelle, Ethnobotanist.)

various restaurants around town. The most regularly updated website on Cayo's businesses and attractions is **www.bestofcayo. com**—start there to see the latest reviews and listings.

SERVICES

Atlantic Bank, Scotia Bank, and **Belize Bank** are all on Burns Avenue, just past the Hawksworth Bridge as you come into town. Martha's Guesthouse (10 West St., tel. 501/804-3647, www.marthasbelize.com) offers daily **laundry** service (7 A.M.–8 P.M.), as does a launderette tucked into a DVD rental place across from the main bus/taxi stand (US$5 for wash, dry, and fold). Across from BTL, **Celina's Super Store** (43 Burns Ave., tel. 501/824-2247) is the largest, best-equipped supermarket in town, but there are many other Chinese shops scattered around as well. **Angelus Press,** on the top floor of the Burns Avenue Mall, also has some books, in addition to copy machines and office supplies. **Venus Photos and Records,** across from the post office, sells camera batteries, memory cards, and some camera equipment.

For travel arrangements, **Exodus International** (tel. 501/824-4400, exodus@ btl.net) is at the beginning of Burns Avenue (near the bridge).

Internet

Many hotels have a computer you can use for free and there are cybercafes around town. **Tradewinds Internet** (7 A.M.–10 P.M. daily, US$2.50/hr) has fast machines, a scanner, free coffee, and a selection of camping gear for sale (not sure why, but it's good stuff).

GETTING THERE AND AWAY

All resorts can arrange for a transfer from the international airport in Belize City, from US$125. A shared shuttle to the Caye Caulker Water Taxi Terminal can be arranged at a number of tour operators, for not much more than an express bus ticket if you have enough people. **Belize San Ignacio Shuttle & Transfer** (tel. 501/620-3055, belizeshuttle@yahoo.com,

US$95 for two people, price drops to US$30 pp for six people) can arrange rides anywhere, including both airports; the owner, William Hoffman, is accommodating and flexible.

By Bus

Westbound buses from Belize City and Belmopan run through the middle of town, stopping at the park as part of the daily runs to Benque. The street next to the main park is the de facto bus station. Expect limited service on Sunday. Expresses take about two hours between Belize City and San Ignacio, including the quick stop in Belmopan. Regular buses leave every hour, and there are a handful of daily expresses 7 A.M.–7 P.M. Check on the express departure times the day before your journey, as the schedule changes from time to time. Bus schedules are constantly changing as companies battle it out over routes and turf. Ask the locals, who will know what is best.

GETTING AROUND

Downtown San Ignacio is tiny and entirely walkable, though there are a few steep hills, including the trek to Cahal Pech. Taxis there or anywhere else within the city limits cost US$3–4 per person. Cheap *colectivo* taxis run from San Ignacio in all directions throughout the day, making it easy to get to towns and destinations in the immediate vicinity (including Bullet Tree, Succotz, and Benque). In addition to the main buses running back and forth on the Western Highway, village buses come into Market Square from most surrounding towns, returning to the hills in the afternoons. To the south, buses only run as far as the village of San Antonio—perhaps someone will think to start public transportation to Caracol once the road is improved.

Car Rentals

Anyone wishing to travel independently to the Mountain Pine Ridge, Caracol, the Hydro Road, or El Pilar might consider renting a car—either in Belize City or at one of the few places in San Ignacio and Santa Elena. Renting in Cayo is cheaper than in Belize (as low as

US$60/day) and a good way to go if you really want to explore this area.

At the top of the Old Benque Road at the western edge of San Ignacio, you'll find **Cayo Rentals** (tel. 501/824-2222, cayorentals@btl. net), with a handful of newish vehicles for rent in the Texaco station parking lot; US$75 per 24 hours *includes* taxes and insurance (which is cheaper than any place in Belize City). There's also **Matus Car Rentals** (tel. 501/663-4702 or 501/824-2089, matuscarrental@yahoo.com), on the hill up from the town center, which offers decent weekly rates. Rent a Land Rover near the airstrip in Central Farm (tel. 501/824-2523).

Vicinity of San Ignacio

ALONG THE WESTERN HIGHWAY

As you drive toward Cayo from Belize City and Belmopan, after passing the Hummingbird Highway junction you are greeted with a jarring series of speed bumps at the roadside village of Teakettle. Turning left at the Pook's Hill sign carries you past cornfields grown atop ancient Maya residential mounds.

Covering 6,741 acres, the **Tapir Mountain Nature Reserve** is one of the newest jewels in the country's crown of natural treasures. The deep, steamy jungle is ripe with an abundance of plant life. Every wild thing native to the region roams its forests, from toucans to tapirs, coatis to kinkajous. At present, the reserve is off-limits to all but scientific expeditions. However, you can see a piece of it by going on an Actun Tunichil Muknal trip.

Pook's Hill Lodge

Once you arrive at the remote clearing that is Pook's Hill Lodge (tel. 501/820-2017, www. pookshillbelize.com, US$198), you'll have a hard time believing that you are only 12 miles from Belmopan and 21 miles from San Ignacio, so dense and peaceful is the forest around you. Towering hardwoods, flowering bromeliads, and exotic birds hem in the accommodations, which are built around a small Maya residential ruin. Pook's Hill is a 300-acre private nature reserve, bordered by the Tapir Mountain Nature Reserve and the Roaring River and offering active travelers 10 thatch-roof cabanas from which to base their Cayo explorations. The cottages have private baths, electricity, and comfortable furnishings. The lounge/bar area overlooks a grassy knoll that gently slopes toward the creek. The dining room is downstairs from the lounge, and good, filling meals are served family style. Vegetarian or other preferences can be accommodated with advance notice. There are plenty of guided walks, birding, tubing, and night walks, all free to guests. Pook's Hill is the only lodge within walking distance of Actun Tunichil Muknal and offers early morning private tours before the crowds arrive. To get there, look for the hand-painted sign at Teakettle Village (around Mile 52.5 of the Western Highway); turn left and follow the signs to Pook's Hill for 5.5 miles (there are a couple of turns). The road can be rough and four-wheel drive is recommended, as is calling ahead so they know to expect you.

Shopping, Accommodations, and Food

Between Pook's Hill and San Ignacio on the Western Highway, **Orange Gifts** (tel. 501/824-2341, www.orangegifts.com) is a popular gift shop, restaurant, bar, and lodging. It's at Mile 60, about 10 miles west of San Ignacio; you can check your email, browse the shop, and then enjoy a glass of wine or a meal in the shaded café. The food (restaurant opens at 6:15 A.M. daily) is fantastic; the menu includes real salads (US$8.50 for the works), shepherd's pie (US$12), and a beef tenderloin for two (US$40), making this an excellent pit stop as you explore the region. Orange Gifts' five clean garden rooms, each with private bath, hot and cold water, tile floors, and ceiling fans, go for US$75.

Spanish Lookout

Turn off the highway at the Spanish Lookout sign and watch the landscape change from ragged forest to neat, rolling green countryside with green lawns and men riding John Deere lawnmowers. Spanish Lookout is one of Belize's largest Mennonite communities, with about 3,000 farmers and builders who supply a large part of the furniture, dairy, and poultry products for the country. Many Mennonites here have embraced organic living, and if you drive around you'll find produce and items that cannot be found anywhere else in Belize. The recent discovery of oil in the area has added a modern twist to this unique scene (you'll pass a few pumps and the refinery on your way in).

Spanish Lookout has no tourist accommodations but has a few excellent places to eat, as well as shopping and services (Scotia Bank has an ATM here and there are three gas stations).

Folks from all over Belize come to shop at places like Farmer's Trading Centre, Reimer's Feeds, the Computer Ranch, and Westrac (the best place for car parts, period). Eat at **The Golden Corral** (tel. 501/823-0421, www.spanishlookout.bz/goldencorral.htm, 10:30 A.M.–2:30 P.M. Mon.–Sat. and 5–8:30 P.M. Thurs.–Sat.), but get there just before noon if you want a seat and first selection. It's about US$7.50 for the all-you-can-eat buffet and all-you-can-drink homemade iced tea! There are also amazing meat pies and other goodies at **Midway Convenience.**

◖ Actun Tunichil Muknal

This is the acclaimed "Cave of the Crystal Maiden," one of the most spectacular natural and archaeological attractions in Central America. The trip to ATM, as the cave is also known, is for fit and active people who do not mind getting wet and muddy—and who are able to tread lightly around ancient artifacts. After the initial 45-minute hike to

Tread lightly around the ancient artifacts in Actun Tunichil Muknal, where the Crystal Maiden was once sacrificed to bring rain.

the entrance (with three river fords) and a swim into the cave's innards, you will be asked to remove your shoes upon climbing up the limestone into the main cathedral-like chambers. The rooms are littered with delicate Maya pottery and the crystallized remains of 14 humans. There are no pathways, fences, glass, or other partitions separating the visitor from the artifacts. Nor are there any installed lights. The only infrastructure is a rickety ladder leading up to the chamber of the Crystal Maiden herself, a full female skeleton that sparkles with calcite under your headlamp's glare, more so during the drier months.

Please be careful—the fact that tourists are allowed to walk here at all is as astonishing as the sights themselves (at the time of this writing, somebody had already trod on and broken one of the skulls). Only a few tour companies are licensed to take guests here; **Pacz Tours** (tel. 501/604-6921 or 501/824-0536, www.pacztours.net) is the most popular provider. The Actun Tunichil Muknal cave is neither for the weak at heart nor recommended for small children or claustrophobics. In fact, children under the age of 8 (or 12, depending on whom you ask) are not permitted inside. Entrance to the site is US$25 per person.

NORTH OF SAN IGNACIO
Bullet Tree Falls

This old, lazy village of a few thousand people is less than three miles out of San Ignacio on the road to El Pilar. Bullet Tree's ultramellow riverbank mood, combined with cheap and easy access to the relative bustle of San Ignacio, makes it a pleasant midrange alternative to the usual Cayo fare of fancy jungle lodges and backpacker camps. Bullet Tree overnighters still have access to the full range of Cayo area activities, right down the road and easily reached by *colectivo* taxi (US$2 pp) or private cab (US$5). Most people like to just sit by the river or float it in a tube. You can also arrange a hike with Don Beto Cocom, a Maya shaman who offers medicinal plant trail walks for donations only. Ask at any local hotel. They can also arrange horseback expeditions to El Pilar and other sites.

ACCOMMODATIONS

Rolling into town, you'll pass the soccer field on your right, then come to a fork in the road; this is the bus stop. Fork left to cross the bridge and reach the turnoff for El Pilar, right to reach **❰ Parrot Nest Lodge** (tel. 501/669-6068 or 501/820-4058, www.parrot-nest.com, US$45–55), which is a unique, rustic hideaway with immediate river access (and free inner tubes). The tropical gardens have remarkable on-site birding. There are six simple, cozy cabins, including two treehouses on stilts under the limbs of a gigantic guanacaste tree. Each cabin has 24-hour electricity, a fan, a linoleum floor, and a simple single or double bed; two have private baths with cold water, four are shared bath. Meals are reasonable: US$4–6 for breakfast and US$11 for dinner.

A stone's throw downstream, **Cohune Palms Cabañas** (tel. 501/824-0166 or 501/669-2738, www.cohunepalms.com, US$89–109) is a class act, beautifully landscaped, right on the riverbank under the shade of plenty of trees. They have just four thatch, bamboo, and wooden structures around a common area with hammocks and an open kitchen. The cabanas have loft bedrooms, colorful paint and tiles, and private baths. The owners will help you plan your time and get to and from San Ignacio, as well as rent you tubes and bicycles with which to explore their backyard. Home-cooked meals are available (US$20 for both breakfast and dinner), and there is plenty of common space in the kitchen or on the wooden yoga deck above the river.

A mile or so upstream (turn left before the the bridge when you enter Bullet Tree Falls), **Mahogany Hall** (Paslow Falls Rd., tel. 501/664-7747, www.mahoganyhallbelize.com, US$175–275) has a spectacular castle-door entrance to a striking view of the Mopan River. In this three-story building, there are six luxurious and stately rooms with heavy wooden furniture, high ceilings, large windows, and French doors, all cradling a pool and restaurant

CAYO

practically on top of the river; it's a good choice for folks who want their air-conditioning and TV but want a lovely, unique setting.

El Pilar Archaeological Site

Seven miles north of Bullet Tree Falls, these jungle-choked Maya ruins are visited by only a handful of curious tourists each day; the rough approach road plus the lack of attention paid to the site by most tour operators helps make El Pilar the excellent, uncrowded day trip that it is. Entrance is US$10. Two groupings of temple mounds, courtyards, and ball courts overlook a forested valley. Aqueducts and a causeway lead toward Guatemala, just 500 meters away. There have been some minor excavations here, including those of illegal looters, but the site is very overgrown, so the ruins retain an intriguing air of mystery. Many trees shade the site: allspice, gumbo-limbo, ramon, cohune palm, and locust. It's a beautiful hiking area and wildlife experience as well.

Even if you book your El Pilar trip in San Ignacio, be sure to start your quest with a visit to the **Amigos de El Pilar** visitors center (9 A.M.–5 P.M. daily) and **Be Pukte Cultural Center** in Bullet Tree Falls. Here you'll find a scale model of the ruins, some helpful booklets and maps, and guide and taxi arrangements (it's about US$25 for a taxi to drive a group out and wait a few hours before taking them back). Or you can rent a mountain bike at Cohune Palms and make a workout of it—the road's so bad, you'll probably beat the cab anyway.

MACAL RIVER JUNGLE LODGES

As you follow the twisting Macal River upstream (south) from San Ignacio, you find an astonishing assortment of mid- to upscale lodges, beginning with the San Ignacio Resort Hotel, which is within the city limits of San Ignacio. They are all small properties, some with as few as two cabins in the forest, others with a dozen or more thatch-roof bungalows under the trees and along the river. Most of the accommodations are small, off the grid, and feel utterly remote, even when they are only a

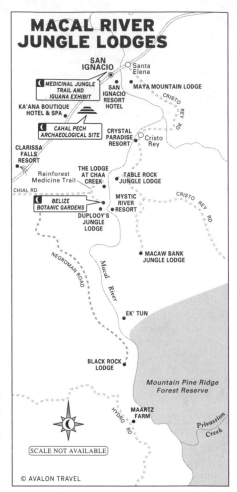

few miles as the crow flies from San Ignacio. They all specialize in arranging tours to area activities, and most offer multiday packages.

Right Bank: Access Via the Cristo Rey Road
ACCOMMODATIONS

Only one mile south of the Western Highway, **Maya Mountain Lodge** (tel. 501/824-2164, www.mayamountain.com, US$59–119) feels remote enough to warrant a listing outside of town (US$5 by taxi from San Ignacio). This is one of the most moderately priced jungle hideaways, operated for the last three decades by Suzi and Bart Mickler, whose knowledge and passion for the area are contagious. The property is 108 acres and it's about a 20-minute walk to the river's edge. A meandering trail through the gardens has signs identifying plants, trees, and birds; there's a nice pool for after your hike. Accommodations range from six simple rooms in a raised wooden building to family cottages and a two-bedroom suite with tiled floors, air-conditioning, and extra bunks and wood furniture. The restaurant features theme nights, homemade bread, and buckets of freshly squeezed orange juice (their Baha'i faith prevents them from selling liquor for profit, but you are welcome to bring your own). Breakfast and lunch cost US$10, and dinner is US$20. Ask about workshops on biodiversity and multiculturalism. This is a great place for families, with discounted (or free) rooms and tours for children and teens.

Before the advent of tourism, the Tut family (Victor and Teresa and their 10 children) grew fruit and vegetables and then transported them by canoe to the town market in San Ignacio. Today, they are the proud owners and operators of **Crystal Paradise Resort** (tel. 501/820-4014, www.crystalparadise.com, US$95–125, rates include breakfast and dinner), a low-key lodge that attracts many satisfied repeat customers. The 21-acre property near Cristo Rey village is a few hundred yards away from the river, and it's an easy walk to a canoe. The Tuts' sons, who are avid birdwatchers and nature lovers, maintain the beautiful grounds and serve as your guides on a variety of tours, including hiking, biking, horseback riding, kayaking, and bird-watching. Find them at **Paradise Expeditions,** which is based at the resort (tel. 501/610-5593 or tel. 501/820-4014, www.birdinginbelize.com). Teresa and her daughters keep the guest rooms clean and comfortable and also cook up the best in traditional Belizean and international cuisine. Accommodations come in several styles on the property; there are 17 units

in all, including simple thatched cabanas near the wide, open dining palapa. These have cement walls, tiled floors, hot and cold showers, and shaded verandas for relaxing. Others are clean and comfortable but more of a clapboard style; all offer ceiling fans and electricity. New additions include a pool and four canopy-level luxury rooms. The Tuts also offer bird-watching, nature walks, and tours.

Table Rock Jungle Lodge (tel. 501/834-4040, www.tablerockbelize.com, from US$150) is an eco-friendly touch of class on a 100-acre preserve. Five gorgeous cabanas (four-poster king and queen beds, private bathrooms with hot water, ceiling fans, private porches) are designed to stay cool the natural way, using adobe construction. There is a beautiful trail leading down a series of stone steps to the Macal River, where guests can go birding, canoeing, swimming, or tubing (all free of charge to guests). The food is fantastic, with unexpected dishes like pan-seared jack with chipotle papaya coconut sauce, cooked in cohune palm oil and served with couscous and okra. The palm-lined entrance through an orange grove is at Mile 5 on Cristo Rey Road.

At **Mystic River Resort** (tel. 501/834-4100, www.mysticriverbelize.com, from US$195), "it's all about the river," say proprietors Tom and Nadege Thomas in their open-air restaurant on a point above the Macal. Guests like to hike or ride upstream, then float back to the lodge in canoe or tube. The six units (so far) are spacious and well furnished, with local tile floors, nice verandas, and fireplaces for cool December nights. The place is a model of sustainable living. They have an on-site stable and organic garden, and raise their own chickens. Tom is still cutting trails and discovering archaeological sites on his property, which you can explore—either by foot or on Tom's ATV. Be sure to make it to Dancing Tree Lookout for sunset views of Guatemala. At the campsite atop this housing mound, you'll admire the same view that Mayan families saw a thousand years ago. By car, Mystic River Resort is accessed at Mile 6 on the Cristo Rey Road.

Macaw Bank Jungle Lodge (tel. 501/603-4825, www.macawbankjunglelodge.com,

US$110–145) occupies an isolated, peaceful clearing in the forest. There are five miles of nature trails on the 50-acre property, many birds and other wildlife, and you can go swimming at a sandy bend on the Macal River, a 5–10 minute walk away. The five comfortable units have wooden bunks and furniture, private bathrooms, hot and cold water, some solar power, and kerosene lanterns. There is a nice restaurant palapa with wireless Internet. Campers are welcome (US$12.50 pp).

Left Bank: Access Via the Chial Road

About five miles west of San Ignacio, look for a turnoff to the left onto a well-maintained dirt road (you will see the hacienda of Belize's "Toilet Paper King" lording over the valley from a hilltop on your left); turn left and the Chial Road will carry you to several worthwhile sites, including some of Belize's most acclaimed accommodations on the banks of the Macal River.

◖ BELIZE BOTANIC GARDENS

Visiting the country's only botanical garden (tel. 501/824-3101, www.belizebotanic. org, entrance US$5, guided walk US$7.50) makes a wonderful full-day activity, no matter where in the area you are staying. Walk through fruit trees, palms, tropical flowers, and native plants of Belize as you learn about the medicinal and ritual "Plants of the Maya" and experience the orchid house with more than 100 species. Botanists' work here has resulted in 20 new orchid records for Belize and one species new to science: *Pleurothallis duplooyii* (named after Ken duPlooy), which has a bloom about the size of a flea! There is also a rainforest trail, a pine forest habitat complete with 30-foot fire tower, a special guidebook for children, education programs for local schoolchildren and visitors, and a sustainably built visitors center for meetings, yoga, and other activities. Belize Botanic Gardens sponsors a program where volunteers pay US$550 for room and board while working on various garden projects for a month. Call to find out

about a shuttle from San Ignacio, or hire your own cab for US$20–25. The gardens' office is in the reception area of duPlooy's Jungle Lodge Resort.

RAINFOREST MEDICINE TRAIL

There are a number of attractions available to nonguests at The Lodge at Chaa Creek (tel. 501/824-2037, entrance US$10 pp), including this short riverside hike, highlighting the medicinal plants of the Maya and their uses. The site also boasts the **Blue Morpho Butterfly Breeding Center**, the **Chaa Creek Natural History Museum** (with exhibit areas that examine ecosystems, geology, and Maya culture in the Cayo area), and a gift shop. Touring all of these can take a half day; the office is at The Lodge at Chaa Creek.

ACCOMMODATIONS

Set on 90 lush acres of rolling countryside on the banks of the Macal River is **duPlooy's Jungle Lodge** (tel. 501/824-3101, www.duplooys.com). The duPlooys have planted thousands of trees, a fruit orchard, and the **Belize Botanic Gardens**. Guests have a number of choices of where to stay, including Jungle Lodge rooms (US$195) and comfy bungalows (US$225, rate includes breakfast, canoes, and entrance to the Botanic Gardens) with king bed, bathtub, full kitchens, and private deck; you'll get to your room via wooden catwalk, which gives you your own canopy tour on the steep riverbank. Other available options are great for families and groups, including La Casita, which sleeps up to eight for US$315 a night. Meal plans, packed lunches, and the dining room provide top-notch, cow-free sustenance—vegetarians are welcome. In addition, duPlooy's offers a sandy river beach with swimming, walks in the garden, horse trails, hiking, orchids, and bird-watching tours. Or you can float in a tube or canoe downstream to other jungle resorts where you'll radio back to duPlooy's for a pickup. In addition to composting, waste reduction, recycling, and the avoidance of the nonsustainable practice of palm frond roof thatching, they also have zero

© JOSHUA EERMAN

The solar array at duPlooy's Jungle Lodge is only one example of sustainable solutions to off-the-grid living in the Macal River Valley. Many properties here have green practices and systems.

chemical use on the vast landscaping—which, considering the 10-foot-deep wee-wee ant complexes that have to be dug up and destroyed by hand, is no small feat in the rainforest. In 2010, they went fully solar (with backup generator).

The Lodge at Chaa Creek (tel. 501/824-2037, www.chaacreek.com, from US$330, breakfast included) is one of the top-rated jungle lodges in Central America. Chaa Creek's 365 acres on the Macal River host the ever evolving vision of owners Mick and Lucy Fleming, an American wife/British husband team who came to Belize in the late 1970s, fell in love with the land, and never left. The 24 palapa-roof cottages have electricity and private verandas for viewing wildlife and are furnished with fine fabrics and works of art from around the world; two "treetop" Jacuzzi suites perch on the riverbank, their wide porches boasting views of iguanas basking in the branches. Chaa Creek guests choose from on-site activities for no extra charge, including daily bird-watching walks, canoeing and swimming in the Macal

River, butterfly farm tour, and medicinal trail. There is a full concierge service to plan your days: mountain biking, horseback riding, and many other tours. The Belizean chef prepares wonderful meals, with many of the ingredients coming from a local Maya farm (which guests can visit); a packed lunch is US$10, dinner US$32.

One of the best deals in the region is Chaa Creek's **Macal River Camp,** where US$65 per person gets you a lantern-lit wall tent, dinner, breakfast, and access to all the main Chaa Creek facilities and activities (located a short 10-minute walk along the medicine trail, right above the river). There are 10 units around a central fire pit and eating area, all with access to a shared bathroom and shower house. Meals are eaten communally under a thatch roof, with a bar available as well.

As you continue upstream on the Macal, **Ek' Tun** (tel. 501/820-3002, www.ektunbelize. com, US$190, plus US$28 for breakfast and dinner) is one of the most remote, romantic

CAYO

© JOSHUA BERMAN

At Black Rock Lodge, there are excellent birding opportunities from the open-air dining lodge, high above the Macal River.

accommodations in Belize, consisting of two quaint, tastefully appointed cottages in the middle of a vast, green chunk of the upper Macal River Valley. The cascade-fed, mineral water swimming pool surrounded by beautiful landscaping and meditation platforms is unique in all of Central America. Excellent meals include Mexican specialties, fresh fruit, spicy local dishes, and desserts; accommodations are rustically elegant and comfortable (there is no electricity). Ek' Tun's intimate atmosphere makes this a favorite for honeymooners (no children, couples only, three-night minimum).

Another couple of river bends later is **Black Rock Lodge** (tel. 501/824-2341, www.blackrocklodge.com, US$135–210 plus meals and taxes), another easy place to recommend for the sheer beauty of its location,

starting with the incredible vista from the open-air dining pavilion. Guests stay in one of 14 units, including a few deluxe options. Meals are communal at long tables with a solid menu that includes four-course dinners for US$22 (breakfast and lunch from US$3–12). There are numerous trips and hikes on the 242-acre property and some unique bird habitats, especially raptors, who love the air currents in front of the big cliffs. There is plenty of wildlife in the area, and it is across the river from Elijio Panti National Park. Black Rock is off the grid and powered by a combination of solar and hydro technology (80 percent of the power comes from a high-pressure mountain spring); they use solar hot-water heating and compost their food and yard waste; they have 30 species of trees in their fruit orchard and a small organic garden.

The Mountain Pine Ridge

Some of Belize's most breathtaking natural and archaeological treasures are found within this vast crinkle of mountains and wildlands, as are a few of the country's most remote and charming accommodations. Despite bark beetle damage to vast tracts of pine trees in the Mountain Pine Ridge (MPR) Forest Reserve, the forests are rebounding, and MPR's waterfalls, swimming holes, and vistas are well worth enduring the rutted roads.

The following points of interest, parks, and accommodations are presented in the order they are found as one travels south from San Ignacio and the Western Highway (along both roads that access the Pine Ridge).

THE CHIQUIBUL/ PINE RIDGE ROAD

The Chiquibul Road begins at Mile 63 on the Western Highway, at Georgeville, and heads south over the Mountain Pine Ridge,

terminating 30-something miles later at Caracol. You'll pass through tropical foothills, citrus farms, and cattle ranches before the terrain rises, gradually changing to sand, rocky soil, red clay, then, finally, groves of sweet-smelling pines. The road is notorious for becoming a slushy mud bed when it rains and a dusty back-breaker when it's dry. Once you start driving, there are few services besides those offered at the resorts, but if you need a drink, beer, meal, supplies, or emergency gasoline, look for the **Junction Store,** a wooden building right where the San Antonio Road meets the Chiquibul Road.

Barton Creek Cave and Outpost

This is a cathedral-like wet cave, once used for ceremonial purposes and human sacrifices by the Maya. A pair of Peace Corps volunteers stumbled on the cave in 1970 and found that it had been looted but still contained an

Pitch a tent at the Barton Creek Outpost, next to the creek that flows out of the sacred Barton Creek Cave.

© JOSHUA BERMAN

CAYO

CAYO

enormous amount of pottery and artifacts. Archaeologists didn't study the cave until 1998; they found large ceramics on high ledges, plus evidence of 20 human remains, including a necklace made of finger bones.

Barton Creek Cave is popular among Cayo visitors who fancy floating through the tall, quiet cavern. The experience is impressive and available to anybody physically able enough to step into a canoe. Contemplate the quiet as your guide slowly paddles you deeper into the earth, the watery sound of his paddle echoing on the limestone. The cave is at least seven miles deep, but tours only go in about a mile or so before turning around.

VISITING THE CAVE

Barton Creek is protected and managed by government archaeologists and is accessed by turning off the Chiquibul Road around Mile 4, then driving 20–30 minutes on a bumpy road through orange groves and a small Mennonite settlement (you'll need to have someone who knows the way with you, as there are many roads and no signs). The visitors center charges US$10 per person, then you'll have to rent canoes (US$7.50 per boat), lights, and a guide, all available at **Mike's Place,** right at the cave's entrance. If you come as part of a prepaid tour, you won't need to worry about such details.

ACCOMMODATIONS AND FOOD

Sleep to the sound of rushing water at **Barton Creek Outpost** (tel. 501/662-4797, www.bartoncreekoutpost.com, from US$10 per person), run by Jacquelyn and Jim Brit, an American couple who met while serving as divers for the U.S. Navy and decided to bring their family to the bush. Jacquelyn is a fantastic cook who serves three meals a day and is happy to do veg/vegan on request. Jim loves to take guests on all-day hikes on their 165-acre property and in the surrounding area. If you bring your own camping gear, you can stay for US$2.50, or they rent tents and mattresses (US$10 per tent). There's a bunkhouse for US$7.50 per person and a single cabana in the orange grove for US$20. Staying here puts you at the end of a very rough road, but there is plenty to do for active nature lovers, as well as discounted access to local tour companies for trips to waterfalls, ruins, horseback riding, and of course, Barton Creek Cave, which is a stone's throw upstream.

Calico Jack's Jungle Canopy and Zip Lining

Located in El Progreso (Mile 7), just off the Chiquibul Road on 365 acres, **Calico Jack's Village** (Belize tel. 501/820-4078, U.S. tel. 305/647-4908, www.calicojacksvillage.com) is an ambitious project to create a full-service adventure resort. For now, Calico Jack's top offerings include a medicinal hiking trail, cave tours, and the "longest, safest, and fastest canopy tour in Belize." Climb and zip between 15 platforms high in the trees; available tours range from a 20-minute "express" experience to the full two-hour exploration (US$35–62). Or try the massive "columpio," a one-of-a-kind jungle swing, which will send you 200 feet in the air after you are hoisted above the top of a re-created Maya pyramid. The cabanas and villas are also being built in Maya temple style, and all have access to a bar, restaurant, and pool.

Green Hills Butterfly Ranch and Botanical Collections

Located at Mile 8, this outstanding butterfly breeding, education, and interpretive center is run by Dutch biologists Jan Meerman and Tineke Boomsma. Green Hills (tel. 501/820-4017, meerman@btl.net, www.green-hills.net, 8 A.M.–4 P.M. daily, US$10). The standard tour of the center takes about an hour. There's also a walk into the forest to see Maya artifacts and the impressive mahogany reforestation project. Your entrance fee (family discounts available) grants you access to the 3,000-square-foot butterfly house, blue morpho breeding facilities, botanical garden (with over 100 labeled species), hummingbird observation spot, and a display on the life cycle of a butterfly (egg-caterpillar-pupa-butterfly). Between 25 and 30 different species are raised at the center, including the tiny glasswing, the banana owl (the largest butterfly in Belize), and of course the magnificent blue morpho. Arrive early enough in the morning and watch a butterfly emerge from a pupa right before your eyes. Or time your visit with "caligo hour"—a unique event that begins one hour before sunset (in December around 4:45 P.M., in summer about 5:45 P.M.) when the owl butterflies become very active and synchronize their flight; owl butterflies can have wing spans of up to seven inches, so it's quite impressive. Jan literally wrote the book on Belizean butterflies (*Lepidoptera of Belize*, Gainesville, Florida: ATL Books, 2000), and both he and Tineke can be available to give lectures to student groups. Green Hills is a must-stop for anyone traveling to and from other sites on the Chiquibul Road; it's worth it for the hummingbird garden alone, where you can watch an amazingly active assortment of hummers buzz in and out all day long. Picnic facilities available.

CAYO

Slate Creek Preserve

A group of local landowners and lodge operators have set aside 3,000 acres as a private preserve. The purpose of the preserve is to protect the watershed, plants, and animals of a valley called the Vega, one of several valleys in the area. The unique ecosystem of limestone karst, which borders the Mountain Pine Ridge Forest Reserve, teems with life. Mahogany, Santa Maria, ceiba, cedar, and cohune palms tower above. Orchids, ferns, and bromeliads are common. Birds such as the aracari, emerald toucanet, keel-billed toucan, keel-billed motmot, king vulture, and various parrots and hummingbirds are to be found here. Pumas, ocelots, coatis, pacas, and anteaters roam the forests.

Accommodations and Food

At **(Mountain Equestrian Trails** (MET, tel. 501/820-4041 or 501/620-4978, U.S. tel. 800/838-3918, www.metbelize.com, US$75–132), the Bevis family keeps 27 sturdy steeds with Endurance saddles. Visitors have a choice of gentle or spirited horses to carry them over 60 miles of trails that to waterfalls, swimming holes, Maya caves, and other sites. Beginners and experienced riders are welcome—children at least 10 years old with previous riding experience are welcome. Riders are required to carry personal liability insurance.

To stay at MET, choose from a range of 10 "safari-style" cabanas of thatch and stucco with exotic wood interiors and private bathrooms with hot and cold water (no electricity—yet). Meals are served in the cozy cantina/restaurant, which offers excellent food (breakfast US$7, lunch US$10, dinner US$18, plus tax). Even though MET's small cantina is a 20-minute drive from San Ignacio, it still attracts visitors and locals from all around for drinks, dinner, and good conversation. All-inclusive, multiday packages are available, riding fees extra.

Their **Chiclero Trails Campsite** offers tents under the rainforest canopy, with beds, mattresses, linens, a private covered deck, and close access to restrooms and showers, for US$20 per person per night. Meals for groups are served in an insulated tent in the camp.

About 200 yards north of the junction with the road to San Antonio, **Moonracer Farm** (U.S. tel. 585/200-5748, www.moonracerfarm.com, US$65–120) provides a pair of comfortable wooden cabins in the forest in one of the best deals in the Mountain Pine Ridge. The cabins are fairly large, with private screened porches. Meals are available for US$30 a day and include the homemade, fresh cooking of owners Marge and Tom. When I visited, the smell of baking granola and brownies emanated from the thatch-roofed kitchen made from an old jaguar cage. Yes, this property used to be the home of a feline rescue center, and the new owners have creatively repurposed some of the hardware. Hiking trails explore their 50 acres and connect to the Mountain Pine Ridge Forest Reserve and Elijio Panti National Park.

THE MOUNTAIN PINE RIDGE FOREST RESERVE

After you steadily ascend along the Chiquibul (Pine Ridge) Road for 21 miles, a gate across the road marks your entrance to Belize's largest and oldest protected area, established in 1944. The 300-square-mile area (126,825 acres) features Caribbean pine and bracken ferns instead of the typical tropical vegetation found in the rest of Belize. It also features a massive granite uplifting; the exposed rocks are some of the oldest formations in the Americas (they make for amazing swimming holes and waterfalls). In fact, some geologists think that the Mountain Pine Ridge (whose highest point is 3,336 feet above sea level at Baldy Beacon) was one of the few exposed islands when the rest of Central America was underwater.

Cycles of Disaster

Shortly after the reserve's creation, the Pine Ridge experienced a huge forest fire, which, combined with the cycles of logging, left an unnaturally uniform population of trees, making the forest further susceptible to disease and insects. In the 1990s, a three-year drought helped establish a disastrous infestation of the

© JOSHUA BERMAN

fire tower in the Mountain Pine Ridge

southern pine bark beetle *(Dendroctonus fron-talis)*, which has wreaked havoc throughout Central and North America.

Today, the forest is coming back wonderfully—thanks to both naturally rich seed sets and a massive replanting campaign (24 million seedlings are required for reforestation of 70,000 acres over four years). It will be another 10–15 years before the new generation of pines fully matures, however. Check out www.reforestbelize.com for an update and to find out how you can help.

Visiting the Reserve

Most San Ignacio tour operators offer day trips to the Pine Ridge's attractions, often combined with a trip to Caracol ruins. There are way more sights than can fit into a day, but a number of lodges can put you right in the thick of it all. You can pitch your tent at Old Mai Gate Village (US$17.50), a barebones site on the road, just a few turns beyond the reserve entrance and gate. There is a well-kept picnic area and they sell drinks and beers.

The forestry station at **Douglas de Silva Reserve** (formerly Augustine) used to be a small village of loggers and forestry workers before the pine beetle and massive layoffs. You can now camp on the mowed grounds of the old school, but the blackflies can be horrendous here. Those interested in camping must get permission from the forest guard at the entrance.

Thousand Foot Falls

Occasionally referred to as "Hidden Valley Falls," this torrent of Roaring Creek is probably a good deal taller than a thousand feet and is considered the highest waterfall in all of Central America. The turnoff to a viewpoint of the falls is a couple of miles beyond the forest reserve gate and is well signed. It's quite a little drive to get all the way there, and though the view is magical, you don't get the reward of being able to jump in. From the turnoff, the road continues down for about four miles and brings you to the falls and a picnic area. View the falls from across the gorge and through

CAYO

© JOSHUA BERMAN

The trailhead to Big Rock Falls is on the road to the Five Sisters Lodge.

breaks in the mist (US$2 pp). A small store and picnic tables can be found at the viewpoint (7 A.M.–5 P.M. daily).

Big Rock Falls

A hand-painted sign on the dirt road to Five Sisters Lodge is your only indicator to the trailhead for Big Rock. You'll park and hike down a fairly steep trail (clinging to a rope at one point) to a series of spectacular pools below the site's namesake. Big Rock Falls is big, loud, impressive, and worth the stop.

Río On Pools and Río Frio Cave

Most Caracol packages try to squeeze in an afternoon stopover at these lovely sites. Continuing south toward Augustine, you will cross the Río On. It's well worth the climb over an assortment of worn boulders and rocks to waterfalls and several warm-water pools. There's a parking area just off the road. Turn right at Douglas de Silva ranger station (the western division of the Forestry Department) and continue for about five miles to reach Río

Frio Cave. Follow the signs to the parking lot. From here, visitors have a choice of exploring nature trails and two small caves on the road or continuing to Río Frio Cave, with an enormous arched entryway into the half-mile-long cave. Filtered light highlights ferns, mosses, stalactites, and geometric patterns of striations on rocks. Watch for sinkholes. At times, a military escort is necessary to Río Frio. Ask at the forest station.

Accommodations and Food

Situated on 7,200 acres of private property in the heart of the Mountain Pine Ridge Forest Reserve, **Hidden Valley Inn** (Cooma Cairn Rd., tel. 501/822-3320, www.hiddenvalley-inn.com, about US$165–205 plus meals and taxes) is a quiet paradise for hikers and birdwatchers, who have a blast exploring the resort's 90-plus miles of walking trails and old logging roads. Later, after dining under the stars, they cozy up in front of their cottage's fireplace. The property encompasses lush broadleaf forest and pine tree habitat, and two diverse ecosystems are divided by a geological fault line, which marks the edge of a towering 1,000-foot escarpment. Birders, be prepared to check off orange-breasted falcons, king vultures, stygian owls, azure-crowned hummingbirds, green jays, and golden-hooded tanagers. Picnic lunches are provided for the myriad day trips available. The main house built of local hardwoods feels more like a ski lodge than a tropical resort, with several spacious common rooms, including a fireside lounge, a card room, bar, library, and the restaurant. The 12 cottages have saltillo tile floors, vaulted ceilings, cypress-paneled walls, fireplaces, ceiling fans, screened louvered windows, comfy beds, and private baths with hot and cold water, some with waterfall orchid showers in a private outdoor bathroom. Hidden Valley Inn is three miles in from the Mile 14 turnoff onto Cooma Cairn Road—just follow the signs.

Five miles beyond the forest reserve gate, you'll find yet another unique hillside lodging with its own primitively comfortable personality. On the banks of Little Vaqueros Creek,

Pine Ridge Lodge (tel. 501/606-4557, U.S. tel. 800/316-0706, www.pineridgelodge.com, US$89) offers six rooms in "forestview, Mayan, and riverview" cottages, all with private bathrooms, hot water, porches, and appealing decor and furnishings. There's no electricity, just quaint kerosene lanterns for reading at night. Owners Vicki and Gary Seewald have done a superhuman job of maintaining the grounds—they've planted bright and beautiful gardens that feature a growing collection of orchids and other epiphytes. Screened-in creekside lounge areas offer shade and a babbling brook, which is great after that bumpy, 32-mile trip back from Caracol—and before your walk down to the Pine Ridge Lodge's 85-foot waterfall. Room rate includes continental breakfast (freshly baked rolls, local honey, coffee, and fresh fruit); lunch is US$8.50, dinner US$25. Catering to vegetarians is a specialty. The lodge is only seven miles north of Río On Pools; ask about tours and transfers.

Francis Ford Coppola first came to Belize just after the country gained independence in 1981; he tried and failed to persuade the new government to apply for a satellite license in order to become a hub of world communications. He did, however, succeed in finding an abandoned lodge on a pine-carpeted bluff overlooking the rocks and falls of Privassion Creek. It served as a private retreat for the film producer until 1993, when he "tricked it open" by flying a group of family and friends down for his 54th birthday. Today, **Blancaneaux Lodge** (tel. 501/824-4912, www.blancaneaux.com, from US$250) remains one of Central America's premier resorts, featuring the design of Mexican architect Manolo Mestre. Splashes of color, dark hardwoods, Central American lines, and soaring thatch ceilings mark Blancaneaux's 10 cabanas and seven luxurious villas. There is a U-shaped hot pool above the river and a spa built in an Indonesian rice house with Thai massage therapists. Blancaneaux's **Ristorante Montagna** offers an exquisite Italian-centric menu, with a range of salads, pastas (US$14), seafood, sandwiches, pizzas (US$18), and, of course, a

selection of wines from Coppola's Napa Valley vineyards—smooth and costly. Two honeymoon cabanas with their own private infinity pools and choice of two views (US$290–390) and the Enchanted Cottage kick things up a notch in luxury. The Enchanted Cottage is also available for a small group of friends looking to celebrate a special event—and who can afford US$1,600 per night. An on-site hydroelectric dam powers the entire operation, and a 3.5-acre organic herb and vegetable garden supplies many of the restaurant's needs (and those of Turtle Inn). They have a stable with 29 healthy horses and a number of guided trail trips. The lodge is at Mile 14½ and has its own airstrip, which many guests prefer to the 2.5-hour drive from Belize City.

Five Sisters Lodge (tel. 501/820-4005, www.fivesisterslodge.com, US$85–150), high above the inviting Privassion Creek, was built in 1991, inspired by the natural beauty Belizean Carlos Popper saw in his property, perched in the Pine Ridge above the famous Five Sisters Falls from which the lodge gets its name. Prices are very reasonable. Rooms and suites are perched on the top of the steep canyon; they range from beautifully thatched cabanas overlooking the river to an exclusive riverside villa—19 units in all. The honeymoon suite has brightly colored bedspreads, mosquito netting, and complete privacy, and a new gazebo is popular for weddings. Restaurant prices are also relatively low, and packages for longer stays are offered. Even if you don't stay here, come by, have a beer on the outdoor deck, and enjoy the commanding view above the river. The hardy can walk the 300 steps down to the river; if you're too tired after splashing around, not to worry—the motorized funicular will carry you back up the hill, at least between 8 A.M. and 4 P.M.

◖ CARACOL ARCHAEOLOGICAL SITE

Archaeologists Diane and Arlen Chase believe that Caracol, one of the largest sites in Belize, is the Maya city-state that toppled mighty Tikal, just to the northwest, effectively

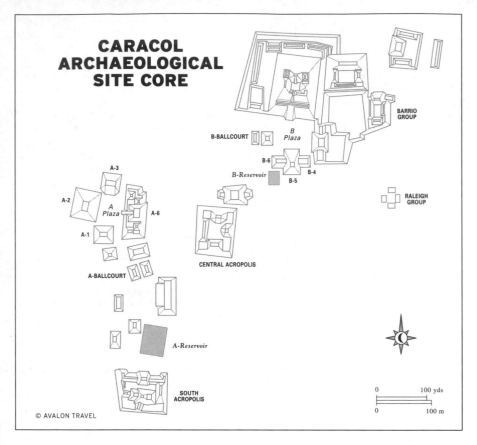

CARACOL
ARCHAEOLOGICAL
SITE CORE

© AVALON TRAVEL

CAYO

shutting it down for 130 years. Located within the **Chiquibul Forest Reserve,** Caracol is *out there,* offering both natural wonders and Maya mystery. To date, only a small percentage of the 177 square kilometers that make up the site has even been mapped, identifying only 5,000 of the estimated 36,000 structures lying beneath the forest canopy.

The centerpiece is no doubt the pyramid of **Canaa,** which, at 136 feet above the plaza floor (roughly two meters higher than El Castillo at Xunantunich), is one of the tallest structures—modern or ancient—in Belize. Canaa was only completely unveiled of vegetation in 2005, by the Tourism Development Project

(TDP), whose work is responsible for most of the structures you see. The vistas from the top of Canaa are extensive and memorable.

In addition to the aforementioned superlatives, Caracol, a Classic Period site, is noted for its large masks and giant date glyphs on circular stone altars. There is also a fine display of the Maya's engineering skills, with extensive reservoirs, agricultural terraces, and several mysterious ramps. Caracol has been studied for more than 20 years by the Chases and their assistants, student interns from Tulane University and the University of Central Florida. According to John Morris, an archaeologist with Belize's Institute of Archaeology, a lifetime of exploration remains to be done for 6–9 miles in every direction of the excavated part of Caracol. It's proving to have been a powerful site that controlled a very large area, with possibly over 100,000 inhabitants. The jungle you see now would have been totally absent in those days, the wood cleared to provide fuel and agricultural lands to support so many people.

Many carvings are dated A.D. 500–800, and ceramic evidence indicates that Caracol was settled around A.D. 300 and continued to flourish when other Maya sites were in decline. Carvings on the site also indicate that Caracol and Tikal engaged in ongoing conflicts, each defeating the other on various occasions. After the war in A.D. 562, Caracol flourished for more than a century in the mountains and valleys surrounding the site. A former archaeological commissioner named the site "Caracol" ("snail" in Spanish) because of the winding logging road to reach it, although some contend it was because of all the snail shells found during initial excavations.

Visiting the Site

Entrance is US$15. The small visitors center presents a scale model and interesting information based mostly on the work of the Chases over the last two decades. A new **Monument Museum** will allow tourists to view a range of artifacts and stelae from the site and will be based on the work of the TDP. There are no official guides on-site, as most groups arrive with their own. However, the caretakers know Caracol well and will be glad to walk you through and explain the site for a few dollars. Most tours start with the Raleigh Group, move by the enormous ceiba trees, then circle through the archaeologists' camp and end with a bang by climbing Canaa. To prepare yourself—and to check on the latest discoveries and trail maps—click over to www.caracol.org.

Most tour operators offer Caracol day trips, often involving stops at various caves and swimming holes on the way back through the Mountain Pine Ridge. A few, like **The Tut Brothers Caracol Shuttle** (tel. 501/610-5593

or 501/820-4014, caracolshuttle@hotmail.com), specialize in it; their shuttle leaves daily from Crystal Paradise Resort near Cristo Rey village and can pick up guests staying elsewhere in the area. The ride should take 2–3 hours, depending on both the weather and the progress made by road improvement crews, who hopefully will not run out of money before you read this. If you're driving, a four-wheel-drive vehicle is a must; gas is not available along the 50-mile road, so carry ample fuel. Camping is not allowed in the area without permission from the Institute of Archaeology in Belmopan. The closest accommodations are those along the Pine Ridge Road.

At times, a military escort is necessary to visit Caracol. Ask at your lodge. Tour operators know to show up at 9:30 A.M. at the Augustine (Douglas de Silva) gate to convoy to the ruins.

THE CRISTO REY ROAD

Heading south from the Western Highway at Santa Elena, this road winds through the villages of Cristo Rey and San Antonio before joining the Chiquibul Road and the Mountain Pine Ridge. It is usually better maintained than the alternative route along the Chiquibul Road, and there are a handful of interesting stops along the way. Village buses that travel the road leave the center of San Ignacio daily, and shared taxis should be available for reasonable rates as well. Most tour operators who travel this road will stop at any of the following places, depending on group size and desires.

Slate Carving Art Galleries

About six miles south, look for the **Sak Tunich Art Gallery,** home of the Magana brothers, Jose and Javier. This indoor-outdoor display is built into the hillside on your left and is worth a look for anyone interested in Maya crafts. These industrious guys are re-creating a Maya temple and cave by carving them into the limestone for the steep hillside next to the road and their home.

A couple miles farther, you'll find more art at **The Garcia Sisters** (tel. 501/820-4023, artistmai1981@btl.net, www.awrem.com/tanah, varying hours and days). These six siblings made a nationwide name for themselves when, in 1981, they turned to their Maya heritage and began re-creating slate carvings reminiscent of those done by their ancestors at Caracol. Their Maya art gallery, shop, and museum are called the **Tanah Mayan Art Museum and Community Collection** (tel. 501/669-4023, 7 A.M.7–P.M. daily), located on the Cristo Rey Road just north of San Antonio. The Tanah Museum is an echo-y one-room affair with long shelves full of fascinating artifacts. The sisters, nieces of the famed healer Don Eligio Panti, are charming and determined ambassadors of San Antonio village. They're also clever artists who make Belizean dolls, native jewelry, and hand-drawn art cards. Ask about the Itzamna Society, a community-based NGO, of which Maria is the chairperson, that works to protect the forest and community. They also sometimes offer language lessons in Yucatecan Maya or cooking classes and can perform blessings, healings, and other ceremonies. The Garcias will be instrumental in organizing a big 2012 Hawk Fire Ceremony with elders from the various Maya groups in Belize.

San Antonio Village

With a population of 2,350 Maya descendants, mostly milpa farmers and, increasingly, employees of nearby lodges, San Antonio has the potential to serve as a low-key gateway to the surrounding wilderness, but as of yet, there are few tourist services in town (there is a new gas station—better fill up before the drive to Caracol). There are horse and hiking trails nearby, as well as several caves, waterfalls, and ruins. Continuing beyond San Antonio, you'll find **Mountain Rider,** a small horseback riding operation.

A women's group has a palapa-roofed shop just off the main road with some nice ceramics for sale. On the way out of town is a little-visited Maya site called Pac Bitun, at the end of an unmarked side road, a mile or so before the T junction.

Noj Kaax Meen Elijio Panti National Park

This 13,000-acre reserve of mountains surrounding the village of San Antonio is filled with trails, waterfalls, and peaks, but there is not much access or tourist development. Go to www.epnp.org, or ask at the Tanah Museum or the women's center if there are any licensed guides taking people into the park.

San Antonio Village, on the way to the Mountain Pine Ridge

West of San Ignacio

Although the chief attraction on this stretch of road between San Ignacio and the Guatemalan border is the Xunantunich archaeological site, there are also resorts, budget lodgings, and campgrounds where some travelers stop in between Guatemalan and Caribbean adventures. Most of these places are close enough to San Ignacio that guests can easily pop into town for dinner and then back out to their tent or cabin in a cheap taxi.

DRIVING WEST FROM SAN IGNACIO TOWARD GUATEMALA
Accommodations and Food

Only a two-minute drive from San Ignacio, **Windy Hill Resort** (tel. 501/824-2017 or 501/824-2598, www.windyhillresort.com, US$100–130) sits on its own lovely rise, just above the Western Highway. You'll find 23 well-appointed, clean, air-conditioned deluxe cottages and standard rooms with private baths, hot and cold water, ceiling fans, private verandas with hammocks, an infinity swimming pool, a fitness center, and a recreation room complete with TV, bar, table tennis, and darts. Windy Hill specializes in tours and multiday packages with meal plans. Guests enjoy canoeing, caving, horseback riding, nature tours, and hiking trails. Meals are served in the casual, thatch-roof Black Orchid Restaurant.

Ka'ana Boutique Hotel & Spa (tel. 501/824-3350, www.kaanabelize.com, US$250–350) opened in 2007 at Mile 69, a few miles west of San Ignacio on the Western Highway. Ka'ana is a small, full-service upscale resort with 15 rooms and 10 fully equipped casitas around a pool, spa, and lounge. The restaurant and bar offer an elite departure from the standard fare in San Ignacio (7 A.M.–9 P.M. daily, dinner entrées US$12–33); at the bar, try the sweet corn colada (cocktails US$5–12). Each evening there are tastings held at 7 P.M. in the well-stocked, climate-controlled wine cellar.

Clarissa Falls Resort (tel. 501/824-3916, www.clarissafalls.com) is at the end of a mile-long dirt road, accessed on the right at Mile 70½ of the Western Highway. This is a laid-back place focused on the river, where guests either camp in their own tents (US$7.50 pp) or stay in an overpriced cottage with private bath (US$75). The shared toilet and shower building has hot and cold water and is cement-basic. The Mopan River is the main attraction here; don't miss the nature trails and a hike (or horseback ride) to Xunantunich, the highest pyramid visible from the cottages. The dining room serves decent food, including a few specialties such as black mole soup and great, cheap Mexican-style tacos or stuffed squash (US$6–9).

SAN JOSÉ DE SUCCOTZ AND XUNANTUNICH
About 6.5 miles from San Ignacio, you'll find this hillside village on your left, above the Mopan River, right where the ferry to Xunantunich is located. In Succotz, the first language is Spanish, and the most colorful time to visit is during one of their fiestas: March 19 (feast day of St. Joseph) and May 3 (feast day of the Holy Cross).

A stroll through the rough village streets is enjoyable if you're into observing village life. **Magana's Art Center** (Western Hwy. across from the Xunantunich ferry) is the workshop of David Magana, who works with the youth of the area, encouraging them to continue the arts and crafts of their ancestors. You'll find the results inside in the form of local wood carvings, baskets, jewelry, and stone (slate) carvings unique to Belize. There are a few taco stands in town, including the popular local eatery **Benny's Kitchen** (Western Hwy. across from the Xunantunich ferry), where one can get a substantial breakfast and other tasty items for low prices. Cold draft Belikin is served in frosty mugs, a nice touch.

◖ Xunantunich Archaeological Site

One of Belize's most impressive Maya ceremonial centers, Xunantunich rests atop a natural limestone ridge with a grand view of the entire Cayo District and Guatemala countryside. The local name for the site, Xunantunich (shoo-NAHN-ta-nich), or "Stone Lady," continues to be used, even after the ancients' own name for the site, Ka-at Witz, or "Supernatural Mountain," was recently discovered, carved into a chunk of stone.

Xunantunich is believed to have been built sometime around 400 B.C. and deserted around A.D. 1000; at its peak, some 7,000–10,000 Maya lived here. Though certainly not the biggest of Maya structures, at 135 feet high, **El Castillo** is the second tallest pyramid in Belize

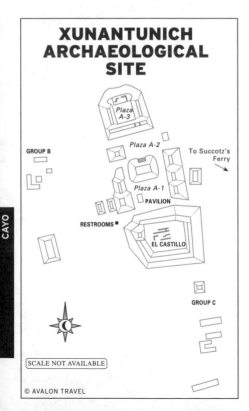

XUNANTUNICH ARCHAEOLOGICAL SITE

Plaza A-3

GROUP B

Plaza A-2

To Succotz's Ferry

Plaza A-1

PAVILION

RESTROOMS

EL CASTILLO

GROUP C

SCALE NOT AVAILABLE

© AVALON TRAVEL

(missing first place by one foot!). The eastern side of the structure displays an unusual stucco frieze (a reproduction), and you can see three carved stelae in the plaza. Xunantunich contains three ceremonial plazas surrounded by house mounds. It was rediscovered in 1894, but not studied until 1938, by archaeologist Sir J. Eric Thompson. As the first Maya ruin to be opened in the country, it has attracted the attention and exploration of many other archaeologists over the years.

In 1950, the University of Pennsylvania (noted for its years of outstanding work across the Guatemala border in Tikal) built a facility in Xunantunich for more study. In 1954, visitors were invited to explore the site after a road was opened and a small ferry built. In 1959, archaeologist Evan Mackie made news in the Maya world when he discovered evidence that part of Xunantunich had been destroyed by an earthquake in the Late Classic Period. Some believe it was then that the people began to lose faith in their leaders—they saw the earthquake as an unearthly sign from the gods. But for whatever reason, Xunantunich ceased to be a religious center long before the end of the Classic Period.

Located eight miles west of San Ignacio, the site is accessed by crossing the Mopan River on the Succotz ferry, easily found at the end of a line of crafts vendors. The hand-cranked ferry shuttles you (and your vehicle, if you have one) across the river, after which you'll have about a mile's hike (or drive) up a hill to the site. The ferry, which operates 8 A.M.–3 P.M. daily, is free, but tipping the operator is a kind and much-appreciated gesture. Don't miss the 4 P.M. return ferry with the park rangers, or you'll be swimming. Be forewarned that during rainy season the Mopan River can rise, run fast, and flood, thus canceling this service until conditions improve.

Entrance to the site is US$10 per person; guides are available for US$20 per group and are recommended—both to learn about what you're seeing and to support sustainable tourism, as all guides are local and very knowledgeable.

© JOSHUA BERMAN

At the top of El Castillo at the Xunantunich Archaeological Site, you can see above the other pyramids and the forest canopy.

Accommodations

Just before entering the roadside village of San José de Succotz, look on your left for the **Trek Stop** (tel. 501/823-2265, www.thetrekstop.com, US$15–38), a backpacker classic offering 10 cabins set in lush gardens on 22 acres of second-growth tropical forest. You can hear the highway, but you can also hear howler monkeys, birds, and the inspired conversation of your hosts and fellow travelers. There are camping facilities (US$5 pp, access to composting toilets and solar showers), a patio restaurant with inexpensive Belizean dishes, and walking access to the Xunantunich ruins. Simple wood cabins have twin or double beds, electricity, porches, and shared bath; a larger, more private cabin with private bath is available. Even if you're not spending the night here, come visit the **Tropical Wings Nature Center,** one of the best and most diverse butterfly ranches in the country. Be sure to leave time for a round on Belize's only **disc golf course,** a nine-basket Frisbee golf game through the jungle, discs available (US$3 per person). The course is a par

31 with narrow and challenging fairways that leave little room for error (wear long pants and closed footwear to retrieve those errant drives). There is a nice view (and sometimes breeze) from the Maya ruins atop hole 6.

BENQUE VIEJO DEL CARMEN

After you drive past the Xunantunich ferry, the village of Succotz creeps over the hill and becomes Benque Viejo del Carmen, the last town in Belize (the border is about one mile farther). Benque Viejo has been greatly influenced by the Spanish, both from its historical past when Spain ruled Guatemala and later when Spanish-speaking *chicleros* and loggers worked the forest. At one time, Benque Viejo ("Old Bank"; riverside logging camps were referred to as "banks") was a logging camp. This was the gathering place for chicle workers, and logs were floated down the river from here for shipment to England.

Benque is a quiet village between the road and river, with a peaceful atmosphere and a handful of shops and Chinese restaurants.

CAYO

Foreign doctors who donate free medical assistance visit the Good Shepherd Clinic in Benque Viejo every year.

Getting There and Away

Buses between Belize City, Benque, and the Guatemala border run daily, starting at ungodly morning hours on both ends. Most bus service to and from San Ignacio also services Benque and the border. The most efficient way to travel to the border from San Ignacio is by *colectivo* taxis, which run in a constant and steady flow roughly 6 A.M.–7 P.M.; the ride should cost approximately US$2, but you take the chance of sharing your cab with as many people as your driver can fit. By private taxi, expect to pay about US$10 per cab for the same trip.

SOUTH ON THE HYDRO ROAD

Look for the left-hand turn in the middle of Benque Viejo, at the top of the hill. It leads south to a few unique attractions and accommodations, all well off the beaten path. The Hydro Road is equipped with mile markers on small white posts. A couple miles in, a right turn leads to the border village of Arenal, where a few *milpero* (corn farmer) families scrape a life from the soils of the Mopan River Valley. The road continues south for 11 miles, where it dead-ends at the Mollejon Dam.

Poustinia Land Art Park

This is a reclaimed cattle ranch, now devoted to the nurturing of art and nature, where foreign and Belizean artists can stay and contribute to the ongoing project, and visitors can come take a look and soak it all in. The lush grounds are part of a 270-acre second-growth forest. Visiting the unique Poustinia Land Art Park (www.poustiniaonline.org, US$10 entrance) is by appointment only and can be arranged at the **Benque Viejo House of Culture** (tel. 501/823-2697). Adjacent to the park is **El Dorado Cabins** (contact Luis Alberto and Deborah Ruiz in Belmopan, tel. 501/822-3532, US$40). The two wooden cabins are each equipped with a kitchenette, a private bathroom with running water, a small dining area, and a deck; limited electricity is available. If you are an artist, ask Luis how you may be able to contribute.

Chechem Ha Cave and the Vaca Plateau

At Mile 8, you'll find a turnoff to the left for **Chechem Ha Farm** (tel. 501/820-4063), a mile or so down a rutted road and belonging to the Morales family. The place is designed to give nature-loving tourists the chance to enjoy the Chechem Ha Spring, Chechem Ha Falls (a 175-foot cascade with a treacherous trail down to its misty bottom), and Chechem Ha Cave, a dry cave—except for the dripping water that has created all the formations over the years. The pottery inside is estimated to be as much as 2,000 years old. You can climb and explore various ledges and passageways, but the highlight is a deep ceremonial chamber in the heart of the hill. In some places, you need a rope to help you get around. While those of average physical abilities can enjoy Chechem Ha Cave, take care when moving amid the pottery.

Stay at the farm in one of several simple cabins made of clay, rock, wood, and thatch; they are well constructed and comfy looking. For US$41 per person, you get a night's stay and three meals (no electricity; outhouses). Camping is US$5 per person; bring your own tent. Individual meals are available (US$5–10), as is an inexpensive transfer from Benque.

Martz Farm

Less than a mile beyond the Chechem Ha road, another left turn will carry you to 【 Martz Farm (tel. 501/614-6462, www.martzfarm. com, US$20–58), a unique and relaxed homestead built and maintained by the hardworking Martinez family. Two good-natured and burly brothers, Joe and Lazaro, hacked this place out of raw bush, and they continue improving their primitive homestead. They've constructed a handful of treehouses and natural cabins (one has a private bath and hot water), each seemingly sprung from wild childhood fantasies. All are open to the forest air (mosquito nets provided), and one is even built over a private dip pool in the passing creek. Joe's German wife, Miriam, cooks family-style meals over a traditional fire hearth in a quaint kitchen, and farm animals wander the grounds with the guests. Home-cooked meal plans and free transfers from San Ignacio or Benque are available. The facilities are slowly improving, with a few new flush toilets and hot water and showers.

THE BORDER AT MELCHOR

The western *frontera* into Guatemala is only 11 miles from San Ignacio, a trip made for around US$3 per person in a *colectivo* taxi, less in a passing bus bound for Benque Viejo. A private taxi from San Ignacio should cost about US$15 total. Be prepared to pay your US$19 exit fee on the Belizean side, which includes the PACT fee (they will ask for exact change); the rest of the money goes to the private "Border Management" company, a point of contention for local tour providers and would-be Guatemalan day-trippers. Expect the usual throng of money changers to greet you on both sides of the border—they're fine to use, as long as you know what rate you should be getting—or you can use the official Casas de Cambio on either side.

If you're driving your own car, make sure you have all the necessary papers of ownership and attendant photocopies of all your documents, including license and passport, which they *will* want to see. You are required by law to have your tires fumigated when entering/exiting Belize and Guatemala, for which the cost is a few Belizean dollars. If driving a private or rental vehicle into Guatemala you will have to pay a "toll" to cross the bridge going over the Mopan into Melchor. If your car has Belize tags, the fee can be as low as 5 quetzales. If your tags are from far away, like Canada or the United States, be prepared to pay Q50 and not one peso more. Save the receipt if you are returning to Belize, as it is good for a two-way crossing. In addition, based on some reports travelers have to ensure that they have received a proper exit stamp when leaving Belize, for both themselves and their vehicle. Double-check your passport before continuing on to Guatemala.

After clearing Guatemalan immigration and shaking off the sometimes aggressive *taxistas,* you'll find yourself on the edge of the Mopan River, across which begins the town of **Melchor de Mencos.** Before crossing the bridge, you'll find the **Río Mopan Lodge** (tel. 502/7926-5196, www.tikaltravel.com, US$20) on your left, a nice riverside hotel and restaurant whose proprietors (a Swiss-Spanish couple) are a wealth of information on remote ruins in the area. There are other places in Melchor if you get stranded in town for some reason or are embarking on your own jungle expedition to unexplored ruins.

Into Guatemala: Tikal National Park

The following text appears in *Moon Guatemala,* by Al Argueta.

TIKAL NATIONAL PARK

Tikal National Park, the oldest and best known of Guatemala's national parks, was created in 1956. It encompasses 575 square kilometers (222 square miles) of primary tropical forest and protects a vast array of wildlife, as well as harboring the remains of one of the Mayan civilization's greatest cities. Tikal is understandably high on the list of priorities for any visitor to Guatemala and shouldn't be missed, as it affords the unique opportunity to combine a visit to a site of mammoth historical importance both in terms of natural and human heritage. Owing to its singular importance in the spheres of natural and human history, UNESCO declared Tikal National Park a World Heritage Site in 1979.

Tikal's towering Temple I dominates the city's Great Plaza and is an icon for

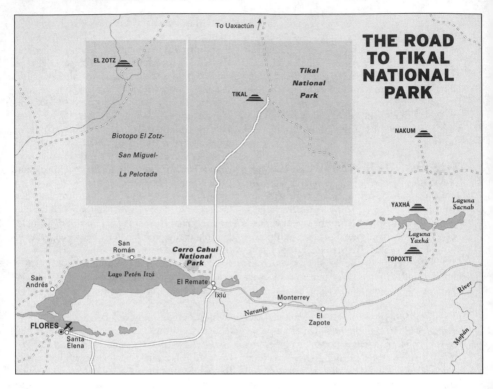

To Uaxactún

EL ZOTZ

Tikal
National
Park

TIKAL

**THE ROAD
TO TIKAL
NATIONAL
PARK**

NAKUM

Biotopo El Zotz-

San Miguel-

La Pelotada

YAXHÁ

Laguna
Sacnab

Laguna
Yaxhá

San
Román

Cerro Cahui
National
Park

TOPOXTE

San
Andrés

Lago Petén Itzá

El Remate

Ixlú

Monterrey

Naranjo

El
Zapote

FLORES

Santa
Elena

River

Mopán

Guatemala itself, much like the Eiffel Tower and Paris. Perhaps not as readily apparent, Tikal National Park also represents the ongoing effort to protect what remains of Petén's tropical forest ecosystem. The park is at the edge, geographically speaking, of the Maya Biosphere Reserve, but at the very heart and soul of what conservationists and archaeologists are trying to protect. The conservation of Petén's rich archaeological and natural treasures has the potential to provide a livelihood to a growing population of *peteneros* long after any perceived benefits from clearing the forests for short-term gain. The lessons learned from Tikal's 50-plus-year existence can help conservationists better manage newer parks deeper inside the forest reserve, which will eventually be open to increasing numbers of visitors. Whatever the approach to managing these newer parks, what is certain is that Petén's vast

wealth as the heartland of the Mayan civilization remains largely untapped.

If you are fortunate enough to visit Tikal, go home with the knowledge that you have been afforded a glimpse into the vast wilderness that remains mostly untouched north of this complex. In the forests beyond Tikal are countless other sites, some still undiscovered, which deserve as much protection and require the vigilance of international travelers and activists to ensure their continued preservation.

History

Tikal was settled somewhere between 900 and 700 B.C. on a site undoubtedly selected because of its position above seasonal swamps that characterize much of the terrain in this part of Peteén, as well as the availability of flint for trade and the manufacture of tools and weapons. It remained little more than

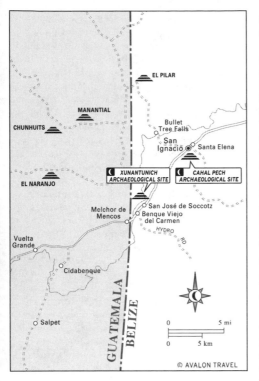

of Tikal until recorded history at the site goes silent in A.D. 869.

The history of Tikal is closely tied to the emergence of Teotihuacán, a powerful city-state to the north in Central Mexico, which it should be noted was completely non-Mayan in origin. Its influence began to be felt during the middle of the 4th century A.D., when Teotihuacán dispatched a warrior by the name of Siyak K'ak' (Born of Fire) to aid Tikal in its war against the neighboring city of Uaxactún. Siyak K'ak' introduced the use of the atlatl, a wooden sling that allowed Tikal's warriors to defeat their enemy by firing arrows without having to engage in hand-to-hand combat. The aid from the north, according to recorded texts chronicling the execution of Tikal's Jaguar Paw I, amounted to a military takeover with the installation of Yax Nuun Ayin I (Curl Nose or First Crocodile), of Teotihuacán royalty, who later married into Tikal's dynasty.

With Teotihuacán hegemony now firmly established, Tikal dominated central Petén for most of the next 500 years. It grew to become one of the richest and most powerful Mayan city-states, aided by its dominance of strategic lowland trade routes. Tikal's influence reached as far south as Copán and as far west as Yaxchilán.

At the same time, the city-state of Calakmul, just north of the Guatemalan border in present-day Mexico, began its assent toward regional dominance. As the power and influence of Teotihuacán waned in the 5th century A.D., Calakmul emerged as a geopolitical force to be reckoned with, incorporating a number of vassal states surrounding Tikal and contesting its dominion over the Mayan lowlands. A key alliance was forged between Calakmul and Caracol, in present-day Belize. Tikal launched a preemptive strike against Caracol in A.D. 556. With backing from Calakmul, Caracol launched a counterattack on Tikal in A.D. 562; the latter suffered a crushing defeat. Desecration of Tikal's stelae and ritual burials, in addition to the destruction of many of its written records, followed.

a small settlement for at least 200 years. By 500 B.C. the first stone temple was erected and later used as the basis for the large Pre-Classic pyramid dominating the complex now known as El Mundo Perdido. Tikal continued its steady progress during the late Pre-Classic Period, sometime around 200 B.C., with the construction of ceremonial buildings found in the North Acropolis and the completion of the pyramid at El Mundo Perdido.

CLASSIC PERIOD

By the time of Christ, Tikal's Great Plaza had begun to take shape, and by the Early Classic Period, around A.D. 250, Tikal was an important religious, commercial, and cultural center with a sprawling population. King Yax Ehb' Xoc established his dynasty at this time, one that was recognized by the 33 subsequent rulers

After this defeat, Tikal underwent a 130-year hiatus from erecting inscribed monuments, though it has recently been discovered that Temple V was constructed during this period. Mayanists now believe Tikal was never completely broken, despite defeat at the hands of its bitter rival.

HEIGHT OF POWER AND DECLINE

Tikal reemerged as a dominant power beginning in A.D. 682 under the new leadership of Hasaw Chan K'awil (Heavenly Standard Bearer), whose 52-year reign was marked by the definitive defeat of Calakmul in A.D. 695 with reassertion of control over regional satellite cities such as Río Azul and Waka' as well as a frenzy of new temple construction. The six great temples dominating Tikal's ceremonial center were reconstructed between A.D. 670 and 810 by Hasaw Chan K'awil and his successors.

At the height of the Classic Period, Tikal covered an area of about 30 square kilometers and had a population of at least 100,000, though some Mayanists believe it may have been much greater.

By the beginning of the 9th century A.D., conditions worsened for many city-states across the Mayan lowlands with the Classic Maya collapse in full swing. Tikal was no exception. The city-state's last inscription is recorded on Stela 24, which dates to A.D. 869. Tikal, like Petén's other Mayan cities, was completely abandoned by the late 10th century A.D. The city would be reclaimed by the jungle and largely forgotten until its rediscovery in the late 17th century.

REDISCOVERY

The Itzá who occupied the present-day island of Flores probably knew about Tikal and may have worshiped here. Spanish missionary friars passing through Peteén after the conquest mention the existence of cities buried beneath the jungle, but it wasn't until 1848 that the Guatemalan government commissioned explorers Modesto Méndez and Ambrosio Tut to visit the site. The pair brought along an artist, Eusebio Lara, to record their discoveries. In 1877, Swiss explorer Dr. Gustav Bernoulli visited Tikal and removed the carved wooden lintels from Temples I and IV. He shipped them to Basel, where they remain on display at the Museum für Völkerkunde.

Scientific study of the site would begin in 1881 with the arrival of British archaeologist Alfred P. Maudslay. His work was subsequently continued by Teobert Maler, Alfred M. Tozzer, and R. E. Merwin, among others. The inscriptions at Tikal owe their decipherment to the work of Sylvanis G. Morley. In the mid-1950s, an airstrip was built, making access to the site much easier. The University of Pennsylvania carried out excavations between 1956 and 1969, along with Guatemala's Institute of Anthropology and History. With help from the Spanish Cooperation Agency, Temples I and V have been restored as part of a project begun in 1991.

A relatively small part of Tikal has been officially discovered and excavated. New discoveries await, along with new information that will undoubtedly continue to shed light on the turbulent history of the Mayan civilization. Among the more recent discoveries are the 1996 unearthing of a stela from A.D. 468 in the Great Plaza and the location of Temple V inscriptions challenging the notion of Tikal's 130-year hiatus after its defeat against Calakmul.

Flora and Fauna

Tikal's abundant wildlife is most active early and late in the day, with birds and forest creatures more easily seen at these times. The summit of Temple IV, Tikal's highest structure, is a particularly popular place at sunrise and sunset. From your position high above the forest canopy, you can watch the sun dip below (or rise above) the horizon of unbroken tropical forest as far as the eye can see, while the chatter of myriad birds and forest creatures permeates the air. The roof combs of the Great Plaza pyramids pop out from the jungle canopy as toucans dart from tree to tree with their curious yellow beaks, like bananas with big black wings. More than 400 species of birds have been recorded at Tikal. *The Birds of Tikal,* by Frank Smithe (Garden City, NY: Natural History Press, 1986), is a useful guide in this regard.

Other animals you may come across during your visit include coatis, which you should refrain from feeding. If you spend the night here, don't be afraid if you awake to a raucous howling roar emanating from the forest. Sometimes confused with wild cats by first-time visitors, the sounds come from the locally abundant howler monkeys. During your explorations in Tikal, you will probably come across the smaller and ever-more-playful spider monkeys, which swing from tree to tree in the forest surrounding the ruins.

Among the park's most fascinating creatures are jaguars. Recent studies done over a two-month span have revealed the confirmed existence of seven of these large spotted cats within the national park's boundaries, and it is thought that at least nine roam its confines.

Exploring the Park

Many visitors come to Tikal on day trips from Belize, Flores, and Guatemala City. While a day at the ruins is adequate for seeing most of the archaeological highlights, staying at the park allows you to enjoy its equally splendid natural setting. After the crowds have departed, you'll be free to wander about the ruins unhurried, and at times you may feel as if you have the site all to yourself. The sunset from the top of Temple IV is truly inspiring but is now only an option in the winter months when the sun sets earlier, as park rangers make sure everyone is out by 6 P.M. For movie buffs, the view from Tikal's Temple IV can be appreciated in *Star Wars: Episode IV*, as the site of the rebels' secret base. The Great Plaza also made an appearance in the more recent movie *2012*.

The park's main gate is found along the road from Flores and El Remate, where there's a checkpoint. From here, it's another 17 kilometers to the main entrance, parking lot, and visitors center. Entrance to the park costs US$19 (US$3 for Guatemalan nationals) and is collected at the gate just opposite the parking lot. The park is open 6 A.M.–6 P.M. daily.

If you arrive after 3 P.M., your ticket should be stamped with the next day's date, allowing you to enter the ruins the next day at no additional cost. Tickets are checked at a booth on the trail between the visitors center and the entrance to the ruins proper, opposite an oft-photographed ceiba tree gracing the side of the road. Sunrise tours, once a popular activity, are no longer an option, as no one is allowed inside the park before 6 A.M.

The visitors center is at the main entrance to the park on your left. It offers a scale model of the site, the Museo Lítico, an overpriced eatery, and a few small shops selling books, souvenirs, snacks, and sundries, including color print film, bug spray, and sunscreen. Nearby are the park campsite, police substation, and a post office. The other museum is farther along, near the airstrip next to the hotels. You can book licensed guides at the visitors center for US$40 for up to four people, plus US$5 for each additional person.

The park website is www.tikalpark.com and has lots of very useful information for planning your visit.

The Ruins of Tikal

There is plenty to explore in this vast Mayan city, which once harbored thousands of people, and you could easily spend several days here taking it all in. The ruins in evidence today are representative of the latter years of Tikal's existence, as the Mayans built on top of existing temples and palaces. Most of the major structures you'll see were built after the time of Tikal's resurgence in the late 7th century A.D. Following is an incomplete list of a few of the attractions.

THE GREAT PLAZA

Most visitors to Tikal head straight from the park entrance to the Great Plaza, and if you are crunched for time this is probably the best approach. A path from the ticket control booth leads you to the plaza in about 20 minutes. You'll gain an appreciation for the site's elevated setting as you walk uphill toward the heart of the ceremonial center. The view

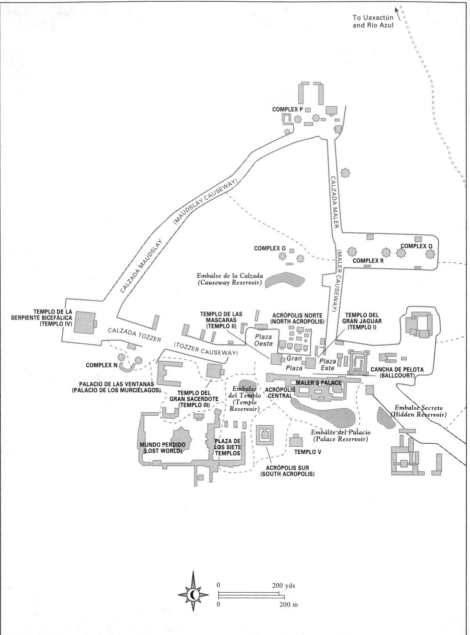

To Uaxactún
and Río Azul

COMPLEX P

(MAUDSLAY CAUSEWAY)

CALZADA MAUDSLAY

CALZADA MALER

(MALER CAUSEWAY)

COMPLEX O

COMPLEX Q

COMPLEX R

Embalse de la Calzada
(Causeway Reservoir)

TEMPLO DE LA
SERPIENTE BICEFÁLICA
(TEMPLO IV)

TEMPLO DE LAS
MASCARAS
(TEMPLO II)

ACRÓPOLIS NORTE
(NORTH ACROPOLIS)

TEMPLO DEL
GRAN JAGUAR
(TEMPLO I)

CALZADA TOZZER

(TOZZER CAUSEWAY)

Plaza
Oeste

Gran
Plaza

Plaza
Este

CANCHA DE PELOTA
(BALLCOURT)

COMPLEX N

PALACIO DE LAS VENTANAS
(PALACIO DE LOS MURCIÉLAGOS)

TEMPLO DEL
GRAN SACERDOTE
(TEMPLO III)

Embalse
del Templo
(Temple
Reservoir)

ACRÓPOLIS
CENTRAL

MALER'S PALACE

Embalse Secreto
(Hidden Reservoir)

Embalse del Palacio
(Palace Reservoir)

MUNDO PERDIDO
(LOST WORLD)

PLAZA DE
LOS SIETE
TEMPLOS

TEMPLO V

ACRÓPOLIS SUR
(SOUTH ACROPOLIS)

| 0 | 200 yds |
| 0 | 200 m |

CAYO

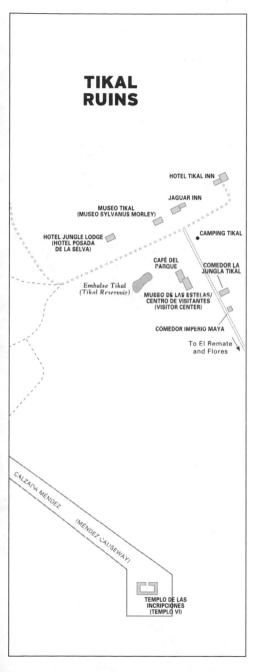

TIKAL
RUINS

HOTEL TIKAL INN

JAGUAR INN

MUSEO TIKAL
(MUSEO SYLVANUS MORLEY)

HOTEL JUNGLE LODGE
(HOTEL POSADA
DE LA SELVA)

• CAMPING TIKAL

CAFÉ DEL
PARQUE

COMEDOR LA
JUNGLA TIKAL

Embalse Tikal
(Tikal Reservoir)

MUSEO DE LAS ESTELAS/
CENTRO DE VISITANTES
(VISITOR CENTER)

COMEDOR IMPERIO MAYA

To El Remate
and Flores

CALZADA MÉNDEZ

(MÉNDEZ CAUSEWAY)

TEMPLO DE LAS
INCRIPCIONES
(TEMPLO VI)

from the back of Temple I as you approach the Great Plaza is always impressive at first sight, as it gives you an idea of the sheer size of the monuments erected by the Mayans. Tourist brochures and posters can never adequately convey just how large and impressive Tikal's temples are.

The path continues alongside the temple and you are at once greeted by the magnificent Temple II, which faces Temple I, as you enter the large, grassy plaza. Also known as "El Gran Jaguar" (The Great Jaguar), Temple I rises to a height of 44 meters (144 feet). The imposing structure was erected to honor Hasaw Chan K'awil (Heavenly Standard Bearer), the ruler who successfully led Tikal to victory against Calakmul. It was built to harbor his remains and was completed shortly after his death in A.D. 721 by his son and successor, Yik'in Chan K'awil, probably with instructions from his father.

The tomb was situated at the temple's core and contained the ruler's remains surrounded by jade, stingray spines, seashells, and pearls, which were typical of Mayan burials. It was believed the instruments would aid the person in his journey into the underworld. This journey is depicted on a bone fragment, also found in the tomb, showing a royal figure in a canoe rowed by mythical animal figures. Tikal's museum harbors a reconstruction of the tomb, known as Tumba 116. The door lintel depicting a jaguar, found at the top of the pyramid and from which the temple gets its name, was carried off to a museum in Basel, Switzerland.

It was once possible to climb Temple I, but this has not been allowed for several years now. The view from the top was truly spectacular, with Temple II in the foreground and the roof combs of Temples III and IV protruding from the jungle behind it. The structure was closed to climbers partly because of damage caused by a chain aiding in this activity, though the death of at least two visitors after tumbling down its steep steps certainly put the final nail in the coffin. The view from the top was popular in tourism posters and brochures from the early

CAYO

© JOSHUA BERMAN

The ruins of Tikal should be seen at dawn, while there is still mist in the trees as the sun hits the temples.

CAYO

1980s, and you can still sometimes see them in unexpected places.

Across the plaza stands the slightly smaller **Temple II,** built to honor Hasaw Chan K'awil's wife, Lady 12 Macaw. Also known as the Temple of the Masks for the large, severely eroded masks flanking its central staircase, it is thought to predate Temple I by a few years. As recently as five years ago, a staircase was constructed on its side to allow access to the top, though you could once climb directly up its central staircase. The view from the top is still as good as ever, with a frontal view of Temple I and the North Acropolis off to the side. Temple II probably once stood at the same height as its counterpart when its roof comb was intact, though its restored height is 38 meters (125 feet).

TEMPLE IV AND COMPLEX N

Continuing along the Tozzer Causeway, which is one of the original elevated walkways connecting various parts of the city, you'll come across Complex N on the left. Complex N is a twin-temple complex of the variety frequently constructed by Tikal's Late Classic rulers, supposedly to commemorate the passing of a katun, or 20-year cycle in the Mayan calendar. Found here is the beautifully carved **Stela 16,** showing Hasaw Chan K'awil in a plumed headdress. The complex was built in A.D. 711 to mark the 14th katun of baktun 9, a baktun being roughly 400 years. **Altar 5,** also found here, depicts Hasaw victoriously presiding over sacrificial skull and bones with a lord from one of Calakmul's former vassal states. The corresponding text also mentions the death of Lady 12 Macaw, Hasaw's wife.

Farther along, you'll come to the colossal Temple IV, the tallest of Tikal's temples at 65 meters (212 feet). Like the Great Plaza's temples, it was completed in A.D. 741 by Yik'in Chan K'awil and may have served as his burial monument, though there is no concrete evidence as of yet. In addition to offering the best views of the site from its summit, it is known as the origin of some excellent lintels depicting a victorious king surrounded by glyphs. As in the case of the lintels from Temple I, you'll now have to travel to Basel if you want to see the originals. A replica of Lintel 3 is in Guatemala City's archaeology museum.

The climb to the top of the temple up a series of wooden ladders attached to its side can be described as simply breathtaking, both for the effort required and for the spectacular views of the forest on all sides.

THE LOST WORLD COMPLEX
Known in Spanish as El Mundo Perdido, this complex is strikingly different from the rest of the site owing to its Pre-Classic origins, which may help to shed light on Tikal's early history. The area is dominated by the presence of a 32-meter pyramid, its foundation dating as far back as 500 B.C., when it served as an astronomical observatory similar to the one found at Uaxactún. The structure now in evidence marks the top of four layers of construction. There are fabulous views of the Great Plaza and Temple IV from the top, though the stone central staircase on the temple's steep face can be slippery after it rains. Exercise due caution.

Museums
Tikal's two museums are, oddly, in different parts of the park. The first of these is the **Museo Lítico** (9 A.M.–noon and 1–4:30 P.M. Mon.–Fri., 9 A.M.–4 P.M. Sat. and Sun., free admission), housing stelae and carved stones from the archaeological site with a scale model outside showing what the city probably looked like around A.D. 800. There are some interesting photos taken by explorers Alfred Maudslay and Teobert Maler showing Tikal's temples overgrown by a tangle of jungle vines and branches as they looked when they were first discovered.

The **Museo Tikal** (9 A.M.–5 P.M. Mon.–Fri., 9 A.M.–4 P.M. Sat. and Sun., US$1.35), across the way next to the Jaguar Inn, has some interesting exhibits, including the burial tomb of Hasaw Chan K'awil found inside Temple I. It may have been renovated by the time you read this.

Recreation
In addition to exploring the ruins, there are recreational opportunities in and around Tikal National Park.

CANOPY TOUR
You have a choice of two zip-line trajectories between raised platforms in the jungle at **Tikal Canopy Tour** (tel. 502/5819-7766, www.canopytikal.com, 7 A.M.–5 P.M. daily, US$30, at the national park entrance). The first of these includes 11 platforms with zip lines ranging in length 75–150 meters while you dangle 25 meters over the forest floor. The second, more adrenaline-inducing option, includes zip lines up to 200 meters long hovering 40 meters above the safety of ground level. Pick your poison.

BIRD-WATCHING
Specialty tours for bird-watchers can be arranged by contacting **La Casa de Don David** (tel. 502/7928-8469 or 502/5306-2190, www.lacasadedondavid.com) in El Remate. The lodge's knowledgeable staff can connect you with good English-speaking local guides who know the park and its birds. Another recommended outfitter is Guatemala City–based **Cayaya Birding** (tel. 502/5308-5160, www.cayaya-birding.com).

Accommodations and Camping
Lodging at Tikal National Park is limited by law to three lodges and a campground. An increasing amount of competition from accommodations at nearby El Remate has spurred the Tikal hotels toward higher standards while keeping prices relatively reasonable. There are few places in the world where you can stay in a comfortable jungle lodge inside a national park just minutes away from a UNESCO World Heritage Site.

Electricity at the park is sporadic, with accommodations and other facilities having to limit the hours during which this convenience is available. Power is usually turned on in the morning for 2–3 hours and then again in the evening shortly after sunset for another three

CAYO

hours. If you need to use a computer provided by one of these facilities for checking email or need to recharge digital/video camera batteries or cell phones, you should plan accordingly. If you absolutely need a fan to cool your room while you sleep overnight in the humid Petén jungle, you may want to stay outside the park, as ceiling fans go silent once the electricity turns off. It can get very hot here, even at night. None of the lodges have air-conditioning.

Coming from the ruins, the first place you'll come across is the **Jungle Lodge** (tel. 502/2476-8775, www.junglelodge.guate.com, US$40–80 d), offering decent bungalows with private hot-water bath, ceiling fan, and two double beds as well as a few very basic, less expensive rooms with shared bath. All are set amid a pleasant tropical garden atmosphere and there is a swimming pool. The restaurant here serves breakfast (US$5), lunch, and dinner (US$8–10). Tour groups often lunch here. Be advised the lodge is closed every year during September. As you head toward the old airstrip just past the museums, you'll reach the friendly **Jaguar Inn** (tel. 502/7926-0002, www.jaguartikal.com), where you can choose from nine comfortable bungalows with small front patios with hammock (US$53 d), a dormitory (US$10 pp), hammocks with mosquito netting (US$5), or camping (US$3.50). You can rent a tent for US$7. The restaurant here is a safe bet, serving adequate portions of good food three meals a day. Dinner is about US$8. There are laptops available for Internet surfing and checking email (US$5/hr), but the electricity shuts off at 9 P.M. Next door, **Tikal Inn** (hoteltikalinn@itelgua.com, US$60–100 d) gets consistent praise for its large, comfortable rooms centered around the swimming pool just behind the hotel's restaurant. You can choose from standard rooms or pricier, more private bungalows; all have ceiling fans and private baths. The restaurant serves three meals a day.

Tikal's **campground** is opposite the visitors center with a spacious grassy area for tents as well as palapa structures for stringing hammocks. There are showering stalls among the bathroom facilities. Hammocks and mosquito netting are available for rent, and there are tiny, two-person basic cabanas (US$6.50 pp). It costs US$4 per person to camp here.

Food

Your best bet for food is at one of the three lodges on-site, but there are *comedores* (eateries) here serving basic yet passable fare in adequate portions for about US$5 for a full meal and a drink. The menus are virtually indistinguishable from one another and are heavy on local staples such as beans, eggs, and tortillas. The restaurant at the visitors center, **Restaurant Café Tikal,** is fancier but a bit overpriced, and you are probably better off eating at one of the lodges if you're not on a small budget. It serves pasta, steaks, chicken, and sandwiches and is open until 6 P.M. daily. The other *comedores* are across from the visitors center on the right-hand side as you enter the park from the main road. They include **Comedor Tikal, Restaurant Imperio Maya,** and **Comedor Ixim K'ua,** all of which open early for breakfast and close at 9 P.M. daily.

As for the hotel restaurants, the large dining room at the **Jungle Lodge** is a popular stop for lunch with tour groups. As such, it tends to offer dependable set-menu lunches of meat or chicken dishes accompanied by rice and salad for about US$8. Dinner options include a varied assortment of meat dishes, pasta, and sandwiches. The **Jaguar Inn** caters largely to the international backpacker crowd and makes a particularly decent place for good-value dinners, including tasty pastas and desserts. The **Tikal Inn** gets props for its hearty breakfasts with good, strong coffee, but there are better options for lunch and dinner.

Getting There and Away
BY AIR

Flights to Flores are available from Belize City, Guatemala City, and Mexico City. Flights from Belize's Philip Goldson International Airport are scheduled on Tropic Air (US$186 round-trip). The airport in Flores is small but modern. From the airport, there are vehicles to drive you to the ruins.

BY GROUND

Most Belize tourists who sign up for a trip to Tikal will have all their transportation taken care of, either in a private shuttle from Belize City or San Ignacio or directly from their resort or lodge. Independent (i.e., patient and tolerant) travelers should also have no problem piecing together their own route to the ruins or to any of the nearby towns.

The road in Guatemala is terrible, and it will take about 1.5 hours to reach the entrance to Tikal National Park, after which the road is excellent for the final 30 kilometers to the site itself. There is no direct public transportation from the Belize border to Tikal (except in chartered taxis and minibuses, a good option for groups). The only bus that runs from the border is a Guatemalan public bus that goes to Flores. You can spend the night there and take the morning bus to Tikal (board in front of the San Juan Hotel). The border-to-Flores bus is usually very crowded with chickens and the works. Or get off at the crossroads in Ixlú, where another northbound bus can whisk you to El Remate or all the way to Tikal.

BY BUS FROM BELIZE CITY

You can always go to Novelo's, catch a local bus to the border, then walk across and go it alone from there, making all your own connections. If, however, you are less confident in your Spanish and would rather go direct for a few dollars more, there are at least four small, private tour companies, all based at various kiosks in the Water Taxi Terminal by the Swing Bridge in Belize City, that offer direct bus service to Chetumal, Mexico, and Flores and Tikal, Guatemala. They are: **S & L Travel and Tours** (tel. 501/227-7593 or 501/227-5145, sltravel@btl.net, www.sltravelbelize.com), **Mundo Maya Deli, Gifts, Travel & Tours** (tel. 502/501/223-1235, mundomayatravel@btl.net), and **Kaisa International** (tel. 501/602-1031). Daily, direct service is available to both Flores (US$15) and Tikal (US$20). It takes about 4.5 hours to either one, although border hassles can increase that time significantly. From Flores, it's another 8 hours or so to Guatemala City, 12 to Antigua.

EL REMATE

El Remate starts about one kilometer past the turnoff to Yaxhá and the Belize border on the road from Santa Elena to Tikal. Once considered a stopping point along this road, El Remate has come into its own in recent years and has begun to pull its fair share of the Petén travel market. Its proximity to Tikal, fabulous lakeside setting, and variety of accommodations makes it a wonderful alternative to staying at Tikal or Flores, or better yet, a destination unto itself worthy of at least one night's stay.

Shopping

El Remate is also a great place to pick up local crafts, consisting of some very attractive wood carvings made from fallen logs and providing a sustainable alternative to wide-scale forest destruction for agriculture. You'll find several handicrafts shops on the main strip along the road to Tikal.

Recreation

Bird-watching tours with knowledgeable, English-speaking local guides can be arranged from La Casa de Don David (tel. 502/7928-8469 or 502/5306-2190, www.lacasadedondavid.com) and cost US$40–75 for a three- to six-hour tour. In addition to Cerro Cahuí, trips are available across the lake to roosting sites and other birding areas up the Río Ixpop and Río Ixlú.

Most of the area lodges can arrange **horseback riding** to Ixlú and Laguna Salpetén for about US$20 per person. Casa Mobego (tel. 502/5909-6999) does **walking tours** to Laguna Salpetén for US$10 per person and rents double **kayaks** for about US$4 for one hour or US$8 for four. Casa de Doña Tonita (tel. 502/5701-7114) also rents kayaks for about US$2 an hour and **mountain bikes** for US$5 a day. Alternatively, La Casa de Don David can arrange almost anything you can think of and also sells discount tickets to area **canopy tours.**

There are some wonderful **swimming** docks around the lake, the best of these at Restaurante El Muelle along the main road, in front of the Cerro Cahui Biotope, and in front of Casa Mobego.

Accommodations

You'll find plenty of accommodations along El Remate's main drag beside the northbound Tikal road as well as along the dirt road diverting west that hugs the lakeshore, including a number of campgrounds and hostels with mats and beds for under US$10.

US$10-25

¶ Hostal Hermano Pedro (tel. 502/2261-4181, www.hhpedro.com) is a charming little place with a friendly Guatemalan owner. Rustically comfortable wooden bedrooms with high ceilings, hot water, and private baths cost US$12 per person, including breakfast. Rooms have patios with chairs and hammocks and there is a small restaurant serving three meals a day. On the ground floor there are several *piletas*, or small pools, for soaking among the tastefully decorated garden festooned with orchids. There is an additional sitting room with hammocks where you can catch the breezes off the lake.

Along the lakeside road toward Cerro Cahuí, at the junction with the road leading to Tikal, is **¶ La Casa de Don David** (tel. 502/7928-8469 or 5306-2190, www.lacasadedondavid.com), a highly recommended establishment owned by a native Floridian transplanted to Guatemala in the late 1970s. His friendly wife and daughter help run the lodge, consisting of 15 rooms with private hot-water bath set amid nicely landscaped grounds. Eleven of the rooms have air-conditioning; all have fans. Rates range from US$32 double for slightly noisier rooms with fan under the restaurant to US$52 double for quieter rooms with air-conditioning set farther back from the main house. All prices include one free meal a day. The restaurant serves delicious international dishes ranging US$4–8 for lunch or dinner. The friendly staff can help you book transportation to virtually anywhere and can answer your travel questions. You can also snag discounted tickets for area canopy tours at the attractive gift shop in the main lobby. The hotel's very informative website is well worth checking out before visiting Petén.

Near the entrance to the Cerro Cahui preserve, my favorite of El Remate's new hotels is **¶ Posada del Cerro** (tel. 502/5376-8722, www.posadadelcerro.com, US$40–56 d). It's a great value and a great place to get away from it all. The comfortably rustic rooms are not lacking anything in style. Some feature cool stonework, while others have angled thatch-roof ceilings. There are also more modern apartments with full kitchen available. There's a small restaurant where guests can enjoy meals or simply hang out under the palapa roof.

US$50-100

Straight out of a West Texas cowboy's dream is **¶ Palomino Ranch Hotel** (tel. 502/7928-8419 or 502/2474-0758, www.hotelpalominoranch.com, US$50 d), with cool western-inspired decor that's tastefully done and includes quirky antiques. There's even an old jukebox. Rooms are housed in a large hacienda-style building centered round a swimming pool and have hot water and air-conditioning. The lodge organizes horse-riding trips to area attractions, and there is a daily horse show in its large horse pen. The lodge is on the Cerro Cahuí road about one kilometer from the junction with the main Tikal-bound highway.

For Petén's ultimate in style and luxury, head to fabulous **¶ La Lancha** (tel. 502/7928-8331, www.blancaneaux.com), farther west along the lakeshore in the village of Jobompiche. Part of movie director Francis Ford Coppola's impressive portfolio of properties, including two other hotels in Belize, La Lancha is Petén's best-kept secret. Its 10 comfortable rooms are housed in lake-view casitas (US$150–210 d) or rainforest casitas (US$120–175 d, depending on season). All rooms have exquisite Guatemalan fabrics and Balinese hardwood furniture. The rooms' wooden decks are graced with hammocks where you can lounge the day away watching the sky's reflection on placid Lake Petén Itzá or order drinks from the bar via your in-room "shell phone." Rates include a continental breakfast, and the restaurant serves gourmet Guatemalan dishes for lunch and dinner for about US$20 per person.

FLORES, GUATEMALA

In the heart of Petén, the twin towns of Flores and Santa Elena are often referred to simply and collectively as "Flores," the latter actually being limited to a small island on Lake Petén Itzá connected to Santa Elena, on the mainland, by a causeway. Flores is a pleasant island town unlike any other in Guatemala, with pastel houses and quiet streets. Santa Elena is a bit noisier and more chaotic because of its prominence as Petén's main commercial center. Farther west, Santa Elena runs into the downright ugly town of San Benito.

Flores is the natural starting point for a visit to Petén's wild interior, as it is the region's transportation and services hub. Many NGOs are based here, and the quiet streets are lined with a variety of shops, restaurants, and comfortable lodgings. While Flores is excellent from a logistical standpoint and entirely attractive, it has been somewhat displaced in recent years by the emergence of El Remate, a lakeside town on the road to Tikal that is convenient for travelers to and from Belize. Still, there are a number of local attractions that make spending at least one day in the Flores area worthwhile.

YAXHÁ-NAKUM-NARANJO NATURAL MONUMENT

This park encompasses the Mayan sites of Yaxhá, Topoxté, Nakum, and El Naranjo. Most prominent of these is Yaxhá, which gained international fame in 2005 with the filming of *Survivor Guatemala*. The park was closed for two months, during which time contestants lived among the ruins eating corn, plotting ways not to get voted off, and fighting off mosquitoes. Only El Mirador and Tikal are bigger than Yaxhá (8 A.M.–5 P.M. daily, US$10 admission includes entrance to Nakum), and

its isolated setting on a limestone ridge overlooking the lagoons of Yaxhá and Sacnab is simply splendid. Despite its TV fame, you can still wander the site with nary another visitor in sight. Don't even think of swimming in the lakes here, as they have a healthy population of rather large crocodiles.

Yaxhá

The relative lack of inscribed monuments found at Yaxhá has made tracking its history a bit of a challenge, though it appears it was a major player during the Classic Period. It is believed Yaxhá was locked into an ongoing power struggle during much of this time with its smaller neighbor, Naranjo, about 20 kilometers northeast. Yaxhá's sphere of influence was almost certainly limited by the proximity of Tikal, and the architecture here shows many similarities to that of Tikal. Naranjo eventually overran Yaxhá in A.D. 799. Spanish friars passed through here in 1618, and Austrian explorer Teobert Maler visited in 1904. Much of the site remained unexcavated until recently. A German-Guatemalan effort is conducting the site's ongoing excavation and restoration. Other worthy archaeological sites in the area are Topoxté and Nakum.

The parking lot and restrooms are on the east side of the park near Plaza C, along with a small museum. There are two boat docks here, one below the parking lot and one at the western end of the site.

Accommodations

You can camp for free at **Campamento Yaxhá,** a designated lakeside campsite below the ruins proper. A more comfortable option is the friendly **Campamento Ecológico El Sombrero** (tel. 502/7861-16878, www.eco-sombrero.com), about 200 meters from the main road before you come to the park entry post. Its 13 comfortable rooms are housed in thatched-roof bungalows fronting the lake. There's a dock, but it's not recommended for swimming because of the crocodiles. A restaurant serves adequate food, with the variety of menu items on offer heavily dependent on

CAYO

whether or not there's a group staying at the lodge. If you're just stopping by, you'll probably end up eating pasta, which actually seems a delicacy when you're in the middle of the jungle. The lodge arranges boat trips to **Topoxté** and guided tours of Yaxhá.

Getting There

A series of roads leads to Yaxhá. About 31 kilometers east of Ixlú, on the road toward the Belize border, a well-marked turnoff leads a further 11 kilometers north to the Yaxhá guardpost, where you pay admission and sign in to the park. It's another three kilometers from here to the actual ruins of Yaxhá. The road is in good condition, even during the rainy season. If traveling by bus, you can get off at the junction to Yaxhá and hitch a ride with an occasional passing pickup truck or fellow travelers. There is some traffic along this route because of the presence of the small village of La Máquina, about two kilometers from the park guardpost.

Several of the Flores tour operators now do Yaxhá with certain frequency. You can also get a minivan from El Remate to the site, but expect to pay about US$60 round-trip. Try to find people to share the ride.

SOUTHERN COAST: DANGRIGA TO PLACENCIA

Stann Creek District is made up of a wide range of habitats. To the east: underwater worlds surrounding scores of Caribbean cayes, or islets. To the west: wildlife, birds galore, rivers, and ruins in the shadow of Belize's highest peaks. Between them: miles of beaches, swamps, citrus plantations, shrimp farms, and—in a few areas—condominium developments aimed at rich foreigners.

The seaside town of Dangriga is home to a third of Stann Creek District's 36,000 inhabitants. Stann Creek's economy is as varied as its culture and geography, with tourism being as important as the orange, banana, and shrimp industries. In Dangriga town and the surrounding villages, the Garinagu (or Garifuna) people survive and thrive as they confront the challenges of maintaining their unique culture. Spanish-speaking fishers paddle through the cayes, diving for lobster and conch for days on end. And this region includes a few full-on tourist destinations like Placencia, with its pleasant village and handful of upscale resorts, or low-key, slack-paced settlements like Hopkins and Sittee River. All of these areas serve the traveler as bases from which to explore nearby cayes, coral, and the Cockscomb Basin and Jaguar Reserve.

PLANNING YOUR TIME

There's not much to see in 'Griga, as the town Dangriga is known, except a typically multiethnic array of Belizeans going about their daily lives. Still, many travelers are glad they chose to spend a night here on their way to or from **Tobacco Caye, South Water Caye, Thatch Caye,** or **Glover's Reef.**

© SCOTT SCHMIDT

HIGHLIGHTS

◖ Gulisi Garifuna Museum: The long-awaited cultural attraction is on the outskirts of Dangriga and offers an interactive history lesson on the proud Garinagu (Garifuna) people (page 176).

◖ Tobacco Caye: Sitting right atop Belize's barrier reef, Tobacco Caye can be as much a social gathering of world travelers as it can an isolated island experience, depending on the time of year (page 180).

◖ Hopkins: This village is on an ultra-tranquil stretch of beach and can serve as a mellow base for kayaking, diving, sailing, windsurfing, fishing, and other trips – or for just doing nothing on the beach (page 185).

◖ Cockscomb Basin Wildlife Sanctuary: Go for a nature hike and river float in this extensive reserve, famous for its multitude of birds, jaguar tracks, and other jungle critters. Stay overnight or do it as a day trip from anywhere in the area (page 191).

◖ The Sidewalk Strip: In Belize's low-key tourist hangout, Placencia, check out the world's narrowest street – it's 4,071 feet long and four feet wide. Walking its length offers ample opportunities for shopping, eating, and getting a sense of village life (page 198).

◖ Laughing Bird Caye: Palms, sand, snorkeling, and sun are found at this national park, part of a 10,000-acre protected marine area (page 210).

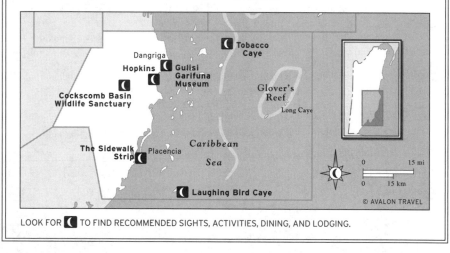

LOOK FOR ◖ TO FIND RECOMMENDED SIGHTS, ACTIVITIES, DINING, AND LODGING.

Want to plant yourself in the sand and have drinks brought to you for a week? Pick a resort, any resort—there are plenty of respected properties throughout the region, covering all budgets. Camp primitively in the jungle or recline in the lap of luxury. There is enough in this one district of Belize to entertain a curious traveler for weeks.

Start in either Dangriga, Hopkins, or Sittee River; take a drumming lesson and sample some home-brewed bitters. Then turn to the hills, trekking to a waterfall in Mayflower Bocawina National Park and spending a night in Maya Centre, a village where you can shop for crafts, converse with herbal healers, and arrange an expedition within the **Cockscomb Basin Wildlife Sanctuary** with a local guide whose last gig was leading a National Geographic team in the same area.

Then pop over to the shoreline and charter

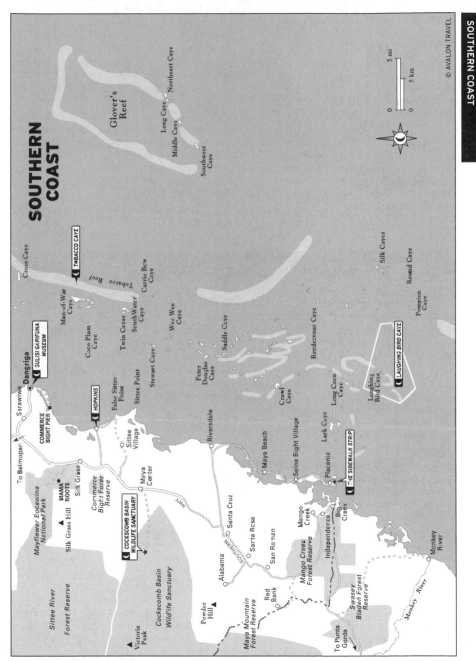

SOUTHERN COAST

Glover's Reef

Northeast Caye
Long Caye
Middle Caye
Southwest Caye

5 mi
5 km
0
0

TOBACCO CAYE

Crose Caye
Tobacco Reef
Carrie Bow Caye
Man-of-War Caye
Coco Plum Caye
Twin Cayes
South Water Caye
Wee Wee Caye
Saddle Caye
Silk Caves
Round Caye
Pompion Caye
Rendezvous Caye
LAUGHING BIRD CAYE
Laughing Bird Caye

GULISI GARIFUNA MUSEUM
Dangriga
Saraviwe
To Belmopan
COMMERCE BIGHT PIER
HOPKINS
False Sittee Point
Sittee Point
Stewart Caye
Peter Douglas Caye
Riversdale
Crawl Caye
Long Coco Caye
Lark Caye
Maya Beach
Seine Bight Village
Placencia
THE SIDEWALK STRIP

Silk Grass
MAMA NOOTS
Commerce Bight Forest Reserve
Sittee Village
Meya Center
Santa Cruz
Mango Creek
Big Creek
Independence
Monkey River

Mayflower Bocawina National Park
Silk Grass Hill
COCKSCOMB BASIN WILDLIFE SANCTUARY
Sarta Rosa
San Ro nan
Mango Creek Forest Reserve
Monkey River

Sittee River Forest Reserve
Cockscomb Basin Wildlife Sanctuary
Victoria Peak
Powder Hill
Alabama
Red Bank
Maya Mountain Forest Reserve
Swasey Bladen Forest Reserve
To Punta Gorda

SOUTHERN HWY

a sailboat or attempt to photograph a whale shark. Finally, run your boat aground on the Placencia Peninsula and rent a cheap cabana in which to recuperate.

HISTORY

The indigenous population of southern Belize dates back 3,600 years, and the Mopan Maya are still well represented, especially in towns like Maya Centre and other villages in these hills. The earliest white settlers were Puritans from the island of New Providence in the Bahamas. These simple-living people began a trading post (also known as a "stand," which over time deteriorated to "Stann") and spread south into the Placencia area. The town's destiny was drastically altered when the first boats of Garifuna people reached the shore from Roatán.

Over the millennia, rivers and streams gushing from the Maya Mountains have deposited a rich layer of soil, making the coastal and valley regions ideal farming areas. A disease called "Panama Rot" wiped out the once-thriving banana industry here, but with new technology, a strain of bananas has been developed that appears to be surviving. Otherwise, it's all about the oranges. Stann Creek's citrus industry produces Valencia oranges and grapefruits, which are then processed (on site) into juice—one of Belize's most important exports.

Dangriga

"Mabuiga!" shouts the sign in Garifuna, welcoming you to this cultural hub and district capital. Built on the Caribbean shoreline and straddling North Stann Creek (or Gumagarugu River), Dangriga's primary boast is its status as the Garifuna people's original port of entry into Belize—and their modern-day ethnic center. But although the majority of Dangriga's 12,500 or so inhabitants are Garifuna descendants of that much-celebrated 1823 landing, the rest are a typically rich mix of Chinese, Creoles, mestizos, and Maya, all of whom can be seen interacting on the town's main drag.

Aside from Dangriga's ideal location for accessing the surrounding mountains and seas—and the limited, barely adequate tourist services available to do so—its chief attraction may just be its total lack of pretense. Dangriga (formerly known as Stann Creek Town) does not outwardly cater to its foreign visitors as does Placencia or San Pedro—there is simply too much else going on in this commercial center, including fishing, farming, and serving the influx of Stann Creek villagers who come weekly to stock up on supplies. Consequently, this area is still relatively undeveloped for tourism, which is either a shortcoming or an attraction, depending on what kind of traveler you are.

If poking around the casually bustling vibe of Dangriga (which, by the way, means something like "sweet, still waters" in Garifuna) sounds intriguing, you'd do well to stay a couple nights. And if it's culture you're looking for, just listen for the drumming.

ORIENTATION

As you pull into town, three massive ceremonial *dugu* drums of iron will greet you. This is the "Drums of Our Fathers Monument," erected in 2003 as a symbol of Garifuna pride—and as a call to war against the ills of society. Turn right to reach the deep dock at Commerce Bight, left (north) to enter Dangriga Town. Heading north from the drums on St. Vincent Street, the old bus terminal is on your left before the first bridge. Continuing, you'll find more shops and eateries, culminating in the center of town on either side of the North Stann Creek Bridge; crossing the bridge, St. Vincent Street turns into Commerce Street and offers an informal market often set up along the north bank of the river. Catch a boat to the cayes from one of several places here. The

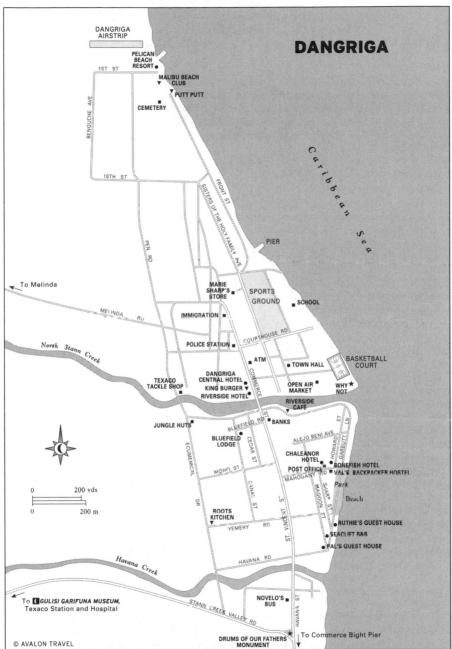

DANGRIGA

DANGRIGA AIRSTRIP

PELICAN BEACH RESORT
1ST ST
MALIBU BEACH CLUB
PUTT PUTT
CEMETERY
BENGUCHE AVE
10TH ST
PEN RD
FRONT ST
SISTERS OF THE HOLY FAMILY AVE

Caribbean Sea

PIER

To Melinda

MELINDA RD

North Stann Creek

MARIE SHARP'S STORE
SPORTS GROUND
SCHOOL

IMMIGRATION

POLICE STATION
COURTHOUSE RD

ATM
TOWN HALL
BASKETBALL COURT

TEXACO TACKLE SHOP
DANGRIGA CENTRAL HOTEL
KING BURGER
RIVERSIDE HOTEL
COMMERCE ST
OPEN AIR MARKET
WHY NOT

RIVERSIDE CAFÉ

JUNGLE HUTS
BLUEFIELD RD
BANKS
BLUEFIELD LODGE
CEDAR ST
ALEJO BENI AVE
CHALEANOR HOTEL
POST OFFICE
BONEFISH HOTEL
VAL'S BACKPACKER HOSTEL
HOWARD ST
GARBUTT LN

ECUMENICAL DR
MOHO ST
CANAL ST
MAHOGANY RD
SHARP ST
MAGOON ST
Park
Beach

0   200 yds
0   200 m

ROOTS KITCHEN
YEMERY RD
ST. VINCENT ST
RUTHIE'S GUEST HOUSE
SEACLIFT B&B
PAL'S GUEST HOUSE

HAVANA RD

Havana Creek

To GULISI GARIFUNA MUSEUM, Texaco Station and Hospital

NOVELO'S BUS
HAVANA ST
STANN CREEK VALLEY RD

To Commerce Bight Pier

DRUMS OF OUR FATHERS MONUMENT

© AVALON TRAVEL

airstrip is a mile or so north of Stann Creek, where you'll also find Pelican Beach Resort, Dangriga's fanciest digs.

SIGHTS

Dangriga does not offer many traditional "sights," per se, but there is plenty going on, and the town makes a good base for excursions around the region. You can browse the few crafts and music stores on St. Vincent Street, and ask around for the drum-making workshops, one of which is sometimes set up at the **Why Not** compound by the beach at Stann Creek. Drums are often heard throughout the town to mark celebrations and funerals; sometimes it's simply a few people practicing the rhythms of their history. Seeking out the town's workshops can be a fun activity, and if you've got the cash, expect to walk away with an instrument of your own. Austin Rodriquez is known for his authentic Garifuna drums. Other local artists of national prominence include painter Benjamin Nicholas and Mercy Sabal, who makes colorful dolls that are sold all over the country.

☾ Gulisi Garifuna Museum

The museum (tel. 501/669-0639, ngcbelize@gmail.com, 10 A.M.–5 P.M. Mon.–Fri., 8 A.M.–noon Sat., US$5) is a mile west of town, on the south side of the highway; you'll see it on your right when driving into Dangriga, next to the thrusting Chuluhadiwa Garifuna Monument (taxi from downtown US$2–3). The small, four-room display is packed with a wealth of information and an interesting collection of artifacts; feel free to talk history with the curator, Peter Ciego. The museum is named after the person thought to be the first Garifuna woman to arrive and settle in Dangriga. She had 13 sons, and many of Dangriga's modern residents believe they are descended from her. In 2008, the "language, dance, and music of the Garifuna" was inscribed on UNESCO's Representative List of the Intangible Cultural Heritage of Humanity.

Marie Sharp's Store and Factory

Be sure to save time to stop by **Marie Sharp's**

Store (in Dangriga, a few blocks north of Stann Creek Bridge, tel. 501/522-2370, 8 A.M.–5 P.M. Mon.–Fri.) to stock up on the area's famous hot sauce and other products; purchase hot sauce for a tiny fraction of the normal retail price. Better yet, make the trip to **Marie Sharp's Factory** (tel. 501/520-2087, www.mariesharps-bz.com), where you'll be offered a free tour of the farm and factory. This is a true Belizean success story: The factory sits on a 400-acre estate. To find it, drive west on the Hummingbird Highway from Dangriga about eight miles and turn right after you cross a bridge and see the White Swan on your left.

Gra Gra Lagoon National Park

This 1,197-acre wetland and mangrove forest reserve includes a 300-acre brackish lagoon that is best explored in a canoe or kayak. Inquire at the **Friends of Gra Gra Lagoon** office (tel. 501/502-0043 or 501/600-6222, gglagoon@yahoo.com), diagonally across from the old bus station.

Tour Operators

A few operators run trips to nearby trails, waterfalls, caves, and other attractions up the Hummingbird Highway, including those at Five Blues Lake and Billy Barquedier National Parks. For ideas of what to do and a wealth of local wisdom, award-winning **C & G Tours and Charters** (29 Oak St., tel. 501/522-3641 or 501/610-2277, www.cgtourscharters.com) will take care of all your needs. C & G is a locally owned and highly recommended tour operator who speaks many languages and is experienced at taking everyone from single travelers to groups around the area.

ENTERTAINMENT AND EVENTS

Dangriga is home to the Warribaggabagga Dancers, the Punta Rebels, the Turtle Shell Band, and the Griga Boyz, among other nationally known party bands. The music and dancing, including syncopated African-flavored rhythms, features interesting mixtures of the various southern Belize cultures.

There is often live music on weekends at **Griga 2000,** right near the main bridge, and sometimes at the **Malibu Beach Club** on the north end of town. Be advised that karaoke, especially to American country music, is very popular 'round these parts.

The biggest celebrations of the year are Garifuna Settlement Day (November 19), Boxing Day (December 26), and New Year's Day, when you'll find plenty of drumming, dancing, and drinking in the streets. Local hotels are often booked up to a year in advance for dates in November, because of Garifuna families visiting from the United States. At other times of the year, many hotels can arrange a special cultural event for you.

ACCOMMODATIONS
Under US$25

Dangriga's main drag has a handful of low-budget options, including the **Riverside Hotel** (north end of bridge on Commerce St., tel. 501/660-1041, US$12.50 pp). Pick one of the front rooms for a chance of a breeze; all have shared bath, wood floor, and fans. A better budget bet is **Val's Backpacker Hostel** (www.valsbackpackerhostel. com, tel. 501/502-3324, valsbelize@yahoo.com, US$11 pp). Val is a cheerful and friendly host who loves meeting her guests from around the world and putting them up in one of her cement bunkrooms; each bed has a fan and locker to stash your gear. The communal lounge area has a chess table, book exchange, and movie library. Amenities include wireless Internet, bikes for rent (US$5/day), and laundry service, and it's all very close to a pleasant park overlooking the ocean. Val can help arrange a fishing trip, transfer to Tobacco Caye, a night wildlife tour, or language and cultural exchange opportunities.

Bluefield Lodge (6 Bluefield Rd., tel. 501/522-2742, bluefield@btl.net, US$15–35) is an excellent choice. The owner, Miss Louise, has six furnished rooms with private baths, TV, fans, and hot and cold water for US$25 double; everything about the place reflects the pride and care Miss Louise takes in her lodge. She also offers great local maps and a helpful information board.

Pal's Guest House (868 Magoon St., tel. 501/522-2095 or 501/522-2365, palbz@btl. net), around the corner from the bus station, has 16 clean, modest cement rooms at the corner of North Havana Road and Magoon Street. Rooms with shared bath in the back building cost US$17.50 for a double and are really basic. Seaside rooms (US$35) are better, with linoleum floors, ceiling fans, hot and cold private showers, TV, and balconies at the ocean's edge; louvered windows on both ends of the rooms create good cross-ventilation; wireless Internet and air-conditioning are available for extra cost. The Raati Grill has breakfast, lunch, and dinner options for guests.

US$25-50

At the towering **Chaleanor Hotel** (35 Magoon St., tel. 501/522-2587, chaleanor@btl.net, US$17–46), friendly owners Chad and Eleanor offer a homey atmosphere in a residential neighborhood. Economy rooms (US$16.50) are equipped with a bed and fan; bath and shower are shared. The well-used standard rooms have private baths with hot water, TV, and fans (air-conditioning optional). Laundry service is available. There's a gift counter in the lobby, and you can help yourself to coffee and bananas all day long. Numerous tour operators book their guests in the Chaleanor, sometimes arranging a drumming or dance session on the roof. Chad maintains an organic garden and tree nursery.

If you'd rather hear the waves lapping below your window, try one of the four stilted wooden cabanas at **Ruthie's** (tel. 501/502-3184, ruthies@btl.net, US$28), a good value if you snag one of the newer cabins. It's a 10-minute walk from the bus station; follow the sign from Magoon Street.

Jungle Huts Resort (4 Ecumencial Dr., tel. 501/522-0185, junglehutsresort@gmail.com) offers 13 rooms (US$39) and three cabanas (US$49) at its riverside location. All rooms have private baths, hot and cold water, cable TV, fans, and/or air-conditioning. Screened porches allow you to listen to the frogs in the evening without mosquitoes. The on-site

Garden of Eden Restaurant serves breakfast, lunch, and dinner to guests.

US$50-100

The **Seaclift Bed and Breakfast** (1738 Southern Foreshore, tel. 501/502-2350, US$75, breakfast included) has three nicely furnished rooms with full kitchen, living and dining room, library, and home gym at guests' disposal. Leonie likes to spoil her guests with breakfast, which includes coffee, juice, fruits, and the daily breakfast special. The place has a very nice, homey feel and is right on the beachfront.

The **Bonefish Hotel** (15 Mahogany St., tel. 501/522-2243, www.bluemarlinlodge.com, US$95) is near the water with seven rooms and a second-floor lobby and bar. It caters to active travelers who want to fish and dive—most guests continue on to **Blue Marlin Lodge** on South Water Caye, which is allied with the Bonefish. Rooms are clean and carpeted with private hot and cold water bathrooms, cable TV, wireless Internet, and air-conditioning.

Over US$100

'Griga's high end is found at the north end of town at the end of Ecumenical Drive, right next to the airstrip: **Pelican Beach Resort** (tel. 501/522-2044, www.pelicanbeachbelize. com, from US$135 plus taxes, includes breakfast) rests comfortably on the Caribbean. Its 17 rooms are open and well lit with wood and tile floors, bathtubs, and porches facing the ocean. Various packages are available that include meal plans, excursions, and time spent at the Pelican's sister resort on South Water Caye. This is a full-service accommodation with many amenities.

FOOD

Most of Dangriga's eateries are open only during meal times, so expect some closed doors in the middle of the afternoon and on Sundays, when only the Chinese restaurants are open. Your best value is probably **King Burger,** on the left as you cross the North Stann Creek bridge from the south (7 A.M.–3 P.M. and 6–10 P.M. Mon.–Sat.). It offers excellent ice cream, breakfast, fresh juices, sandwiches, shakes, and simple comfort dinners.

Another standby is the **Riverside Café** (7 A.M.–9 P.M. daily). It's popular with travelers (boats to the cayes leave from right outside) and a gathering spot for local fishers. Grab a table or belly up to the bar and order a Guinness with your eggs and beans to fit in with the locals.; it's US$4.50 for stew chicken, US$6 and up for fish and shrimp. For something different, try the cassava fries.

If you want cheaper food, walk back to the main drag and grab a fistful of street tacos for a few coins. Street barbecues are another common sight, offering a plate of grilled chicken with flour tortillas, baked beans, and coleslaw for about US$2.50. There are a few local shacks with great dishes for US$3 and under; start with **Roots Kitchen** back on Ecumenical Drive, just a wooden shack with real Belizean food, open all day from 6 A.M.

For Chinese the best are **Starlight** (8 A.M.–11 P.M. daily, closed afternoons), on the north end of Commerce Street, and **Sunlight,** with good food and crappy service on the south end of Commerce Street. There is "fry chicken to take" at any number of Chinese shops.

Dangriga's only proper restaurant is found at the **Pelican Beach Resort** (tel. 501/522-2044, www.pelicanbeachbelize.com) on the north end of town, where delicious food is prepared by Creole cooks and served in the dining room or in an open beachside eating area. The happy hour on Thursday and Friday is 5–9 P.M. and is very popular, especially on the 15th and 30th of each month (paydays).

SERVICES

Belize Bank (8 A.M.–1 P.M. Mon.–Thurs., 8 A.M.–4:30 P.M. Fri.) and **Scotia Bank** (similar hours, but also open 9 A.M.–noon Sat.) are on St. Vincent Street near the bridge, and First Caribbean is across the bridge; all have ATMs. Mail your postcards at the **post office** on Mahogany Road.

Val's Laundry and Internet (tel. 501/502-3324, 7:30 A.M.–7 P.M. Mon.–Sat., plus Sun.

mornings) is near the post office on Sharp Street; laundry is US$1 per pound to wash, dry, and fold. Fast and friendly satellite Internet is available for US$2.50 an hour, as well as FedEx service, local information, and organic, fresh-squeezed juices.

Health and Emergencies

Southern Regional Hospital is just out of town and services the entire population of Stann Creek District (tel. 501/522-2078 or 501/522-2225, dannhis@btl.net).

GETTING THERE AND AWAY

Dangriga is on the coast, only 36 miles south of Belize City as the crow (or local airline) flies. However, the land trip is much longer, roughly 75 miles along the Manatee Road or 100 miles via the Hummingbird Highway.

By Air

Maya Island Air (tel. 501/223-1140, U.S. tel. 800/225-6732, mayair@btl.net, www.mayaislandair.com) and **Tropic Air** (tel. 501/226-2012, U.S. tel. 800/422-3435, reservations@tropicair.com, www.tropicair.com) have a number of daily 20-minute flights between Belize City and Dangriga. It's also possible to fly between Dangriga, Placencia, and Punta Gorda.

By Boat

Boat service from Belize City is entirely custom arranged—they tried running a regularly scheduled shuttle, but it didn't make money. Ask around the docks by the Texaco station, at your hotel, or at the Belize Tourism Board. Expect to pay a decent sum for this trip (probably US$100 each way). Service to and from local cayes or other coastal villages is also dependent on how many people want to go. Only two passengers are required to make the trip to Tobacco Caye (US$35 each); ask around the Riverside Café or Texaco Station Tackle Stop. Captain Doggie will charter 1–3 persons for US$70; groups of 4–12 can expect to pay US$17.50 per person.

By Bus

Bus service between Belize City and Dangriga takes close to three hours, including a stop in Belmopan, and costs US$6 each way; buses run between 4:30 A.M. and 5:30 P.M. There are a few expresses during the day, but the schedule is changing all the time.

There are eight daily southbound buses to Punta Gorda, from 8 A.M. to the day's only express at 5:30 P.M.—a three-hour trip. Buses to PG stop in Mango Creek; from there you can make a connection to Placencia on the water taxi. As of press time, there are three daily buses that go directly to Placencia: 11 A.M., 2 P.M., and 4:40 P.M. (2.5 hours). These buses used to always stop in Hopkins and Sittee River, but that schedule is in question, so ask around the station.

By Car

From Belize City, take the Western Highway to either the Coastal (Manatee) Road or Hummingbird Highway, which you'll follow till it ends. Taking the Coastal Road may shave 20 minutes off the Hummingbird Highway route—but the rutted, red-dirt surface may also destroy your suspension and jar your fillings loose. The unpaved Coastal Road is flat and relatively straight and is occasionally graded into a passable highway, but you'd better have a sturdy ride. Be prepared for lots of dust in the dry season and boggy mud after a rain. Numerous tiny bridges with no railings cross creeks flowing out of the west, and the landscape of pine savanna and forested limestone bluffs has nary a sign of humans (except for the crappy road, of course). About halfway to the junction with the Hummingbird Highway, you'll find a pleasant place to stop and take a dip at Soldier Creek; just look for the biggest bridge of your trip and pull over. Watch out for snakes in the bush, and once you reach your destination try not to spend those hard-earned extra 20 minutes all in one place.

Islands near Dangriga

◖ TOBACCO CAYE

If your tropical island dream includes sharing said island with a few dozen fellow travelers, snorkelers, divers, rum drinkers, and hammock sitters from around the world, then Tobacco Caye is your place. This tiny island, located within South Water Caye Marine Reserve, has long been a popular backpacker and Belizean tourist destination, especially for divers. Tobacco Caye is just north of Tobacco Cut (a "cut" is a break in the reef through which boats navigate). Guesthouse owners have boats to whisk you each day to snorkeling and fishing trips or to Man-O-War Caye and Tobacco Range to look for manatees. Glover's Reef, Blue Hole and Turneffe trips are available for US$150–200; whale shark tours are usually running March–July.

Accommodations

Tobacco Caye's "resorts" offer similar packages but for a range of budgets. All six places are Belizean-run family affairs, each a bit

© SCOTT SCHMIDT

a magnificent frigate bird, Tobacco Caye

different according to the owner's vision, and are comfortably crowded together on the five acres of sand. Apart from some basic differences in room quality, the more you pay, the better food you'll be eating—a pretty important thing when checking into a room that also locks you into a meal plan. Some of the accommodation prices are per person per night and include three meals; always ask to be sure.

Gaviota Coral Reef Resort welcomes you to "the Lifestyle of a Chosen Few" in one of four rooms or five cabanas (tel. 501/509-5032, US$45 pp, shared bath); there are three boats that can be used for visiting the reef and cayes. An on-site marine station often hosts visiting scientists, and you can ask to check out their reference materials on the area's habitats and species. There is also a snack shop and beach volleyball court.

Paradise Lodge (tel. 501/520-5101 or 501/621-1953, resmanagerdean@yahoo.com) occupies the northern tip of the island with rooms for US$12.50 per person and six cabins with porches built over the sea (US$48 pp); **Lana's on the Reef** (tel. 501/520-5036 or 501/522-2571) has four basic rooms for US$40.

Stepping things up a notch, find **Reef's End Lodge** (tel. 501/670-3919 or 501/522-2419, www.reefsendlodge.com) on the southern shore; rooms (US$40, meals not included) and cabanas (US$50) have fans and hot and cold water with private baths. The newest cabana (US$100) is clean, spacious, and has air-conditioning; take in the romantic sunset view from your seaside veranda. There is a bar and restaurant built over the water, and prepaid meal plans are available. Reef's End has the caye's only dive shop, which can be utilized by anyone on the island; this is an excellent location to begin a shore dive or snorkeling adventure. Dive master Eric can take you to his favorite local dive sites; two-tank dives range US$100–150.

Tobacco Caye Lodge (tel. 501/520-5033 or

Paradise Lodge, Tobacco Caye

501/623-0998, www.tclodgebelize.com, US$55 pp) occupies a middle strip of the island and offers three cabins facing the reef. Meals are included and a dinner bell will ring.

On the western side are the Sunset Bar and a popular swimming area. **Fairweather Place** (tel. 501/802-00300 or 660-6870, hevf7@yahoo.com, US$20 pp) has four basic rooms and camping; meals are not included.

Getting There and Away

Water taxis to Tobacco Caye leave when the captain says there are enough passengers—usually around midafternoon from the Riverside Café or the Tackle Stop farther upstream. **Captains Buck** (tel. 501/607-6578) is one option, or try Fermin, a.k.a. Compa (tel. 501/509-5032). The trip costs US$35 round-trip, with a return trip usually made midmorning. **Captain Doggie** (tel. 501/627-7443) is another and will charter 1–3 persons for US$70; groups of 4–12 can expect to pay US$17.50 per person. Compa has the newest, largest, and most comfortable boats. By calling ahead to Gaviota Coral Reef Resort, Reef's End Lodge, or Tobacco Caye Lodge you can arrange a pickup any time from Dangriga and ensure a boat will still be there if you are arriving after midday. Be advised; if you need a boat after 3 P.M., you'll pay a lot more—seas get rough and a private charter is necessary. Plan accordingly.

SOUTH WATER CAYE

South Water Caye is another postcard-perfect, privately owned island 14 miles offshore from Dangriga and 35 miles southeast of Belize City. The reef crests just a stone's throw offshore, sitting atop a 1,000-foot coral wall awash in wildlife. The island stretches three-quarters of a mile from north to south and one-quarter mile at its widest point.

The **Pelican Beach Resort** (tel. 501/522-2044, www.southwatercaye.com, US$258–292, includes three meals) occupies the entire southern end of the island, with five second-story rooms, three duplex cottages, and two single-unit cabanas. The beach is available to other island guests and offers some of Belize's

© SCOTT SCHMIDT

SOUTHERN COAST

best walk-in snorkeling sites. Power is from the sun, and composting toilets help protect the fragile island ecology. The owners also have a strip of island toward the north end that is home to **Pelican's University,** which hosts student research groups throughout the year. Plenty of day trips are available with Pelican's guides or with one of the island dive shops; they charge US$62 per person for the boat transfer to the island.

Lesley Cottages is the common name for **International Zoological Expeditions** (IZE, tel. 501/523-7076, U.S. tel. 800/548-5843, www.ize2belize.com, US$175 pp). Named for an old local fisherman, Dan Lesley, the compound here specializes primarily in student groups and "educational tourism" but also has some nice, exclusive cabins in addition to their own dive shop, dormitory, classroom, and the like. Beautiful rooms are nestled on the shoreline; included are three meals and transport. It's a great spot for couples (but check to see if you'll be sharing with student groups).

Blue Marlin Lodge (tel. 501/520-5104, U.S. tel. 800/798-1558, www.bluemarlin-lodge.com), sister resort of the Bonefish Hotel in Dangriga, offers a variety of rooms, air-conditioned igloos, and cabanas just steps away from the sea. The bar/dining room over the sea serves meals, snacks (included), and drinks (three meals roughly US$60). The Blue Marlin specializes in fishing trips, plus has a full dive shop, cable TV, and Internet. Many packages are available with a three-night minimum stay.

CARRIE BOW CAYE

This dot of sand and palms, close to both the reef and mangrove systems, is home to the Smithsonian Museum of Natural History's **Caribbean Coral Reef Ecosystems Program,** which, since 1972, has produced over 800 published papers. The caye houses up to six international scientists at a time. The public is welcome to check things out, but only if you arrange something first through your host on South Water Caye or elsewhere.

THATCH CAYE

I've heard nothing but excellent reviews from visitors to **Thatch Caye Resort** (tel. 800/435-3145, www.thatchcayebelize.com), an island complex nine miles from Dangriga, within the South Water Marine Reserve. The "handmade eco-resort" consists of four casitas and seven cabanas (with en suite bathrooms, king beds, ceiling fans, and plenty of lounging room), which were constructed without the use of heavy equipment. They're run by solar and wind. There's also a family villa and a soaring thatch-roof dining palapa. Various all-inclusive snorkeling packages requires a three-night minimum stay (US$611–775); that means all meals, three guided snorkeling trips, unlimited use of sea kayaks, and round-trip water transfer from Dangriga. Camping is allowed on the island for US$15 per person; you must have your own equipment and are welcome to join other guests in the dining room for meals.

GLOVER'S REEF ATOLL

The southernmost of Belize's three atolls, Glover's (named for a pirate, of course) is an 80-square-mile nearly continuous ring of brilliant coral, flanked on its southeastern curve by five tiny islands. The atoll is 18 miles long and 6 miles across at its widest point; to the east, the ocean bottom drops sharply and keeps on dropping, eventually to depths of 15,000 feet at the western end of the Caiman Trench, one of the deepest in the world.

The southern section of the atoll around the cayes serves as a protected marine reserve; however, someone should remind the government Fishery Department rangers on Middle Caye of this fact, as they reportedly skip patrols and ignore illegal fishing activity (although they're very efficient at collecting tourist fees).

Divers and snorkelers will find a fabulous wall surrounding the atoll, plus more than 700 shallow coral patches within the rainbow-colored lagoon. There are wreck dives and an abundance of marine life, especially turtles, manta rays, and all types of sharks, including reefs, hammerheads, and whale sharks. The names of the dive sites speak for themselves:

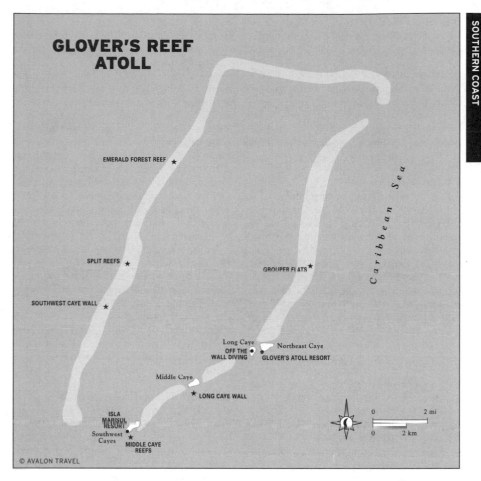

Shark Point, Grouper Flats, Emerald Forest Reef, Octopus Alley, Manta Reef, Dolphin Dance, and Turtle Tavern.

Anglers will have a chance at bonefish and permit, as well as the big trophies, including sailfish, marlin, wahoo, snapper, and grouper. There is also fantastic paddling, sailing, and anything else you can dream up. Glover's is a special place indeed.

Southwest Caye

The first bit of land you'll reach from the mainland is owned by the Usher clan, which runs the high-end, full-service **Isla Marisol Resort** (tel. 501/520-2056, toll-free tel. 866/990-9904, www.islamarisolresort.com) for serious divers and sport fishers. There are comfortable, equipped cabanas, or stay in the reef house. Many all-inclusive packages are available (three-night minimum required).

Island Expeditions (U.S. tel. 800/667-1630, www.islandexpeditions.com) is an adventure travel outfitter with a tent camp on the north tip of Southwest Caye; it's a well-run, professional operation and a great option if you like meeting other travelers and bonding with them on a group trip.

Middle Caye

No accommodations here, unless you're a Belize Fisheries Department ranger or a marine biologist with the Wildlife Conservation Society. If staying on one of the surrounding cayes, ask your host about arranging a trip to see what's going on here.

Long Caye

The 13 acres here form the gorgeous backdrop to **Slickrock Adventures**' thatch-roof base camp (U.S. tel. 800/390-5715, www.slickrock. com); check out the website for a range of active Belize adventures. Slickrock has a veritable armada of kayaks, sailboards, and other water toys; conditions and equipment will cover beginners and experts alike. Guests stay in very private rustic beach cabins overlooking the reef and equipped with kerosene lamps, foam-pad mattresses, and great views. Outhouse toilets are of the *plein air* variety, surrounded by palm leaf "walls"—offering possibly the best views from a WC in the entire country. Book a trip to the island, or link the trip with wild inland adventures as well (call for a catalog).

Off the Wall Dive Center (tel. 501/614-6348, www.offthewallbelize.com) is a PADI 5-Star Resort, where you can stay on Long Caye in an ocean-front rustic cabana with access to a top-notch dive shop, gift shop, and yoga deck. Maximum capacity is only 10 guests. Package prices include seven days' lodging, boat transport, meals, diving, snorkeling, fishing, kayaks, and stand-up paddle board. Whale shark trips and PADI scuba certification courses are popular; yachties are welcome to come ashore and browse the gift shop.

Northeast Caye

This island is owned and run as **Glover's Atoll Resort and Island Lodge**, a primitive island camp run by the Lomont family, which also has **Glover's Guest House** in Sittee River (tel. 501/520-5016 or 501/614-7177, www.glovers.

com.bz). Their 68-foot catamaran takes you from Sittee River to Glover's most remote caye, where you will camp or shack up for the cheapest weekly rates on the atoll: US$149 for a week of camping, US$199 to stay in the dorm, US$249–299 for rustic thatch cabins perched over the water. These per-person prices include transport, a week's worth of primitive lodging, use of the kitchen, and nothing more, not even water. Show up at the guesthouse in Sittee River at 7 A.M. Saturday, and be prepared for the week. It's best to bring your own food, drinking water, and a few camping basics (lighter, can opener, etc.) or pay at least US$30/day to be served. A dive shop and kayak rentals are also available and the snorkeling is out of this world.

Note: According to reader mail I receive—and to the copious online reviews and trip reports about Glover's Atoll Resort—guests either love or hate this experience, and a few have reported safety concerns, hidden charges, and personality clashes with Glover's Atoll Resort staff. However, many of these readers would still recommend the experience because the environment really is that stunning.

OTHER NEARBY CAYES

Man-O-War Caye (Bird Isle) is a bird-choked, raucously chirping clump of protected mangroves that is a crucial nesting site for frigates and brown boobies. Nearby, **Coco Plum Island Resort** (U.S. tel. 512/786-7309, www.cocoplumcay.com) boasts 10 bright cabins on a 16-acre private island that is associated with the Belizean Dreams resort in Sittee; they specialize in exclusive romantic packages.

Wee Wee Caye, affiliated with the Possum Point Biological Station, on the mainland near Sittee River, hosts a tropical field station, marine lab, and educational center, with a neat system of raised catwalks through the mangroves (beautiful, but lots of bugs). The caye also hosts a population of boa constrictors; contact Paul and Mary Shave about bringing your students here (tel. 501/523-7021, www. marineecology.com).

South of Dangriga

◖ HOPKINS

Hopkins was built in 1942 after a hurricane washed away Newtown just up the coast; it is a loose coastal fishing village steering more and more toward tourism. Ignore the monstrous condos going up on either end of the Hopkins coast road—nearly everything in between remains chill, spread out, and reasonably priced. Hopkins's thousand or so inhabitants are mostly Garifuna, making this one of the more exciting places to be for Garifuna Settlement Day (November 19).

With the advent of new resorts and time-share condos in Sittee, and the continual trickle of backpackers that still show up in Hopkins village proper, there are a few decent makeshift art galleries and craft shops along the main drag. Other than that, there really aren't any sights beyond those that make up everyday village life. On a Saturday night, this means drinking beer and bitters, playing drums and dominoes, and laughing away another hot, breezy day. Of course, things pick up considerably on festival days, Christmas, and Easter Week (expect rooms to be in high demand during these times).

Orientation

The road that carries you into town from Dangriga also splits Hopkins into Northside (or "Baila") and Southside (or "False Sittee"). Northside is a bit more dense with local flavor and Southside hosts most of the places to stay and eat.

Recreation

For diving, make plans through the dive shop at **Hamanasi Adventure and Resort** (tel. 501/520-7073, U.S. tel. 877/522-3483, www.hamanasi.com). For snorkeling or fly-fishing, **Noel Nuñez** (tel. 501/523-7219 or 502/609-1991) is your man, located in his tour shack at the Watering Hole. Most guesthouses in Hopkins rent kayaks and other small craft. **Windschief Windsurfing School and Rental** (www.windschief.com, open daily except Thurs. at 1 P.M.) has a nice selection of windsurfing boards of various sizes for rent and offers lessons for all levels.

AN's Snorkeling Gear Rentals (tel. 501/523-7290) has snorkeling gear for US$5 per day and offers snorkeling trips; US$50–75 per person depending on group size. **Bullfrog Tours** (office next to Driftwood Pizza, tel. 501/669-0046) has boat charters and activities such as fishing, snorkeling, and caye hopping. If you want to explore inland, let **Charlton Castillo** (tel. 501/661-8199 or 501/503-7799) be your guide to the Cockscomb or Mayflower Bocawina National Park.

HOPKINS AND SITTEE RIVER

HOPKINS BAY RESORT
DRIFTWOOD BEACH BAR AND PIZZA SHACK
LEBEHA DRUMMING CENTER
To Southern Highway (4 mi)
INTERNET
LARU BEYU
KING CASSAVA'S
RANSOM'S
THONGS CAFE
WINDSCHIEF
HOPKIN'S INN
SEAGULL'S NEST
WHISTLING SEAS
YUGADAH INN & CAFE
WATERING HOLE
TIPPLE TREE BEYA
ALL SEASONS GUESTHOUSE
CHEF ROB'S GOURMET CAFÉ
JUNGLE JEANIE'S BY THE SEA
SCALE NOT AVAILABLE
HAMANASI DIVE & ADVENTURE RESORT
BELIZEAN DREAMS
JAGUAR REEF LODGE
ALMOND BEACH
PARROT COVE LODGE
BEACHES AND DREAMS/ BARRACUDA BAR & GRILL
False Sittee Point
Boom Creek
SITTEE RIVER VILLAGE
TOUCAN SITTEE
BOCATURA
GLOVER'S GUESTHOUSE
INTERNET
To Southern Highway
Anderson's Lagoon
SITTEE RIVER MARINA/ GAS
Sittee Point
Caribbean Sea
© AVALON TRAVEL

Entertainment

King Cassava's (tel. 501/608-6188 or 501/503-7305, 7 A.M.–midnight daily, with a two-hour afternoon break) is at the intersection where the road from Dangriga meets the sea. Here you'll find a bar, restaurant, taxi service, pool hall, and bus stop (when the buses are running, anyway). Lobster dinners go for US$10, shots of bitters are a buck, and they also serve finger-lickin' barbecue. It's a great place to meet the parade of local characters. For karaoke, visit the **New Town Bar** on Back Street. Thursday through Sunday you may find other music or entertainment around Hopkins.

The **Lebeha Drumming Center** (www.lebeha.com, tel. 501/665-9305), way up on Northside (*lebeha* means "the end" in Garifuna), is a notable drumming school, where Garifuna drum master Jabbar Lambey offers both private (US$15/hr) and group lessons (US$12.50 pp for two hours). Call to schedule a lesson, and once you're there, ask about the time Grateful Dead drummer Bill Kreutzmann popped in for a jam.

Shopping

There are many talented wood carvers and drum makers in Hopkins. While strolling through the village you'll find several small shops, including **Joy Jah's Arts Center, David's Woodcarving,** and **Kulcha Gift Shop.**

Save time for a walk or bike ride just south of the village to pay a visit to **Sew Much Hemp,** where Barbara, a dreadlocked Oregonian, will teach you anything you need to know about the plant that can save the world—she's got excellent hemp products for sale as well. If sand flies are out, this is a great place to pick up some natural repellent.

Accommodations

UNDER US$25

In Northside, budget travelers love the **Lebeha Drumming Center** (www.lebeha.com, tel. 501/665-9305), which has campsites (US$5) and a couple of shared-bath stilted wooden rooms (US$15); they are very simple (ceiling fan, no hot water, mosquito net, and tea kettle).

There is wireless Internet. Lebeha also has three furnished cabanas on the beach—with kitchenettes, hot showers, and porches (www.hopkinscabanas.com, US$49–65 plus tax). Ask about dive package opportunities they are forming with local providers. **Yugadah Inn** (yugadahinn@yahoo.com, tel. 501/503-7089, US$15) is another budget option; there are four rooms and a common area.

US$25-50

Walking south from King Cassava's, you'll come across the eccentric, garden-choked **Ransom's Cabana** (cabanabelize@hotmail.com, US$30). A bit farther, there are two very pleasant stilted cabanas at 【 **Windschief** (tel. 501/523-7249, www.windschief.com, US$25–40), right next to owner Oliver's Internet bar and windsurfing school.

From the main junction, head south on the road (or beach), and you'll find several decent clusters of beachside cabins, including **Seagull's Nest** (tel. 501/523-7245 or 501/663-5976, jc-seagulls@yahoo.com, US$27–33) with shared-bath doubles and nice common space, with a full kitchen, dining area, and TV. Guests can rent bikes.

【 **Tipple Tree Beya** (tel. 501/520-7006 or 501/668-3604, www.tippletree.com) is a long-time favorite, a well-maintained spot right on the beach, with rooms from US$40 with private bath, en suite two-bedroom options US$75, or a private cabin with kitchenette US$50. There are lovely hammock-adorned porches and palapas. Half-day or full-day kayak (US$15–20) and bike (US$5–9) rentals available. Ask about inland tours or snorkeling trips.

US$50-100

Whistling Seas Vacation Inn (tel. 501/661-3013 or 501/662-7271, Williams_marcello@yahoo.com) offers three private cement rooms with fridge and fan (US$49; US$54–65 with air-conditioning). Whistling Seas is classy for the neighborhood, with a restaurant and beach bar.

Laru Beya (tel. 501/523-7229 or 501/660-6908, US$50–75), meaning "on the beach" in

Garifuna, is centrally located and offers one of the best deals in the area. There are four cabins with tiled floors, kitchenettes, cable TV, and air-conditioning or a two-bedroom family unit with a full kitchen and living room. The downstairs is a maze of large wood carvings and a small gift shop.

The top of the line for midrange prices is (**€** **Hopkins Inn Bed & Breakfast** (tel. 501/523-7283, www.hopkinsinn.com, US$59), with four fully furnished cabanas (tiled floors, screened windows, fans, hot and cold water, kitchenette) and a nice breakfast of fruits and local pastries. It's a bargain for what you get. You'll also find good value at the **All Seasons Guesthouse** (tel. 501/523-7209, www.allseasonsbelize.com, US$43–75 includes tax and coffee, US$7 more per night if you turn on the air conditioning) It's not right on the beach, but it's not far from it, and the rooms are comfortable and nicely decorated. There's a barbecue pit to cook your own fish at the end of the day.

A short distance after the pavement of Hopkins village runs out, look for the left turn to **Jungle Jeanie's by the Sea** (tel. 501/523-7047, www.junglebythesea.com, US$55–120). This is a wonderful stretch of beach for guests staying in Jeanie's six spacious cabanas. The more secluded cabanas, located along a small network of jungle trails, have kitchenettes, private bathrooms, hot and cold showers, and verandas with a sea view; the Palmetto cabana, with three beds, is ideal for a family; and the treehouse cabana overlooks cocoplum and seagrape trees. Camping is US$15 per person. An on-site restaurant and bar serves breakfast and dinner daily (lunch available upon request), and there's a screened "jungle palapa" for yoga, torchlight drumming ceremonies, or anything else you feel like doing.

OVER US$100

On the northern tip of town, **Hopkins Bay Resort** (tel. 501/523-7320, U.S. tel. 877/467-2297, www.hopkinsbayresort.com, US$179–449) has one- and two-bedroom suites and luxury villas.

Food

There are five groceries and a produce stand in Hopkins, making it easier to stock up on nibbles and booze without breaking the bank; **Dong Lee's Supermarket** has the largest selection. The Garifuna women's group sells johnnycakes, bread, and Creole buns.

There are only a few eateries in Hopkins, most very low-key. Most obvious is **King Cassava's** (tel. 501/503-7305, 7 A.M.–midnight Tues.–Sun.), right at the main junction and providing a central, laid-back atmosphere. A bit south of there, **The Watering Hole** (tel. 501/614-8686), across from Tipple Tree, is very delicious. Down on Southside, you'll find good but slow food at **Innie's** (tel. 501/523-7026); also check out the **Yugadah Café** (tel. 501/503-7089 or tel. 501/503-7255, 6 A.M.–2 P.M. and 5–10 P.M. Thurs.–Tues.) and **Iris's** (tel. 501/523-7019, 8 A.M.–8:30 P.M. daily)—all have similarly relaxed menus and atmospheres.

(**€** **Chef Rob's Gourmet Café** (tel. 501/670-0445, 12:15–9 P.M. Tues.–Sun.) serves up menu items like coconut soup, rib-eye steak, lamb stew in dark beer, and lobster bisque flavored with cognac. Executive chef Rob Pronk also offers a four-course dining experience for around US$25. Full bar and wine list. Also on Hopkins's more upscale side, **Thong's Café** (tel. 501/662-0110, 8 A.M.–2 P.M. and 6–9 P.M. Wed.–Sat., 8 A.M.–2 P.M. Sun., US$3.75–13) serves bruschetta, eggplant parmigiano, and lasagna.

There are always a few fun and funky options on Northside as well, starting with the (**€** **Driftwood Beach Bar and Pizza Shack** (tel. 501/667-4872 or tel. 501/664-6611, www.driftwoodpizza.com, 11 A.M.–10 P.M. Thurs.–Tues., US$8–23), where you can have amazing wood-fired pizza and play beach volleyball. There's also the **Laruni Hati Beyabu Diner** (opens at 10 A.M.), with nice Belizean and Mexican dishes for US$4–6, right on the beach under a cool thatch roof (*laru ni hati* means "clear blue sky" and *beyabu* means "seaside"). Get your Chinese fix at **Rainbow Restaurant.**

Services

The **Windschief Internet** café and cocktail bar is where it's at, though many midrange hotels in Hopkins also offer computers and wireless service. **Inter-Plus Solutions** is a student-run Internet café in a building painted with the blue and yellow European Union colors.

Bring cash, as there are no banking services or ATMs in Hopkins; the closest are in Dangriga.

Getting There and Around

If you have your own transportation, getting to Hopkins is easy: just follow the Southern Highway until you see the well-signed turnoff on your left; from there it's a four-mile straight stretch of dirt road (which can be under water during intense rains). Figure 30–40 minutes' total drive from Dangriga.

There are a few daily buses from Hopkins to Dangriga (10:30 A.M. and 5:15 P.M. Mon.–Sat., US$2.50); buses return to Dangriga at 7 A.M., 7:30 A.M., and 2 P.M. Placencia buses used to go through Hopkins, but currently, there are no buses on the schedule going that route. A popular alternative is to get off the bus at the Hopkins junction and hitch a ride to the village or call for a taxi (tel. 501/669-5499). Otherwise it's an expensive hotel shuttle or local taxi—which can cost up to US$50 from Dangriga. Once in Hopkins, rent a scooter at All Seasons Guesthouse for US$38–50 a day; some people do this to get to the Mayflower reserve or other nearby hiking spots. Bike rentals are also easy to find and good for exploring the village.

FALSE SITTEE POINT

A few minutes' bicycle ride south from Hopkins village will bring you to a small oceanside strip of upscale resorts, restaurants, and condos. The water off the beach resorts at False Sittee can be muddy at times because of the proximity of emptying rivers and streams, and depending on the time of year, sand flies and mosquitoes can get fierce. Still, this is a popular spot to stay because of the quality of the lodges, as well as the location's direct access to so many inland and offshore attractions and activities.

Accommodations and Food

The most low-key option in this stretch of resorts along False Sittee Point is **《 Beaches and Dreams Seafront Inn and Pub** (tel. 501/523-7259, www.beachesanddreams.com, US$125, includes breakfast), whose four ample rooms have tiled floors, porches, and private bathrooms; ask about the new treehouse—great for families. The on-site restaurant, the **《 Barracuda Bar and Grill** (4 P.M. to 9 or 10 P.M. Wed.–Mon., bocce tournaments on Fri.) features chef "Alaska Tony" Marisco's amazing menu, including jerk smoked pork, aged beef, lots of seafood, and some of the best pizza this side of the Sittee River (US$15–25 pp dinner, US$25 for a large lobster pizza, US$12 for a cheese pie).

Another pleasant midrange option is next door at **Parrot Cove Lodge** (tel. 501/523-7225, U.S. tel. 800/207-7139, parrotcovelodge.com, US$130–250), with a handful of standard rooms and suites plus a few homes and villas for rent. Take a kayak out to sea or lounge by the pool. All the standard sea and land tours are available.

Awarded "Hotel of the Year 2010" by the Belize Tourist Board, **Jaguar Reef Resort** (tel. 501/520-7040, U.S. tel. 800/289-5756, www.jaguarreef.com, US$190–275) is a full-service accommodation with an ever-improving variety of spacious, comfortably furnished rooms and cottages. Next door, if you can afford it, there is a selection of ridiculously large luxury suites at **Almond Beach** (U.S. tel. 866/624-1516, www.almondbeachbelize.com, US$180–325). They have a large open dining space shared by the two properties; several pools and bars; plus bikes, kayaks, sand volleyball, and many activity-based packages. The ultra-luxe "beachfront vista suite" costs US$820 a night and includes a private chef. This is a popular spot for fancy weddings, especially with the addition of the **Butterflies Spa** (8 A.M.–7 P.M. daily, tel. 501/523-7291), offering a full range of treatments at about the same rates as back home. **Butterflies Coffee** has grinds from all over Central America, roasted fresh daily.

Belizean Dreams (tel. 501/523-7272, www.

belizeandreams.com, US$285–685) has nine beach villas with one- and two-bedroom suite options, along with two resort restaurants. Area tours are available.

(Hamanasi Adventure and Resort (tel. 501/520-7073, U.S. tel. 877/522-3483, www. hamanasi.com, US$275–350) is the area's premier diving operation. Sitting on 17 acres, including 400 feet of beachfront, Hamanasi offers eight beachfront rooms, four suites (including a honeymoon option), and nine deluxe treehouses tucked away in the littoral forest, all with views and tiled bathrooms, air-conditioning, fans, porches, and colorful Guatemalan bedspreads. Meals include delicious pasta and, of course, fresh seafood. If you're not into dive adventures, there's a pool, kayaks, bikes, and hammocks to use at your leisure. Hamanasi has a high occupancy rate; make reservations ahead of time.

Services
Sittee River Marina (tel. 501/523-7291, www. sitteerivermarina.com, 6 A.M.–6 P.M. daily) has oil, gas, diesel, snacks, and cold beer. They also deliver fuel at sea by request.

SITTEE RIVER
Sittee River is a peaceful, riverine corner of the country with its own calm mood. Sittee River qualifies as a village only in the loosest sense, with a few houses, Reynold's Store, some jungly places to stay, a few resorts, and more often than not, a few insects. Choose from several fully screened accommodations from which to soak up the thick, tropical tranquility. There are dive shops and boats to whisk you out to the cayes, excellent fishing (snook, tarpon, peacock bass, sheepshead, and barracuda), and, only 12 miles by road to the west, the entrance to the Cockscomb Basin Wildlife Sanctuary.

Near the soccer field, you'll find high-speed, air-conditioned Internet—and coffee, juice, beer, and gifts—at **Sittee River Internet** (www.sitteeriver.net).

Sports and Recreation
Sittee River Internet is also where you'll find

famed local guide **Horace Andrews** (tel. 501/603-8358, www.belizebyhorace.com), right across from his dock. Horace does river tours on the Sittee River, snorkel trips to the cayes, fishing trips to the cayes or lagoons, and inland tours such as Cockscomb, Mayflower, and Red Bank to see the scarlet macaws in season.

Bocatura Banks (tel. 501/606-4590 or 501/668-4590, U.S. tel. 207/288-3400, bocaturabank@yahoo.com) runs sailing charters on a 40-foot catamaran named *Toucan Play*. The boat can carry up to 20 people; an all-day snorkeling trip is US$75 per person, with park fees, food, and drinks all included. The owner, Alan Stewart, is a marine biologist, photographer, sailor, and dive master who first came to Belize in the mid-1980s. He also maintains four riverside cottages on his property in Sittee River, where he docks the boat. A restaurant provides meals in a nice setting, and many activities are available.

On the road to Bocatura, you'll also find **Diversity Cafe** (contact Martin or Jeanette at 501/523-7038). Their dive shop, **Second Nature Divers** (www.secondnaturedivers. com), is across from Almond Beach.

Accommodations and Food
Glover's Guest House (tel. 501/509-7099, www.glovers.com.bz) provides cheap, spartan lodging for both passersby and guests of the Glover's Atoll Resort. Stay in a cozy bunkhouse on stilts for US$9 per person, or in one of the private, stilted, screened-in riverside cabins for US$29; meals and a cooking area are available. Camping is US$5, tents provided. You can use the guesthouse's canoes and kayaks to explore the river.

Sir Thomas' at Toucan Sittee (tel. 501/523-7039 or 501/670-4892, www.sir-thomas-at-toucan-sittee.com, US$95) has six unique wood bungalows, including private bathrooms and hot water, comfy mattresses, and nice semi-outdoor jungle showers. The 18-acre property on the bank of the Sittee River is popular with birders, nature lovers, and families. You can camp on the grounds for US$20;

bring your own gear. Accommodations are set amid hundreds of fruit and other trees planted by the previous hosts. Ask about guided river and lagoon canoe trips—for fishing or just nature viewing. A major highlight is the spooky night canoe paddle up Boom Creek; this canopied waterway is filled with wildlife and jaw-dropping vegetation (and insects—be prepared).

Getting There

This area is about a 10-minute drive east of the Southern Highway through mostly orange orchards and riverside lots. There are *usually* two daily buses that drive through Sittee River and False Sittee Point, but this schedule is always up in the air; most accommodations will provide some sort of transfer from Dangriga. Driving south on the road from Hopkins, you'll pass through False Sittee, followed by the village of Sittee River, occupying a few bends of the slow, flat river of the same name.

MAYFLOWER BOCAWINA NATIONAL PARK

More than 7,100 acres of Maya Mountain wilderness were set aside in 2001, to protect and show off the area's waterfalls and green-fringed Maya ruins. The trail system offers excellent hiking and it's an adventurous climb to Antelope Falls. A walk in Mayflower can be combined with a day trip to Cockscomb (just to the south) or can easily fill a whole day or more. There is a campground at the park entrance (US$10 pp); bring your own gear.

The biggest challenge to enjoying Mayflower is simply getting to the trailhead, which lies 4.5 miles west of the Southern Highway with no public transport of any kind making the trip. The turnoff is just north of Silk Grass Village. The park office and interpretive center, where you'll register and pay US$5 per person, greet you when you arrive. The office is open 8 A.M.–4 P.M. daily.

For information, go to **Silk Grass Village**

and seek out Ramon and Doreen Guzman (tel. 501/503-7309). Ramon is a long-time park warden and Doreen is an officer in the **Friends of Mayflower Bocawina National Park,** an organization that co-manages the park with the government. Another contact is Genovivo "Gino" Peck, found in his Tsimin Chac thatch-roof restaurant on the Southern Highway in Silk Grass. Gino (tel. 501/668-7202) is a warden at Mayflower. If he can't take you into the park, he'll find someone who can.

In Dangriga, **C & G Tours and Charters** (29 Oak St., 501/522-3641 or 501/610-2277, www.cgtourscharters.com) can arrange a trip to Mayflower; in Sittee River, Horace Andrews is the best guide around (tel. 501/603-8358, www.belizebyhorace.com).

RED BANK

Tucked away on a red dirt road is the small Maya village of Red Bank. Here, at the edge of the Maya Mountains, rare and impressive scarlet macaws gather to feed on the ripe fruits of polewood trees outside the village. This annual phenomenon was unknown to outsiders until 1997, when conservationists learned 20 birds had been hunted for table fare; at that time it was thought Belize had a population of 30 to 60 scarlet macaws! In response, Programme for Belize worked with the village council to form the Red Bank Scarlet Macaw Conservation Group, led by the village leader Geronimo Sho.

The small community-based ecotourism industry offers visitors accommodations, meals, crafts, and guide services. A reserve has been established about a mile from the village and visitors must pay a small conservation fee; ask around for Mr. Sho. The best time to visit is sometime from mid-January to March, when the annatto fruits are ripe. As many as 100 scarlet macaws have been observed in the morning when the birds are feeding. Dial the Red Bank community phone (tel. 501/503-2233) if you would like to make a reservation at the **Red Bank Bed and Breakfast.**

The Cockscomb Basin

The land rises gradually from the coastal plains to the Maya Mountains; driving south on the Southern Highway, you'll see the highlands to the west and flatlands to the left, mostly covered by orange and banana groves. The highway passes through a few villages and soon delivers you to the area's prime attraction: Maya Centre village and Cockscomb Basin Wildlife Sanctuary. Heavy rain along the peaks of the Maya range (as much as 160 inches a year) runs off into lush rainforest thick with trees, orchids, palms, ferns, abundant birds, and exotic animals, including peccaries, anteaters, armadillos, tapirs, and jaguars.

◪ COCKSCOMB BASIN WILDLIFE SANCTUARY

Also commonly called the "Jaguar Preserve," this is one of the most beautiful natural attractions in the country. A large tract of approximately 155 square miles of forest was declared a forest reserve in 1984, and in 1986 the government of Belize set the region aside as a preserve for the largest cat in the Americas, the jaguar. The area is alive with wildlife, including the margay, ocelot, puma, jaguarundi, tapir, deer, paca, iguana, kinkajou, armadillo (to name just a few), and hundreds of bird species. The park is also home to the red-eyed tree frog and the critically endangered Morelet's tree frog. And though you probably won't spot large cats roaming during the day (they hunt at night), it's exciting to see their prints and other signs—and to know that even if you don't see one, you'll probably *be seen* by one.

Just past the entrance gate into the park is a gift shop and office where you'll be asked to sign in. Visitor facilities include a new interpretive center, picnic area, and outhouse. This protected area is managed by the Belize Audubon Society (www.belizeaudubon.org), which also conducts research and community outreach in support of conservation. Entrance is US$5 for non-Belizeans (pay at the highway, at the Maya Centre Women's Group craft shop

at the head of the access road, immediately off the Southern Highway), and the park is open 8 A.M.–4:30 P.M. daily.

Hiking the Trails

From the visitors center, many trails go off in different directions into the park. There are more than 20 miles of maintained hiking trails, which range from an easy hour-long stroll along the river to a four-day Victoria Peak expedition. An early morning hike on the Wari Loop offers the best chance to see wildlife and to admire the large buttress roots of the swamp kaway *(Pterocarpus officinalis)* trees. At the end of the Tiger Fern Trail you'll find an impressive double waterfall. Check out the front of the visitors center building for a detailed map. If you would like a guide, there are several renowned wilderness guides who grew up in these forests and who can be found up the road in Maya Centre. Bring your swimsuit; you'll find cool natural waterfalls and pools for a refreshing plunge. You can rent an inner tube and float down South Stann Creek. All visitors are also encouraged to bring sturdy shoes, a long-sleeved shirt, long pants, insect repellent, sunscreen, and plenty of water.

If you climb **Ben's Bluff,** you're not just looking out over a park where jaguars live—you're at the entrance of a forest that goes all the way into the Guatemalan Petén, part of the largest contiguous block of protected forest in Central America. The bluff was named after a Ben Nottingham, who monitored radio-collared jaguars with radiotelemetry. From here you can see Outlier Peak, a moderate one-day hike (about 8.5 miles round-trip) and great place to camp.

Victoria Peak

The second highest point in the country is the top of Victoria Peak (3,675 feet). Geologists believe the mountain is four million years old, the oldest geologic formation in Central America. Reportedly, area Maya populations

LOOKING FORWARD: THE JAGUAR'S FUTURE

The first scientist to research the jaguar population in Belize, Dr. Alan Rabinowitz, thought it would take several generations to see any ecological or cultural benefits of the Cockscomb Basin Wildlife Sanctuary's creation – but they occurred much more quickly. This was, he admits, partly due to luck: The formation of a protected area based on the jaguar's natural habitat (which was the first of its kind in the world) happened at a fortuitous time in Belize's history, basically at the very beginning of the country's efforts to attract more tourists. Cockscomb helped set the stage for the local preservation movement, giving a crucial boost to the country's fledgling ecotourism efforts.

Jaguar research continues in the Cockscomb Basin, only now the animals are tracked using infrared-triggered camera traps. Current data supports original density estimates that were based on radiotelemetry, which necessitated the invasive, sometimes harmful practice of physically capturing and collaring the cats and then tracking them from dangerous, low-flying airplanes. "The jaguar's prey are back," reports Rabinowitz, from behind a tiny, cluttered desk in his cramped office at New York's Bronx Zoo, where he is now Director of Science and Exploration for the Wildlife Conservation Society (WCS). "There are peccary all over the place and the jaguars are eating a lot, but their population density has stayed level – it's maxed out – even after 20 years. Also, we've found that the more protected area you give the jaguar, the less complaints there are of jaguars coming out after dogs and cattle – the opposite of what you'd expect."

Rabinowitz also notes that the Maya of the Cockscomb area now show natural curiosity about the big cats, instead of fear. Whereas before locals never entered the bush without a rifle, today they carry binoculars, pointing out jaguar tracks and exotic birds to groups of tourists. "Now I go back to Cockscomb and I see these young adults – sons of people I worked with – working as tour guides. They've known Cockscomb as a protected area since they were children and they realize how important it is, both economically and ecologically. Plus, the women are empowered, with the money from their crafts sales, and you don't see children walking around with parasites and swollen bellies."

Rabinowitz tracked the area's cat population while living in a small clearing of jungle (now the site of the park's visitors center) for nearly two years in the early 1980s and recounted his story in his fascinating "eco-memoir" *Jaguar: One Man's Struggle to Establish the World's First Jaguar Preserve* (reprinted by Island Press in 2000). He has traveled extensively since then, studying jaguars, clouded leopards, tigers, and other large mammal species in Borneo, Taiwan, Thailand, Laos, and Myanmar (Burma).

And while he has moved on from Cockscomb, the restless biologist does not see the Belizean park as a mere thing of the past. Quite the contrary. His ambitious goal now is to save jaguars throughout their entire range – from Mexico to Argentina – by creating and securing a natural, unbroken corridor of wildland on both public and private lands where jaguars can thrive into the future. "We've already made tremendous strides toward that objective," he says, "with jaguar surveys and rancher outreach programs."

The **Save the Jaguar** project is dependent on private and corporate donations (Jaguar Cars has been extremely supportive). You can learn more about current studies and projects – and about how to help – by visiting www.savethejaguar.com and also by checking out WCS's **Adopt-a-Jaguar Project** at www.wcs.org.

thought the peak was surrounded by a lake, unapproachable to man, and occupied by a powerful spirit. The first people (a party led by Roger T. Goldsworth, governor of then–British Honduras) reached the summit in 1888. Today, it is a protected natural monument, managed by the Belize Audubon Society. You can arrange a summit trip in the dry season only (February–May) and must have a permit and licensed guide. This 30-mile round-trip trek takes three or four days; the up-and-down terrain is steep and there are no switchbacks. See the Belize Audubon Society website (www.belizeaudubon.org) for trail and campsite details; entrance is US$5 per person plus camping fees. There are a few reputable mountain guides from the surrounding villages; BAS does not have guides for hire but they can provide a list with contact information. **Marcos Cucul** (tel. 501/670-3116, www.mayaguide.bz) is a renowned guide in this area who can take you rock climbing or on a backcountry trip of a lifetime, including to the top of Victoria Peak (US$500 pp).

Accommodations and Camping

Bring your own tent to stay at one of three well-maintained campgrounds (US$10 pp). The park's overnight accommodations begin with zinc-topped buildings with bunk space for 32 (US$20). You get a bed in a shared "rustic cabin" or a bunk in the main dormitory, clean sheets, shared bathrooms with cold showers, and solar power. There are a few private cabins as well; US$54 gets you six beds and a kitchen. Finally, the "White House," up the road (US$81), features a screened veranda in an isolated jungle setting, a unique experience for a nature-loving family.

Be prepared with food and supplies if you plan to stay a few days; the only food for sale in the visitors center is chips, cookies, candy bars, and soft drinks. There are a couple of small shops in Maya Centre, so feel free to stock up there before catching your cab into the park. You may also be able to arrange for meals to be cooked in Maya Centre and brought in. Otherwise, there is a communal kitchen with

a refrigerator, gas stoves, and crockery and cooking utensils for rent. Again, visitors are required to bring their own food and water. A walled-off washing area has buckets, and a separate cooking area has a gas stove and a few pots and such.

Getting There

Cockscomb is about six miles west of the Southern Highway and the village of Maya Centre (from Dangriga, it's a total of 20 miles). The road can be rough after it rains. By public transport, hop off at Maya Centre from any bus traveling between Dangriga and Punta Gorda. From there, it's a long walk or a US$15–20 taxi ride.

MAYA CENTRE

This small village is at the turnoff to the famous Cockscomb Basin Wildlife Sanctuary. Many of the 400 or so Mopan Maya who live here were relocated when their original home within the Cockscomb Basin was given protected status. Since then, they have had to change their lifestyles; instead of continuing to clear patches of rainforest for short-term agriculture, many men now work as guides and taxi drivers, while the women create and sell artwork. Still, the people of Maya Centre are struggling to support their town with tourism. Ever since they were prohibited from using the now-protected jungle for subsistence farming and hunting, tourism has been their only hope, aside from working for slave wages at the nearby banana and citrus farms. The village has a few places to stay, eat, and experience village life, literally right down the road from the famous reserve.

At the very least, make sure that you— or the driver of your tour bus—stop at one of the three Maya crafts stores, all on the road into the park. At the turnoff from the Southern Highway, you'll find the **Maya Centre Women's Group** (7:30 A.M.–4:30 P.M. daily), which sells local crafts and collects the entrance fee for Cockscomb. The group also offers **Jaguar Mountain Cafe,** which serves traditional Maya food. A quarter mile farther toward the park is the **Nu'uk Che'il Gift Shop,** offering fine jewelry, slate carvings, baskets, herbs, and other crafts. Another small shop is in between.

Right across the road from the women's co-op, look for the sign and trail across the creek to William Sho's **Butterfly Farm** (7 A.M.–5 P.M. daily, US$2.50, possible fee to take photos), boasting several dozen species.

Julio Saqui runs the store next to the women's co-op and offers satellite Internet access (US$4/hr) and taxi service. Julio is also a great guide and offers many services and tours, including Victoria Peak; information is available on his website (www.cockscombmayatours.com).

The Saqui family runs the **Maya Centre Maya Museum** (tel. 501/660-3903 or 501/668-2194, US$10 pp), which provides hands-on cultural activities; learn how to make corn tortillas or process coffee beans, and take home Mayan Coffee to share with friends while you retell your adventures abroad.

Accommodations

There are two guesthouses in Maya Centre, owned by different families that each offer transport in and out of the preserve, guides, meals, and other services.

◖ Nu'uk Che'il Cottages and Hmen Herbal Center (tel. 501/520-3033 or 501/615-2091, nuukcheil@btl.net) offers tranquil accommodations more removed from the highway than the village's other guesthouse. Bunks with shared bath are US$10 per person, and private rooms are US$30 (hot showers available, tax not included). Camping is US$4 per person. There are also a few shared-bath units for US$23. The place is very well kept, with beautifully planted grounds; the guesthouse

has experience hosting student groups and can arrange seminars on herbal medicine, cultural performances, and the like. Proprietress Aurora Garcia Saqui's husband, Ernesto, was director of the Cockscomb Basin Wildlife Sanctuary until 2005 and is extremely knowledgeable about the area. Her late uncle, Don Eligio Panti, was a famous healer; she took over his work when he died in 1996. Aurora offers Mayan spiritual blessings, prayer healings, acupuncture, and massage (each for under US$15). Aurora also has a four-acre botanical garden and medicine trail (US$2.50 entrance), offers herbs for sale, and can arrange homestays in the village (US$30 includes a one-night stay with a local family, one dinner, and one breakfast per person).

Another decent option is right on the highway, about 100 meters north of the entrance to Cockscomb: **Tutzil Nah Cottages** (tel. 501/520-3044, www.mayacenter.com, US$14–22) is owned and operated by the Chun family (they helped Dr. Alan Rabinowitz in his original jaguar studies and appear in his book, *Jaguar*). There are four screened wooden rooms, two with private baths, two with shared bath and shower; all have queen beds, fans, ample space, nice furniture, and a raised deck. Meals are US$6–12, as is camping on the grounds or in a separate campground about a quarter mile into the bush. Inventive trips are available as an alternative to the standard fare, including kayak floats and night hikes.

Getting There

Maya Centre is accessed by hopping off any bus passing between Dangriga and Punta Gorda. Taxis will take you from the village to the Cockscomb Basin Wildlife Sanctuary for about US$15–20 (per cab, not per person).

The Placencia Peninsula

This ribbon of barrier beach and mangroves winds 16 miles southward from the coastal wetlands and shrimp farms near Riverside village all the way to Placencia Village proper, on the tip of the peninsula. The area used to be a forgotten cul-de-sac on the tourist trail, but no more. Traveling to nearby cayes and inland attractions like the Cockscomb Basin Wildlife Sanctuary, Maya villages, and ruins of Toledo District is possible from anywhere on the peninsula. The area offers the full range of accommodations—whether you prefer to mingle with backpackers in Placencia Village or rub elbows with fellow guests at any of a number of beach resorts, each with its own personality. This is also the site of several enormous, ambitious, and controversial development projects, more of which are springing up all over the area every year.

MAYA BEACH

About halfway down the peninsula, you'll enter Maya Beach, which is nothing more than a loose strip of simple, small accommodations. Actually, they're quite nice, in a relaxed, isolated way, offering more value for your money than nearly anything else in the area. The beach here is also more pleasant than many places in Belize. You just have to be content with the relative lack of services in Maya Beach, since getting to and from Placencia Village can be an expensive endeavor, even though it's only seven miles away.

Accommodations

Maya Beach hotels are of the beach cabana variety, with a few furnished apartments, too, many with kitchenettes for cooking on your own. Most of these hotels also manage full houses and a few condos in the area—ask about weekly and monthly rates.

The first place you'll come to from the north is **(Maya Beach Hotel** (tel. 501/520-8040, U.S. tel. 800/503-5124, www.mayabeach-hotel.com, US$90–125), with five well-kept,

immaculate rooms, a few with gorgeous waterfront decks, all with wireless Internet, private baths, hot showers, and a great stretch of sand—oh, and one of the best restaurants in Placencia (the Maya Beach Hotel Bistro). They have a nice pool and one- and two-bedroom beach houses (US$100–180), all with fully equipped kitchens and amenities. A three-bedroom house (US$400), on a private beachfront parcel, has its own infinity pool.

On the lagoon side, **Casa At Last** (www.casaatlast.com, tel. 501/523-3630, US$125–200) is a couples-only resort with four nicely furnished thatch cabanas, a pool, and restaurant. The restaurant serves breakfast, lunch, and dinner for resort guests only.

The Green Parrot Beach Houses (tel 501/523-2488, www.greenparrot-belize.com, US$130–180 plus tax) features eight thatch-roof A-frame cabanas with decks and loft bedrooms facing the ocean. Each sleeps four people and includes multiple beds, couches, a kitchen, and hammocks. There's a restaurant and beach bar.

Catering to relaxed couples and honeymooners, **(Barnacle Bill's Beach Bungalows** (tel. 501/523-8010, www.barnaclebills-belize.com, US$110) consists of two secluded bungalows on the beach, with full kitchen, fans, and hot and cold water. Each sleeps three adults (no children under 12). Tours, free kayaks, and wireless Internet are available, and the staff will stock the fridge prior to your arrival.

Plant and orchid lovers will enjoy **Singing Sands Inn** (tel. 501/520-8022, U.S. tel. 888/201-6425, www.singingsands.com, US$110–150 plus tax). The six thatch-roof oceanfront cabanas have front porches, and the two standard rooms offer ocean and garden views. All units provide private bath, ceiling fan, and constant ocean breezes. Portable air-conditioning is available if desired. Breakfast is served in the open-air restaurant next to the pool; fresh lunches and dinners are served as well at the **Bonefish Grille.** Drinks and light

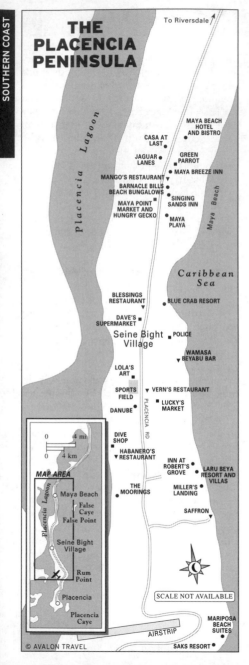

THE PLACENCIA PENINSULA

To Riversdale

Placencia Lagoon

MAYA BEACH HOTEL AND BISTRO

CASA AT LAST

JAGUAR LANES

GREEN PARROT

MAYA BREEZE INN

MANGO'S RESTAURANT

BARNACLE BILLS BEACH BUNGALOWS

MAYA POINT MARKET AND HUNGRY GECKO

SINGING SANDS INN

MAYA PLAYA

Maya Beach

Caribbean Sea

BLESSINGS RESTAURANT

BLUE CRAB RESORT

DAVE'S SUPERMARKET

Seine Bight Village

POLICE

WAMASA BEYABU BAR

LOLA'S ART

SPORTS FIELD

VERN'S RESTAURANT

LUCKY'S MARKET

DANUBE

PLACENCIA RD

DIVE SHOP

HABANERO'S RESTAURANT

INN AT ROBERT'S GROVE

LARU BEYA RESORT AND VILLAS

MAP AREA

THE MOORINGS

MILLER'S LANDING

Placencia Lagoon

Maya Beach

False Caye

False Point

Seine Bight Village

SAFFRON

Rum Point

Placencia

SCALE NOT AVAILABLE

Placencia Caye

MARIPOSA BEACH SUITES

AIRSTRIP

SAKS RESORT

© AVALON TRAVEL

0   4 mi
0   4 km

fare can be enjoyed at **Chez Albert's** bar on the pier, 220 feet out into the Caribbean. Bikes, golf carts, clear-bottomed kayaks, sailboats, and snorkel gear are available, as are snorkeling classes, tours, and transportation. Families, groups, and weddings are welcome.

Food

When you get tired of cooking in your cabana's kitchenette, visit the **Hungry Gecko** (8 A.M.–9 P.M. Mon.–Sat.), which serves a cheap and delicious menu of Honduran and local goodies, fresh seafood, and smoothies. The one store in town, the **Maya Point Market,** is open mornings and afternoons (closed Sun.). **Mango's Beach Bar and Restaurant** (11 A.M.–11 P.M.) has a nice Belizean/Mexican menu and a breezy view to enjoy with your beer. It's popular with the handful of locals, offering darts and poker some nights; Cuban cigars are available.

The 🄲 **Maya Beach Hotel Bistro** (dinner reservations tel. 501/520-8040, opens at 7 A.M. Tues.–Sun., US$16–28) is a breath of fresh, garlic-roasted air on the Belize culinary scene. Just reading the appetizer and meal choices will make your mouth water—few restaurants in the country have a menu this savory and creative. Australian chef John prepares dinner entrées like Sassy Shrimp Pot, Cocoa Pork, and Boathouse Pie (a half-pound fish fillet smothered in truffle and Jim Beam cream sauce, baked into a pie), not to mention fresh bread, an inspired bar food menu (honey-coconut ribs and roasted pumpkin-coconut green chili soup), and a lovely assortment of breakfasts (US$6–11), including homemade bagels and imported lox (smoked salmon).

At the **Bonefish Grille** (7 A.M.–9:30 P.M.), everything is made from scratch: homemade pasta, ricotta cheese, breads, and the salad dressings, and there's no MSG. The menu features Asian and Italian cuisine, prepared with fresh ingredients. This place was Restaurant of the Year runner-up at the 2010 National Tourism Awards.

For all-American fun in the tropics, try bowling at **Jaguar Lanes and Jungle Bar**

(2–10 P.M. Fri.–Wed., US$2.50 per game, US$1.25 shoe rental). There are four nice bowling lanes and a snack bar (US$1.50–5.50) serving hot dogs, onion rings, nachos, and pizza. Outside the air-conditioned alley there's cold beer and mixed drinks.

SEINE BIGHT

Continuing south, a couple more miles of dirt road will put you in the Garifuna village of Seine Bight. In this tiny, unkempt town, most of the men are fishermen and the women tend family gardens. Some are attempting to clean up the town, with hopes it will become a low-key tourist destination, but they've still got a ways to go, as foreign-owned resorts sprout like mushrooms up and down the coast around them. Supposedly, men and women lead split lives here; the women even claim to have their own language that the men don't understand.

Shopping

Lola's Art Gallery is a must-stop (it's behind the soccer field; follow the well-marked signs). Lola sells a selection of bright, inspired artwork, including cards and paintings on canvas; there are lots of cheerful primary colors and village life scenes. Lola's is open 7 A.M.–6 P.M.

Accommodations

On a clean, shallow beach on the very northern end of Seine Bight is **Blue Crab Resort** (tel. 501/523-3544, www.bluecrabbeach.com, US$90–100). American-Belizean-owned, this humble hotel has four rooms with air-conditioning, fridges, coffeemakers, fans, and cable TV, plus two cabanas with high thatch roofs, louvered windows, private baths, and three fans. Blue Crab is on the primitive side, made of mostly wood and thatch, but its new cabanas are more modern, and you're likely to see a few coatimundis foraging among the fruit trees. The hotel's proprietress, Linn, runs their popular restaurant (call for reservations); she brings her Taiwanese ancestry to your Belizean table. Specials include lobster Formosan and Thai shrimp soup. They also run a tiny chocolate factory in the house across the road. **Goss**

Chocolate (www.gosschocolate.com) is made from 100 percent pure organic cacao and is available only in Belize; it costs US$1.50–2.50 for a bar.

Experience southern hospitality at the **Nautical Inn** (www.nauticalinnbelize.com, tel. 501/523-3595, U.S. tel. 800/688-0377, US$70 pp). There are various beachfront accommodations surrounding a pool, and all rooms have air-conditioning, ceiling fans, and cable TV. Basic rooms have a kitchenette, and the two-bedroom suite has a full kitchen and living room. A professional kitchen and thatch palapa can be rented for retreats or conferences. Ask about special group rates.

One of the more exclusive, well-respected resorts on the peninsula, **◖ Robert's Grove Beach Resort** (tel. 501/523-3565, U.S. tel. 800/565-9757, www.robertsgrove.com, from US$215) is a grand affair. Its various structures are situated close together along a short stretch of decent beach, and even though this is one of the most upscale operations in the country, it maintains a very relaxed feel. The various guest rooms, suites, and villas are spacious, with high ceilings, king-size beds, and many updated amenities. There are three pools, a tennis court, spa, gym, a trio of rooftop hot tubs, and an excellent open-air restaurant. Robert's Grove has its own dive shop on the lagoon side (next to its Mexican restaurant, Habanero) and offers all kinds of underwater, offshore, and inland trips and packages. Bikes, kayaks, and sailboats are available for your own explorations. The inn is popular with couples, families, and groups; ask about trips to their private islands.

Laru Beya Resort and Villas (tel. 501/523-3476, U.S. tel. 800/890-8010, www.larubeya.com, US$120–475) has accommodations and amenities similar to Robert's Grove; penthouse suites have a ladder to a private rooftop Jacuzzi with a great view. The **Quarter Deck** restaurant and bar (7 A.M.–10 P.M.) serves international cuisine and caters for destination weddings.

One of Placencia's best kept secrets is **Miller's Landing** (www.millerslanding.net, 501/523-3010, US$85–150). The Millers like to keep things simple and not much has changed since the couple opened their resort. There are three basic rooms and two private cabanas, all with kitchenettes, private baths, hot and cold water, and ceiling fans. This calm and quiet location is surrounded by native vegetation; watch birds and butterflies while having your complimentary breakfast. Lounge by the pool, or if you're feeling more active take out a complimentary bike, kayak, or windsurfing board.

Food

Get a cheery, cheap, home-cooked Honduran meal at an unnamed little **thatch shack** with no sign, about a quarter mile north of Seine Bight, on the west side of the road (6 A.M.–7 P.M.). Fresh, hot tortillas come with your dish. Grab a couple of "dark and love-lies" (bottles of Guinness) or a glass of locally brewed bitters at the reggae-colored **Wamasa Beyabu Bar,** which greets you as you enter town from the north. There is also a taxi stand here. Wamasa just opened a bigger operation on the beach as well, which can be pretty happening on weekends. If you need groceries, the **Peninsula** has the widest selection.

The menu at the **Danube Austrian Restaurant** (south end of Seine Bight, tel. 501/610-0132, 4:30–10:30 P.M. Wed.–Mon.) includes schnitzel, spaetzle, sweet dumplings, and strudels. Call for reservations.

The **Seaside Restaurant** (tel. 501/523-3565, 7 A.M.–9 P.M. daily) at Robert's Grove has an international menu: sandwiches, pizza, wings, and quesadillas for lunch; seafood appetizers and entrées, imported steaks, and à la carte options for dinner. The bar is open till midnight. **Habanero Mexican Café and Bar** (tel. 501/523-3565, noon–10 P.M. daily, closed Jun.–Nov., US$9–15) is an excellent lagoon-side Mexican restaurant across the road from Robert's Grove Marina.

Placencia Village

A fishing village since the time of the Maya and periodically flattened by hurricanes (the last was Iris in 2001), Placencia continues rebuilding and redefining itself, in large part to accommodate the influx of foreigners. Placencia Village is still worlds away from the condo-dominated landscape of San Pedro on Ambergris Caye, and most locals claim it will never go that way, but time will tell. On my last trip to Placencia, I saw plenty of bulldozers, swaths of cut mangroves, and golf carts for rent . . .

Despite area development, this town will remain the *tranquilo*, ramshackle village it is today for years to come. Find a room, book some day tours, pencil in a massage before happy hour, and relax. Oh yeah, and feel free to drink the tap water as you explore: Placencia's *agua* is piped in from an artesian well across the lagoon in Independence, reportedly the result of an unsuccessful attempt to drill for oil, and is clean and pure.

ORIENTATION

The north–south Placencia Road runs the length of the peninsula, doglegs around the airstrip, continues along the lagoon, then parallels the famous central sidewalk as it enters town. You'll see the soccer field on your right before the road curves slightly to the left, terminating at the Shell station and main docks. If there is a "downtown" Placencia, it's probably here, in front of the gas station and dock. This is where buses come and go, taxis hang out, and most dive shops are based.

◖ THE SIDEWALK STRIP

Aside from the beach, the main attraction in Placencia is the world-renowned main-street sidewalk, cited in the *Guinness Book of World Records* as "the world's most narrow street." It's 24 inches wide in spots and runs north–south through the sand for over a mile. Homes, hotels, Guatemalan goods shops, craftmakers, and tour guide offices line both sides.

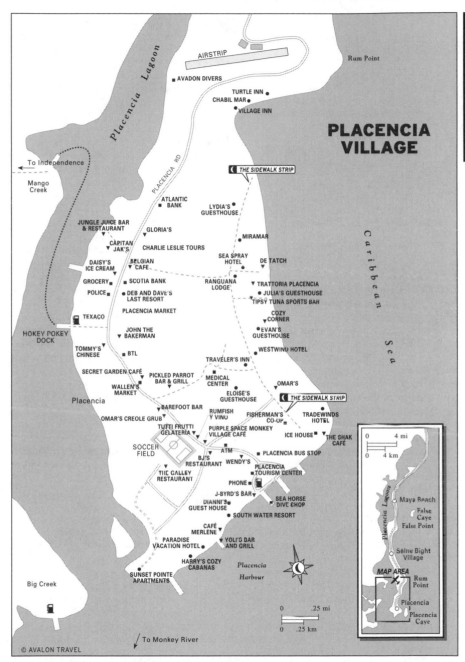

BRING A BOOK TO PLACENCIA

Placencia's school and library are stocked almost entirely by donated books, giving visitors from up north an easy way to contribute something to the children and community. Bring a single book or a whole box and drop them off at the Placencia Tourism office, at Deb & Dave's Last Resort, or with principal Rodney Griffith (find contact information at www.placencia. com or www.placenciabreeze.com). The school also rarely turns away volunteers who'd like to spend time in a Belizean classroom, especially art teachers.

RECREATION
Snorkeling and Diving
Although the beach is usually fine for swimming and lounging, you won't see much with a mask and snorkel except sand, sea grass, a few fish, and other bathers. A short boat ride, however, will bring you to the barrier reef and the kind of underwater viewing you can write home about. Snorkel gear is available for rent everywhere (US$5 per day), and trips to the cayes and reefs cost around US$50 per half day, depending on distance.

Belize's famous barrier reef extends past Placencia and is accessible by boat. There are six dive shops with comparable prices, and you can either let your hotel arrange everything or do it yourself.

Avadon Divers (tel. 501/503-3377, www. avadondiversbelize.com) is run by a brother and sister team with many years of experience; the Belize Tourism Board awarded Avadon in 2010 as one of the top tour operators. They take care of everything (transfer to and from the dive shop, breakfast, lunch, and gear) so that all you have to worry about is seeing the beautiful marine diversity. Call or check with your hotel for a trip schedule.

Seahorse, located on its own dock by the Shell station (tel. 501/523-3166, seahorse@btl. net), is highly recommended for whale shark tours. **Splash Dive Center** (tel. 501/523-3058, www.splashbelize.com) has an office at the south end of the sidewalk; their dive center and retail store are on the north end. Farther north, you'll find a handful of serious dive operations linked to their respective resorts, with professional shops at Robert's Grove Beach Resort and Turtle Inn.

Sea Kayaking
An unforgettable, underrated way to explore the near-shore cayes, mangroves, creeks, and rivers is by paddle. Open plastic kayaks are available to guests at most resorts, and many tour operators and dive shops have some for rent as well. Boats are also available for rent at the **Sugar Reef Bar** and are perfect for putting in and paddling up the lagoon in search of birds, manatees, and dolphins. If you're into extended sea-kayaking expeditions, see Dave Vernon at **Toadal Adventure** (www. toadaladventure.com, tel. 501/523-3207 or 501/600-6044). Dave is one of Belize's premier naturalists and tour guides, and the opportunity to take a personal paddle trip with him is well worth it. He'll take you on any of a number of paddling trips, such as an overnight Monkey River tour, weeklong caye-hopping exploration, or river kayaking through Cockscomb Basin, where you'll encounter a few rapids and possibly a tapir along the calm stretches of South Stann Creek. He also rents kayaks for US$70 a day, with which you can paddle out to any number of cayes and make your own adventure.

Fishing
Placencia has always been a fishing town for sustenance, but with the advent of tourism, it has gained a worldwide reputation for sportfishing. Deep-water possibilities include wahoo, sailfish, marlin, kingfish, and dolphin fish; fly-fishing can hook you a grand slam—bonefish, tarpon, permit, and snook (all catch-and-release). Fortunately, serious angling means serious local guides, several of whom (like the Godfrey brothers, Earl and Kurt) have been featured on ESPN and in multiple

fishing magazines. Hire Earl at **Trip'N Travel Southern Guides Fly Fishing and Saltwater Adventures** (in the Placencia Office Supply building, tel. 501/523-3205, lgodfrey@btl. net). Most tour operators listed throughout this chapter offer fishing trips, and a few specialize in them, like **Kingfisher's Tarpon Caye Lodge,** boasting decades of experience (tel. 501/523-3323 or 501/600-6071, kingfisher@btl.net, www.tarponcayelodge.com). Charlie Leslie Sr., owner and head guide, has a stellar reputation and will take you to a variety of spots, from inshore places that include nearby flats to Tarpon Caye and the remote Ycacos area. Also ask about their island cabanas for rent. Check www.placencia.com for more options.

Sailing

Opportunities abound for day trips, sunset cruises, snorkel voyages, and sail charters. Expensive, high-end **The Moorings** (www. moorings.com, tel. 501/523-3351, U.S. tel. 800/535-7289) has a dock in Placencia for multiple catamaran adventures, based on the lagoon side, north of the airstrip. **Belize Sailing Charters** (www.belize-sailing-charters.com, tel. 501/523-3138) has bareboat and crewed yacht charters. Just across from town, **Placencia Yacht Club** (placenciayachtclub. com) is on Placencia Caye, featuring the Tranquilo Restaurant and Bar.

Massage and Bodywork

Sign up for a massage or other treatment at **The Secret Garden Massage and Day Spa** (behind Wallen's, tel. 501/523-3420, www.secretgardenplacencia.com), where an hour massage costs US$50 and a special four-hands treatment a bit more. If you need relief from the sun and barefooting on the beach, try the sunburn treatment and foot massage for US$50. Secret Garden masseuse Lee Nyhus also works at **Robert's Grove Beach Resort Spa** (tel. 501/523-3565), north of town, where you can get a full range of treatments—for more premium prices, of course. **The Turtle Inn** also has pampering services, as does a **Thai massage** place right in Placencia Village Square, run by experienced Thais who offer seaweed treatments and papaya body polish (massage US$75 per hour). Also check into **Z-Touch Beauty Salon and Massage** (tel. 501/523-3513, massage US$50 per hour).

Tour Guides

There's no shortage of guide services in Placencia, where most tour operators offer service to *all* nearby destinations: Cockscomb Basin Wildlife Sanctuary, Monkey River, snorkeling and fishing trips with lunch on a beautiful caye, Maya ruins of Lubaantun and Nim Li Punit, and a variety of paddling tours. For any of these trips, please also refer to the dive shops and fishing guides listed in this chapter.

Many tour operators have their offices/shacks clustered by the main dock in town, just past the gas station; most are subcontracted by the hotels that offer tours to their guests. If you're going it on your own, ask around and know that prices often rely on a minimum number of passengers, usually four. Prices vary little, but it's definitely worth comparing. Monkey River day trips, for example, range US$40–60 per person, depending on whether lunch is included and the size of the boat. Half-day snorkel trips are about US$35–50 per person. Most tours require that you sign up the day before; reef tours typically leave around 9 A.M. and inland tours around 7 A.M.

Seahorse Dive Shop (tel. 501/523-3166, www.belizescuba.com), by the gas station, is highly recommended for whale shark tours. Right by the main dock, **Nite Wind** (tel. 501/523-3487, renidrag_99@yahoo.com) is very reliable. Just up the sidewalk you'll find **Ocean Motion** (www.oceanmotionplacencia. com, tel. 501/523-3363 or 501/523-3162) and **Placencia Dive School** (tel. 501/628-0911). Hubert and Karen Young's **Joy Tours** (tel. 501/523-3325, www.belizewithjoy.com) is next to Tim's Chinese restaurant. There are also some individual guide gurus lurking around town; ask around your hotel or at restaurants.

ENTERTAINMENT AND EVENTS

Placencia's bars, restaurants, and resorts do a decent job of coordination, so special events like beach barbecues, horseshoe tournaments, karaoke, and live music are offered throughout the entire week—especially during the high season. Your best bet is to check the *Placencia Breeze* (www.placenciabreeze.com) newspaper and look for current schedules.

The **Barefoot Bar** (tel. 501/523-3515, 11 A.M.–midnight) is wildly popular in the high season. Sandy-toed revelers choose from hundreds of froofy cocktails and bar food; there's live music Friday–Sunday and happy hour 5–6 P.M. daily. Another happening bar is **J-Byrd's** (tel. 501/523-3412, 10 A.M.–10 P.M.), right on the water behind the gas station, with live bands most Fridays and Sundays. A bit farther down the harbor, **Yoli's** is a locally popular dock bar and restaurant; they have barbecue and ring toss starting at 3 P.M. on Sunday. Around the corner on the lagoon side is **Sugar Reef,** a relaxed bar a few blocks from the main road. The **Tipsy Tuna** (tel. 501/523-3089, www.tipsytunabelize.com) is popular, with an inside sports bar and outside beach bar with Garifuna drumming on Wednesdays and more live music on weekends from 7 P.M.–midnight.

The biggest party of the year happens the third week of June, during **Lobsterfest.** The whole south end of town closes down for lobster-catching tournaments, costumes, dances, and food booths everywhere. **Easter weekend** is insanely popular as well, as Placencia is a destination for many Belizeans as well as foreign visitors; they typically book their rooms months in advance, so be prepared for the crowds. Look for a Halloween celebration, complete with parade and trick-or-treating (for kids and adults alike). Another annual gig, the **Mistletoe Ball,** wanders to a different hotel before Christmas every year and doubles as a fundraiser for the local Belize Tourism Industry Association chapter. The town humane society organizes various fundraising events as well; keep an eye out.

SHOPPING

Most gift stores feature Guatemalan crafts and clothes, plus local jewelry and sea-inspired artwork. In addition to the numerous shops, stalls, and tables along the sidewalk, **Myrna's** by the gas station has a huge, colorful selection. Happy hunting.

ACCOMMODATIONS

All of Placencia's budget lodgings are found on (or within shouting distance of) the sidewalk, and most of the high-end resorts are strung along the beach north of town. Remember, these are high-season double occupancy prices only! Expect significant discounts and negotiable rates between May and November.

Under US$25

There is one campground on the northern tip of Placencia Village, where you can pitch your tent and use the bathrooms, showers, and grill for US$5 per person; rent gear for another US$5. It's run by a couple from Oregon. Miss Lucille's **Travellers Inn** (tel. 501/523-3190, joytour@btl.net, US$15–23), right in the middle of the village, is a no-frills, bottom-of-the-barrel place to rest, only one lot away from the beach where most guests spend their days. Rooms have either shared or private bath; the wood rooms are hot, the bathrooms grungy.

Right on the sidewalk, **Omar's** is another wooden flophouse, US$15 for a double with private bath. Near the Anglican school, **Eloise Travel Lodge** (tel. 501/523-3299, US$20–25) has four rooms with private or shared bath and a communal kitchen. There is no reception office; ask for Miss Sonia Leslie.

A much better budget bet is **⟨ Lydia's Guesthouse** (tel. 501/523-3117, lydias@btl.net, US$25), toward the north end of the sidewalk. Lydia's is a longtime favorite among backpackers. The eight clean rooms with shared tile-floor bath also share a sociable two-story porch, communal kitchen, fans, hammocks, and a 30-second walk to the beach. Miss Lydia will make you breakfast if you make arrangements the day before; she also makes fresh Creole bread and guava jam. Miss Lydia's son

YOUR OWN ISLAND

Who's never dreamed of starring in his or her own episode of *Castaway* or *Lost?* If you've got the money, you've got access to a handful of Belize's cayes all to yourself (actually, most properties come with at least one caretaker). Though there are a few budget island options, including the Raggamuffin Tours sailing/camping trip from Caye Caulker to Placencia and the budget-oriented Glover's Atoll Resort, it usually costs a pretty penny if you want the island *all* to yourself. If you can't afford the US$12,000 a night to rent **Cayo Espanto** (www.aprivateisland.com, includes personal butler service but *not* wine), then try one of the following.

Most options seem to be based in Placencia, where a few island rentals are available. **Ranguana Caye** (tel. 501/503-8452) is two acres in size and 18 miles (90 minutes by boat) from the mainland. It's managed by Robert's Grove Beach Resort (www.robertsgrove.com), as is **Robert's Caye,** a one-acre island 10 miles from the coast, with four well-appointed thatch-roof cabanas and access to a small bar and restaurant; it's all yours for US$400 per person per night. Robert's and Ranguana are only semiprivate.

French Louie Caye (tel. 501/523-3636, www.frenchlouiecayebelize.com) has its own beach, coral reef, fishing dock, two-bedroom cabin, and a spacious lodge. The caye is about 8 miles off the coast, and the simple wooden cabin has a stocked kitchen and stove. It is very private and the honeymoon experience of a lifetime (I know from experience). Cuisine is "catch and eat"; i.e., meals come from the sea to the grill to your plate, prepared by the cook/caretaker/guide (yes, he stays on the island). He can take you on a night snorkel tour; US$1,150 for a three-night package.

Tarpon Caye Lodge (tel. 501/523-3323, www.tarponcayelodge.com) offers fly-fishing, spin-fishing, and deep-sea fishing from a private island lodge. It also caters to people looking to simply relax on a private Caribbean island.

Reef Conservation International (tel. 501/626-1429, www.reefci.com) offers weekly and monthly dive trips to stay on Tom Owens Caye, a small one-acre private island in the Sapodilla Cayes with incredible snorkeling, off the coast from Punta Gorda. This is one of the best places to view whale sharks, dolphins, and grouper spawning events — and you will most likely be the *only* dive boat in the water. Nondivers are also welcome, and Reef Conservation International offers various packages and degrees of marine conservation work; or just camp on the beach and snorkel the days away. The boat leaves Punta Gorda Monday morning and returns on Friday afternoon.

There are many other islands in the **Sapodilla Cayes** at the southern end of Belize's barrier reef. Ask tour operators in Punta Gorda about exploring **Seal Caye** and others. You may be able to camp on some of them.

---

operates **Pelican Tours** (tel. 501/632-1320 or 501/630-2795, pelicantoursbze@hotmail.com); he'll take you to the reef or Monkey River.

US$25-50

As you enter Placencia there is a gate by the Placencia Bazaar gift shop; **(Deb & Dave's Last Resort** (tel. 501/523-3207 or 501/600-6044, www.toadaladventure.com, US$25) consists of four small, clean rooms surrounding a gorgeous sand courtyard and tropical garden favored by hummingbirds; the common

screened-in porch space is excellent for meeting your neighbors and telling war stories from the day's paddling and snorkeling trips; there are shared bathrooms for all. Owner Dave is head guide for **Toadal Adventures** and is renowned for his local knowledge and trip-leading skills.

Claiming to be the "first established hotel on the Placencia Peninsula" (since 1964), the **(Sea Spray Hotel** (tel. 501/523-3148, www.seasprayhotel.com, US$25–65) is a great choice—30 feet from the ocean, 20 rooms with private bath, refrigerators, hot and cold water, and coffeepots. There are economy rooms and nicer ones closer to the water, where guests can relax in hammocks and chairs under palm trees. **De' Tatch** seafood restaurant on the premises serves breakfast, lunch, and dinner and offers Internet.

US$50-100

Evan's Guest House (tel. 501/523-3127, www.evansplaceplacencia.com, US$75–85) is a clean and well-kept place; standard rooms have a kitchenette, cable TV, ceiling fan and optional air-conditioning; condo units have a full kitchen and private balcony.

At the extreme southern end of Placencia Village, look for the brightly painted **Tradewinds Hotel** (tel. 501/523-3122, trdewndpla@btl.net, US$75–95) on five acres near the sea, offering nine cabanas with spacious rooms, fans, refrigerators, coffeepots, and private yards just feet away from the ocean; there are two new deluxe rooms.

The **Cozy Corner Hotel** (tel. 501/523-3280 or 501/523-3540, cozycorner@btl.net, US$50–70) has 10 decent rooms with private baths and basic amenities, right behind the Cozy Corner bar/restaurant on the beach, with a nice, breezy second-story porch; some rooms have air-conditioning. Next door, the Tipsy Tuna plays loud music at night.

The **Village Inn** (tel. 501/523-3481 or 501/523-3217, www.thevillageinnbelize.com, US$65–150) started before roads or electricity came to the village, and when the children didn't wear shoes to school. Four wooden beach cabanas, located on the cleanest beach around, preserve the simple, yet comfortable barefoot paradise that made Placencia famous. All cabanas have a full kitchen, private bath with hot and cold water, and a cozy veranda. There's a bait and tackle shop on-site; fishing trips and local tours are available.

Dianni's Guest House (www.diannisplacencia.com, tel. 501/523-3159, US$59–85) is a simple, clean, quiet affair, with six rooms with private baths, fans, and coffeemakers, plus wireless Internet, tour service, bikes, and a book exchange.

☾ Paradise Vacation Hotel (tel. 501/523-3179, www.belize123.com, US$59–159) has 12 rooms (all air-conditioned), an on-site restaurant and bar, spa, and gift shop. From the rooftop hot tub you see the Maya Mountains. **Harry's Cozy Cabanas** (tel. 501/523-3234, www.cozycabanas.com) has three simple cabanas with screened porches.

Westwind Hotel (tel. 501/523-3255, www.westwindhotel.com, US$65–150) has 10 rooms with views, light tile floors, sunny decks, private baths, and fans (air-conditioning is optional and costs a little extra if you turn it on); there's wireless Internet too. The family unit goes for US$150 a night. The hotel has a great, friendly vibe and a nice beach to relax on, though it's a little close to the pounding music at Tipsy Tuna. The **Ranguana Lodge** (tel. 501/523-3112, www.ranguanabelize.com, US$85–90) has five private cabanas: three air-conditioned beach cabins and two cabins set back with a garden views. All are spacious with beautiful wood floors, walls, and ceilings.

US$100-150

Captain Jak's (tel. 501/523-3481, www.captainjaksbelize.com, US$90–120) is a quaint lagoon-side resort set in a tropical garden, with cabanas, two-story cottages, and a spacious villa (US$300). Each place has a full kitchen, hot and cold water, and plenty of space to relax. There's an outdoor grill and palapa table where you can feast on the catch of the day; the crow's nest offers a spectacular view of the surrounding area.

South Waters Resort (tel. 501/523-3308, www.southwatersresort.com, US$112–270) has four well-kept cabanas and three air-conditioned suites with a full kitchen, nicely furnished living room, and separate bedroom.

Rent one of four fully furnished, air-conditioned units at **Easy Living Apartments** (tel. 501/523-3481, www.easyliving.bz, from US$125). **Miramar Apartments** (tel. 501/523-3658, www.miramarbelize.com, US$125–235), the hot pink building opposite Lydia's Guesthouse, has studio, one-bedroom, and three-bedroom units. Each has a king-sized bed, full kitchen, air-conditioning, and cable. The three-bedroom unit has hardwood flooring, beautiful decorations, original artwork, and a large seaview balcony. There is a three-night stay minimum, which is flexible depending on the season; it's a great place for a family getaway.

Over US$150

At **Chabil Mar** (tel. 501/523-3606, www. chabilmarvillas.com, US$300–525), the privately owned luxury villas have richly decorated interiors and are furnished with all the modern conveniences one could ask for. Less than a mile north on the beach from the Placencia village, the exclusive Café Mar provides butler service so you can dine where you please: at poolside, on the pier or a private veranda, or in the comfort of your villa.

One of the few truly upscale options actually in Placencia village, **Sunset Pointe Apartments** (U.S. tel. 904/471-3599, www.sunsetpointebelize.com, US$250–275) offers luxury condos for short- or long-term rental. They're back on the lagoon side, but they all have raised roof decks with a breeze. It's only a five-minute walk to the beach from here, and there are many accessible restaurants and shops.

Turtle Inn (tel. 501/523-3244 or 501/523-3150, www.turtleinn.com) is one of the nation's premier luxe destinations, one of U.S. film producer Francis Ford Coppola's two Belizean properties. It is about a mile north of Placencia Village. Prices start at US$375 a night for the Garden View Cottages and go up to US$1,850 a night for the master two-bedroom pavilion house with private entrance, pool, and dining pavilion. Even if you're not staying there, swing by to treat yourself to a fine meal with beautifully framed views of the ocean. Turtle Inn has seven luxury villas and 18 cottages on offer. The rooms are designed along Indonesian and Belizean lines, with lots of natural materials and airy space. The high thatch ceilings absorb the heat, so there are fans only, no air-conditioning (but there are music players for your iPod and fancy shell phones). There are two swimming pools, the über-mellow Laughing Fish Bar on the beach, and one of the peninsula's premier restaurants,

the **Mare Restaurant**. There's also an on-site spa, dive shop, and more dining options; Auntie Luba's Belizean eatery and the Garden Grill are open for dinner (6–9 P.M.) by reservation only.

FOOD

Placencia has a small restaurant offering but enough variety to keep you stuffed during your visit: seafood cooked in coconut milk and local herbs, Creole stews and "fry chicken," sandwiches, burritos, burgers, chow mein, French, and Italian (and adequate vegetarian options nearly everywhere you go).

Cafés, Bakeries, and Ice Cream

John the Bakerman (7 A.M.–close) makes great breads, cinnamon buns, and coffee bread; look for his sign on the sidewalk and get it fresh out of the oven around 5 P.M. Near the Shell station, **Norman's Bakery** (6 A.M.–9 P.M. daily) has cheap breakfasts (including a US$2.50 Backpacker Special) and dinners for US$7.50, not to mention coffee and baked goods.

In Placencia Village Square, **Tutti Frutti Gelatería** (9 A.M.–9 P.M. daily) serves up some of the best homemade Italian ice cream you've ever had in your life (a bold statement, and I stand by it); it's made fresh daily with local fruits and traditional flavors. The fruit sorbets are dairy-free and they serve espresso drinks and iced coffees.

Daisy's (7 A.M.–10:30 P.M.), on the main road, makes its own ice cream and offers cakes, pies, and other goodies, like seaweed shakes and fruit smoothies (about US$4).

The Secret Garden Restaurant and Coffee House (tel. 501/523-3617, www. secretgardenplacencia.com, 7–11 A.M. and 5:30–9 P.M. Tues.–Sat.) has a pleasant shady area and a homey lounge where you can enjoy coffee drinks, free wireless Internet, and yummy burritos, burgers, and Thai curries; Sunday brunch is served during the high season. There is also an on-site day spa. Up the road (past the town dock), look for **The Shak Beach Café** (7 A.M.–7 P.M.), which has

21 smoothie flavors (all with fresh fruits), a healthy vegetarian menu, a view of the water, and good breakfasts (banana pancakes, omelets, coffee, tea for US$5–6).

For early birds, **Sweet Dreams** is a bakery and café with free wireless Internet for customers that opens at 6 A.M. The Swiss family bakery makes a strong cup of coffee and delicious cinnamon rolls. Later in the day there is homemade ice cream and stone-oven-baked pizza; the bakery has a nice variety of specialty bread and pastries using all natural ingredients. It's on the sidewalk in a large concrete building with a few picnic tables for seating.

Michelo's Belgian Café (8 A.M.–2:30 P.M. Mon.–Fri.) offers European street café ambiance, overlooking Placencia Road from a second-story balcony. Here you can find a good cup of coffee and a light menu of waffles, crepes, cream puffs, and sandwiches. Small portions but delicious food made from rich, local ingredients.

Belizean and International

Omar's Creole Grub (7 A.M.–2:30 P.M. and 6–9 P.M. Sun.–Thurs., 6–9 P.M. Sat.) will take care of you all day, with a lobster omelet, handmade tortillas, and guava jelly to start the day off (US$8), then a burrito for lunch (US$4), and creole style barracuda steak (from US$7) for dinner (or pork chops, conch steak, or lobster). Chef Omar Jr. won the 2009 Lobsterfest Cookoff with his stuffed lobster. Come for the food, and stay for the conversation with the vivacious Omar and family. (No alcohol is served.)

BJ's (on the corner of the soccer field, 7 A.M.–7 P.M. Mon.–Sat., closes at 4 P.M. on Sun.), "where good food and God's people meet," has an outdoor porch and cheap fare: sandwiches from US$2.50, seafood and stir-fry dinners from US$9. Next door, [**Wendy's Restaurant and Bar** (tel. 501/523-3335, 7 A.M.–9:30 P.M.) offers a varied menu at reasonable prices, plus a glassed-in, air-conditioned eating area and a full bar. This is a great, cool place to come to for Creole and Mexican cooking, burgers (US$3–7.50),

burritos (US$4.50–8), and fancier steaks and seafood items (US$13–23).

The Cozy Corner (7 A.M.–10 P.M. daily) has a relaxed open-air atmosphere and is one of the nicer beach bars. For breakfast in Belize you can never go wrong with eggs, beans, and fry jacks; they also have a lobster burger for US$7, fish dinners from US$9, and good bar food.

The **Pickled Parrot** (between the sidewalk and main road, just off from the soccer field, 11:30 A.M.–9:30 P.M.) is good for seafood specials (US$11 fish plate, US$15 lobster), burgers, pizza, and blender drinks (including a three-rum "Parrot Piss" cocktail, US$6).

The **Purple Space Monkey Village** (in town across from soccer field, 6 A.M.–midnight) has some of the best pizza, panini sandwiches, and full-belly dishes, including Belizean, bagels, etc.; there's also an espresso bar, free wireless Internet, and laptops for your use.

Fine Dining

Placencia Village's sole Italian restaurant is **La Dolce Vita** (5:30–10:30 P.M. daily, closes the last week of Aug. and reopens in Nov.), with decent pastas and gnocchi (US$8–16) and a wine list; it's above Wallen's Market.

[**Rumfish y Vino Wine and Gastro Bar** (tel. 501/523-3293, www.rumfishyvino.com, 11 A.M.–midnight daily) opened in 2008; the Solomons bought the place while honeymooning. Pamela, a wine specialist, imports Italian and Californian wine; John works his magic in the kitchen. The menu features international comfort food to please any appetite and has a good mix of customers; a sun-beaten tourist bellies up to the bar for a plate of Rumfish tacos and draft beer while at a dinner table a few feet away the prime minister of Belize drinks a glass of wine.

Most of the resorts north of town have fine restaurants to brag about. Grab a fistful of dollars and a taxi and *bon appétit*. At The Turtle Inn's **Mare Restaurant,** the chef prepares meals with greens from his own on-site organic herb garden, as well as those grown in their upland sister resort's extensive organic vegetable garden. In fact, this is the best place to come for a fresh green salad in Placencia—as well as seafood, pasta, and oven-baked gourmet pizza.

Chef Frank de Silva at the **Seaside Restaurant** (reservations tel. 501/523-3565, entrées from US$12, surf-and-turf tenderloin US$28) at Robert's Grove Beach Resort serves mouthwatering seafood and imported U.S. steaks. Don't forget **Habanero Mexican Café and Bar** (3–9 P.M., closed Jun.–Nov., US$9–15) for excellent Mexican food, just south of Seine Bight. A few miles farther north, **Maya Beach Hotel Bistro** (dinner reservations tel. 501/520-8040, open from 7 A.M., closed Mon.) has Placencians raving—and unanimously declaring that the food and experience is well worth the US$15 taxi trip from town (or US$1 on the afternoon bus).

INFORMATION

The Placencia Tourism Center is one of the most organized and useful in the country. Before leaving for your trip, check the website for updates and events: www.placencia.com. Upon arriving in town, head straight to the **Tourism Office** (tel. 501/523-4045, placencia@btl.net, 9 A.M.–5 P.M. Mon.–Fri., closed 1.5 hours at lunchtime) in Placencia Village Square; after reading the various fiesta postings on the wall, pick up a copy of the latest *Placencia Breeze* (www.placenciabreeze.com), a monthly rag with many helpful schedules and listings, including house rentals. The tourism office also sells books, maps, music CDs, and postcards and has a mail drop; the office will *not* recommend one business over another.

SERVICES

The **Shell station,** located at the southern terminus of the road, is open 6 A.M.–7 P.M. **Belize Bank** is across the road and has a 24-hour ATM. **Atlantic Bank** (8 A.M.–3 P.M. Mon.–Thurs., 8 A.M.–4:30 P.M. Fri.) has an ATM in town, across the road from Wendy's. The **Scotia Bank** (8 A.M.–2 P.M. Mon.–Thurs., 8 A.M.–3:30 P.M. Fri., 9–11:30 A.M. Sat.) has an ATM just north of the BTL office, and Belize Bank is there too.

Health and Emergencies

The **Placencia Medical Center** (8:30 A.M.–4:30 P.M. Mon.–Fri.) is behind the school. For after-hour emergencies **Dr. Alexis** (tel. 501/523-4038) makes house calls, should you have a severe shellfish reaction. The **Placencia police station** can be reached at 501/503-3142.

A short boat ride away, the village of Independence has the nearest 24-hour clinic to

HELP THE PLACENCIA HUMANE SOCIETY

The Placencia Humane Society (PHS) was formed in 1999, primarily to respond to the need for regular veterinary care on the peninsula. Today it is one of the country's most successful animal welfare organizations – and it's an entirely volunteer-run organization. In addition to basic veterinary services, the PHS also offers temporary emergency shelter for stray and injured pets, no-interest loans to area residents who need help caring for their pets, and spaying and neutering clinics for feral cats. It is in the process of raising funds to build a permanent clinic facility on land leased from a PHS supporter and donor.

Clinics are held the third weekend of each month at the Placencia Community Center, for surgeries and general appointments. If visitors (especially visiting veterinary surgeons and technicians) are interested in visiting or helping the clinic during their visits to Belize, they should contact the PHS president Mary Smith (tel. 501/523-4306, info@placencia-pets.org, www.placencia-pets.org). PHS accepts donations of medical supplies, pet supplies, and monetary contributions through memberships or donations (or items sold on the website). All monies raised are used for the welfare of animals in the area. The website offers additional descriptions of PHS services, information for volunteers, and a list of PHS-sponsored local events.

Placencia, and if a medevac to Belize City is not possible, this is where a patient will be taken in an emergency. The **private clinic** (tel. 501/601-2769) is on Water Side Street; there is also a public hospital providing health care to the poor.

Communications and Internet

The **BTL office,** at the bottom of the big red-and-white antenna, is open 8 A.M.–5 P.M. Monday–Friday but closes for lunch.

Placencia Office Supply, tucked off the main road in the town center (tel. 501/523-3433, fax 501/523-3205, 8:30 A.M.–7 P.M. Mon.–Sat., closed at lunchtime), has a copy machine, Internet service, fax, and more—they'll let you plug into their Ethernet line or use their wireless Internet as well (US$4/hr). Free wireless broadband is available at the **Secret Garden, Purple Space Monkey Internet Café,** and an ever-growing number of resorts and accommodations.

Groceries

At **Tommy's Market** and **Wallen's Market,** both on the main road, you can fill almost all of your needs, including groceries, dry goods, and sundries. **Everyday Supermarket,** in the center of town, is open 7 A.M.–9 P.M. There is a pharmacy above Wallen's Market (tel. 501/523-3346).

For wine, liquor, deli items, and gourmet groceries, visit **Peckish** (tel. 501/523-3636, www.peckishbelize.com, 8 A.M.–5 P.M.) at Live Oak Plaza, just south of the airstrip; it also offers custom provisioning for boats and condos.

Laundry

Cheaper places usually have someone available to wash clothes by hand. Otherwise, take your load to Omar's Diner and drop it off with Cara (US$10). Nearby, Julia (of Julia and Lawrence Guesthouse) also does laundry (US$5–12). At Live Oak Plaza (near the airstrip), **Cyberwash** is a clean, air-conditioned Laundromat with cable TV and wireless Internet service.

GETTING THERE

There are a number of ways to travel the 100-plus miles between Placencia Village and Belize City. The tip of the long peninsula is not as isolated as it used to be, and various options exist for continuing on to points south and west, including Guatemala and Honduras.

By Air

At last check, there were more than 20 daily flights in and out of Placencia's precarious little airstrip, to and from various destinations throughout Belize. Planes generally hop from either of Belize City's two airports to Dangriga, Placencia, and Punta Gorda (in that order, usually landing at all three), then turn around for the reverse trip north. Ask about service to Belmopan if you are headed to Cayo. For current schedules and fares, check directly with the two airlines: **Maya Island Air** (tel. 501/223-1140, U.S. tel. 800/225-6732, www.mayaislandair.com) or **Tropic Air** (tel. 501/226-2012, U.S. tel. 800/422-3435, www.tropicair.com). There is sometimes air service between nearby Savannah Airport (near Independence Village) and San Pedro Sula in Honduras; three flights a week run about US$160.

By Car

The 21-mile excuse for a road from Placencia village to where the peninsula hits the mainland was a rutted, dusty nightmare for decades. Then, in July 2008 the highest officials in the land gathered at Robert's Grove Beach Resort and signed the papers to begin the paving project that was completed in 2010. And the people rejoiced. It's now about a three- or four-hour drive from Belize City. From Belize City most people drive via the Hummingbird and Southern Highways. About a half hour after turning south before Dangriga, look for a left turn to Riverside, where you'll begin the peninsula road.

By Bus

Placencia Village is serviced by three daily bus departures and arrivals (in high season, anyway; service is spotty the rest of the year). Buses come and go from the Shell station and current schedules are posted on the Placencia Tourism Office door and the Placencia Breeze.

Buses to Dangriga depart Monday–Saturday at 6:30 A.M., 7 A.M., and 1 P.M.; on Sunday the 6:30 A.M. does not run. You'll need to change in Dangriga to reach Belize City. You can change again in Belmopan for a westbound Cayo bus. Cost is about US$5 or less for each leg of the journey. The more common—and quickest—bus route is via the boat to Mango Creek and Independence Village.

By Boat to Mango Creek

For those traveling to points south, like Punta Gorda or Guatemala, or for those who wish to avoid the Placencia Road, a boat-and-bus combo will get you back to the mainland and on your way. **Hokey Pokey Water Taxi** (tel. 501/523-2376 or 501/601-0271) provides regular service between the Texaco station dock and the dilapidated landing at Mango Creek, charging US$5 one-way for the 15-minute trip through bird-filled mangrove lagoons. Boats leave Placencia at 6:45 A.M., 10 A.M., 12:30 P.M., 2:30 P.M., 4 P.M., and 5 P.M.; the same boat turns around for the reverse trip: 6:30 A.M., 7:30 A.M., 8 A.M., 11 A.M., noon, 2:30 P.M., 4:30 P.M., and 5 P.M.

Bus connections to all points are coordinated with the 10 A.M. and 4 P.M. boats from Placencia, so the traveler needs only to worry about stepping onto the correct bus as soon as her boat lands in Independence (after the quick taxi shuttle to the bus depot by Sherl's Restaurant, US$0.50). Hokey Pokey is a reliable family-run operation, proudly steered by captains Pole, Lito, and Caral.

By Boat to Honduras and Guatemala

The ship to Puerto Cortés leaves every Friday at 9:30 A.M., returning Monday afternoon at 2 P.M. (tel. 501/202-4506 or 501/603-7787, Honduras tel. 504/665-1200). The trip costs US$50 and takes roughly four hours, stopping in Big Creek, Belize, for immigration purposes, and carrying a maximum of 50 passengers. Buy tickets at the Placencia Tourism Office. Every now and then (sometimes as often as a couple of times a week), a boatload of passengers arrives in Placencia

from Livingston, Guatemala, and seeks passengers to take with them back to Livingston (with an immigration stop in Punta Gorda). Inquire at Caribbean Tours and Travels.

GETTING AROUND

Placencia Village itself is small enough to walk, and if you're commuting on the sidewalk, walking is your only option (riding a bike on the sidewalk can earn you a US$50 fine). Speaking of two-wheeled options, there are plenty of bicycle rentals in town. If bicycling north on the road, know that Seine Bight is 5 miles from Placencia and Maya Beach another 2.5. The cheapest way (besides walking) to get up and down the peninsula is to hop on a bus as it travels to or from Dangriga.

Taxis

There used to be a free shuttle service up and down the peninsula; perhaps it'll be reinstated after the road is paved. In the meantime, there are at least a dozen green-plated taxis hanging around the Shell station and airstrip. Rides from town to the airstrip cost US$6 for one or two people, to the Seine Bight area one-way US$12, to Maya Beach US$15. Ask around the gas station and tourist office and look for posted rate lists to know what you should be paying. The more trusted and long-standing taxi services are listed in the *Placencia Breeze* and include **Sam Burgess** (tel. 501/523-3310 or 501/603-2819), **Cornell** (tel. 501/609-1077), **Percy Neal** (tel. 501/523-3202 or 501/614-7831), **Radiance Ritchie** (tel. 501/600-6050 or 501/523-3321), and **Traveling Gecko** (tel. 501/603-0553 or 501/523-4078).

Car Rental

Rent a car for do-it-yourself land tours to the Jaguar or Mayflower nature reserves, or for trips to the ruins near Punta Gorda. Otherwise you'll pay US$50–100 per person to join a tour group. **Barefoot Rentals** (tel. 501/523-3438, barefootrentalsbelize.com) has a selection of cars and golf carts (US$25–130 per day for cars; US$65–95 a day for golf carts).

Near Placencia

MONKEY RIVER

An easy 35-minute boat ride from Placencia brings you to the mouth of the Monkey River and the village of the same name. Founded in 1891, Monkey River village was once a thriving town of several thousand loggers, *chicleros,* banana farmers, and fishermen; that was then. Now, the super-sleepy village of 30 families (about 150 people) makes its way with fishing and, you guessed it, tourism. Many villagers are trained and licensed tour guides who work with hotels in Placencia to provide a truly unique wildlife-viewing experience.

Ninety percent of the structures you see have been rebuilt since Hurricane Iris destroyed the town in 2001. The village is accessible by boat—most often through the mangroves from Placencia—but there is also an 11-mile road from the Southern Highway that ends across the river from the village.

If you're on a tour from Placencia, after negotiating the mangrove maze your guide will take you into the river's mouth and dock up in town for a bathroom break and a chance to place your lunch order for later in the day. Then you'll be off upstream, all eyes peeled for animals. You'll beach up at the trailhead to explore a piece of **Payne's Creek National Park,** a 31,000-acre reserve that is surrounded by even more protected area. You'll hike through the dense brush, now a regenerating broadleaf forest that will take decades to reach its pre-Iris glory. Then it's back down the river for lunch and a stroll through the village. Most head back to their rooms in Placencia, but you may wish to consider staying a night or two, either to experience the village life or to get some serious fishing time in.

Accommodations and Food

The options in Monkey River are casual inns, best appreciated by those who enjoy isolation and primitive surroundings. Most offer a set menu (a different entrée served each day). Reservations are required for meals, though all of these small cafés will serve drop-ins something, such as a burger or a beer.

Near the breezy part of town by the mini-basketball court, **Alice's Restaurant** (tel. 501/720-2033) offers meals for about US$6, served in a large dining room with a view of the sea; renting one of her airy wood rooms in a neighboring building costs US$23, with fan and shared bath with hot and cold water. A room with private bath is planned. **Sunset Inn** (tel. 501/720-2028, www.monkeyriverfishing.com, US$50) is a two-story structure with eight musty rooms with private baths, fans, and hot and cold water. Decent meals can be had for about US$8. The **Black Coral Gift Shop, Bar, and Restaurant** offers simple fare, local crafts, and Internet. The family that runs this hotel has an acclaimed guide service too, especially for sportfishing trips.

All hotels and resorts offer sea and land tours and trips. Local guides and fishers are experts. Sorry, there's no dive shop yet, but bring your snorkeling gear. Overnight caye trips are available, as are river camping trips (you're dropped off at the Bladen bridge and canoe down the river, stopping at night to camp).

◀ LAUGHING BIRD CAYE

Managed by the nonprofit **Southern Environmental Association,** a.k.a. SEA Belize, formerly Friends of Nature (office near Placencia Town dock, tel. 501/523-3377, www.seabelize.org), **Laughing Bird Caye National Park** is an important protected area encompassing over 10,000 acres of sea; it's a popular day trip from Placencia. Swaying palms, small beautiful beaches, an absence of biting bugs, shallow sandy swimming areas, and interesting snorkeling and diving all make this an easy must-see.

This particular kind of caye is referred to as a *faro,* and the arms on each end make a kind of enclosure around a lagoon area on the leeward side. In this way, the island acts much like a mini-atoll. That's good news for those wishing to dive the eastern side of the island. You'll find a lot of elkhorn coral and fish life. Grunts, damselfish, parrot fish, houndfish, bonefish, and even rays and nurse sharks are to be found here.

This site was designated in December 1991. The reserve is visited regularly, mostly by researchers and tourists carried out by tour operators from Placencia for picnics, snorkeling, and diving. Previously, the reserve was used for overnight camping, but no longer, because of the lack of toilet or other waste disposal facilities. Some mooring buoys have been installed to prevent anchor damage to the surrounding reef. Private yachts and sea kayaks also use the site regularly. There is one trail through the center of the caye.

SEA Belize also manages the Sapodilla Cayes, Placencia Lagoon, and **Gladden Spit and Silk Cayes Marine Reserve,** a famous whale shark site, where they plan to build a resource center for fishers and tour guides.

MANGO CREEK (INDEPENDENCE VILLAGE)

This coastal population and transport hub began as Mango Creek and later expanded into Independence Village; it is referred to alternately by both names. This is a dispersed community with a sweltering climate and no attractions aimed at tourism, except as a transportation stop. There is also a deep-water port, where Belize's oil is being exported. The only reason a traveler be here for any length of time is if he or she is waiting for a boat or bus or perhaps volunteering in one of the medical facilities. Independence has the area's biggest secondary school, and a boatload of students from Placencia make the daily trip to conduct

their studies, as there is no high school on the peninsula.

Accommodations

There are a few places to stay in Independence if you miss your boat and are stuck here, including 13 rooms at **Ursella's Guest House** (up the street behind the basketball court, tel. 501/503-2062, US$20 shared bath) and **Hotel Hello** (near the bus "station," tel. 501/523-2428, US$25 s, US$40 d), which has a restaurant. The nicest option, **Hotel Cardie's** (tel. 501/523-2421, US$50), is on the main road to the highway. Rooms have air-conditioning, private baths, and TV, and there's also a decent on-site restaurant.

Food

Far at **Sheri's** (Mon.–Sat. 6:30 A.M.–9 P.M.), behind the gas station where you'll board or get off your bus. There are cheap plates of food and a bathroom. Or try the Chinese restaurant by the park.

Services

There is an **Alliance Bank** branch by the park (tel. 501/523-2588, 8 A.M.–2 P.M. Tues.–Fri.).

Getting There and Away

Bus service through Independence is provided on a perplexing timetable. You probably won't have to worry about bus times, though, since your boat will hook you right onto your bus. The best we could make out, the last bus to Punta Gorda leaves at 8 P.M., sometimes later, and the last ride to Dangriga and Belize City is at 5:30 P.M. The earliest northbound bus from PG arrives around 7 A.M. and the James express reaches at 9 A.M.

PUNTA GORDA AND THE TOLEDO VILLAGES

Southern Belize offers wild, remote attractions serviced by a crop of creative accommodations throughout the district. Improvements to the Southern Highway and daily air service to and from Punta Gorda (PG) are helping to put Toledo on the map as the "Unforgettable" corner of Belize, rather than its traditional reputation as "Forgotten" corner. Toledo District's attractions include small, remote villages, caves, waterfalls, and offshore cayes. Still, Toledo remains about as off the beaten track as you can get in Belize.

Toledo District is a blend of many cultures—Q'eqchi' and Mopan Maya, mestizo, Mennonite, Garifuna, Creole, Caucasian, Chinese, Palestinian, and East Indian, to name a few of the local communities. More than 10,000 Q'eqchi' and Mopan Maya are subsistence farmers in the Toledo countryside.

Toledo is the district in Belize with the lowest per capita income, and it is also the most expensive in which to live. Money earmarked for development and tourism rarely finds its way south, although the first signs of growth and real estate swapping around Punta Gorda are showing themselves—the cacao trail, the addition of several upscale lodges, and the cheap hotels and backpacker digs that have been around longer.

Tourism continues to arrive in the region in small, interesting doses: student groups, researchers, botanists, chocolate lovers, and independent travelers interested in the area's world-famous ecotourism programs.

PLANNING YOUR TIME

If you are coming to the area by bus, plan on nearly a full day of travel on either end of your

© JOSHUA BERMAN

HIGHLIGHTS

◖ **The Punta Gorda Waterfront:** It's neither developed nor pristine, but don't miss a casual walk along the Caribbean – then wander to Central Park for ice cream (page 216).

◖ **Lubaantun:** The ancestors of today's Maya used this ceremonial center, which – along with nearby Nim Li Punit and Uxbenka – boasts stunning views, thick forests, and several longstanding legends (page 227).

◖ **Aguacaliente Wildlife Sanctuary:** Swing through the relaxing village of Laguna to access the boardwalks of this premier birding destination (page 229).

◖ **Blue Creek Cave:** Near the village of Blue Creek, the cave of the same name is the source of the Río Blanco – you can swim 600 yards inside it. Also check out nearby Río Blanco National Park (page 233).

◖ **Village Guesthouses and Homestays:** Head upcountry to experience a cultural immersion program in one of a dozen simple country villages. In addition to the cultural adventure, expect guided hiking, swimming, caving, and river trips (page 234).

LOOK FOR ◖ TO FIND RECOMMENDED SIGHTS, ACTIVITIES, DINING, AND LODGING.

trip south (at least five to six hours from Belize City); consider taking the quick flight from Belize City, Placencia, or Dangriga, to Punta Gorda. If you plan on heading into the upcountry Toledo villages, you'll have to come to PG first to set up the trip, usually necessitating at least one night in town, maybe more, depending on the limited village bus schedules. Basically, if you really want to explore Toledo District, one or two days ain't gonna cut it. You'll need to set aside at least four or five days, more if you'd like to get out to the cayes or beyond to Guatemala or Honduras, just across the bay.

HISTORY

Originally, this area served as a coastal trading center for the Maya, who sent trading parties out to sea and guided them back home with hilltop bonfires. In the 1860s, British settlers encouraged Americans to come and begin new lives in Belize. During the American Civil War, arms dealers became familiar with the southern Belizean coast and hundreds of ex-Confederate soldiers arrived and cleared land after the war. Most of the American settlers returned to the United States, though one group of Methodists from Mississippi stayed in Toledo District long enough to develop a dozen sugar plantations. By 1910, most of the Mississippians were gone, but their sugar became popular during U.S. Prohibition; boats decked out as fishing crafts reportedly ran rum from Belize to Florida.

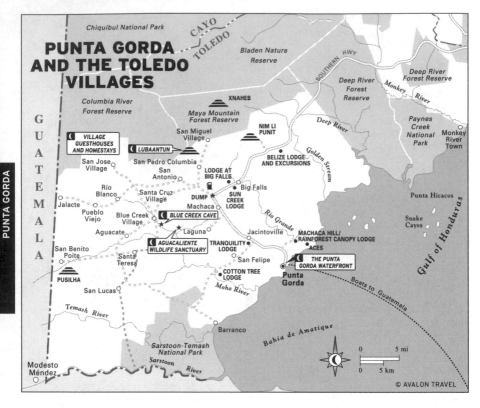

Punta Gorda and Vicinity

Toledo District's county seat and biggest town, PG is simultaneously the lazy end of the road and an exciting jumping-off point to upland villages, offshore cayes, Guatemala, or Honduras. Punta Gorda's 5,000 or so inhabitants live their daily lives, getting by from hurricane to hurricane.

Punta Gorda is a simple port, not superclean, with no real beach, and its crooked streets are framed by many old, dilapidated wooden buildings. The majority of inhabitants in town are of Garifuna and East Indian descent, though there are representatives of most of the groups. Fishing was the main support of

the local people for centuries; today many fishers work for a nearby high-tech shrimp farm. Local farmers grow rice, mangoes, bananas, sugarcane, and beans—mainly for themselves and the local market. Fair trade–certified and organic cacao beans are an important export as well, used to make chocolate by the Green & Black's company in England.

ORIENTATION

Punta Gorda is a casual village with few street names. Arriving from the north, you'll cross a bridge over Joe Taylor Creek, then be greeted by the towering Sea Front Inn, with the

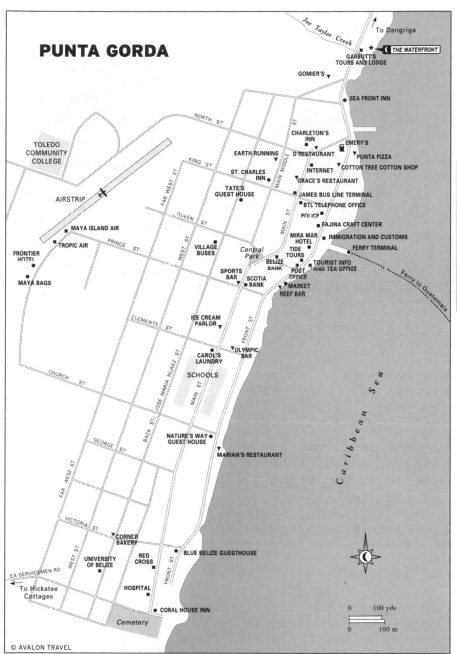

PUNTA GORDA

Joe Taylor Creek

To Dangriga

THE WATERFRONT

GARBUTT'S
TOURS AND LODGE

GOMIER'S

SEA FRONT INN

NORTH ST

CHARLETON'S
INN

EMERY'S

TOLEDO
COMMUNITY
COLLEGE

EARTH RUNNINS

D'RESTAURANT

PUNTA PIZZA

KING ST

INTERNET

COTTON TREE COTTON SHOP

ST. CHARLES
INN

GRACE'S RESTAURANT

AIRSTRIP

TATE'S
GUEST HOUSE

JAMES BUS LINE TERMINAL

BTL TELEPHONE OFFICE

MAYA ISLAND AIR

QUEEN ST

POLICE

FAR WEST ST

FAJINA CRAFT CENTER

TROPIC AIR

PRINCE ST

MIRA MAR
HOTEL

IMMIGRATION AND CUSTOMS

FRONTIER
HOTEL

VILLAGE
BUSES

Central
Park

TIDE
TOURS

FERRY TERMINAL

WEST ST

BELIZE
BANK

POST
OFFICE

TOURIST INFO
AND TEA OFFICE

MAYA BAGS

SPORTS
BAR

SCOTIA
BANK

Ferry to Guatemala

MARKET

REEF BAR

CLEMENTS ST

ICE CREAM
PARLOR

FRONT ST

JOSE MARIA NUÑEZ ST

OLYMPIC
BAR

CAROL'S
LAUNDRY

CHURCH ST

SCHOOLS

MAIN ST

BACK ST

Caribbean Sea

GEORGE ST

NATURE'S WAY
GUEST HOUSE

MARIAN'S RESTAURANT

FAR WEST ST

VICTORIA ST

WEST ST

CORNER
BAKERY

UNIVERSITY
OF BELIZE

RED
CROSS

FRONT ST

BLUE BELIZE GUESTHOUSE

EX-SERVICEMEN RD

To Hickatee
Cottages

HOSPITAL

CORAL HOUSE INN

Cemetery

0   100 yds

0   100 m

© AVALON TRAVEL

TOLEDO'S CHOCOLATE TRAIL

making chocolate the old-fashioned way, Cyrila Cho's kitchen

The cacao tree (*Theobroma cacao* or "food of the gods") has gained renewed importance in the culture and economy of Mayans in southern Belize. Thousands of years ago, Maya kings and priests worshipped the cacao bean, using it as currency and drinking it in a sacred, spicy beverage. Today, farmers sell their cacao crop to the **Toledo Cacao Growers Association (TCGA),** a nonprofit coalition of about a thousand small farms, which, in turn, sells the beans to acclaimed chocolatier Green & Black's, a United Kingdom–based company specializing in fair trade and organic-certified chocolate bars. Some beans remain in Belize, used by a few Maya families and small-batch chocolate makers to produce chocolate for the domestic market. Stop by the **TCGA office** (one block north of the town park on Main Street in Punta Gorda, tel. 501/722-2992, tcga@btl.net) to see if they are offering any tours or products.

Sustainable Harvest International (SHI, tel. 501/722-2010, U.S. tel. 207/669-8254, www.sustainableharvest.org), a nonprofit

Caribbean on your left. After the road splits at a Texaco station, it forms North Park Street (a diagonal street a block long) on the right and Front Street on the left. Following Front Street will take you through town, past the boat taxi pier, the immigration office, the market, and several eating establishments; continue south to Nature's Way Guest House at the bottom of Church Street, followed by Blue Belize. The municipal dock and town plaza, just a couple blocks in from the sea, form the town center.

If arriving by bus, or at the town dock from Guatemala, prepare to be greeted by a few local hustlers; feel free to shake them off by firmly refusing their services.

SIGHTS
C The Waterfront

Even though there is no real lounging beach or developed waterfront, people go swimming off (and sunbathing on) the dock just north of Joe Taylor Creek. The waterfront is rocky, but quiet and tranquil, with small waves lapping the shoreline, and a walk along its length,

organization working to alleviate poverty and deforestation throughout Central America, is active in Belize's Toledo District. The organization works with more than 100 cacao-growing families, helping them develop multistory forest plots that mimic the natural forest; this provides a diversity of food and marketable produce for the families, plus a home for threatened plants and animals. Coffee, plantains, and other shade-loving crops are planted alongside the cacao trees, under a hardwood canopy – sometimes along with spices like turmeric, black pepper, ginger, and vanilla. Sustainable Harvest Belize estimates that for every acre converted to multistory cacao forest, five acres are saved from destructive slash-and-burn practices. The organization offers sustainable chocolate tours and other voluntourism opportunities at work sites in southern Belize. Accommodations range from rustic homestays to the stilted cabins of Cotton Tree Lodge, where SHI maintains a demo garden.

This revival of southern Belize's cacao industry has also led to choco-tourism. A few area lodges and families have found ways to connect ancient cacao farming with the modern craze for high-quality fair-trade food and products. **Cyrila Cho** and her family, in the village of San Felipe (tel. 501/666-3444 or 501/664-3132, chocolatescirila@gmail.com), are one example, offering a five-hour chocolate tour beginning with a visit to an organic cacao farm and continuing with lunch in Cyrila's home, where she and her daughter then lead a chocolate-making session. Sustainable Harvest Belize also offers half-day cacao trips; contact the organization through the website.

Ask your hotel hosts about other cacao day trips and tours. In addition to tours, **Cotton Tree Lodge** offers special weeklong chocolate packages and produces its own small-batch chocolate bars (call 501/621-8776 to visit the mini-chocolate factory in PG). There's also the annual **Cacao Fest,** held in late May, celebrating all things chocolate by offering a host of local products – from cupcakes and kisses to cacao wine and martinis – as well as numerous cultural events. For information, visit www.toledochocolate.com.

MORE BELIZEAN CHOCOLATE

In Placencia, the owners of the Blue Crab Resort make **Goss Chocolate** (www.gosschocolate.com) from 100 percent pure organic cacao, available only in Belize. In San Pedro, "passionate chocolate lovers" Jo and Chris Beaumont created **Kakaw Chocolates** (tel. 501/610-4828 or 501/236-5759, www.belizechocolatecompany.com) to produce small batches of artisan chocolate to order; the beans are grown organically on small family farms in southern Belize and the sugar comes from the north of the country. Kakaw chocolate is available at Wine de Vine in San Pedro in deliciously dark flavors such as orange, cashew, ginger, and mango.

especially at sunrise, should be a top priority of your visit.

Central Park

The town park, on a small triangle of soil roughly in the center of town, has an appropriately sleepy air to it. At the north end is a raised stage dedicated to the "Pioneers of Belizean Independence." In the center of the park is a dry fountain, along with a few green cement benches. A clock tower on the south end of the park has hands everlastingly stuck, as if

holding time at bay. On market days, this is an especially pleasant spot to take a break, enjoy the blue sky, and watch the activities of the villagers who have come in to sell their produce.

Market Days

Although there are four weekly market days, Wednesdays and Saturdays are the biggest. Monday and Friday are smaller but still interesting. Many Maya vendors sell wild coriander, yellow or white corn, chili peppers of various hues, cassava, tamales wrapped in banana leaves, star fruit, mangoes, and much more. Many of the women and children bring handmade crafts as well. Laughing children help their parents. If you're inclined to snap a photo, ask permission first—and perhaps offer to buy something. If refused, smile and put your lens cap in place.

RECREATION
Diving, Snorkeling, and Fishing
The **Sapodilla Cayes** make up the hooked southern end of the Belize Barrier Reef and the continental shelf, and they offer incredible wall dives and very few dive boats. There are also a number of more gradual walls. In general, most sites offer either beautiful coral formations or lots of fish, but rarely both.

For fishing, the waterways and sea around Punta Gorda offer anglers the rare chance to bag a grand slam (permit, tarpon, bonefish, and snook). Fly-fishing is generally possible between November and May, in shallow areas around the cayes, mangroves, and river mouths. Reel fishing is available throughout the year, up the rivers or in the ocean; cast for snapper, grouper, jacks, barracuda, mackerel, or king fish. Most guides help you bring your fish back and find someone to cook it up for you. Fishing trips can run upward of US$400–500 for four people.

Tours
Garbutt's Marine and Fishing Lodge (tel. 501/604-3458), next to Joe Taylor Creek, at the entrance to Punta Gorda, is run by the Garbutt brothers, a local duo who grew up exploring these waters. They offer one of the most reliable ways to get out to the cayes and go sport fishing, diving, or snorkeling; they also maintain a few cabins on Lime Caye, and you can paddle up the creek in a kayak. Another diving option is **Wild Encounters** (tel. 501/722-2716 or 501/722-2300), operating out of the Seafront Hotel.

Reef Conservation International (ReefCI, tel. 501/626-1429, www.reefci.com) offers weekly and monthly dive trips to stay on **Tom Owens Caye**, a small one-acre private island in the Sapodilla Cayes with incredible snorkeling. The boat leaves Punta Gorda Monday morning and returns on Friday afternoon. While you're there, you can take scuba certification courses or help with research projects, always in small groups. It's worth stressing that not only will you be diving in the Sapodilla Cayes—the famous fishhook terminus of the Belize Barrier Reef, internationally renowned for its whale sharks, dolphins, and grouper spawning events—but you will also most likely be the *only* dive boat in the water, an extraordinary opportunity. Nondivers are also welcome. ReefCI offers various packages; there's often a discount for walk-in travelers and last-minute bookings (up to 50 percent). In addition to diving for fun, ReefCI customers have the opportunity to get involved in a number of projects, such as helping with the removal of the invasive lionfish and other preservation projects in the Sapodilla Cayes Marine Reserve (SCMR). They also have the unique opportunity to get involved with the survey work, learn about the environment, and identify fish, coral, and invertebrates—and to combine this with recreational dives and other activities.

BlueBelize Tours (tel. 501/722-0063 or 722-2678, www.bluebelize.com) is owned and run by Dan Castellanos, a local fisherman, guide, and PADI dive master who specializes in fishing and snorkeling tours. You'll have to catch him when he's not staffing biological research or leading National Geographic and BBC film crews around the area.

Toledo Cave and Adventure Tours (tel. 501/604-2124, belizegate@gmail.com or ibtm@gmx.net, www.travelbelize.de) offers trips to to some of Belize's lesser known attractions, including Yok Balum Cave, Tiger Cave, and all other Toledo Caves. Bruno, the German owner, also runs Sun Creek Lodge and offers countrywide tours and pick-up in Belize City.

TIDE Tours (tel. 501/722-2129, www.tide-tours.org) offers numerous inland and sea trips, including river kayaking, snorkeling, fishing, exploring villages, cacao trail tours, and more.

Kayak rentals are US$2.50 per hour. Also ask about multiday tour packages. This is the customer service branch of the Toledo Institute for Development and Environment (TIDE, www.tidebelize.org), Belize's only "ridges to reef" NGO. TIDE does much of the guide training in the area, helping to teach people sustainable, often tourism-related, skills. TIDE staff promote tours to protected areas and give presentations on their work in the Port Honduras Marine Reserve, in Paynes Creek National Park, and on the Private Lands Initiative. They also do tours to archaeological sites, caves, and other inland attractions. Revenue generated from TIDE Tours is used for education and outreach efforts.

ENTERTAINMENT

Nightlife

There are a handful of small bars scattered around town, some with pool tables, all with lots of booze. The best nightlife in PG is at the **Sports Bar** (Main St., closed Mon.–Wed.). Karaoke nights are Thursday and Sunday (9 P.M.–2 A.M.); dance parties are Friday and Saturday until 4 A.M. Locals also gather here for PPV sports and dominoes tournaments. **Waluco's** (it means "son of the soil" in Garifuna) is right across from the ocean, a short walk north of town, and is usually a happening spot, especially during festival times and after soccer games at Union Field. On Friday nights the **Reef Bar** has drumming. The **Olympic Bar** on Clement Street is re-opening soon.

Drumming Lessons

Ray McDonald (corner West St. and Cemetery Ln., "look for the sign by the mango tree and the coconut tree," tel. 501/632-7701), a local musician, offers an introduction to Garifuna drumming class. Learn about the various rhythms, how to produce the correct sound, and then start jamming. Private lessons start at US$7.50 per hour. To continue your drum tour of Belize's south, head up to Emmeth Young's drum-making shop and school in San Pedro Columbia, in the upcountry villages.

© JOSHUA BERMAN

PUNTA GORDA

Take master drumming lessons with Ray McDonald in Punta Gorda, or with Emmeth Young (pictured here) in San Pedro Columbia.

SHOPPING

Start next door to the airstrip, at the **Maya Bags** craft workshop (www.mayabags.org). About 50 area women participate in this craft and export venture. The women make hand-woven bags, embroidered yoga mats, beach bags, jipijapa purses, and other unique products. If you have time, you can order a custom embroidered design; craftsmanship is so good, the bags were featured in *Vogue* magazine in 2010.

Tienda La Indita Maya (24 Main Middle St.) lies just north of Central Park (at the end opposite the clock tower). Also check the **Fajina Women's Group Craft Center** on Front Street near the ferry pier. It's a small co-op for quality Maya crafts run by the Q'eqchi' and Mopan women. You'll find jipijapa baskets, cuxtales, slate carvings, calabash carvings, jewelry, textiles, and embroidered clothes—when they're open, that is. If the door is closed, ask upstairs at the restaurant to get it opened up.

JUNGLE LODGES OF SOUTHERN BELIZE

Toledo District has an eclectic selection of unique outlying resorts and bush camps, spanning all budgets. Discover villages, caves, and ruins by day, then kick back and soak in the surroundings by night, in a hammock or over a candlelit dinner, to the sound of birds and crickets.

NEAR PUNTA GORDA

The area's sole jungle-luxe property is **Machaca Hill Rainforest Canopy Lodge** (tel. 501/722-0050, www.machacahill.com, US$400–565 all-inclusive), located atop a forested perch high above the Río Grande and a gorgeous expanse of rainforest, five miles north of PG. This is a unique spot targeting a unique market. The manager, an "eco-luxury hospitality" expert, is originally from Zimbabwe, and is running the place like a high-end, all-inclusive safari resort. Machaca Hill's property encompasses 12,000 acres of rainforest and organic citrus, coffee, and cacao farms, including 4.5 miles of riverfront and Nicholas Caye, a pristine island in the Sapodilla Cayes. The sea is a 20-minute boat ride down the river, where you'll head for your sportfishing and snorkeling tours. Amenities include a pool, a farm-to-fork restaurant, a break-away sitting room and veranda, and spa, as well as a screened rainforest veranda in your canopy-level treehouse suite (there are 12); you may see a brightly colored toucan from your shower window or get a wakeup call from a howler monkey.

◀ **Cotton Tree Lodge** (tel. 510/670-0557, U.S. tel. 866/480-4534, www.cottontreelodge.com, about US$200 pp all-inclusive) is 12 miles up the Moho River from PG, and is accessed either by boat or via the road to Barranco. Its 11 stilted thatch-roof cabins along the river's edge are connected by a raised plank walkway; ask about the deep-jungle treehouse. The lodge is one of several in the area trying to take "green" to new levels; Cotton Tree conducts voluntourism projects with Sustainable Harvest International, has developed a unique septic system using banana plants, and raises 50 percent of the food it serves in

© JOSHUA BERMAN

cabin at Cotton Tree Lodge

its own organic garden. Available activities include the cacao trail, treks to Blue Creek Cave, mountain hikes, river and village trips, visits to ruins, and the like, plus hands-on classes in subjects like chocolate making and Garifuna drumming. Sportfishing and fly-fishing trips are available as well. There is one honeymoon suite with a Jacuzzi and one cabin with wheelchair access.

NEAR JACINTOVILLE

Tucked away on the San Felipe Road, about eight miles outside Punta Gorda, **Tranquility Lodge** (no phone, www.tranquility-lodge.com, US$100–125) offers four well-appointed rooms popular with avid bird-watchers and orchid lovers; both have plenty to explore right here on Tranquility's 20 lush acres (only five of which are developed at the lodge area). There were 75 species of orchids at last count – both planted and volunteers – and more than 200 identified species of birds. Rates include breakfast; rooms have clean tile floors, private baths, air-conditioning, and fans. When there are no other guests, it's like having your own private lodge. Upstairs from the rooms is a beautiful, screened-in (but very open) dining room, where you'll enjoy gourmet dinners for US$25. All rates are negotiable in the off-season. There's direct access to an excellent swimming hole on the Jacinto River, as well as a number of walking trails.

NEAR BIG FALLS

Hugging a lush bend of the Río Grande as it sweeps near the roadside village of Big Falls, ◖ **The Lodge at Big Falls** (tel. 501/671-7172 or 501/610-0126, www.thelodgeatbigfalls.com, US$140-160) is an elegant and quiet retreat in a peaceful, well-maintained, green clearing. The eight cabanas are ideal for the nature-loving couple looking for a comfortable base from which to explore the surrounding country or just to laze in the pool and listen to the forest sounds. Special rates are offered for multiple nights and for families; it's a 20-minute drive to the town of Punta Gorda, and many day trips are available, as The Lodge at Big Falls is centrally located in the Toledo District.

Sun Creek Lodge (tel. 501/614-2080, www.suncreeklodge.de, US$40-100) offers four octagonal cabanas with center post and thatch roof. Some have shared jungle showers and toilets, a few have private baths, and there is the spacious Sun Creek Suite for families or groups. Sun Creek is popular with European backpackers in that comfy-yet-primitive way. The on-site tour company will take you wherever you want to go in the area, with active hikes being their forte – including trips and expeditions unavailable anywhere else. Car rental is available. Sun Creek Lodge is at Mile 14 on the Southern Highway, about two miles from "Dump." If you haven't arranged for a pickup in PG, look for the broken cement sign with "Sun Creek" painted on it as you drive south on the Southern Highway – get off the bus there.

If you're driving through the area, make time for lunch (or any other meal) at **Coleman's Cafe** in Big Falls (tel. 501/720-2017, 7 A.M.-7 P.M. daily, afternoon break 3-6 P.M.), located just off the highway, on the entrance road to Rice Mill. This is home-cooked Belizean food at its finest, and the restaurant is run by a friendly and accommodating family. Creole dishes, cohune cabbage, and East Indian curries are among the offerings.

NEAR BLUE CREEK

The same outfit that has a resort and research center on South Water Caye also has one in Toledo. **International Zoological Expeditions** (IZE, U.S. tel. 800/548-5843, ize2belize@aol. com, www.ize2belize.com) has a lodge at the Blue Creek Rainforest Station, which can host cottage guests at the rustic site. Guests must hike one-third of a mile up into the rainforest along a trail that borders Blue Creek to reach the group of simple cabins with bunk beds, screens, lights, and electric fans. One cabin has a queen-size bed. Bathrooms are in the main lodge, where meals are served. Your rate of US$115 per person per night covers lodging, three meals, and two daily activities of your choice (for example, guided hikes into the rainforest and cave).

BELIZE LODGE AND EXCURSIONS

This one-of-a-kind operation features a circuit of remote, all-inclusive, upscale safari-style lodges on a vast swath of protected lowland tropical jungle stretching from the Maya Mountain foothills to the sea. (The property was pieced together out of land that otherwise would have gone to shrimp and cattle farms.) **Belize Lodge and Excursions** (BLE, tel. 501/223-6324, U.S. tel. 888/292-2462, www.belizelodge.com, US$450 per day per person) offers a unique three-lodge circuit in an all-inclusive package, modeled after similar circuits in the African safari scene. Guests can land at BLE's private airstrip and begin their eco-adventures at either Indian Creek Lodge, located across the road from the Nim Li Punit archaeological site, or Ballum Na (House of the Jaguar), where guests stay in a unique jaguar enclosure and see big cats out their bedroom windows. They continue their journey by floating down the pristine Golden Stream to accommodations at Jungle Camp, and then on to Moho Caye Lodge, located in the Port Honduras Marine Reserve. Rooms and amenities are quite luxurious, considering how remote they are, yet they are in tune with the surrounding natural landscape.

ACCOMMODATIONS
Under US$25

Punta Gorda's seedier hotels occupy the block of Front Street near the main dock; a good rule of thumb is *not* to book a room that is accessed via a smoky bar and pool hall (e.g., the Mira Mar). Quieter options are only a few blocks off the waterfront.

St. Charles Inn (tel. 501/722-2149, stcharlespg@btl.net, US$25, US$32.50 with a/c) is centrally located, with a dozen rooms and a shady veranda that allows you to observe village life below. Well-kept rooms include springy mattresses, private baths, fans, and small TVs.

You're apt to run into all sorts of interesting travelers from around the world at **(Nature's Way Guest House** (65 Front St., tel. 501/702-2119, natureswayguesthouse@hotmail.com, US$18–23). Six small wooden rooms are basic and fan-cooled in pleasant surroundings; all share a bathroom. There are three rooms with private baths and showers. Nature's Way serves a good breakfast, and you'll have access to all the activities in the area. The place is run by Chet Schmidt and his Belizean wife. Chet is an American expat and Vietnam veteran who has been here for over four decades; he also spent 13 years teaching in the surrounding villages. He can help arrange kayak trips, jungle treks, camping, exploration of uninhabited cayes, visits to archaeology sites, and Maya and Garifuna guesthouse stays with TEA.

A mile and a half outside Punta Gorda, in Cattle Landing, you'll find a uniquely relaxed experience at **Irie Belize** (tel. 501/625-5485, milanusher@yahoo.com, US$18), which offers a few simple rooms by the sea: thatched roof, sand floor, and friendly folks. There's a chill bar and grill, and the owner, Marlon Usher, has a boat for tours and provides shuttle service from the airport or town. He also can set you up in a backabush campground on the Barranco Road, in a cabin or your own tent. To get to Irie Belize, take the last left as you depart PG, before you hit the curve (look for the sign). Then follow the road until you see the bar on your right.

US$25-50

As you step off the tarmac at the airport, you'll see the **Frontier Inn** (3 Airport St., tel. 501/722-2450, frontierinn@btl.net, US$30), a two-story white cement building. Good value, tile-floored rooms have TV, wireless Internet, private bath, and hot water; the place is owned by a local airplane pilot. **(Tate's Guest House** (34 Jose Maria Nunez St., tel. 501/722-0147, tatesguesthouse@yahoo.com, US$23–35) is a comfortable, friendly lodging with five double rooms in a quiet neighborhood setting. Rooms without air-conditioning are considerably cheaper. Ask for room 4 or 5; they are spacious with ceiling fans, TV, sunrooms, louvered windows, and tile floors, and each has an additional entrance through the backyard. Internet and breakfast are available.

Charlton's Inn (tel. 501/722-2197, www.charltonsinn.com, US$40) is close to everything in town, and James buses stop across the street. The 27 rooms are well kept with hot and cold water, private baths, TV, air-conditioning, and fans; there are also five furnished apartments available.

US$50-150

Occupying a breezy, ocean-looking rise next to the hospital, **(Coral House Inn** (151 Main St., tel. 501/722-2878, www.coralhouseinn.net, US$83–100) is an excellent oceanfront bed-and-breakfast with a small pool and bar and a quiet yard, and a view of the sea. It was opened after the owners drove to Belize from Idaho in their VW Microbus (which you'll recognize zipping around town on errands). The four rooms are pleasantly decorated with soft colors, local artwork, and comfortable beds; bicycles and wireless Internet are free for guests. This is where the last prime minister used to stay when in Punta Gorda. Ask about the Seaglass Cottage, a little one-bedroom, one-bathroom, small-kitchen option, pitched on a bluff above the ocean (US$125).

One mile outside Punta Gorda, up Ex-Servicemen Road, **(Hickatee Cottages** (tel. 501/662-4475, www.hickatee.com, US$75–110) is a wonderful option on the edge of the jungle. Your expatriate British hosts are knowledgeable about local flora and fauna, passionate about their "lifestyle business," and strive to run a green hotel and involve the local community as much as possible. After you've settled into your well-appointed wooden cottage (private bathroom, hardwood furniture, ceiling fans, and veranda) or the garden suite (more space, furnishings, and kitchenette), take a walk through the beautiful grounds and nature trail, followed by a dip in the plunge pool. Hickatee Cottages is very popular with birders and naturalists; guests wander on a jungle trail, participate in howler monkey research, watch orchid bees at work while having a cup of Toledo organic coffee, and observe the wild creatures of the night on the bug board. Bicycles are available to get to and from town. Ask about visiting the on-site farm, fruit trees, nursery, and orchid collection (40 native species at last count!); rate also includes a free visit to Fallen Stones Butterfly Farm (Wednesday afternoons, advance reservations required, maximum four people—incredible opportunity!). Also on-site, **Charlie's Bar** offers home-cooked, healthy meals (about US$8 for breakfast and lunch, US$17.50 for dinner). Hickatee sometimes offers cultural nights, including drumming lessons with Ray McDonald, a renowned local musician.

BlueBelize Guest House (tel. 501/722-0063 or 501/722-2678, www.bluebelize.com, US$75–135 plus tax) is owned and operated by marine biologist Rachel Graham. The six furnished apartments are large and tastefully decorated, with one or two bedrooms, en suite bathrooms, kitchenettes or full kitchens, hot and cold water, ceiling fans, and wireless Internet. The rooms open onto verandas or patios—literally a stone's throw from the water's edge. BlueBelize is very popular with visiting doctors, scientists, and volunteers, as well as folks wanting to escape dark cold winters up north.

The **Sea Front Inn** (4 Front St., tel. 501/722-2300, www.seafrontinn.com, US$65–80, continental breakfast) is impossible to miss as you enter town: two towering stone buildings across the street from the sea. The 14 rooms and three apartments are also available for monthly rentals. Guests find comfortable, spacious rooms, no two alike, with TV, fans, air-conditioning, private baths, and handmade furniture built with hardwoods. The third floor is the kitchen/dining room/common area, overlooking the ocean.

Also on the waterfront, **Beya Suites** looks like a giant pink-and-white wedding cake (tel. 501/722-2188, www.beyasuites.com, US$75–87.50). Inside you'll find cheery staff to show you to one of the comfortable, air-conditioned, tile-floored rooms with large bathrooms and a sinus-clearing floral scent. There's a great rooftop, a restaurant (breakfast only), a bar, a conference area, and fast Internet. Ask about apartments and weekly rates.

FOOD

Punta Gorda offers mainly cheap, local eats, with the added benefit of fresh seafood and a few excellent vegetarian options. Many restaurants are closed on Sundays and for a few hours between meals. The town has several good bakeries, and fruit and veggies are cheap and abundant on market days (Monday, Wednesday, Friday, and Saturday). Some of the best breakfast and lunch joints in the market building—the most delicious of which is **Marril's**—are also only open these days. Ask at any corner store for a sampling of the local Mennonite yogurt and bread. Also be sure to try a seaweed shake, which you can buy fresh and cold at Johnson's Hardware Store, across from the market.

Keep an eye out for **Mr. Buns,** who pedals around on his bike with homemade cinnamon rolls and cheese buns. Or stop by the **Corner Bakery** (Mon.–Fri. 7:30 A.M.–9 P.M., Sat. 8 A.M.–2 P.M., and Sun. 5–9 P.M.) on the south end of town by the university. Every day you'll find a variety of baked goods, including brownies, cookies, bagels, creole bread, and honey whole wheat oatmeal bread. Try grilled sandwiches or pizza for lunch and dinner specials such as ginger teriyaki chicken or lasagna; there are also a few vegetarian options on the menu.

PUNTA GORDA

The tortilla factory, just south of the bank, makes fresh tortillas every day; they also make tacos, *panades,* and the like. The shack next to the immigration dock has excellent tacos and sometimes coconut fudge—convenient for that early morning boat trip. The best johnnycakes are baked across the street from the fire station. There are some great fast-food places surrounding Central Park, too, including **Jamal's.**

The **Reef Bar** (tel. 501/631-7968, 11 A.M.–midnight) is a convivial rooftop affair on the water's edge, above the market, with nice views and frequent drum sessions. Lunch and dinner are offered, with a nice selection of fish specials, including conch and lobster in season. There's Garifuna drumming and dancing on Friday nights.

Another popular spot is the **Snack Shack** (near BTL parking lot, 7 A.M.–4 P.M. Mon.–Fri., 7 A.M.–3 P.M. Sat., 7 A.M.–2:30 P.M. Sun.), with breakfast, US$3 burritos, fruit shakes, pancakes, and sometimes bagels.

For Jamaican Ital food, veggie burritos on whole-wheat tortillas, homemade hummus, fish dishes, and a mellow Rasta-flavored bar/lounge scene, stop by (**Earth Runnins Cafe and Bukut Bar** (13 Main Middle St., 7 A.M.–2 P.M. and 5–11 P.M. Wed.–Mon.). There's a barbecue on Sunday and occasionally live music. Earth Runnins has some of the best cocktails in town and offers a few computers for Internet (as well as wireless access). Very *tranquilo* atmosphere.

On the same Ital vibe, but in a smaller, humbler space, (**Gomier's Restaurant** (at the north entrance to town, right across from the Punta Gorda welcome sign, tel. 501/722-2929, www.gomiers.com) offers a delicious veggie and seafood menu oozing with whole grains, homemade tofu, and good karma. The restaurant is tiny and has tasty and creative daily specials, such as barbecued tofu served with baked beans, bread, and coleslaw, plus a veggie grain casserole served with a salad (about US$5), a bulging soysage burger (only US$3), and tofu pizza. There are also fresh fruit juices, soy milk, and soy ice cream. Gomier opens around 8 A.M. and closes around 9 P.M. (though

he often closes up shop at random times). It's closed on Sunday.

Look for the **Cotton Tree Chocolate Shop** (2 Front St., just south of the Texaco Station, tel. 501/621-8772, www.cottontreechocolate. com). They make milk, white, and dark chocolates; in addition to free chocolate samples, tours are available by appointment. A small gift shop sells chocolates, cocoa mix, cocoa butter, whole vanilla beans, and handmade soap by Dawn and Jo's Soap Soap Company, which looks good enough to eat. Upstairs, you'll find **Punta Pizza** (a.k.a. Déja View Café, tel. 501/633-4205, 8 A.M.–9 P.M. Mon.–Sat. and noon–9 P.M. Sun.), offering pizza by the slice or whole pies hot out of the wood-fired oven. Aside from pizza, there's local grown coffee, espresso drinks, brownies, homemade ice cream, and exotic fruit juices. The covered outdoor seating area faces the sea.

Emery's (11:30 A.M.–10 P.M., with a few breaks between meals) serves a solid lunch or dinner when it's open; slow service makes it easy to meet people over daily seafood specials.

An easy place to recommend is (**Marian's Bayview Restaurant** (11 A.M.–2 P.M. and 6–10 P.M. Mon.–Sat., noon–2 P.M. and 6–10 P.M. Sun.), located on a rooftop over the water, on the south edge of Punta Gorda (across from Nature's Way). Marian's serves East Indian cuisine, seafood, or a good ole plate of rice 'n' beans for US$5—all with a view of Guatemala and Honduras across the water.

Nature's Way Guest House (tel. 501/702-2119) and the **Sea Front Inn** (4 Front St., tel. 501/722-2300, www.seafrontinn.com) both serve filling breakfasts, although you need to make a reservation with Nature's Way and the Sea Front may make you wait a while for it. Another option is **D' Restaurant,** in the large corner building by Charlton's Inn, open for breakfast and dinner, with Belizean and American dishes. Around the corner, **El Café** has cheap, diner-style Belizean food all day long.

Merenco's (10 A.M.–2 P.M. and 5:30–10 P.M. Mon.–Sat., 4–10 P.M. Sun.), next to the **Ice**

Cream Parlor (1.5 blocks south of the park), has super-cheap burritos, famous fishbowl-size natural fruit juices, and a selection of dinners, as well as sandwiches and snacks. **Grace's Restaurant** (6 A.M.–10 P.M. daily) is a long-standing joint with typical Belizean fare like stew chicken (US$4), tasty conch soup (US$9), and eggs and beans with fry jacks.

If you don't have the time to visit the Maya villages, be sure to stop by **Fajina Restaurant** for traditional Maya fare, typically a bowl of caldo served with corn tortillas hot off the comal. The restaurant is run by the same women's group that operates the craft shop downstairs. Occasionally you'll find calaloo or cohune cabbage on the daily menu.

A few Chinese restaurants offer reliable chop suey, especially **Tai Song** and **Fei Wang**, although the latter is sometimes frequented by sloppy drunks. Some expats call **Hang Cheon,** on Main Street next to Merenco's, the best Chinese in town.

As you follow the highway north out of Punta Gorda, look for a driveway and sign on your left just as the road is about to turn away from the sea, and you'll find █ **Mangrove Inn and Restaurant** (tel. 501/722-2270 or 501/622-1645, open from 5 P.M. every day). This is a family affair—literally! You have to walk through your hosts' living room to get to the dining balcony. Your cook, Iconie, has worked in fancy resorts across Belize but prefers working at home these days. Expect savory fish dishes, pot pies, lasagna, fresh salads, and rolls; it runs roughly US$6–10 per plate.

INFORMATION

Look for the **Toledo Tourism Information Center** (8:30 A.M.–4:30 P.M. Mon.–Fri., Sat. till noon) on Front Street, not far from the Town Dock. This is a concerted effort by local businesses to provide excellent and organized information to tourists; they'll recommend accommodations, tour companies, transport, and so on. The **Toledo Ecotourism Association** (TEA, tel. 501/722-2531, tea-belize@yahoo.com, www.plenty.org/mayan-ecotours) is based in the information center,

though they rarely have their desk staffed; theoretically, this is where you sign up to stay in one of the seven village guesthouses. Also, pick up a print or PDF copy of *The Toledo Howler* (www.belizenews.com/howler), a local magazine for upcoming events and updated transport schedules.

SERVICES

Near the municipal dock, you'll find the **immigration office** (tel. 501/722-2247). Opposite that are a couple of government buildings, including the **post office. PG Laundry,** across from the Belize Bank, is open 6 A.M.–8 P.M. and charges by the pound. **Carol's Laundry Service,** near St. Peter Claver School, is open 7 A.M.–6 P.M. Fill your gas tank at the **Texaco** station at the north end of Front Street, right across from the ocean; they accept travelers checks and credit cards.

Health and Emergencies

Contact the **police** at 501/722-2022, the **fire department** at 501/722-2032, and the **hospital** at 501/722-2026 or 501/722-2161.

There are several informal tourist information centers in Punta Gorda.

© JOSHUA BERMAN

Money

The **Belize Bank** (tel. 501/722-2326, 8 A.M.–3 P.M. Mon.–Thurs., 8 A.M.–4:30 P.M. Fri.) is right across from the town square and has an ATM. Continue one block south to **Scotia Bank** (8 A.M.–2 P.M. Mon.–Thurs., 8 A.M.–3:30 P.M. Fri., and 9–11:30 A.M. Sat.), which has a 24-hour international ATM. Grace's Restaurant is also a licensed **Casa de Cambio** and can change dollars, quetzales, or travelers checks. You may also find a freelance moneychanger hanging around the dock at boat time.

Internet Access

There are two Internet places just north of the park, both with freezing air-conditioning and decent machines: One is **Dreamlight** (7:45 A.M.–8:45 P.M. Mon.–Sat. and 9 A.M.–3 P.M. Sun.). Two more Internet places are south of Central Park on Main Street.

Groceries

Check at Mel's Mart or one of the two Supaul's stores for local yogurt. Sophia Supaul's store on Alejandro Vernon Street (known locally as "Green Supaul's") carries imported cheeses (French brie in PG!), local jams and honey, a decent wine selection, couscous, white chocolate, vegetables, and fruits.

GETTING THERE
By Air

Daily southbound flights from Belize City to Dangriga continue to Placencia and then to Punta Gorda. This is the quickest and most comfortable way to get to PG. For the return trip, **Tropic Air** (tel. 501/226-2012, U.S. tel. 800/422-3435, www.tropicair.com) and **Maya Island Air** (tel. 501/223-1140, U.S. tel. 800/225-6732, www.mayaislandair.com) each offer five daily flights to Placencia, Dangriga, and Belize City, between 6:45 A.M. and 4 P.M. Tropic is usually more reliable and frequent in southern Belize.

By Land

Punta Gorda is just under 200 miles from Belize City, a long haul by bus, even with the newly surfaced Southern Highway speeding things up. Count on 3–4 hours by car, 5–6 hours by express bus, or seven hours in a nonexpress.

James Bus Lines (tel. 501/702-2049) has a centrally located terminal in Punta Gorda, at King and Main Street, and runs up to 10 daily buses between Punta Gorda and Belize City, departing 3:50 A.M.–3:50 P.M., with one express at 6 A.M. The first departure from Belize City is a 5:30 A.M. express, then service continues until 3:30 P.M. (the only other express is this last bus of the day); the fare is US$11 one-way. The James Bus makes a loop through PG before heading out of town. A few other bus lines make the trip, but much less regularly.

Remember that you can get off in Independence and take a boat to Placencia, or you can get off at any other point, like Cockscomb Maya Centre (Cockscomb Basin Wildlife Sanctuary) or Dangriga.

To the Maya Villages

Every day has a different schedule, but buses go to the Maya villages on Monday, Wednesday, Friday, and Saturday, generally around noon, and depart from Jose Maria Nunez Street (between Prince and Queen Street). From here it's possible to get to **Golden Stream, Silver Creek, San Pedro, San Miguel, Aguacate, Blue Creek, San Antonio,** and other villages. Some buses drop you off at the entrance road, leaving a walk of a mile or two. Check the Toledo Tourism Information Center for updated village bus schedules.

GETTING AROUND

Punta Gorda's taxis will take you anywhere within city limits for about US$3–4; look for their green license plates. It's US$10 to drive the six miles to Machaca Hill and US$12.50 to Jacintoville and the Tranquility Lodge. Or call on **Pablo Bouchub's Taxi and Tour Service** (tel. 501/722-2834 or 501/608-2879); Don Pablo is also a natural healer and can get you all manner of medicinal herbs and roots. Also try **Castro's Taxi** (tel. 501/602-3632) or

Galvez's Taxi Tours (tel. 501/722-2402). Ask your hotel if they provide a free bicycle, or rent one at **Abaisehi** ("One Love") bike rental, on North Street, for US$12.50 per day (less for a few hours). Abaisehi also offers a bike tour of Punta Gorda.

Car Rental

The folks at Sun Creek Lodge will deliver a rental car anywhere in Punta Gorda (if you're not staying with them); it's US$80 per day or US$480 per week for their four-wheel-drive vehicles (tel. 501/604-2124 or 501/665-6778, belizegate@gmail.com).

THE SOUTHERN CAYES

Toledo District is the gateway to the southern hook of the Belize Barrier Reef, a swoosh of tiny cayes and coral that are the least visited of any of Belize's Caribbean islands. There are some 138 islands off the southern coast, although only a handful are actually made of sand and palm trees. The **Port of Honduras**

Marine Reserve (PHMR) is the largest protected area in the country, spanning 160 square miles of ocean in southern Belize. The **Snake Cayes** and a few other gorgeous islands are accessible to travelers with the time and means. There is a week-long raging party on **Hunting Caye** at Easter time, and you'll find camping and simple accommodations on **Lime Caye.**

The **Sapodilla Cayes Marine Reserve** is one of the seven wonders of the Belize Barrier Reef Reserve System, which was declared a World Heritage Site in 1996. The reserve covers 80 square miles and is co-managed by the Fisheries Department and the **Toledo Association for Sustainable Tourism and Empowerment** (TASTE, 53 Main St., Punta Gorda Town, tel. 501/672-0191), a nonprofit organization that focuses on using the reserve to educate local youths about their environment. Contact the office to find out about volunteering or possible tourism-related projects centered around these stunning islands.

PUNTA GORDA

Maya Ruins and Upcountry Villages

The wild, unique, and stunning southwestern chunk of Belize is referred to as "upcountry" or simply "the villages." There are dozens more ruins, waterfalls, caves, trails, and hills to climb than appear in these pages.

MAYA ARCHAEOLOGICAL SITES
Nim Li Punit

At about Mile 75 on the Southern Highway, near the village of Indian Creek, 25 miles north of Punta Gorda Town, Nim Li Punit is atop a hill with expansive views of the surrounding forests and mountains (it's about a half mile west of the highway, along a narrow road marked by a small sign). The site saw preliminary excavations in 1970 that documented a 30-foot-tall carved stela, the tallest ever found in Belize—and among the tallest in all the Maya world. A total of about 25 stelae have

been found on the site, most dated A.D. 700–800. Although looters damaged the site, excavations by archaeologist Richard Leventhal in 1986 and by the Belize Institute of Archaeology (IOA) in the late 1990s and early 2000s uncovered several new stelae and some notable tombs. The stelae and artifacts are displayed in the very nice visitors center built by the IOA. The ruins are open 7 A.M.–5 P.M. daily; entrance is US$5. The small office can be reached at 501/665-5126.

(Lubaantun

On a ridge between two creeks, Lubaantun ("Place of the Fallen Stones") consists of five layers of construction, unique from other sites because of the absence of engraved stelae. The site was first reported in 1875, by American Civil War refugees from the southern United States, and first studied in 1915. It is believed

THE SKULL OF DOOM: MYSTERY SOLVED

In 1924, Anna Mitchell-Hedges, the daughter of explorer F. A. Mitchell-Hedges allegedly found a perfectly formed quartz crystal skull at the Lubaantun archaeological site on her 17th birthday. The object has been the subject of much mystery and controversy over the years. Was it made by the Maya to conjure death? Aliens? Atlanteans? Did Mitchell-Hedges plant it for the pleasure of his daughter? Is the whole story a hoax?

The world got its answer in 2007 when the Smithsonian Institute put the Mitchell-Hedges skull under a scanning electron microscope. Researcher Jane MacLaren Walsh concluded, "This object was carved and polished using modern, high-speed, diamond-coated, rotary, cutting and polishing tools of minute dimensions. This technology is certainly not pre-Columbian. I believe it is decidedly 20th century."

The skull currently resides in North America with the widower of Anna Mitchell-Hedges. Despite the Smithsonian's findings, some still warn of dire consequences if the skull is not returned to Lubaantun by December 21, 2012.

that as many as 20,000 people lived in this trading center.

Lubaantun was built and occupied during the Late Classic Period (A.D. 730–890). Eleven major structures are grouped around five main plazas—in total the site has 18 plazas and three ball courts. The tallest structure rises 50 feet above the plaza, and from it you can see the Caribbean Sea, 20 miles distant. Lubaantun's disparate architecture is completely different from Maya construction in other parts of Latin America.

Most of the structures are terraced, and you'll notice that some corners are rounded—an uncommon feature throughout the Mundo Maya. Lubaantun has been studied and surveyed several times by Thomas Gann and, more recently, in 1970 by Norman Hammond. Distinctive clay whistle figurines (similar to those found in Mexico's Isla Jaina) illustrate lifestyles and occupations of the era. Other artifacts include the mysterious crystal skull, obsidian blades, grinding stones (much like those still used today to grind corn), beads, shells, turquoise, and shards of pottery. From all of this, archaeologists have determined that the city flourished until the 8th century A.D. It was a farming community that traded with the highland areas of today's Guatemala, and the people worked the sea and maybe the cayes just offshore.

To get to Lubaantun from Punta Gorda, go 1.5 miles west past the gas station to the Southern Highway, then take a right. Two miles farther, you'll come to the village of San Pedro. From here, go left around the church to the concrete bridge. Cross and go almost a mile—the road is passable during the dry season.

Uxbenka

Difficult to access and largely unexcavated (actually, some recent excavations were covered back up to protect them), Uxbenka was discovered in 1984 and has more than 20 stelae. The site is perched on a ridge overlooking the traditional Maya village of Santa Cruz and provides a grand view of the foothills and valleys of the Maya Mountains. Here you'll see hillsides lined with cut stones. This construction method is unique to the Toledo District. Uxbenka ("Old Place") was named by the people of nearby Santa Cruz. It's located just outside Santa Cruz, about three miles west of San Antonio village. The most convenient way to see the site is with a rental car. Ask around the village for an experienced guide; you may find someone, or you may not.

Pusilhá

Along the Moho River is a forgotten city, mostly covered by jungle and corn today. Since its discovery in 1927, Pusilhá has received little attention due to the remoteness of the ruins. Early investigations by the British Museum Expedition revealed stelae (stone monuments), extraordinary ceramics, eccentric flints, and the remains of a stone bridge. Pusilhá is near San Benito Poite village, a few miles from the Guatemalan border. In 2001, shortly after a dirt-track road connected the village to the rest of Belize, the Pusilhá Archaeology Project resumed investigations under the direction of Dr. Geoffrey Braswell. Recent analyses of ceramics suggest that Pusilhá was an important regional trading center.

A community-driven project, **Kehil Ha Jungle Lodge** (www.kehilha.com), provides accommodations for researchers, students, and adventurous travelers. Ask around the village for opportunities to explore the ruins, local caves, waterfalls, and the surrounding jungle. One reader had this to say: "Kehil Ha is amazing, I spent a night out there before the place officially opened and I was very impressed. It is easily as nice or nicer then the Toledo Eco-Tourism Association guesthouses that I have stayed in.... The lodge has installed solar panels to provide lights and some basic amenities. FYI the entire village of San Benito Poite runs off of solar power; the previous area representative worked with Cuba to secure a panel and battery for every household. I think this the only village in Belize with this level of solar power."

RÍO BLANCO NATIONAL PARK

Established in 1994 and co-managed by the Río Blanco Mayan Association (composed of seven executives from Santa Elena and Santa Cruz who volunteer their time as the park wardens) and by the government, the park provides amazing scenery and natural beauty for the tourist and an alternative income for members of neighboring villages. Río Blanco National Park is 105 acres and encompasses a spectacular waterfall that is 20 feet high and ranges from a raging 100 feet wide during the rainy season to about 10 feet during the dry season.

Locals say the pool under the waterfall is bottomless (one claims to have dived 60 feet and never touched bottom). If you are adventurous, you can jump off of the surrounding rocks and fall 20 feet into the crystal-clear water. There are also two miles of nature trails, which include the cave where the Río Blanco river enters the mountain and a suspended cable bridge over the river.

Surrounding the falls is a beautiful forest with thriving flora and fauna populations and a possibility of jaguar sightings. Because the park is a community-based effort, 10 percent of all entrance fees collected at the park go back to the villages.

The surrounding villages are made up of indigenous Maya, and a trip to the park allows visitors to drive through Santa Cruz, a very typical village with thatch huts and no electricity, where women wear traditional dresses.

Accommodations and Services
Camping and **furnished dorms** are available at Río Blanco National Park. Visit the **Craft & Snack Shop,** run by the Río Blanco Women's Association. They have everything from baskets to jewelry to embroidery, plus the only cold beverages in the area! A picnic area is under the visitors center.

Getting There
The park is about 30 miles west of Punta Gorda, between the villages of Santa Cruz and Santa Elena on the road to Jalacte. Three small bus companies serve the village of Jalacte daily at 6 A.M., and on Monday, Wednesday, Friday, and Saturday, leaving from Jose Maria Nunez Street in Punta Gorda at 11 A.M., 11:30 A.M., and noon; they return from the village on the same days at 5:30 A.M. and 3 P.M.

◖ AGUACALIENTE WILDLIFE SANCTUARY
The Aguacaliente Wildlife Sanctuary comprises a myriad of ecosystems, including rainforests, lagoons, and grasslands found nowhere else in Belize and hosting an incredible variety of flora and fauna. The richness of its native

SPEAKING Q'EQCHI':
IS THERE HAPPINESS IN YOUR HEART?

Most of southern Belize's people of indigenous descent speak Q'eqchi' Maya – though some communities speak the Mopan language instead, which is more closely related to Yukatek or Itzá Maya.

In Belize, you may see the word Q'eqchi' spelled different ways. "Kekchi" is how Protestant missionaries labeled the Maya of southern Belize, and British colonial officials wrote "Ketchi." Today, in neighboring Guatemala, the indigenous leaders of the Guatemalan Academy of Maya Languages (ALMG) have developed a standard Maya alphabet that the Q'eqchi' leaders in Belize have begun to use as well.

Making even a small attempt to speak and learn the language of your Maya hosts will deepen your experience. Never mind the laughs your funny accent will attract – your noble attempts are an amusing novelty, and no one means any harm. Persist, and you will be rewarded in ways you would never have expected – indeed, learning another language in such an immersive setting is one of the most humbling and empowering experiences a traveler can have.

Should you want to learn more than the few words presented here, track down the grammar book and cassette tapes by Q'eqchi' linguist Rigoberto Baq, available in Guatemala City at the Academia de Lenguas Mayas (www. almg.org.gt) or at their regional offices in Coban, Alta Verapaz (in the municipal palace), or Poptán, Petén.

BASIC PHRASES

All Q'eqchi' words have an accent on the last syllable. One of the first things you will probably be asked is, *"B'ar xat chalk chaq?"* (bar shaht chalk chok), to which you can respond, *"Xin chalk chaq sa'* New York" (sheen chalk chok sah New York, or wherever you are from).

In Q'eqchi', there are no words for "good morning," "good afternoon," or "good evening." You simply use the standard greeting, *"Ma sa sa' laa ch'ool"* (mah sah sah lah ch'ohl), literally, "Is there happiness in your heart?" (In Q'eqchi', however, you wouldn't use a question mark because the "Ma" indicates a question.) A proper response would be *"Sa in ch'ool"* (sah een ch'ohl), "Yes, my heart is happy."

Although it is falling out of custom with the younger generation, if you are speaking with an older woman or man, she or he would be delighted to be greeted with the terms of respect for the elderly: "Nachin" (nah cheen) for an elder woman, and "Wachin" (kwah cheen) for an elder man.

and migratory bird species makes it an excellent destination for birdwatching. During the dry season, hike through lush seasonal grasslands to see the great jabiru stork, the roseate spoonbill, or any of the other 150 bird species that call Aguacaliente home. During the rainy season, take a canoe through the lagoons to see four-foot tarpon and flowering orchids.

From Punta Gorda, take the Southern Highway north until the turnoff to Laguna Village (approximately 10 miles, to just before the Toledo Forest Department Machaca Station), then turn left and travel about three miles into Laguna; bear right and look for the Aguacaliente Wildlife Sanctuary.

The suggested donation is US$5 per person, payable in neighboring Laguna Village; visitors must sign in by the church. Complimentary use of dories is included.

UPCOUNTRY VILLAGES

This is a loose term used to describe the Toledo District settlements to the west of Punta Gorda. Most villagers are Q'eqchi' or Mopan Maya, whose descendants fled to Belize to escape oppression and forced labor in their native Guatemala. Anthropologists now believe that the Mopan were probably the original inhabitants of Belize, but that they were forcibly removed by the Spanish in

If you decide to go swimming in one of Toledo's beautiful rivers, you might want to ask first, "Ma wan li ahin sa' li nima'" (mah kwan lee aheen sa le neemah), which means "Are there crocodiles in the river?"

"Ani laa kab'a?" (anee lah kabah) means "What's your name?" You can respond: "Ix [woman's name] in kab'a" (eesh . . . een kabah) or "Laj [man's name] in kab'a" (lahj . . . een kabah).

MORE PHRASES AND VOCABULARY

Chan xaawil? (chan shaa kwil) – What's up?
Jo xaqa'in (hoe shakaeen) – Not much, just fine.
B'an usilal (ban ooseelal) – Please.
B'antiox (ban teeosh) or T'ho-kre (ta HOH cree) – Thank you.
Us (oos) – Good.
Ylb' I r u (yeeb ee rue) – Bad, ugly.
Hehe (eheh) – Yes.
Ink'a (eenk'ah) – No.
K'aru? (kaieeroo) – What?
B'ar? (har) – Where?
Joq'e? (hoekay) – When?
Jarub?' (hahrueb) – How many?
Jonimal tzaq? (hoeneemahl ssahq) – How much does it cost?
Chaawil aawib (chah kwil aakweeb) – Take care of yourself (a good way to say goodbye).

Jowan chik (hoek wan cheek) – See you later.
Wi chik (kwee cheek) – Again.
wa (kwah) – tortilla
kenq (kenk) – beans
molb' (mohlb) – eggs
kaxlan wa (kashlan kwah) – bread
tib' (cheeb) – meat
tzilan (sseeelan) – chicken
kuy (kue-ee) – pork/pig
kar (car) – fish
chin (cheen) – orange
kakaw (cacao) – chocolate
ha' (hah) – water
woqxinb'il ha' (kwohk sheen bill hah) – boiled water
cape (kahpay) – coffee
sulul (suelul) – mud
ab' (ahb) – hammock
chaat (chaht) – bed
nima' (neemah) – river
kokal (kohkahl) – children
chaab'il (chahbill) – good
kaw (kauw) – hard
najt (nahjt) – far
nach (nahch) – close

(Special thanks to Clark University anthropologist Liza Grandia, PhD, who spent four years among the Maya.)

the late 17th century. The Q'eqchi' were close neighbors with the Mopan and the Manche Ch'ol, a Maya group completely exterminated by the Spanish. The older folks continue to maintain longtime traditional farming methods, culture, and dress. Modern machinery is sparse—they use simple digging sticks and machetes to till the soil, and water is hand-carried to the fields during dry spells. It's not an easy life.

On the outskirts of each town, the dwellings are relatively primitive; they often have open doorways covered by a hanging cloth, hammocks, and dirt floors. Chickens and sometimes dogs wander through the houses in search of scraps. People use the most primitive of latrines or just take a walk into the jungle. They bathe in the nearest creek or river, a routine that becomes a source of fun as much as cleanliness.

As you walk into town, past the thatched homes on each side of the road, it becomes apparent that the effects of modern conveniences are only beginning to arrive. When a family can finally afford electricity, the first things that appear are a couple of lights and a refrigerator—the latter allows the family to earn a few dollars by selling chilled soft drinks and such. After that, it's a television set; you can see folks sitting in open doorways, their faces lit by the light inside.

Laguna

Laguna is a small Q'eqchi' Maya village of around 250 people, living against a backdrop of limestone karst hills. The scenery is also home to howler monkeys and many types of parrots, which can be seen flying over the village daily. The village's namesake lagoon is now a protected area called **Aguacaliente Wildlife Sanctuary** and is one of the best spots in Toledo to go birding. With the new mile-long boardwalk, it is easily accessible (except for the first five minutes of the walk, which can get a bit muddy). Laguna is also home to a loosely organized women's crafts group that produces *cuxtales* (traditional woven Maya bags, pronounced "CUSH-tal-les"), table mats, beading, baskets, embroidery, beaded necklaces, and earrings.

There is also a long muddy farmers' road that leads to the confluence of Blue Creek and the Moho River; this two- to three-hour flat hike is very beautiful but only recommended in the dry season (March–May). There's also a super-cool cave about a 20-minute hike away;

ask your guide. To get to the village, take the Laguna bus directly to the village, or take any bus that can drop you at the Laguna junction (10 miles from Punta Gorda). It is only about three miles to the village from the highway. Laguna is the oldest member of the TEA guesthouse program, and there is a guesthouse with a nice veranda; beds are equipped with mosquito nets. A TEA guesthouse stay includes all meals and the opportunity to interact and cook or farm with local Q'eqchi' indigenous people. Local tours, craft demonstrations, and cultural performances are available at an additional cost.

San Pedro Columbia

To get there, take the main road in Punta Gorda, which goes inland about 10 miles toward San Antonio. Just before you get to San Antonio, a dirt track to the right breaks off to the village of San Pedro. San Pedro is one of the biggest of the villages. A small Catholic church in town has an equally small cemetery. It sits on a hilltop surrounded by a few

children in San Pedro Columbia, one of many upcountry villages in the Toledo District

thatched dwellings. Not far away is a prefab-looking school that was erected with the assistance of National Guards from the United States who were getting jungle training.

This village is home to well known Mayan musicians, and also to Emmeth Young, a Creole drum master who offers drum-making classes and music lessons. Emmeth's sambai rhythms, which can be heard on the full moon if he is performing, can be traced half a millennium back to the Ibo tribe in Nigeria—Emmeth is a talented man whose drumming and efforts to preserve Belizean culture have been featured on the Travel Channel and elsewhere. His **Maroon Creole Drum School,** previously located in Gales Point, is now re-established on the beautiful grounds of the **Columbia River Co-operative** (tel. 501/632-7841, pricklypeartat2@hotmail.com, www.columbiarivercooperative.com). There, in addition to the drumming school, you'll find a small culture museum, gift shop, gallery, medicinal garden, and place to eat. Stay in the two-story bunkhouse with fans, electricity, wireless Internet, and a shared bathroom (US$10 pp) or camp out on the grounds (US$5 pp). The Columbia River Co-operative is a quarter-mile down a little farm road just before the turnoff to Lubaantun from San Pedro Columbia. Emmeth's wife, Jill, writes, "There's a botanical loop to walk with some additional art that explains ancient Maya cosmology and rituals. We will be adding paintings and sculptures of Belizean mythological creatures as we go along. We are right on the Columbia River so it makes a great little half-day addition to a trip to Lubaantun. Get a drum lesson, hang out, walk through the garden and butterfly house, and then cool off with a shake or a dip in the river."

Near San Pedro Columbia

Two miles upriver from the village of San Pedro Columbia, situated on 70 acres, you'll find **Maya Mountain Research Farm (MMRF)** (www.mmrfbz.org), a registered NGO and working demonstration farm that promotes sustainable agriculture, renewable energy, appropriate technology, and food security using permaculture principles and applied biodiversity. The farm also lives on solar power and offers a number of courses. The property has over 500 species of plants (including lots of cacao), and the staff are working to establish an ethnobotanical garden of useful plants with their Q'eqchi' Maya names and uses. The farm suffered a devastating fire in 2008 but quickly recovered. Accommodations are simple rustic affairs, with solar lighting and Internet access.

San Antonio

After leaving San Pedro and returning to the main road, make a right turn and you'll soon be in San Antonio, just down the road. The village of San Antonio is famous for its exquisite traditional Q'eqchi' embroidery. However, the younger generation is being whisked right along into 21st-century Belizean society, so who knows how much longer it will survive.

There should be a local tourism representative in San Antonio who can give helpful advice about the area and direct you to an experienced guide to take you to **Blue Creek Cave** (bring a swimsuit). This is great bird-watching country.

From here the road is passable as far as Aguacate (another Q'eqchi' village). But if you intend to visit the ruins at **Pusilhá,** near the Guatemala border, you must travel to San Benito Poite via the Santa Teresa Road. Another ruin, **Uxbenka,** is west of San Antonio near the village of Santa Cruz and is easy to get to via the trucks that haul supplies a couple of times a week. Not known by anyone but locals until 1984, Uxbenka is where seven carved stelae were found, including one dating from the Early Classic Period.

[Blue Creek Cave

This village of some 275 Q'eqchi' and Mopan Maya was first settled in 1925 and is also called Ho'keb Ha, "the place where the water comes out," describing this spot where the Río Blanco emerges from the side of a mountain, becoming Blue Creek and home to an extensive cave system. You'll need a guide who's familiar with these caves; ask at Punta Gorda or at one of the nearby Maya villages. Many of these folks know the nearby caves well. Go prepared with flashlights. You can swim up to 600 yards into the cave; it's pretty stunning. Ack's bus leaves PG at noon on Monday, Wednesday, Friday, and Saturday.

San Miguel

This friendly Q'eqchi' Maya village has a village guesthouse, a nearby river, thatched houses, traditional dress, and children carrying dishes and clothes in buckets on their heads from the swiftly flowing river. San Miguel is also experiencing intense change with recent access to electricity, water, better roads, and increased educational opportunities.

During times when the villagers are harvesting coffee, you can witness the process of picking, shelling, drying, and grinding organic coffee. Tours of the village, cave, and *milpa* are also available. All activities are US$3.50 per hour. The Mayan site of Lubaantun, famous for the discovery of the Crystal Skull and unique architectural features, is about three miles from San Miguel. You can either walk to the site or charter a vehicle (US$7.50). The village does not have a restaurant, but meals are cooked and served at local homes (US$3.25 breakfast or supper, US$4 for lunch).

San Miguel is home to one guesthouse, run by Maria Ack and her family, who live across the street from the accommodations. The guesthouse is a traditional thatch structure comprising a bedroom, which may be shared among multiple travelers (although it is likely you will be the only one there); a main living area with a desk, chair, and hammock; and a covered outdoor veranda with hammocks. They also provide electricity, linens, and mosquito nets, and a shower and toilet are on the premises. Rates are under US$10 for a dorm bed. The family offers cooking lessons where you can learn to make corn tortillas (*xoroc li cua* in Q'eqchi'), along with *caldo* and other traditional dishes. They also offer handicraft lessons on calabash carving and traditional embroidery.

San Miguel buses leave from Punta Gorda two times a day, Monday–Saturday. You can catch the village bus on Jose Maria Nunez Street. The first bus leaves at 11:30 A.M. and is marked "Silver Creek." The bus has a 30-minute layover in Silver Creek before heading on to San Miguel. The second is marked "San Miguel" and leaves the park at 4:30 P.M. The bus ride is about an hour and 15 minutes (the 11:30 bus ride is half an hour longer due to the layover). Buses leave San Miguel for Punta Gorda at 5:15 A.M. and 12:45 P.M.

Barranco

Barranco is an isolated Garifuna village, where activities include fishing along the river as well as traveling by dugout canoe up the river into the Sarstoon-Temash National Park to see howler monkeys, hickatees, and iguanas. Return for a refreshing glass of *hiu* (a spicy drink made of cassava and sweet potato) and an evening of drumming. Get there by bus from the park in Punta Gorda, or by boat from the Punta Gorda dock. Ask for times, as transportation is scarce; charter boats can be arranged.

Numerous individuals of Barranco's 600 inhabitants have traveled far from their village to become some of Belize's most renowned musicians, painters, and researchers; many have earned advanced degrees in their fields, giving Barranco one of the highest per capita PhD percentages in Central America.

◖ VILLAGE GUESTHOUSES AND HOMESTAYS

For the culturally curious traveler who doesn't mind using an outhouse, the unique experiential accommodation programs in the Toledo District offer a three-fold attraction: 1) firsthand observation of daily rural life in southern Belize; 2) a chance to interact with one of several proud, distinct cultures while participating in a world-renowned model of ecotourism; and 3) a unique way to go deep into the lush, natural world of the forests, rivers, caves, and waterfalls of southwestern Belize.

Simple guesthouse and family home

networks in participating villages offer a range of conditions and privacy, but most are simple, primitive, and appreciated most by those with an open mind. Activities include tours of the villages and surrounding natural attractions. For nighttime entertainment, traditional dancing, singing, and music can usually be arranged; otherwise it's just stargazing and conversation.

These are poor villages, and the local brand of ecotourism provides an alternative to subsistence farming that entails slashing and burning the rainforest. Additionally, the community-controlled infrastructure helps ensure a more equitable distribution of tourism dollars than most tour operations (members rotate duties of guiding, preparing meals, and organizing activities).

Dem Dats Doin' (office in Punta Gorda next to Scotia Bank, demdatsdoin@btl.net) has maintained the Maya Village Homestay Network since 1991, offering traditional village accommodations, in which you stay in a Maya home, maybe in a hammock (not much privacy, but plenty of cultural exchange). The office in Punta Gorda is open only on Wednesday and Friday mornings. It's less than US$20 per person per night for homestays and all meals; families are in the villages of Aguacate, Na Luum Ca, and San José. The same folks run the Toledo Botanical Arboretum (US$5 pp).

Food

You'll usually pay about US$11 for three meals. Breakfast in Maya villages is generally eggs, homemade tortillas, and coffee or a cacao drink. All meals are ethnic and lunch is the largest meal of the day; it is often chicken *caldo* (a soup cooked with Maya herbs) or occasionally a local meat dish like iguana ("bush chicken") or gibnut (paca, a large rodent). Fresh tortillas round out the meal. Supper is the lightest meal of the day and generally includes "ground" food (a root food such as potatoes) that the guide and visitors might "harvest" along the jungle trail. The *comal* (tortilla grill) is always hot, and if you're invited to try your hand at making tortillas, go ahead—this is a

wonderful way to break the ice with the usually shy Maya women. In a Garifuna village, be prepared for simple but traditional cooking, like *sere,* or fish in coconut milk. If you have special dietary needs your hosts will do their best to accommodate you.

Practicalities

For the **Toledo Ecotourism Association** (TEA) program, a registration fee, one night's lodging, and three meals run US$28 per person per night. Other activities, like storytelling, crafts lessons, and village tours are US$3.50 per hour. Prices are standardized throughout the participating villages. Other activities, such as paddling trips, forest and cave tours (US$14 pp), and music/dance sessions cost more, but will be extremely reasonable—especially with a group. If visiting during the rainy season, be advised that trails and caves may be inaccessible.

TEA is the umbrella organization for the guesthouse program, which is cooperatively managed and includes village representatives in their respective towns. At last count, there were 7 participating villages, down from 12 a few years ago. Participants must arrange their visits from the central TEA office in Punta Gorda (tel. 501/722-2096, teabelize@yahoo.com, www.plenty.org/mayan-ecotours), where you will pay the registration fee (US$5), be briefed about the program, and told how to get out to the village (the villages are on a rotating basis). One full day may be sufficient, as the villages are quiet small; if you would like to explore the surrounding landscape, plan an extra day.

Bring comfortable walking shoes, bug repellent, a poncho, a swimsuit, a flashlight with extra batteries, and lightweight slacks and a long-sleeved shirt. Photos of your own family and home—or postcards of your hometown—are appreciated and good icebreakers. Be sure to fill out the evaluation form afterwards to help TEA improve the program.

TEA is doing the best it can in the face of relatively low interest in the program. Though TEA still successfully hosts travelers from all over the world, the overall low number of visitors makes it difficult to properly maintain some facilities—not to mention villagers' interest. In addition, TEA doesn't have funding for a person to work at the Punta Gorda office full-time (it's too much of a commitment for farmers and housewives); the position is sometimes filled by international volunteers. If there is nobody at the TEA desk in the BTIA office, contact Chet Schmidt at **Nature's Way** (tel. 501/702-2119). Despite these challenges, TEA is an engaging community-based tourism project that is well worth supporting and experiencing.

GETTING THERE

To get to Maya country from Punta Gorda, you have several choices. If you plan an overnight with the homestay or guesthouse programs, TEA will assist you. They may simply direct you to the appropriate village bus from Punta Gorda.

The **Chun Bus** (tel. 501/722-2666) makes the run to San Antonio Monday, Wednesday, Friday, and Saturday (about US$4 round-trip). This bus doesn't stop in San Pedro; instead you will have to leave the bus at the road and trek in several miles. You can also catch a bus as far as Pueblo Viejo, "the edge of the known world." Catch the Chun Bus at Jose Maria Nunez Street to ensure getting a seat. Remember: No buses run on Sunday.

If traveling by car, you have the option of exploring every little road you see (four-wheel drive recommended). From the turnoff for Punta Gorda at Mile 86 on the Southern Highway, take the road north. At about Mile 1½, there will be a turnoff on the right that heads for San Pedro and other villages.

Across the Border to Guatemala and Honduras

One of the many Central American backpacker routes involves entering Belize after a visit to Tikal, then re-entering Guatemala via boat from southern Belize. From there, one can travel up the Río Dulce, take a bus to Guatemala City, or take a series of hired cars to the Honduran border. Conversely, some backpackers do a loop from Punta Gorda that includes Livingston, Río Dulce, and Tikal, then heads into Belize again. Below are some tips to get you started, including top picks from some traveling friends and from the author of *Moon Guatemala,* Al Argueta.

LIVINGSTON

A day trip or overnight to the coastal vacation town of Livingston can be an exciting breath of activity after sleepy Punta Gorda. Livingston is situated on the Caribbean shore and the wide mouth of the Río Dulce, making it an ideal base for upriver jungle tours. The Social Travel tour company offers a number of trips worth taking.

Livingston is a popular destination for vacationing Guatemalans and foreign tourists alike. There are many restaurants, open-air street cafés, and a rich Garifuna presence (most readily experienced at the Rasta-colored **Abafu Bar,** where you'll find live drumming, potent bitters, and lots of reggae).

Midpriced hotels are abundant and close to the pier; expect to pay US$15 for a double with private bath. In fact, prices of everything from beer to hotel rooms are less than half of what they are in Belize, and many budget accommodations are available as well. **The African Place** is a real bargain; it's a 10-minute walk out of "downtown," and US$7.50 gets you a double room in a fantastically decorated mosaicked castle-like structure. Highly recommended by one friend is **Casa Rosada** (US$20): "Good food, great coffee, shared bath, very clean."

There is an ATM in Livingston, but it is unreliable. Keep a stash of cash.

Up the Río Dulce

You can also catch a boat up the river to **El Hotelito Perdido** (www.hotelitoperdido.com, dorm US$6, bungalows US$18–24), in the middle of the rainforest on Río Lampara, a small river connected to Río Dulce. It is popular with backpackers, run by a Polish couple, and located in the deep bush. There's no beach on the river, just a dock. Another option up the Río Dulce is **Texan Bay Marina** (www.texanbaymarina.com), which is always a good time, serving Texas-sized burgers in the middle of the jungle.

Up the Río Tatin (a tributary of Río Dulce like Lampara) you'll find the backpacker hangout at **Finca Tatin**. In Río Dulce proper **Hacienda Tijax** and **Tortugal** are both recommended as great places to stay. Ask about getting to the white-sand beach of Playa Blanca and the biological station at Río Sarstun.

PUERTO BARRIOS, GUATEMALA

This trash-strewn, rough-and-tumble port town is primarily a deep-water banana-loading dock and not much more. Puerto Barrios has a reputation for hard drugs, prostitution, and bar fights. Many travelers stop only as long as necessary to make their boat connections and get the hell out of Dodge. Express buses to Guatemala City leave the **Terminal de Autobuses Litegua** (eight blocks from the dock in Puerto Barrios, a 10-minute walk or US$1.50 cab ride); the 5.5-hour ride costs about US$5.

To escape the scene painted above, stay at the **Amatique Bay Resort** (tel. 502/7931-0000, www.amatiquebay.net), an upscale resort. Cerro San Gil and Rio Las Escobas are popular day-trip destinations for cruise ship travelers, but only on certain days. They are in a beautiful, well-managed rainforest preserve with a series of travertine pools and hiking trails, in neighboring Puerto Santo Tomas de Castilla.

To Guatemala City, take a Litegua double-decker *Clase* bus; they are quite comfortable (US$12). Book the trip on www.litegua.com.

TO LIVINGSTON AND PUERTO BARRIOS BY BOAT

Before leaving Punta Gorda, you'll get your passport stamped at the customs office at the municipal dock; you'll also be charged a US$4 PACT fee to help support Belize's protected areas—or maybe you won't. If traveling directly to Livingston, be sure to walk up the hill from the dock to check in at the **Migración Office,** where you'll get stamped and pay a tiny fee (less than US$2); if you fail to do this, you'll have problems leaving Guatemala. In Puerto Barrios, Migración is located 1.5 blocks east of the dock and is open 24 hours. If leaving for Belize, you'll need to pay a US$10 exit fee here when you get your passport *ponchada* (stamped). Be sure to do this *before* buying your boat ticket to Punta Gorda. There is no fee to enter Belize.

A triangular boat run between the municipal docks of Punta Gorda, Puerto Barrios, and Livingston shuttles travelers across this section of Central American coastline. The trip is done in rather small boats with minimal shelter, so prepare for cold, wet, and rough seas during the rainy season. The direct leg between Livingston and Punta Gorda runs only Tuesdays and Fridays, leaving at 7 A.M. from Livingston, then shoving off from Punta Gorda at 10 A.M. If you miss that boat, you'll have to travel first to Puerto Barrios (the hour-long trip costs US$25), then catch a regular *colectivo* water taxi to Livingston (leaves about every hour, 40-minute trip, under US$4).

There are three trips every day between Punta Gorda and Puerto Barrios, one based in Belize (**Requena's Charter Service,** tel. 501/722-2070, watertaxi@btl.net) and the others based in Guatemala: **El Chato** (tel. 501/722-2870, Guatemala tel. 502/7948-5525, www.transporteselchato.com.gt, pichilingo2000@yahoo.com) and **Marisol Tours.** Boats leave Punta Gorda around 9:30 A.M., 2 P.M., and 4 P.M. daily and depart from Puerto Barrios at 10 A.M., 1 P.M., and 2 P.M. Another boat man is **Memo's,** with daily departures to Puerto Barrios and Livingston and also Río Dulce tours (tel. 501/630-5889). The cost is US$20–25 one way.

TO HONDURAS

There is no legal direct boat service to Puerto Cortés, Honduras, from the Punta Gorda

PUNTA GORDA

docks, but there is service from Placencia and Dangriga, and those boats stop in Punta Gorda for immigration purposes. Otherwise, to get to Honduras from Punta Gorda, first take a daily boat shuttle from Punta Gorda to Puerto Barrios. Buses and taxis in Puerto Barrios can whisk you to the Honduran border. Look for one of the many minivans trolling for passengers around the docks and market; it's about an hour to the border at Corinto, then another 1.5 hours to the coastal backpacker hideout of Omoa, Honduras. From there, it is under an hour to Puerto Cortés and San Pedro Sula, where you'll find connecting buses and flights to Copan, the Bay Islands, and points farther south. There are direct flights from Belize international to San Pedro Sula (and possibly Roatán) for around US$250 one-way; inquire at **Maya Island Air** (www.mayaairways.com).

NORTHERN BELIZE

The Orange Walk and Corozal Districts are overlooked by most tourists, even though the area's protected areas are home to as much wildlife as anywhere else in Central America, including populations of jaguars and regionally endemic birds (Yucatán jay and occelated turkey). In addition, the extensive coastal lagoons of Shipstern and Sarteneja are largely undeveloped, and home to manatees, dolphins, and flocks of native and migratory birds.

The second-largest district of Belize, Orange Walk encompasses vast tracts of wilderness, peaceful waterways, and Maya ruins; Orange Walk Town is the area's hub, a small commercial and farming center on the Northern Highway.

New River Lagoon, which you must navigate to reach the Lamanai ruins, is Belize's largest body of fresh water—28 miles long. Its dark waters are smooth, changing with every cloud that passes. Morelet's crocodiles and Mesoamerican river turtles, locally known as "hickatee" turtles, inhabit these waters, along with abundant fish, wading birds, and waterfowl.

The north's largest town is the bayside town of Corozal, 96 miles north of Belize City and just nine miles from the Río Hondo and the Mexican border. In Corozal, you'll enjoy a peaceful stroll along the seawall as you plot where to go next: North to Mexico? East by boat to Sarteneja and San Pedro? Or south to Lamanai?

PLANNING YOUR TIME

Few travelers choose to stay in Orange Walk or Corozal Town, even though both have

© JOSHUA BERMAN

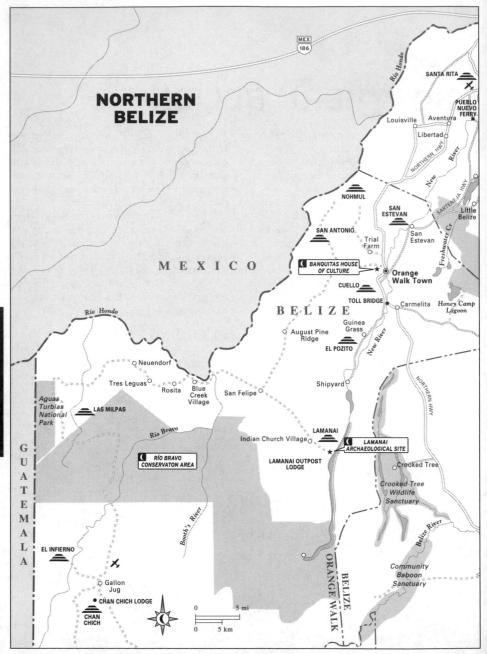

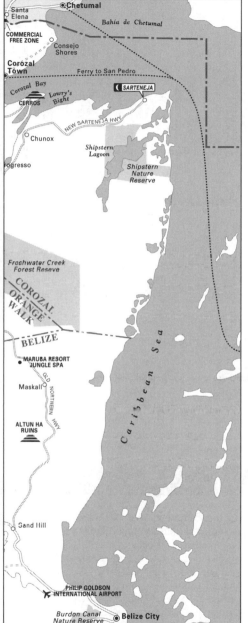

decent budget and midrange options. Both towns are small enough to be explored in a couple hours each. There are day trips from either town, to Chetumal (Mexico), Lamanai, and Cerro Maya (commonly known as "Cerros") archaeological sites. To really dig into the north, plan on at least a night or two at the Lamanai Outpost Lodge or in Indian Church village; by being situated so close to the ruins and not having to travel hours to reach them, this is the best, fullest way to experience Lamanai and the jungle surrounding it. Add an extra couple of days if you attempt to venture to the Río Bravo Conservation Area or Gallon Jug Estate. Some travelers link Corozal into a loop that includes Ambergris Caye, using the boat service between Corozal and San Pedro, with a chance to stop off at Sarteneja, a remote fishing village.

HISTORY

Belize's northern region was settled in the 19th century by refugees from southern Mexico during the Caste War, and you'll still hear more Spanish than English here. What's left of three forts (Mundy and Cairns in Orange Walk Town, and Fort Barley in Corozal) reminds one that this was the scene of violent battles between Belizean settlers and war-minded Maya trying to rid the area of outsiders. The last battle took place in 1872.

For centuries, before settlement by farming-inclined mestizo refugees from Yucatán (Mexico) in 1849, this was timber country. Logs from the north and middle districts of Belize were floated down the New River to Corozal Bay, and then to Belize City; from there they were shipped all over the world. If you travel about two miles south past Orange Walk Town, you'll find a toll bridge over the New River. Tree harvesting is still going on, and you'll encounter large logging trucks crossing the toll bridge.

At one time, sugarcane was the most important Belizean crop, then oranges. Today, local farmers grow more papaya than citrus, and beef producers are tapping into the export

HIGHLIGHTS

◖ Banquitas House of Culture: Located in Orange Walk Town, this exhibition hall features displays on history, industry, and culture (page 244).

◖ Lamanai Archaeological Site: Lamanai is arguably one of the top attractions in all of Belize, and is certainly the most popular site in the region; its network of trails leads you through a semi-excavated city on the shore of the beautiful New River Lagoon (page 248).

◖ Río Bravo Conservation Area: Participate in a variety of research projects at Programme for Belize's field stations, deep in Belize's northwest wilds (page 252).

◖ Sarteneja: This remote village of fishers and boat builders is the perfect off-the-beaten-path destination for curious travelers (page 262).

LOOK FOR ◖ TO FIND RECOMMENDED SIGHTS, ACTIVITIES, DINING, AND LODGING.

market. Caribbean rum (a product of sugarcane) is still big business in this area. During the cane harvest, the one-lane highway is a parade of trucks stacked high with sugarcane and waiting in long lines at the side of the road to get into the Tower Hill sugar mill. Night drivers beware: The trucks aren't new and often have no lights.

Orange Walk Town

Located 66 miles north of Belize City and 30 miles south of Corozal, Orange Walk is one of the larger communities in Belize. Its 16,700 inhabitants work in local industry and agriculture. If passing through, stop and look around. The town has three banks, a few hotels, and a choice of small, casual eateries. Roads stemming from Orange Walk access 20 villages and a handful of small, lesser known archaeological sites.

Outside of town, you'll find historic sites including **Indian Church village;** a 16th-century Spanish mission; and the ruins of Belize's original sugar mill, a 19th-century structure built by British colonialists. Heading west and then southwest, you'll find **Blue Creek,** a Mennonite development where Belize's first hydroelectric plant was built. This is also your gateway to New River Lagoon and the Lamanai ruins.

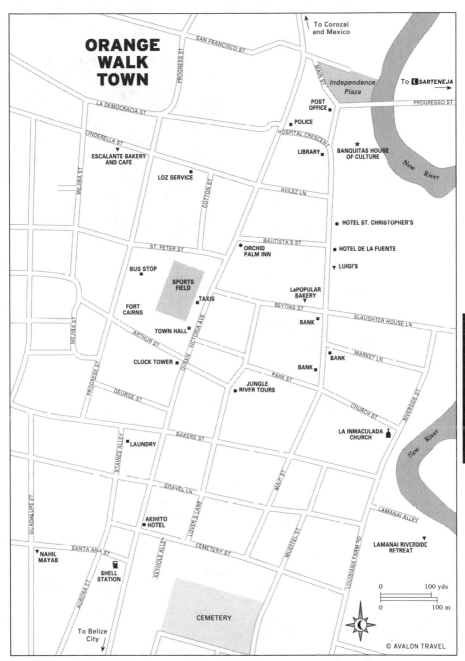

ORANGE WALK TOWN

SAN FRANCISCO ST

PROGRESS ST

MAIN ST

To Corozal and Mexico

Independence Plaza

To ◀ SARTENEJA ➡

LA DEMOCRACIA ST

PROGRESO ST

POST OFFICE ■

POLICE ■

New River

CINDERELLA ST

HOSPITAL CRESCENT

LIBRARY ■

★ BANQUITAS HOUSE OF CULTURE

MEJIBA ST

ESCALANTE BAKERY AND CAFE ▼

LOZ SERVICE ■

COTTON ST

AVILEZ LN

● HOTEL ST. CHRISTOPHER'S

BAUTISTA'S ST

ST. PETER ST

● ORCHID PALM INN

● HOTEL DE LA FUENTE

▼ LUIGI'S

BUS STOP ■

SPORTS FIELD

LaPOPULAR BAKERY ▼

FORT CAIRNS

TAXIS ■

BEYTIAS ST

SLAUGHTER HOUSE LN

ARTHUR ST

TOWN HALL ■

QUEEN VICTORIA AVE

BANK ■

MEJIBA ST

CLOCK TOWER ■

MARKET LN

BANK ■

PROGRESS ST

PARK ST

BANK ■

JUNGLE RIVER TOURS ■

GEORGE ST

CHURCH ST

RIVERSIDE ST

BAKERS ST

STAINES ALLEY

LAUNDRY ■

LA INMACULADA CHURCH ⛪

New River

GRAVEL LN

MAIN ST

LAMANAI ALLEY

GUADALUPE ST

AKIHITO ● HOTEL

LOVER'S LANE

LAMANAI RIVERSIDE RETREAT ▼

NAHIL MAYAB ▼

SANTA ANA ST

CEMETERY ST

MUEFFEL ST

LOUISIANA FARM RD

KEYHOLE ALLEY

SHELL STATION ⛽

AURORA ST

CEMETERY

To Belize City

0   100 yds
0   100 m

© AVALON TRAVEL

SIR BARRY BOWEN: 1945-2010

The man behind Gallon Jug Estate and Chan Chich Lodge in Orange Walk District was a larger-than-life figure in the Belizean spheres of business, politics, agriculture, and beyond. Bowen's dealings extended far beyond the northwest corner of Belize. The following account of his life is excerpted with the permission of the author.

SIR BARRY BOWEN KILLED IN AIR CRASH IN SAN PEDRO: AN OBITUARY, WITH A PRELIMINARY LOOK AT HIS PLACE IN MODERN BELIZE HISTORY

Sir Barry Mansfield Bowen, 64, a seventh-generation Belizean, the country's most prominent entrepreneur, and one of Belize's wealthiest men, a former senator and financier of the People's United Party, died Friday, February 26, 2010, in the crash of a private airplane he was piloting.

The accident occurred on approach to the airstrip at San Pedro, Ambergris Caye. Four other people also died in the crash: Michael Casey and Jill Casey, both teachers at Gallon Jug Community School on the Gallon Jug Estate, the Bowen property in northwestern Belize, and their two young children, two-year-old Makayla and seven-month-old Bryce. The Caseys, from Albany, New York, had been teachers at Gallon Jug for nine years. [The Gallon Jug Community School was renamed Casey Community School, in their honor.]

© LADY BOWEN

Barry M. Bowen at his farm Gallon Jug Estate, Orange Walk District

The Bowens' business interests in Belize are extensive. They include Bowen and Bowen, Ltd., founded by Barry Bowen's father, Eric Bowen, which became the exclusive Belize bottler for Coca-Cola soft drinks and Crystal bottled water; Belize Brewing Company, which brews Belikin, Lighthouse, and Belikin Supreme lager beers, Belikin stout and, under license, Guinness stout, and almost completely dominates the beer market in Belize; Belize Aquaculture Ltd., a large shrimp farm near Placencia in Stann Creek District; Gallon Jug Estate, a 130,000-acre tract in Orange Walk District that includes Chan Chich Lodge, a world-renowned jungle lodge, and Gallon Jug Agro-Industries, a

SIGHTS AND RECREATION

◖ Banquitas House of Culture

Banquitas Plaza (tel. 501/322-0517, 8:30 A.M.–4:30 P.M. Mon.–Fri., free) is an exhibition hall that presents a broad exhibit about Orange Walk–area history, culture, and industry, and the work of local artisans. The hall also hosts special traveling exhibits on Maya and African archaeology and the modern culture of Central America. The plaza comes alive on Friday and Saturday nights, when young Orange Walk couples stroll the river walk enjoying the cool evening together. The nearby amphitheater hosts monthly cultural activities.

New River and New River Lagoon

Trips up and down the New River and around the New River Lagoon are adventures for the entire family, with a chance to see Morelet's crocodiles and iguanas sunning on the bank. By day you'll see the sights of verdant jungle and wildlife along the river. Most people combine a river trip with a visit to the ruins of Lamanai. It is the most impressive way to

3,000-acre experimental farm that produces organic coffees (the only commercial coffee production in Belize), cacao, and cattle; and Belize Estate Co., the Ford auto and truck dealership in Belize City.

Over the years, Barry Bowen had many other business interests, including an import business, a bakery, a quarry and aggregates business, and a cargo business. He always invested in Belize, not taking his money outside of his native land.

Sir Barry, who was knighted by Queen Elizabeth II in 2008 and was Honorary General Consul to Belize for the Kingdom of Norway, is survived by his wife, Dixie Summerscales Bowen, six children, ten grandchildren, and other family members.

A state funeral took place on March 2, 2010, at St. John's Cathedral in Belize City. Sir Barry was interred next to his mother at a family plot in a cemetery in Cayo.

A CENTRAL FIGURE IN BELIZE'S MODERN HISTORY

Barry Bowen not only was the most prominent and best-known businessman in Belize, whose products touched nearly every Belizean and every visitor to Belize, but he also was a central figure in the political and economic history of modern Belize and a key link to the British Honduras past. In fact, Bowen could trace his roots in Belize back to the middle of the 18th century, when the first Bowen, from England, disembarked from a British ship and joined the ragtag band of Baymen at an encampment at the mouth of the Belize River.

Although only 64 – he was born September 19, 1945, in Belize City – Bowen's career connected in some way to nearly every major development in the history of Belize. He owned the most storied (and also at times the most hated) business enterprise in the country's history, Belize Estate and Produce Company; he was a pioneer in the two industries that now dominate commerce in Belize, agriculture and tourism; he was a supporter, leader, and major financier of the most powerful political party in the country, the People's United Party, although he also had close friends and associates in the United Democratic Party; and he proved himself one of the toughest and most capable entrepreneurs in modern Belize, using a combination of savvy marketing, hardball tactics, and government connections to make Belikin beer and Coca-Cola soft drinks his personal cash cows.

Admired or distrusted, envied or loved, Sir Barry Bowen was one-of-a-kind. He made his mark on nearly every major event in his lifetime. Bold and full of life, ambitious and willing to take a risk, a man of vision and large plans, he was a multimillionaire who achieved things. There will be none like him again in Belize.

(Contributed by Lan Sluder, editor of Belize-First.com and author of more than half a dozen books on Belize.)

approach the site, and a time-saver, as well, compared to going by land. Bob the crocodile and a group of spider monkeys have become regular tour stops, as they are accustomed to feeding routines. Some boats invite spider monkeys on board to eat bananas, which should be discouraged; they can become aggressive toward people and cause serious injury.

Your Orange Walk hotel or any of the local guide companies can arrange a trip up the lagoon. Night safaris can be especially exciting, offering a chance to see the habits of animals that come out to play only after the sun sets; you'll need the help of a good guide and a spotlight.

Honey Camp Lagoon

About 20 minutes south of Orange Walk Town, on the old Northern Highway, you can join the locals to indulge in white sandy beaches and shady coconut trees as nice as any on the cayes. It's mostly a locals' picnic spot, and you'll find some basic food services and tons of people during Semana Santa (Easter week).

Nohmul Archaeological Site

This major Maya ceremonial center means "Great Mound," and the top of the pyramid is the highest point in the Orange Walk and Corozal Districts. Twin ceremonial groups are connected by a *sacbe* (raised causeway). The center catered to a thriving population in the Late Pre-Classic and Late Classic Periods (350 B.C.–A.D. 250 and A.D. 600–900, respectively) and controlled an area of about 12 square miles. Nohmul was named by the people living in the vicinity of the site.

Not much has been consolidated for tourists here. The entrance to the site is about 10 miles north of Orange Walk Town, in the sugarcane fields west of the village of San Pablo; it is one mile from the center of the village. Public transportation from Belize City, Orange Walk Town, and Corozal passes through the village of San Pablo several times daily.

Tour Operators

All regional tour operators in Orange Walk, Corozal, and Belize City offer tours to Lamanai. Ask about night safaris, bird-watching tours, and sunrise trips up and down the New River. Most hotels can arrange tours with licensed guides. Most tours include entrance fee, drinks, and a catered lunch as part of the deal; prices range US$40–60 per person.

Freddy Gomez, owner of **Transport Services** (21 St. Peters St., tel. 501/322-2037 or 501/609-9641), has a 15-passenger van and a Crown Vic and is a highly knowledgeable guide who can arrange insightful tours anywhere in Orange Walk District. **Elvis Usher** (tel. 501/669-6686, elvisusher31@hotmail.com) is another notable guide and is available for group or private tours.

Jungle River Tours (20 Lovers Ln., tel. 501/302-2293 or 501/615-1712) is the oldest operating guide service, with a reputation for giving the best tours of Lamanai. Jungle River boats leave from a landing near the historic La Inmaculada Catholic Church. **Errol Cadle Eco Tours** (errolcadle1@yahoo.com) is a top-notch guide service and will cater to travelers who wish for a less frenetic pace when it

comes to their boat trips; meals and drinks are provided. **Lamanai EcoAdventures** (tel. 501/322-3653 or 501/610-1753) also has a dock just south of the Tower Hill Toll Bridge, as does **New River Cruises.**

ACCOMMODATIONS

Orange Walk has a combination of well-equipped, business-oriented hotels and a few old budget standards.

Under US$25

Akihito Hotel (tel. 501/302-0185 or 501/322-3018, akihitolee@yahoo.com, www.akihito-hotel.com) charges US$23–25 for standard rooms, more for air-conditioning; most rooms have shared bath. Dorm beds go for US$7.50–9 per person. The hotel tax is included in all room rates. Run by the Lees, this is a good sleep for the dollar. It's clean, with cool tiled interiors and a downstairs shop serving beverages and a few necessities, and offers just about every basic amenity the traveler needs: laundry service, credit-card phone calls, high-speed wireless Internet, and cable television. The Lees are an excellent source of information about the Orange Walk area, including which restaurants are good and which bars to avoid.

Lucia's Guesthouse (68 San Antonio Rd., tel. 501/322-2244, US$11) is a basic traveler's rest house; most rooms have private baths. Air-conditioning is available. Coming from Belize City, hang a left at the fire station downtown and continue a half mile.

US$25-50

Named after the patron saint of travelers, **Hotel St. Christopher's** (tel. 501/302-1064 or 501/322-2420, www.stchristophershotel-bze.com) is an ideal setting for large groups; it has 22 colorful, traditional Spanish-feeling rooms with tiled floors and private baths for US$30 with fan, US$45 with air-conditioning. Amenities include wireless Internet, laundry service, private parking, and complimentary coffee in the lobby. A conference room, which seats 70, is available for meetings or catered meals. Located on the riverfront, the hotel has plenty of space for recreation: kayak and paddle rentals, volleyball court, picnic tables, and greenery to attract birds and other wildlife. A few of the rooms have shared balconies with a view of the river.

You'll find great value at **Hotel de la Fuente** (tel. 501/322-2290, www.hoteldelafuente.com, US$45–65), where 22 varied rooms offer a range of amenities, including fully equipped apartments and free wireless Internet; it's great for business travelers. All rooms are nonsmoking and have airconditioning. By press time they should have 10 new rooms completed.

Orchid Palm Inn (22 Queen Victoria Ave., tel. 501/322-0719, fax 501/322-3947, www.orchidpalminn.com, US$40–60) offers similar amenities, including a nice lobby, airconditioning, and wireless Internet. All these places are centrally located.

Lamanai Riverside Retreat (tel. 501/302-3955, lamanairiverside@hotmail.com, US$40) is a small family-run business located on the New River. It has four basic rooms with fans (a/c is also available), cable TV, and private baths. The Pelayos can take care of all your needs with a nice open-air bar and restaurant on-site and a variety of tour offerings.

FOOD

Orange Walk may actually have the highest per capita number of Chinese restaurants in all of Central America, but **Tan's Delight** is probably your best bet. Or maybe **Lee's Chinese Restaurant,** near the fire station, with passable versions of chicken chow mein (US$3.25), sweet and sour fish (US$7.50), or black soybean lobster (US$12).

Central Park Restaurant (New Market near the bus terminal, a.k.a. "Fort Cairns") is actually a collection of six restaurants styled after the old-school open market located next door. They serve everything a hungry traveler could want: burgers, tacos, empanadas, pizza, hot dogs, bacon and eggs breakfasts, sweet cakes, waffles, and the usual assortment of

beverages, all for a couple of bucks. You'll find basic Belizean meals at **Luigi's,** next door to Hotel de la Fuente.

Lamanai Riverside Retreat is open daily for breakfast, lunch, and dinner. It's a nice setting to relax after a long day of traveling and sightseeing. Their midrange dinner menu includes burgers, fajitas, burritos, and seafood dishes; fresh fruit juices and a full bar are also available. Karaoke nights (Friday and Sunday) attract a local crowd and occasionally there is live music.

Nahil Mayab (tel. 501/322-0831, www.nahilmayab.com, 10 A.M.–3 P.M. Mon., 10 A.M.–10 P.M. Tue.–Sat., 10:30 A.M.–3 P.M. Sun.) offers a great dining atmosphere; the outdoor patio is set in a beautiful tropical garden and the air-conditioned restaurant has an attractive Maya theme. The food is here is excellent; the menu includes seafood, steak, and pasta, with a daily happy hour 5–7 P.M.

Panificadora La Popular (6:30 A.M.–8 P.M.) is regarded as the best bakery in town. They have a large selection of breads and pastries. Get pizza by the slice starting at 3 P.M. or have a whole pizza ready in 15 minutes (tel. 501/322-3229 to place an order). **Escalante Bakery and Café** on Cinderella Street serves espresso drinks and freshly baked goods, including sweet breads, cinnamon rolls, muffins, and brownies.

For a cold treat, try **IceBreak** by Scotia Bank or **Loz Service Internet Café and Snack Shop** on Cinderella Street.

Orange Walk's fanciest meals are found outside of town at **El Establo.** Ask any taxi driver to take you there.

SERVICES

This is the commercial center of the district, so there are many small shops selling all kinds of merchandise, including agricultural supplies, local cookware (like a cast-iron comal or tortilla press, both heavy but useful souvenirs), and many used American clothing shops. There are three major banks on Main Street, a few Internet cafés, and basic traveler services, like laundry and cheap food.

GETTING THERE AND AWAY
By Bus
There is no main station, but the buses traveling between Corozal and Belize City all stop to idle next to Fort Cairns (the site is supposedly temporary, but nobody knew where the bus station was moving) for a few minutes before lumbering on—they pass about every hour until 6 P.M. Buses passing through town after 6 P.M. usually stop by Town Hall briefly. The last bus to Belize City will pass around 6:45 P.M. and service to Corozal continues hourly until about 9 P.M. Some of the buses are express, but it's hard to tell which ones, unless they are the comfy, air-conditioned charter buses. Sunday service is about every two hours. Buses to Indian Church village (near Lamanai) leave only on Friday, returning Monday. There are hourly buses to San Felipe to the west and Sarteneja to the east. Buses to Sarteneja can be found across the street from Banquitas House of Culture by the Zeta Ice Factory.

By Boat
Going by boat is a pleasant way to get anywhere, especially up the New River to Lamanai. Enjoy nature's best along the shore of the river and the labyrinthine passageways through the wetlands. You never know what you'll see next—long-legged birds, orchids in tall trees, hummingbirds, crocs—it's like a treasure hunt. Bring your binocs. Ask anywhere for directions to the boat dock. Some boat operators depart from the New Hill Toll Bridge south of town.

GETTING AROUND
There are a few taxi stands located on Queen Victoria Avenue, next to the sports field. Fares around the central part of Orange Walk Town are US$2.50; US$7.50 to the toll bridge; and US$10 to the airstrip.

Lamanai Archaeological Zone

Set on the edge of a forested broad lagoon are the temples of Lamanai. One of the largest and longest-inhabited ceremonial centers in Belize, Lamanai is believed to have served as an imperial port city encompassing ball courts, pyramids, and several more exotic Maya features. Hundreds of buildings have been identified in the two-square-mile area. Archaeologist David Pendergast headed a team from the Royal Ontario Museum that, after finding a number of children's bones buried under a stela, presumed that human sacrifice was a part of the residents' religion. Large masks that depict a ruler wearing a crocodile headdress were found in several locations, hence the name Lamanai ("Submerged Crocodile").

The ruins of Lamanai huddle to one side of New River Lagoon and sprawl westward through the forest and under the village of **Indian Church** (which was relocated by the government from one part of the site to another in 1992). It is reachable by boat from Orange Walk or by road from San Felipe. The Institute of Archaeology has done a great deal of work at this site, and the main temples are impressive even to the uneducated eye. The High Temple can be climbed to yield a 360-degree view of the surrounding jungle and lagoon.

With the advent of midday cruise ship tours, the site boasts a new dock, visitors center, craft shops, and museum. Lamanai is also a popular site for day-trippers from Ambergris Caye and can be quite crowded in the middle of the day, especially during the week. If you want a more solitary experience, go early in the morning or late in the afternoon, as cruise ship crowds arrive at noon and disappear in less than two hours. The reserve is open to the public 8 A.M.–5 P.M. daily. Entrance to the site is US$10 per person.

◖ LAMANAI ARCHAEOLOGICAL SITE
Lamanai consists of four large temples, a residential complex, and a reproduction stela of a Maya elite, Lord Smoking Shell. Excavations

A guide points out the jaguar face on the Jaguar Temple at the Lamanai Archaeological Site.

reveal continuous occupation and a high standard of living into the Post-Classic Period, unlike in other colonies in the region. Lamanai is believed to have been occupied from 1500 B.C. to the 19th century—Spanish occupation is also apparent, with the remains of two Christian churches and a sugar mill that was built by British colonialists.

The landscape at most of Lamanai is forest, and trees and thick vines grow from the tops of buildings. The only sounds are birdcalls and howler monkey voices echoing off the stone temples. These are some of the notable sites:

• **The Mask Temple N9-56:** Here two significant tombs were found, as well as two Early Classic stone masks. It was built around A.D. 450. The second mask on the temple was exposed in late 2010.

• **The High Temple N10-43:** At 100 feet high, this is the tallest securely dated Pre-Classic structure in the Maya area. Among many findings were a dish containing the skeleton of a bird and Pre-Classic vessels dating to

100 B.C. The view above the canopy is marvelous, and on a clear day you can see the hills of Quintana Roo, Mexico.

• **The Ball Court:** The game played in this area held great ritual significance for the Maya, though because of the small size of Lamanai's court, some think it was just symbolic. In 1980, archaeologists raised the huge stone disc marking the center of the court and found lidded vessels on top of a mercury puddle. Miniature vessels inside contained small jade and shell objects.

• **Royal Complex:** Excavated in 2005, this was the residence of up to two dozen elite Lamanai citizens; you can see their beds, doorways, and the like.

• **Jaguar Temple N10-9:** Dated to the 6th century A.D., this temple had structural modifications in the 8th and 13th centuries. Jade jewelry and a jade mask were discovered here, as was an animal motif dish. Based on the animal remains and other evidence, archaeologists now believe that this was the site of an enormous party and feast to celebrate the end of a drought in A.D. 950.

• **The Stela Temple N10-27:** In 1983, archaeologists began an investigation of structure N10-27, where they discovered a large stone monument, designated Stela 9. The elaborately carved stela depicts Lord Smoking Shell in ceremonial dress. Hieroglyphic text of Stela 9, while incomplete, indicates that this monument was erected to commemorate the accession of Smoking Shell, the Lord of Lamanai. Further excavations near the base of the monument revealed a cache of human remains and artifacts, believed to be associated with a dedication ritual. Today, a replica stands at the stela temple; the original can be viewed in the museum at Lamanai.

Wildlife and Birding

The trip to the site up the New River Lagoon is its own safari; once you're at the ruins, you'll see numbered trees that correspond to an informational pamphlet available from the caretakers at the entrance of Lamanai Reserve.

NORTHERN BELIZE

Birders, look around the Mask Temple and High Temple for Montezuma oropendolas and their drooping nests. Black vultures are often spotted slowly gliding over the entire area. A woodpecker with a distinct double-tap rhythm and a red cap is the male pale-billed woodpecker. Near the High Temple, small flocks of collared aracaris, related to the larger toucan, forage the canopy for fruits and insects. The black-headed trogon is more spectacular than its name implies, with a yellow chest, a black-and-white tail, and iridescent blue-green back. Though it looks as if the northern jacana is walking on water, it's the delicate floating vegetation that holds the long-toed bird above the water as it searches along the water's edge for edible delicacies.

Other fauna spotted by those who live there are jaguarundis, agoutis, armadillos, Central American river turtles, and roaring howler monkeys. Up in the village, pay a visit to the **Xochil Ku Butterfly Farm,** an effort by Don Guillermo Melchor Ramos.

Indian Church Village Artisans Center

Contribute directly to the local economy by shopping at this community-based organization, founded in 2000 with the assistance of professional archaeologists, artisans, and architects working at the nearby Lamanai site. The center provides workspace, tools, material, craft training, English classes, and a computer center to interested villagers. The center has a small shop at the Lamanai site, or you can check out the artisans' wares at their workshop in the village. Artisans produce silver and bronze jewelry, hand-sewn purses, bags, embroidered pillowcases, slate carvings, and fired clay statues. Most of the artwork emulates artifacts found at the Lamanai site, including silver pendants of the Lord Smoking Shell stela. Stop by the village workshop yourself or ask your guide to take you by the shop at the Lamanai site.

Getting There

Most visitors use one of the tour companies based in Orange Walk or the transfer services

of their lodge, but it is possible to do it yourself as well. A two-person boat transfer from Orange Walk should cost about US$125, less if you can get in with a bigger group. You can drive the San Felipe road in about 1.5 hours, depending on road conditions. Or you can take the village bus to Indian Church, which leaves Orange Walk at 5–6 P.M. on Fridays and Mondays. The same buses depart Indian Church at 5–5:30 A.M. on the same days, so you'll have to make a weekend out of it—or more. On the opposite end of the time, comfort, and price spectrum, you can charter a 15-minute flight from Belize City to Lamanai Outpost Lodge's airstrip with one of Belize's private charter services.

ACCOMMODATIONS

The Indian Church villagers have been hosting groups of foreign archaeologists, anthropologists, and biologists (and the odd gringo volunteer) for decades. In addition to the places listed, there are a few informal homestay options available. Find out the latest developments in the village's foray into tourism by calling the community phone at 501/309-1015, or just wander into town and see what you find. Note that Indian Church is off the electricity and telephone grid, and solar panels and gasoline generators provide power. All budget options provide meals and cultural activities and can hook you up with local guides for the ruins and wildlife tours.

US$25-50

Olivia and David Gonzalez (tel. 510/603-1068, 510/660-3826, or 510/309-1015, from US$20–30 per person) have moved up from rustic wooden rooms connected to their home to a row of modern cement rooms with private baths and basic amenities, including a few hours of electricity each evening. **Doña Blanca Hotel** (tel. 501/603-7243 or 501/309-1015, from US$25) has 15 rooms with private bath, solar power, and hot and cold showers.

Lamanai Outpost Lodge

About a half mile up the bank of the lagoon from

the Lamanai archaeological site, [Lamanai Outpost Lodge (tel. 501/223-3578, U.S. tel. 888/733-7864, www.lamanai.com) is one of Belize's premier jungle retreats. From the moment the staff greet you at the dock, you know you're in capable, welcoming hands. The lodge boasts 17 elegantly rustic thatch-roof, rough-hewn wood cabanas detailed with converted brass oil lamps and other amenities that contribute to an old-fashioned feel (although a couple of rooms add plasma-screen TV, air-conditioning, and wireless Internet access to the old-timey mix). Outside, lush, landscaped grounds of orchids, ceiba trees, and palmettos provide cooling shade as you walk the gravel paths. Below the resort's lodge and dining room (which are the only parts of the complex visible from the river) lies the shore of the lagoon, where you'll find a dock, a swimming area, canoes, boats of various types, and an assortment of deck chairs. The dock is particularly peaceful at sunset. Activities keep you busy from pre-dawn hikes and canoe trips to nighttime "spotlight cruises." All-inclusive packages start at US$676; there's a two-night minimum stay, and rates transfer to and from Belize City, meals, and two guided adventure activities per night booked. See the website for summer specials and individual pricing options.

The owners of Lamanai Outpost are involved in several scientific research projects that also allow nature-study opportunities for guests. Study topics include local bats, archaeology, howler monkeys, Morelet's crocodiles, and ornithology. Guests with some group programs can participate in the work.

Lamanai Outpost offers a low-key, escape-to-nature kind of setting, perfect for the bird-watcher, Mayaphile, naturalist, or traveler who wants to get away from the tourist trail for a while. The area is rich in animal life, including close to 400 species of birds, as well as crocodiles, margays, jaguarundis, anteaters, tayras, arboreal porcupines, and the fishing bulldog bat.

FOOD
In Indian Church village, you'll find cheap local food (about US$5 a meal) at the **Grupo de Mujeres Las Orquidias Restaurant.** This is a communal effort of nine women from nine families who are adept at dealing with both groups and individuals. **Doña Blanca** (tel. 501/603-7243 or 501/309-1015) also serves food at her hotel.

West of Orange Walk Town

CUELLO RUINS
Four miles west of Orange Walk on Yo Creek, on the property of a Caribbean rum warehouse, are the minor ruins of Cuello. Check in at the gate office (tel. 501/322-2141, 8:30 A.M.–4:30 P.M. daily), then investigate these relatively undisturbed ruins, consisting of a large plaza with seven structures in a long horizontal mound. There are three temples; see if you can find the uncovered ones. These structures (as in Cahal Pech) have a different look than most Maya sites. They are covered with a layer of white stucco, as they were in the days of the Maya.

The ruins of Cuello were studied in the 1970s by a Cambridge University archaeology team led by Norman Hammond. A small ceremonial center, a proto-Classic temple, has been excavated. Lying directly in front is a large excavation trench, partially backfilled, where the archaeologists gathered the historical information that revolutionized previous concepts of the antiquity of the ancient Maya. Artifacts indicate that the Maya traded with people hundreds of miles away. Among the archaeologists' out-of-the-ordinary findings were bits of wood that proved, after carbon testing, that Cuello had been occupied as early as 2600 B.C., much earlier than ever believed. Archaeologists now find, however, that these tests may have been incorrect, and the age is in dispute.

Also found was an unusual style of pottery

—apparently in some burials, clay urns were placed over the heads of the deceased. It's also speculated that it was here, over a long period, that the primitive strain of corn seen in early years was refined and developed into the higher-producing plant of the Classic Period. Continuous occupation for approximately 4,000 years was surmised, with repeated layers of structures all the way into the Classic Period.

CONTINUING WEST

As the road meanders west from Cuello, numerous small villages dot the border region. Occasionally you see a soft drink sign attached to a building, but there's not much in the way of facilities between Orange Walk and Blue Creek. Heading west from San Felipe, you soon find flat, open farmland, with Mennonite accoutrements, dominating the landscape. Low, open rice paddies provide great bird-watching opportunities as well as placid scenery.

Soon, however, you hit the foothills of the Maya highlands near **Blue Creek** village. Climbing up into the foothills you can see the flatlands of the Río Hondo and New River drainages to the east. The small village to the right is **La Union,** on the other side of the Mexico border. This part of Orange Walk District is much hillier and has an increasingly wild feel to it.

In the village of Blue Creek, **The Hillside Bed & Breakfast** (tel. 501/323-0155, bchillsideb_b@yahoo.com, US$50) is an incredibly unique and peaceful place to stay, about 30 miles west of Orange Walk, on the left coming up the hill. Experience Belizean Mennonite hospitality and life on a working farm. Rate includes breakfast in the kitchen, and the rooms have all basic amenities, including air-conditioning. As far as I know, this is the only tourist accommodation offered in a Mennonite community in Belize.

At the top of the hill is the **Linda Vista Credit Union** and a gas station/general store. Fill the tank if you're driving on to Río Bravo or Chan Chich, as this is the last gas station until you come back this way.

As you continue farther west, the area becomes progressively more forested until you reach the dramatic boundary of the Programme for Belize Río Bravo Conservation Area. Here, the cleared pastureland runs smack-dab into a wall of jungle, and there is a gate at the border. If you aren't expected, the guard won't let you pass. Once inside the gate, you've entered the Río Bravo Conservation Area.

◖ RÍO BRAVO CONSERVATION AREA

Programme for Belize is a Belizean nonprofit organization, established in 1988, to promote the conservation of the natural heritage of Belize and wise use of its natural resources, centering on the Río Bravo Conservation and Management Area (RBCMA), a 260,000-acre chunk of Belize where Programme for Belize demonstrates the practical application of its principles (the land was originally slated for clearing). The RBCMA represents approximately 4 percent of Belize's total land area and is home to a rich sample of biodiversity, which includes 392 species of birds, 200 species of trees, 70 species of mammals, 30 species of freshwater fish, and 27 species of conservation concern.

Within the conservation area, the research station is housed in a cluster of small thatch-roof buildings. Programme for Belize is dedicated to scientific research, agricultural experimentation, and the protection of indigenous wildlife and the area's Maya archaeological locations—all this while creating self-sufficiency through development of ecotourism and sustainable rainforest agriculture such as chicle production. A scientific study continues to determine the best management plan for the reserve and its forests.

Ongoing projects include archaeological research at the La Milpa Maya Site and other sites on the RBCMA in conjunction with Boston University and the University of Texas; timber and pine savanna research programs aimed at identifying the most optimal approach to sustainable timber extraction on the RBCMA; a carbon sequestration pilot program, the first of seven globally approved projects to start on-the-ground research on how forest conservation could combat global warming; ecological research and monitoring of migratory and resident avifauna, such as the yellow-headed parrot; a freshwater management program, which looks at the New River Lagoon, its tributaries, and the New River; and the biological connectivity program, which looks at the RBCMA and the critical links it forms with other protected areas in northern Belize.

Scientists, research volunteers, donors, and interested travelers are encouraged to contact **Programme for Belize** (1 Eyre St., Belize City, tel. 501/207-5616 or 501/227-1020, U.S. tel. 617/259-9500, www.pfbelize.org).

La Milpa Field Station

Programme for Belize's La Milpa Field Station lies nestled deep in the forests of northwestern Belize. This field station is only three miles from the third-largest archaeological site in Belize. The La Milpa archaeological site is only one of at least 60 archaeological sites found on the Río Bravo. Hiking nature trails, jungle trekking, and birding are the order of the day at La Milpa. Spend a day in the nearby mestizo and Mennonite villages for a taste of Belizean culture. Tour breathtaking and majestic ancient Maya sites. Birders can compile a list of more than 150 species during a three-day trip to La Milpa.

For accommodations, guests can choose between charmingly rustic thatch-roof cabanas (US$50–55 pp) with private baths or a comfortable and tastefully decorated dormitory (US$41 pp) featuring state-of-the-art "green" technology with shared baths. The La Milpa venue has meeting facilities, telephones, and dining facilities and is family oriented, with 24-hour electricity and hot and cold water. All-inclusive packages start at US$140 per person, which includes accommodations, three buffet-style meals, and two guided tours on the property. Contact Programme for Belize for details.

Hill Bank Field Station

Located on the banks of the New River Lagoon, the Hill Bank Field Station serves as a research base for sustainable forest management and specialized tourism, which incorporates research activities into the visitors' forest experience. Hill Bank, an important site in Belize's colonial history, served as a center of intensive timber extraction for more than 150 years, commencing in the 17th century. The Hill Bank experience brings to life the architecture and artifacts of colonial land use, such as the quaint wooden buildings of logging camps, antique steam engines, and railroad tracks.

Explore the wilds of Hill Bank by canoeing, crocodile spotting, hiking nature trails, birding, and jungle trekking. The scenic boat ride, replete with wildlife sightings along the New River Lagoon, is a great experience in itself. For accommodations, guests stay in Hill Bank's Caza Balanza, which features 100 percent solar power, no-flush composting toilets, and a rainwater collection system with shared baths. Or choose a charming double cabana with private baths with verandas overlooking the New River Lagoon. Rates are the same as at La Milpa. Contact Programme for Belize for details.

CHAN CHICH
Chan Chich Ruins

As recently as 1986, the only way in to the Maya site of Chan Chich (Kaxil Uinich) was with machete in hand and a canoe to cross the swiftly flowing rivers. Most people making the trip were either loggers, pot farmers, or grave robbers. Then, in the northwestern corner of Belize in Orange Walk District, near the Guatemala border, an old overgrown logging road, originally blazed by the Belize Estate and Produce Company (logging operators), was reopened, and consequently, the site of Chan Chich was rediscovered.

When found, three of the temples showed obvious signs of looting with vertical slit trenches—just as the looters had left them. No one will ever know what valuable artifacts were removed and sold to private collectors all over the world.

NORTHERN BELIZE

The large main temple on the upper plaza had been violated to the heart of what appears to be one or more burial chambers. A painted frieze runs around the low ceiling. Today, the only temple inhabitants greeting outsiders are armies of small bats and spider monkeys.

The ruins provide opportunity for discovery and exploration, and the population and diversity of wildlife here is probably greater than anywhere else in Belize. The nine miles of hiking trails wind through the verdant jungle and give ample chance to sight wildlife, including big cats.

This is not a public archaeological site and the ruins are unexcavated. Chan Chich Lodge looks after the site.

Gallon Jug Village and Estate

Originally the hub of the British Belize Estate and Produce Company's mahogany logging operation, the land was purchased by Barry Bowen. Gallon Jug Village and Estate (tel. 501/227-7031 ext. 5251, www.gallonjug.com) is now a privately owned diverse working farm, ranch, and community, with an airstrip, post office, coffee-roasting facility, and school. The scientific research conducted here, led by Bruce and Carolyn Miller, has focused on jaguars and neotropical bats.

Chan Chich Lodge

A dozen upscale thatch-roof cabanas rest inside a peaceful Maya plaza. Though decried by some archaeologists when it was built, the presence of Chan Chich Lodge serves as a deterrent to temple looters and marijuana traffickers (both of whom used to thrive in northern Belize).

This elegant and luxurious retreat is surrounded on all sides by unexcavated pyramids and the second largest tropical forest in the Americas. The landscaped grounds, subtly lit pool and Jacuzzi, and sunset views from the tops of the mounds complement the spacious cabanas, which have modern amenities like water coolers, refrigerators, huge tiled bathrooms, and natural insulation and ventilation.

Guests spend their days exploring the ruins and hiking trails, canoeing at the nearby Laguna Verde, or horseback riding from the Gallon Jug stables. Birding opportunities include seeing trogons, ocellated turkeys, toucans, and hundreds of other birds. All five species of Belizean cat live in the surrounding forest. Tours of the coffee plantation and experimental farm at Gallon Jug provide the opportunity to learn all the steps in the coffee-making process as well as about other sustainable agricultural initiatives taking place here. And the day doesn't end at the peaceful dining veranda. If you're not signed up for the night safari, then you can finish off at the Looter's Trench Bar.

The Chan Chich office in Belize City is near the water (1 King St., tel. 501/223-4419, U.S. tel. 800/343-8009, www.chanchich.com, info@chanchich.com). Considering the logistics of running a lodge so far out in the forest, it's not such a bad deal: rooms from US$205, plus US$70 per day for meals, plus tours, guides, and taxes. Ask about inclusive packages to lower costs.

Chan Chich is 130 miles from Belize City, an all-day drive from the international airport or (much easier) a 30-minute charter flight to Gallon Jug. Call or write for more information; the lodge can make all your travel arrangements.

Corozal and Vicinity

Corozal Town's 9,000 or so inhabitants casually get by while the bay washes against the seawall running the length of town. While English is the official language, Spanish is just as common, since many residents are descendants of early-day Maya and mestizo refugees from neighboring Mexico. Historically, Corozal was the scene of attacks by the Mayans during the Caste War. What remains of Fort Barlee can be found in the center of town (west of Central Park).

The town was almost entirely wiped out during Hurricane Janet in 1955 and has since been rebuilt. As you stroll through the quiet streets, you'll find a library, a museum, town hall, government administrative offices, a Catholic

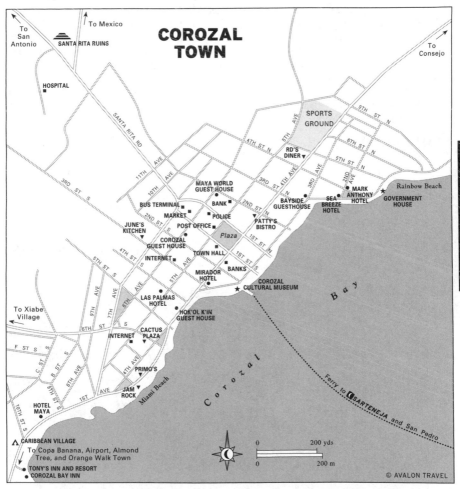

NORTHERN BELIZE

church, two secondary schools, five elementary schools, one gas station, a government hospital, a clinic, a few small hotels, a couple of bars, and several restaurants. There's not a whole lot of activity here, unless you happen to be in town during the Mexican-style "Spanish" fiestas of Christmas, Carnival, and Columbus Day; there are also a few local events in mid-September.

ORIENTATION
Visitors enter Corozal from the north (from Mexico), from the south on the Northern Highway, or from Ambergris Caye to the east by boat or plane. Getting oriented to Corozal is easy, since it's laid out on a grid system with avenues running north and south (parallel to the seawall) and streets running east and west. Corozal's two primary avenues, 4th and 5th, run the length of town. The majority of restaurants and stores of interest to travelers lie on, or adjacent to, these streets.

SIGHTS AND RECREATION
There are no tourist attractions, per se, in Corozal, but it's an unassuming base for fishing trips, nature watching, and tours of a few nearby ruins and waterways. Wander through the town square, stroll the waterfront, and strike up a conversation with the locals or expats who've come to love the laid-back lifestyle. The seaside park, called Miami Beach, is a popular hangout on the weekend and holidays.

In the town hall, you'll find a dramatic historical **mural** painted by Manuel Villamour. The bright painting depicts the history of Corozal, including the drama of the downtrodden Maya, the explosive revolt called the Caste War, and the inequities of colonial rule.

Some trips include day trips to the Shipstern Wildlife Nature Reserve, Sarteneja village, and the Maya sites of Cerros and Santa Rita.

Local Guides and Tour Companies
One of the best independent guides around is **Vital Nature and Mayan Tours,** also known as Vitalino Reyes (tel. 501/602-8975, www.cavetubing.bz), whose years of experience qualify him to teach and certify many of Corozal's other guides. Vital will take you to local ruins,

Corozal is a small town that hugs the bay.

© JOSHUA BERMAN

ARCHAEOLOGICAL SITES NEAR COROZAL

The nearby ruins of Cerros and Santa Rita are not as immediately awe-inspiring as, say, Lamanai or Caracol, but they are still interesting and easy to visit.

CERRO MAYA

Commonly referred to as "Cerros," the Cerro Maya ("Maya Hill") archaeological site lords over both sea and jungle on a peninsula across from Corozal called Lawry's Bite. Cerros was an important coastal trading center during the Late Pre-Classic Period (350 B.C.-A.D. 250) and was occupied as late as 1300 A.D. Magnificent frescoes and stone heads were uncovered by archaeologist David Friedel, signifying that elite rule was firmly fixed by the end of the Pre-Classic Period. The tallest of Cerros's temples rises to 70 feet, and because of the rise in the sea level, the one-time stone residences of the elite Maya are partially flooded.

It would appear that Cerros not only provisioned oceangoing canoes, but also was in an ideal location to control ancient trade routes that traced the Río Hondo and New River from the Yucatán to Petén and the Usumacinta basin. A plaster-lined canal for the sturdy, oversized ocean canoes was constructed around Cerros. Archaeologists have determined that extensive fishing and farming on raised fields took place, probably to outfit the traders. But always the question remains: Why did progress suddenly stop?

Be prepared for vicious mosquitoes at Cerros, especially if there's no breeze. You can reach the site by boat in minutes — hire one at **Tony's Inn** in Corozal or check with a travel agent. If you travel during the dry season (Jan.-Apr.), you can get to Cerros by car; it

takes up to 45 minutes, and you'll have to employ the hand-cranked Pueblo Nuevo Ferry. Admission to the ruins is US$10 per person. Guests at **Cerros Beach Resort** (tel. 501/623-9763 or 501/623-9530, www.cerrosbeachresort.com, US$40-60) can bike to the ruins; keep an eye out for jaguarundis, gray foxes, and coatimundis along the way. Cerros Beach Resort is a quiet, off-the-grid location with four screened-in thatch cabanas with private bathrooms and hot water.

SANTA RITA

This site, one mile northeast of Corozal, was still a populated community of Maya when the Spanish arrived. The largest Santa Rita structure was explored at the turn of the 20th century by Thomas Gann. Sculptured friezes and stucco murals were found along with a burial site that indicates flourishing occupation in the Early Classic Period (about A.D. 300), as well as during the Late Post-Classic Period (A.D. 1350-1530). Two significant burials were found from distant periods in the history of Santa Rita: one from A.D. 300 was a female and the other was a king from a period 200 years later.

In 1985, archaeologists Diane and Arlen Chase discovered a tomb with a skeleton covered in jade and mica ornaments. It has been excavated and somewhat reconstructed under the Chases' jurisdiction; only one structure is accessible to the public. Post-Classic murals, mostly destroyed over the years, combined Maya and Mexican styles that depict the ecumenical flavor of the period. Some believe that Santa Rita was part of a series of coastal lookouts. Santa Rita is probably more appealing to archaeology buffs than to the average tourist.

to the caves at Jaguar Paw, to the Belize Zoo, on night safaris, or anywhere else you want to go. **Belize VIP Transfer Services** (tel. 501/422-2725, www.belizetransfers.com or menziestours@btl.net) is your best bet for charter transportation, using brand-new vehicles that are great for groups. Belize VIP specializes in local tours (including a day tour of Corozal and Cerros), Lamanai trips, Chetumal transfers (and other Mexican attractions), and Tikal/Flores trips to Guatemala. **George & Esther Moralez Travel Service** (tel. 501/422-2485, www.gettransfers.com) offers transfer services and tours. They will also help you with hotel and local flight bookings. Dial 00 before the phone number when calling from Mexico to

Belize. **Hok'ol K'in Guest House** handles all such trips as well, especially to local villages. For travel agencies or local flight bookings, go to the **Hotel Maya.** International flights, ADO bus tickets, and other travel reservations can be booked through **Cruzob Travel** (33 3rd Ave., tel. 501/607-7930), which is next door to Bayview Guest House.

SHOPPING

Corozal has lots of little shops, grocery stores, bookstores, and a few gift shops. You'll find locally made jewelry, pottery, wood carvings, clothing, textiles, and a host of other mementos here and there, but the place is not overrun with gift shops yet. **White Sapphire,** south of the Texaco station on 7th Avenue, has a large selection of local crafts and jewelry. **D's Superstore,** on College Road, is the largest grocer in town; **Family Supermarket,** by Fort Barlee, is an option that is more centrally located. Gifts, books, postcards, and other supplies can be obtained at **A&R,** on 4th Avenue near Patty's Bistro.

ACCOMMODATIONS
Under US$25

Maya World Guest House (tel. 501/666-3577 or 501/627-2511, byronchuster@gmail.com, from US$22.50) has clean rooms that surround a well-kept, cheery garden. It features a communal kitchen, common areas, and veranda with hammocks. The central location and conveniences such as bike rental and laundry service attract backpackers. **Caribbean Village RV Park and Campground** (tel. 501/422-2725, menziestours@btl.net) offers full RV hookups for US$20 a night and camping for US$5 per person.

(Sea Breeze Hotel (tel. 501/422-3051 or 501/605-9341, www.theseabreezehotel.com, gwyn_lawrence@yahoo.com, US$18–30) offers the best budget accommodations in Corozal. Rooms have cable TV, fans (a/c for additional cost), hot water, and wireless Internet. The seaside location of this hotel offers a cooling breeze in the evening. Call ahead or email as this place has only seven rooms and gets

busy. The second-floor bar (for guests only) is a great place to meet other travelers and is a quick walk from the main thoroughfares. Bikes are available for guests to explore the town by day. Enjoy a freshly brewed cup of coffee in the morning and breakfast upon request.

US$25-50

Just two blocks south of the town center, and right across from the water, the **(Hok'ol K'in Guest House** (tel. 501/422-3329, maya@btl.net, www.corozal.net, US$21–65) was begun by an ex–Peace Corps volunteer with the intention of supporting local Maya community endeavors. In Yucateca Mayan, "Hok'ol K'in" means "Coming of the Rising Sun," a sight you'll see from your window if you're up early enough—follow your sun salutations with an excellent breakfast (and real coffee!) on the patio downstairs. Hok'ol K'in's 10 immaculate rooms have private baths, verandas, cable TV, and fans; free wireless Internet is available. Ask about available trips and homestays (or visits) with local families; the staff are very helpful in arranging things to do. This is one of the few lodgings in Belize equipped to handle a wheelchair (one room only, so be sure to specify if it's needed). The restaurant serves a variety of good meals (7 A.M.–7 P.M. daily).

The Mark Anthony Hotel (2nd Ave. N. at 4th St. N., tel. 501/422-3141 or 501/631-4803), overlooking Corozal Bay, has nine rooms with cable, hot and cold water, and queen beds starting at US$35 (a/c available for additional cost). A wide selection of souvenirs is available and the bar and restaurant has some of the best food to be had in town. **The Oasis** (2nd St., off Northern Highway, tel. 501/402-0391, darlenebartlett@gmail.com) is an affordable option geared toward both long- and short-term stays. Rooms are about US$30; apartments start at US$300 a month. A communal kitchen is onsite as well as a lovely swimming pool and tranquil garden area.

Hotel Mirador (tel. 501/422-0189, www.mirador.bz, US$35–75) is a 24-room lodging across from the main dock and seawall, whose rooftop boasts the best views in town.

The rooms are sparkling and spotless, with private baths and hot and cold water, and the hallways are cavernous. There's cable TV and wireless Internet, plus you'll get lots of friendly help from your hosts, Jose and Lydia Gongora. Deluxe rooms with air-conditioning start at US$50.

On the road leading into town from the south, the **Hotel Maya and Apartments** (tel. 501/422-2082 or 501/422-2874, www.hotel-maya.net, US$35–50 offers 20 rooms with air-conditioning, TV, and private baths; the restaurant serves breakfast only. There is also a gift shop and travel agency that can arrange trips to local destinations as well as transport across the borders to Tikal, Chetumal, or even Cancún. Furnished apartments with air-conditioning start at US$300 per month.

Las Palmas Hotel (formerly Nestor's, but completely rebuilt, tel. 501/422-0196, www.laspalmashotelbelize.com, US$45 and up) is in the heart of town, with 25 full-service rooms that include air-conditioning, private baths, hot and cold water, wireless Internet, parking, 24-hour security, and a backup generator.

Bayside Guest House (31 3rd Ave., tel. 501/625-7824, US$45) has four rooms with hot and cold water, ceiling fan, cable TV, Internet, and air-conditioning for an additional cost. There's a free continental breakfast. The terrace bar and restaurant is open to guests for an evening meal or drink.

US$50-100

Three seaside options reside on the south end of town, clustered together on what is locally known as "Gringo Lane." At **Tony's Inn and Beach Resort** (tel. 501/422-2055 or 501/422-3555, tonys@btl.net, from US$85), "beach" may be stretching it a bit, and the 24 rooms are set up more like a Motel 6 than a resort. Still, the large rooms have air-conditioning, private baths, and hot and cold water. The Y-Not Bar and Grill is in a nice setting on the water, and the hotel has its own marina and runs a variety of local trips.

Right next door to Tony's Inn, you'll find the **Corozal Bay Inn** (tel. 501/422-2691, www.

corozalbayinn.com, from US$100), a couples-oriented cluster of 10 cute thatch-roof cabanas set around 396 truckloads of sand imported from Belize's Pine Mountain Ridge; the inn offers a swimming pool, a lively bar, and rooms with air-conditioning, big-screen TV, private baths, and fridges. A bit more to the south, in a very quiet, out-of-the-way spot, the **Copa Banana** (tel. 501/422-0284, www.copabanana.bz, US$55) has lovely, tropical-decor rooms and suites open to the sea breeze (but also air-conditioned), with a shared living room and kitchen area and lots of space, plus free bikes, coffee, tea, and juices.

Corozal's newest offering is **[Almond Tree Hotel Resort** (425 Bayshore Dr., tel. 501/628-9224, www.almondtreeresort.com), in a quiet location down the road from Tony's Inn. Each of the six rooms has its own elegant decor and comfortable beds; larger units are equipped with a kitchenette and living room. Downstairs is a bar and restaurant where breakfast is available upon request and cold Belikin is on tap. Outside, you can relax at poolside, walled by a tropical garden, or talk to the owner, Lynn, about arranging an activity that suits your interests: fishing by dory, a trip to the cayes, or inland tours.

Serenity Sands Bed and Breakfast (three miles north of Corozal and one mile off of Consejo Rd., www.serenitysands.com, tel. 501/669-2394, Canada tel. 250/992-6583, US$90) has four tastefully decorated upper-level rooms with queen or twin beds, air-conditioning, and private balconies over Corozal Bay. The two-bedroom guest house can accommodate a family of six for US$125. The hotel is off the grid and uses organic products as often as possible. There's complimentary Internet access and a well-stocked library.

FOOD AND NIGHTLIFE

The town market has a selection of cheap eats and is your best bet early in the morning if you have to eat and run to catch a bus just up the street.

For solid, super-cheap Mexican snacks and meals, **Cactus Plaza** has a very popular streetside café; drinks, beers, and juices are served all night (till the club inside closes, anyway). This is also the center of the nightlife on weekends. The club is open Friday–Sunday from 6 P.M. There are plenty of Chinese options, but **Chon King,** near the park, is said to be the best. The Japanese seaweed salad and homemade dim sum make this a stand-out option. A close runner-up is the **Romantic Bar and Restaurant,** on the ground floor of the Mirador Hotel. Their diverse menu features daily specials such as curry masala gibnut, cowfoot soup, and lasagna. The restaurant has second sign that reads RD's, not to be confused with **RD's Diner** (tel. 501/422-3796) on 4th Avenue by the sports ground, which serves Belizean and American food, including seafood and pasta. On 5th Avenue across from the immigration office is **Venky's** (tel. 501/402-0536), a takeout place for curries and other East Indian foods.

Ⓒ Patty's Bistro (tel. 510/402-0174, 10 A.M.–10 P.M., dine in or take out) is a nice little option for authentic Belizean lunches and dinners, where the conch soup has a unique hint of coconut, as does the curry shrimp entrée (US$7.50). Fajitas and chicken dishes cost less.

Try the home-cooked daily specials in **June's Kitchen** (tel. 510/422-2559), where rice 'n' beans with stew chicken will set you back only US$4; breakfasts are huge and famous. You're basically eating in Miss June's living room or on her porch; breakfast and lunch daily, dinner by reservation only. The **Purple Toucan Restaurant Bar and Grill,** beside Atlantic Bank on 4th Avenue, features *cochinita pibil, poc chuc,* and other Yucatecan specialties. Also on 4th Avenue is Marcello's Pizza (tel. 501/422-3275).

If hamburgers are your fancy, head to **Ⓒ Butchies Bar and Grill** (Mark Anthony Hotel, 2nd Ave. N. at 4th St. N., tel. 501/422-3141 or 501/631-4803, 10:30 A.M.–9 P.M.). The Belizean food is on par with Patty's and their ceviche is fantastic; the view is of the sea.

For bars, try **Machie's** (2nd St. N. near 4th Ave. N.) for billiards and dominoes tournaments. On the south end of town, at Miami Beach, are two popular open-air bars; swing at **Jam Rock** while the bartender mixes a michelada, or have a cold drink and botanas at **Primo's Casita Bar** across the street.

INFORMATION AND SERVICES

Nearly all of the businesses mentioned in this chapter have websites found on Corozal's main portals: www.corozal.bz is more tourist- and business-related; www.corozal.com offers many local resources.

For other needs, Corozal has several ATMs and branches of **Belize Bank, Nova Scotia Bank,** and **Atlantic Bank** (all 8 A.M.–2 P.M. Mon.–Thurs., 8:30 A.M.–4:30 P.M. Fri.).

Emergency numbers are **fire** (tel. 501/422-2105); **police** (tel. 501/422-2022); and **hospital** (tel. 501/422-2076).

The main places to get online are the Hotel Mirador and **M.E. Computer Systems** (3rd St. S., 9 A.M.–9 P.M. Mon–Sat.). There are a few other Internet places around the central plaza.

GETTING THERE
By Air

There are five inexpensive daily flights on each airline between Corozal and San Pedro only. Call **Tropic Air** (tel. 501/226-2012, U.S. tel. 800/422-3435, www.tropicair.com) or **Maya Island Air** (tel. 501/223-1140, U.S. tel. 800/225-6732, mayair@btl.net, www.mayaislandair.com) for schedules.

By Bus

Buses are in disarray, so check the schedule at Corozal's **Northern Transport Bus Station** before departure. Northbound buses from Belize City alternate final destinations between Corozal and Chetumal, taking three hours to Corozal and leaving Belize City frequently 5:30 A.M.–7:30 P.M. (US$6). Southbound buses from Corozal leave regularly between 3:45 A.M. and 7 P.M., all of them originating 15 minutes or so earlier in Santa Elena. If you have connections to make in Chetumal, be aware that, unlike Belize, Mexico practices daylight saving time.

© JOSHUA BERMAN

The *Thunderbolt* boat has daily service between Corozal and Ambergris Caye.

NORTHERN BELIZE

By Boat

The *Thunderbolt* (tel. 501/422-0026 or 501/610-4475) departs daily for San Pedro at 7 A.M. for US$23 per person. Special promotions are often run during peak holiday times, so call ahead. The boat leaves San Pedro's Westside dock at 3 P.M. The trip takes about two hours, and stops in Sarteneja are possible on request.

GETTING AROUND

There are a few taxi stands in town: **Baldi Taxi Service** (tel. 501/604-7940) and **Los Toucanes Taxi Union** (tel. 501/402-2070) are by the market, a few steps away from the bus station; **Corozal Central Park Taxi Union** (tel. 501/422-2035) is by the plaza. You can get around town for US$2.50, to the border for US$10, or to Chetumal and Cerros for US$30, all convenient ways to go if you have a few people to split the costs. Or check with the tour companies.

CONSEJO VILLAGE

Nine miles north of Corozal, the tiny fishing village of Consejo is home to a beach hideaway,

an upscale hotel, a nine-hole golf course, and a retirement community of some 400 North Americans called **Consejo Shores** (www.consejoshores.com).

Rent one of three bayside units at **Smuggler's Den** (two miles northwest of Consejo, tel. 501/600-9723, http://smugglersdenbelize.tripod.com, US$40–65), nicely furnished and with hot and cold water—quite a bargain if you're looking for isolation. Two have private baths and kitchenettes; the unit without a kitchen is cheaper. Discounts can be had if requested. Smuggler's is locally famous for its Sunday afternoon roast beef dinners; reserve in advance.

Right in Consejo, **Casablanca by the Sea** (tel. 501/423-1018, U.S. tel. 781/235-1024, www.casablanca-bythesea.com, from US$65) is an intimate hotel with lovely grounds and views of the Bay of Consejo. Casablanca has eight stately rooms with queen-size beds, private bathrooms, air-conditioning, hot and cold water, and TV. The bar and dining room offer excellent seafood dishes and other meals, eaten while watching the lights of Chetumal, just across the bay. There's rooftop stargazing, volleyball, and top-notch conference/group facilities.

The **New Millennium Restaurant,** in the heart of Consejo village, is a friendly watering hole and eatery serving up daily specials at great prices (closed Tues.). **Derricks Cozy Bar** is a popular hangout in the afternoons, and you can meet other expats. Challenge Mr. Derrick to a game of dominoes, as he is a wily player.

SHIPSTERN NATURE RESERVE

In Corozal District, Shipstern is in the northeastern corner of the Belize coast. Thirty-two square miles of moist forest, savanna, and wetlands have been set aside to preserve as-yet-unspoiled habitats of well-known insect, bird, and mammal species associated with the tropics. The reserve encompasses the shallow **Shipstern Lagoon,** dotted with mangrove islands, which creates wonderful habitat for many wading birds. The reserve is home to about 300 species of birds, 70 species of reptiles and amphibians, and over 270 species of butterflies (they began the production of live butterfly pupae through intensive breeding).

The International Tropical Conservation Foundation has been extremely generous in supporting Shipstern. As at most reserves, the objective is to manage and protect habitats and wildlife, as well as to develop an education program that entails teaching the local community and introducing children to the concept of wildlife conservation in their area. Shipstern, however, goes a step further by conducting an investigation of how tropical countries such as Belize can develop self-supporting conservation areas through the controlled, intensive production of natural commodities found within such wildlife settlements. Developing facilities for the scientific study of the reserve area and its wildlife is part of this important program.

It's essential that visitors go first to the visitors center. The admission fee of US$5 includes a guided tour of the visitors center, butterfly garden, botanical trail, and observation tower.

The forest is alive with nature's critters and fascinating flora, and the guides' discerning eyes spot things that most city folk often miss, even though they are right in front of them. Hours for touring are 9 A.M.–noon and 1–3 P.M. daily except for Christmas, New Year's Day, and Easter. While accommodations are available by special request, visitors are encouraged to stay overnight in Sarteneja village. **Sarteneja Adventure Tours** (tel. 501/669-4911, www.sartenejatours.com) provides standard tours and overnight camping trips, with opportunities to explore Shipstern's trails by day or night and visit local caves, Maya ruins, and nesting bird colonies.

Botanical Trail

This lovely trail starts at the parking lot by the visitors center and meanders through the forest. You will have the opportunity to see three types of hardwood forests with 100 species of trees. Many of the trees are labeled with their Latin and Yucatec Maya names. Before starting your 20- to 30-minute walk, pick up a book with detailed descriptions of the trail and the trees at the park's visitors center, about three miles outside of Sarteneja.

Getting There

It is easiest to take a boat from Corozal or to hire a local tour guide to arrange travel. From Corozal and Orange Walk, figure a little more than an hour to drive there. The road takes you through **San Estevan** and then to **Progresso.** Turn right just before entering Progresso, to **Little Belize** (a Mennonite community). Continue on to **Chunox. Sarteneja** is three miles beyond Shipstern. Don't forget a long-sleeved shirt, pants, mosquito repellent, binoculars, and a camera for your exploration of the reserve.

(SARTENEJA

From the Maya "Tzaten-a-ha" or "give me the water," Sarteneja was named after the 13 Maya wells found in the area, carved into limestone bedrock and providing potable water. In addition to being a picturesque fishing village,

Sarteneja is the only place on mainland Belize where you can watch the sun set over the water.

The spot was first settled by the Maya as an important trading area. It is thought to have been occupied from 600 B.C. to A.D. 1200, and gold, copper, and shells continue to turn up in the area. Mexican refugees from the Yucatán Caste Wars settled here in the mid-19th century, again attracted by the availability of drinking water. The village took a pounding from Hurricane Janet in 1955 but rebounded and became known for its boat builders and free-diving lobster and conch fishers.

Today, 80 percent of Sarteneja's households remain reliant on the resources of the Belize Reef. Tourism is creeping in, and Sarteneja offers one of the more off-the-beaten-path experiences in the country. Located on Corozal Bay, it is a well-kept secret in Belize, and few tourists have heard about its breathtaking sunsets, sportfishing, and importance as a protected area for manatees and bird-nesting colonies in the **Corozal Bay Wildlife Sanctuary.** It is also known for the annual regatta that takes place each Easter, with newly painted sailboats of the artisan fishing fleet, crewed by local fishers, racing against each other in a tradition that has continued since 1950. Master boat builders Juan Guerrero and Jacobo Verde handcraft traditional wooden vessels at their workshops in Sarteneja. During fishing season, these boats dock in Belize City, by the Swing Bridge.

With access to nearby Maya sites and ties to the barrier reef at Bacalar Chico, Sarteneja has a lot to offer the adventurous tourist in search of the real Belize. The community is aware of its resources, and community groups have joined forces to form the **Sarteneja Alliance for Conservation and Development,** which co-manages Corozal Bay Wildlife Sanctuary. Local fishers, now trained as tour guides, offer a number of guided tours—both marine and inland. Sarteneja is also the location of the Manatee Rehabilitation Centre, run by **Wildtracks,** a local NGO, which takes in and rehabilitates orphan manatee calves as part of a national program to protect this threatened

species. The center isn't open to visitors unless by special arrangement—check with the **Sarteneja Tour Guide Association** (www. sartenejatours.com, tel. 501/669-4911) for details; their office is on the seafront. They can also help visitors find licensed local tour guides. The region can get pretty buggy, so take precautions.

Accommodations

There are 13 participating families in the **Sarteneja Homestay** program (tel. 501/669-3020 or 501/662-6860, sartenejahomestay@gmail.com, US$25 pp includes meals), a unique village opportunity. Stay for a night or a week in a safe, comfortable, private room with shared indoor toilet. Eat three home-cooked meals, learn how to make tortillas, and practice your Spanish.

Most accommodations, eateries, and bars can be found along Front Street, abutting the sea and dock. For US$25 per night (including meals and hotel tax), you can experience local culture through the **Sarteneja Homestay Program** (tel. 501/669-4911 or 501/423-2677).

Backpackers Paradise (http://bluegreenbelize.org) is right outside Sarteneja; it's a funky, laid-back, rustic, and friendly hangout where accommodations range from campgrounds (US$3.25 pp) to a few private cabanas (US$11–19). Also on-site, **Nathalie's Restaurant** serves up wonderful and cheap dishes, including crepes made by the Vietnamese/French proprietress. Free wireless Internet is available for customers; bicycles, horses, and guided day trips are available as well. You can use the communal kitchen to prepare your own meals; Sarteneja has a few grocery shops and *tortillerias.*

☾ Fernando's Seaside Guesthouse (tel. 501/423-2085, www.cybercayecaulker.com/sarteneja.html, US$30–40 plus tax) has rooms with private baths (and optional a/c); a larger cabana is also available. Like most folks in Sarteneja, the owner, Fernando Alamilla, was once a full-time fisherman who used to sail and fish for up to 10 days at a time. You can also stay at **Candelie's Sunset Cabanas** (tel. 501/423-2005 or 501/660-8795, candeliescabanas@yahoo.com, US$60–80), with three well-appointed cabins with air-conditioning, double beds, cots, and minifridges. The neighboring **Krisami's Bayview Lodge** (tel. 501/423-2283, US$60) is managed by the same family.

Food

Ritchie's Place (Front St., tel. 501/423-2031) has a good selection of fresh dishes, prepared by his wife, featuring fish empanadas. Owner Ritchie Cruz will also arrange fishing trips. **Liz's Fast Food,** two streets back from the seafront, serves tasty, traditional food in a friendly, snack-stall setting: tacos, empanadas, and *garnaches,* as well as rice and beans. The homemade *horchata* (rice-based drink) is well worth trying. Another local favorite, **Estrella del Mar Restaurant and Bar,** on Carlos Street, has burritos, tacos, and *salbutes; lobster* is available seasonally. **Chez Didi** offers French cuisine, freshly baked bread, and butter from a Mennonite dairy farm.

Getting There and Away

Sarteneja has been linked to the rest of Belize by land for less than 40 years—roads are rugged and dusty, and during rainy season often flooded and rutted. The road from Corozal to Sarteneja was recently upgraded through a European Union funded project. Although the road remains unpaved, it was a significant improvement; still, expect a few rough spots after a heavy rain.

BY BOAT

Most visitors get to Sarteneja by boat from Corozal or San Pedro. *Thunderbolt* water taxi (www.ambergriscaye.com/thunderbolt) will stop in Sarteneja on its once-daily Corozal–San Pedro run. They depart Corozal at 7 A.M., arriving in Sarteneja 40 minutes later before heading on to San Pedro. The San Pedro–Corozal boat (about 90 minutes) departs at 3 P.M. from San Pedro, stopping at Sarteneja at approximately 4:30 P.M. Sarteneja is a request stop only, so purchase a ticket from Tino at Tiny's Internet Café on Front Street in advance if you want to be sure of leaving Sarteneja by boat (US$12.50 to Corozal, US$22.50 to San Pedro).

BY AIR

Tropic Air has two flights a day that will stop at Sarteneja's tiny airstrip on request. Flights leave San Pedro at 7 A.M. and 4:45 P.M., arriving in Sarteneja 10 minutes later, as part of the San Pedro–Corozal schedule. Flights will stop later in the day if there is more than one passenger requesting to be dropped off or picked up in Sarteneja.

BY BUS

The bus from Belize City is often full of returning fishermen and is the most exciting way to get here. The distinctive light-blue Sarteneja buses leave Belize City daily except Sunday, from a riverside lot next to the Supreme Court Building. Four buses make the three-hour ride each day (US$5 one-way), the first at noon and the last at 5 P.M. All stop just before the bridge at the Zeta Ice Factory in Orange Walk to pick up more passengers. Buses depart Sarteneja for Belize City (via Orange Walk) between 4 and 6:30 A.M. There is a direct bus from Chetumal, via Corozal and Orange Walk, which runs every day (including Sundays), leaving Chetumal at midday or 1 P.M. (depending on whether or not Mexico is on daylight saving time). It departs for Corozal and Chetumal at 6 A.M. every morning. Buses from Corozal are intermittent, so it's best to check with the Corozal bus station first. There is also local traffic going to Sarteneja from Orange Walk via San Estevan.

BY CAR

From Corozal, head south and turn left at the sign for Tony's Inn. Follow this road, veering right until you come to a stone wall; then go left. Follow this road until you reach the first ferry across the New River, an experience in itself and free. Sometimes there are lineups on Fridays and Mondays, so anticipate a bit of a wait. After crossing, continue on the unsurfaced road until you reach a T junction. Turn left toward Copper Bank, Cerros, and the ferry to Chunox. Upon entering Copper Bank, keep driving until you see the signs for Donna's Place (an excellent eatery) and the Cerros ruins. If you're not stopping to eat or visit the ruins, turn left at the ruins sign and proceed until you see the sign for the ferry crossing. After crossing, continue until you reach another T junction. Turn left for Sarteneja, or right for Chunox and the grinding drive through Little Belize back to Orange Walk.

Chetumal, Mexico

An exciting dose of culture shock is an easy 15 miles from Corozal. Chetumal, capital of the Mexican state of Quintana Roo, is a relatively modern, midsize city of more than 200,000—nearly as many people as in the entire country of Belize! If you don't come for the culture (wonderful museums, a few parks, a zoo, and a delicious seafront), then you must be here to shop in the new American-style mall or see a first-run film in Chet's brand-new air-conditioned Cineplex, located in the **Plaza de las Americas** mall.

Chetumal can be seen as a day trip from Corozal or used as a base from which to visit the many Yucatecan archaeological sights, like Tulum, just up the coast. It's also a gateway to Mexico's well-known Caribbean resort areas: Cancún, Cozumel, Playa del Carmen, and Akumal. Chetumal presents the businesslike atmosphere of a growing metropolis, without the bikini-clad, touristy crowds of the north. A 10-minute walk takes you to the waterfront from the marketplace and most of the hotels. Modern, sculpted monuments stand along a breezy promenade that skirts the broad crescent of the bay. Also explore the back streets, where worn, wooden buildings still have a Central American/Caribbean look. The largest building in town—white, three stories, close to the waterfront—houses most of the government offices. Wide, tree-lined avenues and sidewalks front dozens of small variety shops.

SIGHTS

Do not miss the **Museo de la Cultura Maya** (9 A.M.–7 P.M. Sun. and Tues.–Thurs.,

9 A.M.–8 P.M. Fri. and Sat., US$5), located at the new market; it is an impressive and creative experience by any standards. The **Museo Municipal** is excellent as well, with a great deal of contemporary Mexican art.

On Avenida Heroes, five miles north of the city, is **Calderitas Bay,** a breezy area for picnicking, dining, camping, and RVing. Tiny **Isla Tamalcas,** 1.5 miles off the shore of Calderitas, is the home of the primitive capybara, the largest of all rodents.

Twenty-one miles north of Chetumal (on Highway 307) is **Cenote Azul,** a circular cenote over 200 feet deep and 600 feet across and filled with brilliant blue water. This is a spectacular place to stop for a swim, lunch at the outdoor restaurant, or just to have a cold drink.

ACCOMMODATIONS AND FOOD

Chetumal has quite a few hotels in all price categories (including a Holiday Inn near the new market), as well as many fine cafés specializing in fresh seafood. Check out *Moon Yucatán Peninsula* for details.

My favorite budget hotel in Chetumal is the vibrantly decorated **Hotel Ucum** (US$20; parking, pool, and hot showers included). **Hotel Brasilia** (US$18, limited on-street parking only) is another option. Both are visible from Avenida Heroes, the main street, which is home to most of the city's other hotels and the Museo Mundo Maya. If your bus from Cancún or Playa del Carmen arrives late at night, **Hotel Santa Teresa** (US$42) is conveniently located one block from the ADO bus terminal.

GETTING THERE

Buses between Belize City, Corozal, and Chetumal travel throughout the day, taking you all the way through the border (you'll need to get off twice to pass through Immigration and pay a US$19 exit fee) to the Nuevo Mercado Lazaro Cardenas in Chetumal. A local Chetumal bus from Corozal costs US$1.25, a taxi to the border US$10. If it is running, the express bus to Chetumal from Belize City takes about four hours and costs US$11. Also check with the various kiosks and travel agents in and near the Water Taxi Terminal by the Swing Bridge in Belize City for direct bus service to Chetumal.

Also, Corozal-based **Belize VIP Transfer Services** (tel. 501/422-2725, www.belizetransfers.com) or **George & Esther Moralez Travel Service** (tel. 501/422-2485, www.gettransfers.com) will arrange Chetumal transfers (and other Mexican attractions) and trips to local ruins. Also check other Corozal travel folks at the **Hok'ol K'in Guest House** (tel. 501/422-3329, maya@btl.net, www.corozal.net) or with **Herman Pollard** (tel. 501/422-3329). For travel agencies, stop by the **Hotel Maya** (tel. 501/422-2082 or 501/422-2874, www.hotelmaya.net) or **Jal's Travel Agency** (tel. 501/422-2163, ligializama@hotmail.com).

By Boat from San Pedro, Ambergris Caye, Belize

Chetumal can also be reached by water taxi on the **San Pedro Belize Express** (www.sanpedrobelizeexpress.com, US$30 one-way), which departs for Chetumal at 7:15 A.M. and returns

at 3 P.M. **San Pedro Water Jets Express** (www.sanpedrowatertaxi.com, US$35 one-way) leaves San Pedro at 8 A.M. and returns from Chetumal at 3:30 P.M.

Continuing North from Chetumal

A good paved road connects Chetumal with Mérida, Campeche, Villahermosa, and Francisco Escarcega; Highway 307 links all of the Quintana Roo coastal cities. Expect little traffic, and you'll find that gas stations are well spaced if you top off at each one. Car rentals are scarce in Chetumal; go to the Hotel Los Cocos for Avis. Chetumal is an economical place to rent your car (if one is available), since the tax is only 6 percent. If you're driving, watch out for No Left Turn signs in Chetumal. It's about a 22-hour bus ride to Mexico City.

GETTING AROUND

If traveling by bus from Belize, you will pass the main ADO bus terminal on Avenue Insurgentes; ask the driver to stop at the Pemex gas station on the corner of Insurgentes and Heroes Avenues. Bus travel is a versatile and inexpensive way to travel the Quintana Roo coast—there are frequent trips to Playa del Carmen and Cancún, and a new fleet of luxury express buses are a treat after Belize's school bus system. Chetumal is part of the loop between Campeche, Cancún, and Mérida. Fares and schedules change regularly; currently the fare to Cancún is about US$30. Taxis in Chetumal should not be more than a couple dollars if you're within the city limits.

BACKGROUND

The Land

GEOGRAPHY

Belize lies on the northeast coast of Central America, above the corner where the Honduran coast takes off to the east. Belize's 8,866 square miles of territory are bordered on the north by Mexico, on the west and south by Guatemala, and on the east by the Caribbean Sea and the Belize Barrier Reef. From the northern Río Hondo border with Mexico to the southern border with Guatemala, Belize's mainland measures 180 miles long, and it is 68 miles across at its widest point. Offshore, Belize has more than 200 cayes, or islands. Both the coastal region and the northern half of the mainland are flat, but the land rises in the south and west to over 3,000 feet above sea level. The Maya Mountains and Cockscomb range form the country's backbone and include Belize's highest point, **Doyle's Delight** (3,688 feet). Mangrove swamps cover much of the humid coastal plain.

In the west, the Cayo District contains the **Mountain Pine Ridge Reserve.** At one time a magnificent Caribbean pine forest, it has, over the decades, been reduced by lumber removal, fires, and the pine bark beetle. Despite vast beetle damage, the upper regions of Mountain Pine Ridge still provide spectacular scenery, with sections of thick forest surrounding the **Macal River** as it tumbles over huge granite

CAVES AND THE MAYA

MYTHOLOGY

Large populations of Maya were concentrated in the limestone foothills, where water supplies and clay deposits were plentiful. Caves were a source of fresh water, especially during dry periods. Clay pots of grain were safely stored for long periods of time in the cool air and, thousands of years later, can be seen today. Looting of caves has been a problem for decades, and as a result, all caves in Belize are considered archaeological sites.

The Maya used caves for utilitarian as well as religious and ceremonial purposes. The ancient Maya believed that upon entering a cave, one entered the underworld, or Xibalba, the place of beginnings and of fright. The Maya believed there were nine layers of the underworld, and as much as death and disease and rot were represented by the underworld, so was the beginning of life. Caves were a source of water – a source of life – for the Maya. Water that dripped from stalactites was used as holy water for ceremonial purposes. The underworld was also an area where souls had hopes of defeating death and becoming ancestors. As a result, rituals, ceremonies, and even sacrifices were performed in caves, evidenced today by many pots, shards, implements, and burial sites.

Caves were important burial chambers for the ancient Maya, and more than 200 skeletons have been found in more than 20 caves. One chamber in Caves Branch was the final earthly resting spot for 25 individuals. Many of these burial chambers are found deep in the caves, leading to speculation that death came by sacrificing the living, as opposed to carrying in the dead. Some burial sites show possible evidence of commoners being sacrificed to accompany the journey of an elite who had died – but who really knows?

SPELIO-ARCHAEOLOGY

The first written accounts related to cave archaeology began in the late 1800s. A British medical officer by the name of Thomas Gann wrote of his extensive exploration of caves throughout the country. In the late 1920s, he was also part of the first formal study of some ruins and caves in the Toledo District, and his papers provide insight no one else can give to modern-day archaeologists.

Little else was done until 1955, when the Institute of Archaeology was created by the government of Belize. Starting in 1957, excavations were organized throughout the years under various archaeologists. Excavations in the 1970s led to many important archaeological discoveries, including pots, vessels, and altars. In the 1980s, a series of expeditions was undertaken to survey the Chiquibul cave system. Other finds during this time period include a burial chamber and one cave with over 60 complete vessels and other ceremonial implements.

Today, projects are underway in many caves around the country. The Institute of Archaeology does not have a museum – yet. They've been talking about one for years. In the meantime, you may have to get a little wet and dirty to go visit some of these artifacts yourself. Start by calling up a cave specialist tour guide in Cayo, like River Rat or Belizean Sun Tours.

The Maya used caves for utilitarian, religious, and ceremonial purposes.

© JOSHUA BERMAN

boulders (except where the river was dammed at Chalillo). **Thousand Foot Falls** plunges 1,600 feet to the valley below and is the highest waterfall in all of Central America. The **Río Frio** cave system offers massive stalactites and stalagmites to the avid spelunker. The diverse landscape includes limestone-fringed granite boulders.

Over thousands of years, what was once a sea in the northern half of Belize has become a combination of scrub vegetation and rich tropical hardwood forest. Near the Mexican border, much of the land has been cleared, and it's here that the majority of sugar crops are raised, along with family plots of corn and beans. Most of the northern coast is swampy, with a variety of grasses and mangroves that attract waterfowl and wading birds. Rainfall in the north averages 60 inches annually, though it's generally dry November–May.

CLIMATE

The climate in Belize is subtropical, with a mean annual temperature of 79°F, so you can expect a variance between 50 and 95°F. The dry season generally lasts from Decemberish through May and the wet season June through November, although it has been known to rain sporadically all the way into February.

Rainfall varies widely between the north and south of Belize. Corozal in the north receives 40–60 inches a year, while Punta Gorda averages 160–190 inches, with an average humidity of 85 percent. Occasionally during the winter, "Joe North" (a.k.a. cold fronts) sweeps down from North America across the Gulf of Mexico, bringing rainfall, strong winds, and cooling temperatures. Usually lasting only a couple of days, they often interrupt fishing and influence the activity of lobster and other fish. Fishers invariably report increases in their catches several days before a norther.

The "mauger" season, when the air is still and the sea is calm, generally comes in August; it can last for a week or more. All activity halts while locals stay indoors as much as possible to avoid the onslaught of mosquitoes and other insects.

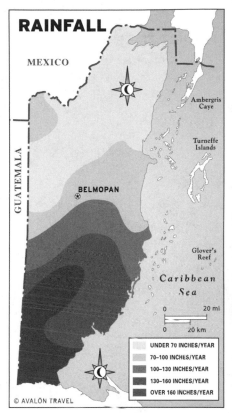

Hurricanes

Since record keeping began in 1787, scores of hurricanes have made landfall in Belize. In an unnamed storm in 1931, 2,000 people were killed and almost all of Belize City was destroyed. The water rose nine feet in some areas, even onto Belize City's Swing Bridge. Though forewarned by Pan American Airlines that the hurricane was heading their way, most of the townsfolk were unconcerned, believing that their protective reef would keep massive waves away from their shores. They were wrong.

The next devastation came with Hurricane Hattie in 1961. Winds reached a velocity of 150 mph, with gusts of 200 mph; 262 people drowned. It was after Hurricane Hattie that the capital of the country was moved from

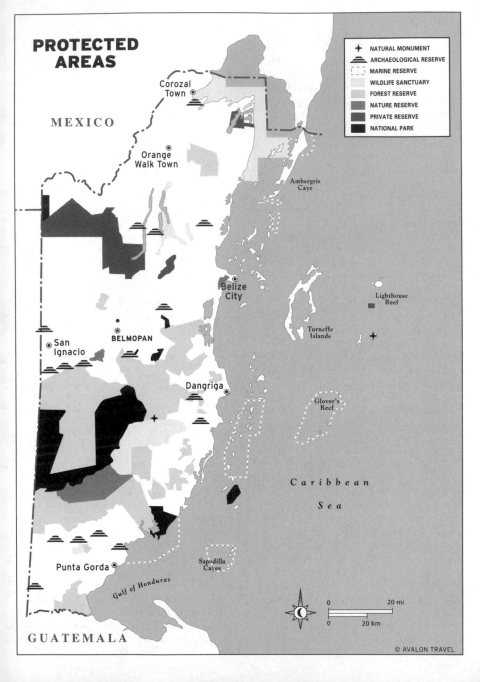

Belize City (just 18 inches above sea level) to Belmopan. Then, in 1978, Hurricane Greta took a heavy toll in dollar damage, though no lives were lost. More recent serious hurricanes affecting Belize include Mitch in 1998, Keith in 2000, Iris in 2001, and Dean in 2007. There have also been a number of less serious "northers." In the summer of 2008, Tropical Storm Arthur caused severe flooding throughout the country and major bridges were washed out. In 2010 Hurricane Richard did an unexpected two-step into the Cayo District, destroying the Belize Zoo and a swath of forest canopy in the center of the country.

ENVIRONMENTAL ISSUES

Because of the country's impressive network of protected areas and relatively low population density, the widespread deforestation that occurs in other parts of Central America is not nearly as big a problem in Belize. However, Belize faces its own set of challenges. Perhaps the biggest problem is improper disposal of solid and liquid wastes, both municipal and industrial, particularly agro-wastes from the shrimp and citrus industries.

Mining of aggregates from rivers and streams has negative impacts on local watersheds and the coastal zones into which they empty, where sedimentation can be destructive to reef and other marine systems. Unchecked, unplanned development, especially in sensitive areas like barrier beaches, mangroves, islands, and riverbanks, where changes to the landscape often have wide and unanticipated effects, is another problem.

Energy—or lack thereof—is a major issue for Belize, which has historically had to buy expensive power from neighboring Mexico. The controversial construction of the Chalillo Dam on the upper Macal River brought all of Belize's energy and environmental issues to the forefront (the saga of Chalillo is told in *The Last Flight of the Scarlet Macaw*, by Bruce Barcott).

The discovery of oil in 2005 near Spanish Lookout fueled a market of foreign prospectors hoping to tap into new petroleum resources. Oil exploration concessions have been granted for most of Belize's land and marine areas, which has caused much concern among environmental groups.

Meanwhile, the Belize Barrier Reef Reserve System was added to the "List of World Heritage Sites in Danger" in 2009 due to concerns over mangrove cutting and excessive development—and efforts to begin offshore oil drilling.

The Sea

CAYES AND ATOLLS

More than 200 cayes (pronounced "keys" and derived from the Spanish *cayo* for "key" or "islet") dot the blue waters off Belize's eastern coast. They range in size from barren patches that are submerged at high tide to the largest, Ambergris Caye—25 miles long and nearly 4.5 miles across at its widest point. Some cayes are inhabited by people, others only by wildlife. The majority are lush patches of mangrove that challenge the geographer's definition of what makes an island (that's why you'll never see a precise figure of how many there are).

Most of the cayes lie within the protection of the Belize Barrier Reef (almost 200 miles long), which parallels the mainland. Without the protection of the reef—in essence a breakwater— the islands would be washed away. Within the reef, the sea is relatively calm and shallow.

Beyond the reef lie three of the Caribbean's four atolls: **Glover's Reef, Turneffe Islands,** and **Lighthouse Reef.** An atoll is a ring-shaped coral island surrounding a lagoon, always beautiful, and almost exclusively found in the South Pacific. The three types of cayes are **wet cayes,** which are submerged part of the time and can support only mangrove swamps; **bare coral outcroppings** that are equally uninhabitable;

SWIM LIGHTLY: REEF ETIQUETTE

Belize's world-class reefs are being impacted by overfishing, coastal development, sewage and sedimentation, coral bleaching, and inappropriate and uninformed marine tourism practices. That's where you come in! Divers and snorkelers can be strong and effective advocates for coral reef conservation.

When I asked top Belizean naturalist Dave Vernon about the number one way people can be responsible tourists, his response was, "Leave the fins at home!" Beginning snorkelers, he explained, panic when they come up to clear their masks, automatically standing on the coral or kicking it with their fins. When boat propellers and careless snorkelers stir up bottom sediment, corals may become smothered and die. Linda Searle, Belize Coral Watch Program Coordinator and founder of ECO-MAR, says that when you touch coral, you are destroying the thin layer of living tissue that keeps the coral healthy. It is like when people get a cut on their skin, she explains; the area becomes more susceptible to invasion by bacteria and disease. When a "cut" on a coral does not heal, this space can become invaded by a disease that can spread to the rest of the coral head, killing the entire colony.

Your guide is not exempt from these rules! Some guides (mostly hot-shot younger guys bucking for a tip) snorkel like they're in a race and stir up plenty of sediment with their fins, especially when they lift their heads out of the water to talk. Such guides end up doing more damage to the coral than the tourists themselves, both by their actions and example. Experienced divers know the best way to enjoy a reef is to slow down, relax, and watch as the creatures go about their daily lives undisturbed. Learn all you can about coral reefs and follow these simple guidelines to be a "coral-friendly" diver.

PREPARING FOR YOUR DIVE TRIP

Support coral reef conservation by choosing your resort with care and being a "green consumer" with your vacation dollars. Look for coral parks and other marine reserves, and pay user fees that support marine conservation. Keep your diving skills finely tuned, and be sure to practice them away from the reef. When it's time to get in the water, choose coral-friendly dive operations that practice reef conservation by:

- Giving diver orientations and briefings.

- Holding buoyancy control workshops.

- Actively supporting local marine protected areas.

- Using available moorings − anchors and chains destroy fragile corals and seagrass beds.

- Using available wastewater pump-out facilities.

- Making sure garbage is well stowed, especially light plastic items.

- Taking away everything brought on board, such as packaging and used batteries.

and **sandy islands** with littoral forest, which is the most endangered habitat in Belize due to development pressure. The more inhabited cayes lie in the northern part of the reef and include Caye Caulker, Ambergris Caye, St. George's Caye, and Caye Chapel.

REEFS

Reefs are divided into three types: atoll, fringing, and barrier. An **atoll** can be formed around the crater of a submerged volcano. The polyps begin building their colonies on the round edge of the crater, forming a circular coral island with a lagoon in the center. Thousands of atolls occupy the world's tropical waters. Only four are in the Caribbean Sea; three of those are in Belize's waters.

A **fringing reef** is coral living on a shallow shelf that extends outward from shore into the sea. A **barrier reef** runs parallel to

IN THE WATER

- Never touch corals; even a slight contact can harm them, and some corals can sting or cut you (coral cuts take a long time to heal and become infected easily).

- Carefully select points of entry and exit to avoid walking on corals (remember, corals also live within seagrass beds).

- Make sure all of your equipment is well secured.

- Make sure you are neutrally buoyant at all times.

- Maintain a comfortable distance from the reef, so that you're certain you can avoid contact.

- Learn to swim without using your arms.

- Move slowly and deliberately in the water – relax and take your time.

- Practice good finning and body control to avoid accidental contact with the reef or stirring up the sediment.

- Know where your fins are at all times and don't kick up sand.

- Stay off the bottom and never stand or rest on corals.

- Avoid using gloves and kneepads in coral environments.

- Take nothing living or dead out of the water, except recent garbage.

- Do not chase, harass, or try to ride marine life.

- Do not touch or handle marine life except under expert guidance and following established guidelines. Never feed marine life.

- Use photographic and video equipment only if you are an advanced diver or snorkeler; cameras are cumbersome and affect a diver's buoyancy and mobility; it is all too easy to touch and damage marine life when concentrating on "the shot."

- Remember, look but don't touch.

These guidelines were developed by the Coral Reef Alliance (CORAL, www.coral.org), © CORAL.

BECOME A BELIZE CORAL WATCH VOLUNTEER

As a Belize Coral Watch Volunteer, you'll learn how to identify coral species, coral reef ecology, coral disease, and coral bleaching. After attending a training session you will be equipped with the knowledge needed to help identify resilient reefs in Belize. Divers and snorkelers are asked to monitor sites and submit reports on line. Look for a dive or snorkel center or resort that participates in "Adopt a Reef" with ECOMAR and help them complete surveys! For more information on becoming a Coral Watch Volunteer contact ECOMAR (www.ecomarbelize.org).

the coast, with water separating it from the land. Sometimes it's actually a series of reefs with channels of water in between. This is the case with some of the larger barrier reefs in the Pacific and Indian Oceans.

The Belize Barrier Reef is part of the greater Mesoamerican Barrier Reef, which extends from Mexico's Isla Mujeres to the Bay Islands of Honduras. The Belizean portion of the reef begins at Bacalar Chico in the north and ends with the Sapodilla Cayes in the south. This 180-mile-long reef is the longest reef in the Western and Northern Hemispheres.

Coral

Coral is a unique limestone formation that grows in innumerable shapes, such as delicate lace, trees with reaching branches, pleated mushrooms, stovepipes, petaled flowers, fans, domes, heads of cabbage, and stalks of broccoli. Corals are formed by millions of tiny carnivorous polyps that feed on minute organisms and live in large colonies of individual species. Coral polyps have cylinder-shaped bodies, generally less than half an inch long. One end is attached to a hard surface (the bottom of the sea, the rim of a submerged volcano, or the reef itself). The mouth at the other end is encircled with tiny tentacles that capture the polyp's minute prey with a deadly sting. At night, coral reefs really come to life as polyps emerge to feed. Related to the jellyfish and sea anemone, polyps need sunlight and clear saltwater not colder than 70°F to survive. Symbiotic algal cells, called zooxanthellae, live within coral tissues and provide the polyps with much of their energy requirements and coloration.

How a Reef Grows

The polyps of reef building corals deposit calcium carbonate around themselves to form a cup-like skeleton or corallite. As these small creatures continue to reproduce and die, their sturdy skeletons accumulate. Over eons, broken bits of coral, animal waste, and granules of soil contribute to the strong foundation for a reef that will slowly rise toward the surface. In a healthy environment, it can grow 1–2 inches a year.

ESTUARIES

The marshy areas and bays at the mouths of rivers where saltwater and fresh water mix are called estuaries. Here, nutrients from inland

---

FISHING REGULATIONS

BONEFISH *(ALBULBA VULPES)*
Also known locally as *macabi*. No person shall buy or sell any bonefish.

CONCH *(STROMBUS GIGAS)*
Shell length should exceed seven inches, and market clean weight should exceed three ounces, no diced or fillet. The season is closed July 1–September 30.

CORAL
It is illegal for any person to take, buy, sell, or have in his or her possession any type of coral. An exception is made in the case of black coral (order *Antipatharia*), which may only be bought, sold, or exported with a license from the Fisheries Administrator.

HICKATEE *(DERMATEMY MAWII)*
No person shall have in his or her possession more than three, or transport on any vehicle more than five such turtles, or fish for female hickatee that are greater than 43 centimeters (17.2 inches) or smaller than 38 centimeters (15.2 inches). The season is closed May 1–31.

LOBSTER *(PANULIRUS ARGUS)*
Minimum cape length is three inches, minimum tail weight is four ounces; no diced or fillet. The season is closed February 15–June 14.

MARINE TURTLES
No person should interfere with any turtle nest. No person may take any turtle unless with a license from the Fisheries Administrator (traditional use only). No person shall buy, sell, or have in his or her possession any articles made of turtle shell.

NASSAU GROUPER *(EPINEPHELUS STRIATUS)*
No person shall take in the waters of Belize, or buy, sell, or have in his or possession, any Nassau grouper between December 1 and March 31, except from Maugre Caye at Turneffe Islands and Northern Two Caye at Lighthouse Reef. At these two places a special license is granted to traditional fishers.

SHRIMP
Trawling: The season is closed April 15–August 14. No one should fish using scuba gear except under license from the Fisheries Administrator. Contact the Fisheries Department for further information: P.O. Box 148, Belize City, tel. 501/223-2623, 501/224-4552, or 501/223-2187, species@btl.net.

are carried out to sea by currents and tides to nourish reefs, sea grass beds, and the open ocean. Many plants and animals feed, live, or mate in these waters. Conch, crabs, shrimp, and other shellfish thrive here, and several types of jellyfish and other invertebrates call this home. Seabirds, shorebirds, and waterfowl of all types frequent estuaries to feed, nest, and mate. Crocodiles, dolphins, and manatees are regular visitors. Rays, sharks, and tarpon hunt and mate here. During the wet season, the estuaries of Belize pump a tremendous amount of nutrients into the sea.

MANGROVES

The doctor on Christopher Columbus's ship reported in 1494 that mangroves in the Caribbean were "so thick that a rabbit could scarcely walk through." Mangroves live on the edge between land and sea, forming dense thickets that act as a protective border against the forces of wind and waves. Four species grow along many low-lying coastal areas on the mainland and along island lagoons and fringes. Of these, the red mangrove and the black mangrove are most prolific. Red mangrove in excess of 30 feet high is found in tidal areas, inland lagoons, and river mouths, but always close to the sea. Its signature is its arching prop roots, which provide critical habitat and nursery grounds for many reef fish. Black mangrove grows to almost double that height. Its roots are slender, upright projectiles that grow to about 12 inches, protruding all around the mother tree. Both types of roots provide air to the tree.

Mangrove Succession

Red mangroves *(Rhizophora mangle)* specialize in creating land—the seedpods fall into the water and take root on the sandy bottom of a shallow shoal. The roots, which can survive in seawater, then collect sediments from the water and the tree's own dropping leaves to create soil. Once the red mangrove forest has created land, it makes way for the next mangrove in the succession process. The black mangrove *(Avicennia germinans)* can actually out-compete the red mangrove at this stage, because of its ability

© JOSHUA BERMAN

Mangroves are essential to marine ecology.

to live in anoxic soil (without oxygen). In this way, the red mangrove appears to do itself in by creating an anoxic environment. But while the black mangrove is taking over the upland of the community, the red mangrove continues to dominate the perimeter, as it continuously creates more land from the sea. One way to identify a black mangrove forest is by the thousands of dense pneumataphores (tiny air roots) covering the ground under the trees.

Soon, burrowing organisms such as insects and crabs begin to inhabit the floor of the black mangrove forest, and the first ground covers, *Salicornia* and salt wart *(Batis maritima)* take hold—thereby aerating the soil and enabling the third and fourth mangrove species in succession to move in: the white mangrove *(Laguncularia racemosa)* and the gray mangrove *(Conocarpus erectus),* also known locally as buttonwood.

Desalinizers

Each of the three primary mangrove species lives in a very salty environment, and each has its own special way of eliminating salt. The red mangrove concentrates the salt taken up with seawater into individual leaves, which turn bright yellow and fall into the prop roots, thereby adding organic matter to the system. The black mangrove eliminates salt from the underside of each leaf. If you pick a black mangrove leaf and lick the back, it will taste very salty. The white mangrove eliminates salt through two tiny salt pores located on the petiole (the stem that connects the leaf to the branch). If you sleep in a hammock under a white mangrove tree, you will feel drops of salty water as the tree "cries" upon you! The buttonwood also has tiny salt pores on each petiole.

Importance of Mangroves

Mangrove islands and coastal forests play an essential role in protecting Belize's coastline from destruction during natural events such as hurricanes and tropical storms. Along with the sea grass beds, they also protect the Belize Barrier Reef by filtering sediment from river runoff before it reaches and smothers the delicate coral polyps. However, dense mangrove forests are also home to mosquitoes and biting flies. The mud and peat beneath mangrove thickets is often malodorous with decaying plant matter and hydrogen sulfide–producing bacteria. Many developers would like nothing better than to eliminate mangroves and replace them with sandy beaches surrounded by seawalls. But such modification to the coastline causes accelerated erosion and destruction of seaside properties, especially during severe storms.

Birds of many species use the mangrove branches for roosting and nesting sites, including swallows, redstarts, warblers, grackles, herons, egrets, osprey, kingfishers, pelicans, and roseate spoonbills. Along the seaside edge of red mangrove forests, prop roots extend into the water, creating tangled thickets unparalleled as nurseries of the sea. Juveniles of commercial fisheries, such as snapper, hogfish, and lobster, find a safe haven here. The flats around mangrove islands are famous for recreational fisheries such as bonefish and tarpon.

The three-dimensional labyrinth created by expanding red mangroves, sea grass beds, and bogues (channels of seawater flowing through the mangroves) provides the home and nursery habitat for nurse sharks, American crocodiles, dolphins, and manatees.

Snorkeling among the red mangrove prop roots is a unique experience where you can witness the abundant marine life that grow on prop roots and live between the roots. It is within the algae, plants, corals and sponges that grow on the roots that juvenile spiny lobsters and sea horses can be found.

Destruction of mangroves is illegal in most of Belize; cutting and removal of mangroves requires a special permit and mitigation.

SEA GRASS BEDS

Standing along the coast of Belize and looking seaward, many tourists are surprised to see something dark in the shallow water just offshore. They expect the sandy bottom typical of many Caribbean islands. However, it is this "dark stuff" that eventually will make their day's snorkeling, fishing, or dining experience more enjoyable. What they are noticing is sea grass, another of the ocean's great nurseries.

Sea grasses are plants with elongated, ribbon-like leaves. Just like the land plants they evolved from, sea grasses flower and have extensive root systems. They live in sandy areas around estuaries, mangroves, reefs, and open coastal waters. Turtle grass has broader, tapelike leaves and is common down to about 60 feet. Manatee grass, found to depths of around 40 feet, has thinner, more cylindrical leaves. Both cover large areas

of seafloor and intermix in some areas, harboring an amazing variety of marine plants and animals. Barnacles, conch, crabs, and many other shellfish proliferate in the fields of sea grass. Anemones, seahorses, sponges, and starfish live here. Grunts, filefish, flounder, jacks, rays, and wrasses feed here. Sea turtles and manatees often graze in these lush marine pastures.

These beds and flats are being threatened in some areas by unscrupulous developers who are dredging sand for cement and landfill material (especially on Ambergris Caye).

Flora and Fauna

Belize's position at the biological crossroads between North and South America has blessed it with an astonishingly broad assortment of wildlife. Belize's wide-ranging geography and habitat have also been a primary factor in the diversity and complexity of its ecosystems and their denizens.

FLORA

Belize is a Garden of Eden. Four thousand species of native flowering plants include 250 species of orchids and approximately 700 species of trees. Most of the country's forests have been logged off and on for more than 300 years (2,000 years, if you count the widespread deforestation during the time of the ancient Maya). The areas closest to the rivers and coast were the hardest hit, because boats could be docked and logs easily loaded to be taken farther out to sea to the large ships used to haul the precious timber.

Forests

Flying over the countryside gives you a view of the patchwork landscape of cleared areas and secondary growth. Belize consists of four distinct forest communities: pine-oak, mixed broadleaf, cohune palm, and riverine forests. Pine-oak forests are found in sandy, dry soils. In the same areas, large numbers of mango, cashew, and coconut palm are grown near

homes and villages. The mixed broadleaf forest is a transition area between the sandy pine soils and the clay soils found along the river. Often the mixed broadleaf forest is broken up here and there and doesn't reach great height; it's species-rich but not as diverse as the cohune forest. The cohune forest area is characterized by the cohune palm, which is found in fertile clay soil where a moderate amount of rain falls throughout the year. The cohune nut was an important part of the Maya diet. Archaeologists say that where they see a cohune forest, they know they'll find evidence of the Maya.

The cohune forest gives way to the riverine forest along river shorelines, where vast amounts of water are found year-round from excessive rain and from the flooding rivers. About 50–60 tree varieties and hundreds of species of vines, epiphytes, and shrubs grow here. Logwood, mahogany, cedar, and pine are difficult to find along the easily accessible rivers because of extensive logging. The forest is in different stages of growth and age. To find virgin forest, it's necessary to go high into the mountains that divide Belize. Because of the rugged terrain and distance from the rivers, these areas were left almost untouched. Even today, few roads exist. If left undisturbed for many, many years, the forest will eventually regenerate itself.

Among the plant life of Belize, look for mangroves, bamboo, and swamp cypresses, as well as ferns, bromeliads, vines, and flowers creeping from tree to tree, creating a dense growth. On topmost limbs, orchids and air ferns reach for the sun. As you go farther south, you'll find the classic tropical rainforest, including tall mahoganies, *campeche, sapote,* and ceiba, thick with vines.

Orchids

In remote areas of Belize, one of the more exotic blooms, the orchid, is often found on the highest limbs of tall trees. Of all the orchid species reported in Belize, 20 percent are terrestrial (growing in the ground) and 80 percent are epiphytic (attached to a host plant—in this case trees—and deriving moisture and nutrients from the air and rain). Both types grow in many sizes and shapes: tiny buttons, spanning the length of a long branch; large-petaled blossoms with ruffled edges; or intense, tiger-striped miniatures. The lovely flowers come in a wide variety of colors, some subtle, some brilliant. The black orchid is Belize's national flower. All orchids are protected by strict laws, so look but don't pick.

FAUNA

A walk through the jungle brings you close to myriad animal and bird species, many of which are critically endangered in other Central American countries—and the world. Bring your binoculars and a camera, and be vewy, vewy quiet.

Following is a short introduction to a few of the creatures you are likely to see in the wild if you spend any amount of time outside your hotel room. This is an incomplete, random selection; for more detailed information, pick up one of the many field guides to the flora and fauna of Belize.

Birds

If you're a serious birder, you know all about Belize. Scores of species can be seen while sitting on the deck of your jungle lodge: big and small, rare and common, resident and

© JOSHUA BERMAN

The black orchid is the national flower of Belize.

migratory—and with local guides aplenty to help find them in all the vegetation. The **keel-billed toucan** is the national bird of Belize and is often seen perched on a bare limb in the early morning.

Cats

Seven species of felines are found in North America, five of them in Belize. For years, rich adventurers came to Belize on safari to hunt the jaguar for its beautiful skin. Likewise, hunting margay, puma, ocelots, and jaguarundis was a popular sport in the rainforest. Today, hunting endangered cats (and other species) in Belize is illegal, and there are many protected areas to help protect their wide-ranging habitats.

The **jaguar** is heavy-chested with sturdy, muscled forelegs; a relatively short tail; and small, rounded ears. Its tawny coat is uniformly spotted and the spots form rosettes: large circles with smaller spots in the center. The jaguar's belly is white with black spots. The male can weigh 145–255 pounds, females 125–165 pounds. Largest of the cats in Central America and third-largest cat in the world, the jaguar is about the same size as a leopard. It is nocturnal, spending most daylight hours snoozing in the sun. The male marks an area of about 65 square miles and spends its nights stalking deer, peccaries, agoutis, tapirs, monkeys, and birds. If hunting is poor and times are tough, the jaguar will go into rivers and scoop fish with its large paws. The river is also a favorite spot for the jaguar to hunt the large tapir when it comes to drink. Females begin breeding at about three years old and generally produce twin cubs.

The smallest of the Belizean cats is the **margay,** weighing in at about 11 pounds and marked by a velvety coat with exotic designs in yellow and black and a tail that's half the length of its body. The bright eye shine indicates it has exceptional night vision. A shy animal, it is seldom seen in open country, preferring the protection of the dense forest. The "tiger cat," as it is called by locals, hunts mainly in the trees, satisfied with birds, monkeys, and insects as well as lizards and figs.

Larger and not nearly as catlike as the margay, the black or brown **jaguarundi** has a small flattened head, rounded ears, short legs, and a long tail. It hunts by day for birds and small mammals in the rainforests of Central America. The **ocelot** has a striped and spotted coat and an average weight of about 35 pounds. A good climber, the cat hunts in trees as well as on the ground. Its prey include birds, monkeys, snakes, rabbits, young deer, and fish. Ocelots usually have litters of two kittens but can have as many as four. The **puma** is also known as the cougar or mountain lion. The adult male measures about six feet in length and weighs up to 198 pounds. It thrives in any environment that supports deer, porcupines, or rabbits. The puma hunts day or night.

Primates

In Creole, the **black howler monkey** (*Alouatta caraya*) is referred to as a "baboon" (in Spanish, *saraguate*), though it is not closely related to the African species with that name. Because the howler prefers low-lying tropical rainforests (under 1,000 feet of elevation), Belize is a perfect habitat. The monkeys are commonly found near the riverine forests, especially on the Belize River and its major branches. The adult howler monkey is entirely black and weighs 15–25 pounds. Its most distinctive trait is a roar that can be heard up to a mile away. A bone in the throat acts as an amplifier; the cry sounds much like that of a jaguar. The howler's unforgettable bark is said by some to be used to warn other monkey troops away from its territory. Locals, on the other hand, say the howlers roar when it's about to rain, to greet the sun, to say good night, or when they're feeding. The **Community Baboon Sanctuary** is the best place to see howler monkeys in the wild in Belize, though they are very common in the forests around many jungle lodges throughout the country.

Spider monkeys (*Ateles geoffroyi*) are smaller than black howlers and live in troops of a dozen or more, feeding on leaves, fruits, and flowers high in the jungle canopy. Slender limbs and elongated prehensile tails assist them as they

FOUR WAYS THAT TRAVELERS CAN HELP ENDANGERED WILDLIFE

You are guaranteed to see animals in Belize, whether in the wild or in captivity. When captive animals are held at a Belize Forestry Department-permitted research, rescue, or educational facility, it's okay to view them, to learn about them, and to take a photo or two. Often, however, these facilities are not licensed and should be avoided.

This is particularly a big a deal for the yellow-headed Amazon parrot (*Amazona oratrix*), a gorgeous species under serious threat of extinction in the world. Its numbers have plummeted from 70,000 to 7,000 in the last two decades. Human encroachment on their habitat fuels nest robbing for the illegal pet trade. **Belize Bird Rescue** (www.belizebirdrescue.com), a nonprofit organization operating on a private reserve in western Belize, reports that 65 percent of all wild-caught captive birds die before they reach sale. Of those that make it, most are sold to people who have no idea how to raise a baby parrot, so the majority die in their first year or grow up with leg, foot, or wing deformities due to malnutrition.

In Belize, some poached birds are sold on the international market, while others end up in Belizean homes or in businesses who want to add "color" to attract tourists. That's where you and I come in. The following guidelines were provided by Jerry Larder, Director of Belize Bird Rescue, on what travelers can do to discourage the illegal trade in parrots and other animals. Here are his recommendations.

DOS AND DON'TS WHILE TRAVELING

- Do not have your photograph taken with captive indigenous wildlife. By encouraging the keepers of the wildlife, more will be taken from the wild.

- Do not patronize establishments with captive wildlife on display unless they are government sanctioned as a breeding or educational facility such as a zoo. There is no educational value to a single monkey or bird in a restaurant.

- Do not believe anyone who tells you that he "rescued" an orphan animal or bird, unless they are licensed rescue facility. The vast majority of these animals were captured from the wild and/or bought from dealers. If people really want to rescue a bird or animal, they will turn them over to a proper rescue/rehab facility.

- Never buy goods made from animal hides, skins, teeth or claws, or exoskeletons such as bugs and corals. Some leather goods are okay but exotic ones (crocodile, snake, etc.) normally are not. Jewelry made from jaguar teeth has also appeared on the streets being offered to tourists. Buying them contributes to the decline of the remaining jaguar population. In Belize it is also prohibited to sell any products made out of sea turtle.

REPORTING VIOLATIONS

If you observe any conditions where endangered terrestrial animals are being held in captivity or offered for sale, contact the Belize Forest Department (tel. 501/822-2079). If you observe the sale of turtle meat or jewelry, report the location and date immediately to the Belize Fisheries Department (tel. 501/224-4552).

---

climb and swing from tree to tree. Though not as numerous in Belize as howler monkeys because of disease and habitat loss, they remain an important part of the country's natural legacy.

Rodents of Unusual Size

A relative of the rabbit, the **agouti** or "Indian rabbit" has coarse gray-brown fur and a hopping gait. It is most often encountered scampering along a forest trail or clearing. Not the brightest of creatures, it makes up for this lack of wit with typical rodent libido and fecundity. Though it inhabits the same areas as the paca, these two seldom meet, as the agouti minds its

WILDLIFE VIEWING GUIDELINES

It takes many years of practice to fine-tune your wildlife-viewing skills, hours upon hours of patient sitting and walking sessions to learn some of Mother Nature's more subtle communication skills. Growing up and living off the forest helps – that's why hiring a native guide will guarantee you more sightings than going it on your own. Spending years in the Belizean bush studying jaguars and other cats is a good method as well, the one employed by biologist Alan Rabinowitz in his landmark studies of the Cockscomb Basin. He shares some of his hard-won knowledge in the following passage from his book *Jaguar*:

The forest is teeming with wildlife, but you see and hear very little just by walking through it. It often seems simply a quiet, green darkness, but that appearance is deceiving. When you learn to read the signs of an animal's passing, it's like watching the wildlife. A nibbled twig tells you a red brocket deer has been feeding; a muddy wallow says a tapir has been by; chewed nuts from the cohune palm tree indicate that a paca has fed the night before; and a musky smell warns you that a group of peccaries may be closer than you'd like.

The following Wildlife Viewing Guidelines guidelines are derived from the International Ecotourism Society and are courtesy of the American Crocodile Education Sanctuary (ACES). They are intended to help you enjoy watching wildlife without causing them harm or placing one's personal safety at risk.

- **Keep your distance.** International policy is to remain at least 100 yards from all protected wildlife species, and time spent observing animals should be limited to avoid causing stress.

- **Never harass the wildlife.** If your presence disturbs an animal from its activity, then you are harassing that animal. No animal should ever be encircled or trapped; this includes between boats, or between a boat and shore. If you are approached by an animal, allow it to pass and do not obstruct its path of travel. Boaters are to put their engine in neutral. Causing an animal to move from an area, or flee, may result in an unsuccessful mating or aborted nesting. This can lead to a species' extinction.

- **Hands off.** Do not touch or interact with wild animals. Wildlife can behave unpredictably and may transmit disease. Handling any protected species without a scientific permit is illegal.

- **Do not feed wildlife.** Attempting to attract wildlife with food disrupts normal feeding cycles and may cause sickness or death from unnatural or contaminated food items. Offering wildlife any food products, including discarded waste, is prohibited.

- **Help keep wildlife habitats clean.** Please pick up all trash. Garbage, particularly plastic, is one of the greatest threats to wildlife, which may view the garbage item as food or become entangled.

business during the day and the paca prefers nighttime pursuits. The agouti is less delectable than the paca. Nonetheless, it is taken by animal and human hunters and is a staple food of jaguars.

The **paca**, or **gibnut**, is a quick, brownish rodent about the size of a small dog, with white spots along its back. Nocturnal by habit and highly prized as a food item by many Belizeans, the gibnut is more apt to be seen by the visitor on an occasional restaurant menu than in the wild.

A member of the raccoon family, the **coatimundi**—or "quash"—has a long, ringed tail, a masked face, and a lengthy snout. Sharp claws aid the coati in climbing trees and digging up insects and other small prey. Omnivorous, the quash also relishes jungle fruits. Usually seen in small troops of females and young, coatis have an amusing, jaunty appearance as they cross a jungle path, tails at attention.

Tapirs

The national animal of Belize, the **Baird's tapir** *(Tapirus bairdii)* is found from the southern part of Mexico through northern Colombia. It is stout-bodied (91–136 pounds), with short legs, a short tail, small eyes, and rounded ears. Its nose and upper lip extend into a short but very mobile proboscis. Totally herbivorous, tapirs usually live near streams or rivers in the forest. They bathe daily and also use the water as an escape when hunted either by humans or by their prime predator, the jaguar. Shy, nonaggressive animals, they are nocturnal with a definite home range, wearing a path between the jungle and their feeding area.

Reptiles
IGUANAS

Found all over Central America, lizards of the family *Iguanidae* include various large planteaters, in many sizes and typically dark in color with slight variations. The young iguana is bright emerald green. The common lizard grows to three feet long and has a blunt head and long flat tail. Bands of black and gray circle its body, and a serrated column reaches down the middle of its back, almost to its tail. During mating season, it's common to see brilliant orange males on sunny branches near the river. This reptile is not aggressive, but if cornered it will bite and use its tail in self-defense.

Though hawks prey on young iguanas and their eggs, the human still remains its most dangerous predator. It is not unusual to see locals along dirt paths carrying sturdy specimens by the tail to put in the cook pot. Iguana stew is believed to cure or relieve various human ailments, such as impotence. Another reason for their popularity at the market is their delicate white flesh, which tastes so much like chicken that locals refer to iguana meat as "bamboo chicken."

CROCODILES

Though they're often referred to as alligators,

© JOSHUA BERMAN

There are 59 species of snakes in Belize, but only nine of them are poisonous.

Belize has only crocodiles, the American (*Crocodylus acutus*, up to 20 feet) and the Morelet's (*Crocodylus moreletii*, up to 8 feet). Crocodiles have a well-earned bad reputation in Africa, Australia, and New Guinea as man-eaters, especially the larger saltwater varieties. Their American cousins are fussier about their cuisine, preferring fish, dogs, and other small mammals to people. But when humans feed crocs, either intentionally or by tossing food wastes into the waters, the animals can acquire a taste for pets, making them extremely dangerous. When apex predators become fearless of man, they are more prone to attack, especially small children. The territories of both croc species overlap in estuaries and brackish coastal waters. They are most abundant in the rivers, swamps, and lagoons of Belize City and Orange Walk Districts. Able to filter excess salt from its system, only the American crocodile ventures to the more distant cayes, including Turneffe Islands. Endangered throughout their ranges, both crocs are protected by international law and should not be disturbed. Often seen floating near the edges of lagoons or canals during midday, they are best observed at night with the help of a flashlight. When caught in the beam, their eyes glow red (LED flashlights make white eye-shine).

SNAKES

Of the 59 species of snakes that have been identified in Belize, at least nine are venomous, notably the infamous fer-de-lance (locally called a "Tommygoff") and the coral snake.

MARINE LIFE

Belize is world famous for the diversity of its rich underwater wildlife, primarily due to its unique geology, the barrier reef lagoon system, and a government that actively works to protect marine habitat. There is also a great deal of marine research in Belize, often with opportunities for tourists to get involved. While all the standard Caribbean species are found in Belizean waters, there are a few animals in particular worth noting.

Manatees

These "gentle giants of the sea" are large and bulky—weighing 600–1,200 pounds. Manatees belong to the taxonomic order Sirenia, a group of four species that represents the only herbivorous marine mammals living today. There are three species of manatees: the Amazonian manatee (*Trichechus inunguis*), the West African manatee (*Trichechus senegalensis*), and the West Indian manatee (*Trichechus manatus*). The two subspecies of the West Indian manatee are the Florida manatee (*T. m. latirostris*) and the Antillean manatee (*T. m. manatus*). Belize has long been considered the last stronghold for West Indian manatees in Central America and the Caribbean. West Indian manatees are also found year-round in Florida, and are sparsely distributed throughout Central America and the Caribbean, and occur as far south as Brazil. The Antillean subspecies (which excludes the Florida animals) is red-listed by the World Conservation Union (IUCN) as endangered, in continuing decline, with severely fragmented populations.

With a relatively short coastline extending from the Gulf of Honduras in the south to Chetumal Bay in the north, Belize reports the greatest density of Antillean manatees in the Caribbean region, perhaps because of the extensive sea grass, mangrove, coastal, and riverine habitat within the Belize Barrier Reef Lagoon system or perhaps because manatees have been protected by local laws since the 1930s and are currently listed as endangered under the Wildlife Protection Act of 1981.

Belize has designated several wildlife sanctuaries and protected areas for the benefit of manatees and other marine life, including Swallow Caye Wildlife Sanctuary, Southern Lagoon Wildlife Sanctuary, Corozal Bay Wildlife Sanctuary, Bacalar Chico National Park and Marine Reserve, South Water Caye Marine Reserve, Burden Canal (part of the Belize River system), and Port Honduras Marine Reserve. Many foreign researchers, including Caryn Self-Sullivan, PhD, and James A. "Buddy" Powell, PhD, as well as Belizean biologists, including manatee researcher

LIONFISH: HOW BELIZE IS MANAGING AN INVASIVE SPECIES IN ITS WATERS

As if Caribbean coral reefs did not have enough problems – overfishing, mangrove cutting, pollution, and climate change, to name a few – they now face invasion by a voracious, venomous, and predatory fish that has the potential to devastate their delicate ecological balance.

Lionfish are members of the scorpionfish (Scorpaenidae) family and have long lacy spines capable of injecting venom into a potential predator. Scientists, dive operators, fishers, and everyone else in Belize's tourism and fishing industries are worried that the lionfish could overwhelm native species, destroying both the reef ecology and their livelihoods.

The campaign to fight the lionfish is led by ECOMAR, a nongovernmental organization in Belize. Linda Searle, founder of ECOMAR's Belize Lionfish Project, stresses, "the best way to control this invasion is to educate the public and restaurants that lionfish is really tasty and good to eat. By creating a demand for lionfish, fishermen will put time and effort into managing the lionfish population."

This "get in my belly" approach is being embraced by chefs and diners throughout Belize. It also has a multifaceted impact, reducing the lionfish population while simultaneously taking pressure off other stressed fisheries.

To learn more about lionfish in Belize, I turned to Linda Searle, and asked her a few questions:

WHAT ARE LIONFISH AND HOW DID THEY GET INTO THE CARIBBEAN?

Lionfish are native to the Indian and Pacific Oceans and have been introduced into the Atlantic Ocean and Caribbean Sea, where they are reported to grow larger since there are not many natural predators. There are several theories on how lionfish got into the Atlantic Ocean. The most common hypothesis is that when Hurricane Andrew hit Miami in 1992 an aquarium with six lionfish was destroyed and the lionfish entered the sea. Aquarium hob-

the infamous invasive lionfish, spotted near Glover's Reef Atoll

© KENDRA SCHOFIELD/OFF THE WALL DIVE CENTER & RESORT

byists are also suspected to have contributed to the introduction of lionfish after releasing them into the ocean since they could no longer afford the loss of expensive aquarium fish to the voracious lionfish. Lionfish eggs, larvae, and fish could have also come into the Atlantic Ocean through the bilge water of large ships.

WHEN DID LIONFISH FIRST APPEAR IN BELIZE AND WHY IS EVERYONE CONCERNED?

The first recent sighting of lionfish took place in December 2008 at a dive site off the eastern side of Turneffe. Shortly thereafter, lionfish were sighted at Glover's Atoll, then Lighthouse Reef Atoll and along the Belize Barrier Reef. However, while recording the locations of the observations, a report was made by a long-time diver to Belize, Bobby Sutton from Texas, that he had sighted a lionfish in 2001 at a dive site near Gladden Spit. Upon returning to the dive shop they had looked through the Caribbean Reef Fish ID book and did not see this fish. It was not until the sightings became more frequent in 2009 that Bobby and Sea Horse Dive Shop realized what they had seen in 2001.

Lionfish are reported to be voracious predators and have been shown to consume prey over half their size, and some have been found with more than 15 prey in their stomachs. They also spawn more than 10,000 eggs every 4-5 days! Fishermen are concerned that lionfish will eat juvenile native fish like grouper and snapper and the spiny lobster. Indeed, a report came in from a fisherman where he witnessed a lionfish eating the eggs from a gravid female lobster!

To encourage the participation of dive leaders throughout Belize, ECOMAR is launching its "Adopt A Reef" program, where specific dive and snorkel sites can be adopted and kept clean of lionfish.

IS THERE ANY MEASURABLE IMPACT ON BELIZEAN ECOLOGY YET?

It is too early to tell since quantitative studies have not been done over a period of time to compare reef fish abundance at sites. Anecdotal reports from divers and fishermen indicate that lionfish are becoming abundant on the reef and that in places where lionfish are sighted there are no lobsters.

WHAT IS BELIZE LIONFISH PROJECT?

The program targets local fishermen, who comb the reef from north to south and are Belize's secret weapon for controlling lionfish populations. The Belize Lionfish Project aims to increase awareness of this introduced species through a media campaign, outreach workshops in coastal communities, and by promoting capture and consumption of lionfish.

By partnering with the Belize Fisheries Department and other NGOs in Belize, the Belize Lionfish Project has raised the level of awareness of lionfish in Belize. The monthly lionfish tournaments that were conducted from May through November 2009 resulted in more than 5,000 fish being captured, and many were analyzed, providing important baseline data on size, distribution, and prey. Tissue samples sent to colleagues at the United States Geological Survey in Florida have provided preliminary details on the lionfish in Belize that will be used to identify the path taken to Belize.

In January 2011, the first lionfish tournament was held in San Pedro, Ambergris Caye, co-sponsored and organized by Coral Reef Alliance, Hol Chan Marine Reserve, San Pedro Tour Guide Association, Wahoo's Lounge, and ECOMAR. Over 600 lionfish were caught in one day. Free barbecued and fried lionfish samples were offered at the end of the event.

ARE DIVERS ALLOWED TO HUNT LIONFISH?

Scuba divers are reminded that it is illegal to harvest marine life while on scuba. However, the Fisheries Department has approved a "trident" made locally by Adolpho Ayuso, a divemaster in San Pedro, for harvesting lionfish while scuba diving. There are many other devices available that can be used while snorkeling, but before you head on your dive with the goal of catching and handling lionfish, be sure that you are doing it legally and safely!

Do your part by participating in lionfish tournaments and asking for it at restaurants. Look for T-shirts that say, "Saving the Reef One Taco at a Time" and "Lionfish Hunter." To learn more about the Belize Lionfish project and how you can help, contact **ECOMAR Belize** at www.ecomarbelize.org.

(Caryn Self-Sullivan, PhD, also contributed to this article.)

SWIMMING WITH BELIZE'S WHALE SHARKS

© SCOTT SCHMIDT

Swimming with whale sharks is an extraordinary opportunity.

An opportunity to share the water with a creature larger than a school bus does not come often in life – and is not soon forgotten. If you're diving in southern Belizean waters between March and June, especially after the full moon, you may be lucky enough to encounter a whale shark.

Biologist Dr. Rachel Graham researches sharks for the Wildlife Conservation Society and lives in Punta Gorda where she runs Blue-Belize Guest House. Dr. Graham has spent literally thousands of hours in the water with whale sharks around the world. I asked her about swimming with the world's biggest fish.

WHY ARE WHALE SHARKS IMPORTANT?

Whale sharks are iconic creatures that put our relatively small lives and aspirations into perspective. They fly the banner for many less charismatic species, and their movements weave a pattern across our tropical ocean landscapes, linking sites and making them true ambassadors of the seas. I truly believe that the world would be a poorer place without whale sharks, which is why we must protect them.

WHAT ARE SOME IMPORTANT THINGS TO REMEMBER WHEN SNORKELING OR DIVING WITH WHALE SHARKS?

The key rule is not to touch, chase, ride, or harm whale sharks in any way. Stay at least three meters away from the shark unless it comes up to you, in which case do nothing and enjoy the unforced close encounter. I ask boat drivers to not cut off the path of a whale shark when it's moving and to drop guests off 15 meters away from the shark (as opposed to right on top of the animal). We also strongly recommend not using flash photography or underwater motorized vehicles.

Nicole Auil (EcoHealth Alliance) and Jamal Galves, have dedicated years of work to a countrywide research program, aerial surveys, and the stranding network through Coastal Zone Management Institute (www.coastalzonebelize.org). Orphaned manatees in Belize are cared for by Wildtracks in Sarteneja, where volunteer positions are often available. For more information about manatees, visit www.sirenian.org.

Sharks and Rays

There are at least 42 species of sharks and rays in the waters of Belize. Most people get a good close glimpse of nurse sharks and southern stingrays on their trip to Hol Chan, and divers occasionally spot other species as well,

such as the Caribbean reef shark or the great hammerhead, especially on trips to the farther atolls, particularly Lighthouse Reef. (The only recorded shark attacks in Belizean waters were due to sheer stupidity: a spearfisherman who refused to give up a fish to a curious shark, and a tour guide who pulled a nurse shark by the tail and wouldn't let go.) To learn more about sharks in Belize and how you can help them, check out www.belizesharks.org.

WHALE SHARKS

Although Belize is home to many species of sharks, the biggest and most notable is the whale shark (*Rhincodon typus*). Like all sharks it has a cartilaginous skeleton and visible gill slits, yet feeds on zooplankton like a whale,

WHAT CURRENT RESEARCH HAS BEEN DONE WITH THE BELIZE WHALE SHARK POPULATION?

Much of the work on whale sharks in Belize was undertaken between 1998 and 2004. Their movements, site fidelity, feeding behavior, tourism value, and population size and structure were researched. I found at least 106 individuals identified from over 580 encounters. The majority of sharks encountered were immature males with an average length of six meters. The whale sharks visiting Gladden Spit are capable of arriving exactly when the snappers spawn and leave when spawning ceases to provide enough food. After this, they move to other feeding sites along the Mesoamerican Barrier Reef, such as Holbox/Isla Contoy and into the Gulf of Mexico to the north; to the south and southeast, they travel to Utila (Honduras) and beyond. Since these studies, SEA Belize, a conservation organization in Placencia, is noting the number of whale sharks encountered and the number of tourists visiting Gladden Spit.

WHAT IS THE MOST AMAZING EXPERIENCE YOU'VE EVER HAD SWIMMING WITH WHALE SHARKS?

Probably with a whale shark named "Mr. Facey," whose name comes from a Creole word for someone with an attitude. Mr. Facey is a young male (about six meters) who reveled in surprising divers, doing "peekaboo" moves behind them and swimming up to them and placing his snout in their midriffs. In my case, Mr. Facey swam up to me at 25 meters depth and parked his snout at the level of my stomach. We sat there for a while not really knowing what to do as this was a bit facey for a first date. Since I could not move sideways or downwards, I eventually crawled on top of his head and pushed away against his dorsal fin. He came back several more times, always gently, always hanging in the water. In the end I almost ran out of air and had to surface.

ANY SCARY MOMENTS?

Never a scary moment. Whale sharks are gentle giants, and even though I have encountered many in my 14 years of diving with them, I remain in awe of their grace, docility, and curiosity.

For more information on Belize's whale sharks and other sharks and rays please visit **www.belizesharks.org** and **www.marine meganet.org**.

and is the largest fish in the sea (up to 20 meters in length and over 15 tons!). Whale sharks bear live young (up to 300 have been found in one female) and are believed to be long-lived—living more than 60 years—and may require up to 30 years to mature. According to biologist Rachel Graham, PhD, who has been studying whale sharks since 1998, Belize hosts the only known aggregation of whale sharks that feeds on the eggs of large schools of reproducing snappers. Although this must occur elsewhere in the world, to date Belize is the only known site where it has been observed.

History

Early recorded comments following Columbus's fourth voyage to the New World led the Spaniards to hastily conclude that the swampy shoreline of what is now Belize was unfit for human habitation. Someone should have told that to the Maya, who had been enjoying the area for quite some time. The pre-Columbian history of Belize is closely associated with that of its nearby neighbors: Mexico, Guatemala, and Honduras. The Maya were the first people to inhabit the land. They planted *milpas* (cornfields), built ceremonial centers, and established villages with large numbers of people throughout the region.

ANCIENT CIVILIZATION
Earliest Humans
During the Pleistocene epoch (about 50,000 B.C.), when the level of the sea fell, people and animals from Asia crossed the Bering land bridge into the American continent. For nearly 50,000 years, humans continued the epic trek southward.

As early as 10,000 B.C., Ice Age people hunted woolly mammoth and other large animals roaming the cool, moist landscape of Central America. Between 7000 and 2000 B.C., society evolved from hunters and gatherers to farmers. Such crops as corn, squash, and beans were independently domesticated in widely separated areas of Mesoamerica after about 6000 B.C. The remains of clay figurines presumed to be fertility symbols marked the rise of religion in Mesoamerica, beginning about 2000 B.C. Archaeologists believe that during this Archaic Period (3400–1000 B.C.) some hunter-gatherer communities made temporary settlements in Belize.

Around 1000 B.C., the Olmec culture, believed to be the earliest in the area and the predecessors to the Maya, began to spread throughout Mesoamerica. Large-scale ceremonial centers grew along Gulf Coast lands, and much of Mesoamerica was influenced by the Olmecs' religion of worshipping jaguarlike

BELIZE: WHAT'S IN A NAME?

No one knows for sure where the name Belize originated or what it means. The country was called Belize long before the British took the country over and renamed it British Honduras. In 1973, the locals changed it back to the original Belize as a first step on the road to independence. There are several well-known theories about its meaning. Some say it's a corruption of the name Wallis (wahl-EEZ), from the pirate (Peter Wallace) who roamed the high seas centuries ago and visited Belize. Others suggest that it's a distortion of the Maya word *belix*, which means "muddy river." Still others say it could be a further distortion of the Maya word *belikin*, the modern name of the local beer.

gods. The Olmecs also developed the New World's first calendar and an early system of writing.

The Classic Period
The Classic Period, beginning about A.D. 250, is now hailed as the peak of cultural development among the Maya. For the next 600 years, until A.D. 900, the Mayans made phenomenal progress in the development of artistic, architectural, and astronomical skills. They constructed impressive buildings during this period and wrote codices (folded bark books) filled with hieroglyphic symbols that detailed complicated mathematical calculations of days, months, and years. Only the priests and the privileged held this knowledge and continued to learn and develop it until, for some unexplained reason, the growth suddenly halted. A new militaristic society was born, built around a blend of ceremonialism, civic and social organization, and conquest.

Maya Society Collapses

All evidence points to an abrupt work stoppage. After about A.D. 900, no buildings were constructed and no stelae, which carefully detailed names and dates to inform future generations of their roots, were erected.

What happened to the priests and noblemen, the guardians of religion, science, and the arts, who conducted their ritual ceremonies and studies in the large stone pyramids? Why were the centers abandoned? What happened to the knowledge of the intelligentsia? Theories abound. Some speculate about a social revolution—the people were tired of subservience and were no longer willing to farm the land to provide food, clothing, and support for the priests and nobles. Other theories include population pressure on local resources, i.e., that there just wasn't enough land to provide food and necessities for the large population. Others believe drought, famine, and/or epidemics were responsible.

Whatever happened, it's clear that the special knowledge concerning astronomy, hieroglyphics, and architecture was not passed on to Maya descendants. Why did the masses disperse, leaving once-sacred stone cities unused and ignored?

COLONIALISM

In 1530, the conquistador Francisco de Montejo y Alvarez attacked the Nachankan and Belize Maya, but his attempt to conquer them failed. This introduction of Spanish influence did not have the impact on Belize that it did in the northern part of the Caribbean coast until the Caste War.

Hernán Cortés and Other Explorers

After Columbus's arrival in the New World, other adventurers traveling the same seas soon found the Yucatán Peninsula. In 1519, 34-year-old Cortés sailed from Cuba against the will of the Spanish governor. With 11 ships, 120 sailors, and 550 soldiers, he set out to search for slaves, a lucrative business with or without the blessings of the government. His search began on the Yucatán coast and eventually encompassed most of Mexico. However, he hadn't counted on the resistance and cunning of the Maya. The fighting was destined to continue for many years—a time of bloodshed and death for many of his men and for the Maya. Anthropologists and historians estimate that as many as 90 percent of Mayans were killed by diseases such as smallpox after the arrival of the Spaniards.

Catholicism

Over the years, the majority of Maya were baptized into the Catholic faith. Most priests did their best to educate the people, teach them to read and write, and protect them from the growing number of Spanish settlers who used them as slaves. The Maya practiced Catholicism in their own manner, combining their ancient beliefs, handed down throughout the centuries, with Christian doctrine. These mystic yet Christian ceremonies are still performed in baptism, courtship, marriage, illness, farming, house building, and fiestas.

Pirates and the Baymen

While all of Mesoamerica dealt with the problems of economic colonialism, the Yucatán Peninsula had an additional problem: harassment by vicious pirates who made life in the coastal areas unstable. In other parts of the Yucatán Peninsula, the passive people were ground down, their lands taken away, and their numbers greatly reduced by the European settlers' epidemics and mistreatment.

British buccaneers sailed the coast, attacking the Spanish fleet at every opportunity. These ships were known to carry unimaginable riches of gold and silver from the New World back to the king of Spain. The Belizean coast became a convenient place for pirates to hole up during bad weather or for a good drinking bout. And, though no one planned it as a permanent layover, by 1650 the coast had the beginnings of a British pirate lair/settlement. As pirating slacked off on the high seas, British buccaneers discovered they could use their ships to carry logwood back to a ready market in England (logwood is a low-growing tree that provided rich dyes for Europe's growing textile industry until man-made dyes were developed). These early settlers were nicknamed the Baymen.

For 300 years, the Baymen of Belize cut the logwood and then, when the demand for logwood ceased, they starting cutting down mahogany trees from the vast forests. For three centuries, the local economy depended on exported logs and imported food.

Agreement with Spain

In the meantime, the Spanish desperately tried to maintain control of this vast New World across the ocean. But it was a difficult task, and brutal conflicts continually flared between the Spanish and either the British inhabitants or the Maya. The British Baymen were continually run out but always returned. Treaties were signed and then rescinded. The British, meanwhile, made inroads into the country, importing slaves from Africa (beginning in the 1720s) to help cut and move the trees.

Politically, Belize (or, more to the point, its timber) was up for grabs, and a series of treaties did little to calm the ping-pong effect between the British and the Spanish over the years. One such agreement, the Treaty of Paris, did little to control the Baymen—or the Spanish.

In 1763, Spain "officially" agreed to let the British cut logwood. The decree allowed roads (along the then-designated frontiers) to be built in the future, though definite boundaries were to be agreed upon later. For nearly 150 years, the only "roads" built were narrow tracks to the rivers; the rivers became Belize's major highways. Boats were common transport along the coast, and somehow road building was postponed, leaving boundaries vaguely defined and countrymen on both sides of the border unsure. This was the important bit of history that later encouraged the Spanish-influenced Guatemalans to believe that Belize had failed to carry out the 1763 agreement by building roads, which meant the land reverted back to Spain. Even after Spain vacated Guatemala, Guatemalans tried throughout the 20th century to claim its right to Belizean territory.

BELIZE HISTORY IN A NUTSHELL

The peaceful country of Belize is a sovereign democratic state of Central America located on the Caribbean. The government is patterned on the system of parliamentary democracy and experiences no more political turmoil than any other similar government, such as Great Britain or the United States.

IMPORTANT DATES

- 1798: Battle of St. George's Caye
- 1862: Became a British colony
- 1954: Attained universal adult suffrage
- 1964: Began self-government
- 1973: Name of the territory changed from British Honduras to Belize
- 1981: Attained full independence

The Battle of St. George's Caye

The Baymen held on with only limited rights to the area until the final skirmish on St. George, a small caye just off Belize City. The Baymen, with the help of an armed sloop and three companies of a West Indian regiment, won the battle of St. George's Caye on September 10, 1798, ending the Spanish claim to Belize once and for all. After that battle, the British Crown ruled Belize until independence was gained in 1981.

Land Rights

In 1807, slavery was *officially* abolished in Belize by England. This was not agreeable to the powerful British landowners, and in many quarters it continued to flourish. Changes were then made to accommodate the will of the powerful. The local government no longer "gave" land to settlers as it had for years (the British law now permitted former slaves and

FROM A 19TH-CENTURY TRAVEL WRITER

The next day we had to make preparations for our journey into the interior, besides which we had an opportunity of seeing a little of Balize. The Honduras Almanac, which assumes to be the chronicler of this settlement, throws a romance around its early history by ascribing its origin to a Scotch bucanier named Wallace. The fame of the wealth of the New World, and the return of the Spanish galleons laden with the riches of Mexico and Peru, brought upon the coast of America hordes of adventurers – to call them by no harsher name – from England and France, of whom Wallace, one of the most noted and daring, found refuge and security behind the keys and reefs which protect the harbour of Balize. The place where he built his log huts and fortalice is still pointed out; but their site is now occupied by warehouses. Strengthened by a close alliance with the Indians of the Moscheto shore, and by the adhesion of numerous British adventurers, who descended upon the coast of Honduras for the purpose of cutting mahogany, he set the Spaniards at defiance. Ever since, the territory of Balize has been the subject of negotiation and contest, and to this day the people of Central America claim it as their own. It has grown by the exportation of mahogany; but, as the trees in the neighbourhood have been almost all cut down, and Central America is so impoverished by wars that it offers but a poor market for British goods, the place is languishing, and will probably continue to dwindle away until the enterprise of her merchants discovers other channels of trade.

John L. Stephens, *Incidents of Travel in Central America, Chiapas and Yucatán*, 1841

other "coloureds" to hold title). The easiest way to keep them from possessing the land was to charge for it—essentially barring the majority in the country from landownership. So, in essence, slavery continued.

Caste War

It was inevitable that the Maya would eventually erupt in a furious attack. This bloody uprising in the Yucatán Peninsula in the 1840s was called the Caste War. Though the Maya were farmers and for the most part not soldiers, in this savage war they took revenge on every white man, woman, and child by rape and murder. When the winds of war reversed themselves and the Maya were on the losing side, vengeance on them was merciless. Some settlers immediately killed any Maya on sight, regardless of his beliefs. Some Maya were taken prisoner and sold to Cuba as slaves; others left their villages and hid in the jungles, in some cases for decades. Between 1846 and 1850, the population of the Yucatán Peninsula was reduced from 500,000 to 300,000. Guerrilla warfare ensued, with the escaped Maya making repeated sneak attacks upon the white settlers. Quintana Roo, adjacent to Belize along the Caribbean coast, was considered a dangerous no-man's-land for more than a hundred years until, in 1974, with the promise of tourism, the territory was admitted to the Federation of States of Mexico. The "war" didn't *really* end on the peninsula until the Chan Santa Cruz people finally made peace with the Mexican federal government in 1935, more than 400 years after it had begun.

Restored Maya Pride

Many of the Maya who escaped slaughter during the Caste War fled to the isolated jungles of Quintana Roo and Belize. The Maya revived the religion of the "talking cross," a pre-Columbian oracle representing gods of the four cardinal directions. This was a religious/political marriage. Three determined survivors of the Caste War—a priest, a master spy, and a ventriloquist—all wise leaders, knew their people's desperate need for divine leadership. As a result of their leadership and advice from the talking cross, the shattered people came together in large numbers and began to organize. The community guarded the location of the cross, and its advice made the Maya strong once again.

They called themselves Chan Santa Cruz ("People of the Little Holy Cross"). As their confidence developed, so did the growth and power of their communities. Living very close to the Belize (then British Honduras) border, they found they had something their neighbors wanted. The Chan Santa Cruz Maya began selling timber to the British and in return received arms, giving the Maya even more power. Between 1847 and 1850, in the years of strife during the Caste War in neighboring Yucatán, thousands of Maya, mestizo, and Mexican refugees who were fleeing the Spaniards entered Belize. The Yucatecans introduced the Latin culture, the Catholic religion, and agriculture. This was the beginning of the Mexican tradition in northern Belize, locally referred to as "Spanish tradition." The food is typically Mexican, with tortillas, black beans, tamales, squash, and plantain (a type of banana that can be cooked). For many years, these mestizos kept to themselves and were independent of Belize City.

They settled mostly in the northern sections of the country, which is apparent by the Spanish names of the cities: Corozal, San Estevan, San Pedro, and Punta Consejo. By 1857, the immigrants were growing enough sugar to supply Belize, with enough left over to export the surplus (along with rum) to Britain. After their success proved to the tree barons that sugarcane could be lucrative, the big landowners became involved. Even in today's world of low-priced sugar, the industry is still important to Belize's economy.

INDEPENDENCE

In 1862, the territory of British Honduras was officially created, even though it had been ruled by the British Crown since 1798. The average Belizean had few rights and a very low living standard. Political unrest grew in a stifled atmosphere. Even when a contingent of Belizean soldiers traveled to Europe to fight for the British in World War I, the black men were scorned. But when these men returned from abroad, the pot of change began to boil. Over the next 50 years, the country struggled through power plays, another world war, and economic crises. But always

THE BELIZE NATIONAL ANTHEM

"LAND OF THE FREE"

O, Land of the Free by the Carib Sea,
Our manhood we pledge to thy liberty!
No tyrants here linger, despots must flee
This tranquil haven of democracy.
The blood of our sires which hallows the sod,
Brought freedom from slavery oppression's rod,
By the might of truth and the grace of God.
No longer shall we be hewers of wood.
Arise! ye sons of the Baymen's clan,
Put on your armours, clear the land!
Drive back the tyrants, let despots flee –
Land of the Free by the Carib Sea!
Nature has blessed thee with wealth untold,
O'er mountains and valleys where prairies roll;
Our fathers, the Baymen, valiant and bold
Drove back the invader; this heritage bold
From proud Río Hondo to old Sarstoon,
Through coral isle, over blue lagoon;
Keep watch with the angels, the stars and moon;
For freedom comes tomorrow's noon.

the seed was there—the desire to be independent. The colonial system had been falling apart around the world, and when India gained its freedom in 1947, the pattern was set. Many small, undeveloped countries began to gain independence and started to rely on their own ingenuity to build an economy that would benefit their people.

Even though Belize was self-governing by 1964, it was still dominated by outside influences until September 1981, when it gained its independence from the British Crown. In September 1981, the Belizean flag was raised for the first time—the birth of a new country. Belize joined the United Nations, the Commonwealth of Nations, and the Non-Aligned Movement. The infant country's first parliamentary elections were held in 1984. You can see that original Belizean flag at the George Price Centre in Belmopan.

Government and Economy

GOVERNMENT

The Government of Belize, or "GOB," as you'll see it referred to in the newspapers, is directed by an elected prime minister. The bicameral legislature, or National Assembly, comprises an appointed senate and elected house of representatives. Belize has two main political parties, PUP (People's United Party) and UDP (United Democratic Party). As in most democracies, the political rhetoric can get very animated, but political-based violence is unheard of.

The current prime minister, Dean Barrow of the UDP, took the post from long-time PUP frontman Said Musa in 2008. Barrow's party had been gaining ground in recent years, especially as PUP rulers became increasingly implicated in various corruption scandals.

The official GOB website is www.governmentofbelize.gov.bz. The country's constitution, judicial code, and other legal documents are explained and can be downloaded at the Ministry of the Attorney General's homepage, www.belizelaw.org.

ECONOMY

The economy of Belize was traditionally based on the export of logwood, mahogany, and *chicle* (the base for chewing gum, from the *chicle* tree). Today, tourism, agriculture, fisheries, aquaculture (shrimp farming), and small manufactured goods give the country an important economic boost, but it is still dependent on imported goods to get by. The main exports are sugar, citrus, bananas, lobster, and timber. Overall, domestic industry is severely constrained by relatively high labor and energy costs, a very small domestic market, and the "brain drain" of Belize's most qualified managers, health professionals, and academics to the United States and Europe.

In general, and despite books by PUP economists declaring that all is well, Belize's economy is a mess, and the GOB has been on the verge of bankruptcy for years. In 2004, the government was rocked by a scandal over the use of millions of dollars of pension funds to pay the foreign debts of bankrupt companies controlled by government insiders. This led to

GEORGE PRICE

George Price was Belize's first prime minister upon independence in 1981, then served the position again from 1989-1993. Born in 1919, Price entered politics in 1944 and never looked back. He did not step down from the leadership of the People's United Party which he founded in 1950 until 1996 when he retired in Belize City. Price also served as the mayor of Belize City several times. The **George Price Centre for Peace and Development** (www.gpcbelize.com) in Belmopan is a must-see to learn more about Price's central role in Belizean history.

CRUISE SHIP TOURISM

The image of numerous hulking cruise ships on the watery eastern horizon, as seen from Belize City, is striking. The sheer scale of these ships so dwarfs anything that exists in Belize that the effect cannot but be impressive, especially when the tenders arrive in streams, carrying thousands of cruise passengers to a specially designated "Tourism Village" in the Fort George area of the city.

The arrival of the cruise industry to Belize's shores in the 1990s was both much-hailed and a highly contentious event. It happened quickly and Belize soon recorded the highest growth in cruise ship arrivals in the entire Caribbean region: Annual cruise visitor arrivals grew from 14,183 in 1998 to a peak of more than 851,000 in 2004. The year 2010 saw 767,000 cruise visits, according to the Belize Tourism Board.

The Belize Tourism Board officially promotes cruise ship visits. Director Seleni Matus told me there are 2,000 people in Belize City who rely on cruise visits for their livelihoods, most of whom work in Tourism Village shops and restaurants. She acknowledges the need to balance cruise ship tourism with overnight tourism, making sure that one does not take over the other, as has happened in Cozumel, just to the north.

In Belize City, cruise ship arrival days are boom days for taxi drivers, hair braiders, some tour operators, and generic Viagra sellers. But critics of allowing the industry to operate in Belize say that's not enough. Stewart Krohn, an esteemed Belizean journalist, writes that inviting cruise tourism is the equivalent of selling Belize cheaply. In one editorial, he wrote, "Tourism, at its heart, is a cultural encounter. Long, relaxed, unhurried stays by visitors who have time to meet, interact with, and understand Belizeans and Belize not only means more money in our pockets for beds, food, drinks and tours; it produces the kind of relationships that small countries in a highly competitive world find increasingly necessary."

Such meaningful encounters are impossible with hurried bus-loads of day-trippers from the ship, he argues. "Cruise tourism at best

© JOSHUA BERMAN

According to the Belize Tourism Board, in 2010 nearly 767,000 cruise ship passengers visited Belize.

produces a few pennies for a few people; at worst a negative impression born of an impersonal encounter."

Other critics cite cruise visits' impact on Belize's tiny and fragile infrastructure – damage to roads by cruise bus traffic, maxed-out septic systems, trash on the trails and in the caves, etc. I once witnessed a cruise ship offloading trash onto a tiny barge outside Belize City. Passengers don't spend much, if anything, onshore, and few of their dollars trickle very far from the pockets of those who own Tourism Village and the cruise concessions.

One thing is for certain: If you bring up cruise tourism at a Belizean barbecue, get ready to hear some fiery opinions, especially if you mention the proposal to expand cruise visits into Placencia and southern Belize. The government says it is considering all its options in that area. Land has already been sold where the passengers will dock, leading some to believe it is a done deal. However, a vocal grassroots campaign of Placencians – including many small business owners – is fighting to keep the ships out. On their website (www.nocruises.org), they say, "Many people in Placencia fear that mass cruise ship tourism will destroy not only the responsible tourism Placencia has worked so hard to build, but also the quality of life of local residents and the natural resources that are an integral part of that quality of life and Placencia's overnight tourism."

© JOSHUA BERMAN

government buildings in Belmopan, in the style of a Maya pyramid

the collapse of the overextended Development Finance Corporation (DFC), the effects of which are still being felt and evaluated today.

Thanks to tax concessions given to foreign investors, Belize has attracted new manufacturing industries, including plywood, veneer, matches, beer, rum, soft drinks, furniture, boat building, and battery assembly.

TOURISM

No longer the unknown backwater it once was, Belize is now a common destination for North American and European travelers. Tourism is one of the most critical economies in the country, responsible for about 1 in 7 jobs and 22 percent of the country's GDP. The **Belize Tourism Board** (BTB, tel. 501/227-2420, www.travelbelize.org) has gotten the word "Belize" buzzing on the lips of millions of potential visitors who, only a few years ago, had

never even heard of the tiny country. Today, roughly 250,000 overnight visitors come to Belize each year; the majority (about 150,000) are from the United States.

In 2010, 664 registered hotels were providing jobs to nearly 5,000 Belizeans, and that's not counting restaurant employees, guides, transport services, etc. Tourism has encouraged the preservation of vast tracts of forests and reefs; it has helped the Institute of Archaeology enhance and develop Belize's archaeological sites as destinations, making possible astounding excavations and discoveries at the Caracol, Xunantunich, Lamanai, Altun Ha, and Cahal Pech ruins.

Of course, tourism can be a double-edged sword, and Belize's founding father, George Price, warned against it. Price said tourism would make Belizeans indentured servants to rich foreigners.

People and Culture

The extraordinary diversity of Belize's tiny population (about 320,000) allows Belizeans to be doubly proud of their heritage—once for their family's background (Maya, Creole, Garifuna, Mennonite, etc.) and again for their country. The mestizo (mixed Spanish and indigenous descent) population has risen to about 50 percent of the country's total, with Creoles making up about 25 percent, Maya 10–12 percent, Garifuna 6 percent, and others 9 percent (2000 census).

Here's a bit of background about Belize's diverse demography, but keep in mind that every one of these groups continues to mingle with the others, at least to some extent, ensuring continuing creolization.

CULTURAL GROUPS
Creoles
Creoles share two distinctive traits: some degree of African-European ancestry and the use of the local English-Creole dialect. Skin color runs from very dark to very light, but some old trace of English logger or buccaneer is back there. Many Creoles are also descended from other groups of immigrants.

The center of Creole territory is Belize City. Half of Belize's ethnic Creoles live here, and they make up more than three-fourths of the city's population. Rural Creoles live along the highway between Belmopan and San Ignacio, in isolated clusters in northern Belize District, and in a few coastal spots to the south—Gales Point, Mullins River, Mango Creek, Placencia, and Monkey River.

Cheap labor was needed to do the grueling timber work in thick, tall jungles. The British failed to force it on the maverick Maya, so they brought slaves from Africa, indentured laborers from India, and Caribs from distant Caribbean islands, as was common in the early 16th and 17th centuries. "Creolization" started when the first waves of British and Scottish began to intermingle with these imported slaves and servants.

Mestizos
Also referred to as "Ladinos" or just "Spanish," mestizos make up the quickest-growing demographic group in Belize and encompass all Spanish-speaking Belizeans, descended from some mix of Maya and Europeans. These immigrants to Belize hail from the nearby countries of Guatemala, El Salvador, Honduras, and Mexico. Once the predominant population (after immigration from the Yucatecan Caste War), mestizos are now the second most-populous ethnic group of Belize. They occupy the old "Mexican-Mestizo corridor" that runs along New River between Corozal and Orange Walk. In west-central Belize—Benque Viejo and San Ignacio—indigenous people from Guatemala have recently joined the earlier Spanish-speaking immigrants from Yucatán.

The Maya
Small villages of Maya—Mopan, Yucatec, and Q'eqchi'—still practicing some form of their ancient culture dot the landscape and comprise roughly 10–12 percent of Belize's population. After the Europeans arrived and settled in Belize, many of the Maya moved away from the coast to escape hostile Spanish and British intruders who arrived by ship to search for slaves.

Many Maya communities continue to live much as their ancestors did and are still the

SUNDAY: DAY OF REST

Belize is serious about its Sundays. Expect businesses in most parts of the country – even restaurants and cafés – to close on Sundays. The streets empty as well, giving a ghost-town feeling to places like downtown Belize City. Usually, the only stores and eateries open are Chinese shops and maybe a few taco stands on the street.

most politically marginalized people in Belize, although certain villages are becoming increasingly empowered and developed, thanks in part to tourism (although some would argue at a cultural cost).

Most modern Maya practice some form of Christian religion integrated with ancient beliefs. But ancient Maya ceremonies are still quietly practiced in secluded pockets of the country, especially in southern Belize.

Garifuna

The Garifuna, also called "Garinagu," came to exist on the Lesser Antillean island of San Vicente, which in the 1700s had become a refuge for escaped slaves from the sugar plantations of the Caribbean and Jamaica. These displaced Africans were accepted by the native Carib islanders, with whom they freely intermingled. The new island community members vehemently denied their African origins and proclaimed themselves Native Americans. As the French and English began to settle the island, the Garifuna (as they had become known) established a worldwide reputation as expert canoe navigators and fierce warriors, resisting European control. The English finally got the upper hand in the conflict after tricking and killing the Garifuna leader, and in 1797, they forcefully evacuated the population from San Vicente to the Honduran Bay Island of Roatan. From there, a large part of the Garifuna migrated to mainland Central America, all along the Mosquito Coast.

On November 19, 1823, so the story goes, the first Garifuna boats landed on the beaches of what is now Dangriga, one of the chief cultural capitals of the people. They landed in Belize under the leadership of Alejo Beni, and a small Garifuna settlement grew in Stann Creek, where they fished and farmed. They began bringing fresh produce to Belize City, but were not welcome to stay for more than 48 hours without getting a special permit—the Baymen wanted the produce but feared that these free blacks would help slaves escape, causing a loss of the Baymen's tight control.

The Garifuna language is a mixture of Amerindian, African, Arawak, and Carib, dating from the 1700s. The Garifuna continued to practice what was still familiar from their ancient African traditions—cooking, dancing, and especially music, which consisted of complex rhythms with a call-and-response pattern that was an important part of their social and religious celebrations. An eminent person in the village is still the drum maker, who continues the old traditions, along with making other instruments used in these singing and dancing ceremonies that often last all night.

There are a number of old dances and drum rhythms still used for a variety of occasions, especially around Christmas and New Year's. If you are visiting Dangriga, Hopkins, Seine Bight, Punta Gorda, or Barranco during these times (or on Settlement Day, November 19), expect to see (and possibly partake in) some drumming. Feel free to taste the typical foods and drinks. If you consume too much "local dynamite" (rum and coconut milk) or bitters, have a cup of strong chicory coffee, said by the Garifuna "to mek we not have goma" (prevent a hangover).

East Indians

From 1844 to 1917, under British colonialism, 41,600 East Indians were brought to British colonies in the Caribbean as indentured workers. They agreed to work for a given length of time for one "master." Then they could either return to India or stay on and work freely. Unfortunately, the time spent in Belize was not as lucrative as they were led to believe it would be. In some cases, they owed so much money to the company store (where they received half their wages in trade and not nearly enough to live on) that they were forced to "re-enlist" for a longer period. Most of them worked on sugar plantations in the Toledo and Corozal Districts, and many of the East Indian men were assigned to work as local police in Belize City. In a town aptly named Calcutta, south of Corozal Town, many of the population today are descendants of the original indentured East Indians. Forest Home near Punta Gorda also has a large settlement. About 47 percent of the ethnic group live in these two locations. The East Indians usually have large families and live on small farms with orchards adjacent to their homes. A few trade in pigs and dry goods in mom-and-pop businesses. Descendants of earlier East Indian immigrants speak Creole and Spanish. A few communities of Hindi-speaking East Indian merchants live in Belize City, Belmopan, and Orange Walk.

Mennonites

Making up more than 3 percent of the population of Belize, German-speaking Mennonites are the most recent group to enter Belize on a large scale. This group of Protestant settlers from the Swiss Alps wandered over the years to northern Germany, southern Russia, Pennsylvania, and Canada in the early 1800s, and to northern Mexico after World War I. For some reason, the quiet, staid Mennonites disturbed local governments in these other countries, and restrictions on their isolated agrarian lifestyle led to a more nomadic existence.

Most of Belize's Mennonites first migrated from Mexico between 1958 and 1962. A few came from Peace River in Canada. In contrast to other areas where they lived, the Mennonites bought large blocks of land (about 148,000 acres) and began to farm. Shipyard (in Orange Walk District) was settled by a conservative wing; Spanish Lookout (in Cayo District) and Blue Creek (in Orange Walk District) were settled by more progressive members. In hopes of averting future problems with the government, Mennonites made agreements with Belize officials that guarantee them freedom to practice their religion, use their language in locally controlled schools, organize their own financial institutions, and be exempt from military service.

Over the 30-plus years that Mennonites have been in Belize, they have slowly merged into Belizean activities. Although they practice complete separation of church and state (and do not vote), their innovations in agricultural production and marketing have advanced the entire country. Mennonite farmers are probably the most productive in Belize; they commonly pool their resources to make large purchases such as equipment, machinery (in those communities that use machinery), and supplies. Their fine dairy industry is the best in the country, and they supply the domestic market with eggs, poultry, fresh milk, cheese, and vegetables.

Belizeans Abroad

By some estimates, there are more Belizeans living in the United States than there are in Belize. They are concentrated mostly in New York City, Chicago, Los Angeles, and New Orleans. Of these, many young Belizeans have served in the U.S. armed forces. The money these emigrants send home is an important source of income for their Belizean families. Some Belizean expats stay in the States, but many return with new skills. On the flip side are those who have been deported back to Belize because of illegal activities in the United States, bringing the negative impacts of U.S. gang culture with them, a problem plaguing Belize City.

LANGUAGE

There are more than eight languages commonly spoken in Belize! English is the official language, although Belizean Creole (or "Kriol") serves as the main spoken tongue among and between groups. There are an increasing number of Spanish speakers in Belize, as Central American immigrants continue to arrive. Spanish is the primary language of many native Belizean families, especially among descendants of Yucatecan immigrants who inhabit the Northern Cayes, Orange Walk, and Corozal Districts. As a tourist, there are only a few areas of Belize, mainly rural outposts in northern and western Belize, where knowing Spanish is essential to communicate. The Garinagu people speak Garifuna, and the various Mennonite communities speak different dialects of Old German. Then there are Mopan, Yucateca, and Q'eqchi' Mayan tongues. Still other immigrant groups, like Chinese and Lebanese, also often speak their own languages amongst themselves.

BELIZEAN CONCEPT OF TIME

As in many other Central American and Caribbean cultures, the Belizean clock is not as rigidly precise as it is in other parts of the world. "Nine o'clock A.M." is not necessarily a moment in time that occurs once a morning, as it is a general guideline that could extend an hour or two in either direction (usually later). Creoles say, "Time longa den da roop, mon" ("time is longer than the rope"), which means the same as the Spanish *"Hay mas tiempo que vida"* ("there is more time than there is life")—both of which boil down to the unofficial motto of Caye Caulker: "Go slow!"

A great deal of patience is required of the traveler who wishes to adapt to this looser concept of time. Buses generally leave when they are scheduled, but may stop for frustratingly long breaks during the journey. Don't use Belize Time as an excuse to be late for your tour bus pickup, and don't get angry when your taxi driver stops to briefly chat and laugh with a friend.

THE ARTS

Belize has a fairly rich art scene for such a small country. Several painters and visual artists from Belize have made a name for themselves internationally. Start your research of Belizean art by looking up the work of Gilvano Swasey, Pen Cayetano, Michael Gordon, Benjamin Nicholas, Carolyn Carr, Chris Emmanuel, and Yasser Musa, to name only a couple.

There are many more artists out there, of course. Start in Belize City, at the **Museum of Belize,** the **Belize Centre for Art Education,** and the **House of Culture,** all with space for exhibits, concerts, and exchanges. The **Bliss Centre for the Performing Arts** hosts performances in music, dance, and drama. The **Image Factory Art Foundation** (www.imagefactorybelize.com) has a gallery and store on Front Street and hosts many art projects and showings.

The government ministry responsible for the arts is the **National Institute for Culture and History** (NICH), which encompasses four organizations: The Institute of Creative Arts (based at the Bliss Centre for the Performing Arts on Southern Foreshore in Belize City); Museum of Belize and Houses of Culture (MOB is on Gaol Lane in front of the Central Bank of Belize; Houses of Culture are in Belize City, Orange Walk, Benque Viejo del Carmen, and San Ignacio Town Hall); the Institute of Archaeology (in the Belmopan NICH Headquarters Building), which manages all archaeological sites in the country; and the Institute for Social & Cultural Research (Belmopan, NICH Headquarters Building). Find out more at www.nichbelize.org.

CRAFTS

You'll have a selection of Belizean and Guatemalan crafts to choose from when visiting any archaeological site, as vendors typically set up rows of stalls with similar gifts, crafts, textiles, and basketwork. You'll also see slate carvings, a recently resurrected skill of the Maya. Among the leading slate carvers are **the Garcia Sisters, Lesley Glaspie,** and the **Magana family.** Their work can be found in several Cayo shops as well as elsewhere in the country (especially Aurora's shop near the entrance to Cockscomb). The Garcia sisters helped revive the slate craze, and their quality has always been high. **Mennonite furniture pieces** like hardwood chairs and small tables make possible take-home items. Orange Gifts (in Cayo and San Pedro) has the best selection of crafts for sale in the country.

MUSIC

The music of Belize is heavily influenced by the syncopated beats of Africa as they combine with modern sounds from throughout Latin America, the Caribbean, and North America.

The most popular Belizean music is ***punta,*** a fusion of traditional Garifuna rhythms and modern electric instruments. The "Ambassador of Punta Rock" was Andy Palacio, a prolific musician from the southern village of Barranco, who died in 2008 and was honored as a national hero. The newer form of *punta* is characterized by driving, repetitive dance rhythms and has its acoustic roots in a type of music called ***paranda.*** A recent PBS special described

SPEAKING BELIZEAN KRIOL

If you think Belize Kriol refers to nothing more than the exotic Caribbean accent of your Belizean hosts, think again. Better yet, *listen* as they talk casually with each other; you'll hear an entirely different language than the Rasta-tinted English Belizeans reserve for foreigners. Belize Kriol, or "Creole" in its English spelling (not to be confused with the French Creole of New Orleans, which is completely different), is a Belize-ified version of the greater Caribbean pidgin conglomerations heard elsewhere in the region. It's a rare and dedicated foreigner who learns to speak fluent Belize Kriol, but trying out a few local phrases, proverbs, and dirty words can go a long way to getting laughs and making friends.

The National Kriol Council of Belize created the Belize Kriol Project to help you do just that – and to promote the unique culture and language of the Kriol people of Belize. In their Belize City office (next to the House of Culture), pick up one of several publications in written Kriol, including dictionaries, phrasebooks, poetry, and prose (my favorite is the *Chravl Buk eena Kriol ahn Inglish*, or "Travel Book in Kriol and English"). For an introduction to Belize Kriol before your trip, subscribe to a mailing list or online forum, where you can see the language as it is used in active conversation (do an online search to find these).

SPEAKING THE LANGUAGE

To speak Kriol, listen to the spoken language. If you are comfortable doing so, ask the speaker to slow it down and explain the words and phrases to you. Writing these down phonetically and practicing saying them, over and over, is the best, most humbling way to learn any language. Here are a few facts and phrases to get you started.

For one thing, there is no past tense in Belize Kriol, which explains menu items like "fry chicken" and "stew fish." You should also be aware of a few Kriolized English phrases. For example, "right now" means "just a moment," or "coming right up," and despite its promise of promptness, actually refers to a time period between the present moment and three to four lazy hours into the future. Also, money and numbers are expressed as "Wan dollah, two dollah, chree dollah, etc." A "five dollah" bill, by the way, is also known as a "red bwai" (red boy). Another expression is, "Life without a wife, is like kitchen without a knife."

GREETINGS

- **Weh yu nayhn?** – What is your name?
- **Ah nayhn** (or) **Mee naym** – My name is . . .
- **Weh di go aan?** – What's up? Hello.

paranda as "nostalgic ballads coupling acoustic guitar with Latin melodies and raw, gritty vocals...which can feature traditional Garifuna percussion like wood blocks, turtle shells, forks, bottles, and nails." A few of the original *paranda* masters, like Paul Nabor in Punta Gorda, can still be found in their hometowns throughout Belize. Several excellent compilation albums of Belizean and Honduran *punta* and *paranda* music are available from Stonetree Records.

Brukdown (or "Bruckdong") began in the timber camps of the 1800s, when the workers, isolated from civilization for months at a time, would let off steam by drinking a full bottle of rum and then beating on the empty bottle— or the jawbone of an ass, a coconut shell, or a

wooden block—anything that made a sound. Add to that a harmonica, guitar, and banjo, and you've got the unique sound of *brukdown*. This is a traditional Creole rhythm kept alive by the legendary Mr. Peters and his **Boom and Chime** band until Mr. Peters passed away in 2010 at the age of 79.

Over the last five years, dub-poetry has emerged as an important format for musical expression in Belize. The most popular artist of this is **Leroy "The Grandmaster" Young**, whose album *Just Like That* is a wonderful listening experience and has been acclaimed by numerous international reviewers.

In the southern part of Belize, you'll likely hear the strains of ancient Maya melodies

- *Gud maanin* – Good morning.
- *Da how yu di du?* – How are you?
- *Aarait* – Fine, thank you.
- *Weh taim yu gat?* – What time is it?

EXCLAMATIONS

- *Choh!* – Exasperated expression; "I don't want to hear it!"
- *Haul your rass!* – Get the hell out of here!
- *Dat da lone rass!* – That's bull!
- *Belly full, boti glad!* – Declaration after a good meal.
- *Stap u rass!* – Shut your mouth; stop your foolishness.
- *Kohn ya!* – Come here!
- *Madda Fiyah!* – Gosh darnit!
- *Cheese 'n rice!* – A way of saying "Jesus Christ" without using the Lord's name in vain.

OTHER USEFUL PHRASES

- *Gud-gud!* – Good, fine.
- *Ah sari.* – I am sorry.
- *Dat okay.* – It's okay.

- *Fa tru?* – For true? Really?
- *Dis meet ya haaf raa.* – This meat isn't done.
- *Yu da lamp up.* – You are lazy.
- *Mek ah tel yu sumting.* – Let me tell you something.
- *We gwan bash tonight.* – We're gonna party tonight.
- *How much pikni yu got?* – How many children do you have?
- *Jook.* – To fornicate.
- *Hamahingi* – A well-endowed male member. Synonym: "anaconda."
- *You da bleech out.* – You've been drinking a lot.
- *Scrapist* – A man who dates different types of women.
- *She a proppah like a snappah* – She's good looking.
- *Icky de bolla.* – Foul-smelling genitals.
- *Luk pon de!* – Look at those idiots.

This random selection of Belize Kriol was contributed by a mix of Belizean and gringo friends. You know who you are. Thank you!

played on homemade wooden instruments, including Q'eqchi' harps, violins, and guitars. In Cayo District in the west, listen for the resonant sounds of marimbas and wooden xylophones—from the Latin influence across the Guatemala border. In the Corozal and Orange Walk Districts in the north, Mexican *ranchera* and *romantica* music is extremely popular. Of course reggae is popular throughout the country, especially on the islands (Bob Marley is king in Belize).

Stonetree Records (www.stonetreerecords. com) has the most complete catalogue of truly Belizean music, covering a wide range of musical genres and styles. This author's favorite is *Belize City Boil-Up,* an incredibly funky collection of remastered vintage Belizean soul tracks from the 1950s, '60s, and '70s, featuring The Lord Rhaburn Combo, Jesus Acosta and the Professionals, The Web, Harmonettes, Nadia Cattouse, and Soul Creations. From the record's description, "In a Belizean musical landscape that is currently dominated by *punta,* rap, and reggae, it's easy to forget that there was actually a time when the Belizean scene was alive with cool jazz, smooth rhythm and blues, and even psychedelic funk."

In addition to recording and marketing dozens of albums, Stonetree, based in Benque Viejo in western Belize, is also very active in encouraging new Belizean musicians to experiment and develop their individual sounds. Buy albums online, or pick up a couple of CDs at any gift shop during your visit.

FESTIVALS AND EVENTS

When a public holiday falls on Sunday, it is celebrated on the following Monday. If you plan to visit during holiday time, make advance hotel reservations—especially if you plan to spend time in Dangriga during Settlement Day on November 19 (the area has limited accommodations).

Note: On Sundays and a few holidays (Easter and Christmas), most businesses close for the day, and some close the day after Christmas (Boxing Day); on Good Friday most buses do not run. Check ahead of time.

Garifuna Settlement Day

On November 19, Belize recognizes the 1823 arrival and settlement of the first Garifuna in the southern districts of Belize. Belizeans from all over the country gather in Dangriga,

Greasy pole contests are common at some Belizean festivals. The goal is to reach the prize at the top.

© SCOTT SCHMIDT

NATIONAL HOLIDAYS IN BELIZE

January 1 – New Year's Day
March 9 – National Heroes and Benefactors Day (formerly Baron Bliss Day)
March or April – Good Friday
March or April – Easter Sunday
May 1 – Labour Day
May 25 – Commonwealth Day
September 10 – National Day
September 21 – Independence Day
October 12 – Columbus Day
November 19 – Garifuna Settlement Day
December 25 – Christmas Day
December 26 – Boxing Day

Hopkins, Punta Gorda, and Belize City to celebrate with the Garifuna. The day begins with the **reenactment** of the arrival of the settlers and continues with all-night dancing to the local Garifuna drums and live *punta* bands. Traditional food—and copious amounts of rum, beer, and bitters—is available at street stands and local cafés.

St. George's Caye Day

On September 10, 1798, at St. George's Caye off the coast of Belize, British buccaneers fought and defeated the Spaniards over the territory of Belize. The tradition of celebrating this victory is still carried on each year, followed by a weeklong calendar of events from religious services to carnivals. During this week, Belize City feels like a carnival with parties everywhere. On the morning of September 10, the whole city parades through the streets and enjoys local cooking, spirits, and music with an upbeat atmosphere that continues well into the beginning of Independence Day on September 21.

National Independence Day

On September 21, 1981, Belize gained independence from Great Britain. Each year, Belizeans celebrate with carnivals on the main streets of downtown Belize City and district towns. Like giant county fairs, they include displays of local arts, crafts, and cultural activities, while happy Belizeans dance to a variety of exotic rhythms from *punta* to *soka* to reggae. Again, don't miss the chance to sample local dishes from every ethnic group in the country. With this holiday back to back with the celebration of the Battle of St. George's Caye, Belize enjoys two weeks of riotous, cacophonous partying.

National Heroes and Benefactors Day (formerly Baron Bliss Day)

On March 9, this holiday is celebrated with various activities, mostly water sports. English sportsman Baron Henry Edward Ernest Victor Bliss, who remembered Belize with a generous legacy when he died, designated a day of sailing and fishing in his will. A formal ceremony is held at his tomb below the lighthouse in the Belize Harbor, where he died on his boat. Fishing and sailing regattas begin after the ceremony.

Ambergris Caye Celebration

If you're wandering around Belize near June 26–29, hop a boat or plane to San Pedro and join the locals in a festival they have celebrated for decades, **El Día de San Pedro,** in honor of the town's namesake, St. Peter. This is good fun; reservations are suggested. **Carnaval,** one week before Lent, is another popular holiday on the island. The locals walk in a procession through the streets to the church, celebrating the last hurrah (for devout Catholics) before Easter. There are lots of good dance competitions.

Maya Dances

If traveling in the latter part of September in San Antonio Village in the Toledo District, you have a good chance of seeing the **deer dance** performed by the Q'eqchi' Maya villagers. Dancing and celebrating begins around the middle of August, but the biggest celebration begins with a *novena,* nine days before the feast day of San Luis.

Actually, this festival was only recently revived. The costumes were burned in an accidental fire some years back at a time when (coincidentally) the locals had begun to lose interest in the ancient traditions. Thanks to the formation of the **Toledo Maya Cultural Council,** the Maya once again are realizing the importance of recapturing their past. Some dances are now performed during an annual Cacao Festival in Toledo District during the last weekend in May.

ESSENTIALS

Getting There

BY AIR

To Belizeans, flying was a far-fetched idea when American hero Charles Lindbergh paid a dramatic visit to the small Caribbean nation as part of his ongoing effort to promote and develop commercial aviation. At the time (1927), Lindbergh had just completed his famous nonstop flight across the Atlantic. On his visit to Belize, the Barracks Green in Belize City served as his runway, and the sound of his well-known craft, *The Spirit of St. Louis,* attracted hundreds of curious spectators.

Today, dozens of daily international flights fly in and out of the country, served by a growing number of major carriers. In general, airfares to Belize range from expensive to exorbitant, though rates occasionally dip throughout the year.

Philip Goldson International Airport

Most travelers to Belize arrive at Philip Goldson International Airport (BZE), nine miles from Belize City, outside the community of Ladyville. The medium-size airport (by Central American standards) offers basic services like gift shops, currency exchange, and two restaurants; Internet is available in the **Sun Garden Restaurant** upstairs from the American terminal. Check out the "waving

© JOSHUA BERMAN

deck" upstairs by the other bar/restaurant for exciting farewell/hello energy. The airport is named after Philip Stanley Wilberforce Goldson (1923–2001), a respected newspaper editor, activist, and politician. The airport's ongoing runway and apron expansion is hoping to attract new carriers from farther away, particularly the European market.

Arriving in Belize

After clearing customs, you'll be besieged by taxi drivers offering rides into town for a fixed US$25; split the cost with fellow travelers if you can. If you are not being picked up by a resort or tour company and you choose to rent a car, look for the 11 rental car offices, all together on the same little strip, across the parking lot from the arrival area.

If you're continuing to the cayes, you can fly directly to Caye Caulker or San Pedro, or take a taxi into town and get on a boat for about half the price and a few hours longer.

When it's time to go, don't forget to carry enough U.S. dollars for your US$36 departure fee (if it's not already included in your ticket).

BY BOAT

Daily boats to Punta Gorda travel back and forth from Puerto Barrios, Guatemala, and there are two boat services to Puerto Cortés, Honduras (one leaves from Placencia, the other from Dangriga). Vessels traveling to the area must have permission from the Belize Embassy in Washington, D.C.

VIA MEXICO

Because airfares to Belize are so high, a few travelers choose to fly into the Mexican state of Quintana Roo on the Yucatán Peninsula, especially to Cancún, where discounted airfares are common. By bus from Mexico is a cinch; many daily buses travel from the main terminal in Chetumal all the way to Belize City and back. You'll have to get out to wait in various customs and immigration lines, but just follow the crowd and you'll be fine. There are also several Mexican lines that run daily between Chetumal, Belize City, Cayo (Benque), and Guatemala.

By Bus from Cancún

After passing through customs at the airport, you will find service desks for shuttle transport and the ADO bus ticket agent. You want to go Playa del Carmen, an hour south, where you will make a connection to Chetumal. It costs about US$23 for a shared shuttle to Playa del Carmen; private shuttle service is US$70–80 depending on group size. Visit the airport's website (www.cancun-airport.com) to search for rates and reserve shuttle transport. The airport personnel are very helpful in directing you where you need to go and ensuring you have transportation from the airport; shuttle vans are immediately outside and buses are located to the right.

A bus to Playa del Carmen (about US$10) is the most economical route. Riviera buses are comfortable and air conditioned; if you're the type of person who packs a sweater for your tropical vacation it may be useful. After arriving at the station, a few blocks from an amazing beach, you have two options: continue immediately to Chetumal near the Belize border, or overnight in Playa del Carmen. Playa del Carmen has two bus stations: Terminal Alterna on Calle 20 and Terminal Touristica (a.k.a. Terminal Riviera, 5th Ave. and Ave. Juarez); you can buy tickets for any destination at either station, so always double-check where your bus departs from when you buy a ticket.

If you continue directly to Chetumal, check the bus schedule; you may need to take a taxi (US$2.50) to Terminal Touristica. Buses to Chetumal (US$13.50–20) depart every hour until 5:15 P.M.; the trip takes 5–6 hours and has a few stops in between if you need to grab a snack or use the restroom. Chances are you'll arrive in Chetumal later in the evening, and public transportation options to Belize may not be available.

If you'd rather linger in Playa Del Carmen, you won't be sorry; find a hotel, head to the beach, or stroll along 5th Avenue. You can book a morning bus to Chetumal and most likely, it will be departing from Terminal Touristica.

The main ADO bus terminal in Chetumal is not too far from the Neuvo Mercado, where local buses to Belize depart. Outside the station you can find a taxi or continue walking across the plaza to Avenue Insurgentes. Continue left toward the Pemex gas station on the corner and turn right onto Avenue Heroes. Continue two blocks to Calle Segundo Circuito Periferico and turn left. You'll see the repainted school buses waiting at Nuevo Mercado Lazara Cardenas, in a parking lot on the right side of the street.

Driving from Cancún

Yes, it is possible to rent a car in Cancún and continue south on a Belizean adventure, but it'll cost you both money and patience. Still, with the money you save with the cheaper airfare into Cancún, the mobility may be worth it. Cancún is 369 kilometers from the border at Santa Elena, roughly 4.5 hours in a car on Route 307. Corporate international rental companies will not let you take their vehicles across the border, so you'll have to find a more accommodating Mexican company, like **J.L. Vegas,** with one office near the airport and another in the Crystal Hotel. Next, you'll need to "make the papers," as the car guy will surely remind you. Another company that says they'll let you drive into Belize is **Caribbean Rent A Car** (U.S. tel. 866/577-1342, Mexico tel. 800/633-7799, www.cancunrentacar.com).

Driving from the United States

The road from Brownsville, Texas, to the border of Belize is just under 1,400 miles. If you don't stop to smell the cacti, you can make the drive in three days, especially now that there is a toll-road bypass around Veracruz and the Tuxtla mountains. The all-weather roads are paved, and the shortest route through Mexico is by way of Tampico, Veracruz, Villahermosa, Escarcega, and Chetumal. There often is construction on Mexican Highways 180 and 186. Lodging is available throughout the drive, although it is most highly concentrated in the cities and on the Costa Esmeralda, a beautiful strip of mostly deserted beach near Nautla (prices start at around US$20 for a very simple double). If attempting this trip, be sure you have a valid credit card, Mexican liability insurance, a passport, and a driver's license—all original documents and one set of photocopies.

Driving Across the Border

The most crucial part of driving into Belize from Mexico is having a letter of permission from the car's owner; customs will scrutinize this document. Next, to avoid being turned back at the border, be sure to get the vehicle sprayed with insecticide from one of the roadside sprayers near the border—it's tough to pick them out, but look for a little white shack past the bridge after leaving Mexico and keep your receipt for when you reach customs/immigration (fumigation costs US$5). After passing through Mexican immigration (have your passport stamped and hand in your tourist card), you will cross a bridge welcoming you to Belize. On the righthand side, you will see two unsigned buildings where you must purchase insurance. The tire fumigation is near the fork in the road before the free zone. You will likely be greeted when you first pull over by men offering to help you through the stations, but their services are unnecessary. Still, it can be wise to befriend these touts, as many of them are related to the officers at the border. Give a small tip and ask them to clean your windows while you are getting insurance at the Atlantic house (you must have insurance before you enter immigration).

Although in Mexico proof of registration suffices as proof of ownership, in Belize you may be asked to show a title. You will not need a Temporary Vehicle Importation permit if entering for one month or less; for more time, you may need to post a bond on your vehicle (in greenbacks, to be refunded in Belizean dollars later). One very important detail when entering Mexico from the United States is to request a "doble entrada" on your passport to avoid steep fees. This should only cost 100 pesos, if it's available. Returning to Mexico from Belize, you'll pay a US$19 Belizean exit tax, per person.

Getting Around

BY AIR

It is very reasonable and common to get around the country in puddle jumper planes. Some Belizean airstrips are paved and somewhat official-looking (Belize City and San Pedro, for example); the rest are more like short abandoned roadways or strips of mown grass, but they work just fine. Because such small planes are used, you not only watch the pilot handling the craft, you may also get to sit next to him or her if the flight is full (which is easy in a 12-seater). Best of all, flying low and slow in these aircraft allows you to get a panoramic view of the Belize Barrier Reef, cayes, coast, and jungle (keep your camera handy).

Two airlines offer regularly scheduled flights to all districts in Belize, from both the international and municipal airports: **Tropic Air** (tel. 501/226-2012, U.S. tel. 800/422-3435, reservations@tropicair.com, www.tropicair. com) and **Maya Island Air** (tel. 501/223-1140, U.S. tel. 800/225-6732, mayair@btl. net, www.mayaislandair.com). Daily flights are available from Belize City to Caye Caulker, San Pedro, Dangriga, Placencia, Punta Gorda, and a handful of other tiny strips around the country. The Maya and Tropic flights usually combine several destinations in one route, so if you're traveling to PG, you may have to land and take off in Dangriga and Placencia first. Ditto for Caulker and San Pedro, the two of which are linked together. There are also regular flights to Flores, Guatemala, and you can fly between Corozal and San Pedro. If your scheduled flight is full, another will taxi up shortly and off you go.

Several charter flight companies will arrange trips to remote lodges like Lighthouse Reef Resort, Blancaneaux Lodge in the Mountain Pine Ridge, and Gallon Jug airstrip near Chan Chich. **Javier's Flying Service** (municipal airport, tel. 501/223-1029) is one such charter, offering local and international flights, air ambulance, and day tours.

By Helicopter

Charter a chopper for a transfer, adventure tour, filming/photography assignment (e.g., the cover of this book!), aerial property survey, search and rescue mission, or medevac with **Astrum Helicopters** (Mile 3½ on Western Highway, near Belize City, tel. 501/222-9462, www.astrumhelicopters.com); expect to pay around US$1,000 per hour (US$250 per person for most sightseeing tours). Astrum is a modern, professional outfit with new aircraft and a very skilled father-son pilot team.

BY BUS

Save money, meet Belizeans, and see the countryside in an untouched trip between towns. The motley fleet of buses that serves the entire country ranges from your typical rundown, recycled yellow school bus to plush, air-conditioned luxury affairs. Belize buses are relatively reliable, on time, and less chaotic than the chicken-bus experience in other parts of Central America and Mexico. Even so, buses make many extra stops, including a requisite break in Belmopan for anywhere from 5 to 30 minutes for all buses traveling between

ROAD DISTANCES FROM BELIZE CITY

Belmopan	55 miles
Benque Viejo	81 miles
Corozal Town	96 miles
Dangriga	105 miles
Orange Walk Town	58 miles
Punta Gorda	210 miles
San Ignacio	72 miles

Belize City and points west and south; it's a good bathroom and taco break.

Your best up-to-date resource for all Belize bus schedules and information is www.belizebus.wordpress.com, an independent website that pays impressive attention to travel details. Another website with bus schedules is www.guidetobelize.info. Travel time from Belize City to Corozal or San Ignacio is about two hours, to Dangriga 2–3 hours, and to Punta Gorda 5–6 hours. Fares average US$2–4 to most destinations, US$7–12 for the longer routes.

In Belize City, nearly all buses still begin and end at the **Novelo's Terminal** (it's still called that even though the company no longer exists; tel. 501/207-4924, 501/207-3929, or 501/227-7146), located on West Collett Canal Street in Belize City. Reach it by walking west on King Street, across Collett Canal, and into the terminal—definitely use a taxi when departing or arriving at night. Another walking route from the downtown area and water taxi is to go west along Orange Street, cross over the canal, then turn left and continue a short distance to the terminal.

James Bus runs the most reliable daily Punta Gorda service, using the block in front of the Shell station on Vernon Street (two blocks north of the Novelo's) as its terminal.

There are at least a dozen booths to buy a ticket on the various international express bus services **to Guatemala and Mexico.** All are located inside or in front of the Caye Caulker Water Taxi Terminal and Swing Bridge. Boat-bus connections are convenient and easy to make, but it all happens in the middle of one of Belize's busiest intersections.

BY RENTAL CAR

Driving Belize's handful of highways gives you the most independence when traveling throughout the country, but it is also the most expensive. Rental fees were running US$75–125 per day and gasoline was approaching US$6 per gallon at press time. You'll also have to be adept at avoiding careless drivers and obstacles like pedestrians, farm animals, cyclists,

Many travelers rent a car and drive Belize's countryside on their own.

iguanas, and the occasional moped-riding cruise ship passengers.

In some areas, like the Mountain Pine Ridge and other hinterlands, there is no public transportation, and a sturdy rental car is a good way to go if you're into traveling on your own schedule.

Rental Cars in Belize City

One of the first things you'll see upon walking out of the arrival lounge at the international airport is a strip of about a dozen car rental offices offering small, midsize, and four-wheel-drive vehicles. Vans and passenger cars are also available, some with air-conditioning. Insurance is mandatory but (like taxes) not always included in the quoted rates. If you know exactly when you want the car, it's helpful (and often cheaper) to make reservations. Note the hour you pick up the car and try to return it before that time: A few minutes over could cost you another full day's rental fee. Also take the vehicle inspection seriously to make sure you don't get charged for someone else's dings. And don't forget to fill the tank up before giving it back.

DRIVING IN BELIZE

Rule number one: Drive defensively! Expect everyone out there to make stupid passes and unexpected turns – they probably will and it's your job to stay out of their way (especially when they are bigger than you, like the buses and oil trucks that speed crazily around blind curves and over one-lane bridges).

Valid U.S. (or other nationality) driver's licenses and international driving permits are accepted in Belize for a period of three months after entering the country. Try not to drive at night if you can avoid it. Besides the additional hazards of night driving in general, some Belizean drivers overuse their high beams and many vehicles have no taillights. Watch out for unmarked speed humps. Driving rules are U.S.-style with one very strange exception: Sometimes a vehicle making a left-hand turn is expected to pull over to the right, let traffic behind pass, and then execute the turn. This practice is being phased out, but you can still get a ticket – or rear-ended – so be careful.

Tires frequently pop, so make sure you have a good spare to get you to the nearest used-tire dealer. New tires may be hard to come by, but Belizeans are geniuses with a patch kit. A decent used spare can be had for around US$30, a patch job about US$5. If you plan on traveling during the rainy season and/or without a four-wheel-drive vehicle, make sure you are prepared in the event you get stuck in the mud. In general, road conditions may

In Belize, speed bumps are called "sleeping policemen."

dictate where you can and cannot go, and it is always best to ask around town if you plan to go off the beaten path. Watch out for speed bumps, even on the highways – no matter how slow you drive, on some, you may bottom out. If you're going to the cayes and leaving a vehicle on the mainland, be sure to seek out a secure pay parking lot in your city of departure, especially if it's Belize City (the municipal airport is probably the best choice).

Expect police checkpoints anywhere around the country: They'll check your seat belt (US$25 fine), car papers, and driver's license, and, courtesy of the U.S. Drug Enforcement Agency, dogs will sniff for that dime bag of weed in your shaving kit (apparently, these small busts are as big a priority as the tons of cocaine flowing northward through the country).

Crystal Auto Rental (tel. 501/223-1600, www.crystal-belize.com) has the largest, newest, most reliable fleet of cars in Belize. It is also the only company that will allow you to drive across the border into Guatemala or Mexico, but you won't be insured. **Jabiru Auto Rental** (tel. 501/224-4680, www.jabiruautorental. bz) is also reliable and has low Internet rates. **Budget Rent a Car** (tel. 501/223-2435, www. budget-belize.com) offers new cars that are well maintained. You'll find a few other international brands with local Belizean branches, including **Avis**.

Rental Cars in Cayo

If you plan on traveling in the Cayo region, it's cheaper to use one of the San Ignacio–based car rental options. Start with **Cayo Rentals** (at Texaco station at top of hill, tel. 501/824-2222, cayorentals@btl.net); US$75 per 24 hours *includes* taxes and insurance. Also in Cayo, **Matus Car Rentals** (tel. 501/663-4702 or 501/824-2089, matuscarrental@yahoo.com) is another option with a handful of sturdy cars, and there is a Land Rover rental place in Central Farm, just east of San Ignacio (tel. 501/824-2523), if you really planning on going off-road.

Visas and Officialdom

U.S. citizens must have a passport valid for the duration of their visit to Belize; U.S. citizens, British Commonwealth subjects, and citizens of Belgium, Denmark, Finland, Greece, Iceland, Italy, Liechtenstein, Luxembourg, Mexico, Spain, Switzerland, Tunisia, Turkey, and Uruguay do not need a visa. They are automatically granted a 30-day tourist pass and technically must have onward or return air tickets and proof of sufficient money (though I've never heard of anyone checking this). Visitors for purposes other than tourism, or who wish to stay longer than 30 days, need to visit an immigration office of the Government of Belize.

If you are planning on staying more than 30 days, you can ask for a new stamp at any immigration office in the country, or you can cross the border and return. The first few times are free, then there may be various fees to extend (the

EMBASSIES AND CONSULATES OF BELIZE

For the most recent update on Belize's diplomatic corps abroad, check the Ministry of Foreign Affairs website: www.mfa.gov.bz.

CANADA
Belize does not have an embassy or an ambassador in Canada, only a few honorary consul:

**Bob Dhillon, Honorary Consul
to Belize in Alberta**
305 10th Ave. SE, Calgary, AB T2G 0W2
tel. 403/215-6072, 403/560-6520, or
403/215-6063
bdhillon@mainst.biz

**David W. Smiling, Honorary Consul
to Belize in Vancouver, British Columbia**
belize@smilingassociates.com
tel. 604/306-7645

COSTA RICA
Consulate of Belize in San José
Apartado Postal 11 121-1000
36th St., 7th and 9th Aves.
San José, Costa Rica
tel. 506/2223-1037 or 506/2223-6654
fax 506/2233-6587
jgamboa@gamboaydengo.com

EUROPE
Belize High Commission in London
45 Crawford Place, 3rd Floor
London, W1H 4LP, United Kingdom

tel. 44/20-7499-9728, fax 44/20-7491-4139
bzhc-lon@btconnect.com
www.belizehighcommission.com

**Embassy of Belize and Mission of Belize
to the European Communities**
Boulevard Brand Whitlock 136
1200 Brussels, Belgium
tel. 32/2-732-6204
fax 32/2-732-6246
embelize@skynet.be

**Permanent Delegation of
Belize to UNESCO**
1 Rue Miollis, Office M. 345-346
75015 Paris, France
tel. 33/1-45-68-32-11
fax 33/1-47-20-18-74
dl.belize@unesco-delegations.org

**Permanent Mission of Belize
to the United Nations**
7 Rue du Mont-blanc
CH 1201 Geneva, Switzerland
tel. 022/906-8420
mission.belize@ties.itu.int

GUATEMALA
Embassy of Belize
5 Avenida 5-55, Zona 14
Edificio Euro Plaza, Torre 2, Oficina 1502
Ciudad de Guatemala
tel. 502/2367-3883 or 502/2367-3885

most I've been charged was US$12.50 for an extra 30 days).

U.S. citizens are strongly encouraged by the State Department to register their trip, no matter how short, online at www.travel.state.gov, so that the local embassy has emergency contact information on file.

FOREIGN EMBASSIES IN BELIZE

Only a handful of countries have embassies in Belize. The **United States Embassy** (Floral Park Rd., Belmopan, tel. 501/822-4011, fax 501/822-4012, embbelize@state.gov, http://belize.usembassy.gov) is open for U.S. citizen services 8 A.M.–noon and 1–4 P.M. Monday–Thursday and 8 A.M.–noon on Friday in its brand-new fortified US$50 million building. The after-hours emergency number for American citizens is 501/610-5030. For inquiries pertaining to American citizens, email ACSBelize@state.gov.

The **British High Commission** (Embassy Square, P.O. Box 91, Belmopan, tel. 501/822-2146, brithicom@btl.net, www.britishhighbze.com) is open 8 A.M.–noon and 1–4 P.M.

---

fax 502/2367-3884
embelguat@yahoo.com
www.embajadadebelize.org

HONDURAS
Embassy of Belize
Hoteles de Honduras
R/do Hotel Honduras Maya
Tegucigalpa, Honduras, C.A.
tel. 504/238-4614
fax 504/238-4617
consuladobelice@yahoo.com

MEXICO
Consulate of Belize in Cancún
Avenida Nader 34
Cancún, Quintana Roo, Mexico
tel. 52/555-520-1274 or 52/555-520-1346
telefax: 52/555-520-6089
embelize@prodigy.net.mx
nel.bel@prodigy.net.mx

Embassy of Belize in Mexico
215 Calle Bernardo de Galvez, Col. Lomas de Chapultepec
Mexico D.F. 11000
tel. 52/5-520-1274
embelize@prodigy.net.mx

UNITED STATES
In addition to the listings below, there are a number of honorary consulates to Belize throughout the United States, including in Illinois, Florida, California, Louisiana, Michigan, Nevada, and North Carolina. Check www.mfa.gov.bz for the latest list.

Consulate General of Belize
Korean Trade Center Park Mile Plaza
4801 Wilshire Blvd., Ste. 250
Los Angeles, CA 90010
tel. 323/634-9900
belizeconsulate@sbcglobal.net

**Debbie M. Schell, Honorary
Consul to Belize in Chicago**
780 Lee St., Ste. 109
Des Plaines, IL 60016
tel. 847/759-9833
dschell@bzconsulchicago.org

Embassy of Belize
2535 Massachusetts Ave. NW
Washington, DC 20008, USA
tel. 202/332-9636
belize@oas.org
www.embassyofbelize.org

**Permanent Mission of Belize
to the United Nations**
675 3rd Ave., Ste. 1911
New York, NY 10017
tel. 212/593-0999
fax 212/593-0932
blzun@belizemission.com
www.un.int/belize

Monday–Thursday and 8 A.M.–2 P.M. Friday. El Salvador and India also have embassies in Belmopan.

Countries with embassies in Belize City include China, Cuba, Mexico, Colombia, Holland, Sweden, and Taiwan.

MOVING TO BELIZE

It's a typical story—the foreigner who vacationed in Belize and never left. There are a number of ways to do it, from starting a business, investing in land, retiring, or working online. Just be sure to do your homework before deciding to move to Belize, as it's more of a lifestyle change than you might realize.

Visit during different seasons of the year, and start your research by listening to Jerry Jeff Walker's song, "Just Another Gringo in Belize."

Retiring in Belize

Anyone 45 years or older with a monthly income of no less than US$2,000 through a pension, annuity, or other retirement benefit generated outside of Belize can apply for the **Qualified Retired Persons Incentives Program** (tel. 800/624-0686, shauma@travelbelize.org, www.belizeretirement.org), which greatly facilitates the process of retiring in Belize.

Accommodations

Of the 664 licensed hotels in Belize, the vast majority are very small and boutiquey. Large foreign-owned hotel chains are few and far between in Belize. Most accommodations are simple, local affairs. Average room rates have been creeping up year after year; in 2007, the average rate was US$103. (If the descriptions in this book don't mention "tax included," it may be added on top of the advertised rate; it's worth asking about tax when booking your

room.) I've selected the most well-kept, comfortable, friendly, family-run operations I could find throughout Belize. If you find any properties that deserve to be in these pages but aren't (or ones I've listed that you think should be removed), please let me know.

The Belize Hotel Association (BHA, 13 Cork St., Belize City, tel. 501/223-0669, www.belizehotels.org) is a nonprofit, nongovernmental organization of some of the country's most

UNDERSTANDING HOTEL RATES

Exact hotel rates are an elusive thing in Belize; seasonal pricing fluctuations are compounded by various hotel taxes and service charges, sometimes as much as 25-30 percent above the quoted rate. Using a credit card can add another 3-5 percent. Universal standards for presenting prices are absent in Belize's hotel industry. Always make sure the rate you read about or are quoted is actually the same amount you will be asked to pay.

The high season is loosely considered to be mid-December through the end of April, and it is marked by a rise in both the number of visitors

and the price of most accommodations. Some places kick their rates up even higher during Christmas, New Year's, and Easter, calling these "holiday" or "peak" rates. A minority of hotels keep their rates the same year-round, but it's rarely that simple. *Moon Belize* quotes **high-season double occupancy** rates only! Expect lower rates (30-40 percent lower than what is quoted in this book) if traveling during the low/rainy season (May-November) and/or on your own. Occasionally walk-in discounts are given, when hotels are eager to avoid empty rooms and you stumble along at the right time.

respected resorts and lodges. They work with the Belize Tourism Board and handle much of the global marketing for Belize; they also have a helpful listing of accommodations on their website.

BUDGET HOTELS

Budget accommodations are ample in Belize, as long as you have a flexible idea of what's "cheap." In this book, nightly rates under US$25 are reasonable, though value varies like anywhere else. In Belize, hostels and dormitories for under US$10 per person per night may mean a sacrifice in safety or cleanliness. At press time, US$10–15 is the bottom line for low-cost lodging, and it'll get you anything from a cramped concrete box to a generous wooden cabin like those found at the Trek Stop and other backpacker hot spots. Guesthouses and budget hotels sometimes offer a dormitory or bunkroom, shared among fellow travelers; this option is cheaper, but obviously you give up privacy and maybe security—and you'll enjoy shared bathrooms and cold water (assume that accommodations described in this book have hot water unless otherwise noted). Sometimes, nicer hotels offer a few "economy rooms," which are considerably cheaper than normal rates.

Great deals are abundant in the low season, when room rates plummet across the board, and walk-in specials can save you as much as 50 percent off normal winter (high-season) rates.

Some villages around the country are trying to emulate the guesthouse and homestay networks available in the southern Toledo villages. Sometimes calling themselves "bed-and-breakfasts," such options are usually primitive, often lacking electricity, running water, and flush toilets. Look for them along the Hummingbird Highway and in some outlying Cayo villages. Sarteneja has a homestay program too.

UPSCALE

The sky's the limit when it comes to midrange and high-end accommodations in Belize. From business traveler standards to the chic lap of luxury, Belize has it all—if you've got the cash. A great many Belizean families and foreign investors have attempted to bring their personal visions of paradise to life throughout this class, and Belize's amazing selection of creative resorts and lodges has been featured in international travel magazines around the world. For the latest in luxe, click on "Belize" at Luxury Latin America (www.luxurylatinamerica.com).

Food and Drink

Throughout this book (and throughout Belize), you will find references to "Belizean" food, often preceded by words like "simple" and "cheap." It should be noted that the very idea of a national cuisine is as new as every other part of Belizean identity. Since the times of the Baymen, Belize has been an import economy, surviving mostly on canned meats like "bully beef" and imported grains and packaged goods. With independence, however, came renewed national pride, and with the arrival of tourists seeking "local" food, the word "Belizean" was increasingly applied to the varied diet of so many cultures. Anthropologist Richard Wilk wrote about the process in his

book, *Home Cooking in the Global Village: Caribbean Food from Buccaneers to Ecotourists.*

The common denominator of Belizean food is **rice and beans,** a starchy staple pronounced as one word with a heavy accent on the first syllable: *"RICE-'n'-beans!"* Belizeans speak of the dish with pride, as if they invented the combination, and you can expect a massive mound of it with most midday meals. Actually, Belizean rice and beans *is* a bit unique: They use red beans, black pepper, and grated coconut, instead of the black beans and cilantro common in neighboring Latin countries. The rest of your plate will be occupied by something like **stew beef, fry chicken,** or a piece of fish, plus a small mound of either potato or cabbage salad. Be sure to take advantage of so much fresh fruit: oranges, watermelon, star fruit, soursop, mangoes, and papaya, to name a few.

For breakfast, try some **fry jacks** (fluffy fried-dough crescents) or **johnnycakes** (flattened biscuits) with your eggs, beans, and bacon.

One of the cheapest and quickest meal options, found nearly everywhere in Belize, is Mexican "fast-food" snacks, especially **taco stands,** which are everywhere you look, serving as many as five or six soft-shell chicken tacos for US$1. Also widely available are **sal-butes,** a kind of hot, soggy taco dripping in oil; **panades,** little meat pies; and **garnaches,** which are crispy tortillas under a small mound of tomato, cabbage, cheese, and hot sauce.

Speaking of hot sauce, you'll definitely want to try to take home **Marie Sharp's** famous habanera sauces, jams, and other creative products. Marie Sharp is a classic independent Belizean success story, and many travelers visit her factory and store just outside Dangriga. (Her products are available on every single restaurant table and in every gift shop in the country.) Her sauce is good on pretty much everything.

Then, of course, there's the international cuisine, in the form of many excellent foreign-themed restaurants. San Pedro and Placencia, in particular, have burgeoning fine-dining scenes.

Many restaurants in Belize have flexible hours of operation, and often close for a few hours between lunch and dinner. The omnipresent **Chinese restaurants** provide authentic Chinese cuisine of varying quality. Most Chinese places sell cheap "fry chicken" takeout and are often your only meal options on Sundays and holidays.

GIMME DOLLAH! WHAT A BUCK BUYS IN BELIZE

Food in Belize often goes by dollar amounts. In marketplaces you can determine the price of bananas, limes, or oranges by asking, "How much fi dalla?" You can get 8-10 bananas for a one Belize dollar, or 4-6 limes depending on the season and vendor. While much of the produce is sold by the pound, some fruits and vegetables are packed in dollar bags for a quick sale.

Street food, such as tacos and panades, is also sold by the dollar, usually "three fi dalla" (three for a dollar). If you're craving six tacos for breakfast you could say, "Gimme two-dalla tacos." You will also learn that patience does not pay off; there are no waiting lines when ordering food, and although it seems rude, you often have to shout over a crowd to get any service.

(Contributed by Scott Schmidt.)

SEAFOOD

One of the favorite Belize specialties is fresh fish, especially along the coast and on the islands, but even inland Belize is never more than 60 miles from the ocean. There's lobster, shrimp, red snapper, sea bass, halibut, barracuda, conch, and lots more prepared in a variety of ways.

Conch (pronounced "KAHNK") has been a staple in the diet of the Maya and Central American communities along the Caribbean coast for centuries. There are conch fritters, conch steak, and conch stew; it's also often used in *ceviche*—uncooked seafood marinated in lime juice with onions, peppers, tomatoes, and a host of spices. In another favorite, conch is pounded, dipped in egg and cracker crumbs, and sautéed quickly (like abalone steak in California) with a squirt of fresh lime. Caution: If it's cooked too long, it becomes tough and rubbery. Conch fritters are minced pieces of conch mixed into a flour batter and fried—delicious.

On many boat trips, the crew will catch a fish and some conch and prepare them for lunch, either as *ceviche,* cooked over an open

Roadside casual eateries are called "cool spots," like this one in Roaring Creek.

beach fire, or in a "boil up," seasoned with onions, peppers, and *achiote*, a fragrant red spice grown locally since the time of the early Maya.

Responsible Seafood Eating

Don't order seafood out of season! Closed season for lobster is February 15–June 15, and conch season is closed July 1–September 30. The ocean is being overfished, due in large part to increasing demand from tourists. The once-prolific lobster is becoming scarce in Belizean waters. And conch is not nearly as easy to find as it once was. Most reputable restaurateurs follow the law and don't buy undersize or out-of-season seafood; however, a few have no scruples.

Small snappers are great fish to eat. Not only are they delicious, but they are one of the most sustainably caught finfish in Belize, often caught locally with hook and line. You also get positive ecological karma points for every invasive lionfish you eat in the Caribbean.

When dining out (especially in one of Belize's many, many Chinese restaurants), do *not* patronize any restaurant offering shark fin soup, *panades* made with shark meat, or live reef fish. Not only are sharks critical to a functional marine ecosystem, but the meat is high in methyl mercury so it's bad for you, too. Also avoid any restaurant that displays endangered reef fish like the Nassau grouper or Goliath grouper in tanks as meal choices. In fact, stay away from grouper in general, especially Goliath grouper (*Epinephelus itajara*, locally known as "jewfish"), a critically endangered species that is also high in methyl mercury. In addition, do not buy marine curios such as shark teeth or jaws, starfish, coral, etc.

NONALCOHOLIC BEVERAGES

There are wonderful natural fruit drinks to be had throughout Belize. Take advantage of fresh lime, papaya, watermelon, orange, and other healthy juices during your travels—they are usually made with purified water, at least in most tourist destinations.

© JOSHUA BERMAN

You'll find a unique combination of ingredients at sidewalk markets in Belize City, such as pig snout, bitters, shark oil, and pineapples.

ALCOHOLIC BEVERAGES

Beer

Perhaps the most important legacy left by nearly three centuries of British imperialism is a national affinity for dark beer. Nowhere else in Central America will you find ale as hearty and dark as you do any bar, restaurant, or corner store in Belize, where beer is often advertised separately from stout, a good sign indeed for those who prefer more bite and body to their brew.

At the top of the heap are the slender, undersized (280 ml) bottles of **Guinness Foreign Extra Stout,** known affectionately by Belizeans as "short, dark, and lovelies." Yes, Guinness—brewed in Belize under license from behind the famous St. James's Gate in Dublin, Ireland, and packing a pleasant 7.5 percent punch of alcohol. No, this is not the same sweet nectar you'll find flowing from your favorite Irish pub's draft handle at home, but c'mon, you're in Central America. Enjoy.

Next up is **Belikin Stout,** weighing in with a slightly larger bottle (342 ml) and

distinguishable from a regular beer bottle by its blue bottle cap. Stouts run 6.5 percent alcohol and are a bit less bitter than Guinness, but still a delicious, meaty meal that goes down much quicker than its caloric equivalent of a loaf of bread. **Belikin Premium** (4.8 percent alcohol) boasts a well-balanced body and is brewed with four different types of foreign hops; demand often exceeds supply in many establishments, so order early.

Asking for a "beer" will get you a basic **Belikin,** which, when served cold, is no better or worse than any other regional draft. Lastly, the tiny green bottles belong to **Lighthouse Lager,** a healthy alternative to the heavies, but packing a lot less bang for the buck with only 4.2 percent alcohol and several ounces less beer (often for the same price).

All beer in Belize is brewed and distributed by the same company in Ladyville, just north of Belize City (Bowen and Bowen Ltd. also has the soft drink market cornered). Some batches are occasionally inconsistent in quality—if you get skunked, send back your mug and try

BITTERS: LOVE POTION NUMBER NINE

"It's good for your penis!" boomed Doctor Mac, extolling the wonders of bitters — that age-old Garinagu herbal tonic, aphrodisiac, and more. Mac poured a measured portion of yellowed liquid through a funnel into a recycled pint bottle. "It's good for making babies!" He laughed and clenched a fist atop an upraised forearm to emphasize his point — Central American sign language for "virility." Bitters are made by soaking herbs like *palo del hombre* (man-root) and jackass bitters in 80-proof white rum or gin. They are available under the counter of many a bar and corner store, a liquid baby-maker known in Garifuna as *"gífiti."* Bitters are a cure-all used to treat everything from the common cold to cancer, sometimes taken as a daily shot to keep your system clean and your urine clear. And of course, bitters are a sure cure for impotency and infertility, according to any vendor of the stuff.

Belizean and Honduran Garinagu expats bring bitters back to the United States by the gallon (or did until the airlines' ban on liquids, anyway). Until he moved to Chicago, the most famous bitters maker in the country was Doctor Mac, a formidable man, also known as "Big Mac," who was credited with the births of many local babies for the fertility juice he proffered. He used to make a version for women, the bottles labeled either "boy" or "gal."

Last time I was in the area, looking for the new king of the bitters crown, I was told "There's a new kid on the block," but not given any names. I did however, discover the bitters of "Kid B," a spry 76-year-old from Silk Grass Village, who spent 36 years as a welterweight prize fighter in Chicago. Find him at **Kid B's Cool Spot** in Silk Grass, just off the Southern Highway, north of the Hopkins turnoff.

Don't forget; in addition to curing what ails ya, bitters can get you really, really wasted. Be careful with long-term, regular use, both for your liver's sake and because some say the ingredients carry trace amounts of arsenic. Talk about a hangover.

again. You'll see most Belizeans vigorously wipe the rust and crud from the open bottle mouths with the napkin that comes wrapped around the top—you'd be smart to do the same. Beers in Belize cost US$1.50–3 a bottle, depending on where you are.

Rum

Of all the national rums, **One Barrel** stands proudly above the rest. Smooth enough to enjoy on the rocks (add a bit of Coca-Cola for coloring if you need to), One Barrel has a sweet, butterscotchy aftertaste and costs about US$8 for a liter bottle, or US$3 per shot (or rum drink). The cheaper option is **Caribbean Rum,** which is fine if you're mixing it with punch, cola, or better yet, coconut water *in* the coconut. Everything else is standard, white-rum gut rot.

Tips for Travelers

PAPERWORK

Make a photocopy of the pages in your passport that have your photo and information. When you get the passport stamped in the airport, it's a good idea to make a photocopy of that page as well, and store the copies somewhere other than with your passport. This will facilitate things if your passport ever gets lost or stolen. Also consider taking a small address book, credit cards, a travel insurance policy, and an international phone card for calling home. Be discreet when using a money belt—the best option is to buy one that looks like a regular belt, where you can zip the folded bills inside, and don't open it in public. A separate passport pouch can be used for documents, but make sure it's waterproof so it won't get soggy from your sweat.

ALTERNATIVE TRAVEL

By "alternative," I mean anyone traveling to Belize to teach, study, learn, volunteer, research, or work—instead of or in addition to traditional tourist activities. Following are a few options for alternative travel that I've come across—be sure to research more deeply on your own before committing. Some organizations offer full funding and support; others expect you to pay tuition to participate. For these, find out how much (if any) money you are expected to pay and, of that, how the money is divided between the community where you'll be working and the organization's overhead costs. Look for specific opportunities that may suit your skills and experience; check www.transitionsabroad.com. There are numerous other websites, magazines, and books that specialize in volunteering and studying abroad, including the author's home page and blog, www.joshuaberman.net.

Field Research and Educational Travel

Belize shines in this category. There are many opportunities to learn, teach, and volunteer at the **Belize Zoo and Tropical Education Center** (tel. 501/220-8004, www.belizezoo. org). The **Oceanic Society** (U.S. tel. 800/326-7491, www.oceanic-society.org), a nonprofit conservation organization, maintains a field station in the Turneffe Islands Atoll and invites curious travelers to participate in educational marine ecotourism activities, such as snorkel and kayak programs to learn about coral reef ecology and whale shark research projects (about US$2,000 includes everything for eight-day trips). The family program includes interaction with Belizean and American researchers.

Get involved with **ACES/American Crocodile Education Sanctuary** (tel. 501/666-3871 or 501/631-6366, acesnpo@ hughes.net, www.americancrocodilesanctuary.org), a nonprofit conservation organization licensed by the Belize Forest Department to protect Belize's critical habitats and protected species, especially *Crocodilians,* through scientific research and education. Anyone wishing to learn, observe, or help biologist Cherie Chenot-Rose collect data and conduct research is welcome, including students; 100 percent of their donations and proceeds go to croc care, croc rescues, research, and education.

WHAT TO TAKE

Pack for hot weather (80-95°F, both humid and dry), as well as the occasional cool front (60-80°F). At least one pair of **pants** and a **light shell jacket** are recommended, as rainy season can push all the way into February, and June through November it's guaranteed to be damp. **Long sleeves** are helpful for avoiding mosquito bites and sunburn. Cayo and the Mountain Pine Ridge can drop to sweater weather in any part of the wet season. Bring a small **first-aid kit, a flashlight or headlamp,** and **waterproof plastic bags** for protection during rain or boat travel.

REDUCE AND RE-USE THOSE PLASTIC BOTTLES

Consider the ecological footprint you leave in Belize after your vacation is over. Chances are that, after the jet fuel burned, your footprint's chief component is a huge pile of plastic water bottles. If you'd rather not contribute to Belize's volume of unnecessary solid waste (which, many agree, is the country's top environmental problem), think about ways to make that pile smaller. Do you order a new half-liter bottle with every meal instead of bringing your own larger one? Do you throw away every single bottle you buy, or do you refill them with purified water from the five-gallon jug in your hotel lobby? Consider bringing your own reusable water bottle to Belize and reduce that pile of trash to nothing but banana peels and mango pits. When reusing a plastic bottle, you'll want to disinfect it with a drop of bleach every couple of days (or ask your hosts to wash it with soap). Many health buffs say you should scrap the plastic altogether and only drink out of stainless steel water bottles.

Until 2000, beer and soda came in reusable glass bottles in Belize. That changed with the introduction of soft drinks in plastic bottles by the country's only major beverage distributor. Bowen & Bowen, Ltd. promised a recycling center to address the tonnage of plastic bottles bound to end up in landfills, along roads, and in the ocean, but has done little to make this happen.

Reports of plastic collection points and a Belizean recycling program come and go, though it is possible that someone is sending scraps to Mexico. Keep an eye out and follow the folks in Belize City with sacks of empties slung over their shoulders. Some businesses, especially in the Cayo District, refuse to sell plastic bottles at all until they can be properly disposed of or reused throughout Belize, as glass beer bottles still are. And no, drinking beer instead of water is not a sustainable solution.

Global Vision International (www.gvi-usa.com) offers 4- to 12-week opportunities around the country—assisting wildlife rangers at Cockscomb Basin Wildlife Sanctuary, conducting marine surveys for dive masters at Blue Hole and Half Moon Caye Natural Monuments, and assisting Institute of Archaeology staff in site management of archaeological reserves, including at Caracol.

Volunteer opportunities are also available at **Wildtracks** (tel. 501/614-8244, www.wildtracksbelize.org), which hosts both Belize's Manatee Rehabilitation Centre and Primate Rehabilitation Centre, in partnership with the Belize Forest Department. Volunteer placements are normally for one month or more, and volunteers need to apply in advance through Global Nomadic or Global Vision International.

The St. George's Caye Research Station & Field School was founded by ECOMAR in 2009. **ECOMAR** (17 Princess Margaret Dr. LF, P.O. Box 1234, Belize City, tel. 501/223-3022, www.ecomarbelize.org) hosts archaeology students and also high school and university professors interested in bringing their students to study marine ecosystems in the area. Other groups stay on St. George's Caye to participate in the Coral Watch Program and learn how to identify coral bleaching.

Want to be a behavioral ecologist or marine mammal biologist? Join Caryn Self-Sullivan, PhD (U.S. tel. 540/287-8207, caryns@sirenian.org), and her research team for two intense weeks of total immersion in the world of animal behavior, ecology and conservation, Antillean manatees, bottlenose dolphins, coral reefs, mangrove forests, and seagrass beds in Belize. Earn up to four credit hours during this total immersion field course where you will live, work, and study from a marine science field station on a pristine, private island off the coast of Belize (Spanish Bay Conservation & Research Center at Hugh Parkey's Belize Adventure Lodge, www.belizeadventurelodge.com, course is generally held in May of each year).

KEEPING THE "ECO" IN TOURISM

Belize is generally acknowledged as one of the world's freshest and most successful models of ecotourism. The word "ecotourism" was created in the 1980s with the best of intentions – ostensibly, to describe anything having to do with environmentally sound and culturally sustainable tourism. It was the "business" of preventing tourism from spoiling the environment and using tourism as an economic alternative to spoiling the environment for some other reason.

The success of the concept – and its marketing value – led to a worldwide surge in the usage of that prefix we know so well, even if its actual practice may sometimes fall short of original intentions. Indeed, "eco" has been used, abused, prostituted, and bastardized all over the world, and Belize is no exception. Some word-savvy tourism marketers have tried to freshen things up by using "alternative" or "adventure" tourism, but, when trying to describe an operation that practices the original definition of ecotourism mentioned above, I prefer "sustainable," "responsible," "ethical," or even "fair trade" tourism.

In 2009, Belize hosted the **Third Annual World Conference for Responsible Tourism.** The conference featured experts from around the world speaking on local economic development through tourism, the impact of mass tourism on local communities, and climate change.

The **Belize Eco-Tourism Association** (BETA, www.bzecotourism.org) and **Belize Audubon Society** (BAS, www.belizeaudubon.org) are two organizations concerned with keeping the "eco" in tourism – and in keeping pressure on the government of Belize to do the same. BETA was created on Earth Day in 1993 by a small group of members of the Belize Tourism Industry Association.

In Toledo District, the **Belize Foundation for Research and Environmental Education** (BFREE, www.bfreebz.org) offers student programs from one week to a whole semester, with lots of activities and cultural immersion programs available. BFREE has spearheaded amphibian research and monitoring in the Maya Mountains as a participant in the Maya Forest Anuran Monitoring Project, among other things. Also, the **Belize Rainforest Institute** (www.mayamountain.com) provides weeklong courses and workshops on such topics as rainforest ecology, butterflies, cultures of Belize, and ecotourism. You've also got the huge array of research and educational programs at **Monkey Bay Wildlife Sanctuary** (tel. 501/820-3032, www.monkeybaybelize.org), which specializes in groups and classes.

Look up the summer workshops and other educational trips offered by **International Zoological Expeditions** (U.S. tel. 800/548-5843, www.ize2belize.com); they've got bases and considerable experience in South Water Caye and Toledo District.

Programme for Belize (1 Eyre St., Belize City, tel. 501/227-5616, U.S. tel. 617/259-9500, www.pfbelize.org) is the group that manages the 260,000-acre Río Bravo Conservation Area and has a full menu of ecology and rainforest workshops.

Two miles upriver from the village of San Pedro Columbia, in southern Belize, the **Maya Mountain Research Farm** (www.mmrfbz.org) is a registered NGO and working demonstration farm that promotes sustainable agriculture, appropriate technology, and food security using permacultural principles and applied biodiversity, and it offers hands-on coursework in all of the above.

Maya Study and Archaeological Field Work

For Mayaphiles and archaeology students, the **Belize Valley Archaeology Reconnaissance Project** (BVAR, www.bvar.org) conducts research and offers field schools at several sites in western Belize. Expect BVAR and other organizations to be offering a host of opportunities throughout 2012, at which academics, researchers, archaeologists, and other professionals from around the world will present the teachings of the Maya.

Volunteer Opportunities

There are many opportunities for volun-tourists to get their feet wet in the world of international development and resource conservation work throughout Belize. Some regional chapters throughout this book offer local volunteer opportunities or ways to help the community. For those interested in spending some time lending a hand, sharing their expertise, or supporting community efforts, there's plenty to choose from. Some of these programs cost money and some don't; be sure you know exactly what you're getting into when you sign up. Also, be clear on what kind of work your position will entail, as well as your host organization's expectations and Belizean legal requirements. Speaking of which, Belizean immigration officially requires long-term volunteers to apply for special visas, a process that takes months and is not cheap. Some NGOs get around this (for short-term assignments, anyway) by calling their volunteers "interns."

The **Belize Audubon Society** (BAS, www.belizeaudubon.org) accepts qualified volunteers and interns for a variety of land and marine projects, with a three-month minimum (less for marine). Past skilled BAS volunteers have worked in community education; helped create trail signs, brochures, and management guidelines for protected areas and wardens; and analyzed the effectiveness of BAS gift shops. **Habitat for Humanity Belize** (tel. 501/227-6818), a world leader in providing low-income housing, operates in Belize City and beyond and accepts qualified volunteers and church groups to help erect home projects.

Cayo-based **Pro-Belize** (tel. 501/601-9121, www.myproworld.org) is part of ProWorld, an international placement organization that offers study and volunteer abroad experiences from two weeks to six months or longer. Your weekly tuition covers room, board, work

---

GETTIN' HITCHED AND HONEYMOONIN'

Belize's reputation for romance is growing, and an increasing number of resorts cater to exotic weddings and honeymoon packages, including ceremonies conducted underwater, atop Maya pyramids, or in caves. Actually, I don't think anyone's been married in a cave yet, but someone's bound to do it. Most couples, however, are quite content with a bare-foot beach ceremony.

For a US$50 marriage license, the couple must arrive in Belize three business days before submitting marriage paperwork to the Registrar General's office on the fourth business day. A rush job costs US$250 and allows you to obtain your marriage license before arriving in Belize, in which case you can get married on your first day in country, if you so wish. For this service, you'll need a travel agent or wedding planner to act on your behalf in Belize.

The **Registrar General of Belize** (tel. 501/227-2053, www.belizelaw.org) handles marriage licenses. You'll need to show proof of citizenship (i.e., a valid passport), proof that you're over 18, and, where applicable, a certified copy of a divorce certificate or death decree to annul a previous marriage. Forms can be obtained at two locations: the General Registry, Supreme Court Building, Belize City and the Solicitor General's Office, East Block Building, Belmopan. No blood test is required.

A few select Belize wedding specialists can help you facilitate the paperwork, find ministers, and handle your party's flowers, accommodations, receptions, and everything else. Contact **Iraida Gonzales** on San Pedro (www.belizeweddings.com), **Lee Nyhus** in Placencia (www.secretgardenplacencia.com), and **Katie Valk**, who provides services anywhere in the country (www.belize-trips.com).

TRAVEL SPECIALISTS AND TOUR COMPANIES

BELIZE TRAVEL SPECIALISTS

More than a travel agent, not quite a tour operator, Belize country specialists are small, independent operations that work directly with their clients to arrange all kinds of niche, group, and solo travel within Belize. There is usually no charge for their services, so you really can't go wrong by letting them handle some of the planning and booking. **Belize Trips** (tel. 501/610-1923, U.S. tel. 561/210-7015, www.belize-trips.com) helps you arrange active itineraries, weddings, and honeymoons, and can book you at the best mid- to upscale accommodations in the country. Owner Katie Valk finds out exactly what kind of experience her clients want and then, through her vast network of friends and colleagues across the country, makes that experience happen. Katie is a self-described "music business refugee from New York City" who has lived full time in Belize for 20-odd years, and you'll often find her swinging a machete through the bush or paddling her kayak as she seeks out and test-drives every adventure she promotes.

Barb's Belize (U.S. tel. 888/321-2272, www. barbsbelize.com) is another small operation that offers custom itineraries for any budget, from backpacker to decadent. Barb's specializes in unique interests such as traditional herbal medicine, jungle survival, and extreme adventure expeditions. She charges US$50 for her planning services and advice, which she credits to your invoice if you book through her.

ADVENTURE TRAVEL

Dangriga- and Vancouver-based **Island Expeditions** (U.S. tel. 800/667-1630, www.islandexpeditions.com) has been leading exciting sea kayaking, rafting, ruins, nature, and snorkeling adventures in Belize since 1987. It's a very experienced and professional outfit, and they have stunning island camps in Glover's Reef and Lighthouse Reef Atolls with canvas-wall platform tents. They also offer popular lodge-to-lodge sea kayaking trips and inland river adventures, and can help you outfit your own kayak expedition.

Slickrock Adventures (U.S. tel. 800/390-5715, www.slickrock.com), based on their primitively plush camp on a private island in Glover's Reef Atoll, offers paddling trips of various lengths and specializes in sea kayaking, windsurfing, and inland activities like mountain biking.

With decades of experience as a premier land operator in Belize, **International Expeditions** (U.S. tel. 800/633-4734, belize@ietravel.com, www.ietravel.com) has a full-time office in Belize City. They offer group and independent nature travel in sturdy, comfortable vehicles and are staffed by travel and airline specialists, naturalists, and an archaeologist. Trips run 7-14 days with two- and three-day add-ons available.

You'll also find an interesting menu of tours offered by **Intrepid Travel** (tel. 800/970-7299, intrepidtravel.com), an Australian company that runs trips around the world and has a

---

placement, donation, and weekend excursions. The work in Belize can be in health, environment, micro-business, youth sports, fine arts, journalism, or women's issues. Semester-length courses are available.

In San Pedro, **Green Reef** (100 Coconut Dr., San Pedro Town, tel. 501/226-2833, www.greenreefbelize.org) is a nonprofit conservation organization that works to protect Belize's barrier reef and associated environment; they're always interested in hearing from

potential volunteers, especially those who have skills in web design, photography, fund-raising, community outreach, and environmental education.

Itzamna Society (tel. 501/820-4023, www.epnp.org) is based in San Antonio, Cayo District, and was set up "for the protection and conservation of the environment and cultural patrimony" of the local Maya community and national park.

The **Belize Botanic Gardens** (www.

dozen trips that include Belize, some Maya-themed.

TOUR OPERATORS

For those interested in letting someone else do the driving (and planning, booking, etc.), various tour operators are reliable. In Belize City, Sarita and Lascelle Tillet of **S & L Travel and Tours** (91 N. Front St., tel. 501/227-7593 or 501/227-5145, www.sltravelbelize.com) operate as a husband/wife team. They drive late-model air-conditioned sedans or vans and travel throughout the country with airport pickup available. The Tillets have designed several great special-interest vacations and will custom design to your interests, whether they be the Maya archaeological zones (including Tikal), the cayes, or the caves and the countryside.

InnerQuest Adventures (www.innerquest.com) has over 14 years of experience leading wildlife-viewing trips with local guides around the country. They've been featured in dozens of magazines. Minnesota-based **Magnum Belize Tours** (U.S. tel. 800/447-2931, www.magnumbelize.com) is one of the biggest, most longstanding tour operators, with an extensive network of resorts across the country; the staff is very experienced and can customize every aspect of your trip.

Sea & Explore (U.S. tel. 800/345-9786, www.seaexplore.com) is run by owners Sue and Tony Castillo, native Belizeans who take pleasure and pride in sharing their country

with visitors by the means of customized trips. They know every out-of-the-way destination and make every effort to match clients with the right areas of the country to suit their interests. Susan worked with the Belize Tourism Board prior to coming to the United States.

Mary Dell Lucas of **Far Horizons Archaeological and Cultural Trips** (U.S. tel. 800/552-4575, www.farhorizon.com) is known throughout the Maya world for her excellent archaeological knowledge and insight. Her company provides trips into the most fascinating Maya sites, regardless of location. Although Mary is an archaeologist herself, she often brings specialists along with her groups.

Also check **Jaguar Adventures Tours and Travel** (4 Fort St., tel. 501/223-6025, www.jaguarbelize.com), located in Belize City and offering night walks at the Belize Zoo, cave tubing trips, visits to Maya ruins, snorkeling the reef, and diving the atolls, to name a few adventures.

Belize Travel Representatives (www.belizetravelrepresentatives.com) specializes in tour packages to the cayes, Placencia, and most of the mainland resorts and lodges. They also have some of the most extensive archaeological-themed tours in Belize. Contact **The Mayan Traveler** (www.themayantraveler.com, tel. 888/843-6292 or 713/299-5665); they can satisfy even the most serious temple junkie, going to some of the most spectacular sites in the region.

---

belizebotanic.org) sponsors a program where volunteers pay US$550 for room and board while working on various garden projects.

The **Cornerstone Foundation** (tel. 501/824-2373, www.peacecorner.org/cornerstone.htm) is a humanitarian NGO based in the Cayo District, whose volunteer opportunities include HIV/AIDS education and awareness, special education, adult literacy, working with youth or women, and teaching business skills.

Teachers for a Better Belize (TFABB,

www.tfabb.org) is a partnership of educators from North America and Belize who volunteer their time to improve the training of Belizean teachers and the education of children in rural Toledo villages. During summers, TFABB invites 5–10 experienced North American K–8 teachers to Belize for 1–2 weeks to partner with Belizean teachers in presenting lessons at a teacher-training workshop in Punta Gorda. Every few years, they also need construction volunteers (no experience necessary). TFABB accepts donations of children's storybooks to ship to Belize.

Trekforce Belize (8 Saint Mark St., Belize City, tel. 501/223-1442, www.trekforce.org.uk) offers challenging conservation, community, and research trips from two weeks to five months long, including "jungle survival," Spanish school in Guatemala, and a teaching assignment in a rural Belizean school.

Aspiring organic farmers will want to check up on the few Belize listings for the **World Wide Opportunities on Organic Farms** (www.wwoof.org) network, which at last check had five independent host opportunities in Belize. You can often work on the farm in exchange for room and board, but conditions vary from site to site. **Barton Creek Outpost** in Cayo (bartoncreekoutpost.com) offers other kinds of work/trade opportunities to stay in this backpacker's paradise.

Sustainable Harvest International's **Smaller World Program** (U.S. tel. 207/669-8254, shi@sustainableharvest.org, www.sustainableharvest.org) has an office in Punta Gorda, where they coordinate sustainable agriculture projects with 100 area farmers. SHI offers service trips for groups, staying in rustic homestays or the relatively upscale Cotton Tree Lodge. Typical service trips for volunteers are 10 days long and include side trips to natural and cultural sites. Some projects they've done include organic gardens, multistory cacao and coffee plots, composting latrines, organic fertilizers and pesticides, biodigestors, and wood-conserving stoves. In Belize, the trips include sustainable chocolate tours and family voluntourism trips.

U.S. Peace Corps

The Peace Corps (www.peacecorps.gov) is a U.S. government program created by John F. Kennedy in 1961, whose original goal was to improve America's image in the Third World by sending volunteers deep into the countryside of developing countries. Fifty years later, some 8,000 volunteers are serving in more than 70 countries around the world. Accepted participants serve a two-year tour preceded by three months of intensive language and cultural training in the host country; they receive a bare-bones living allowance and earn a nominal "readjustment allowance" at the completion of their service.

The first group of Peace Corps volunteers arrived in Belize in 1962. Since that time, more than 1,700 volunteers have worked in Belize in a variety of projects. Currently, there are about 70 volunteers providing assistance in education, youth development, rural community development, environmental education, and HIV/AIDS prevention. Pre-service training is conducted in rural Creole and mestizo villages and includes Spanish, Q'eqchi', and Garifuna language classes, depending on where the volunteer is being sent. Volunteers are placed throughout the country's six districts to work with government agencies and NGOs.

SPECIAL CONCERNS
Travelers with Children

Children love Belize and Belizeans love children. At least, this was my experience the last time I traveled with my family; the Belizeans we met couldn't get enough of my 9-month-old daughter, Shanti. For one, she was snatched away by every one of our restaurant servers, allowing us to eat in peace while Shanti and the restaurant staff entertained one another.

A select few romantic resorts do not allow children, but most do. Any place offering a special "family package" is a place to start your research. Always check in advance and tell the staff the ages of your children. You'll find most resorts are quite experienced at dealing with all ages.

For babies, be prepared with your own travel kit, but don't stress it too much if you forget something. There is a modern selection of jarred food, diapers, bottles, formula, and the like at Brodie's supermarkets in Belize City. If you're short on jars, or if baby wants more than breast milk, you'll find enough fresh fruit and fish to keep your baby growing the whole time you're in Belize. A few resorts can provide a crib in your room if you want one, but make sure you verify this in advance; otherwise bring

© JOSHUA BERMAN

It's easy to travel with children in Belize, especially when they're still portable.

the country. You'll meet many fellow travelers at the small inexpensive inns and guesthouses. Belizeans are used to seeing all combinations of travelers; solo women are no exception.

That said, sexual harassment of females traveling alone or in small groups can be a problem, although most incidents are limited to no more than a few catcalls. Just keep on walking; usually, some minor acknowledgment that you have heard them will shut harassers up more quickly than totally ignoring them. Although violent sexual assault is not a common occurrence, it does occur (like anywhere in the world). Several American travelers were the victims of sexual assaults in recent years. At least one of these rapes occurred after the victim accepted a ride from a new acquaintance, while another occurred during an armed robbery at an isolated resort. Never give the name of your hotel or your room number to someone you don't know.

Wearing revealing clothes *will* attract lots of gawking attention, possibly more than you want. Most of the small towns and villages are safe even at night, with the exception of Belize City—don't walk anywhere there at night, even with friends.

A few international tour companies specialize in trips for independent, active women. For "uncommon advice for the independent woman traveler," pick up a copy of Thalia Zepatos's *A Journey of One's Own* (Eighth Mountain Press), a highly acclaimed women's travel resource.

your own fold-up contraption, which can be great for the beach too, especially since you can easily drape a mosquito net over the top.

Once in Belize, a visit to the zoo is a must. There are a few kid-friendly cave trips, and, of course, scrambling on the pyramids at any of the archaeological sites is heaven for young explorers. Just be extra careful about covering them up with loose, long clothing against the sun and mosquitoes, and make sure they stay hydrated while they rage through the jungle. Also, during the rainy season, it's best to steer clear of river activities like cave tubing, since rivers can be unpredictable when they swell with rain.

Women Travelers

For the independent woman, Belize is a great place for group or solo travel. Its size makes it easy to get around, English is spoken everywhere, and if you so desire, you won't be lacking for a temporary travel partner in any part of

Senior Travelers

Active seniors enjoy Belize. Some like the tranquility of the cayes, others the bird-watching in the Maya ruins. Many come to learn about the jungle and its creatures or about archaeology. **Elderhostel** (U.S. tel. 877/426-8056, www.elderhostel.org) has a number of tours to Belize, including dolphin and reef ecology projects.

Gay and Lesbian Travelers

Although there are plenty of out-and-about gay Belizean men (in Kriol, "Batty-Men" or "Benque Boys"), there is no established community or any gay clubs, per se. The foreign gay travelers we've seen were totally accepted by both their fellow lodge guests and Belizean hosts. Still, the act of "sodomy" (between men) is officially illegal in Belize, so a bit of discretion is advised.

Travelers with Disabilities

There are probably about as many wheelchair ramps in all of Belize as there are traffic lights (three); disabled travelers will generally be treated with respect, but expect logistics to be a bit challenging in places. **Experience Belize Tours** (tel. 501/225-2981, U.S. tel. 205/383-2921, www.experiencebelizetours.com) offers wheelchair-accessible tours for seniors, slow walkers, and disabled travelers. You can also try **Belize Special Tours** (tel. 501/600-4284 or 501/824-4748, belizeanlove@yahoo.com), catering specifically to travelers with disabilities, which offers tours of the Belize Zoo, Belize City, and the Altun Ha ruins. Hok'ol K'in Guest House in Corozal and Red Jaguar Lodge in San José Succotz both have nice wheelchair-accessible suites and facilities. There is also a "Belize disabled travel holiday" listed on responsibletravel.com.

CAMERAS AND PHOTOGRAPHY

Cameras can be a help or hindrance when trying to get to know the locals. When traveling in the backcountry, you'll run into folks who don't want their pictures taken. Keep your camera put away until the right moment. *Always* ask permission first, and if someone doesn't want his or her picture taken, accept the refusal with a gracious smile and move on. Especially sensitive to this are Mennonites and Mayans, who often specifically request that you not take their photos.

Many Internet cafés have readers for your digital camera card, so you can make CD backups as you go. To be safe, travel with extra cards, readers, and cables.

Underwater Photography

Most travelers use disposable underwater cameras, which may have depth limits, but if you're looking to publish something in *Dive Fever* magazine, you'll need a bit more under the hood. Some hotels, resorts, and shops in Belize rent underwater DSRL cameras or housings for your own camera. Don't expect a large selection. A strobe or flash is a big help if shooting in deep water or into caves. Natural-light pictures are great if you're shooting in fairly shallow water. It's best to shoot on an eye-to-eye level when photographing fish. Be careful of stirring up silt from the bottom with your fins and try to hold very still when depressing the shutter; if you must stabilize yourself, *don't* grab onto any live coral—you will kill it and you may hurt yourself as well.

Health and Safety

BEFORE YOU GO
Resources

Staying Healthy in Asia, Africa, and Latin America, by Dirk G. Schroeder (Avalon Travel Publishing, 2000), is an excellent and concise guide to preventative medicine in the developing world and small enough to fit in your pack. Same goes for *The Pocket Doctor: A Passport to Healthy Travel,* by Stephen Bezruchka (Mountaineers Books, 1999). A bit more unwieldy but a standard in the field is David Werner's *Where There Is No Doctor* (Hesperian Foundation, 1992).

For up-to-date health recommendations and advice, consult the "Mexico and Central America" page of the U.S. Centers for Disease Control and Prevention (CDC) at www.cdc.gov/travel/camerica.htm, or call their International Travelers Hotline at 404/332-4559 or 877/394-8747. Another excellent resource is the Belize page of www.mdtravelhealth.com. You can also call the Belizean embassy in your country for up-to-date information about outbreaks or other health problems.

STAYING HEALTHY

Ultimately, your health is dependent on the choices you make, and chief among these is what you decide to put in your mouth. Expect your digestive system to take some time getting accustomed to the new food and microorganisms in the Belizean diet. During this time (and after), use common sense: wash your hands with soap often; alcohol-based hand sanitizers are less effective at removing germs from your hands. Eat food that is well cooked and still hot when served. Be wary of uncooked foods, including shellfish and salads.

Most importantly, be aware of flies, the single worst transmitter of food-borne illnesses. Prevent flies from landing on your food, glass, or table setting. You'll notice Belizeans are meticulous about this, and you should be too. If you have to leave the table, cover your food with a napkin or have someone else wave a hand over it slowly.

Drinking the Water

Even though most municipal water systems are well treated and probably safe, there is not much reason to take the chance, especially when purified bottled water is so widely available and relatively cheap. Canned and bottled drinks, including beer, are usually safe, but should never be used as a substitute for water when trying to stay hydrated, especially during a bout of traveler's diarrhea or when out in the sun.

If you plan on staying awhile in a rural area of Belize, check out camping catalogs for water filters that remove chemical as well as biological contamination. Alternatively, six drops of liquid iodine (or three of bleach) will kill everything that needs to be killed in a liter of water—good in a pinch (or on a backcountry camping trip), but not something you'll find yourself practicing on a daily basis. Also, bringing any water to a full boil is 100 percent effective in killing bacteria.

Oral Rehydration Salts

Probably the single most effective preventative and curative medicine you can carry is packets of powdered salt and sugar, which, when mixed with a liter of water (drink in small sips), is the best immediate treatment for dehydration due to diarrhea, sun exposure, fever, infection, or hangover. Particularly in the case of diarrhea, rehydration salts are essential to your recovery. They replace the salts and minerals your body has lost due to liquid evacuation (be it from sweating, vomiting, or urinating), and they're essential to your body's most basic cellular transfer functions. Whether or not you like the taste (odds are you won't), consuming enough rehydration packets and water is very often the difference between being just a little sick and feeling really, really awful.

Sport drinks like Gatorade are super-concentrated mixtures and should be diluted with water to make the most of the active ingredients. If you don't, you'll pee out the majority of the electrolytes. Rehydration packets are available from any drugstore or health clinic. They can also be improvised, according to the following recipe: mix a half teaspoon of salt, a half teaspoon baking soda, and four tablespoons of sugar in one quart of boiled or carbonated water. Drink a full glass of the stuff after each time you use the bathroom. Add a few drops of lemon juice to make it more palatable.

Sun Exposure

Belize is located a scant 13–18 degrees of latitude from the equator, so the sun's rays strike the earth's surface at a more direct angle than in northern countries. The result is that you will burn faster and sweat up to twice as much as you are used to. Did we mention that you should drink lots of water?

Ideally, do like the majority of the locals do, and stay out of the sun between 10 A.M. and 2 P.M. It's a great time to take a nap anyway. Use sunscreen of at least SPF 30, and wear a hat and pants. Should you overdo it in the sun, make sure to drink lots of fluids—that means water, not beer (or at least water and beer). Treat sunburns with aloe gel, or better yet, find a fresh aloe plant to break open and rub over your skin.

DISEASES AND COMMON AILMENTS

Diarrhea and Dysentery

Generally, simple cases of diarrhea in the absence of other symptoms are nothing more serious than "traveler's diarrhea." If you do get a good case, your best bet is to let it pass naturally. Diarrhea is your body's way of flushing out the bad stuff, so constipating medicines like Imodium A-D are not recommended, as they keep the bacteria (or whatever is causing your intestinal distress) within your system. Save the Imodium (or any other liquid glue) for emergency situations like long bus rides or a hot date. Most importantly, drink lots of water! Not replacing the fluids and electrolytes you are losing will make you feel much worse than you need to. If the diarrhea persists for more than 48 hours, is bloody, or is accompanied by a fever, see a health professional immediately. That said, know that all bodies react differently to the changes in diet, schedule, and stress that go along with traveling, and many visitors to Belize stay entirely regular and solid throughout their trips.

Pay attention to your symptoms: Diarrhea can also be a sign of amoebic (parasitic) or bacillic (bacterial) dysentery, both caused by some form of fecal-oral contamination. Often accompanied by nausea, vomiting, and a mild fever, dysentery is easily confused with other diseases, so don't try to self-diagnose. Stool-sample examinations are cheap, can be performed at most clinics and hospitals, and are your first step to getting better. Bacillic dysentery is treatable with antibiotics; amoebic is treated with one of a variety of drugs that kill off all the flora in your intestinal tract. Of these, Flagyl is the best known, but other non-FDA-approved treatments like tinidazole are commonly available, cheap, and effective. Do not drink alcohol with these drugs, and eat something like yogurt or acidophilus pills to refoliate your tummy.

Malaria

By all official accounts, malaria is present in Belize, although you'll be hard-pressed to find anybody—Belizean or expat—who has actually experienced or even heard of a case of it. Still, many travelers choose to take a weekly prophylaxis of chloroquine or its equivalent. The CDC specifically recommends travelers to Belize to use brand-name Aralen pills (500 mg for adults), although you should ask your doctor for the latest drug on the market. A small percentage of people have negative reactions to chloroquine, including nightmares, rashes, or hair loss. Alternative treatments are available, but the best method of all is to not get bitten by mosquitoes, which transmit the disease.

Dengue Fever

Dengue, or "bone-breaking fever," is a flulike, mosquito-carried illness that will put a stop to your fun in Central America like a baseball bat to the head. Dengue's occurrence is extremely low in Belize, but a couple dozen cases are still reported each year. There is no vaccine, but dengue's effects can be successfully minimized with plenty of rest, Tylenol (for the fever and aches), and as much water and *hydration salts* as you can manage. Dengue itself is undetectable in a blood test, but a low platelet count indicates its presence. If you believe you have dengue, you should get a blood test as soon as possible, to make sure it's not the hemorrhagic variety, which can be fatal if untreated.

Ciguatera

This is a toxin occasionally found in large reef fish. It is not a common circumstance, but it is possible for grouper, snapper, and barracuda to carry this toxin. If after eating these fish you experience diarrhea, nausea, numbness, or heart arrhythmia, see a doctor immediately. The toxin is found in certain algae on reefs in all the tropical areas of the world. Fish do nibble on the coral, and if they happen to find this algae, over a period of time the toxin accumulates in their systems. The longer they live and the larger they get, the more probable it is they will carry the toxin, which is not destroyed when cooked.

Other Diseases

There is moderate incidence of hepatitis B in

Belize. Avoid contact with bodily fluids or bodily waste. Get vaccinated if you anticipate close contact with the local population or plan to reside in Central America for an extended period of time.

Get a rabies vaccination if you intend to spend a long time in Belize. Should you be bitten by an infected dog, rodent, or bat, immediately cleanse the wound with lots of soap, and get prompt medical attention.

Tuberculosis is spread by sneezing or coughing, and the infected person may not know he or she is a carrier. If you are planning to spend more than four weeks in Belize (or plan on spending time in the Belize jail), consider having a tuberculin skin test performed before and after visiting. Tuberculosis is a serious and possibly fatal disease but can be treated with several medications.

No cases of cholera have been reported in Belize since 2000.

BITES AND STINGS

Thousands of people dive in Belize's Caribbean and hike its forests every day of the year without incident. The information on possible bites and stings is only to let you know what's out there, not to scare you into remaining in your resort. Know what you're getting into and be sure your guide does as well, and then get into it.

Mosquitoes and Sand Flies

Mosquitoes are most active during the rainy season (June–Nov.) and in areas with stagnant water, like marshes, puddles, and rice fields. They are more common in the lower, flatter regions of Belize than they are in the hills, though even in the highlands, old tires, cans, and roadside puddles can provide the habitat necessary to produce swarms of mosquitoes. The mosquito that carries malaria is active during the evening and at night, while the dengue fever courier is active during the day, from dawn to dusk. They are both relatively simple to combat, and ensuring you don't get bitten is the best prophylaxis for preventing the diseases.

First and foremost, limit the amount of skin you expose—long sleeves, pants, and socks will do more to prevent bites than the strongest chemical repellent. Choose accommodations with good screens, and if this is not possible, use a fan to blow airborne insects away from your body as you sleep. Avoid being outside or unprotected in the hour before sunset, when mosquito activity is heaviest, and use a mosquito net tucked underneath your mattress when you sleep. Consider purchasing a lightweight backpackers' net, either freestanding or to hang from the ceiling, before you come south—mosquito nets are more expensive in Belize than at home. Some accommodations provide nets; others are truly free of biting bugs and don't need them. If you know where you're staying, ask before you arrive whether you'll need a net.

Once in Belize, you can purchase mosquito coils, which burn slowly, releasing a mosquito-repelling smoke; they're cheap and convenient, but try to place them so you're not breathing the toxic smoke yourself.

Sand flies don't carry any diseases that we know about, but, man, do they *suck!* Actually, these tiny midges, or no-see-ums, bite. Hard. They breed in wet, sandy areas and are only fought by the wind (or a well-screened room). Don't scratch those bites! For prevention, any thick oil is usually enough of a barrier—most people like baby oil or hempseed oil, and some swear that a hint of lavender scent in the oil keeps sand flies away too.

Scorpions, Spiders, and Snakes

Scorpions are common in Belize, especially in dark corners, at beaches, and in piles of wood. Belizean scorpions look nasty—black and big—but their stings are no more harmful than that of a bee and are described by some as what a cigarette burn feels like. Your lips and tongue may feel a little numb, but the venom is nothing compared to that of their smaller, translucent cousins in Mexico. Needless to say, to people who are prone to anaphylactic shock, it can be a more serious or life-threatening experience. Everyone has heard that when in a jungle, never put on your shoes without checking the insides—good advice—and always give your clothes a good visual going-over and a vigorous shake before putting them on. Scorpions occasionally drop out of thatch ceilings.

Don't worry; despite the prevalence of all kinds of arachnids, including big, hairy tarantulas, spiders do not aggressively seek out people to bite and do way more good than harm by eating things like Chagas bugs. If you'd rather the spiders didn't share your personal space, shake out your bedclothes before going to sleep and check your shoes before putting your feet in them.

Of the 59 species of snakes that have been identified in Belize, at least nine are venomous, most notably the fer-de-lance (locally called a "Tommygoff") and the coral snake. The chances of the average tourist being bitten are slim. Reportedly, most snakebite victims are children. However, if you plan on extensive jungle exploration, check with your doctor before you leave home. Antivenin is available, doesn't require refrigeration, and keeps indefinitely. It's also wise to be prepared for an allergic reaction to the antivenin—bring an antihistamine and epinephrine. The most important thing to remember if bitten: *Don't panic and don't run.* Physical exertion and panic cause the venom to travel through your body much faster. Lie down and stay calm; have someone carry you to a doctor. Do not cut the wound, use a tourniquet, or ingest alcoholic beverages.

Botfly

Worst. Souvenir. Ever. Also known as *torsalo,* screw-worm, or *Dermatobia hominis,* this insect looks like the common household fly. The big difference is that the botfly deposits its eggs on mosquitoes, which then implant them in an unsuspecting warm-blooded host. Burrowing quickly under the skin, the maggot sets up housekeeping. To breathe, it sticks a tiny tube through the skin, and there it stays until one of two things happen: you kill it, or it graduates and leaves home (to witness this, Google "botfly removal" and get ready for an eyeful).

A botfly bite starts out looking like a mosquito bite, but if the bite gets red and tender instead of healing, get it checked out. Though uncomfortable and distasteful, it's not a serious health problem if it doesn't get infected. A tiny glob of petroleum jelly or tobacco over the air hole often works to draw out or suffocate the creature; just make sure you squeeze all of it out.

Marine Hazards

Anemones and sea urchins live in Belize waters. Some can be dangerous if touched or stepped on. The long-spined black sea urchin can inflict great pain, and its poison can cause an uncomfortable infection. Don't think that you're safe in a wetsuit, booties, and gloves. The spines easily slip through the rubber and the urchin is encountered at all depths. If you should run into one of the spines, remove it quickly and carefully, disinfect the wound, and apply antibiotic cream. If you have difficulty removing the spine, or if it breaks, see a doctor—*pronto!* Local remedies include urinating on the wound if nothing else is available.

Tiny brown gel-encased globules called *picapica* produce a horrible rash; look for clouds of these guys around any coral patch before getting in. Avoid the bottom side of a moon jellyfish, as well as the Portuguese man-of-war (usually only in March). Sea wasps are tiny four-tentacled menaces that deliver a sting.

For the hundredth time, don't touch the coral! Many varieties of fire coral will make you wish you hadn't. Cuts from coral, even if just a scratch, will often become infected. If you should get a deep cut, or if bits of coral are left in the wound, see a doctor.

MEDICAL CARE

Although there are hospitals and health clinics in most urban areas and towns, care is extremely limited compared with more developed countries. Serious injuries or illness may require evacuation to another country, and you should consider picking up cheap travel insurance that covers such a need—otherwise, you're looking at US$12,000 just for the medevac transport.

Many Belizean doctors and hospitals

require immediate cash payment for health services, sometimes prior to providing treatment. Uninsured travelers or travelers whose insurance does not provide coverage in Belize may face extreme difficulties if serious medical treatment is needed. **International Medical Group** (www.imglobal.com) is one reliable provider that offers short-term insurance specifically for overseas travelers and expats for very reasonable rates.

Belize Medical Associates (5791 St. Thomas St., tel. 501/223-0302, 501/223-0303, or 501/223-0304, bzmedasso@btl.net, www.belizemedical.com) is the only private hospital in Belize City. They provide 24-hour assistance and a wide range of specialties. Look under "Hospitals" in the BTL yellow pages for an updated listing of other options. In San Ignacio, **La Loma Luz Hospital** (tel. 501/824-2087) offers primary care as well as 24-hour emergency services and is one of the best private hospitals in the country.

Medications and Prescriptions

Many medications are available in pharmacies in Belize. Definitely plan on the conservative side: Bring adequate supplies of all your prescribed medications in their original containers, clearly labeled and in date; in addition, carry a signed, dated letter from your physician describing all medical conditions and listing your medications, including their generic names. If carrying syringes or needles, carry a physician's letter documenting their medical necessity. Pack all medications in your carry-on bag and, if possible, put a duplicate supply in the checked luggage. If you wear glasses or contacts, bring an extra pair. If you have significant allergies or chronic medical problems, wear a medical alert bracelet.

Female travelers taking contraceptives should know the generic name for the drug they use. Condoms are cheap and easy to find. Any corner pharmacy will have them, even in small towns of just a few thousand people.

Bring a Small Medical Kit

At the very minimum, consider the following items for your first-aid kit: rehydration salts, sterile bandages/gauze, moleskin for blister prevention, antiseptic cream, strong sunblock (SPF 30), aloe gel, some kind of general antibiotic for intestinal trouble, acetaminophen (Tylenol) for pain/fevers, eyedrops (for dust), and antifungal cream (clotrimazole).

CRIME

Most of the crime in Belize (besides drug possession and trafficking) is petty theft and burglary, though gang-related violence in Belize City is a worsening problem.

Staying Safe

It's best not to wear expensive jewelry when traveling. And don't carry large amounts of money, your passport, or your plane tickets if not necessary; if you must carry these things, wear a money belt under your clothes. Most hotels have safe-deposit boxes. Don't flaunt cameras and video equipment or leave them in sight in cars when sightseeing, especially in some parts of Belize City. Remember, this is a poor country and petty theft is its number-one crime—don't tempt fate.

It is generally not wise to wander around alone on foot late at night in Belize City. Go out with others if possible, and take a taxi. Most Belizeans are friendly, decent people, but, as in every community, a small percentage of unscrupulous crackheads will steal anything, given the opportunity. To many Belizeans, foreigners come off as "rich," whether they are or not. The local hustlers are quite creative when it comes to thinking of ways to con you out of some cash. Keep your wits about you, pull out of conversations that appear headed in that direction, don't give out your hotel name or room number freely or where they can be overheard by strangers.

In emergencies, dial 911 or 90 for police assistance. The number for fire and ambulance is also 90.

If You Are Robbed

If you are the victim of a crime while overseas, in addition to reporting it to local police, contact your embassy or consulate as soon as possible. The embassy or consulate staff can, for example, assist you in finding appropriate medical care and contacting family members or friends and will explain how funds can be transferred to you. Although the investigation and prosecution of the crime is solely the responsibility of local authorities, consular officers can help you to understand the local criminal justice process and to find an attorney if needed. From my experience, Belize police detectives respond quickly and take these matters—even near misses—seriously.

Police

Belizean police can hold somebody for 48 hours with no charges; one U.S. embassy warden called prison conditions in Belize "medieval," though this situation is improving. Some police officers have been arrested for rape and routinely beat and torture detainees (usually Belizeans). On the whole, though, most officers are good folks, making the best of a poorly paying job with very few resources. Don't try to bribe them if you're in trouble—you'll only contribute to a more corrupt system that does not need any encouragement.

Illegal Drugs

Belize's modern history began with law-breaking pirates hiding out among the hundreds of cayes, lagoons, and uninhabited coastlines of the territory. The same natural features have made Belize a fueling stopover for Colombian cocaine traffickers. The drug runners' practice of paying off their Belizean helpers with product (in addition to irresistible sums of cash) has created a national market for cocaine and crack with devastating effects, especially in Orange Walk Town and numerous coastal communities.

According to the U.S. State Department, Colombian narcotraffickers increasingly use maritime operations in conjunction with aircraft "wet-drops" or off-loads from sea vessels to smuggle drug shipments into Belizean waters. Cocaine, air-dropped off the coast of Belize, is transported to the Belizean mainland

or Mexico by small "go-fast" boats, stored, and then shipped onward to the United States. Occasionally, unintended recipients find this "sea lotto." Also known as "square grouper" and "white lobster," these bales of uncut cocaine are also sometimes dumped overboard by traffickers who are about to get busted.

The U.S. Drug Enforcement Agency (DEA) is active in Belize—as it is throughout Central America—to battle the flow of cocaine and other illegal drugs; the agency provides boat patrols, overflights, drug war technology and herbicides, and sniffing dogs at roadside checkpoints.

Marijuana

Cannabis sativa, or ganja, grows naturally and quite well in the soils and climate of Belize, although the country is no longer the major producer it once was. In the early 1980s, "Belizean Breeze" was smuggled in massive enough quantities to make Belize the fourth-largest marijuana exporter to the United States. In the early 1980s, the DEA put an end to that with chemical-spraying programs, seizing and destroying 800 tons of marijuana in one year. Today, small-scale production continues, primarily for the domestic market. Some argue that the job vacuum created by marijuana suppression led directly to Belize's role in the trafficking of cocaine and the subsequent entrance of crack into Belizean communities.

Foreign, hip-looking tourists like yourself will most likely be offered pot (locally known as "ta-boom-boom") at some point during your visit. Be careful: The proposal may be a harmless invitation to get high on the beach, or it may be coming from a hustler or stool pigeon who is about to rip you off and/or get you arrested. Legally, marijuana prohibition is alive and well in Belize, despite widespread use of the herb throughout the population (not just among Rastas). The anti-ganja policy allows harsh penalties for possession of even tiny quantities for both nationals and tourists alike. Tightly wrapped nuggets of buds, usually under two grams, are referred to as "bullets," and possessing even one of these can bring a fine of hundreds of dollars and possible incarceration. Also, watch out for guys selling pre-rolled joints called *serias,* as they may be laced with crumbled crack cocaine.

Prostitution

Although illegal in Belize, the sale of sex is alive and well at a handful of brothels throughout the country, usually on the highways outside major towns. Prostitutes are rarely Belizean and are often indentured sex slaves unwittingly recruited from Honduras, Guatemala, or El Salvador with false promises of legitimate employment. It is undeniable that foreign johns contribute to Belize's sex economy, especially on cruise ship arrival days.

Information and Services

MONEY

Automated teller machines (ATMs) are available in nearly all major Belizean towns, but they may operate on different card networks (Plus, Cirrus, etc.), so you may have to try a few to get your card to work. They're also often out of order.

Currency

The currency unit is the Belize dollar (BZE$), which has been steady at BZE$2 to US$1 for some years. While prices are given in U.S. dollars in this book, travelers should be prepared to pay in Belizean currency on the street, aboard boats, in cafés, and at other smaller establishments. Everyone else accepts U.S. dollars.

When you buy or sell currency at a bank, be sure to retain proof of sale. The following places are authorized to buy or sell foreign currency: Atlantic Bank Ltd., Bank of Nova Scotia, Barclays Bank, Belize Bank of Commerce and Industry, and Belize Global Travel Services Ltd. All are close together near the plaza in Belize City and in other cities. Hours are till 1 P.M. Monday–Friday, till 11 A.M. Saturday. You can also change money, sometimes at a rate a bit better than 2:1, at Casas de Cambio. But because Casas de Cambio must charge the official rate, many people still go to the black market, which gives a better rate.

At the Mexico-Belize border, you'll be approached by money changers (and you can bet they don't represent the banks). Many travelers buy just enough Belize dollars to get themselves into the city and to the banks. Depending on your mode of transport and destination, these money changers can be helpful. Strictly speaking, though, this is illegal—so suit yourself. The exchange rate is the same, but you'll have no receipt of sale. If selling a large quantity of Belize dollars back to the bank, you might be asked for that proof.

Tipping

Most restaurants and hotels include a 10–15 percent service charge on the bill; if they don't, you should pay this amount yourself. It is not customary to tip taxi drivers unless they help you with your luggage. Always tip your tour guide 10–15 percent if he or she has made your trip an enjoyable one.

Costs

Make no mistake: Belize vies with Costa Rica for being the most expensive country in Central America, and backpackers entering Belize from Mexico, Guatemala, and Honduras can expect some serious sticker shock after crossing the border. This was true even before the advent of tourism, because of the import-reliant economy and whatever other invisible market hands guide such things. Shoestring travelers squeaking by on US$25–50 per person per day in Belize are most likely stone sober and eating street tacos three times a day; they are not paying for tours or taxis, and they are surely not diving in the Blue Hole. They can still have a grand old time though, camped out in the bush (or in a US$10 room), doing lots of self-guided hiking, paddling, and cultural exploring. It's possible to travel on this little—but it depends on your comfort zone and definition of a good time.

If you've only got a seven-day vacation, you won't have to stretch your dollars over as many weeks or months as Jimmie Backpacker and his dog, Dreddie, and can thus spend more on lodging and activities. Figure at least US$100 per person per day if you want to pay for day trips and don't want to share a bathroom; serious divers or anglers should add a bit more. Weeklong packages at many dive and jungle resorts run US$1,000–US$1,600 and go up from there.

There are usually low-budget, decent quality exceptions to the rule across Belize, and I've tried to point all of those out in each region. In general though, prices are high and getting higher. Many mid- and upscale accommodations have raised their rates by as much as 20–40 percent since the last edition of *Moon Belize*—and not all have increased the quality of their service to match. Alcohol is always a good indicator: A bottle of One Barrel Rum is peaking at US$12 in most stores; a six-pack of Belikin beer can go for US$10.

Be prepared for some additional taxes and service charges on your bill, which sometimes are and sometimes are not included in quoted rates:

- General sales tax (GST): 10 percent
- Hotel tax: 9 percent
- Service charge (often placed on bill): 10–15 percent
- Airport departure tax: US$20

If you use your credit card, it will cost you a little more at most businesses, sometimes an extra 3–5 percent of the bill.

Bank Hours

Many banks are only open till 1 P.M. or 2 P.M. Monday–Thursday (staying open a bit later on Fridays), are often closed for lunch, and are always closed Saturday afternoons and Sundays.

TIME, WEIGHTS, AND MEASURES

The local time is Greenwich mean time minus six, the same as U.S. central time, year-round (there is no daylight saving time). The electricity is standard 110/220 volt, 60 cycles. Most distances are measured in inches, feet, yards, and miles, although there is some limited use of the metric system.

COMMUNICATIONS AND MEDIA
Mail

Posting a letter or postcard is easy and cheap, costing well under US$1, and the stamps are gorgeous. If you visit the outlying cities or cayes, bring your mail to Belize City to post—it's more apt to get to its destination quickly.

Post offices are located in the center of (or nearby) all villages and cities in Belize, although they usually don't look too post-officey from the outside. You can receive mail in any town without getting a P.O. Box—just have the mail addressed to your name, care of "General Delivery," followed by the town, district, and "Belize."

FedEx, DHL, and other international couriers are widely available, and the Mailboxes, Etc. in Belize City (on Front St., just up from the Water Taxi Terminal) can take care of most of your mailing and package needs.

Sending mail within Belize, you can use either the post office system or hand your package to a bus driver or go through the bus station office.

Public Telephones

Buy a prepaid phone card from Belize Telecommunications Limited (BTL) and punch in the card's numbers every time you borrow a phone or use a pay phone. All towns also have a local BTL office, usually identified by a giant red and white radio tower somewhere very nearby; they can place calls anywhere in the country or world for you and will assign you to a semiprivate booth after they've dialed the number. They can also connect you to your homeland phone carrier. See www.btl.net for more information.

It's cheap to mail postcards; find the local post office and send a few home.

One reader gave the following warning: "*Do not* use the blue and yellow plastic hotel phones for international calls! I was charged US$42 for a one-minute phone call not once, but twice for the same call! After visiting BTL offices in Belize City, San Ignacio, and Punta Gorda, I could not get a refund, and the company claimed to have no record of the transaction (even though my credit-card company surely did)." According to a BTL employee, credit-card calls made through these phones are so expensive because the touch-tone "international operator" charges US$16 per minute.

Cell Phones

Some car rental companies offer a free cell phone; always ask. If not, they'll rent you one. Otherwise, **DigiCell** (www.digicell.bz) offers prepaid temporary service to tourists. Get it at BTL's Airport Service Center, or bring your own GSM 1900 MHz handset and purchase a SIM pack from any DigiCell distributor nationwide. There are several local cellular services, both analog and digital, and coverage

along roadways and in major towns is decent but still improving.

Smart Phones (Mile 1½ Northern Hwy. in Belize City, tel. 501/280-1010, www.smart-bz.com) is more user-friendly and cheaper than BTL and the rest, offering roaming service on your CDMA 800 MHz phone from home (including Verizon and Sprint). Activation fee is US$20, then you use prepaid cards available throughout the country.

International Calls

To call out of Belize, find a phone with international direct dialing service, then dial the international access code 00, followed by your country code, and then the city or area code and the number. The country code for Canada and the United States is 1 and England's is 44. Australia is 61. BTL's telephone directory has a complete listing of country codes. An (often cheaper) alternative is to dial 10-10-199 instead of 00, followed by your country code, etc. Although they are not toll-free from Belize, 800 numbers are dialed as they are written, preceded by the 00.

USEFUL NUMBERS

- Police, fire, ambulance: 90 or 911

- Directory assistance: 113 or 115

- To report crimes: 0/800-922-8477

- To report child abuse: 0/800-776-8328

- Operator assistance: 114 or 115

- Date, time, and temperature: 121

Belize's country code is 501. To receive a call in Belize from the United States, for example, tell the caller to dial 011 to tap into the international network, followed by 501 and your seven digit number. To call collect to Belize from other countries, dial the MCI operator at 800/265-5328.

VOIPs

Some Internet cafés have found ways around BTL's efforts to block VOIPs (voice over Internet protocols), while some haven't, so VOIP services are still not 100 percent reliable in Belize. Free VOIPs (like Skype) offer dirt-cheap rates on international calls and are getting better to use by the day. If you have a laptop, be sure to install some sort of VPN (virtual private network) to encrypt the data coming in and out of your computer, thus bypassing BTL's VOIP jams. Feel free to join the "Unblock Skype in Belize" Facebook group.

Internet Access

Web access is widely available throughout the country and is improving all the time. Crappy dial-up connections are now the exception rather than the norm, and broadband (DSL, cable, and satellite) is springing up everywhere. If you're in town for a while, many Internet businesses have monthly memberships that include unlimited access. You are welcome to sign up for a BTL account if you don't have your own ISP (Internet service provider), but that may lead to more headaches then you need, and there are many other options.

Wireless Internet (Wi-Fi) access is increasingly available in Belize's accommodations, bars, and restaurants. I won't go so far as to tell you to *expect* wireless access yet, but if it's a concern of yours, definitely inquire whether your hotel has it or not. Most of these connections are free—with the exception of BTL Hotspots, which are US$16 per 24-hour period (plus tax!), and it's your only option at a handful of upscale hotels, including the Radisson and the Inn at Robert's Grove.

Local Newspapers and Magazines

Four weekly, highly politicized Belizean newspapers come out on Fridays, with occasional midweek editions, and you'll find many a Belizean conducting the weekly ritual of reading his favorite over a cup of instant coffee, and then going to happy hour to yap away about the latest scandal. *Amandala* and the *Reporter* seem to be the most objective and respected of these rags. The other two are *The Belize Times* and *The Guardian*. There are also publications in San Pedro and Placencia.

The Image Factory in Belize City is a good place for books and periodicals, and there are only a couple of other book shops in the country. In most hotel gift shops, you'll find at least a few colorful Belizean history and picture books put out by Cubola Productions, a local publisher specializing in all things Belize, including maps, atlases, short stories, novels, and poems written by Belizeans. Cubola's publications give great insight into the country.

Foreign News

You will not find the *International Herald Tribune* on every newsstand like in other destinations. In fact, you probably won't find it at all. Check with the Radisson Hotel or Fort Street Guest House in Belize City, where you can sometimes find the *Miami Herald,* a relatively recent *Newsweek,* or if you're lucky, the *New York Times* or *London Times.* **Brodie's** and **The Book Center** also carry American magazines.

Maps

The most readily available and up-to-date map to Belize is published by International Travel Maps, whose 1:250,000 map of Belize makes a useful addition to any guidebook (or wall). The best, biggest country map to hang on your wall at home, or in your classroom (it's way too big to use as a travel guide) is a physical/political 1:265,000 scale, distributed by Cubola Productions and available at Angelus Press in Belize City for US$40.

All of Belize's most heavily touristed areas create updated town maps, found most often at tourist information booths and car (or golf cart) rental places.

The **Government of Belize Land Department** in Belmopan has detailed topographic maps for the entire country—spendy at US$40 per quad, but vital if you're doing any serious backcountry travel. The British Army and United Kingdom Ordinance Survey have created a number of map series of various scales, but tracking them down will be a challenge.

Tourist Information

The **Belize Tourism Board** (BTB, 64 Regent St., tel. 501/227-2420, U.S. tel. 800/624-0686, info@travelbelize.org, www.travelbelize.org) has a central office in Belize City, near the Mopan Hotel. The **Belize Tourism Industry Association** (10 N. Park St., tel. 501/227-5717 or 501/223-3507, www.btia.org) can also answer many of your questions and give you lodging suggestions. **The Belize Hotel Association** (BHA, 13 Cork St., Belize City, tel. 501/223-0669, www.belizehotels.org) is a nonprofit, nongovernmental organization of some of the country's most respected resorts and lodges. The BHA can help you decide where to stay.

You'll find more information at the **Embassy of Belize** in the United States (2535 Massachusetts Ave. NW, Washington, D.C. 20008, U.S. tel. 202/332-9636, www.embassyofbelize.org) and also the **Caribbean Tourism Association** (20 E. 46th St., New York, NY 10017, U.S. tel. 212/563-6011 or 800/624-0686, www.onecaribbean.org).

RESOURCES
Suggested Reading and Films

Start with Belizean writers, particularly the novels of Zee Edgell, then continue with the catalog of **Cubola Productions** (www.cubola. com), a publishing company whose Belizean writers series includes six anthologies of short stories, poetry, drama, folk tales, and works by women writers. Cubola also publishes sociology, anthropology, and education texts; seek them out at any bookstore or gift shop in Belize, or order a few titles before your trip. **Angelus Press** (www.angeluspress.com) is the other main publisher of Belizean writers. You'll also want to read a book—or six—by **Emory King** (www.emoryking.com); King arrived in Belize in 1953 when his yacht crashed on the reef at English Caye and has been talking and writing about his adopted country ever since.

FICTION
Edgell, Zee. *Beka Lamb*. Portsmouth, New Hampshire: Heinemann, 1982. The first internationally recognized Belizean novel, this story of a girl named Beka who is growing up with her country is required reading for all Belizean high schoolers and offers an excellent view of Belizean family life, history, and politics.

Lukowiak, Ken. *Marijuana Time*. Orion, 2000. Follow the author's experiences on a six-month "hardship posting" to Belize in 1983 with the British military: "The long days are palliated by a constant and increasingly compulsive supply of drugs and japes, until he starts using his position in the army postroom to send improbably large bundles of the stuff home—to his army flat in Aldershot."

Miller, Carlos Ledson. *Belize: A Novel*. Xlibris. com: 1999. This history-laden piece of fiction offers an impressively thorough snapshot of Belize over the last 40 years.

Westlake, Donald. *High Adventure*. Tor Books, 1986. Another marijuana-smuggling action thriller: "You are in the jungles of Belize. You pick your way carefully along the overgrown trail until you come to the clearing. There, above you, rest the ruins of a Mayan pyramid. Is that a stone whistle at your feet? An idol of the bat-god? Riches surround you and Kirby Galway will be more to happy to smuggle your finds to the United States in a bale of marijuana. Aren't you glad you met Kirby?"

HEALTH AND PRACTICAL
Arvigo, Rosita. *Sastun: One Woman's Apprenticeship with a Maya Healer and Their Efforts to Save the Vani*. San Francisco: Harper, 1995. One of the better-known books about Belize, which tells the story of the American-born author's training with 87-year-old Elijio Panti, the best-known Maya medicine man in Central America. It takes place in the remote, roadless expanse of Cayo District in western Belize.

Schroeder, Dirk. *Staying Healthy in Asia, Africa, and Latin America*. Emeryville, California: Avalon Travel Publishing, 2000. An excellent resource that fits in your pocket for easy reference.

NATURE AND FIELD GUIDES

As Belize is one of the most exhaustively studied tropical countries in the world, there are innumerable references that span every conceivable niche of flora, fauna, and geology. They come in massive, coffee-table sizes with color plates, as well as in pocket-size field guides: Tarantulas of Belize, Hummingbirds of Belize, Orchids of Belize, and so on. Following are a few titles that make up the tip of the iceberg for this category.

Arvigo, Rosita, and Michael Balick (foreword by Mickey Hart). *Rainforest Remedies: 100 Healing Herbs of Belize.* Wisconsin: Lotus Press, 1998.

Beletsky, Les. *Belize and Northern Guatemala: The Ecotravellers' Wildlife Guide.* San Diego, California: Academic Press, 1999. One of the best reasonably-sized general nature guides to the area, with abundant color plates for all types of fauna.

Chalif, Edward L. and Roger Tory Peterson. *Peterson Field Guide to Mexican Birds.* Mexico, Guatemala, Belize, El Salvador: Houghton Mifflin Harcourt, 1999. This is one of the best birder bibles for this region.

Dunn, Jon L. and Jonathan Alderfer. *National Geographic Field Guide to the Birds of North America.* National Geographic, 2006. A gorgeous field guide worth lugging to the jungle.

Jones, H. Lee, and Dana Gardner (illustrator). *Birds of Belize.* Christopher Helm Publishers Ltd., 2004. This is the long-awaited, much-acclaimed bible of Belize birding (say *that* three times fast); it's a big book (445 pages, 56 color plates, 28 figures, 234 maps), prompting some birders I met to cut out all the plates and travel with those only.

Sayers, Brendan, and Brett Adams. *Guide to the Orchids of Belize.* Benque Viejo del Carmen, Belize: Cubola Productions, 2009. This is an excellent field guide to the many orchids found throughout Belize.

Stevens, Katie. *Jungle Walk: Birds and Beasts of Belize, Central America.* Belize: Angelus Press, 1991. Order through International Expeditions, tel. 800/633-4734.

ARCHAEOLOGY AND MAYA CULTURE

Carrasco, David. *Religions of Mesoamerica: Cosmovision and Ceremonial Centers.* San Francisco: Waveland Press, 1998. Carrasco details the dynamics of two important cultures—the Aztec and the Maya—and discusses the impact of the Spanish conquest and the continuity of native traditions.

Coe, Michael D. *The Maya,* 8th ed. New York: Thames and Hudson, 2011. This updated classic, which has been in print for nearly 50 years, attempts to understand the "most intellectually sophisticated and aesthetically refined pre-Columbian culture." The new edition has information on new discoveries, including the polychrome murals of Calakmul and evidence of pre-classic sophistication. Coe, an archaeologist, anthropologist, epigrapher, and author, is a forefather of Maya studies. This book is mandatory reading for both amateur Mayanists and pros.

De Landa, Friar Diego. *Yucatán: Before and After the Conquest.* New York: Dover Publications, 1978 (translation of original manuscript written in 1566). The same man who provided some of the best, most lasting descriptions of ancient Maya also singlehandedly destroyed the most Maya artifacts and writings of anyone in history.

Stephens, John L. *Incidents of Travel in Central America, Chiapas and Yucatán.* New York: Dover Publications, Inc., 1969 (originally Harper & Bros., New York, 1841). In this classic 19th-century travelogue, Stephens's writing is wonderfully pompous, amusing, and incredibly astute—with historical and archaeological observations that still stand today. If you can, find a copy with the original set of illustrations by Stephens's expedition partner.

2012

On December 21, 2012, a Maya calendar cycle of 5,125 years that began in 3114 B.C. will end and another era of 13 baktuns will begin (a baktun is a time span of roughly 400 years). The implications of this transition are discussed in hundreds of books. Here are a couple of recent titles I recommend to get a grasp on the entire 2012 phenomenon, from different perspectives. This is only the tiny tip of an enormous iceberg.

Berman, Joshua. *Moon Maya 2012: A Guide to Celebrations in Mexico, Guatemala, Belize & Honduras.* Berkeley, CA: Avalon Travel, 2011. This book is a 100-page companion guide for anyone traveling in the Mundo Maya in the year 2012, when year-long celebrations of all things Maya will take place in Belize and beyond. Find out how to witness a solstice sunrise from atop a Maya temple, visit an archaeological dig, stay with a family in a traditional Maya village, or experience multi-country 2012 Maya tours. Visit www.moon.com for more information.

González, Gaspar Pedro. *13 B'aktun: Mayan Visions of 2012 and Beyond.* North Atlantic Books, 2010. González is a Q'anjobal Maya novelist, philosopher, and scholar from Guatemala. This book (translated to English by Dr. Robert Sitler) is unlike any other you'll read on the subject. It is written as a deep, lyrical dialogue—not just about 2012, but about all of creation, blending "past and present thought into a persuasive plan for moving into the new era."

Jenkins, John Major. *The 2012 Story: The Myths, Fallacies, and Truth Behind the Most Intriguing Date in History.* Tarcher, 2009. Jenkins is one of the most prolific, passionate 2012-ologists out there. *2012 Story* is his most all-encompassing book yet, covering the entire story—from the ancients' forward-reaching stone inscriptions to the modern-day 2012 meme, to a summary of his and others' work on the subject.

Sitler, Robert, PhD. *The Living Maya: Ancient Wisdom in the Era of 2012.* North Atlantic Books, 2010. This book begins with the Yucatec Maya greeting *"Bix a bel?"* which means, "How is your road?" And that's right where the author puts us—on the road in the Guatemalan highlands and southern Mexico. Robert Sitler, PhD, is a professor at Stetson University in DeLand, Florida. In *The Living Maya,* he draws lessons from his four decades studying Maya culture and traveling in the Mundo Maya. The most important messages we can take from the Maya, he writes, are: "Cherish our babies, connect with our communities, revere the natural world that sustains us, seek the wisdom of humanity's elders, and immerse ourselves in direct experience of this divine world."

MORE NONFICTION

Barcott, Bruce. *The Last Flight of the Scarlet Macaw: One Woman's Fight to Save the World's Most Beautiful Bird.* Random House, 2008. Fantastic nonfiction narrative about the Chalillo Dam in western Belize, a highly contentious construction project on the upper Macal River in Cayo. The author skillfully lays out the story and characters around the dam business, while providing a sweeping panoramic snapshot of a unique country as it makes its debut in the new global economy.

Bolland, O. Nigel. *Belize: A New Nation in Central America.* Boulder, Colorado: Westview, 1986. This book is one of many sociopolitical analyses by this prolific author.

Duffy, Rosaleen. *A Trip Too Far: Ecotourism, Politics and Exploitation*. Earthscan, 2002. A critical look at the impacts of ecotourism, using Belize as a case study.

Fry, Joan. *How to Cook a Tapir: A Memoir of Belize*. University of Nebraska Press, 2009. The story of a young teacher's year abroad, living among the Maya in southern Belize in 1962. The author offers an intimate glimpse at Maya village life in this heartfelt, oftentimes funny story of how she "painstakingly baked and boiled her way up the food chain" to gain acceptance among her neighbors and students.

Jovaisa, Marius. *Heavenly Belize*. Lithuania: Unseen Pictures, 2009 (www.heavenlybelize. com). This is a magnificent coffee table tome of aerial photography. The Lithuanian author is an ultra-light aircraft pilot who wanted to share the extraordinary vistas he had discovered. If you don't pick it up in Belize, download the iPad version from iTunes, with more multimedia features than just the book.

Pattullo, Polly. *Last Resorts: The Cost of Tourism in the Caribbean*, 2nd edition. London: Latin America Bureau, 2005. Pattullo provides an interesting breakdown of how the Caribbean tourism industry is structured, as well as a hard-hitting commentary on who benefits and how, providing numerous examples from Belize.

Rabinowitz, Alan. *Jaguar: One Man's Struggle to Establish the World's First Jaguar Preserve*. Washington, D.C.: Island Press/Shearwater Books, 2000 (originally 1986). If you've only got time to read one book on Belize, I recommend this excellent eco-memoir. In addition to telling the true story of his jaguar work in Belize, Rabinowitz gives an alluring glance at Belize's wild post-independence, pre-tourism phase.

Shoman, Assad. *13 Chapters of a History of Belize*. Belize City: Angelus Press, Ltd., 1994. A no-nonsense history of Belize from a Belizean perspective.

Sutherland, Anne. *The Making of Belize: Globalization in the Margins*. London: Bergin & Garvey Paperback, 1998. The British Bulletin of Publications calls this "an enjoyable mixture of academic research, anecdotal insights and strong, even controversial opinion.… This book deserves to be read by any visitor to Belize, whether arriving as a tourist or as a volunteer with one of the many international conservation organizations now operating there."

Wilk, Richard. *Home Cooking in the Global Village: Caribbean Food from Buccaneers to Ecotourists*. Palgrave Macmillan, 2006. Using food to describe Belize's longtime struggle within "the great paradox of globalization," Wilk raises questions like "How can you stay local and relish your own home cooking, while tasting the delights of the global marketplace?" Includes menus, recipes, and "bad colonial poetry."

FILMS

There are many excellent short films on Belize, on both the natural world and cultural issues. Look up Richard and Carol Foster's *Path of the Rain Gods* and Channel 5's *The Sea of Belize* and *The Land of Belize*. Then tune in to www.trphoto.blip.tv, which has some gorgeous educational shorts on Belize; these would be excellent for families to watch together before or after their trip to Belize.

Punta Soul is a 2008 documentary film produced and directed by Nyasha Laing, a Belizean who wanted to tell the story of Garifuna music as it evolved with the Garifuna people's journey from the Caribbean islands to Central America. Laing addresses how the rhythms continue to influence the cultural revival of the ethnic communities in Belize. Learn more at www.parandamedia.com or buy the DVD at the Image Factory in Belize City.

Three Kings of Belize is a 2007 film by Katia Paradis. *Three Kings* is a beautiful, poignant tribute to Belizean musicians Paul Nabor, Wilfred Peters, and Florencio Mess, who represent Garifuna, Creole, and Mayan music traditions, respectively. Though their music is internationally recognized, they live humble lives in Belizean villages. The film moves at the slow, relaxed pace of Belize itself. To find a copy, go to the Image Factory in Belize City, or contact Stonetree Records.

Internet Resources

The first page you bookmark should be **www.belizesearch.com,** the premier search engine for all things Belize, with access to 250,000 Belizean web pages and documents (and growing).

Ambergris Caye
www.ambergriscaye.com
Official site of Ambergris Caye and a lot more, with links to the whole country and a hugely popular user forum (10,000 unique visits a day).

Belize Audubon Society
www.belizeaudubon.org
Belize Audubon manages a number of national parks and protected areas throughout the country and is the place to go for basic info on visiting them. It also has background information on birding and checklists.

Belize First Magazine
www.belizefirst.com
The online exploits of Lan Sluder, a long-time travel writer on Belize with many books under his belt, including *San Pedro Cool,* which you can download.

The Belize Forums
www.belizeforum.com
This is one of the more popular forums, inhabited by many prolific and colorful Belize-a-philes.

Belize Tourism Board
www.travelbelize.org
The official BTB website is quite helpful for anyone planning a trip, and it's filled with gorgeous photography as well.

Best of Cayo
www.bestofcayo.com
Constantly updated reviews of Cayo businesses and activities. These are also the folks behind the "Official San Ignacio & Santa Elena Town Cayo Transactor" page on Facebook.

Centers for Disease Control
www.cdc.gov
Check here for the latest health recommendations for travelers by the U.S. government.

Government of Belize
www.belize.gov.bz
The official page of the GOB, an informative portal to the country.

Naturalight
www.belizenet.com
This is the main portal to the vast Naturalight network, which hosts a variety of sites and forums.

Planeta
www.planeta.com
This is one of the premier ecotourism sites around; look up the Belize page for all kinds of wikis, current events, and interesting articles.

San Pedro Sun
www.sanpedrosun.net
Belizean news and links from this island newspaper, in addition to the latest Ambergris scoop.

Transitions Abroad
www.transitionsabroad.com
Information on working, studying, and volunteering abroad, including updated listings of available positions.

United States Embassy in Belize
www.belize.usembassy.gov
Official site of the United States Embassy in Belize.

Index

List of Maps

Acknowledgments

My sincerest gratitude to Chicki Mallan, who wrote the first five editions of *Moon Belize*. She began this journey in 1990, I took it over in 2003, and I am honored to continue the tradition with this ninth edition.

This book would not have been possible without the hard work, hard traveling, and hard writing of my research assistant, Scott Schmidt. Scott's experience in Belize includes years working with Peace Corps Belize and Belize Audubon Society. He enjoys sharing his experiences of Belize through photography, stories, and homemade shrimp *ceviche*.

Joni Miller also helped with the research of this book. Joni founded the Caye Caulker Ocean Academy, the island's first high school. Contact her to see how you can contribute to the school or help out. It is a worthy effort.

To Al Argueta, author of *Moon Guatemala*, who graciously shared his write-up of Tikal, *Gracias, compañero!* I'll buy you a beer in Flores one of these days. Thanks to Lan Sluder for letting me reprint his obituary of Sir Barry Bowen, and also to Dixie, Lady Bowen, for the photo of Sir Barry and for her blessings.

During the mad pre-deadline scramble of the 8th edition of *Moon Belize*, I egregiously forgot to mention Rosey "Drivegoddess" Goodman, one of my researchers for that edition. My apologies for this omission and thank you for your work on that book.

My friends at the Belize Tourism Board were very helpful and supportive during the research of this edition. I appreciate all your patient responses to my erratic queries, and for your help during my trip to Belize.

Additional thanks to Carrie Tengler-Stuart, Kelly McDermott Kanabar, Mr. B, Marcus "Dr. Feel Awesome" Horton, and to all my biologist and wildlife friends: Caryn Self-Sullivan, PhD; Rachel Graham, PhD; Cherie Rose, Zoe Walker, Sharon Matola, Linda Searle, Robby Thigpen, Jerry Larder, and Nikki Buxton.

To my wife and daughters, thank you for your patience and understanding of the ridiculous hours of a guidebook writer. I wrote an enormous chunk of this book in Boulder coffee shops, including many hours at Logan's and Amante North, my North Boulder offices with a view. Thanks to the stomach flu for infecting my 3-year-old daughter and me only two weeks before my deadline—no, seriously, that wasn't cool, don't do that again.

Thanks to photographer Tony Rath for a gorgeous cover. And finally, to my colleagues and editors at Avalon Travel—Bill Newlin, Donna Galassi, Grace Fujimoto, Kevin McLain, Erin Raber, Darren Alessi, Mike Morgenfeld, Jen Rios, Jodee Krainik, and the rest of the team.

www.moon.com

DESTINATIONS | ACTIVITIES | BLOGS | MAPS | BOOKS

MOON.COM is ready to help plan your next trip! Filled with fresh trip ideas and strategies, author interviews, informative travel blogs, a detailed map library, and descriptions of all the Moon guidebooks, Moon.com is all you need to get out and explore the world—or even places in your own backyard. While at Moon.com, sign up for our monthly e-newsletter for updates on new releases, travel tips, and expert advice from our on-the-go Moon authors. As always, when you travel with Moon, expect an experience that is uncommon and truly unique.

KEEP UP WITH MOON ON FACEBOOK AND TWITTER
JOIN THE MOON PHOTO GROUP ON FLICKR